Historical Writing in England

Historical Writing
in England *c.* 550 to *c.* 1307

Antonia Gransden

Reader in Medieval History, University of Nottingham

Routledge & Kegan Paul

London

First published 1974
by Routledge & Kegan Paul Ltd
Broadway House, 68-74 Carter Lane
London EC4V 5EL
Printed in Great Britain by
William Clowes & Sons, Limited
London, Beccles and Colchester

ISBN 0 7100 7476 x

To K. W. G.

Contents

Plates

[ix]

a. The single combat of Edmund Ironside and King Canute at Deerhurst, 1016.

b. The siege of Damietta, 1219.

XI Possible examples of the revision of chronicles because of political circumstances.

a. The erasure in John de Taxter's chronicle of the sentence stating that Simon de Montfort worked miracles posthumously. Reproduced with the permission of the Trustees of the British Museum.

b. The Chronicle of London, showing the word 'insane' (before 'Parlamentum') written on an erasure. Reproduced with the permission of the Corporation of London.

XII Coronation pictures from the 'Merton' *Flores Historiarum*. Reproduced with the permission of the Provost and Fellows of Eton .

Introduction

This book is a survey of chronicles and biographies written in England to the end of Edward I's reign. It also includes works which though not written in England are of primary importance for English history. I intend to continue the survey until the Reformation in a second volume.

Despite the interest of the subject nearly a century has passed since a survey of this kind was attempted. James Gairdner published his book on English chroniclers, in the series 'Early Chroniclers of Europe', in 1879. Inevitably England occupies only a small place in J. W. Thompson, *A History of Historical Writing* (New York 1942), which covers all periods from the earliest times to the nineteenth century, on a world scale. Nevertheless there are useful studies of certain categories of historical writing, which include material relating to England, for example R. L. Poole's *Chronicles and Annals* (Oxford 1926). And recently much work has been done on individual literary sources of English history – for example by Professor Alistair Campbell (on the Anglo-Saxon Chronicle and the *Encomium Emmae Reginae*), by Dr R. W. Southern (on Eadmer) and by Professor V. H. Galbraith (on the St Albans chronicles and others).

My approach to each author is pragmatic, not theoretical. I have based this survey on the texts themselves correlated with the secondary sources, which, however, I cannot claim to have exhausted. I have borne in mind the interests of students using chronicles and biographies as historical sources. Therefore I have tried to indicate what the student can expect to find in a specific work and what possible misrepresentations, resulting for example from political bias, local loyalties or literary mode, he must guard against.

The production of a survey of this sort is made more difficult because a number of important chronicles, such as those of Florence of Worcester and Henry of Huntingdon, the Lanercost and Melrose chronicles, Fitz Thedmar's chronicle of London and the historical works of Nicholas Trevet, are still only available in antiquated editions (the projected publication of William of

Malmesbury's *Gesta Regum* and *Gesta Pontificum* is still awaited). As I have tended to give proportionately more space to authors who have been neglected by recent scholars, the amount of space devoted to a writer does not necessarily imply a value-judgment.

Although I have sometimes had recourse to the manuscripts themselves, I have not undertaken detailed research on individual works. Nevertheless it has been possible to make a few new suggestions. For example my emphasis on Matthew Paris's debt to Ralph Diceto and my interpretation of some aspects of his historiographical motivation are, I think, new. Similarly I have made suggestions concerning the authorship of some of the chronicles written at Bury St Edmunds, and indicate that Robert of Gloucester wrote for a lay patron. Moreover, I suggest that the so-called 'Merton' *Flores Historiarum* was in fact written in Westminster abbey, perhaps for Edward II on his coronation.

NOTE ON THE ARRANGEMENT OF THIS BOOK

The contents of the chapters have been determined by various factors. The three most important writers, Bede, William of Malmesbury and Matthew Paris, have been given chapters on their own. The remaining writers are grouped roughly in chronological order, but also sometimes according either to the nature of their works (namely whether general histories, local histories or biographies), or to the authors' status in society (for example monastic chroniclers may be dealt with in one chapter, mendicants in another, and so on). This arrangement has the result that material on a particular reign is scattered. Therefore, so that the reader may discover the principal sources for the Anglo-Saxon period, and, from 1066, for each reign, I have appended a chronological list of the relevant works (Appendix D).

Acknowledgments

In the course of writing this book my greatest debt has been to Professor M. D. Knowles who has encouraged me throughout the undertaking, and has read a number of chapters in typescript, making valuable suggestions. It is also a pleasure to express my gratitude to my former tutor, Dr J. N. L. Myres, who read the first three chapters in typescript and made a number of useful criticisms and comments. In addition I am deeply indebted to Professor Sir J. Goronwy Edwards and Dr R. W. Southern who very kindly read the typescript of the other chapters, pointing out some errors and causing me to reconsider some of my judgments. I must, however, emphasize that I am responsible for any remaining mistakes and omissions, and for the opinions expressed.

Other scholars have helped me by answering queries on particular points. I have usually acknowledged such help in footnotes, but I must thank here Dr Wolfgang van Emden for reading the sections on the Anglo-Norman chronicles, Miss Gay Clifford for reading the section on the chronicle in Middle English by Robert of Gloucester, Dr Marjorie Chibnall for recommending a page from the autograph manuscript of Orderic Vitalis, in the Bibliothèque Nationale, for reproduction, and my colleague Professor R. L. Storey who read the book in proof and saved me from a number of small mistakes. I also owe a debt to the staff of the following institutions for assistance when consulting manuscripts and/or printed books in their custody: Nottingham University Library, the British Museum, the Bodleian Library, the library of the Dean and Chapter of St Paul's, the Corporation of London Record Office, the College of Arms, and the libraries of Magdalen College, Oxford, and of Eton College. And I should like to record my obligation to Messrs Routledge & Kegan Paul for their co-operation and courtesy in the preparation of this volume.

Finally, I must thank my husband, to whom this book is dedicated: without his patience and help, both intellectual and domestic, it would never have been written.

Abbreviations

This list is restricted to those abbreviations used in the footnotes.

A St. E: *The Annals of Bury St. Edmunds*, printed in F. Liebermann, *Ungedruckte Anglo-Normannische Geschichtsquellen* (Strasburg 1879), pp. 107–55.

ASC: *The Anglo-Saxon Chronicle*, a revised translation ed. D. Whitelock with D. C. Douglas and S. I. Tucker (London 1961).

Ab.:   *Chronicon Monasterii de Abingdon*, ed. Joseph Stevenson (RS, 1858, 2 vols).

Abbo: Abbo of Fleury, *Passio Sancti Edmundi*, printed in *Memorials of St. Edmund's Abbey*, ed. Thomas Arnold (RS, 1890–6), vol. 1, pp. 3–25.

Adelard: Adelard, *Life of St. Dunstan*, printed in *Memorials of St. Dunstan*, ed. William Stubbs (RS, 1874), pp. 53–68.

Æthelweard: *The Chronicle of Æthelweard*, ed., with an English translation, Alistair Campbell (Nelson's Medieval Texts, 1962).

Ailred, *Relatio* or *Relatio*:   Ailred of Rievaulx, *Relatio de Standardo*, printed in *Chronicles of the Reigns of Stephen, Henry II, and Richard I*, ed. Richard Howlett (RS, 1884–9), vol. 3, pp. 179–99.

Am. Hist. Rev.:   *American Historical Review*.

Ambroise: *L'Estoire de la Guerre Sainte: Histoire en vers de la Troisième Croisade (1190–1192) par Ambroise*, ed. Gaston Paris (Paris 1897).

An. Boll.:   *Analecta Bollandiana*.

Ann. Mon.:   *Annales Monastici*, ed. H. R. Luard (RS, 1864–9, 5 vols).

Asser: *Asser's Life of King Alfred together with the Annals of Saint Neots erroneously ascribed to Asser*, ed. W. H. Stevenson (Oxford 1904, reprinted 1959 with an article (pp. cxxxii–clii), 'Recent work on *Asser's Life of Alfred*', by Dorothy Whitelock).

BC: *Bartholomaei de Cotton Monachi Norwicensis Historia Anglicana*, ed. H. R. Luard (RS, 1859).

BIHR: *Bulletin of the Institute of Historical Research.*

BJRL: *Bulletin of the John Rylands Library.*

BM: British Museum.

BP: *The Chronicle of the Reigns of Henry II and Richard I, A.D. 1169–1192, known commonly under the name of Benedict of Peterborough*, ed. W. Stubbs (RS, 1867, 2 vols).

'*Barn.*': *The continuation of Roger of Howden commonly called the 'Barnwell' chronicle*, printed in *Memoriale Fratris Walteri de Coventria*, ed. W. Stubbs (RS, 1872, 1873, 2 vols), vol. 1.

Battle: *Chronicon Monasterii de Bello*, ed. J. S. Brewer (Anglia Christiana, London 1846).

Blair, 'Observations': P. H. Blair, 'Some observations on the *Historia Regum* attributed to Symeon of Durham' in *Celt and Saxon* . . ., ed. N. K. Chadwick (Cambridge 1963), pp. 63–118.

Burt.: *The chronicle of Burton 1004 to 1262*, printed in *Annales Monastici*, ed. H. R. Luard (RS, 1864–9), vol. 1, pp. 183–500.

Bury Chron. or *Bury*: *The Chronicle of Bury St. Edmunds 1212–1301*, ed., with an English translation, Antonia Gransden (Nelson's Medieval Texts, 1964).

CCR: *Calendar of Close Rolls.*

CM: *Matthaei Parisiensis, Monachi Sancti Albani, Chronica Majora*, ed. H. R. Luard (RS, 1872–83, 7 vols).

CPR: *Calendar of Patent Rolls.*

Carmen de HP: *Carmen de Hastingae Proelio*, printed in *Scriptores Rerum Gestarum Willelmi Conquestoris*, ed. J. A. Giles (London 1845).

Chadwick, *Celt and Saxon*: *Celt and Saxon, Studies in the Early British Border*, ed. N. K. Chadwick (Cambridge 1963).

Cheney, 'The Dunstable annals': C. R. Cheney, 'Notes on the making of the Dunstable annals, A.D. 33 to 1242' in *Essays in Medieval History presented to Bertie Wilkinson*, ed. T. A. Sandquist and M. R. Powicke (Toronto 1968), pp. 79–98.

Chibnall, *OV*: *The Ecclesiastical History of Orderic Vitalis, Books III to VI*, ed., with an English translation, Marjorie Chibnall (Oxford 1969, 1972: only vols 2 and 3 published to date; vol. 1 will appear last).

Chrons. and Mems. Ric. I: *Chronicles and Memorials of the Reign of Richard I*, ed. W. Stubbs (RS, 1864–5, 2 vols).

Chrons. Stephen, Henry II, and Richard I: *Chronicles of the Reigns of Stephen, Henry II, and Richard I*, ed. Richard Howlett (RS, 1884–9, 4 vols).

Colgrave, *Lives*: *Two Lives of St. Cuthbert: A Life by an Anonymous Monk of Lindisfarne and Bede's Prose Life*, ed., with an English translation, Bertram Colgrave (Cambridge 1940).

Cont. GC: *The continuation of the chronicle of Gervase of Canterbury, to 1327*, printed in *The Historical Works of Gervase of Canterbury*, ed. W. Stubbs (RS, 1879, 1880), vol. 2, pp. 106–324.

Councils and Synods: *Councils and Synods with other Documents relating to the English Church*, ed. F. M. Powicke and C. R. Cheney (Oxford 1964, only vol. 2 published to date).

DNB: *Dictionary of National Biography*.

DTR: Bede, *De Temporum Ratione*, printed in W. C. Jones, *Bedae Opera de Temporibus* (Cambridge, Mass. 1943), pp. 177–291, excluding the chronicle which is printed in *MGH, Auctorum Antiquissimorum*, xiii: *Chronica Minora Saeculi iv–vii*, vol. 3, ed. T. Mommsen (Berlin 1898), pp. 247–327.

De Ant. Glast.: William of Malmesbury, *De Antiquitate Glastoniensis Ecclesiae* printed in *Adami de Domerham Historia de Rebus Gestis Glastoniensibus*, ed. T. Hearne (Oxford 1727), vol. 1, pp. 1–122.

De Ex.: Gildas, *De Excidio Britanniae et Conquestu*, printed in *MGH, Auctorum Antiquissimorum*, xiii: *Chronica Minora Saeculi iv–vii*, vol. 3, ed. T. Mommsen (Berlin 1898), pp. 3–85.

Dean, 'Relations': R. J. Dean, 'Cultural relations in the middle ages: Nicholas Trevet and Nicholas de Prato' in *Studies in Philology*, xlv (1948), pp. 541–64.

Denholm-Young, 'Winchester-Hyde chron.': N. Denholm-Young, 'The Winchester-Hyde chronicle', in his *Collected Papers on Medieval Subjects* (Oxford 1946), pp. 86–95, reprinted from *EHR*, xlix (1934), pp. 85–93.

Douglas and Greenaway, *Documents*: *English Historical Documents*, vol. 2, *1042–1189*, ed. D. C. Douglas and G. W. Greenaway (London 1953).

Dunst.: *The Dunstable chronicle*, printed in *Annales Monastici*, ed. H. R. Luard (RS, 1864–9), vol. 3, pp. 3–408.

EETS: Early English Text Society.

EH: *Electio Hugonis*, printed in *Memorials of St. Edmund's Abbey*, ed. Thomas Arnold (RS, 1890–6), vol. 2, pp. 29–130.

EHR: *English Historical Review*.

Eadmer, *HN*: *Eadmeri Historia Novorum in Anglia*, ed. Martin Rule (RS, 1884).

Eddius: *The Life of Bishop Wilfrid by Eddius Stephanus*, ed., with an English translation, Bertram Colgrave (Cambridge 1927).

Enc.: *Encomium Emmae Reginae*, ed., with an English translation, Alistair Campbell (Camden Soc., 3rd series, lxxii, 1949).

Eve.: *Chronicon Abbatiae de Evesham ad annum 1418*, ed. W. D. Macray (RS, 1863).

FH: *Flores Historiarum*, ed. H. R. Luard (RS, 1890, 3 vols).

FW: *Florentii Wigorniensis Monachi Chronicon ex Chronicis*, ed. Benjamin Thorpe (English Historical Soc., 1848, 1849, 2 vols).

Felix: *Felix's Life of Saint Guthlac*, ed., with an English translation, Bertram Colgrave (Cambridge 1956).

Foedera: *Foedera, conventiones, litterae* . . . , ed. T. Rymer (Record Commission ed., 1816–69, 4 vols).

Furness: *The Furness chronicle*, printed in *Chronicles of the Reigns of Stephen, Henry II, and Richard I*, ed. Richard Howlett (RS, 1884–9), vol. 2, pp. 503–83.

GASA: *Gesta Abbatum Monasterii Sancti Albani*, ed. H. T. Riley (RS, 1867–9, 3 vols).

GC: *The Historical Works of Gervase of Canterbury*, ed. W. Stubbs (RS, 1879, 1880, 2 vols).

GEC, *Peerage*: G.E.C[ockayne], *The Complete Peerage of England, Scotland, Ireland and Great Britain and the United Kingdom*, new edition, by Vicary Gibbs *et al.* (London 1910–59, 13 vols).

GGDN: *Guillaume de Poitiers, Histoires de Guillaume le Conquérant* [*i.e. Gesta Guillelmi Ducis Normannorum*], ed., with a French translation, Raymonde Foreville (Les Classiques de l'Histoire de France au Moyen Age, xxiii, Paris 1952).

GND: *Guillaume de Jumièges, Gesta Normannorum Ducum*, ed. Jean Marx (Société de l'Histoire de Normandie, Rouen 1914).

GS: *Gesta Stephani*, ed., with an English translation, K. R. Potter, with contributions to the introduction by R. A. B. Mynors and A. L. Poole (Nelson's Medieval Texts, 1955).

GW: *Giraldi Cambrensis Opera*, ed. J. S. Brewer and others (RS, 1861–91, 8 vols).

Garmonsway, *ASC*: *The Anglo-Saxon Chronicle*, ed. G. N. Garmonsway (Everyman's Library, London 1953, corrected edition 1955).

Giso: *The Autobiography of Giso, bishop of Wells (1060–1088)*, printed in *Ecclesiastical Documents: viz. I. A Brief History of the Bishoprick of Somerset from its Foundation to the Year 1174* . . ., ed. Joseph Hunter (Camden Soc., 1840).

Greenaway, *Becket*: *The Life and Death of Thomas Becket Chancellor of England and Archbishop of Canterbury based on the account of William Fitz-Stephen his Clerk with Additions from other Contemporary Sources*, translated and ed. G. W. Greenaway (Folio Soc., 1961).

Grosjean, 'Notes': P. Grosjean, 'Notes d'hagiographie Celtique' in *An. Boll.*, lxxv (1957), pp. 158–226.

Guernes: Guernes de Pont-Sainte-Maxence, *La Vie de Saint Thomas Becket*, ed. Emmanuel Walberg (Paris 1936).

HA: *Matthaei Parisiensis, Monachi Sancti Albani, Historia Anglorum*, ed. F. Madden (RS, 1866–9, 3 vols).

HB: Nennius, *Historia Brittonum*, printed in *MGH, Auctorum Antiquissimorum*, xiii: *Chronica Minora Saeculi iv–vii*, vol. 3, ed. T. Mommsen (Berlin 1898), pp. 113–222.

HBS: Henry Bradshaw Society.

HC: *The Chronicle of Hugh Candidus*, ed. W. T. Mellows (Oxford 1949).

HE: Bede, *Historia Ecclesiastica Gentis Anglorum*. Two editions cited: *Bede's Ecclesiastical History of the English People*, ed., with an English translation, Bertram Colgrave and R. A. B. Mynors (Oxford Medieval Texts, 1969) and
Venerabilis Baedae Historiam ecclesiasticam gentis Anglorum, Historiam abbatum, epistolam ad Ecgberctum una cum Historia abbatum auctore anonymo . . ., ed. C. Plummer (Oxford 1896).

HGM: *L'Histoire de Guillaume le Maréchal*, ed., with a translation into modern French, Paul Meyer (Société de l'Histoire de France, Paris 1891–1901, 3 vols).

HH: *Henrici Archidiaconi Huntendunensis Historia Anglorum*, ed. Thomas Arnold (RS, 1879).

HRB: *The Historia Regum Britanniae of Geoffrey of Monmouth*, ed. Acton Griscom (London 1929).

Hardy, *Catalogue*:   T. D. Hardy, *Descriptive Catalogue of Materials Relating to the History of Great Britain and Ireland to the end of the Reign of Henry VII* (RS, 1862–71, 3 vols).

Hist. Abb.:   Bede, *Historia Abbatum*, printed in *Venerabilis Baedae Historiam ecclesiasticam gentis Anglorum, Historiam abbatum, epistolam ad Ecgberctum una cum Historia abbatum auctore anonymo . . .*, ed. C. Plummer (Oxford 1896), vol. I, pp. 364–87.

Hist. SC: *Historia de Sancto Cuthberto*, printed in *Symeonis Monachi Opera Omnia*, ed. Thomas Arnold (RS, 1882, 1885), vol. I, pp. 196–214.

Holt, 'St. Albans chroniclers':   'The St. Albans chroniclers and Magna Carta' in *TRHS*, 5th series, xiv (1964), pp. 67–88.

Hugh the Chantor: *Hugh the Chantor: The History of the Church of York*, ed., with an English translation, Charles Johnson (Nelson's Medieval Texts, 1961).

IP^1:   *Das Itinerarium Peregrinorum. Eine zeitgenossische englische Chronik zum dritten Kreuzzug in ursprünglicher Gestalt*, ed. H. E. Mayer (Schriften der Monumenta Germaniae Historica, 18, Stuttgart 1962). IP^1 virtually corresponds to Book I of IP^2 (see p. 239 and n. 159 below).

IP^2:   *Itinerarium Peregrinorum et Gesta Regis Ricardi*, printed in *Chronicles and Memorials of the Reign of Richard I*, ed. W. Stubbs (RS, 1864–5), vol. I.

JB: *Chronicle of Jocelin of Brakelond Concerning the Acts of Samson Abbot of the Monastery of St. Edmund*, ed., with an English translation, H. E. Butler (Nelson's Medieval Classics, 1949).

JF: Jordan Fantosme, *Chronique de la Guerre entre les Anglois et les Ecossois en 1173 et 1174*, printed, with an English translation, in

Chronicles of the Reigns of Stephen, Henry II, and Richard I, ed. Richard Howlett (RS, 1884–9), vol. 3, pp. 202–377.

JH: The chronicle of John of Hexham, printed in *The Priory of Hexham, its Chroniclers, Endowments and Annals*, ed. James Raine (Surtees Soc., xliv, xlvi, 1864–5), vol. 1, pp. 107–72.

JO: *Chronica Johannis de Oxenedes*, ed. H. Ellis (RS, 1859).

JW: The Chronicle of John of Worcester, *1118–1140*, ed. J. R. H. Weaver (Anecdota Oxoniensia, Oxford 1908).

Knowles, 'Becket': 'Archbishop Thomas Becket: a character study' in M. D. Knowles, *The Historian and Character and other Essays* (Cambridge 1963), pp. 98–128, reprinted from *Proceedings of the British Academy*, xxxv, pp. 177–205.

L de AL: De Antiquis Legibus Liber: Cronica Maiorum et Vicecomitum Londoniarum, ed. Thomas Stapleton (Camden Soc., 1846).

LE: *Liber Eliensis*, ed. E. O. Blake (Camden Soc., 3rd series, xcii, 1962).

Lan. or *Lanercost*: Chronicon de Lanercost *1201–1346*, ed. Joseph Stevenson (Maitland Club, Edinburgh 1839).

Legge, *A-N Lit.*: M. D. Legge, *Anglo-Norman Literature and its Background* (Oxford 1963).

Liebermann, *U A-N G*: F. Liebermann, *Ungedruckte Anglo-Normannische Geschichtsquellen* (Strasburg 1879).

Life of Leofric: Life of Leofric, *bishop of Exeter (1046–1072)*, printed in *The Exeter Book of Old English Poetry*, ed. R. W. Chambers, M. Förster and R. Flower (limited edition, London 1933), pp. 8–9.

Little, 'Authorship': A. G. Little, 'The authorship of the Lanercost chronicle' in his *Franciscan Papers, Lists, and Documents* (Manchester 1943), pp. 42–54.

—, 'Chronicles': A. G. Little, 'Chronicles of the mendicant friars' in his *Franciscan Papers, Lists, and Documents* (Manchester 1943), pp. 25–41.

—, *Studies*: A. G. Little, *Studies in English Franciscan History* (Manchester 1917).

MF: Memorials of the Abbey of St. Mary of Fountains, ed. J. R. Walbran (Surtees Soc., xlii, 1863).

MGH: *Monumenta Germaniae Historica*.

MGH, Scriptores: Monumenta Germaniae Historica: Scriptores, ed. G. H. Pertz *et al.* (Hanover 1826–).

MTB: Materials for the History of Thomas Becket, ed. J. C. Robertson and J. B. Sheppard (RS, 1875–85, 7 vols).

Memorials SD: Memorials of St. Dunstan, ed. W. Stubbs (RS, 1874).

Memorials SE: Memorials of St. Edmund's Abbey, ed. Thomas Arnold (RS, 1890–6, 3 vols).

Migne, *PL*: Patrologiae cursus completus, series Latina, ed. J. P. Migne (Paris 1852–1904, 221 vols).

Mommsen: *MGH, Auctorum Antiquissimorum*, xiii, Chronica *Minora Saeculi iv–vii*, vol. 3, ed. T. Mommsen (Berlin, 1898).

Mon. Angl.: W. Dugdale, *Monasticon Anglicanum*, ed. J. Caley, H. Ellis and B. Bandinel (London 1817–30, 6 vols).

Moor, *Knights*: C. Moor, *Knights of Edward I* (Harleian Soc., lxxx–lxxxiv, 1929–32, 5 vols).

NT: *Nicholai Triveti Annales*, ed. Thomas Hog (English Historical Soc., 1845).

OV: *Orderici Vitalis Historiae Ecclesiasticae Libri Tredecim*, ed. A. Le Prévost and L. Delisle (Société de l'Histoire de France, Paris 1838–55, reprinted London and New York 1965, 5 vols).

Osney: *The chronicle of Osney*, printed in *Annales Monastici*, ed. H. R. Luard (RS, 1864–9), vol. 4, pp. 3–352.

PL: *The Chronicle of Pierre de Langtoft*, ed. T. Wright (RS, 1866–8, 2 vols).

Pastoral Care, ed. Sweet: *King Alfred's West-Saxon Version of Gregory's Pastoral Care*, ed., with a translation into modern English, H. Sweet (EETS, xlv, l, 1871, 2 vols).

Pet.: *Chronicon Petroburgense*, ed. Thomas Stapleton (Camden Soc., 1849).

Plummer: *Venerabilis Baedae Historiam ecclesiasticam gentis Anglorum, Historiam abbatum, epistolam ad Ecgberctum una cum Historia abbatum auctore anonymo . . .*, ed. C. Plummer (Oxford 1896, 2 vols, reprinted 1961).

—, *SC*: *Two of the Saxon Chronicles Parallel*, ed. C. Plummer (Oxford 1892, 1899, 2 vols, reprinted 1952 with a bibliographical note and a note on the commencement of the year (see ii. xv, cx–cxlii *d*, 316 *a–e*) by D. Whitelock).

RC: *Radulphi de Coggeshall Chronicon Anglicanum*, ed. Joseph Stevenson (RS, 1875).

RD: *The Historical Works of Master Ralph de Diceto, Dean of London*, ed. W. Stubbs (RS, 1876, 2 vols).

—, *Ab.*: Ralph Diceto, *Abbreviationes Chronicorum*, printed in *The Historical Works of Master Ralph de Diceto, Dean of London*, ed. W. Stubbs (RS, 1876), vol. 1, pp. 3–263.

—, *Ym.*: Ralph Diceto, *Ymagines Historiarum*, printed in ibid.; vol. 1, pp. 291–440; vol. 2, 3–174.

R. Dev.: *The Chronicle of Richard of Devizes of the Time of King Richard the First*, ed., with an English translation, J. T. Appleby (Nelson's Medieval Texts, 1963).

RG: *The Metrical Chronicle of Robert of Gloucester*, ed., with a translation into modern English, W. A. Wright (RS, 1887, 2 vols).

RH: *Chronica Magistri Rogeri de Houdene*, ed. W. Stubbs (RS, 1868–71, 4 vols).

RS: Rolls Series.

RT: *Chronique de Robert de Torigni*, ed. Léopold Delisle (Société de l'Histoire de Normandie, Rouen 1872–3, 2 vols).

RW: *The Flowers of History by Roger of Wendover*, ed. H. G. Hewlett (RS, 1886–9, 3 vols).

Raine, *Hexham*: *The Priory of Hexham, its Chroniclers, Endowments and Annals*, ed. James Raine (Surtees Soc., xliv, xlvi, 1864, 1865, 2 vols).

Ram.: *Chronicon Abbatiae Rameseiensis*, ed. W. Dunn Macray (RS, 1886).

Relatio: see Ailred.

Ric. H.: *The Chronicle of Richard of Hexham*, printed in *Chronicles of the Reigns of Stephen, Henry II, and Richard I*, ed. Richard Howlett (RS, 1884–9), vol. 3, pp. 139–78.

Robinson, 'St. Oswald': J. Armitage Robinson, 'St. Oswald and the church of Worcester' in *British Academy Supplemental Papers*, v (London 1919).

SD: *Symeonis Monachi Opera Omnia*, ed. Thomas Arnold (RS, 1882, 1885, 2 vols).

—, ed. Hinde: *Symeonis Dunelmensis Opera et Collectanea*, ed. H. Hinde (Surtees Soc., li, 1868, only vol. 1 published).

Stan.: *The Stanley chronicle*, printed in *Chronicles of the Reigns of Stephen, Henry II, and Richard I*, ed. Richard Howlett (RS, 1884–9), vol. 2, pp. 503–58.

Stenton, 'Medeshamstede': F. M. Stenton, 'Medeshamstede and its colonies' in *Historical Essays in Honour of James Tait*, ed. *J. G.* Edwards, V. H. Galbraith and E. F. Jacob (Manchester 1933).

Stubbs, *Charters*: *Select Charters and Other Illustrations of English Constitutional History*, ed. W. Stubbs (Oxford 1870; 9th ed. revised by H. W. C. Davis, Oxford 1913, reprinted 1946).

—, *FWA*: *The Foundation of Waltham Abbey*, ed. W. Stubbs (Oxford and London 1861).

TE: *Fratris Thomae vulgo dicti de Eccleston Tractatus de Adventu Fratrum Minorum in Angliam*, ed. A. G. Little (Manchester 1951).

TRHS: *Transactions of the Royal Historical Society*.

TW: *The chronicle of Thomas Wykes*, printed in *Annales Monastici*, ed. H. R. Luard (RS, 1864–9), vol. 4, pp. 6–319.

Tatlock, *The Legendary History of Britain*: J. S. P. Tatlock, *The Legendary History of Britain: Geoffrey of Monmouth's 'Historia Regum Britanniae' and its early vernacular versions* (Berkeley and Los Angeles 1950).

Thompson, *Bede*: *Bede, his Life, Times and Writings*, ed. A. Hamilton Thompson (Oxford 1935, reissued New York 1966).

V et M SG: *Libellus de Vita et Miraculis S. Godrici, heremitae de Finchale, auctore Reginaldo Monacho Dunelmensis*, ed. Joseph Stevenson (Surtees Soc., xx, 1845).

VAAR: *The Life of Ailred [Abbot] of Rievaulx by Walter Daniel*, ed., with an English Translation, F. M. Powicke (Nelson's Medieval Classics, 1950).

VCH: *Victoria County History*.

VER: *The Life of King Edward who rests at Westminster attributed to a monk of St. Bertin*, ed., with an English translation, Frank Barlow (Nelson's Medieval Texts, 1962).

VSA: *The Life of St. Anselm Archbishop of Canterbury by Eadmer*, ed., with an English translation, R. W. Southern (Nelson's Medieval Texts, 1962).

VSC (Anon.): The Anonymous *Life of St. Cuthbert*, printed in *Two Lives of St. Cuthbert: A Life by an Anonymous Monk of Lindisfarne and Bede's Prose Life*, ed., with an English translation, Bertram Colgrave (Cambridge 1940), pp. 61–139.

VSC (Bede): Bede, *Life of St. Cuthbert*, in prose, printed in ibid., pp. 142–307.

VSC (*met.*): *Bedas metrische Vita Sancti Cuthberti*, ed. Werner Jaager (Palaestra no. 198, Leipzig 1935).

VSD: *Life of St. Dunstan*, by 'B', printed in *Memorials of St. Dunstan*, ed. W. Stubbs (RS, 1874), pp. 3–52.

VSE (Ælfric): Ælfric, *Life of St. Ethelwold*, printed in *Chronicon Monasterii de Abingdon*, ed. Joseph Stevenson (RS, 1858), vol. 2, pp. 255–66.

VSG: *The Earliest Life of Gregory the Great*, ed., with an English translation, Bertram Colgrave (Kansas 1968).

VSH: *Magna Vita Sancti Hugonis. The Life of St. Hugh of Lincoln*, ed., with an English translation, D. L. Douie and Hugh Farmer (Nelson's Medieval Texts, 1961, 1962, 2 vols).

VSO: The Anonymous *Life of St. Oswald*, printed in *Historians of the Church of York*, ed. James Raine [jun.] (RS, 1879–94, 3 vols), vol. 1, pp. 399–475.

VW: *The Vita Wulfstani of William of Malmesbury*, ed. R. R. Darlington (Camden Soc., 3rd series, xl, 1928).

WC: *Memoriale Fratris Walteri de Coventria*, ed. W. Stubbs (RS, 1872, 1873, 2 vols).

WG: *The Chronicle of Walter of Guisborough*, ed. Harry Rothwell (Camden Soc., 3rd series, lxxxix, 1957).

WM, *GP*: *Willelmi Malmesbiriensis Monachi de Gestis Pontificum Anglorum Libri Quinque*, ed. N. E. S. A. Hamilton (RS, 1870).

—, *GR*: *Willelmi Malmesbiriensis Monachi de Gestis Regum Anglorum Libri Quinque: Historiae Novellae Libri Tres*, ed. W. Stubbs (RS, 1887, 1889, 2 vols).

—, *HN*: *The Historia Novella of William of Malmesbury*, ed., with an English translation, K. R. Potter (Nelson's Medieval Texts, 1955).

WN: William of Newburgh, *Historia Rerum Anglicarum*, printed in

Chronicles of the Reigns of Stephen, Henry II, and Richard I, ed. Richard Howlett (RS, 1884–9), vol. 1, pp. 11–408; vol. 2, pp. 416–583.

Walberg, *Tradition*: Emmanuel Walberg, *La Tradition hagiographique de Saint Thomas Becket avant la fin du xiie siècle* (Paris 1929).

Wav.: *The Waverley chronicle*, printed in *Annales Monastici*, ed. H. R. Luard (RS, 1864–9), vol. 2, pp. 129–411.

Wharton, *Anglia Sacra*: Henry Wharton, *Anglia Sacra, sive, Collectio Historiarum...*, *de Archiepiscopis et Episcopis Angliae, a prima fidei Christianae susceptione ad annum 1540* (2 pts, London 1691).

Wilmart, 'Adam': A. Wilmart, 'Maître Adam chanoine tréprémon devenu Chartreux à Witham' in *Analecta Praemonstratensia*, ix, fasc. 3–4 (1933), pp. 209–32.

Wint.: *The Winchester chronicle*, printed in *Annales Monastici*, ed. H. R. Luard (RS, 1864–9), vol. 2, pp. 3–125.

Worc.: *The Worcester chronicle*, printed in *Annales Monastici*, ed. H. R. Luard (RS, 1864–9), vol. 4, pp. 355–62.

Gildas and Nennius

Gildas stood between two worlds, his back to the Roman past and his face to the Anglo-Saxon England of the future. It was partly a consciousness of this transition which caused him to write his work on the fall and conquest of Britain, the *De Excidio Britanniae et Conquestu* (*The Ruin and Conquest of Britain*). He can claim the distinction of being the first man in Britain to write history (the pre-history of Britain and the history of the Roman occupation have to be written from archaeological and place-name evidence, and from continental literary sources).

Gildas was born probably in the last decade of the fifth century, nearly a century after the Roman troops finally left Britain, and apparently lived somewhere in south-west Britain.[1] He probably wrote before 547,[2] visited Ireland in 565 at the invitation of the over-king Ainmire,[3] and died in 570.

The *De Excidio*[4] is in two parts, with a preface. He says in the preface that

---

[1] There is evidence in a late *Life of St. Gildas*, which could be interpreted as suggesting that Gildas came from Strathclyde; see F. Lot, 'La Vie de Saint Gildas' in *Annales de Bretagne*, xxiii (1907–8), p. 286. However, in view of Gildas's excellent Latin education (which surely must have been acquired in the lowland zone of sub-Roman Britain) and his interest in south Wales and Brittany, a home in one of the latter areas seems more likely. Lot (op. cit., pp. 246–99, 364–88) discusses the value of the eleventh-century *Life of St. Gildas*, and the twelfth-century one; neither contain much truth. Both are printed by T. Mommsen in *MGH*, *Auctorum Antiquissimorum*, xiii, *Chronica Minora*, vol. 3, pp. 91–110. For the legends connecting Gildas with Brittany see also R. Largillière, 'La Topographie du culte de Saint Gildas' in *Mémoires de la Société d'Histoire et d'Archéologie de Bretagne*, v (1924), pt 1, pp. 3–25. Gildas's name and work were known in Brittany by the late ninth century; see *Vita S. Winwaloei*, printed in *Cartulaire de l'Abbaye de Landévennec*, ed. A. de la Borderie (Société Archéologique du Finistère, Quimper 1888), and *Vita S. Pauli Aureliani*, ed. C. Cuissard in *Revue Celtique*, v (1881–3), p. 421. O. Chadwick, 'Gildas and the monastic order' in *Journal of Theological Studies*, new series, v (1954), pt 1, pp. 78–80, points out that there is no good evidence that Gildas was a monk, and suggests that he was a deacon. For Gildas in general see W. F. Bolton, *A History of Anglo-Latin Literature 597–1066*, vol. 1 (Princeton 1967), pp. 27–37, and R. W. Hanning, *The Vision of History in Early Britain* (New York 1966), pp. 44–62 (see the review of the latter by J. N. L. Myres in *History*, liii (1968), pp. 65–7).

[2] One of the princes denounced by Gildas in the second part of the *De Ex.* was Maglocanus, who died in 547 according to the tenth-century *Annales Cambriae*, ed. E. Phillimore in *Y Cymmrodor*, ix (1888), p. 154.

[3] A version of the *Annales Cambriae*, ed. J. Williams ab Ithel (RS, 1860), p. 5, and the twelfth-century *Life of Gildas* (Mommsen, p. 94) record Gildas's visit to Ireland. The *Annales* supply the date. See Lot, op. cit., p. 286.

[4] The standard edition is by Mommsen, op. cit., pp. 3–85. For a Latin text with an English translation see *Gildae de Excidio Britanniae*, ed. H. Williams (*Cymmrodorion Record Series*, no. 3 (1899, 1901), 2 pts). For some corrections to Mommsen's edition see P. Grosjean, 'Remarques

'it is not so much my purpose to narrate the dangers of savage warfare incurred by brave soldiers, as to tell of the dangers caused by indolent men'. He lived in a period of comparative peace between the Britons and the Anglo-Saxons. In the year of his birth forty-four years earlier, he relates, the Britons won a famous victory at Badon Hill.[5] The significance of this victory in Gildas's view was that it made possible the preservation of government, justice and truth.[6] The victory and subsequent peace were 'God's gift in our time'.[7]

The preface and second section of the work are devoted to admonishing the Britons, and especially the five British princes named, to abandon their lives of luxury, lust and petty strife, and use the peace to its best advantage. It has been argued that the first section of the work, which is a history of Britain from the Roman occupation to the coming of the Anglo-Saxons, is a later addition and not by Gildas.[8] There is, however, very strong evidence that the work is one. All the manuscripts contain the whole (but this evidence on its own is weak as none is earlier than the eleventh century), linguistically there is no significant difference between the sections,[9] and, finally, the historical section fits in with Gildas's argument.

---

sur le *De Excidio* attribué à Gildas' in *Bulletin du Cange, Archivum Latinitatis Medii Aevi,* xxv (1955), pp. 155–76, and P. Grosjean, 'Notes d'hagiographie Celtique' in *An. Boll.,* lxxv (1957), pp. 188, 189, 194–202 *passim,* 212. The earliest manuscript of *De Ex.* is BM MS. Cotton Vitellius A VI. It is a tenth-century volume written probably for St Augustine's abbey, Canterbury, and is probably no. 88 in the catalogue of the library of that house; M. R. James, *The Ancient Libraries of Canterbury and Dover* (Cambridge 1903), pp. lxx, 293, and see P. Grosjean, 'Notes', pp. 186–7. It was badly damaged in the fire in the Cottonian library in 1731. As a result the text to the beginning of c. 8 is wanting and the first and last twelve leaves are hard to read and partly illegible. The pages were mounted and bound in a quarto volume in the nineteenth century. The text was printed, before it was damaged, by Polydore Vergil in 1525 and John Joscelin in 1568. Mommsen collated the text as well as he could in its present condition.

[5] This is the meaning accepted by most scholars of a textually obscure passage in *De Ex.,* c. 26. Vitellius A VI (for which see the previous note) gives the passage as follows: 'usque ad annum obsessionis Badonici montis, novissimaeque ferme de furciferis non minimae stragis, quique quadragesimus quartus ut novi orditur annus mense iam uno emenso, qui et meae nativitatis est'; the other manuscripts give slightly different readings, all apparently corrupt. For the problems relating to the date of the battle and of Gildas's birth see R. G. Collingwood and J. N. L. Myres, *Roman Britain and the English Settlements* (Oxford 1936), p. 460, and C. E. Stevens, 'Gildas Sapiens' in *EHR,* lvi (1941), p. 370.

[6] *De Ex.,* c. 26; 'ob hoc [i.e. the battle of Badon Hill] reges, publici, privati, sacerdotes, ecclesiastici, suum quique ordinem servarunt'.

[7] *De Ex.,* c. 2; it seems a safe assumption that the victory here mentioned but not named ('postrema patriae victoria, quae temporibus nostris dei nutu donata est') is that of Badon Hill which is noticed by name in c. 26 and described in c. 25 as 'victoria domino annuente'.

[8] See Mommsen, p. 11. W. A. Wade Evans, *Nennius's History of the Britons* (London 1938), postulates an early eighth-century date for the authorship of the first section: his views are severely dealt with by J. N. L. Myres in *Journal of Theological Studies,* xli (1940), pp. 196–8. Stevens, 'Gildas Sapiens', pp. 353–4, regards the first section as an afterthought of the author.

[9] The philology of *De Ex.* has been exhaustively studied by F. Kerlouégan who has established that the Latin could well belong to the sixth century and that there is no significant linguistic difference between the sections; F. Kerlouégan, 'Le Latin du *De Excidio Britanniae* de Gildas' in *Christianity in Britain, 300–700* (Papers presented to the Conference on Christianity in

In the first section Gildas traces the events leading up to the present peace. Orosius had accused the pagans of forgetting or never having known about the past, and countered their argument that Christianity had brought disaster on the world by recalling the calamities of the pre-Christian era.[10] Similarly Gildas tried to urge his contemporaries to repentance by reminding them of the long struggle that the peace had cost and of God's previous punishments for their wickedness. The only men Gildas excepted from these comminations were a few who remembered the days of their grandfathers and followed Christ.[11]

Gildas is only concerned with the history of Christian Britain and purposely omits the pagan period.[12] He praised Roman rule because Christianity flourished in organized society. Like Orosius he appreciated that the boundaries of the church were those of the Roman empire.[13] He follows his account of the Claudian conquest of Britain[14] with one of St Alban and other British martyrs, whom, he observes, God had sent to prevent Britain being enveloped in darkness.[15] He notes the church-building after the Diocletianic persecution and deplores the heresy which followed.[16]

Nostalgia for the Roman past is evident in the historical section. Gildas refers to his countrymen as *cives*,[17] to Latin as 'our language'[18] and quotes Virgil and other Latin authors.[19] He distinguishes the legitimate rule of the Roman emperors from the illegal one of usurpers like Maximus.[20] In praising the British leader Ambrosius Aurelianus he remarks that the latter's parents, who died fighting the Saxons, were born in the purple, and laments the degeneracy of his descendants.[21] He observes that formerly foreign luxuries were imported by the Thames and Severn,[22] and that in his day Roman cities lay ruined and deserted.[23]

Gildas was a historian with ideas, not a mere recorder of information. On the whole his approach to history is rational. He mentions only one miracle, and that relates to a saint[24] and not to general history, and attributes one

---

Roman and sub-Roman Britain held at the University of Nottingham in 1967), ed. M. W. Barley and R. P. C. Hanson (Leicester 1968), pp. 151–76.

[10] Orosius, *Seven Books of History against the Pagans*, translated into English with an introduction and notes by I. W. Raymond (Records of Civilization, no. 26, New York 1936), p. 30.

[11] *De Ex.*, c. 26. cf. c. 17. Stevens, 'Gildas Sapiens', p. 354, expresses the contrary view that the historical section has no relevance to the denunciatory section.

[12] *De Ex.*, c. 4; 'Igitur omittens priscos illos communesque cum omnibus gentibus errores, quibus ante adventum Christi in carne omne humanum genus obligabatur astrictum'.

[13] Probably Orosius is his source for the notice of the Romans' treaty with the Parthians in *De Ex.*, c. 5. See Stevens, 'Gildas Sapiens', p. 355.

[14] *De Ex.*, c. 7. See Stevens, 'Gildas Sapiens', p. 355.

[15] *De Ex.*, c. 10.   [16] Ibid., c. 12.   [17] e.g. *De Ex.*, cc. 19, 20, 26.

[18] *De Ex.*, c. 23; 'tribus, ut lingua eius exprimitur, cyulis, nostra longis navibus'. But cf. c. 32; 'Cuneglase, Romana lingua lanio fulve?' See Mommsen, p. 10.

[19] Juvenal, Persius or Martial, and Claudian; Mommsen, p. 6. Philo of Alexandria; P. Grosjean, 'Notes', p. 193.

[20] *De Ex.*, c. 13.   [21] Ibid., c. 25.   [22] Ibid., c. 3.   [23] Ibid., c. 26.

[24] Ibid., c. 11.

plague and one defeat to God's vengeance.[25] He associates cause with effect: he asserts that the Britons' faithlessness and cowardice resulted in total subjugation by the Romans,[26] and their cowardice and incompetence in defeats by the barbarians;[27] he suggests that Roman *civitates* were built in the north as a defence against the Picts.[28]

Gildas interprets his sources and does not copy them word for word, which makes them hard to identify. He writes that he used continental sources, as he could find no British books on the subject, for these, if they ever existed, had been destroyed in barbarian raids or carried abroad by his fleeing countrymen.[29] He probably means Orosius, Jerome's translation of Eusebius, and Rufinus.[30] As he gives the number of cities and *castella* in Britain, it has been suggested that he used a Notitia Britanniarum, now lost, like the surviving *Notitia Galliarum*.[31] He also appears to have used a lost Life of St Alban[32] and one of Maximus, also unknown today. Personal observation and folk-lore no doubt provided some information.

Folk-lore may partly account for his failure to interpret correctly the evidence about the Roman walls. His tripartite interpretation is reminiscent of a Celtic triad.[33] The walls were built, he relates, as a result of British appeals to Rome for help against the Picts and Scots. They appealed three times. First, during the raids which followed the withdrawal of troops by Maximus in 383: the Romans sent a legion, drove back the barbarians and told the Britons to build a wall; this they did, but as it was of turf the barbarians broke through. This seems to be a reference to the Antonine wall, built more than two centuries earlier (A.D. 143), though Gildas may have meant the *vallum* of Hadrian's wall (as this is south of Hadrian's wall he may have assumed that it was built first). Possibly he associated Maximus with wall-building because Hadrian's wall was restored in 369 after a campaign in which Maximus took part.

When the Britons appealed a second time, the Romans sent cavalry troops[34] and built a stone wall and forts on the south-west coast. Gildas must be referring to the reorganization of Britain by Stilicho in 398: there is archaeological evidence that the Saxon shore forts were restored at this time, though Hadrian's wall was finally abandoned soon after 383. The third

---

[25] Ibid., cc. 22, 24.   [26] Ibid., cc. 6, 7.   [27] Ibid., cc. 17, 18.   [28] Ibid., c. 18.
[29] Ibid., c. 4.
[30] Mommsen, p. 7; Stevens, 'Gildas Sapiens', p. 356.
[31] C. E. Stevens, 'Gildas and the Civitates of Britain' in *EHR*, lii (1937), pp. 193–201.
[32] Printed by W. Meyer, 'Die Legende des h. Albanus des Protomartyr Angliae in Texten vor Beda' in *Abhandlungen der Königlichen Gesellschaft der Wissenschaften zu Göttingen*, philol.-hist. Klasse, n.f., Bd viii, 1904/5 (1905).
[33] For Welsh triads see J. Loth, *Les Mabinogion*, vol. ii, pp. 199 et seq. in H. D'Arbois de Jubainville and J. Loth, *Cours de Littérature Celtique*, iv (Paris 1889). For Gildas's account of the Roman walls see Stevens, 'Gildas Sapiens', pp. 353–62.
[34] Gildas was correct in saying that cavalry units, not a legion, came to Britain in Stilicho's time; Stevens, 'Gildas Sapiens', p. 360.

appeal was to Aetius in his third consulship (A.D. 446–50). This time no help was sent and no wall built.

To the historian today Gildas's work has shortcomings. Besides misinterpreting some of his evidence, he is vague, giving no precise dates and few names. His knowledge is confined mainly to west Britain and he knows little of the Anglo-Saxon settlements in the east. Nevertheless his work is an important historical source. It contains a number of statements that can be verified from other evidence. Some of these statements relate to Roman Britain. Thus Gildas correctly states that Roman coins were first struck in Britain under Claudius,[35] and that the stone wall was built by private and public subscription.[36]

But the principal value of the *De Excidio* is for the period within Gildas's own memory.[37] He is the only authority who was in any sense contemporary with the period of the Anglo-Saxon invasions: grandparents of old people living in the mid-sixth century would have been alive at the time (it should be remembered that Bede's account of the fifth century is largely based on Gildas). For this period many of Gildas's statements, though few can be corroborated, are likely to be true: for example that the Britains appealed to Aetius against the Picts and barbarians in general,[38] and that a British prince (the 'proud tyrant') called in the Saxons to defend his people against the same barbarians, in return for supplies and land (like *foederati* of the late Roman empire)[39] and that these settlers eventually rebelled, forcing many Britons to take refuge beyond the sea, though others rallied under Ambrosius Aurelianus. Gildas's picture of west Britain in the second section, of the British princes torn by civil war and weakened by depravity, is no doubt exaggerated, but may contain enough truth to help to account for their ultimate defeat by the Anglo-Saxons. The importance of the *De Excidio* as a historical source was already recognized in the twelfth century by the historian William of Newburgh. He challenged the authenticity of the Arthurian legends because they were not in it.[40]

Arthur and his twelve battles first appear in the *Historia Brittonum* (*The History of the Britons*) of Nennius.[41] The *Historia* is a miscellaneous collection of material relating mainly to Britain. It has a section on the chronology

---

[35] *De Ex.*, c. 7. See C. H. V. Sutherland, *Coinage and Currency in Roman Britain* (Oxford 1937), p. 9. Perhaps Gildas obtained his information from a hoard of Roman coins.

[36] *De Ex.*, c. 18; 'sumptu publico privatoque'. See Stevens, 'Gildas Sapiens', p. 356 n. 5.

[37] See John Morris, 'Dark Age dates' in *Britain and Rome: Essays presented to Eric Birley*, ed. M. G. Jarret and Brian Dobson (privately printed, Kendal 1965), pp. 151–2.

[38] For the significance of this statement in relation to the problem of the date of the coming of the Saxons see Collingwood and Myres, op. cit., p. 354.

[39] *De Ex.*, c. 23. See Collingwood and Myres, op. cit., p. 359.

[40] See pp. 264–5 below and *Chrons. Stephen, Henry II and Richard I*, vol. 1, p. ii.

[41] The standard edition is by Mommsen, pp. 113–219. For another edition see F. Lot, *Nennius et l'Historia Brittonum*, Bibliothèque de l'École des Hautes Études, fasc. 263 (Paris 1934). Lot has a long introduction and copious footnotes but some modern scholars do not regard his edition as being as good as Mommsen's; see *Celt and Saxon: Studies in the Early British Border*, ed. N. K. Chadwick (Cambridge 1963), pp. 21 n. 1, 33 n. 3, 36 n. 1, 46.

of the six ages of the world; a description of Britain; a history of the Britons from their pagan origins to the death of St Cuthbert in 687; a Life of St Patrick; Arthuriana; royal genealogies; a list of the cities of Britain and an account of its marvels. Nennius wrote about 830, probably in south Wales,[42] and was, he states in the preface, a pupil of Elfodd, who introduced the Roman Easter into Wales.[43]

Whether Nennius was the reviser of an existing *Historia Brittonum* or the author of the work as it survives today is uncertain. The evidence in the work itself for Nennius's authorship is the preface, which occurs in only four of the thirty-three manuscripts known to modern editors;[44] and of these four manuscripts only two are of textual value.[45] However, this evidence receives some support from the fact that a scholar in the eleventh century, Gilla Coemain, translated the *Historia* into Irish under Nennius's name.[46] It has been argued that Nennius was no more than the interpolator of a pre-existing *Historia Brittonum*.[47] But against this it can be argued that the existing work has a stylistic unity and contains no mention of such a British source – on the contrary Nennius in the preface accuses the Britons of slothfully neglecting their past.[48] Moreover no manuscript of an earlier *Historia* is known. On the whole it seems most likely that Nennius was the author of the *Historia* as we have it, although he undoubtedly used native sources (notably as will be seen, some northern British work).[49]

Nennius writes in the preface:'I have heaped together all I have found in Roman annals and in the chronicles of the holy fathers, that is Jerome, Eusebius, Isidore and Prosper, and of the Scots and Saxons, and from ancient

---

[42] Lot, *Nennius*, p. 115.

[43] For Elfodd, see J. E. Lloyd, *A History of Wales* (London 1939, 2 vols), vol. 1, pp. 203–4.

[44] The MSS. are described by Mommsen, pp. 113–24, and Lot, *Nennius*, pp. 1 et seq.

[45] These two MSS. are Durham MS. B II. 35, a late twelfth-century volume from Durham cathedral priory, and Corpus Christi College Cambridge MS. 139, a late twelfth-century volume probably from Hexham priory: see N. R. Ker, *Medieval Libraries of Great Britain* (London 1941), p. 55 (Mommsen, p. 124, and Lot, *Nennius*, p. 3, attribute this MS. to Sawley).

[46] The Irish text is published by J. H. Todd and A. Herbert, *Leabhar Breathnach. The Irish version of the Historia Brittonum of Nennius* (Irish Archaeological Soc., Dublin 1848). Mommsen published a Latin translation by H. Zimmer of the Irish text in the right-hand column of his edition. See Lot, *Nennius*, p. 5.

[47] This is the view held by Lot who prints the hypothetical *Historia Brittonum* (which he extracted from the existing work) separately: Lot, *Nennius*, pp. 219–25.

[48] This is the view held by Kenneth Jackson, *Language and History in Early Britain* (Edinburgh 1953), pp. 47 et seq. See also F. Liebermann, 'Nennius the author of the *Historia Brittonum*' in *Essays in Medieval History presented to Thomas Frederick Tout*, ed. A. G. Little and F. M. Powicke (Manchester 1925), pp. 25–44.

[49] The preface to *HB* begins; 'Ego Nennius Elvodugi discipulus aliqua excerpta scribere curavi, quae hebitudo gentis Britanniae deiecererat, quia nullam peritiam habuerunt neque ullam commemorationem in libris posuerunt doctores illius insulae Britanniae. ego autem coacervavi omne quod inveni tam de annalibus Romanorum quam de cronicis sanctorum patrum, id est Hieronymi Eusebii, Isidori, Prosperi et de annalibus Scottorum Saxonumque et ex traditione veterum nostrorum. quod multi doctores atquel ibrarii scribere temptaverunt, nescio quo pacto difficilius reliquerunt, an propter mortalitates frequentissimas vel clades creberrimas bellorum.'

tradition.' But as he did not acknowledge his authorities in the text of his history, nor cite them *verbatim*, it is seldom clear what his sources were, especially as many of them are now lost. However, it is fairly certain that he was indebted to Gildas for part of his account of Roman Britain, the rule of the British princes and the coming of the Anglo-Saxons. Scholars are not agreed as to whether he used Bede's *Historia Ecclesiastica Gentis Anglorum* (*Ecclesiastical History of the English People*).[50] Felix Liebermann and others maintained that he used a common source (or sources), but Ferdinand Lot believed that he used Bede himself. Collation of the passages in chapters 63 to 66, which resemble those in Bede, does not prove that Nennius was citing him, as Nennius has additional information[51] and makes some slightly different statements.[52] These may be due to his own knowledge and to misunderstanding of Bede. However, it is hard to believe that his chronology would have been so chaotic had he known Bede's work.

Nennius had no satisfactory chronological system. For clear chronology and comparative history it is necessary to adopt one era – one important event (such as the Passion or Incarnation) from which to date all other events. Nennius used no less than twenty-eight eras. The confusion is made worse by the fact that sometimes he or the scribes who copied his work gave the wrong era for the date. This apparently is the cause of the year 401 of the Incarnation for the coming of the Saxons: 401 of the Passion (i.e. A.D. 428–9) must have been intended.[53] Often Nennius used what may be described as a 'stepping-stone' method of dating: the number of years between a series of events is given. For example the opening section on the six ages of the world, based on Jerome, has the number of years from Creation to the Flood, from the Flood to Abraham, and so on. Similarly chapter 66 links the Creation by a series of events to Vortigern and Ambrosius. As Nennius's work stops in 687, about a century and half before he wrote, none of the dates has the authority of contemporaneity.

The *Historia Brittonum* has numerous errors, inconsistencies and obscurities. Nennius often misunderstood or misread his sources. He records that Claudius was buried at Monza (Mongantia) in Lombardy, probably because he misread Jerome's statement that Claudius's nephew Drusus was buried at Mainz (Moguntiacum).[54] He gives the name of a settler in Scotland as Damhoctor, which is a misreading of 'dām ochtair', the Irish

---

[50] See Lot, *Nennius*, p. 72 n. 6, and *HB*, cc. 63–6 *passim*. Lot gives the relevant references to Bede in footnotes. Cf. Liebermann, op. cit., pp. 25–8.

[51] e.g. *HB*, c. 63, names the king who gave Bamburgh to his wife but Bede, *HE*, iii. 6, does not.

[52] e.g. cf. the accounts in *HB*, c. 63, and Bede, *HE*, ii. 9 and v. 24, of Eanfleda's and Edwin's baptism.

[53] See *HB*, c. 66, and Lot, *Nennius*, p. 101. For a similar mistake made by a copyist of Nennius's work see I. Williams, 'Mommsen and the Vatican Nennius' in *Bull. of the Board of Celtic Studies*, xi (London 1944), p. 47. For the eras used by Nennius, see Mommsen, pp. 118–19.

[54] *HB*, c. 21. Lot, *Nennius*, p. 165 n. 5, unjustly accuses Nennius of confusing Mainz with Milan (Mediolanum). For Nennius's errors see Lloyd, *History of Wales*, vol. 1, pp. 224–6.

for a party of eight people.[55] Sometimes he was misled by a corrupt passage in his source; Bellinus son of Minocannus entered history in this way. Suetonius wrote 'Adminius Cynobellini Britannorum regis filius'. Orosius, misreading the passage, wrote 'Minocynobellinus Britannorum regis filius', and Nennius misread Orosius as 'Minocanni Bellinus Britannorum regis filius'.[56] Nennius made no attempt to reconcile apparently contradictory evidence, giving, for example, two distinct dates for the coming of the Saxons, 375[57] and 428.[58]

Nennius's love of legends was a factor contributing to his historical inaccuracy. It caused him to give an inconsistent account of the parentage of Ambrosius Aurelianus. The legend in question was that of Vortigern's tower,[59] which related how Vortigern tried to build a citadel on a certain spot in Wales, but wise men told him that it would not stand for ever unless he sprinkled the site with the blood of a fatherless boy. Vortigern found such a boy, who told him that two dragons, one red and the other white, lived in a lake under the place, in two tents which were in two jars. The boy prophesied that the red dragon, symbolizing the Britons, would drive the white dragon, symbolizing the Saxons, from the lake—which symbolized the world. The boy said he was called Ambrosius, and Nennius, turning to Gildas's account of Ambrosius Aurelianus, asserts, contrary to his previous statement that the boy had no father, that Ambrosius's father was a Roman of consular descent.

The legend of Vortigern's tower derives from various primitive pantheistic beliefs. Nennius probably partly included it because it was a good story. But he may also have intended it to explain the origin of a place name (just as Virgil had told the story of Romulus and Remus to explain the derivation of the name Rome). The identification of the boy as Ambrosius could have been an attempt to account for the name of a fifth or sixth century hill fort in Snowdonia, Dinas Emrys.[60] Nennius was fond of such eponyms. He gives a legend concerning Vortigern's death in the Arx Guorthigirni on the river Teivi: the place can be identified as a vast Iron Age earthwork called Craig

[55] HB, c. 14. See Lot, Nennius, p. 157 n. 2 (who gives the Irish as dam octòr), and H. Zimmer, Nennius Vindicatus (Berlin 1893), pp. 221–2. The actual Irish words (dām ochtair) occur in connection with the mythical invader of Ireland, Partholon: see ibid., p. 217; Edward Gwynn, 'The metrical Dindshenchas', pt iii (Royal Irish Todd Lecture series, x, 1913), p. 419, line 15; Whitley Stokes, 'The prose tales in the Rennes Dindshenschas' in Revue Celtique, xvi (1895), p. 141; Lebor Gabála Érenn, the Book of the Taking of Ireland, ed., with an English translation, R. A. S. Macalister (Irish Text Soc. xxxiv, xxxv, xxxix, xli, xliv, 1938–56, 5 vols), vol. 3, pp. 5, 39. I owe these references to Professor D. A. Binchy.

[56] HB, c. 19. See Zimmer, op. cit., pp. 272–3.   [57] HB, c. 31. See Lot, Nennius, pp. 41–2.

[58] HB, cc. 28, 66. See Lot, Nennius, pp. 97–103.

[59] HB, cc. 40–2. For this legend see L. A. Paton, 'The story of Vortigern's tower' in Studies in English and Comparative Literature presented to Agnes Irwin (Radcliffe College Monographs, no. 15, Boston and London 1910), pp. 13–23, A. H. Krappe 'Note sur un épisode de l'Historia Brittonum de Nennius' in Revue Celtique, xli (1924), pp. 181–8, and Lot, Nennius, pp. 178 et seq.

[60] HB, c. 42. See Lot, Nennius, p. 90. For Dinas Emrys see L. Alcock, Dinas Powys, an Iron Age, Dark Age and Early Medieval Settlement in Glamorgan (Cardiff 1963), pp. 65–70 passim.

Gwrtheyrn.[61] And he says that Gloucester took its name from Glovus, an ancestor of Vortigern,[62] and that a tumulus was called Cairn Cabal after King Arthur's dog Cabal (he alleges that the imprint of the dog's paw was on one of the stones).[63] Similar eponyms occur in the Anglo-Saxon Chronicle and are particularly characteristic of another writer with a taste for legend, the twelfth-century romance historian Geoffrey of Monmouth.

The errors, obscurities and legends in the *Historia Brittonum* have caused historians in the past to regard it as almost worthless as a historical source. However, it has been partially rehabilitated by recent scholars. Research has revealed that much truth is preserved in Nennius's heap of material, partly because he did not synthesize his evidence, but narrated with uncritical diligence what he read, heard and saw. Even some of his errors when traced to their sources contain interesting information. Moreover the *Historia Brittonum* is more than a repository of facts. It throws light on how at least one man, Nennius, thought in one of the darkest periods of history.

There is little doubt that Nennius used earlier sources, most of which are now lost, and many of which contained valuable historical information. Some of these sources were of British, and some of Anglo-Saxon origin. Because Nennius made no attempt to synthesize his sources, the British and Anglo-Saxon elements can often be distinguished. His information on St Patrick must derive from earlier British material.[64] There is evidence suggesting that the section from the end of chapter 56 to the end of chapter 65 is based on a lost British chronicle written in about 750, perhaps at Whithorn or Glasgow, which itself derived from earlier material, perhaps dating back as far as the sixth century (Nennius or a reviser inserted the Anglo-Saxon genealogies in chapters 56 to 61).[65] This section has a passage recording that a tribe from Manaw Gododdin, an area in southern Scotland, settled in Wales: modern scholars accept the likelihood of such a settlement which they date about A.D. 400.[66] Moreover these chapters have valuable information about the relations between the Northumbrians and the Britons of southern Scotland in the sixth and seventh centuries. They suggest that during this period the two peoples were not constantly at war, as appears in Bede's *Ecclesiastical History*, but were sometimes on more friendly terms. For example they state that Oswy king of Bernicia (641–70) was married to a British princess, Rieinmelth, daughter of Royth, son of Rum, before he married Eanfled the daughter of Edwin king of Deira.[67] They also state that

---

[61] This earthwork and its legendary connection with Vortigern is noticed by J. E. Lloyd, *A History of Carmarthenshire* (Cardiff 1935–9), vol. I, p. 115. See also Royal Commission on the Ancient and Historical Monuments . . . , v, *County of Carmarthen* (London 1917), no. 393.

[62] *HB*, c. 49.   [63] *HB*, c. 73.

[64] *HB*, cc. 50–5. For these chapters see R. P. C. Hanson, *Saint Patrick, his Origins and Career* (Oxford 1968), p. 82.

[65] See K. Jackson in Chadwick, *Celt and Saxon*, pp. 20–62.

[66] *HB*, c. 62. See Collingwood and Myres, op. cit., p. 289, and P. Hunter Blair, *An Introduction to Anglo-Saxon England* (Cambridge 1959), p. 41.

[67] *HB*, c. 57. See Jackson in *Celt and Saxon*, pp. 21, 42, 50, 56.

Edwin (616–32) was baptized by a Briton, Rum map Urbgen, before his baptism by Bishop Paulinus.[68] However, this last statement could be due to a desire on the part of a British historian to claim for the Britons the credit for the conversion of the northern Angles, perhaps in conscious opposition to the account of the Roman mission used by Bede.

Nennius used two main sources (which he made no attempt to correlate) for the Anglo-Saxon invasions, one British and one Anglo-Saxon, giving virtually two accounts of the invasions.[69] He told the story from his British source which is in accordance with Gildas's account – the Saxons were invited to Britain by the British king, here named Vortigern, to defend the Britons and subsequently revolted, sending home for reinforcements. But, using a Saxon source, Nennius states elsewhere that Hengist and Horsa came as exiles, seeking refuge with the British king. He ascribes the Britons' initial defeat by the Saxons to trickery. Vortigern tricked a Kentish ruler by making a treaty behind his back, ceding Kent to Hengist. And Hengist and his men tricked Vortigern by arriving at a banquet with daggers concealed in their boots with which they attacked their hosts. This account, though not identical with the British version, can be harmonized with it, and may preserve genuine tradition. Vortigern could well have settled the exiles as federates, and the treachery at the banquet could have taken place sometime after the settlement. Probably also of Saxon origin is Nennius's statement, which receives some support from archaeology, that Hengist's son and nephew, Octha and Ebissa, were the first Anglo-Saxons to settle in Northumbria.[70] The Anglo-Saxon royal genealogies in chapters 56 to 61 probably derived from a late eighth-century Mercian document, now lost, and are of considerable value to historians today.[71]

Nennius's ideas appear in a number of passages in the *Historia*. The main characteristics of his thought were pride in the British people and a keen interest in the surrounding countryside, its landmarks and ancient monuments. His pride in the Britons was tempered by an objective interest in the Anglo-Saxon invaders, and his interest in his surroundings was often moulded by superstition.

Nennius tried to prove that the Britons had a long and famous history, comparable to the history of biblical peoples and of the Greeks and Romans. He tells legends of the early invaders of Ireland and Scotland. Though the Irish arrived in pre-Christian times, the legends associate their first arrival with biblical events: they were descendants of a Scythian prince who had

---

[68] *HB*, c. 63. See Jackson in *Celt and Saxon*, pp. 32–3, 42, 46, 50, 55, 59. See also N. K. Chadwick in *Celt and Saxon*, pp. 156–64 *passim*.

[69] *HB*, cc. 31, 36–46 *passim*. For Nennius's account see H. M. Chadwick, *The Origin of the English Nation* (Cambridge 1924), pp. 37 et seq.

[70] *HB*, c. 38. See Collingwood and Myres, op. cit., p. 412, and J. N. L. Myres, 'The Teutonic settlement of northern England' in *History*, xx (1935), p. 261.

[71] See Jackson in *Celt and Saxon*, pp. 21–5, 39–46, 55–61.

fled from the Egyptians after crossing the Red Sea.[72] Nennius was attempting to fit Britain into the history of the world as conceived by Jerome and others. He proposed to correlate events in Britain with those on the continent – partly to prove that Britain had as long a history as anyone, but also to provide it with a chronology. In Nennius's day Rome had become a distant memory (he had forgotten that the Britons were once Roman citizens), but he tried to link British with Roman history. Dolabella, whom Orosius mentions as a naval commander in Illyria, appears as a Roman proconsul in Britain.[73] The first inhabitant of Britain was Aeneas's grandson Brutus, who was driven from Italy because he accidentally killed his father: to give him a biblical connection, Nennius provided him with a family tree back to Noah.[74]

Nennius is less critical of the Britons of his day than Gildas had been of his contemporaries. Although he has no good word for Vortigern, he ascribes one defeat of the Britons by the Anglo-Saxons to God's will[75] and others to Anglo-Saxon cunning.[76] He believed that one day the Britons would be victorious under Arthur,[77] but he does not say when or how the victory was to be achieved. Meanwhile he accepted the Anglo-Saxons, regarding them with some interest. He names a Briton who acted as an interpreter in an Anglo-Saxon court,[78] he gives genealogies of their kings, and Anglo-Saxon place-names and the corresponding British ones.[79]

Nennius had an antiquarian interest in the countryside. He seems to have attempted to explain archaeological finds. He alleges that Constantius Chlorus was buried at Cair Segeint (Segontium, near Caernarvon), 'as the inscription on a tombstone near the town testifies', and that he had buried gold, silver and bronze under the pavements of the town.[80] As Constantius was probably buried at York, it is likely that Nennius was deceived by the tombstone of some other Constantius, by a hoard of coins,[81] and by an association in his mind of Constantius with Segontium (the town was evacuated while Constantius was emperor).[82]

The section on the marvels of Britain (natural and man-made landmarks with supernatural qualities) shows not only Nennius's interest in the countryside but also his superstition. Clearly his Christian faith had been eroded by pagan pantheism. Of the twenty-one marvels, only two have a Christian connection.[83] Nennius claims to have seen two of them himself.[84] All of the marvels were in Celtic areas – twelve in south Wales and its vicinity, four in Anglesey, two in Ireland and one in Scotland. A typical example was the

---

[72] *HB*, cc. 13, 15.   [73] *HB*, c. 19.   [74] *HB*, cc. 10, 11, 18.   [75] *HB*, c. 45.
[76] *HB*, cc. 37, 46.
[77] *HB*, c. 27; after noting that Maximian drained Britain of troops, Nennius remarks: 'propter hoc Brittannia occupata est ab extraneis gentibus et cives expulsi sunt, usque dum deus auxilium dederit illis.' See also the prophecy in the legend of Vortigern's tower, cc. 40–2.
[78] *HB*, c. 37.   [79] See *HB*, cc. 31, 37, 43, 61.   [80] *HB*, c. 25.
[81] For hoards of coins found at Segontium in 1921–3 see R. E. M. Wheeler, 'Segontium and the Roman occupation of Wales' in *Y Cymmrodor*, xxxiii (1923), pp. 111 et seq.
[82] Collingwood and Myres, op. cit., p. 278.   [83] *HB*, c. 71.   [84] *HB*, cc. 72, 73.

piece of wood on which people stood to wash in a spring by the river Severn: the tidal river periodically bore the beam away and returned it four days later.[85] Another example was the burial place of Arthur's son which could not be measured accurately.[86]

Both Gildas and Nennius were Christian Celts of west Britain, living in a rural society partially isolated from the Anglo-Saxons by hills and mountains, and remote from the continent. Two centuries divided them: Gildas was on the whole a rational historian, strongly influenced by the Roman tradition; Nennius was the product of a society where the Roman past was a fading memory and paganism flourished alongside Christianity. Their works raise many problems but are important as the only contemporary historical sources of early British history.

[85] *HB*, c. 72.   [86] *HB*, c. 73.

2

Bede

Bede's mind was dominated by the Christian religion – the Roman past and pagan superstitions were unimportant memories. His world contrasted with that of Nennius, his contemporary. He lived in Northumbria, one of the seven Anglo-Saxon kingdoms which together covered an area roughly corresponding with present-day England excluding the Cornish peninsula. Northumbria itself was hilly and sparsely populated in Bede's day, but it was not isolated. The Anglo-Saxon kingdoms were united by rivers and, in most areas, by valleys and plains, while the Britons were cut off from outsiders by mountains and moorlands. Geographically the Anglo-Saxons were closer to the centres of European civilization; only a narrow sea divided them from Gaul and the Rhenish route to Italy. From the sixth century they were in close touch with Gaul (Ethelbert king of Kent, 560 to 616, married a Frankish princess) and in the late seventh and eighth centuries they sent missionaries to the Low Countries, to convert the Frisians and Old Saxons, men of their race, to Christianity. The Anglo-Saxon church established by Augustine who had been sent by Pope Gregory the Great and accepted papal surveillance, was closely connected with Rome. However, Northumbria itself also came under another influence, that of the Celtic missionaries from Iona.

The cultural streams from Italy, Gaul and Iona met in the monasteries which were founded in seventh-century Northumbria and became the centres of a cultural renaissance. One of the best known monasteries was the twin foundation of Wearmouth and Jarrow, founded by Benedict Biscop in 674 and 681 (or 682) respectively. These houses were within five miles of each other and were ruled by one abbot. Benedict Biscop endowed his foundation with books and works of art he brought back from Rome,[1] and the library[2] and *scriptorium*[3] of Wearmouth/Jarrow were among the best in the country.

The most famous monk of Jarrow was the Venerable Bede, whose work

---

[1] See Bede's *Hist. Abb.* (for which see pp. 14–15, 73–4), §§ 4, 6, 11, 15. See also Plummer's introduction to his edition of Bede's *HE*; *Venerabilis Baedae Historiam ecclesiasticam gentis Anglorum . . .*, ed. C. Plummer (Oxford 1896, 2 vols, reprinted 1961), vol. 1, pp. xviii–xix, with references.

[2] For the library at Wearmouth/Jarrow, see M. L. W. Laistner, *A Hand-List of Bede Manuscripts* (New York 1943), p. 1, and Laistner, 'The library of the Venerable Bede', in *Bede, his Life, Times and Writings*, ed. A. Hamilton Thompson (Oxford 1935, reissued New York 1966), pp. 237–66.

[3] E. A. Lowe, 'A key to Bede's scriptorium', in *Scriptorium*, xii (1958), pp. 182–90. See p. 16 and n. 30 below.

was the supreme achievement of Northumbrian learning. He was born in 672 or 673 on land later owned by Wearmouth. When he was seven years old his parents sent him to Wearmouth to be educated. He transferred to Jarrow soon after its foundation, was ordained deacon in 691 or 692 and priest in 702 or 703. He died on Ascension day 735. As far as is known he had only left Jarrow twice, once to visit Lindisfarne, and once to visit York.[4]

Bede was a man of profound religious conviction. His personal piety appears very vividly in the contemporary account of his last hours: he died at peace, having distributed his few personal possessions (pepper, napkins and incense) to his fellow monks, on the floor of his cell singing 'Glory be to the Father, and to the Son, and to the Holy Ghost'.[5] The sincerity of his religious feeling is also shown in the long letter he wrote to Egbert, later archbishop of York. In it he expresses his deep concern for the state of the Northumbrian church and of the monasteries in his day.[6]

Bede's deathbed scene also illustrates his devotion to learning. He spent his last hours translating the Gospel of St John into Anglo-Saxon, telling the scribe to write quickly. Throughout his life Bede devoted his time, when not engaged on the divine office, to 'teaching, study and writing'.[7] His range of studies was for those days encyclopaedic.[8] He wrote on theology, hagiography, geography (of the Holy Land), science, chronology and history, composed homilies and poems, compiled school books and translated Latin works into English. He was probably best known to his contemporaries as a biblical scholar and his commentaries on the bible give him some claim to be called the last Father of the Church.[9] Bede's historical works were a by-product of his religious preoccupation.[10] He wrote four history books and two biographies. Two of his works on history were chronicles of the world, one to 703 and the other to 725.[11] He also wrote the *Historia Abbatum* (the

[4] For Bede's account of his life, see *HE*, v. 24. For Bede's life see also Plummer, vol. 1, pp. ix–lxxii *passim*, and C. E. Whiting, 'The life of the Venerable Bede' in Thompson, *Bede*, pp. 1–38.

[5] Bede's death is fully described in a contemporary letter of Cuthbert, later abbot of Wearmouth and Jarrow, to Cuthwin; printed in Plummer, vol. 1, pp. clx–clxiv (in Latin), lxxii–lxxviii (in an English translation), and in *Bede's Ecclesiastical History of the English People*, ed., with an English translation, B. Colgrave and R. A. B. Mynors (Oxford Medieval Texts, 1969), pp. 580–7.

[6] Bede's letter to Egbert is printed in Plummer, vol. 1, pp. 405–23.

[7] *HE*, v. 24; 'atque inter obseruantiam disciplinae regularis, et cotidianam cantandi in ecclesia curam, semper aut discere, aut docere, aut scribere dulce habui.'

[8] For lists of Bede's works see Plummer, vol. 1, pp. cxlv–clix, and Laistner, *Bede MSS.*, *passim*.

[9] For Bede's place in the patristic tradition see Beryl Smalley, *The Study of the Bible in the Middle Ages* (Oxford 1952), pp. 35–6. For Bede's biblical criticism see M. L. W. Laistner, 'Bede as a classical and patristic scholar' in *TRHS*, 4th series, xvi (1933), pp. 69–94.

[10] For an excellent and detailed account of Bede as a historian, with numerous bibliographical references, see W. Levison, 'Bede as historian' in Thompson, *Bede*, pp. 111–51. For a more recent survey of Bede's historical work, see James Campbell, 'Bede' in *Latin Historians*, ed. T. A. Dorey (London 1966), pp. 159–90. For Bede's scholarship in general, see W. F. Bolton, *A History of Anglo-Latin Literature 597–1066*, vol. 1 (Princeton 1967), pp. 101–85.

[11] The chronicle to 703 forms the last part of Bede's chronological work *De Temporibus* and is printed by Mommsen, pp. 247–317. That to 725, which is the last part of *De Temporum Ratione*, is printed by Mommsen, pp. 247–327.

History of the Abbots of Wearmouth and Jarrow)[12] and the *Ecclesiastical History of the English People.*[13] His biographies were two Lives of St Cuthbert, one in prose and one in verse.[14]

As a historian Bede was influenced by three main academic disciplines, historiography, chronology and hagiography. He was well equipped for these studies by the resources of Wearmouth/Jarrow, and augmented its library facilities by borrowing books from other monasteries. He could consult such historical works as Jerome's translation of Eusebius's *Chronicle*, Orosius's *History against the Pagans*,[15] and Gildas's *De Excidio Britanniae*. He used the monastic archives for documentary evidence (from which he derived the privilege granted by Pope Agatho to Benedict Biscop for his new foundation,[16] and by Pope Sergius to Ceolfrid, abbot of Wearmouth/ Jarrow from 681 to 716).[17] For chronology he could draw on Isidore of Seville,[18] and various computistical tables, including those for calculating the date of Easter. And for hagiography he could use such saints' Lives as Constantius's *Life of St. Germanus*[19] and a now lost Life of St Alban.[20] Moreover Northumbria already had a flourishing school of hagiography which Bede plundered and developed. The earliest known Northumbrian hagiography was the *Life of St. Cuthbert* written by an anonymous monk of Lindisfarne between 699 and 705.[21] The next was the *Life of Bishop Wilfrid* written by Eddius Stephanus, a monk of Ripon, within ten years of the date of Wilfrid's death (709).[22] A *Life of Gregory the Great* was written at Whitby between 704 and 714,[23] and at Wearmouth/Jarrow itself an anonymous monk wrote a *Life of Abbot Ceolfrid.*[24]

Bede's two world chronicles were in the tradition of the early historians

---

[12] Printed by Plummer, vol. 1, pp. 364–387, as *Historia Abbatum Auctore Baeda*. There is evidence (see Levison, 'Bede', p. 129 and n. 1) suggesting that Bede used for this abbatial history the anonymous biography of Ceolfrid, abbot of Wearmouth and Jarrow (d. 716), printed by Plummer, vol. 1, pp. 388–404 as *Historia Abbatum Auctore Anonymo*. Whiting, op. cit., pp. 22–3, expressed the contrary view that the *Life of Abbot Ceolfrid* was later than and partly based on Bede's work.

[13] Plummer's edition (see n. 1) contains the *textus receptus* of *HE*. However the recent edition, with an English translation, by the late Bertram Colgrave and R. A. B. Mynors, includes a collation of the manuscript of *HE* in the Leningrad Public Library (see p. 16 n. 30 below), which Plummer neglected. The passages here quoted from *HE* are based on the translation in Colgrave and Mynors.

[14] For an edition of the metrical *Life of St. Cuthbert* see 'Bedas metrische Vita Sancti Cuthberti', ed. Werner Jaager, in *Palaestra*, cxcviii (Leipzig 1935). For an edition, with an English translation, of the prose *Life* see *Two Lives of St. Cuthbert*, ed. B. Colgrave; for a review of the latter see M. L. W. Laistner in *Am. Hist. Rev.*, xlvi (1941), pp. 379–81.

[15] For the numerous books available to Bede, including Jerome and Orosius, see Laistner, 'Library', *passim*.

[16] *Hist. Abb.*, § 6, and *HE*, iv. 18. [17] Noticed in *Hist. Abb.*, § 15.

[18] See Levison, 'Bede', p. 116, and Laistner, 'Library', pp. 241, 243, 244.

[19] See Levison, 'Bede', p. 134, and Laistner, 'Library', p. 244.

[20] See Levison, 'Bede', p. 135.

[21] Printed in Colgrave, *Lives*. Cf. Levison, 'Bede', pp. 126–8.

[22] For Bede's use of Eddius see Levison, 'Bede', p. 138.

[23] See pp. 72–3. [24] See p. 73 and n. 43.

and chronologers. They are part of his own works on chronology, the *De Temporibus* (*On Time*) and *De Temporum Ratione* (*On the Reckoning of Time*). They briefly note important events in world history in a chronological framework (both works were popular with medieval chroniclers who copied and continued them). The longer of the two chronicles, to 725, shows Bede's theological outlook. It is arranged in eight ages, corresponding to the seven days of the Creation and the seven periods of man's life on earth (his babyhood, childhood, adolescence and so on). The eighth age represents man's eternal life in heaven or hell, thus illustrating the Augustinian concept that all life on earth is but a journey to eternal happiness or damnation.[25]

The *History of the Abbots of Wearmouth and Jarrow* and the Lives of St Cuthbert (both of which will be discussed more fully in a later chapter) belong to the Northumbrian hagiographical tradition. The former, following the anonymous *Life of Abbot Ceolfrid*, is remarkably free from the miraculous element and is a business-like record of the abbey's history from its foundation to 716.[26] Bede probably wrote it between 725 and 731. The Lives of of St Cuthbert, written in 721, are based partly on the anonymous Lindisfarne Life.[27]

The historiographical, chronological and hagiographical influences combine in Bede's most important work, the *Ecclesiastical History of the English People*, completed in 731. It is in five books. The first half of Book I is introductory; it contains a geographical description of the British Isles, and accounts of its prehistoric inhabitants, the Roman invasion and occupation, the British church, and of the Anglo-Saxon invasion and settlement. The work's main theme is the history of the Anglo-Saxon church from St Augustine's mission to 731. It is in literary form, arranged in chronological order which is broken to some extent by saints' lives and because phases in the history of the Anglo-Saxon kingdoms are described in turn. Prominence is given to Northumbria which Bede regarded as the glory of Anglo-Saxon England, a land of saints protected by pious kings.[28] Bede ends with a brief chronological summary of the important events noticed in the body of the work, an account of his life and writings, and a prayer.

Bede's permanent reputation rests on the *Ecclesiastical History*. It was widely read and respected in the dark and middle ages, and has retained a pre-eminent place in English historiography to the present day. Its great reputation in early times is shown by the number of medieval copies which survive – over a hundred and fifty[29] – the earliest two written in Northumbria, probably at Wearmouth/Jarrow, within a decade of Bede's death.[30] In the

---

[25] See Levison, 'Bede', pp. 122–3.   [26] See p. 73.   [27] See pp. 69–70.
[28] For Bede's love of Northumbria, see B. Colgrave, 'Bede's miracle stories' in Thompson, *Bede*, p. 216.
[29] Listed Laistner, *Bede MSS.*, pp. 94–103.
[30] These two early MSS. are: (1) the Moore MS. (CUL MS. Kk. 5. 16); printed facsimile in *The Moore Bede*, ed. P. H. Blair, with a contribution by R. A. B. Mynors (Early English MSS. in

eighth century it was one of England's chief literary exports, at first for the use of Anglo-Saxon missionaries on the continent.[31] Its reputation soon spread over Europe (about half of the known medieval copies are in foreign libraries).[32] It was translated into English in King Alfred's reign,[33] and borrowed and extracted from by chroniclers and hagiographers in England and abroad.[34] The text presents no problems because of the excellent manuscript tradition. It was treated as a classic and not tinkered with in the middle ages.[35] And today it is regarded as the most important source for early English history.

The *Ecclesiastical History* owed its early reputation to rather different qualities than those for which it is valued in modern times. Then it appealed to people's piety[36] and to the Anglo-Saxons' love of their own race. Now it appeals to scholars' respect for historical thoroughness and competence. But at all periods readers have appreciated Bede's literary skill – his ability to describe people and events, and to expound ideas. The reception given to the *Ecclesiastical History* in the early period shows that Bede succeeded in his objectives for writing. He had proposed to write a pious work for the edification of his audience, and one which would please the Anglo-Saxons by recording their achievements.

Facsimile, ix, Copenhagen 1959); for its date see Blair, 'The Moore memoranda on Northumbrian history' in *Early Cultures of North-West Europe: H. M. Chadwick Memorial Studies*, ed. C. F. Fox and B. Dickens (Cambridge 1950), pp. 247–8; (2) the Leningrad MS. (Latin MS. Q. v. I. 18 in the Leningrad Public Library), printed facsimile in *The Leningrad Bede*, ed. O. Arngart (Early English MSS. in Facsimile, ii, Copenhagen 1952). For its provenance see Lowe, 'A key to Bede's scriptorium'. For a reproduction of a page see Plate 1. This MS. is collated in Colgrave and Mynors (but not in Plummer) without reference to the much-debated colophon at the end of this MS. ('Beda famulus X̅p̅i indig[nus]'), presumably because Sir Roger Mynors (who edited the text for the edition), accepts that it cannot be Bede's autograph. E. A. Lowe, 'An autograph of the Venerable Bede?' in *Revue Bénédictine*, lxviii (1958), pp. 200–2, suggested that the colophon is in Bede's hand; but D. H. Wright, 'The date of the Leningrad Bede' in *Revue Bénédictine*, lxxi (1961), pp. 265–73, argued convincingly that the Leningrad MS. is to be dated 746, thus precluding the possibility of the colophon being Bede's autograph. See also P. Meyvaert in *Revue d'Histoire Ecclésiastique*, liv (1959), p. 632. For Bede's arrangements for the copying of his works at Jarrow and elsewhere see *The Complete Works of the Venerable Bede . . .* , ed. J. A. Giles (London 1843–4, 12 vols), vol. 10, p. 268; Plummer, vol. 1, p. 3; and *Bedae Venerabilis Expositio Actuum Apostolorum et Retractatio*, ed. M. L. W. Laistner (Medieval Academy of America, publication no. 35, 1939), p. 3; for their revision, at Bede's request, by his friends, etc., see *HE*, preface, and Colgrave, *Lives*, p. 145.

[31] Levison, 'Bede', pp. 149–51. For appeals to its authority in ecclesiastical disputes in the middle ages see W. Levison, *England and the Continent in the Eighth Century* (Oxford 1946, reprinted 1956), pp. 183–224 *passim*, 241.

[32] Laistner, *Bede MSS.*, p. 3. An even greater proportion of copies of some of Bede's other works were written abroad; ibid., p. 2, and C. W. Jones, *Bedae Opera de Temporibus* (Cambridge, Mass. 1943), p. 142.

[33] *The Old English Version of Bede's Ecclesiastical History of the English People*, ed. T. Miller (EETS, old series, nos 95, 96, 110, 111, 1890–1).

[34] For the use of *HE* by later English chroniclers see the index to the present volume under 'Bede'.

[35] For evidence that Bede himself recast the text see Plummer, vol. 1, pp. xciv–xcvii.

[36] There are over a hundred medieval volumes containing extracts from *HE* – nearly all the extracts are of events in saints' lives, visions etc. See Laistner, *Bede MSS.*, pp. 103–11.

Bede was preoccupied with the salvation of mankind:[37] he wrote in a missionary period; Northumbria itself was not yet fully converted[38] and Anglo-Saxon missionaries had gone to convert the Old Saxons. His theological point of view permeates the *Ecclesiastical History* and explains the touch of morbidity and intolerance in the work. Death as the gateway to heaven should have no terrors for the pious[39] (the sincerity of Bede's faith was shown by his cheerfulness and contentment when dying). Bede likes to write of prophecies of death,[40] visions of the after-world,[41] death-bed scenes,[42] coffins[43] and corpses.[44] Only twice does he express pleasure at the recovery of the sick, and then it is because the patients' salvation was in jeopardy – one being unbaptized[45] and the other uncanonically baptized.[46]

The way to heaven was a narrow one. The pope held the keys, and salvation was likely only in the Roman church. This view led Bede to take a rather intolerant attitude to people observing customs different from those of Rome. Thus he was totally committed to the Roman cause in the Northumbrians' dispute with the Celtic church (the church of the Britons of Wales and Cornwall, and of the Irish and Picts of Scotland) over various observances, but primarily over the method of calculating the date of Easter.[47] From the time of St Augustine of Canterbury throughout the seventh century the Celts defended their customs against the Roman church. The controversy was particularly acute in Northumbria where Celtic customs had gained ground because of the work of the missionaries from Iona. King Oswy had been baptized by a Celt: Bede records that as a result of the different methods of calculation of Easter, Oswy kept Easter while his queen Eanfled, who observed the Roman customs, was fasting in Lent.[48] The controversy was only settled, in favour of the Roman party, at the

---

[37] For assertions that his purpose was edification see *HE*, the preface and iii. 19; iv. 22; v. 13.

[38] See *HE*, iii. 30; iv. 27.

[39] e.g. the nun of Barking and a crippled girl longed to die (*HE*, iv. 9) and the two princes of the Isle of Wight went happily to martyrdom after baptism (*HE*, iv. 16).

[40] e.g. Earcongota (*HE*, iii. 8), Chad (*HE*, iv. 3), a nun of Barking (*HE*, iv. 8), Sebbi (*HE*, iv. 11) and Etheldreda (*HE*, iv. 19) foresaw their own deaths.

[41] e.g. Fursey (*HE*, iii. 19) and Drythelm (*HE*, v. 12) had visions of the afterworld.

[42] e.g. the death of a nun of Barking; *HE*, iv. 9. Cf. the account of the deaths of Eosterwini and Benedict Biscop in *Hist. Abb.*, §§ 8, 14.

[43] e.g. the miraculous alteration in the size of Sebbi's coffin so that it fitted him (*HE*, iv. 11) and the discovery of a Roman sarcophagus for Etheldreda's body (*HE*, iv. 19).

[44] An incorruptible corpse was regarded as a sign of holiness. E.g. Cuthbert's body was found incorrupt; *HE*, iv. 30.

[45] *HE*, iii. 23.   [46] *HE*, v. 6.

[47] cf. *HE*, iii. 25; 'grauior de obseruatione paschae, necnon et de aliis ecclesiasticae vitae disciplinis controuersia nata est. Unde merito mouit haec quaestio sensus et corda multorum, timentium, ne forte accepto Christianitatis uocabulo, in uacuum currerent aut cucurrissent.' For the controversy see Plummer, vol. 1, pp. xxxix–xl and nn. It should however be noted that Bede's attitude to the Celts observing their own customs was much less intolerant than that found in the *Life of Bishop Wilfrid* attributed to Eddius Stephanus. Bede had the highest regard for Aidan (see pp. 19 and nn. 54, 56, 22 below) and apparently rather disliked Wilfrid.

[48] *HE*, iii. 25.

synod of Whitby in 664. Most of the Irish accepted the Roman customs in the course of the eighth century, the last being the monks of Iona in 716.[49] The Britons of Wales still observed the Celtic customs in Bede's day.

Bede devoted much space to the paschal controversy. It interested him intellectually because of his technical interest in dating systems – he did not agree on a purely intellectual level with anyone who reached a different conclusion on the matter. Moreover, he wrote partly to defend the Roman position; from one point of view, the *Ecclesiastical History* can be seen as a *pièce justificative* for the Roman party. He gives a very full account of the synod of Whitby, quoting the speeches of the two advocates, Wilfrid for Rome and Colman for the Celts.[50] He gives the full arguments, culminating in Wilfrid's statement that as the pope represents Peter, to whom the keys of heaven were entrusted, the customs sanctioned by the pope must be right: the reader (or listener) is meant to understand that the synod marked the triumph of the Roman church, and the triumph was just, because the Roman customs, founded on papal authority, were correct.

Bede returns to the paschal controversy towards the end of the *Ecclesiastical History*, with two long chapters on it.[51] One includes a copy of a letter from Ceolfrid, abbot of Wearmouth/Jarrow, to the king of the Picts arguing the case for the Roman date of Easter. The letter is very technical and there can be little doubt that Bede drafted it.[52] The other chapter describes how Egbert, an Anglo-Saxon, went to Iona and persuaded the monks to accept the Roman Easter. It was a cause of great satisfaction to Bede that an Anglo-Saxon converted the Iona monks to the Roman usage, for the Northumbrians owed their conversion to Christianity partly to the monks of Iona: the wheel had come, as it were, full circle. As this chapter virtually ends the historical narrative in the *Ecclesiastical History*,[53] the Easter controversy has the last word.

The controversy to some extent conditioned Bede's attitude to the Celts. On the whole he liked the Irish.[54] The dispute with them was in the past at the time of writing so that he could see them fairly objectively. He regarded Ireland as a very holy place[55] and he admired the austerity, piety and missionary zeal of the Irish. He was particularly grateful to the monks of Iona, men such as Aidan, for their part in the conversion of Northumbria.[56]

---

[49] *HE*, v. 22.   [50] *HE*, iii. 25.   [51] *HE*, v. 21, 22.

[52] See Plummer, vol. 2, p. 332, and Levison, 'Bede', p. 139.

[53] After this chapter are two final chapters, one on the condition of England in Bede's time, and the other containing the chronological summary etc. (see p. 16 above).

[54] Bede's attitude to the Irish is typified in his attitude to Aidan: 'immo hoc [i.e. the customs relating to Easter etc.] multum detestans ... sed quasi uerax historicus, simpliciter ea, quae de illo siue per illum sunt gesta, describens, et quae laude sunt digna in eius actibus laudans, atque ad utilitatem legentium memoriae commendans'; *HE*, iii. 17. Bede observed that though Aidan kept Easter on the wrong day he worked for the salvation of mankind: *HE*, iii. 19.

[55] *HE*, i. 1.

[56] Bede wrote of the conversion of the monks of Iona to the Roman Easter by the Anglo-Saxon Egbert: 'Quod mira diuinae constat factum dispensatione pietatis, ut quoniam gens illa, quam

He recognized that they had observed the Celtic customs later than some of the other Irish because of the geographical isolation of Iona from Rome[57] and their understandable loyalty to the customs of such a famous monastery.[58]

Bede's attitude to the Britons of Wales was different. Here he was quite intolerant. Not only were they still observing the Celtic customs in his day, but also they had not tried to convert the Anglo-Saxons.[59] He gives little information about them, beyond a misleading attempt to describe their monastery at Bangor.[60] One of the most unpleasant passages in the *Ecclesiastical History* is the account of the British defeat at Chester when the army of Ethelfrith king of Bernicia (592 or 593 to 616) slaughtered about twelve hundred of the monks of Bangor who had come to pray for victory.[61] Bede regards the defeat as a divine judgment on the Britons for not accepting St Augustine's authority. As Ethelfrith was a pagan, Bede seems in this instance to prefer heathenism to non-Roman Christianity. No doubt he was partly influenced by his loyalty to the Northumbrians and his belief that a strong Northumbria was ultimately to the church's advantage. The Britons were the Northumbrians' enemies – and when they defeated the Northumbrians in 632, killing King Edwin, the latter reverted to paganism.

Bede's concern for his readers' salvation is demonstrated by the miraculous element in the *Ecclesiastical History*. The reader was to be shown God's power on earth by numerous examples of divine rewards and punishments, and the power of God's saints to suspend the laws of nature. Bede related some miracles to convince men of the superiority of the Roman to the Celtic church. For example he describes how St Augustine, to persuade the Britons of Wales that the Roman church was the true church, cured a blind man whom the British bishops had failed to cure.[62]

The miraculous element in the *Ecclesiastical History* raises the question whether Bede was credulous and his account of events irrational, neglecting the idea of cause and effect as historians see it today. It is true that Bede gives a few miracles which are miraculous in the strict sense, involving the suspension of natural laws without reasonable explanation. For example the bodies of the two martyred Ewald brothers were borne by the water nearly forty miles *up* the Rhine.[63] But it should be noted that Bede copied some of

---

nouerat scientiam diuinae cognitionis libenter ac sine inuidia populis Anglorum communicare curauit; ipsa quoque postmodum per gentem Anglorum in eis, quae minus habuerat, ad perfectam uiuendi normam perueniret'; *HE*, v. 22. Cf. the account of Aidan's missionary work; *HE*, iii. 17.

[57] Bede wrote that the monks of Iona 'in tempore quidem summae festiuitatis dubios circulos sequentes, utpote quibus longe ultra orbem positis nemo synodalia paschalis obseruantiae decreta porrexerat'; *HE*, iii. 4.

[58] *HE*, iii. 4, 17, 25.

[59] *HE*, ii. 2; v. 22. For the Britons' hatred of the Anglo-Saxons and the Roman church see *HE*, v. 23. Bede followed Gildas closely in his account of the Anglo-Saxon conquest, reiterating his invective against the Britons.

[60] *HE*, ii. 2.   [61] Ibid.   [62] Ibid.

[63] *HE*, v. 10. The miracle of Tunna (*HE*, iv. 22) is also hard to explain scientifically. Cf. Colgrave, 'Bede's miracle stories', p. 201.

his miracle stories straight from his sources, and he would have thought it wrong to tamper with such authorities. For example the miracle of the river drying up so that St Alban could cross to his place of martyrdom and of his executioner's eyes dropping out, comes from a lost Life of St Alban.[64] Similarly Bede borrowed the story of St Germanus and the Alleluia victory from Constantius's *Life of St. Germanus*.[65]

Nevertheless Bede derived most of his miracle stories at first hand, from, as he considered, reliable witnesses. But the *Ecclesiastical History* is not full of incredible happenings and irrational statements. On occasion it is clear that Bede appealed to the supernatural for explanations because of ignorance. In his day scientific knowledge was almost non-existent,[66] and occurrences which struck Bede as miraculous may seem to the modern reader, on Bede's own evidence, to be normal events or coincidences. The sick may recover naturally, storms blow over and fires die down, people may dream and corpses be mummified. Moreover Bede was on the whole a rational historian and obviously regarded rational causation as compatible with divine intervention. He often puts a pious interpretation on an event which he must have recognized as normal – he sometimes explicitly offers a rational explanation for a miracle.

A good example of a miracle explicable in rational terms is John of Beverley's cure of a dumb boy with a scabby head.[67] The cure of the dumbness, which Bede regarded as a miracle, was achieved, according to Bede's own account, by John's patience and understanding – by what we should call speech therapy. First John taught the boy to say 'yes', and then to pronounce syllables and finally words and phrases. John's physician treated the scabs. Thus, Bede wrote, the boy gained 'a clear complexion, ready speech, and beautiful curly hair, whereas he had once been ugly, destitute and dumb.'

An example of an event which Bede explains both as divine retribution and on rational grounds, is King Egfrith's defeat by, and death at the hands of, the Picts in 685.[68] Bede says that this was a punishment for the king's making war against the Irish. He also says that Egfrith was defeated because of a trick played by the Picts, who pretended to retreat so that he followed them into the inaccessible mountains of Scotland, and then they ambushed

[64] *HE*, i. 7. Cf. Plummer, vol. 2, pp. 17–18.
[65] *HE*, i. 20. Cf. Plummer, vol. 1, p. xxiv n. 1; vol. 2, pp. 31–2.
[66] For Bede's knowledge of natural science see Jones, *Bedae Opera de Temporibus*, pp. 125–9.
[67] *HE*, v. 2.
[68] *HE*, iv. 26. Other examples of divine rewards and punishments occurring through the agency of natural laws are: St Germanus defeated the Picts and Scots (a) with God's help (b) by sending out scouts and choosing a good place for the battle (*HE*, i. 20); the monastery of Coldingham was burnt down (a) as a divine punishment for the self-indulgent lives of its inmates (b) through carelessness (*HE*, iv. 25); Cenwalh king of Wessex was attacked by Penda (a) as a divine punishment for refusing to become a Christian (b) because he had angered Penda by putting away his wife, Penda's sister (*HE*, iii. 7); Sigeberht king of the East Saxons was murdered (a) as a divine punishment for dining with an excommunicate (b) because his murderers were exasperated by his lenient treatment of criminals etc. (*HE*, iii. 22).

him. An example of an event which Bede calls a miracle and yet explains rationally is how Bishop Mellitus put out a fire at Canterbury.[69] The bishop went to where it raged the worst and prayed. 'Immediately,' Bede writes, 'the south wind, which had spread the conflagration over the city, veered round to the north and first of all prevented the fury of the flames from destroying those places which were in its path; then it soon ceased entirely and there was a calm, and at the same time the flames sank and died out.' He tells a similar story about Aidan who on seeing flames leaping from Bamburgh, which had been fired by Penda, said, '"Oh Lord, see how much evil Penda is doing!" As soon as he had uttered these words, the winds turned away from the city and carried the flames in the direction of those who had kindled them.'[70]

Bede's subject was ecclesiastical history but he interpreted it widely, to include much secular history. He dedicated the work to Ceolwulf king of Northumbria. He recorded not only the succession of Anglo-Saxon bishops,[71] but also the succession and genealogies of the kings.[72] The inclusion of secular history reflects the inextricably close connection of church and state in Anglo-Saxon times. Bede thought that kings should be the servants of the church, taking its advice, protecting and endowing it,[73] and helping its missionary work.[74] In return God rewarded good kings with victory and prosperity,[75] and punished bad ones with earthly calamities.[76] Just rule was Christian rule:[77] Bede omitted from his list of the seven Anglo-Saxon kings

[69] *HE*, ii. 7.   [70] *HE*, iii. 16.

[71] e.g. *HE*, ii. 3–9 *passim*. In the early period of Anglo-Saxon history the question of the episcopal succession was acute because the British church was schismatic. Thus when Chad was consecrated there was only one canonically consecrated bishop in Britain, and two of the bishops assisting at this consecration were British (*HE*, iii. 28). Therefore Chad himself was not canonically consecrated and Archbishop Theodore deposed and reconsecrated him (*HE*, iv. 2). To overcome the difficulty Wilfrid had been consecrated in Gaul (*HE*, iii. 28).

[72] e.g. *HE*, ii. 5, records Ethelbert of Kent's death, length of reign, pedigree and the succession of his son Eadbald, and *HE*, ii. 15, the succession and pedigree of Earpwald, king of the East Angles. See G. H. Wheeler, 'The genealogy of the early West Saxon kings' in *EHR*, xxxvi (1921), p. 165 (with reference to *HE*, iv. 12 and 24); Wheeler states: 'The rule of succession to the old English kingdoms is no longer understood, but it is clear that in Bede's opinion there was a rule.'

[73] He praised Eadbald king of Kent for consulting the church (*HE*, ii. 6) and blamed Egfrith king of Northumbria for neglecting Cuthbert's advice – God punished him by defeat and death (*HE*, iv. 26). He recorded that Ethelbert king of Kent legislated to protect the church from theft (*HE*, ii. 5), and Earconbert king of Kent enforced Lenten observance and the destruction of idols (*HE*, iii. 8). He recorded that Sigeberht king of the East Angles (*HE*, iii. 18), Ethelwald king of Deira (*HE*, iii. 23), Æthelwalh king of the South Saxons (*HE*, iv. 13) and others endowed religious houses.

[74] He recorded that Oswy was responsible for the conversion of Peada of Mercia, and of the East Saxons; *HE*, iii. 21, 22.

[75] e.g. Bede asserted that the earthly power of Edwin and Oswald, kings of Northumbria, increased after their conversion (*HE*, ii. 9; iii. 6), and that Oswy and Aldfrith, though their forces were outnumbered, defeated the pagan Mercians because they were strong in faith (*HE*, iii. 24). Cf. Coifi's argument in favour of Christianity; *HE*, ii. 13.

[76] e.g. Bede attributed the British defeat at Chester to their refusal to co-operate with Augustine; *HE*, ii. 2.

[77] Cf. Pope Gregory's letter to King Ethelbert stating that God makes good men rulers so that through them He may distribute His gifts to their subjects; *HE*, i. 32.

having overlordship throughout England two pagan kings who are known to have exercised as widespread powers.[78] Bede's idea of a united England was dominated by his belief in the church: he noted that Theodore of Canterbury was the first prelate obeyed by the whole English church[79] and that all the races in the British Isles were united by the study of the scriptures.[80] His work as a pioneer in translating Latin works (hymns, the creed, the Gospel of St John, part of Isidore) into English was due less to patriotic feeling for the vernacular than to a wish to help priests save souls.[81]

And yet there are indications that Bede recorded secular history because he loved England and the Anglo-Saxon people for themselves, not only as parts of the church. In *De Temporum Ratione* he gave an account of pagan Anglo-Saxon festivals, because, he said, he was unwilling to omit the customs of his own race while including those of the Greeks, Romans and Hebrews.[82] The introductory chapters in the *Ecclesiastical History* on the period before the conversion of the Anglo-Saxons suggest that he thought of England as a land with a history worthy of record from the earliest times.

Bede's sources for the pre-conversion period were scanty and it was beyond living memory. He adds little to his written authorities (such as Pliny, Orosius, Gildas, Constantius's *Life of St. Germanus*, the Life of St Alban[83] and the *Liber Pontificalis*[84]). There is little evidence that Bede made use of his own observation of ancient remains as a source of evidence[85] – he copied Gildas's errors concerning the Roman wall.[86] However, he did have a sense of geography. He realized the importance of geography in early history, putting events in their geographical setting. He demarcated the areas occupied by the Angles, Saxons and Jutes on the continent before the invasion of Britain and the subsequent areas of settlement in England. Bede was here reading history backwards, trying to account for the territories of the

[78] *HE*, ii. 5. See P. H. Blair, 'The Moore memoranda on Northumbrian history', p. 249.

[79] *HE*, iv. 2. Theodore enjoined ecclesiastical unity in the Council of Hertford in 673; *HE*, iv. 5. Bede particularly hated the Britons for disrupting the unity of the church; *HE*, v. 22, 23.

[80] *HE*, i. 1. Cf. iii, 6.

[81] Plummer, vol. 1, pp. lxxv, 409; Levison, 'Bede', p. 134; V. H. Galbraith, 'Nationality and language in medieval England' in *TRHS*, 4th series, xxii (1941), p. 119.

[82] *DTR*, c. 15 and pp. 211–13.

[83] See p. 4 and n. 32 above and Levison, 'Bede', p. 135 and nn. 3, 4.

[84] Led astray by the *Liber Pontificalis* (the official collection of Lives of the popes), Bede introduced (*HE*, i. 4) the non-existent Lucius, first Christian king of the Britons, into English history; see Levison, 'Bede', p. 135 and n. 2.

[85] For notices of Roman remains still to be seen in Bede's day see *HE*, i. 11, 12, 15. Bede noted the survival of Paulinus's church at Lincoln; *HE*, ii. 16. For a description of a guided tour attended by St Cuthbert of the Roman walls of Carlisle in Bede's prose *Life of St. Cuthbert*, see p. 70 below.

[86] *HE*, i. 5, 12. Bede also accepted (*HE*, i. 7) Gildas's apparently groundless attribution of the martyrdom of St Alban to the time of Diocletian (*De Ex.*, cc. 9, 10; cf. Levison, 'Bede', p. 135 n. 4). He uses (*HE*, i. 15 and v. 24) Gildas's statement for the date of the Anglo-Saxon invasion (*De Ex.*, c. 26) in *HE*, although in *DTR*, § 489 (Mommsen, p. 304) he gives another date; see R. G. Collingwood and J. N. L. Myres, *Roman Britain and the English Settlements* (Oxford 1936), p. 354.

Anglo-Saxon kingdoms of his own day and thinking in terms of boundaries (which did not exist in the migration period). He did not know that these peoples were to some extent mixed just before the invasions and remained so afterwards. The intermixture has been shown by modern archaeology. However, he was on the whole right about the continental origins of the Angles, Saxons and Jutes, and in connecting the settlers in Kent with those in the Isle of Wight and the part of Hampshire opposite.[87]

Bede's sense of geography also appears in his description of the British Isles, with which he begins his work, and in other descriptions (for example of the islands of Thanet,[88] Wight,[89] Anglesey,[90] Man[91] and Lindisfarne.[92] He noted that the Humber formed the dividing line of north and south England,[93] and that the Trent divided the northern from the southern Mercians.[94] Besides his geographical sense, Bede recognized the value of another source of evidence much used by modern scholars – the study of place-names. He gives place-name derivations, and his derivation of 'Ely' (as the district of eels, from the Old English ēl, an eel, and gē, a district) is accepted today as correct.[95]

Bede loved the Anglo-Saxon people in general, but he loved the Northumbrians in particular. He devoted a disproportionate amount of space to Northumbria, partly because he knew a lot about it, but partly because of an especial interest. In places his work reads like a panegyric on Northumbria. But it is a nostalgic panegyric. It is clear that Bede regarded the reign of King Edwin (616–32) as a golden age, with which his own times compared unfavourably (he deplored the contemporary civil wars and worldly monasteries[96]). Under King Edwin, he says, a mother with a new-born baby could walk from sea to sea without fear. And the king put drinking cups by springs for travellers.[97]

As has been said, the *Ecclesiastical History* owes its lasting reputation to Bede's ability as a historian. His grasp of historical method was unique in the middle ages. It appears in his chronology and in the competence with which

---

[87] *HE*, i. 15. On the truth of Bede's account of the continental origins of the Angles and Saxons and the areas of their settlement see Collingwood and Myres, op. cit., pp. 336–49 *passim*. Recent excavations have shown that contrary to the tentative statement in ibid., pp. 345–6, there are significant cultural links between Jutland and Kent; see J. N. L. Myres, *Anglo-Saxon Pottery and the Settlement of England* (Oxford 1969), pp. 95–6, map 7 and fig. 40, and Myres, 'The Angles, the Saxons and the Jutes' in *Proceedings of the British Academy*, lvi (1970), pp. 28–31.

[88] *HE*, i. 25.   [89] *HE*, iv. 16. For a description of Selsey see *HE*, iv. 13.

[90] *HE*, ii. 9.   [91] Ibid.   [92] *HE*, iii. 3.   [93] *HE*, i. 25; ii. 5, 9.

[94] *HE*, iii. 24.

[95] *HE*, iv. 19. See P. H. Reaney, *The Place-Names of Cambridgeshire and the Isle of Ely* (English Place-Name Soc., xix, 1943), p. 214. Cf. Bede on the name 'Augustine's Oak' (*HE*, ii. 2) and 'Tunnacaester' (*HE*, iv. 22), both now unidentified. For 'Inderauuda' (i.e. Beverley, *HE*, v. 2) see A. H. Smith, *The Place-Names of the East Riding of Yorkshire and York* (English Place-Name Soc., xiv, 1937), p. 12.

[96] See *HE*, v. 23, and Bede's letter to Egbert archbishop of York, printed in Plummer, vol. 1, pp. 405–23.

[97] *HE*, ii. 16.

he collected data. He was the first historian to date consistently by the era of the Incarnation—the system of dating A.D. and B.C. in use today. Bede's interest in chronology partly derived from study of the controversy over the calculation of Easter. He may have used as a source historical notes entered on paschal tables[98] (the tables used by priests to find the date of Easter), and these by their nature began at the Incarnation. Moreover Bede knew the work of Dionysius Exiguus, a Spaniard who two hundred years earlier had invented the system of dating from the Incarnation.[99] Bede was the first man to popularize the system: through his work it spread throughout western Europe in the eighth century.

It is hard to overemphasize the importance of this chronological achievement. Previously the Anglo-Saxons had usually dated by the regnal years of their kings, or by the indiction. Both systems had disadvantages: the regnal years of one Anglo-Saxon kingdom were inapplicable in another and incomprehensible abroad; as the indiction was a cycle of only fifteen years it was not always clear which cycle was intended.[100] Thus Bede solved a problem which had defeated Gildas (who gave only one date) and Nennius (who used no less than twenty-eight different eras).[101]

To obtain information, Bede exploited all resources. He ransacked the library and archives at Wearmouth/Jarrow, asked his friends to search for documents, and questioned people he met. Unlike most medieval writers he meticulously named most of his sources of information, literary, documentary and oral, giving a survey of some in the preface and mentioning others in the course of the work (his recognition of the importance of naming authorities also appears in two of his biblical commentaries: in the prefaces he instructed scribes to copy the authorities' names into the margin).[102] He mentions in the preface to the *Ecclesiastical History* that he used, for example, Gildas, Adamnan (*On the Holy Places*),[103] a book on the vision of

---

[98] On the question whether Bede used annals entered on paschal tables, see D. P. Kirby, 'Bede and Northumbrian chronology' in *EHR*, lxxviii (1963), pp. 514–27, and Levison, 'Bede', pp. 136–7. Scholars are not in agreement as to the date on which Bede began the year; see J. B. Wynn, 'The beginning of the year in Bede and the Anglo-Saxon Chronicle' in *Medium Ævum*, xxv (1956), pp. 70–8.

[99] The era was known to some historians of Bede's day but was not in general use: it was used once in the anonymous *Life of Abbot Ceolfrid* (c. 7), and in the calendar of Willibrord of 728 (see *The Calendar of St. Willibrord*, facsimile ed. H. A. Wilson, HBS, lv (1918), pp. 13, 42–3).

[100] For eras in use in the early middle ages see R. L. Poole, *Chronicles and Annals* (Oxford 1926), pp. 124–78.

[101] See p. 7 and n. 53 above.

[102] For the survival today of some of these marginalia see M. L. W. Laistner, 'Source marks in Bede MSS.' in *Journal of Theological Studies*, xxxiv (1933), pp. 350–5. Bede's biblical commentaries also show that he could spot textual corruptions; see *Bedae Venerabilis Expositio Actuum Apostolorum et Retractatio*, ed. Laistner, pp. 13, 88, 145. He also recognized the value of the Septuagint as the version of the Old Testament nearest to the Hebrew, and therefore collated it with the Vulgate; see Plummer, vol. 1, p. liv, and Levison, 'Bede', pp. 116–17, 120.

[103] *HE*, v. 16–17. Bede recorded that Aldfrith, king of Northumbria 685–704, circulated Adamnan's work, which is printed P. Geyer, *Itinera Hierosolymitana* (Corpus Scriptorum Ecclesiasticorum Latinorum, xxxix, Vienna 1898), pp. 221–97. Bede (*HE*, v. 16–17) conflated Adam-

Fursey (now lost)[104] and one on the miracles at Barking (also lost).[105] But he did not name all his literary sources – for examples his own work on the Holy Places and his *Life of St. Cuthbert*,[106] and Eddius Stephanus's *Life of Bishop Wilfrid*.[107]

Bede also states where he obtained his documents. Thus he records that Nothelm, later archbishop of Canterbury, searched the papal archives and brought back to Canterbury letters of Gregory the Great and other popes, which, on the advice of Albinus abbot of St Augustine's, Canterbury, he sent to Bede. Albinus himself searched the archives of Kent for documents about St Augustine's mission and sent them to Bede. So Bede was able to copy *verbatim* into the *Ecclesiastical History* such important and otherwise unknown documents as Augustine's letter asking Pope Gregory for advice on the mission and Gregory's long reply. The practice of copying documents *in extenso* into narrative works had been adopted in Northumbria before Bede wrote: Eddius Stephanus includes the text of a few in the *Life of Wilfrid*.[108]

Bede's preface acknowledges written information from various quarters.[109] Daniel bishop of Winchester sent information about Wessex, Bishop Cynebert sent some about Lindsey, Abbot Esi supplied facts on the history of East Anglia and the monks of Lastingham on Mercia. For the history of Northumbria, Bede relied on 'countless faithful witnesses who either know or remember facts, apart from what I know myself'. Here he was drawing on evidence by word of mouth. He makes frequent references throughout the work to oral information, particularly for the acts of saints.[110] The practice of naming a witness was widely accepted by hagiographers. It had become a convention and did not always reflect the truth (for example the ninth-century author of the *Life of St. Hubert* claimed to have himself witnessed events which took place two centuries earlier).[111] But when Bede cites a witness he is probably to be believed, because most of the men he names were well known and it seems unlikely that Bede would have spread false reports about them. The events he heard of through talk had taken place within living memory (that is within the century). Thus Bede says that he heard from Deda abbot of Partney how Paulinus baptized men in the Trent, and Deda had heard it from a very old man who had been baptized on that occasion. This must have

---

nan's work with his own work on the Holy Places, printed Geyer, op. cit., pp. 301–24. See Laistner, *A Hand-List of Bede MSS.*, p. 83. For the written sources of *HE*, see Plummer, vol. 1, p. xxiv n. 1, and pp. 15, 23 above.

[104] *HE*, iii. 19.   [105] *HE*, iv. 7–11.

[106] Bede's prose *Life of St. Cuthbert* is based on the anonymous *Life*. He implies in the preface to *HE* that he used the anonymous *Life* for *HE*, although he quotes passages (*HE*, iv. 27–30) word for word from his own *Life*.

[107] See *Eddius*, p. xii, and Levison, 'Bede', p. 138 and n. 1.

[108] See e.g. *Eddius*, cc. 30, 51.

[109] *HE*, preface. Cf. Plummer, vol. 1, p. xliv n. 3.

[110] For examples in *HE* see Plummer, vol. 1, p. xliv n. 3.

[111] See Colgrave, 'Bede's miracle stories', pp. 224–6.

happened before Paulinus left the north for Kent in 633.[112] The *Ecclesiastical History* is therefore a valuable repository of oral tradition.

Bede's qualities as a writer have been appreciated by readers at all periods. He can describe a man's appearance and character, convey an idea and stir the imagination. He was the first Englishman (and the last for many centuries) to say what someone looked like. He writes that Paulinus was 'tall, with a slight stoop, black hair, a thin face, a slender aquiline nose; he was at once both venerable and awe-inspiring in appearance.'[113] He throws light on King Edwin's character in the passage describing his ruminations on whether to become a Christian: 'He himself being a man of great natural sagacity would often sit alone for long periods in silence, but in his innermost thoughts he was deliberating with himself as to what he ought to do and which religion he should adhere to.'[114]

One of Bede's most famous passages is the speech he attributes to a chief man of Edwin's witan giving reasons in favour of the adoption of Christianity. It conveys an idea clearly and imaginatively.

'This is how the present life of man on earth, King, appears to me in comparison with that time which is unknown to us. You are sitting feasting with your ealdormen and thegns in winter time. The fire is burning on the hearth in the middle of the hall and all inside is warm, while outside the wintry storms of rain and snow are raging; and a sparrow flies swiftly through the hall. It enters in at one door and quickly flies out through the other. For the few moments it is inside, the storm and wintry tempest cannot touch it, but after the briefest moment of calm, it flits from your sight, out of the wintry storm and into it again. So this life of man appears but for a moment; what follows, or indeed what went before, we know not at all. If this new doctrine brings us more certain information, it seems right that we should accept it.'[115]

Finally an example can be taken of Bede's best descriptive writing – Drythelm's vision of heaven, hell, limbo and purgatory, which belongs to the same literary tradition which later produced Dante's *Divine Comedy*. It illustrates well Bede's concern with life and death. Drythelm, according to Bede, died one evening and came alive next day and described the 'many things to be dreaded or desired' which he had seen. Of purgatory he said:

'As we walked we came to a very deep and broad valley of infinite length. It lay on our left and one side of it was exceedingly terrible with raging fire, while the other was no less intolerable on account of the violent hail and icy snow which was drifting and blowing everywhere. Both sides were full of the souls of men which were

[112] *HE*, ii. 16.   [113] Ibid.   [114] *HE*, ii. 9 (cf. ii. 12).   [115] *HE*, ii. 13.

apparently tossed from one side to the other in turn, as if by the fury of the tempest. When the wretched souls could no longer endure the fierceness of the terrific heat, they leapt into the midst of the deadly cold; and when they could find no respite there, they jumped back only to burn once again in the midst of the unquenchable flames.'[116]

---

[116] *HE*, v. 12. For a similar vision, allegedly experienced by a boy near Durham in the eleventh century, see H. Farmer, 'The vision of Orm' in *An. Boll.*, lxxv (1957), pp. 72–82.

3

Anglo-Saxon Chronicles

Bede's two world chronicles[1] and the summary of events at the end of the *Ecclesiastical History*[2] are a different kind of historical writing from the rest of the *Ecclesiastical History* and the *History of the Abbots*. They are chronicles, recording briefly the events of each year in chronological order. Such chronicles are not in a literary form. A literary history has a sustained theme and the subject matter often overrides the chronological sequence of events. The distinction between the chronicle and literary history goes back to ancient times: Jerome's translation of Eusebius's *Chronicle* typifies the chronicle and Caesar's *Gallic War* literary history. Although this distinction was recognized throughout the middle ages,[3] it was not a rigid one. The yearly entries (that is the annals) in chronicles are sometimes detailed and well composed, so that they are almost literary in form.

Chronicles themselves can be divided into two groups, 'dead' chronicles and 'living' ones. 'Dead' chronicles were compiled by one man from earlier chronicles and histories. Bede's world chronicles belong to this group. 'Living' chronicles were composed by one man until his own time and then continued, altered and interpolated by him and/or by others. They were not regarded as complete, like literary works. Bede's chronological summary to the *Ecclesiastical History* was a 'living' chronicle. Possibly Bede himself added the annals to it for the years from 731 to 734,[4] and another man or men added more for some of the years from 735 to 766:[5] these annals are known as the Appendix to the *Ecclesiastical History*.

The appearances of 'living' chronicles is determined by their nature. The date of the year A.D. is in the left-hand margin. One line is usually left blank for each annal: the framework for the annals is sometimes drawn up for many years after the author's time,[6] in rather the same way as a

---

[1] See pp. 15–16.   [2] See p. 16.
[3] For references see C. W. Jones, *Bedae Opera de Temporibus* (Cambridge, Mass. 1943), p. 119 n. 2; cf. W. Stubbs in *GC*, vol. 2, p. 4.
[4] Plummer, vol. 2, p. 345.   [5] Printed in Plummer, vol. 1, pp. 361–3.
[6] e.g. one scribe of the copy of the Anglo-Saxon Chronicle in the Parker MS. (see p. 38) set out in advance the year-dates 924–30, and another scribe those for 1002–69: see *The Parker Chronicle and Laws*, ed. R. Flower and H. Smith (EETS, Oxford 1941), ff. 26, 31, 31ᵛ. There are numerous other examples of the chronological framework being constructed for the insertion of annals in future years. See e.g. BM MSS. Cotton Caligula A XV, ff. 132ᵛ–8 (11th c., printed in Liebermann, *U A-N G*, pp. 1–8), Royal 8 E XVIII, ff. 94–6 (annals of Reading or Leominster, 12th c., printed in ibid., pp. 9–12), Egerton 3142, ff. 83ᵛ–104ᵛ (the annals of Hickling, 13th-

modern diary provides for the future. Some annals cover more than their allotted space and overflow into the next year-space,[7] and annals are not entered for every year. As the author nears his own time he often devotes much more than one line – even a page or more – to a year, particularly if the framework is not already fixed. Often various hands of different dates have made entries, particularly towards the end of the chronicle.[8]

The earliest 'living' chronicles were written in the margins of tables drawn up to give the date of Easter for a series of years.[9] In England through-out the middle ages Easter tables were used as the framework for chronicles: either the table was set out with a space of one line ruled especially for an annal, on the right opposite each Easter date, or, more rarely, the annalist fitted his entries as best he could into the margins of a table written simply to give the dates of Easter.[10]

The purpose of chronicles was primarily to record events. The first Anglo-Saxon chronicles, which originated in the eighth century or before, were probably intended to remind readers of important events so that the full stories and related facts would come to mind.[11] Thus the annals of early chronicles are often cryptic and their significance sometimes lost today because of the passage of time. Just as a modern diary amuses its writer, although many entries are incomprehensible to the outsider, so a chronicle appealed to those who shared its author's folk memory. As the written record gained in importance over oral traditions, chronicles became more detailed and specific. Besides noting natural phenomena such as eclipses and storms, chronicles record the succession and genealogies of kings, their battles, and the succession of bishops. Probably such entries were made partly because the authors intended to support the established order by emphasizing its anti-quity and continuous history and the prowess and success of some rulers.

15th cc., printed in *JO*, pp. 417–39), Additional 47214, ff. 2ᵛ–20 (the annals of the Grey Frairs of Lynn, 14th c., printed by A. Gransden in *EHR*, lxii (1957), pp. 270–8).

[7] e.g. see Flower and Smith, op. cit., ff. 26, 31, 31ᵛ. For a later example see the fifteenth-century chronicle of Croxden (for which see C. Lynam, *The Abbey of St. Mary, Croxden, Staffordshire*, London 1911) in BM MS. Faustina B VI, pt i, ff. 41–65ᵛ *passim*, where the scribe had to rewrite many year-dates because annals took up more than the space allotted to them in the chrono-logical framework already drawn up.

[8] e.g. see Flower and Smith, op. cit., *passim*, and *The Chronicle of Melrose*, a facsimile, ed. A. O. and M. O. Anderson (limited edition, London 1936), *passim*.

[9] For the importance of Easter tables in the evolution of chronicles, see R. L. Poole, *Chronicles and Annals* (Oxford 1926), pp. 5 et seq.; see also P. Grosjean, appendix, 'Sur les annales anglaises du VIIᵉ siècle jointes à des tables pascales', to his 'La date du Colloque de Whitby' in *An. Boll.*, lxxviii (1960), pp. 255–60. The practice of entering annals on Easter tables continued throughout the middle ages: see e.g. BM MS. Cotton Caligula A XV, ff. 132ᵛ–8 (11th c., noticed in Gar-monsway, *ASC*, p. xxii and n. 2, and two pages reproduced after p. xxiii), the Reading/Leominster annals (see n. 6 above), Cotton Cleopatra D III, ff. 59–72 (annals of Hailes abbey, 13th–14th cc., extracts printed *MGH, Scriptores*, xvi, 482–3) and see the next note.

[10] e.g. BM MS. Cotton Nero C VII, ff. 80–84ᵛ, an early 12th c. Easter table for 961–1421, with 12th–15th cc. annals of Thorney abbey entered in the margins (extracts printed in *Mon. Angl.*, vol. 2, pp. 611–12).

[11] See Plummer, *SC*, vol. 2, p. xix.

The very second-rateness of chronicles gives them a value to the historian today. The author of a literary history arranged and selected his facts, working them into his theme. Few medieval historians approached Bede's skill in the assembling of data and in their judicious handling: many omitted facts which now seem important and emphasized others which today appear to be of little significance. But the chronicler was less selective and although a chronicle is jerky to read it is a mine of information. A chronicler was not necessarily a man of great gifts. All he required was an accurate eye and a lively interest in events. Very few good histories were written in the middle ages, but numerous useful chronicles were compiled from at least the eighth century until the end of the period. Many more were written than have survived. As chronicles are rough and unfinished they were not preserved with the same care as literary histories. Some were plundered by other chroniclers and then lost.[12]

Chronicles could be written when disturbed political conditions made the pursuit of scholarship and the composition of literary histories difficult. In Northumbria such a period followed Bede's death. Ceolwulf was forced from the throne and into a monastery in 737 and the kingdom began to disintegrate in civil strife. Viking attacks on Northumbria were frequent from the last half of the ninth century. In 867 the Danes attacked York, killing the king and his rival for the throne, and conquered the country.

Besides the Appendix to the *Ecclesiastical History*, a chronicle later known as the *Gesta Northanhumbrorum (Deeds of the Northumbrians)* was written in eighth-century Northumbria.[13] It was a history of the Northumbrian kings from 732 until about 802, beginning with a genealogy of the royal house. The chronicle is now lost and its text can only be recovered from the works of later chroniclers who extracted from it. It was apparently used as a source by a late tenth century Northumbrian compiler,[14] whose work was embodied in the early twelfth century *Historia Regum (History of the Kings)* attributed to Symeon of Durham. It was also used by the author of the chronicle compiled at Melrose and by the author of the so-called *Historia post Obitum Bedae*, both writing in the twelfth century. It is impossible to be certain of the text because of its later accretions, and no attempt has been made to print it. However, some of the annals can be identified with certainty and a few of these appear to have been written soon after the events recorded; for example eclipses and other natural phenomena are noted,

---

[12] e.g. the Northumbrian annals noticed below. For the loss of copies of the Anglo-Saxon Chronicle see Plummer, *SC*, vol. 2, pp. xxxviii–cii *passim*, and D. Whitelock, a review of Smith and Flower, op. cit., in *EHR*, lvii (1942), 120–2.

[13] For this work and its use by the later authors mentioned below see *RH*, vol. 1, pp. xxvi–xxxi; *SD*, vol. 2, pp. xvii–xix; P. H. Blair, 'Some observations on the *Historia Regum* attributed to Symeon of Durham' in Chadwick, *Celt and Saxon*, pp. 86–99.

[14] Arnold (*SD*, vol. 2, pp. xvii–xxv) postulated that this compiler was a 'Cuthbertine' of Chester-le-Street, writing in the mid-tenth century. However, there is no evidence supporting this view; see H. S. Offler, *Medieval Historians of Durham* (Durham 1958), p. 9, and *Asser*, p. lix.

and the month and day of the week given for events which someone living much later would not have remembered. The late tenth century Northumbrian compiler also seems to have used another lost Northumbrian chronicle for the years from 888 to 957.[15] This was apparently a very brief chronicle of the Viking kingdom of York, but as far as the text is known it is of considerable value to the historian today as the only contemporary work throwing light on Northumbrian history in this period.

While Latin historical writing was struggling for survival in Northumbria, the first vernacular annals were written in Wessex. The Anglo-Saxon Chronicle was begun in King Alfred's reign. The Alfredian chronicle covered the period from the Creation of the world to 891, having as its main theme the history of Wessex.[16] It has continuations, of varying length and content in the different manuscripts (the longest reaches to the accession of Henry II). The Chronicle is an invaluable source for the historian today because it is an almost contemporary record of events for about five hundred years. Usually it is factual – although sometimes it gives rational explanations for events[17] – and on the whole it is remarkably accurate. Nevertheless it must be used with caution. For example, its estimate of the number of ships in several Viking fleets is probably not reliable,[18] and its chronology is in places baffling: this is partly because the copyists were sometimes misled by the annalistic arrangement (failing to notice blank annals and so dating events too early),[19] and partly because it is not always clear on what day the chronicler began the year.[20] Moreover not all the continuations are of equal

15 See Blair, 'Observations', pp. 104–6.

16 The most recent edition of the Anglo-Saxon Chronicle, in all its versions, in an English translation with a definitive introduction, is *The Anglo-Saxon Chronicle*, ed. D. Whitelock, with D. C. Douglas and S. I. Tucker (London 1961): the passages cited below from ASC are based on this edition. The edition by G. N. Garmonsway, *The Anglo-Saxon Chronicle* (Everyman's Library, London 1953, corrected ed. 1955), is also excellent and has an interesting introduction. For a standard edition of two of the original texts, see *Two of the Saxon Chronicles Parallel*, ed. C. Plummer on the basis of an edition by J. Earle (Oxford 1892, 1899, 2 vols, reprinted 1952, with two notes by D. Whitelock). For editions of the different versions see pp. 38 nn. 55–8, 39 n. 59 below.

17 e.g. *s.a.* 839 (Ā C) Beorhtric king of the West Saxons helped Offa because he had married his daughter: *s.a.* 894 (895 C D) the Danes could not remain in Wirral as the cattle and corn had been ravaged: *s.a.* 914 (917 Ā, 915 C D) the king guarded the south side of the Severn estuary so that the Danes could not land: *s.a.* 1037 (C D) Harold was chosen king, and Harthacanute deserted because he was too long in Denmark.

18 See P. H. Sawyer, *The Age of the Vikings* (London 1962), pp. 120–3. For the value of the Chronicle as a source for the Viking raids and settlement in general, see ibid., pp. 13–25, 143–8.

19 e.g. from 754 to 845 Ā dates events two and even three years too early; Plummer, *SC*, vol. 2, pp. cii–ciii. A scribe who continued Ā copied the year-dates for 924 to 932 but omitted 930; J. A. Robinson, *The Times of St. Dunstan* (Oxford 1923), pp. 19–20. For the reason why the annals for 916–20 in Ā are dated three years too late, see D. Whitelock in *EHR*, lvii (1942), p. 120.

20 See M. L. R. Beaven, 'The beginning of the year in the Alfredian chronicle (866–87)' in *EHR*, xxxiii (1918), pp. 328–42, R. H. Hodgkin, 'The beginning of the year in the English chronicle' in *EHR*, xxxix (1924), pp. 497–510, A. J. Thorogood, 'The Anglo-Saxon Chronicle in the reign of Ecgberht' in *EHR*, xlviii (1933), pp. 353–63. For further references see *English*

value (of the five now extant, two are post-Conquest in their present form).[21] I shall discuss the Alfredian chronicle first, and then the continuations (but the latters' accounts of the Norman Conquest and settlement will be considered in more detail in later chapters).[22]

Apart from its historical importance, the Chronicle made a significant contribution to the development of the English language. It starts with short, simple statements. For example under 702 it records: 'In this year Coenred of the Southumbrians succeeded to the kingdom' and under 703: 'In this year bishop Haedde died, and he held the bishopric of Winchester for twenty seven years.' Towards the end the annalists were writing expressive English prose. There is, for example, the first character-sketch of a king of England (excluding Bede's account of Edwin of Northumbria). It says of William the Conqueror: 'He was a very wise, and very powerful and more worshipful man and stronger than any predecessor of his had been. He was gentle to good men who loved God, and stern beyond all measure to those who resisted his will. . . . Amongst other things the good security he made in this country is not to be forgotten – so that any honest man could travel over his kingdom without injury with his bosom full of gold.'[23]

The problem arises why the Chronicle was written in the vernacular, as Latin was the language of educated men. And, although vernacular chronicles were common after 1200, they were extremely rare before that date. Apart from the Anglo-Saxon Chronicle, the only vernacular chronicles were some Irish annals and the Russian chronicle of Novgorod.[24] One explanation for the use of the vernacular is that it was part of the Alfredian cultural revival – a product of King Alfred's policy of promoting the vernacular. Under his rule the English writ was increasingly used,[25] and Alfred himself collected together into one book the Old Engish laws of his predecessors. His enthusiasm for English appears in his translations of standard Latin works – Gregory's *Pastoral Care*, Orosius's *History against the Pagans*, Boethius's *Consolation of Philosophy* and St Augustine's *Soliloquies*.[26] Alfred justified his translations on historical grounds: the Greeks and Romans had translated the Hebrew bible, so it was right for him to translate important books 'into the language we can all understand'.[27] But the practical reason for the use of the vernacular lay in the conditions of his own times. Though he used English partly to enable his nobles to read or hear famous works, his main purpose

Historical Documents, vol. 1, *c. 500–1042*, ed. D. Whitelock (London 1955), p. 130, and J. B. Wynn, 'The beginning of the year in Bede and the Anglo-Saxon Chronicle' in *Medium Ævum*, xxv (1956), pp. 70–8.

[21] Plummer, *SC*, vol. 2, pp. cxxii–cxxiv.

[22] See pp. 92–4, 142–3.   [23] ASC (E), pp. 163–4. Cf. p. 93 below.

[24] See Garmonsway, *ASC*, pp. xv–xvi.

[25] For the growth of the practice of writing legal memoranda in English see F. M. Stenton, *The Latin Charters of the Anglo-Saxon Period* (Oxford 1955), pp. 43–9.

[26] See F. M. Stenton, *Anglo-Saxon England* (Oxford 1947), pp. 267–70, 273.

[27] See the preface to Alfred's translation of the *Pastoral Care*, ed. Sweet. For another modern English rendering, with further references, see Whitelock, *Documents*, pp. 818–19.

was to help the clergy as administrators and pastors. There was a shortage of good Latin scholars. As he says of the time before his accession, with some exaggeration, in the preface to the *Pastoral Care*: 'So completely had learning decayed in England that there were very few on this side of the Humber who could understand their services in English or even translate a letter from Latin into English, and I think there were not many beyond the Humber. There were so few of them that I cannot recall even a single one south of the Thames when I succeeded to the kingdom.'[28]

There is the problem whether the Anglo-Saxon Chronicle was written at the command of Alfred.[29] If, as is likely, Asser's *Life of King Alfred* is genuine,[30] Alfred probably commissioned it in 893; it is not therefore unlikely that two years earlier he commissioned someone to write the history of the West Saxon dynasty to 891. It is well established that Alfred was interested in history. This is shown by the fact that he translated Orosius and by the frequent references to Anglo-Saxon history in his translation of the *Pastoral Care* (Alfred was not a literal translator; he paraphrased and interpolated comments). His reliance on historical precedent appears in the argument he uses to justify translating, and in his law code, which is a collection of earlier material and also mentions great law-makers of the past.[31]

Alfred's claim to be patron of the Chronicle is strengthened by the fact that the Alfredian chronicle is essentially a history of Wessex told with a touch of propaganda in favour of the ruling dynasty. The propagandist element appears in the story of Cerdic and Cynric, the West Saxon leaders of the late fifth and early sixth centuries and founders of the royal house. The Chronicle records that they conquered Wessex from southern Hampshire.[32] But the weight of modern archaeological evidence shows that the earliest Anglo-Saxon settlements in Wessex were in the upper Thames valley,[33] not in southern Hampshire, and took place at least half a century before the dates given by the Chronicle for Cerdic and Cynric.[34] Similarly the propagandist motive must surely account for the total suppression of any reference to the part played in the settlement by the Jutes – which was well known to Bede

---

[28] *Pastoral Care*, ed. Sweet, p. 3. For the element of exaggeration in Alfred's statement see Stenton, *Latin Charters*, p. 49. Alfred had at his court Mercian scholars such as Werferth; see Stenton, *Anglo-Saxon England*, p. 268.

[29] This view was firmly held by Plummer, *SC*, vol. 2, p. civ, and recently has been adopted by R. H. C. Davis, 'Alfred the Great: propaganda and truth' in *History*, lvi (1971), pp. 173-7.

[30] See pp. 47-51.

[31] See the preface to King Alfred's law-code, printed F. Liebermann, *Die Gesetze der Angelsachsen* (Halle 1903-16, 3 vols), vol. 1, pp. 26-47 *passim*. Cf. Whitelock, *Documents*, pp. 332, 372-3.

[32] ASC, s.a. 495, 508, 519, 527, 530, 534.

[33] For a summary of the evidence supporting the theory that the earliest settlements were in the upper Thames valley see J. N. L. Myres, 'Wansdyke and the origin of Wessex' in *Essays in British History presented to Sir Keith Feiling*, ed. H. R. Trevor-Roper (London 1964), pp. 11-12 and nn.

[34] There has recently been discovered some evidence of Anglo-Saxon settlement in south Hampshire in the period when, according to ASC, Cerdic and Cynric lived; see ibid., p. 13 and nn.

and is mentioned by Asser.[35] A propagandist element seems to occur also in the genealogies of the West Saxon kings in the Chronicle: the latter gives two versions of the royal pedigree, one old and one new.[36] The most ancient, copied from a now lost source, traces the ancestry back to Woden. But apparently such a heathen origin did not suit the chronicler of Alfred's day, for he included another, more modern, version which extended the genealogy back from Woden to Adam, thus giving the West Saxon kings a biblical ancestry.

Although the Alfredian chronicle has a strong bias in favour of the West Saxon dynasty, it is not an official history in the worst sense. Its bias does not, as far as is known, amount to the conscious suppression of some facts and overemphasis of others to give a calculated impression. In view of Alfred's stand against the Danes, at a time when the other Anglo-Saxon kingdoms had succumbed, a certain patriotic fervour was justified (incipient national feeling also appears in the English translation of Bede's *Ecclesiastical History* made in Alfred's reign though not by him personally: the translator omitted material not connected directly with England).[37] But in the reign of Alfred's successor Edward the Elder (899–924), a version of the Chronicle was produced which was very like official history of the dishonest kind. The Chronicle was not only continued under Edward, but also the account of the last years of Alfred's reign was revised. The purpose of the revision was to give a slant in favour of Edward instead of Alfred. The original of this revised version is lost, but its contents can be inferred from the chronicle of Æthelweard the ealdorman, who used it in the late tenth century.[38]

A comparison of the annal for 893 in the Alfredian chronicle with Æthelweard's version shows significant differences. The Edwardian chronicle suppresses all mention of King Alfred. Instead it gives prominence to the young Edward who was ignored in the Alfredian chronicle under this year. The Edwardian version omits Alfred's activities as army commander, including his division of the forces into two rotas. But it is fuller on the subsequent campaign against the Danes, centring events on Edward, not on Alfred as does the original version. Edward, hearing that the Danes had ravaged Northamptonshire and Berkshire, goes to Farnham (the Alfredian

---

[35] See *HE*, i. 15. *Asser* (c. 2) states that Alfred's own mother was descended from the Jutish chieftains who led the Jutish migration.

[36] ASC, *s.a.* 597, 855. For the West Saxon genealogy see H. M. Chadwick, *The Origin of the English Nation* (Cambridge 1924), pp. 56 et seq., 252–83. F. M. Stenton, 'The south-western element in the Old English chronicle' in *Essays in Medieval History presented to Thomas Frederick Tout*, ed. A. G. Little and F. M. Powicke (Manchester 1925), p. 23 n. 3, suggests that the descent from Adam was added after the Chronicle was sent to the monasteries for copying (soon after 891).

[37] See D. Whitelock, 'The Old English Bede' in *Proceedings of the British Academy*, xlviii (1962), p. 62. Professor Whitelock argues convincingly that there is no good evidence associating the English Bede with Alfred's scheme for translating standard works into English; ibid., pp. 57–78 *passim*.

[38] For the 'official' element in the ASC used by Æthelweard, see A. Campbell, *Æthelweard*, pp. xxviii–xxix. For other aspects of the version of *ASC* used by Æthelweard see p. 44 below.

chronicle merely records that the English army defeated the Danes at Farnham – making no reference to Edward). And on his arrival the English soldiers 'exulted, being set free [from care] by the prince's arrival, like sheep brought to the pastures by the help of the shepherd'.[39]

There can be little doubt, therefore, that the Anglo-Saxon Chronicle to the death of Edward the Elder was a court production, at least to the extent that it was intended to please the king. It had no edificatory purpose in a religious sense. It was primarily a secular record, although, because of the close connection of church and state, it recorded important ecclesiastical events (such as the succession of archbishops and bishops). However, there is no conclusive evidence that King Alfred actually commissioned the Chronicle. In fact there is evidence which could be interpreted as contrary to the theory of Alfred's direct patronage. The Alfredian chronicle shows west country affinities.[40] It is particularly well informed about Somerset and Dorset. Under 867 it records exactly where a bishop of Sherborne was buried ('in the cathedral cemetery'). Under 878 it has a detailed account of Alfred's retreat to Athelney, the expedition to the now unidentified Egbert's stone (near Frome), Guthrum's baptism at Aller, and the chrism-loosing at Wedmore. Obviously the annalist had minute knowledge of the topography of the region. Æthelweard's chronicle provides additional evidence connecting the Chronicle with the west country. Æthelweard, an ealdorman of the south-western shires, used a version of the Chronicle with a number of facts not found in the surviving copies, and many of these additions relate to his own neighbourhood.[41] It therefore seems likely that the author of the Alfredian chronicle was from the west country. It has been argued that the author's patron was a west country nobleman.[42] But equally well King Alfred, who employed scholars from many places, could have commissioned a west-countryman to write the Chronicle.

The Alfredian chronicle itself can be compared with a Russian doll: it incorporates earlier annals which in their turn incorporated still earlier ones, and so on.[43] These early Wessex annals, all of which are now lost, may well have been in Latin. The latest such chronicle to be copied into the Alfredian chronicle was probably compiled in about 855, after the death of Alfred's

---

[39] *Æthelweard*, p. 49.

[40] See Stenton, 'The south-western element in the Old English chronicle', *passim*. Stenton (*Anglo-Saxon England*, p. 683) dismisses the argument put forward by some scholars that Alfred himself wrote the chronicle, on the ground that ASC, *s.a.* 853, states that Pope Leo consecrated Alfred king when he first came to Rome as a child; Stenton comments: 'It is incredible that Alfred himself should have confused decoration, or even the rite of confirmation at the pope's hands, with an anointing to kingship.'

[41] See *Æthelweard*, pp. xxvii–xxxii *passim*.

[42] Stenton, 'The south-western element in the Old English chronicle', pp. 22–4.

[43] For various views on the earlier chronicles incorporated in the Alfredian chronicle see F. M Stenton, 'The foundations of English history' in *TRHS*, ix (1926), pp. 163–7, Chadwick, *Origin*, pp. 23–5, and G. H. Wheeler, 'The genealogy of the early West Saxon kings' in *EHR*, xxxvi (1921), pp. 161–71 *passim*.

father Æthelwulf. The 'Æthelwulf chronicle' was apparently made up of various sources such as Bede's chronological summary, lists and genealogies of kings, lists of bishops and the like, and also, it seems, a series of West Saxon annals covering the period from the mid-seventh to the mid-eighth century.[44] These hypothetical West Saxon annals appear to have been written up fairly close to the events they record. This is suggested by details in the Chronicle which could hardly have been retained in folk memory. For example under 661 the Chronicle records that Cenwalh fought at 'Posentes-byrig' (the place is unidentified), and under 671 that 'there was a great mortality of birds' (such an event does not seem important enough to have been remembered for many years).

The sources of the Anglo-Saxon Chronicle for the period from the landing of Cerdic and Cynric in 495 to the mid-seventh century are obscure.[45] Clearly this section was compiled in Alfred's time but it probably used oral traditions, partly in the form of epic poems. Thus the entries about Ceawlin in the Chronicle between 550 and 593 are clearly derived from a separate saga about this king. The use of poetry is also suggested by the occurrence of alliterative words (Cerdic and Cynric, Cuthwine and Ceawlin, and the rest). Such alliteration is particularly noticeable in the royal genealogies. It is therefore problematical how much truth the genealogies contain. For example the occurrence of Giwis after Wig (the 'wi' alliterates) is suspect: the personal name may well have been invented from Geuissae, the generic name of the West Saxons in ancient times.[46] Only two of the names in the genealogies (Wig and Freawine) can apparently be verified from other sources.[47]

Another reason for suspecting the historical accuracy of the early part of the Chronicle is the frequent appearance of eponyms. Here one must distinguish between personal names related to pre-Saxon place-names, and those related to place-names of the post-migration period. Thus the warrior leader called 'Port' obviously never existed: the name is an eponym to explain the name Portsmouth where, according to the Chronicle, he first landed. And the name 'Wihtgar' who, the Chronicle records, settled in the Isle of Wight, was invented to explain the name Wight.[48] Nevertheless, the author of the eponyms may of course have been finding suitable names for the real heroes whose deeds were remembered in folk tradition. The case with place-names containing the element 'Cerdic' is different. The Chronicle mentions places with this element in connection with the hero; thus Cerdic fought at 'Cerdi-

---

[44] For doubts about the previous existence of these early chronicles see D. P. Kirby, 'Problems of early West Saxon history' in *EHR*, lxxx (1965), p. 10 and nn. for further references.

[45] For the possibility that ASC incorporates material of earlier date than the mid-seventh century see Stenton, 'The foundations of English history', p. 164, and Wheeler, op. cit., pp. 167–71. R. G. Collingwood and J. N. L. Myres, *Roman Britain and the English Settlements* (Oxford 1936), pp. 327–8, 396–410 *passim*, indicate the necessity of treating this part of ASC with caution. Some of the questions it raises are discussed by Kirby, 'Problems of early West Saxon history', pp. 10–29.

[46] See Chadwick, *Origin*, p. 31.   [47] Ibid., pp. 115 et seq., 125 et seq., 136, 252.

[48] See Collingwood and Myres, op. cit., p. 398 and n. 5.

cesora' and 'Cerdicesford'.[49] As there is no evidence for the existence of these place-names in pre-Saxon times, they strengthen the case for a historic Cerdic. A final problem in assessing the value of the Chronicle is chronological. The dates tend to be arbitrary, as if the compiler had tried to distribute his material fairly evenly among the years.[50] However, though the exact attribution of events to particular years may be wrong, the general chronological picture is probably correct.[51]

When the Alfredian chronicle was completed to 891 it was sent to monasteries throughout England for copying (Alfred's translation of the *Pastoral Care* was distributed in the same way[52]). The Chronicle was continued by the addition of instalments which the monasteries received from some source or sources now unknown.[53] These covered the periods from 894 to 924, 925 to 975 and 983 to 1018. The Mercian Register, a brief chronicle of the Mercian kingdom from 902 to 924, was also incorporated.[54] From the beginning of the tenth century the text of the Chronicle varies greatly in the different manuscripts. This was partly due to the way the chroniclers treated the new instalments as they arrived, adapting them to suit their own interests by inserting local material. And it was partly because some instalments did not reach them at all. The chroniclers left blank or provided their own material for periods not covered by the instalments.

Probably the full story of the writing of the Chronicle will never be known because many manuscripts are now lost. The extant manuscripts are commonly designated as $\bar{A}$ (the 'Parker manuscript', Corpus Christi College, Cambridge, MS. 173),[55] B (BM MS. Cotton Tiberius A VI), C (BM MS. Cotton Tiberius B I),[56] D (BM MS. Cotton Tiberius B IV),[57] E (Bodleian Library, Oxford, MS. Laud 636),[58] and F (BM MS. Cotton

---

[49] See Chadwick, *Origin*, pp. 19 et seq.

[50] See ibid., pp. 21 et seq.

[51] See J. N. L. Myres's review of V. I. Evison, *The Fifth-century Invasions South of the Thames* (London 1965) in *EHR*, lxxxi (1966), pp. 344–5.

[52] *Pastoral Care*, ed. Sweet, p. 8.

[53] For the continuations to the Alfredian chronicle, see Plummer, *SC*, vol. 2, pp. xxxviii–cxxii *passim*. For a short and very lucid account of them, see J. A. Robinson, op. cit., pp. 16–24. See also for the question of the source of the instalments *The Battle of Brunanburh*, ed. A. Campbell (London 1938), pp. 1–7, 34–5.

[54] The Mercian Register is printed in *ASC* pp. 59–68.

[55] Part of $\bar{A}$ is printed in *The Parker Chronicle* (832–900), ed. A. H. Smith (London 1939). For a facsimile see Flower and Smith, op. cit. $\bar{A}$ is not the author's first draft but is a copy of an earlier manuscript; see Plummer, *SC*, vol. 2, pp. cii–civ.

[56] Printed in *The C-Text of the Old English Chronicles*, ed. H. A. Rositzke (Beiträge zur englischen Philologie, xxxiv, Bochum-Langendreer 1940). The continuation in C relating to the reign of Ethelred II is printed in *English and Norse Documents relating to the Reign of Ethelred the Unready*, ed. M. Ashdown (Cambridge 1930).

[57] Printed in *An Anglo-Saxon Chronicle from British Museum Cotton MS., Tiberius B IV*, ed. E. Classen and F. E. Harmer (Manchester 1926).

[58] Printed in Plummer, *SC*, vol. 1 and *The Peterborough Chronicle, 1070–1154*, ed. C. Clark (2nd ed., Oxford 1970). A facsimile edition is by D. Whitelock, *The Peterborough Chronicle* (Early English Manuscripts in Facsimile, iv, Copenhagen 1954).

Domitian A VIII).[59] The first five of these are of textual importance and Ā is the earliest. Ā provides the evidence that the Chronicle originally extended to 891; to that date Ā is in one hand of about 900, which ends at 891, writing the year-date 892 below. Ā was continued apparently at Winchester in a number of tenth-century hands until 924, incorporating the 894 to 924 continuation and the Mercian Register. It was laid aside until 958 when it was continued, probably still at Winchester, until 1001; it included the 925 to 975 continuation and annals relating to Winchester. Immediately after the Norman Conquest Ā was at Christ Church, Canterbury, where it was continued from 1066 until 1070 (it does not have the 983 to 1018 continuation). A copy of Ā was made at Winchester before it was transferred to Canterbury.[60]

Soon after the Chronicle to 891 was completed a copy went to some northern monastery, perhaps Ripon. It was there revised: Bede's preface to the *Ecclesiastical History* was substituted for the genealogy of the West Saxon royal house and material from Bede's chronological summary was inserted into the annals. It was continued to 1023; although it did not have the 894 to 924 continuation or the Mercian Register, it did have the 925 to 975 and 983 to 1018 continuations. It incorporated annals from the *Gesta Northanhumbrorum* and from continental chronicles (the Annals of Rouen and the Norman Annals).

Probably by 977 a copy of the Chronicle to that date was at Abingdon.[61] This version had the first continuation from 894 until 917 (but not the section from 918 to 924), and that from 925 to 975. It is now lost and known only from its descendants, B and C. B is a copy of it to 977 made in about 1000, which was not continued. C was written in the mid-eleventh century and was continued at Abingdon to 1066, incorporating the 983 to 1018 continuation.

No manuscript survives of the northern, 'Ripon', version of the Chronicle. It is known only from two manuscripts which descended from it, D and E, both of comparatively late date. The provenance of D is uncertain: York, Worcester and Evesham have all been suggested.[62] The earliest hand in it is mid-eleventh century and the latest twelfth century. It was continued in southern England until 1079. The text in E is post-Conquest. It was written for Peterborough abbey, in one hand to 1121 and in other hands contem-

[59] Printed *Annales Domitiani Latini: an Edition*, ed. F. P. Magoun, jun. (Medieval Studies of the Pontifical Institute of Medieval Studies, ix (Toronto 1947), pp. 235–95).

[60] BM MS. Cotton Otho B XI, written *c.* 1025, almost totally destroyed in the 1731 Cottonian fire; Plummer, *SC*, vol. 2, xxviii, xcviii–ci. For the possibility that there was another copy of ASC in the tenth century, at Winchester, see D. Whitelock in *EHR*, lvii (1942), p. 121.

[61] By that date Abingdon abbey had been revived under St Ethelwold. This version of ASC has entries relating to Abingdon 971–1050.

[62] A York provenance is supported by Stenton, *Anglo-Saxon England*, p. 681, and by Whitelock, *Peterborough Chronicle*, pp. 29 et seq. Garmonsway, *ASC*, pp. xxxvii–xxxix, takes the claims of Worcester seriously. Plummer, *SC*, vol. 2, pp. lxxvi–lxxvii, suggests Evesham.

porary with the annals to 1154. In the pre-Conquest section it has interpolated passages relating to Peterborough and some Latin annals. It is based on early material: to 1023 E is very like D, and is a descendant of the northern recension of the Chronicle; from 1023 to the early twelfth century it has a version of the Chronicle written at St Augustine's, Canterbury. Both C and E survived the Conquest and their frequent agreement until D ends in 1079 suggests that they received information for their continuations from a common source. Moreover traces in later works of lost versions of the Chronicle suggest that the common source survived well into the twelfth century.[63]

Although both D and E survived the Norman Conquest, ultimately the Conquest killed the Chronicle, mainly because English was no longer the language of the ruling class (the Peterborough version survived the longest presumably because it was written in an area which became a centre of English resistance). Norman French was spoken by the secular magnates and Latin was the language of the church. The interpolation of Latin annals in E reflects the transition to Latin.[64] The change is shown even more clearly in F, a bilingual version of the Chronicle written at St Augustine's, Canterbury. The English text, which is paraphrased, is in the left-hand column and the Latin one in the right. Significantly the marginal signs made in the middle ages to draw attention to particular passages are all next to the Latin translation.

The nature of the Chronicle gradually changed from the early tenth century onwards. The second instalment, from 925 to 975, was brief. So to supplement it the chronicler inserted a number of verses into the annals. These poems are virtually panegyrics on royal persons, celebrating some particular event connected with royalty – a coronation or a victory. A well-known example is the poem on the battle of Brunanburh. As literature these verses are in the ancient style and tradition of Norse sagas. Poems of this type must have appealed to the audience of the Chronicle because not only were four included in the tenth century portion,[65] but another, as late as 1065, was inserted to commemorate the death of Edward the Confessor.

Although these archaic poems in general praise the achievements, especially military ones, of the Anglo-Saxon kings, representing them as heroic warriors, a gradual alteration in the attitude to the ruling house can be detected. As the unification of England proceeded, the Chronicle began to reflect incipient national feeling. This could involve criticism of the king. Thus the poem on King Edgar, under 959, criticizes him for inviting foreigners to England and being too fond of 'evil foreign customs'. The Chronicle identifies itself with the English people rather than the king. The annal for 1009, for example, combines both criticism of the king and a sense of

[63] Whitelock, *ASC*, pp. xvii, xix, xx.
[64] See Plummer, *SC*, vol. 2, pp. xxxviii–lxvii *passim*, and J. A. Robinson, op. cit., pp. 22–3.
[65] ASC, *s.a.* 937, 942, 973, 975. For these poems see Campbell, *Brunanburh*, pp. 36–8 and *passim*.

national interest. It blames King Ethelred for the loss of the English fleet, which he abandoned, and comments that on the withdrawal of the ships 'the toil of all the nation was lightly brought to nought – no better than this was the victory which all the English people had expected'. And so the Chronicle developed an objective attitude to the 'establishment'. And it maintained a fair degree of impartiality even after the Norman Conquest.[66]

The Chronicle's increasing objectivity was undoubtedly partly due to the process of localization which began towards the end of the tenth century. The authors of the different versions were attached to the interest of their own monasteries and (except for the chronicler writing at Winchester) had no close connection with the royal court. They inserted entries of local interest – the Winchester chronicler inserted the succession of the bishops of Winchester, the Abingdon one inserted the succession of the abbots of Abingdon. The most extreme example of localization is the Peterborough copy of the Chronicle: not only did the post-Conquest writer interpolate the previous section with local material, but also after the Conquest local news gained almost equal importance with national information.[67]

The localization of the Chronicle had one good result: it ensured the Chronicle's lasting influence. The Chronicle became part of the historiographical tradition of the monasteries where it had taken root. Although it came to an end in the course of the twelfth century, Latin chronicles grew from it. The process of translating the Anglo-Saxon Chronicle into Latin had begun early. Asser (if he was the author of the *Life of Alfred*) used the Chronicle, translating it into Latin.[68] Æthelweard, in the late tenth century, was heavily indebted to the Chronicle – also translating it into Latin.[69] After the Conquest it was extensively used, translated into Latin, by Anglo-Norman chroniclers such as Florence of Worcester and 'Symeon of Durham'. Not only was it plundered and translated by post-Conquest writers, but it also helped determine the type of their chronicles: like the Anglo-Saxon chroniclers they kept to the strictly annalistic form, emphasized local events, and had an objective attitude to the ruling classes.

[66] See p. 93. [67] See pp. 142–3. [68] See p. 46.
[69] The question of the influence of ASC after the Conquest is discussed more fully on pp. 142–8 *passim*.

4

Anglo-Saxon
Secular Narrative History and
Royal Biography

As has been pointed out above, the Anglo-Saxon Chronicle and the earlier Latin chronicles written in England belong to a specific historiographical type. They are brief annalistic records. Though the Anglo-Saxon Chronicle included historical poems and some passages of excellent narrative, the tradition of creative historical writing was so slender in Anglo-Saxon England after Bede as to be almost non-existent. It is true that historical narrative occurs in the three surviving biographies of Anglo-Saxon kings, *De Rebus Gestis Ælfredi* (the *Life of King Alfred*), the Life of King Canute (which goes under the name *Encomium Emmae Reginae*) and the *Vita Ædwardi Regis* (the *Life of King Edward*, the Confessor). But none of these works was by an Englishman. A Welshman, Asser, was almost certainly the author of the *Life of King Alfred*, and the other two Lives were by Flemings. Perhaps, however, it was an Anglo-Saxon who wrote the now lost Life of King Athelstan in Latin verse, parts of which are preserved in William of Malmesbury's *Gesta Regum Anglorum*.

The only serious attempt by an Anglo-Saxon, after Bede, at historical composition in Latin was the chronicle written in the late tenth century by Æthelweard.[1] Æthelweard was a layman of some standing, being related to the West Saxon royal family and an ealdorman of Wessex from about 975 to 1002. The Anglo-Saxon Chronicle records that in 994 he went with Ælfheah, bishop of Winchester, to negotiate peace on behalf of King Ethelred I with Olaf Tryvasson. His son Æthelmar probably succeeded him as ealdorman and was also an important man: it was probably he who led the west country thegns to submit to the Danish King Swein at Bath in 1013.

Æthelweard has the distinction of being the first layman to write history in England. He exemplifies the growing interest of the lay nobility in intel-

---

[1] Printed *The Chronicle of Æthelweard*, ed., with an English translation, A. Campbell (Nelson's Medieval Texts, 1962). For the facts known about his life, see ibid., pp. xii–xvi, and E. E. Barker, 'The Anglo-Saxon Chronicle used by Æthelweard' in *BIHR*, xl (1967), pp. 85–91. It should be noted that Æthelweard the chronicler is not identified as the ealdorman beyond doubt; see ibid., p. xxxvi.

lectual matters. The scholar Ælfric was on friendly terms with a number of thegns. A letter of his survives to a Warwickshire thegn, Wulfgeat of Ilmington.[2] Ælfric dedicated some of his works to thegns. His commentaries on the Old and New Testaments are dedicated to Sigeweard of Astall (in Oxfordshire).[3] But Ælfric's best-known lay patron was Æthelweard.[4] He translated into English parts of the Pentateuch at Æthelweard's request,[5] and gave him a copy of his *Catholic Homilies*.[6] Ælfric mentions in his prefaces to the *Lives of Saints* that Æthelweard had asked him to write the work in English, and that both Æthelweard and his son were avid readers of Ælfric's translations.[7] Moreover, Æthelmar continued his father's patronage of Ælfric. He founded the abbeys of Cerne and Eynsham, in both of which Ælfric worked.[8]

Æthelweard obviously preferred to read works in an English translation. This makes it the more remarkable that he should have undertaken to write a chronicle in Latin. Knowledge of Latin was extremely rare among the laity. Possibly Æthelweard had a secretary to help him, perhaps a Celt.[9] This is suggested by the fact that the chronicle is in the convoluted, ornate type of Latin written by Aldhelm, with its proclivity for recondite words, and not in the lucid classical style of Bede.[10] Æthelweard had three apparent motives for writing: love of history, family feeling, and patriotism.

Æthelweard's chronicle covers the period from the Creation to 975. It deals briefly with the ages preceding the arrival of the Anglo-Saxons in Britain, and once the latter appear on the scene they dominate it. The chronicle is mainly a compilation (with short insertions by Æthelweard) from well-known sources – from Bede and, to 893, the Anglo-Saxon Chronicle.[11] From 893 to 946 Æthelweard used some other short annals, now lost,[12] and then returned to the Anglo-Saxon Chronicle: presumably he stopped in 975 because his version of the Chronicle ended at that date and he felt unequal to the task of writing his own contemporary annals.[13] Æthelweard

---

[2] See *Ælfric's Lives of Saints*, ed. W. W. Skeat (EETS, lxxvii, lxxxii, xciv, cxiv, 1881, 1900, 2 vols), vol. 2, p. xxxiii.

[3] See *The Old English Version of the Heptateuch, Aelfric's Treatise on the Old and New Testament and his Preface to Genesis*, ed. S. J. Crawford (EETS, clx, 1922), pp. 15–16.

[4] See *Æthelweard*, pp. xiv–xv.

[5] See Crawford, op. cit., p. 32. Apparently Æthelweard also asked Ælfric to translate the Life of St Thomas of India; ibid., p. 76.

[6] See *The Homilies of the Anglo-Saxon Church*, pt i, *The Sermones Catholici or Homilies of Ælfric*, ed., with a rendering in modern English, Benjamin Thorpe (Ælfric Soc., London 1844, 2 vols), vol. 1, p. 8. Cf. K. Sisam, *Studies in the History of Old English Literature* (Oxford 1953) p. 161.

[7] See Skeat, op. cit., vol. 1, p. 5.   [8] *Æthelweard*, p. xv.   [9] Ibid., pp. xxxvi–xxxvii.

[10] On Æthelweard's latinity, see ibid., pp. xlv et seq., and, for a defence of his latinity, Michael Winterbottom, 'The style of Aethelweard' in *Medium Ævum*, xxxvi (1967), pp. 109–18. On noting Aldhelm's death (ibid., p. 21), Æthelweard comments: 'Men read his works, which are composed with wondrous skill.'

[11] On the whole Æthelweard's translation of ASC is good; see *Æthelweard*, pp. xxiii, xxxvii.

[12] Ibid., pp. xxix–xxxi.

[13] E. E. Barker, 'The Cottonian fragments of Æthelweard's chronicle' in *BIHR*, xxiv (1951), pp. 46–62, argues that Æthelweard continued the work for the reigns of Edward the Martyr

tried to make his compilation readable by breaking down the annalistic arrangement of the chronicles he used, in order to produce a continuous narrative. He adopts the 'stepping-stone' method of chronology ('in the next year', 'two years later', and so on). The result is often chronological confusion, although some errors in dates were probably due to obscurities and mistakes in the copy of the Anglo-Saxon Chronicle Æthelweard used.[14]

The version he used is now lost and its contents are only known from him. The information given by Æthelweard about it is the main reason why his work is an important historical source. As has been shown above,[15] the lost version of the Anglo-Saxon Chronicle contained a revised text made probably in the reign of Edward the Elder. It not only rewrote the annal for 893, to give a pro-Edwardian bias, but it also had additional information, much of it relating to the west country. Presumably many of these additions represent the reminiscences of veterans of the Danish wars. A similar type of addition was in the version of the Anglo-Saxon Chronicle, also lost, used in the *Life of King Alfred*.[16]

Æthelweard wrote his chronicle, as he says in the preface, for his cousin Matilda abbess of Essen (the implication that the chronicle was not intended for a wide audience is corroborated by the fact that only one medieval manuscript of it is known to have survived the Reformation).[17] Æthelweard wanted to reaffirm for Matilda her kinship with himself – she was descended from King Alfred, and he was descended from Alfred's brother King Ethelred. His purpose was to glorify their family by telling its history, set against the background of national events. So Æthelweard wanted to tell Matilda about the origin of the Anglo-Saxons, 'especially the arrival of our ancestors in Britain from Germany' and about 'our family in modern times'. Thus family pride led to an interest in national history. In return Æthelweard wanted Matilda to send him information about the continental relatives of the royal family, 'for you have not only the family connection, but the capacity, since distance does not hinder you.'

The result of Æthelweard's researches into the genealogy of the West

---

and Ethelred II. The basis of his argument is Æthelweard's list of contents which includes these reigns. He also argues that H. Savile, in *Rerum Anglicarum Scriptores post Bedam praecipui* (London 1696), pp. 473–83, printed from some other manuscript than the only one now known, BM MS. Cotton Otho A X (more fragments of the same text are in Otho A XII), which was almost totally destroyed in the Cottonian fire of 1731. However A. Campbell, *Æthelweard*, pp. xi–xii and xii n. 1, is not convinced by Barker's arguments and considers that the contents list merely indicates Æthelweard's *intention* to continue.

[14] For a full discussion of Æthelweard's chronology, see *Æthelweard*, pp. xxxviii–xliv.

[15] See pp. 35–6.

[16] For the version of ASC used by Æthelweard see *Æthelweard*, pp. xix–xxxvii *passim* and E. E. Barker, 'The Anglo-Saxon Chronicle used by Æthelweard', pp. 74–91, where some of Professor Campbell's views are questioned. See also F. M. Stenton, 'Æthelweard's account of the last years of King Alfred's reign' in *EHR*, xxiv (1901), pp. 79–84; Stenton, 'The Danes at Thorney Island in 893' in *EHR*, xxvii (1912), pp. 512–13, and Stenton 'The foundations of English history' in *TRHS*, ix (1926), pp. 167–8.

[17] See n. 13.

Saxon kings is seen in the preface. He thought that Matilda would be particularly interested to know about West Saxon princesses who had been married abroad. He states that Alfred's daughter Ælfthryth married Baldwin II count of Flanders (Æthelweard names their children). And he records that Edward the Elder's daughter Eadgifu married Charles the Simple king of France, and his daughter Eadhild married Hugh the Great 'dux Francorum'. Moreover, according to Æthelweard, King Athelstan sent one sister, Eadgyth, to marry Otto the Great, and another, Ælfgifu, to marry 'a certain king near the Alps'. Other records show that Æthelweard's family history is here remarkably correct, and he is the only independent authority for Ælthfryth's marriage to Count Baldwin.[18] Æthelweard's interest in royal genealogy also appears in his revision of Bede's version of the West Saxon pedigree.[19]

Æthelweard's concern for his and Matilda's ancestry expanded into an interest in English history. He probably meant to edify Matilda as well as to inform her. He sought to demonstrate the power of God in English history, 'with examples of wars, massacres and shipwrecks',[20] and the virtues of saints (some of his additions to the Anglo-Saxon Chronicle are miracles worked by saints).[21] Æthelweard's general interest in English history is shown by the fullness with which he treats it, and his excursus on the derivation of place-names[22] and on geographical features.[23]

Æthelweard's chronicle has some features in common with the royal biographies of the Anglo-Saxon period. As with two of the biographies (the *Encomium Emmae Reginae* and the *Life of King Edward*), he addressed his work to a woman. The dedication of these works to women is symptomatic of the respected position of women in Anglo-Saxon society. The survival of Æthelweard's chronicle in only one manuscript (now almost totally destroyed) is also paralleled by the secular biographies. There is evidence for the existence of only two copies of the *Life of King Alfred* before the Conquest (none is extant now).[24] No manuscript at all has survived of the Life of King Athelstan, although one was available to William of Malmesbury. One early manuscript survives of the *Encomium* and one, written a generation after the work, of the *Life of King Edward*. Moreover, the biographies seem to have been practically unknown before the Conquest. Most writers in the Anglo-Saxon period ignored them.

The thin manuscript tradition of the biographies has significance. It partly accounts for the fact that the authenticity of two of the works, the *Life of King Alfred* and the *Life of King Edward* has been questioned in modern times: scholars believing that they are genuine have been unable to point to

---

[18] *Æthelweard*, pp. xix–xx, 2. [19] Ibid., pp. xx, 9, 18. [20] Ibid., p. 1.
[21] See ibid., pp. xxxv, 17, 54.
[22] For eponyms used by Æthelweard to explain names see ibid., pp. 11, 18.
[23] See e.g. the description of Thanet, Aller and Thorney; *Æthelweard*, pp. 31, 43, 49 (cf. ibid., p. xxxv).
[24] See p. 47 and n. 31.

early copies. Furthermore, the dearth of manuscripts indicates that the Anglo-Saxons were not interested in royal biographies. If they wanted to read biographies they read saints' Lives. If they wanted to read secular history they read the Anglo-Saxon Chronicle.

Lack of interest in royal biographies had a corollary – the absence of a tradition in England for this type of literature. Æthelweard could use Bede and the Anglo-Saxon Chronicle as models. The secular biographer had to model his work mainly on hagiography and on foreign secular biographies. All the Anglo-Saxon royal biographies have shortcomings by modern standards. They are, in varying degrees, imprecise and chronologically uncertain. These features are partly deliberate. In accordance with current literary modes, the authors tried to convey, often with considerable literary elaboration, a picture of the hero which was true in its general purport – which captured his essential qualities; they were not interested in accuracy of detail. Thus they might include information which they knew to be false, but they did not necessarily intend to deceive. The works were also inaccurate because the sources of information were imperfect. Moreover, as they were all probably command biographies, they were intended to please the patrons, and therefore eulogize them. And to some extent the heroes were idealized in order to portray the perfect Christian king, as an example to all rulers. The four biographies will be considered in chronological order: first, the *Life of King Alfred*; second, the lost Life of King Athelstan; third, the *Encomium*; and fourth, the *Life of King Edward*.

The *Life of King Alfred*[25] consists of brief annals, mostly derived from a lost version of the Anglo-Saxon Chronicle, to 887, into which are fitted passages of narrative biography. It is a jejune compilation. The marriage of annals and biographical narrative is clumsily done, without attempt at synthesis or much regard for chronological order.[26] The biographical passages, though remarkably vivid and detailed, have a romantic, often laudatory, tone and contain some statements which are hard to believe and impossible to verify; they suggest that King Alfred was already the subject of legend.

The *Life* purports to have been written in 893[27] by Asser, who as the Anglo-Saxon Chronicle records, died, as bishop of Sherborne, in 910. It is also known, from Alfred's preface to the *Pastoral Care*, that Asser was one of

---

[25] The standard edition is *Asser's Life of King Alfred together with the Annals of St. Neots . . .* ed. W. H. Stevenson (Oxford 1904; a new impression, with an article, 'Recent work on Asser's Life of Alfred,' by D. Whitelock, 1959). For some emendations to Stevenson's text see G. H. Wheeler, 'Textual emendations to Asser's Life of Alfred' in *EHR*, xlvii (1932), pp. 86–8. A good English translation is by A. S. Cook, *Asser's Life of King Alfred translated from the text of Stevenson's edition* (Boston 1906); that by L. C. Lane (King's Classics, 1908) is less useful than Cook's, as it does not retain the chapter divisions.

[26] For examples of biographical narrative entered under years to which it does not belong see *Asser*, pp. lxxii, xc, 294–6.

[27] Ibid., c. 91.

the scholars who helped Alfred in his literary activities.[28] The preface to the *Life* proclaims that 'Asser, the least of all the servants of God', dedicates the work 'to my venerable and most pious lord, Alfred ruler of all Christians in the British Isles and King of the Anglo-Saxons'. In the course of the *Life* there are details about Asser's career and association with Alfred. He was a monk of St David's in south Wales, met Alfred at 'Dene' (the place is unidentified) and was asked by the king to teach him for a part of each year. On Asser's return to Wales he fell ill for a year at 'Wintonia' (probably Caerwent).[29] He finally joined Alfred at 'Leonaford' (the place is unidentified) and supervised his studies, being rewarded with various gifts.[30]

But at the outset the reader is faced with the problem of the authenticity of the *Life of King Alfred*. The work's romanticism and possible inaccuracy, combined with men's apparent ignorance of it for nearly a century after Asser's death,[31] led some scholars in the nineteenth century and more recently to conclude that it was a forgery and no earlier in date than the sole surviving manuscript, Cottonian MS. Otho A XII in the British Museum which, like Æthelweard's chronicle, was almost totally destroyed in the fire of 1731. The *Life* was further discredited, unjustly, because of the unscholarly nature of the early printed editions. The first editor, Archbishop Parker, who published it in 1574, inserted from a twelfth-century source the famous story of King Alfred burning the cakes, which formed no part of the original work.[32] William Camden, in his edition of 1602 interpolated a passage of his own, concocted to prove that Oxford university was founded in Alfred's reign and so was older than Cambridge.[33]

W. H. Stevenson did much to re-establish the authority of the *Life* in his definitive edition of 1904. He published the original text, stripped of its later accretions. Moreover, in a learned introduction he countered the arguments brought against the *Life*'s authenticity. But, while strongly disposed to accept it as genuine, he admitted that there is 'no very definite proof that the work was written by Bishop Asser', and warned readers not to be blind to the difficulties it presents.[34] No conclusive new evidence has since come to light to alter the position though scholars have continued to debate the issue. The attitude of qualified acceptance has recently been adopted by Professor Alistair Campbell.[35] On the other hand, Professor Stenton accepted it as 'a very naïve, but sincerely intimate biography'.[36] And it has recently been de-

[28] *Pastoral Care*, ed. Sweet, p. 7.   [29] *Asser*, c. 79.   [30] Ibid., c. 81.

[31] Only one medieval writer corroborates that Asser wrote a *Life of King Alfred* and his evidence is unsatisfactory; Gerald of Wales (?d. 1220) in his (lost) Life of St Ethelbert cites him ('historicus veraxque relator gestorum regis Alfredi') as the authority for some miracles – but they are not in the *Life of King Alfred* as we have it: see *GW*, vol. 3, pp. 420 and note b, 422, and *Asser*, pp. lxiii–lxiv. For evidence that a copy of the *Life* was extant about 900 see p. 48 and n. 42 below, and for the possibility that it was used by the eleventh-century secular biographers see pp. 56 and n. 111, 60–1 below.

[32] See *Asser*, c. 53, 53b, and pp. 136, 256.   [33] See ibid., pp. xxiii–xxvi.

[34] See ibid. pp. vii, cxxix.   [35] *Æthelweard*, pp. xxxiii–xxxiv.

[36] F. M. Stenton, *Anglo-Saxon England* (Oxford 1947), p. 268.

fended at length by Professor Whitelock[37] against renewed attacks on its authenticity by Professor V. H. Galbraith.[38]

Professor Galbraith argues that the work is an eleventh-century forgery, perhaps by Leofric, bishop of Exeter (1046–72). The *Life* was forged, he suggests, to provide a historical justification for the removal of the see of Crediton to Exeter in 1050. For the *Life* apparently provides evidence that Exeter was an episcopal see in Alfred's time: it states that Alfred gave Asser 'Exeter with all its *parochia*'.[39] However, Professor Whitelock effectively disposes of Leofric's claim to authorship.[40] One cogent piece of evidence is the date of Otho A XII; palaeographers agree that it was written in about 1000,[41] too early for Leofric. And there is evidence that an even earlier manuscript, of about 900, once existed.[42]

But the question remains whether anyone else forged the *Life*. Does it have stylistic features or anachronisms betraying post-ninth-century work? Professor Galbraith emphasizes the fact that it contains a mixture of past and present tenses. He suggests that the forger first wrote as if Alfred were dead, and then, having stopped at 887, rather haphazardly revised the work to make it seem as if Alfred were still alive.[43] But the changes of tense can be otherwise explained. They could be due to limited literary ability.[44] Or perhaps Asser while at court kept a notebook in which he noted, in the present tense, anecdotes about the king (the *Life* itself states that Alfred had a pocket commonplace book[45]); and he incorporated these notes, still in the present tense, into the final work when writing it up, in the past tense, after he returned to Wales.

With regard to anachronisms, it is hard to prove that the *Life* has any. The author wrote in a romantic style and exaggerated to praise his hero; as he was concerned to represent the general truth about King Alfred, not to record accurate details, the *Life* should not be submitted to too close critical scrutiny. Furthermore, Alfred's reign was in the dark ages: confirmatory evi-

---

[37] D. Whitelock, *The Genuine Asser* (Stenton Lecture, 1967, University of Reading 1968).

[38] V. H. Galbraith, 'Research in action: who wrote Asser's Life of Alfred?' in his *An Introduction to the Study of History* (London 1964), pp. 85–128.

[39] *Asser*, c. 81.　　　　　　　　　[40] Whitelock, *Genuine Asser*, pp. 6–8.

[41] Humphrey Wanley, a very accurate palaeographer, saw the manuscript, Otho A XII, before it was burnt and dated it 'about 1000 or 1001'. See *Asser*, p. xliv and nn. For the agreement of modern palaeographers see Whitelock, *Genuine Asser*, p. 17.

[42] P. Hunter Blair suggests that the source of the section from 849 to 887 of the *Historia Regum* ascribed to Symeon of Durham was a copy of the *Life of King Alfred* written in about 900, and not, as Stevenson believed, the text now Otho A XII. He reached this tentative conclusion on the basis of variant readings in Symeon which seem to represent an older textual tradition than those in Otho A XII. However, certainty is impossible as the Otho text cannot be established beyond doubt, nor is it possible to be sure how much Symeon tinkered with his exemplar. See P. H. Blair, 'Some observations on the *Historia Regum* attributed to Symeon of Durham' in Chadwick, *Celt and Saxon*, pp. 99–104, 116.

[43] Professor Galbraith suggests the author first wrote in the past tense because he was modelling himself on Einhard (see pp. 51–2 below); Galbraith, op. cit., pp. 110 et seq.

[44] See Whitelock, *Genuine Asser*, pp. 6–7.　　　　　[45] *Asser*, cc. 24, 88.

dence is often scarce and hard to interpret. To take two instances. Professor Galbraith, translating *parochia* as bishopric, points out that there was no bishopric of Exeter until 1050: therefore, he concludes that the statement in the *Life*, that Alfred gave Asser 'Exeter with all its *parochia*', is anachronistic. But there is no evidence that *parochia* at this date always meant bishopric – it could refer to the area attached to the monastery of St Peter's at Exeter, in the Celtic fashion. And even if *parochia* does mean bishopric, it is by no means unlikely, in view of the large size of Wessex, that the monastery at Exeter temporarily became an episcopal see.[46] Similarly, Professor Galbraith regards as suspect the *Life*'s description of King Alfred as 'ruler of all Christians in the British Isles' (which he never was) and 'King of the Anglo-Saxons' (a title which he did not use, according to Professor Galbraith).[47] But both titles are in keeping with the eulogistic tone of the *Life*[48] – and in a *general* sense they are accurate enough.[49]

There are strong arguments in favour of Asser's authorship of the *Life of King Alfred*. It was obviously by a Briton, either of Wales or Cornwall. Like Nennius, whose work the author probably knew, the author gave British equivalents for Anglo-Saxon place-names.[50] His knowledge of Anglo-Saxon was imperfect,[51] and he had unique information about Cornwall and Wales: he states that St Neot was buried with St Gueriir in a Cornish church,[52] has details of the attacks on St David's property by the Welsh king Hemeid, and gives a list of the Welsh princes who put themselves under

[46] H. P. R. Finberg, 'Sherborne, Glastonbury and the expansion of Wessex' in *TRHS*, 5th series, iii (1953), p. 115, argues that Alfred's intention (if rightly described in the *Life*) was that Asser should act as an auxiliary to the bishop of Sherborne, exercising episcopal functions in Devon and Cornwall and drawing his revenues from the monastery at Exeter. Cf. Whitelock, *Genuine Asser*, p. 14.

[47] See Galbraith, op. cit., pp. 91–3. Whitelock, *Genuine Asser*, p. 15, points out that Alfred is styled REX ANGLO in a coin legend (cf. *Asser*, pp. 151–2).

[48] Einhard called Charlemagne 'rex Francorum'.

[49] See Asser's account (c. 80) of Alfred's overlordship of the Welsh princes, and the treaty between Alfred and Guthrum; *English Historical Documents*, vol. 1, c. 500–1042, ed. D. Whitelock (London 1955), pp. 380–1. Cf. also ASC, *s.a.* 886, and *Asser*, pp. 69, 324.

[50] *Asser*, cc. 30³⁻⁴, 49⁷·²³, 52⁶, 55⁸, 57⁵. For an example apparently taken from Nennius see c. 9⁴ and Stevenson's note, p. 186. See cc. 21⁷, 69³, for names qualified with 'Saxonice dicitur'.

[51] See *Asser*, pp. lxxvii–lxxviii.

[52] *Asser*, c. 74¹⁷⁻²¹; 'Sed quodam tempore, divino nutu, antea, cum [Alfredus] Cornubiam venandi causa adiret, et ad quandam ecclesiam orandi causa divertisset, in qua Sanctus Gueriir requiescit et nunc etiam Sanctus Niot ibidem pausat.' Stevenson, pp. xlix, 297–8, dismissed 'et nunc etiam Sanctus Niot ibidem pausat' as a late tenth-century interpolation in the text, but there is no evidence for this view. On the contrary the statement that St Neot was buried in the same church as St Gueriir is so explicit as to carry conviction. Presumably the writer intended to tell readers that St Gueriir, about whom almost nothing is known, was buried at St Neot in Cornwall, which was well known. The passage is good evidence that the Lives of St Neot (all twelfth century) are correct in saying that St Neot lived in Alfred's time in Cornwall. The Lives conflate two St Neots, this one who was a Celt and lived in Cornwall, and an Anglo-Saxon one who probably lived in Huntingdonshire. I owe these suggestions to Mr Christopher Hohler. See also G. H. Doble, *St Neot* (privately printed, 'Cornish Saints' series no. 21, with notes by C. Henderson), and Bollandists, *Acta Sanctorum*, 31 July, pp. 325–40.

King Alfred's protection.[53] He also shows particular knowledge of Gaul;[54] it is quite credible that Asser could have obtained such news from one of the continental scholars at Alfred's court.

If the *Life* is a forgery it is a very clever one. As far as can be seen the author used no post-Alfredian material, and had access to quite a wide variety of information, some, such as the Welsh king-list and the facts about St Gueriir, both abstruse and ancient. It is hard to explain why a forger used the Anglo-Saxon Chronicle to only 887 in a work purporting to be written in 893. Surely a copy to 893, which would have included Alfred's successes against the Danes in those years, would have been available to him.

The arguments for the authenticity of the *Life* are strengthened by the fact that some of the statements which at first sight seem unlikely prove on examination to be plausible, while the accuracy of others can be corroborated by independent evidence. For example the *Life*'s statement that Asser fell ill at 'Wintonia' on the way back from his first meeting with Alfred is very improbable if one takes 'Wintonia' to mean Winchester which was so called in the middle ages. However, the author may have meant Caerwent,[55] which like Winchester was called 'Venta' in Roman Britain: perhaps it was a witticism in the dark ages to call both places 'Wintonia'. And there is no reason why Asser should not have gone to Caerwent *en route* from England to St David's.

There is independent evidence confirming the statement in the *Life* that the wives of the kings of Wessex before Æthelwulf's wife Judith were not called queen,[56] that Judith when a widow married her stepson,[57] that King Alfred forced his subjects to build fortresses,[58] that Offa built a dyke between England and Wales,[59] and that the first settlers of the Isle of Wight were Jutes (and not as the Anglo-Saxon Chronicle asserts West Saxons).[60] All these statements show that the author was remarkably well informed. Moreover, the picture he gives of Alfred as a Christian and a scholar is confirmed by the preface to the translation of the *Pastoral Care* (if the latter is an

[53] *Asser*, c. 80, and p. lxxv. J. E. Lloyd, *A History of Wales* (London 1939), vol. i, pp. 215, 226–8 and n., considers that the details about Welsh history are evidence of Asser's authorship (see also below). N. K. Chadwick, 'The Celtic background of early Anglo-Saxon England' in her *Celt and Saxon*, pp. 350–1, points out that Asser could have copied the chapter from a contemporary political poem or other source. Therefore, having admitted that the passage may not be the author's own work, it follows that anyone, not necessarily Asser, might have plundered its source. The most that the chapter suggests is that the author was a Briton interested in Welsh history.

[54] See *Asser*, p. xciii.   [55] See ibid., pp. 313–14.

[56] Ibid., c. 13[9]. This statement is confirmed by Prudentius of Troyes; see Stevenson in *Asser*, pp. 200–2, citing *Annales Bertiniani*, ed. G. Waitz (octavo, Hanover 1883) in G. H. Pertz, *Scriptores Rerum Germanicarum* (Hanover 1839–1921, 64 vols), p. 47, *s.a.* 856.

[57] *Asser*, c. 17. This statement is also confirmed by Prudentius of Troyes: see Stevenson in *Asser*, p. 212, citing Waitz, op. cit., p. 49, *s.a.* 858.

[58] *Asser*, c. 91[49–73] *passim*; see Stenton, *Anglo-Saxon England*, pp. 262–3.

[59] *Asser*, c. 14[3]; see Stenton, *Anglo-Saxon England*, p. 211.

[60] *Asser*, c. 2[5]; see R. G. Collingwood and J. N. L. Myres, *Roman Britain and the English Settlements* (Oxford 1936), p. 366 and n.

independent authority), and the account of Alfred as a humane law-giver is corroborated by Alfred's law-code.[61]

One curious characteristic of Alfred as represented in the *Life* is his predilection for dividing things into fractions. He divided his household (the members were to serve in three annual rotas),[62] his money,[63] and, by time-measuring candles, the day.[64] The same characteristic appears in the Anglo-Saxon Chronicle: it records, under 894, Alfred's division of the army into two rotas. As the author of the *Life* apparently had a copy of the Chronicle only to 887, the Chronicle can here be regarded as an independent authority. It therefore confirms the *Life*'s information that Alfred had a taste for fractions.

To say that the *Life of King Alfred* is genuine is not to say that it is a good piece of *reportage*. It is true that the author was not without historical talent. He had serious antiquarian tastes, evinced, for example, by his descriptions of towns,[65] antiquities[66] and topographical features, and his interest in the derivation of place-names (some of which are accepted by modern scholars).[67] And sometimes he gave a rational explanation of events.[68] But it was not his intention to give a true-to-life portrait of Alfred (there is no account of his physical appearance), but to praise him and to edify readers. Therefore a little exaggeration was not out of place. The author was influenced by Einhard's *Life of Charlemagne* and by the hagiographical tradition. The one gave him a model for a great Christian ruler, the patron of scholars, himself with intellectual interests. The other provided models for an exemplary Christian through whom God demonstrated his power.

Einhard's *Life of Charlemagne* in its turn was influenced by Suetonius's *Lives of the Twelve Caesars*, especially that of Augustus: therefore the *Life of Alfred* has a classical prototype. The author arranged his work roughly like Einhard, devoting the first half to Alfred's immediate predecessors on the

---

[61] For evidence supporting this description of Alfred in the *Life* and other statements in it, see Whitelock, *Genuine Asser*, pp. 9–11. I believe the point I make in the next paragraph is new.

[62] *Asser*, c. 100.   [63] Ibid., cc. 99, 102.   [64] Ibid., c. 104.

[65] For descriptions of towns etc. see *Asser*, c. 4[4] (London, probably derived from Bede, *HE*, ii. 3), 26[4] (York), 35[5] (Reading), 49[8, 22] (Thorney and Exeter), 54[6] ('arx Cynuit'), 55[6] ('Petra Ægbryhta'), 57[4] (Cirencester), 66[6] (Rochester), 92[8] (Athelney), 3[6] (Isle of Sheppey), 5[2] (Surrey). Cf. 82[6] (Paris).

[66] See *Asser*, cc. 27[16] (the walls of York), 35[9] (the Danish *vallum* at Reading).

[67] His derivation of Berkshire (c. 1[4]) and of the Isle of Sheppey (c. 3[6]) are accepted by E. Ekwall, *The Concise Oxford Dictionary of English Place-Names* (Oxford 1960, 4th ed.), pp. 39, 416. Although the form Asser gives of Ashdown (c. 37[3]) is wrong, the derivation is right; see *Asser*, pp. 234–8, and A. Mawer and F. M. Stenton, *The Place-Names of Buckinghamshire* (English Place-Name Soc., vol. 2, 1925), p. 102. The derivations of 'Aclea' (c. 5[6]) and Englefield (c. 35[13]) are probably wrong; see J. E. B. Gover, A. Mawer and F. M. Stenton, *The Place-Names of Surrey* (English Place-Name Soc., vol. 11, 1934), pp. 276, 120. That for Nottingham (c. 30[3]) is certainly wrong; see *Asser*, p. 231, and J. E. B. Gover, A. Mawer and F. M. Stenton, *The Place-Names of Nottinghamshire* (English Place-Name Soc., vol. 17, 1940), p. 13: the mistakes are probably due to the author's imperfect knowledge of Anglo-Saxon.

[68] For example *Asser*, c. 12[12–15], suggests reasons for the revolt against King Æthelwulf and, c. 93, gives reasons for the decline of monasticism before Alfred's accession.

throne and to his military victories, and the second part to Alfred's character and family life and to the internal history of the reign. He borrowed one passage (without acknowledgment) almost *verbatim* from Einhard[69] and probably had other passages in mind when writing. The account of the piety of Alfred's predecessor as king,[70] Alfred's help to him,[71] Alfred's honours from the pope,[72] his victories[73] and the voluntary submission of foreign princes,[74] his arbitration of disputed legal cases,[75] his building activities,[76] his love of hunting,[77] his piety,[78] his generosity to foreigners and to the poor,[79] his solicitude for his children[80] and their education,[81] his love of learning[82] and interest in the vernacular,[83] are all paralleled in Einhard. It would be rash to conclude, on the evidence of these similarities, that the author's statements are untrue (Alfred himself may have been influenced by Charlemagne's example), but they do suggest that he was painting a conventional portrait of Alfred. Hagiographical influence is particularly apparent in the account of Alfred's illnesses and their miraculous cure by St Gueriir.[84] As the passage

---

[69] *Asser*, c. 73. See Einhard's preface in *Éginhard Vie de Charlemagne*, ed. Louis Halphen (Les Classiques de l'Histoire de France au Moyen Age, Paris 1947), p. 2. For the influence of Einhard on the *Life of King Alfred* see Marie Schütt, 'The literary form of Asser's "Vita Alfred"' in *EHR*, lxxii (1957), pp. 209–20. For the possible influence of Thegan's *Life of Louis the Pious* see D. A. Bullough, 'The educational tradition from Alfred to Aelfric: teaching *utriusque*' in *XIX Settimana di Studi del Centro Italiano di Studi sull'Altomedioevo: La Scuola* (Spoleto 1972), p. 454–5 and n. 2.

[70] *Asser*, c. 37, records how King Ethelred, Alfred's brother, finished mass after the battle of Ashdown had begun; Einhard, c. 2, records that Carloman who shared the office of Mayor of the Palace with Pippin, became a monk in Rome.

[71] *Asser*, cc. 29³, 38⁸, 42², records that Alfred was 'secundarius' in the government of the kingdom under Ethelred; Einhard, c. 2, records that Charlemagne's father Pippin exercised power as Mayor of the Palace when Charles Martel was king.

[72] *Asser*, c. 8; 'Leo papa... infantem Ælfridum oppido ordinans unxit in regem, et in filium adoptionis sibimet accipiens confirmavit'. Einhard, c. 28, records that the pope made Charlemagne Emperor and Augustus.

[73] Cf. the account in *Asser*, c. 56, of King Guthrum's defeat at Edington, with the account in Einhard, c. 7, of the defeat of the continental Saxons by Charlemagne; in both cases the vanquished gave hostages and promised to adopt Christianity. Cf. also *Asser*, c. 70 and Einhard, c.12.

[74] *Asser*, c. 80; Einhard, cc. 5–16 *passim*.   [75] *Asser*, c. 106; Einhard, c. 24.

[76] *Asser*, c. 91¹⁸⁻²⁵, ⁴⁹⁻⁷¹ *passim*; Einhard, cc. 17, 26. Asser's statement, c. 91¹⁹⁻²¹, that Alfred built buildings with gold and silver ('De aedificiis aureis et argenteis incomparabiliter, illo edocente, fabricatis?') has a counterpart in Einhard, c. 26, who states that Charlemagne decorated his chapel at Aachen with gold and silver ('plurimae pulchritudinis basilicam Aquisgrani extruxit auroque et argento et luminaribus atque ex aere solido cancellis et ianuis adornavit').

[77] *Asser*, c. 76⁴; Einhard, c. 22.

[78] *Asser*, cc. 74²², ⁴⁷⁻⁹, 76¹⁵, ²⁶⁻⁹, 92¹⁻¹⁷, 102¹⁻⁴, 103¹⁻¹¹; Einhard, cc. 17, 26.

[79] *Asser*, cc. 76¹⁶⁻¹⁷, ²¹⁻⁹, 101⁸⁻¹³; Einhard, cc. 21, 27.

[80] *Asser*, c. 75²¹⁻⁴, records that Alfred kept his sons with him at court; Einhard, c. 19, records that Charlemagne had his sons and daughters with him at meals and on journeys.

[81] *Asser*, c. 75¹¹⁻³¹ *passim*; Einhard, c. 19.

[82] *Asser*, c. 76³⁹⁻⁴³ (cf. 106⁵⁴⁻⁶¹); Einhard, c. 25.

[83] *Asser*, cc. 22, 23, 75¹⁷, ²⁹⁻³¹; Einhard, cc. 24, 29.

[84] *Asser*, c. 74. For an attempt to rationalize the account of Alfred's illnesses see Marie Schütt, 'The literary form of Asser's "Vita Alfredi"', p. 215.

reads like a saint's life, perhaps modern scholars have worried unnecessarily about its factual accuracy: it was meant to be read, like the rest of its genre, for edification not information.

It is likely that the author was sometimes inaccurate because he loved a good story. His powers as a raconteur were considerable, and the *Life* is far more readable than, say, Æthelweard's chronicle. Some passages, such as the account of the lamps Alfred invented, have become a well-known part of English literature. Particularly famous is the passage describing how Alfred's mother taught him to read (its factual content is problematical: Alfred's mother, Osburh, died when he was seven years old and the *Life* indicates that the incident happened when he was twelve or more – perhaps the lady referred to was his stepmother, Judith):[85]

> When one day his mother was showing him and his brothers a certain book of Saxon poetry, which she held in her hand, she said, 'I shall give this book to which ever of you can learn it most quickly.' Moved by these words or rather by divine inspiration, and attracted by the beauty of the initial letter of the book, Alfred said to his mother, forestalling his brothers who were his elders in years though not in grace: 'Will you really give this book to one of us, to the one who can first understand and repeat it to you?' And she, pleased and smiling, confirmed it saying, 'To him will I give it.' Then taking the book from her hand, he immediately went to his master and read it. And when it was read he went back to his mother and repeated it.

The next royal biography, the Life of Alfred's grandson, King Athelstan (924–40), presents even more problems than Asser, because no manuscript of it has survived. However, William of Malmesbury, writing in about 1124, included two sections from the Life of King Athelstan in the *Gesta Regum*: one describes the coronation feast on Athelstan's accession, and the other the defeat of the Danes by Athelstan in 937 at the battle of Brunanburh.[86] William says that he had found the work 'a little while ago' in 'a very old book'.[87] He did not copy it out in full for two reasons: it was written, he asserts, in 'bombastic' Latin ('the writer struggles with the difficulty of his subject, unable to express his views as he wished'); and it was excessively eulogistic of Athelstan. William excuses the over-eloquent style because it was customary at that time, and he excuses the eulogy on account of good-will towards Athelstan 'who was still living'.

Besides copying the two passages of verse, William used the Life, rendered into 'familiar language', for his prose account of the reign. Some of the

---

[85] *Asser*, c. 23 and pp. 221–5.
[86] WM, *GR*, vol. 1, pp. 145–6, 151–2. Cf. p. 54 n. 93 below.
[87] Ibid., p. 144.

material he borrowed can be isolated with fair certainty because of its style and content. And some of William's own interpolations can be easily isolated: for example, he added a topographical account of Exeter (Athelstan's noble fortifications 'are better described by the conversation of the inhabitants than in our narrative'),[88] and a copy of a charter supposed to have been granted by Athelstan to Malmesbury.[89] Nevertheless one cannot be certain about the derivation of a few passages in the prose.[90]

The exact date of the poem cannot be established. William's statement that Athelstan was alive when it was written seems to be contradicted by a line cited from the work by William: it says that Olaf, having had the good fortune to avoid death in the battle of Brunanburh in 937, 'would again play an important part in affairs after Athelstan's death'.[91] It is hard to reach a conclusion about the date by comparing the extant verses, which are in rhymed hexameters, with other Latin poems of the first half of the tenth century. For Latin verse was extremely rare in England at that time. The only surviving parallel to this work is the *Breviloquium* on the *Life of St. Wilfrid* by Frithegode, a monk of Canterbury.[92] But the latter is primarily a hagiography and not like what survives of the Life of King Athelstan.

Nevertheless there seems no reason to doubt that the Life was written soon after Athelstan's death.[93] It obviously belonged to the epic literature popular in the tenth century. As has been seen above,[94] heroic poems were inserted into the Anglo-Saxon Chronicle which were of the same genre as *Beowulf* and the *Battle of Maldon*. Such verses shared the same literary tradition as the Norse sagas, by which, moreover, they were often directly influenced. The Life of King Athelstan, though in Latin, shows the characteristics of this type of literature – love of the generous lord and the heroic warrior. The verses on the coronation feast give a picture of life in a great hall: the festive fire leaps, wine flows, the hall echoes with noise, bellies are filled with deli-

---

[88] Ibid., pp. 148–9.

[89] Ibid., p. 153. For this spurious charter see P. H. Sawyer, *Anglo-Saxon Charters: An Annotated List and Bibliography* (Royal Historical Soc., 1968), no. 436.

[90] For an example see n. 100 below. I am not convinced that the list of Hugh the Great's gifts to Athelstan (see p. 55 and n. 102) derived from the poem.

[91]   'Fugit Analafus, de tot modo milibus unus,
       Depositum mortis, fortunae nobile munus,
       Post Ethelstanum rebus momenta daturus.'

   GR, vol. 1, p. 152. Olaf Guthfrithson, not Olaf Sihtricson, is almost certainly intended (*The Battle of Brunanburh*, ed. A. Campbell (London 1938), pp. 49 and n. 5, 50), for whose career see Stenton, *Anglo-Saxon England*, pp. 338–9, 352–4.

[92] The *Breviloquium* is in the style of Latin used by Aldhelm, using words of Greek derivation. See *Frithegodi Monachi Breviloquium Vitae Beati Wilfredi et Wulfstani Cantoris Narratio Metrica de Sancto Swithuno*, ed. Alistair Campbell (Thesaurus Mundi Bibliotheca Scriptorum Latinorum Mediae et Recentioris Aetatis, Zurich 1950), p. vii–x.

[93] The Life of King Athelstan as cited by William of Malmesbury is accepted as authentic by Stenton, *Anglo-Saxon England*, pp. 315 n. 1, 335 and n. 1, 686, 688, and by Campbell, *The Battle of Brunanburh*, pp. 45 n. 1, 49 and n. 5 (William of Malmesbury's account of the poem and the text of the verses on the battle of Brunanburh are cited in ibid., pp. 154–5).

[94] See p. 40.

cacies and ears with song.[95] Emphasis is laid on Athelstan's generosity to his followers and others. His 'rule of conduct was never to hoard riches, but to give all his gains liberally to monasteries or to his faithful followers'.[96] He is shown as an invincible warrior, terrible to rebels and other enemies. His victories over the Danes, 'with banners flying' and 'warlike din', are described[97] – he was feared and respected by all his neighbours.[98] At least one passage seems to show the direct influence of Norse literature, with its love of the sea. It describes the ship Harold king of Norway sent to Athelstan, 'with golden prow and purple sail, armed within by a dense row of gilded shields'.[99]

There would be nothing surprising in the preservation of an ancient Life of King Athelstan in Malmesbury abbey, for Athelstan was buried there[100] and his tomb was one of its chief pilgrim attractions. William of Malmesbury was able to describe the colour of Athelstan's hair because he had seen his remains when the tomb was opened.[101] And the abbey possessed relics, part of the true cross and of the crown of thorns which according to William had belonged to Athelstan: the king acquired them, together with other rich gifts described by William, from Adolf son of Baldwin count of Flanders when he came on an embassy to ask for the hand of one of Athelstan's sisters for Hugh the Great of France.[102]

The poet no doubt partly intended to show that Athelstan was a worthy descendant of King Alfred. He was presumably the authority for two unique pieces of information preserved by William about Athelstan's relations with Alfred and other members of the royal family.[103] William states that Alfred bestowed on Athelstan as a boy 'a scarlet cloak, a jewelled belt and a Saxon sword with a golden scabbard'.[104] William says that thus Alfred 'made him a knight': it seems fair to assume that William here put a twelfth-century interpretation on the ancient ceremony of the bestowal of arms. As William states that Athelstan was thirty at his accession,[105] he cannot have been more than five at the time of the ceremony. William is also the sole authority for the information that Athelstan was educated in the court of his aunt, Alfred's daughter Æthelflaed, and her husband Ethelred ealdorman of Mercia.

[95] *GR*, vol. 1, p. 146. [96] Ibid., p. 147; cf. p. 150. [97] Ibid., p. 152.
[98] Ibid., pp. 147, 149. [99] Ibid., p. 149.
[100] Ibid., p. 157. William also alleges (ibid., p. 151) that two cousins of Athelstan, Elwin and Ethelwin, were buried at Malmesbury. But Professor Campbell questions whether the poem is his authority for this statement; see Campbell, *The Battle of Brunanburh*, p. 54 and n. 6.
[101] *GR*, vol. 1, p. 148.
[102] Ibid., pp. 149–51. For the story of the gift of relics etc. to Athelstan by Hugh the Great of France, with some general remarks on the Life of King Athelstan, see L. H. Loomis, 'The holy relics of Charlemagne and King Athelstan: the lances of Longinus and St. Mauricius' in *Speculum*, xxv (1950), no. 4, pp. 437–56. For the use of this 'gift story' by later writers see L. H. Loomis, 'The Athelstan gift story: its influence on English chronicles and Carolingian romances' in *Publications of the Modern Language Association of America*, lxvii (1952), pp. 521–37, reprinted in L. H. Loomis, *Adventures in the Middle Ages* (New York 1962), pp. 254–73.
[103] See *GR*, vol. 1, p. 145 n. 2. [104] Ibid., p. 145. [105] Ibid.

The two other royal biographies, the *Encomium Emmae Reginae*[106] and the *Life of King Edward*,[107] both written in the eleventh century, have some characteristics in common. They were both by inmates of religious houses at St Omer, in Pas de Calais. Both authors wrote to please a queen, Emma and Edith. And they tried to please them primarily by narrating the exploits and describing the characters of their husbands. They probably knew the *Life of King Alfred* and were influenced by hagiography and by continental secular biographies, and both decorated their prose with rather inaccurate references to, and with unacknowledged borrowings from the classics.

The *Encomium* was written at the command of Emma, the Norman queen (?1002–16) of King Ethelred II and then (1017–35) of King Canute. The author was probably a monk of St Bertin's at St Omer (perhaps Bovo, the author of a number of hagiographies, who became abbot in 1142 or 1143).[108] He seems to have written during Emma's exile from England from 1037 to 1040, when she lived in Flanders under Count Baldwin's protection. The *Encomium* is in three books: the first two are virtually a biography of King Canute; the third concerns Emma and Harthacanute, her son by Canute, from 1035 to the accession of Harthacanute as sole ruler of England in 1040 and the consequent restoration of Emma's power and fortunes.[109] The encomiast does not in fact devote much attention to Emma's career. He justifies his concentration on King Canute's life by saying that to praise the queen's family was to praise her, strengthening this argument with a classical allusion: Virgil, he points out, wrote the *Aeneid* to praise Octavian – without mentioning him.[110]

There are two indications that the encomiast knew the *Life of King Alfred*. Possibly he adopted the bipartite arrangement from it. He divided the biography of Canute in the *Encomium* roughly into two parts; the first mainly concerns Canute's wars, conquests and secular activities, and the second his moral stature, spiritual life and relations with the church. Moreover, possible traces of borrowing from the *Life of King Alfred* can be detected in three passages – notably in the story of the Danes' raven banner.[111] Only the prologue of the *Encomium* shows signs of hagiographical influence – the author

---

[106] The standard edition is *Encomium Emmae Reginae*, ed., with an English translation, Alistair Campbell (Camden Soc., 3rd series, lxxii, 1949).

[107] The standard edition is *The Life of King Edward who rests at Westminster* . . . , ed., with an English translation, Frank Barlow (Nelson's Medieval Texts, 1962).

[108] See *Enc.*, pp. xx–xxi.

[109] The *Encomium* was known as *Gesta Cnutonis Regis* in the late middle ages. The present title was adopted by its first modern editor (A. Duschene in *Historiae Normannorum Scriptores Antiqui*, Paris 1619, pp. 161–78); see *Enc.*, pp. xi, xviii.

[110] See *Enc.*, pp. xxiii, 7 (Argument).

[111] *Enc.*, ii. 9. This description agrees exactly with that in *Asser*, c. 54b, which Stevenson regarded as an interpolation by Archbishop Parker from the Annals of St Neots; however, if the encomiast was using *Asser* he must have had a version which included the passage, i.e. not the version in Otho A XII which did not have it; see *Enc.*, p. xxxvii. The two other passages in the *Encomium* which may derive from *Asser* are in ii. 8 (cf. *Asser*, c. 3⁷) and ii. 9 (cf. *Asser*, c. 37⁴).

declares himself inadequate to the task, undertakes it at the order of a superior and is hampered not by lack of material but of time. Such protestations belong to the hagiographical tradition, originating with Athanasius's *Life of St. Antony* and Sulpicius Severus's *Life of St. Martin*.[112]

Perhaps the encomiast and his patroness may have decided on the writing of a work to praise the queen because of the example of the *Epitaphium Adelheide Imperatricis*.[113] This was written by Odilo, abbot of Cluny (995–1049) in praise of his friend Adelheide, widow of Otto I, soon after her death in 999. The *Epitaphium* was quite popular on the continent, particularly in the monasteries founded by Adelheide. But its content does not resemble the *Encomium*: it is a biography of the empress, from her birth to her death, recounting her virtues and religious foundations.

Another continental work which could have influenced the encomiast was the *History of the Dukes of Normandy* by Dudo of St Quentin.[114] Emma's father, Richard I duke of Normandy, commissioned it in about 994 (Dudo finished writing in about 1015).[115] Like the encomiast, Dudo's purpose was eulogy of his patron, and like the encomiast his treatment of the patron is disappointingly slight. He praised Richard by writing about his family – his predecessors as dukes of Normandy. But as the work is mainly a narrative history of the duchy, beginning with a geographical description of it, and as Dudo wrote of events which happened before his time and about which he knew very little, the likeness to the *Encomium* should not be exaggerated.

The text of the *Encomium* itself shows Norse influence. This appears, for example, in the vivid description of the fleet with which King Swein set out to conquer England in 1013. It reads:[116]

> When at last the soldiers were all assembled, they went on board the towered ships, each man having picked out by observation his own leader on the brazen prows. On one side lions moulded in gold were seen on the ships, on the other birds on the tops of the masts indicated by their movements the winds as they blew, or dragons of various kinds poured fire from their nostrils. Here there were glittering men of solid gold or silver almost like living people, there bulls, with arched necks and legs outstretched, were carved like real ones. . . . But why should I now dwell upon the sides of the ships, painted in bright colours and covered with gold and silver figures? The royal vessel excelled the others in beauty just as the king excelled the soldiers in the honour of his proper dignity,

[112] See *Enc.*, p. xxxiv, and Colgrave, *Lives*, p. 310.

[113] Printed in Migne, *PL*, vol. cxli, coll. 910–35.

[114] Printed *De Moribus et Actis Primorum Normanniae Ducum auctore Dudone Sancti Quintini*, ed. J. Lair (Caen 1865). See *Enc.*, pp. xxii, xxxiv–xxxv, xxxix.

[115] See H. Prentout, *Étude Critique sur Dudon de Saint-Quentin et son Histoire des premiers ducs normands*, Memoires de l'Académie Nationale des Sciences, Arts et Belles-Lettres de Caen (Caen 1915), p. 14.

[116] *Enc.*, i. 4.

concerning which it is better for me to be silent than to speak in-adequately. Placing their confidence in such a fleet, when the signal was suddenly given, they set out joyfully, and, as commanded, placed themselves around the royal vessel, with steady prows, some in front and some behind. The blue water, smitten by many oars, might be seen foaming far and wide, and the sunlight, reflected in gleaming metal, gave out a doubled radiance.

Despite the realistic touches in this description, which suggest that the author had seen a Viking fleet, it is a rhetorical set-piece. Another passage, the graphic account of King Canute's visit to the abbeys of St Omer and St Bertin, is in a similar style. Because of the rhetoric it is impossible to be certain that the author wrote this passage from personal observation; he may have been merely describing how a king like Canute would behave on such an occasion:[117]

When Canute entered the monasteries and had been received with great honour, he advanced humbly and prayed with complete concentration and wonderful reverence for the intercession of the saints, his eyes fixed on the ground and overflowing with a veri-table river of tears. And when the time came for heaping the altars with royal offerings, how often did he first press kisses with tears on the pavement! how often did self-inflicted blows punish that re-verent breast! what sighs he gave! how often did he pray that the heavenly mercy should not disdain him! At length at his request his offering was supplied to him by his followers, no one, nor such that could be enclosed in a purse, but a man brought it, something very large, in the ample folds of his cloak, and this the king placed on the altar with his own hands, a cheerful giver according the apostolic admonition. But why do I say altar when I remember seeing him going round every corner of the monasteries and pass-ing no altar, however small, without giving a gift and pressing a sweet kiss on it?

The rhetorical element detracts from the value of the *Encomium* as a historical source. The author wrote to praise, and to give a general impres-sion of Emma, Canute and Harthacanute, not to record details accurately. Moreover he knew little about English politics; literally and figuratively he wrote at a distance from events – he was not involved, and he lived in Flanders. His information was patchy and often vague. He gave no dates and sometimes the order of the events he records is unclear; this was partly because gaps in his knowledge led him to try to fill gaps in time,[118] and

[117] *Enc.*, ii. 21. Cf. ibid., pp. lxii, lxix.
[118] See the account of Canute's war against the English, 1015–16, in Bk II; cf. *Enc.*, p. lxi.

partly because he treated events according to subject, not chronological sequence.[119] He relied for information to a considerable extent on hearsay – he believed rumours and tall stories. One of his best pieces of narrative tells how the usurper Harold used a forged letter purporting to be from Emma to entice two of her sons by Ethelred II, Edward and Alfred, to come to England. Harold wanted to secure his position by killing them, and on arrival Alfred was murdered at Guildford by Godwin's men.[120] Contemporary accounts differ, but it is certain that the story of the forged letter is untrue.[121]

The encomiast's desire to praise Emma and her family led him beyond harmless eulogy. His honesty is questionable, despite his protests that he, like any other reputable historian, sticks strictly to the truth.[122] He does not actually write a lie, but some of his omissions and turns of phrase could mislead a reader. He does not mention Emma's marriage to King Ethelred, contriving to give the impression that she was a single woman when she married Canute. Presumably this was because it was not altogether to her credit that she married Ethelred's enemy. Thus the encomiast makes nonsense of his own claim that her marriage helped to reconcile the English to Danish rule.[123] He also manages to give the impression that Edward and Alfred, sons of her first marriage, were younger than Harthacanute,[124] and so disposes of any doubt the reader might have about the claim of Emma's eldest sons to the throne.

Nevertheless the *Encomium* is not without historical value. The general impression it gives of the chief characters is plausible; at the least it probably reflects contemporary opinion. Emma emerges, despite flattering remarks about her piety and popularity, as vain and inordinately ambitious for herself and her sons. Canute appears cautious almost to cowardice, Edmund Ironside brave and Eadric treacherous. Textually the *Encomium* is unproblematical. A very early manuscript survives, probably a copy of the author's own draft. It is carefully written and has a drawing of a queen crowned and enthroned, with two men standing beside her, being presented with a book by a kneeling ecclesiastic. This suggests that the volume itself was expressly

---

[119] Because the encomiast mentions Canute's pilgrimage to Rome (*Enc.*, ii. 23) after the account of his conquest of the five realms, including Scotland (*Enc.*, ii. 19), does not mean that he visited Rome after the submission of the Scottish kings in 1031; the order is due solely to the fact that the encomiast treats Canute's secular affairs first and then his ecclesiastical ones; see *Enc.*, pp. lxii–lxiii.

[120] *Enc.*, iii. 2. Cf. pp. lxiv–lxvii.

[121] See *Enc.*, p. lxvii.

[122] See *Enc.*, Prologue and i. 1. For further examples of the author giving false impressions see: the account of Canute's voluntary return to Denmark (ii. 1) – in fact he was forced to leave England by the English resistance (*Enc.*, p. liv); the suggestion that Thurkill was at that time loyal to Canute (ii. 1) – in fact he was in alliance with the English (*Enc.*, pp. liv, lvii); the account of Canute's voluntary retreat from London (ii. 7) – in fact the English drove him out (*Enc.*, p. lix); and the account of Emma's voluntary removal to Flanders after Alfred's murder (iii. 7) – the Anglo-Saxon Chronicle records that she was exiled (*Enc.*, p. lxvii).

[123] *Enc.*, p. 7 (Argument) and ii. 16; cf. p. xlvi.

[124] *Enc.*, ii. 18; cf. p. xlvi.

written for Emma.[125] The *Encomium* is the only biography of an Anglo-Saxon king which does not present textual problems.

The *Life of King Edward* has, like the *Life of King Alfred* and the Life of Athelstan, a weak textual tradition. The only known manuscript was written in about 1100,[126] a generation after the work claims to have been composed. The *Life* was, the author says, written to please Queen Edith, wife of Edward the Confessor and daughter of Godwin earl of Essex.[127] Therefore, on its own showing, it must have been written before 1075, the date of her death. And statements in the *Life* suggest that it was written between 1066 and January 1067, in stages, as events happened.[128] However, it was argued by Marc Bloch, for reasons discussed below, that it was written between 1103 and 1120.[129] If so, the work would be a forgery, a deliberate attempt of a later writer to deceive the reader into believing that the *Life* was contemporary with the Norman Conquest. This argument (which neglects the approximate date of the manuscript) has been satisfactorily disposed of, in my opinion, by a number of scholars.[130]

Like the *Life of King Alfred*, the *Life of King Edward* is arranged in two parts (here they are distinct books), the first mainly dealing with Edward's public, political life, and the second with his spiritual, personal life, and relations with the church. It has a feature not found in the two earlier royal biographies: the two books begin with quite long poems, dialogues between poet and muse. Each chapter also begins with verses. The author was fond of classical references (like the encomiast), and had a sense of style; for example he puts his account of Edith's foundation of Wilton in juxtaposition to Edward's building of Westminster abbey.[131] In places he writes with power, giving the impression that he cared deeply about the problems of the age. The end of Book I conveys the tragedy of Edward's last years with force and feeling.

The author was subject to various literary influences. It is likely that he knew the *Encomium*, especially as it was written for Edward's mother, Emma. He probably also knew the *Life of King Alfred*. He could well have derived the bipartite arrangement from it (unless he got it direct from Einhard's *Life of Charlemagne*). Possibly he consciously made his portrait of Edward resemble the portrait of Alfred in the *Life of King Alfred*. The

---

[125] The manuscript is BM MS. Additional 33241. Described in *Enc.*, pp. xi–xiii. See Plate 3.

[126] BM MS. Harley 526, ff. 38–57, probably written at Christ Church, Canterbury. Described in *VER*, pp. lxxix–lxxxi. For losses of leaves in the MS. see ibid., pp. xv, xxxviii and n. 1, lxxx.

[127] *VER*, pp. 2–5. The purpose of the *Vita Edwardi Regis* is fully discussed in Frank Barlow, *Edward the Confessor* (London 1970), pp. 291–300.

[128] For the date of the *Life*, see *VER*, pp. xxv et seq.

[129] This was argued by Marc Bloch, 'La vie de S. Édouard le Confesseur par Osbert de Clare' in *An. Boll.*, xli (1923), pp. 5–131.

[130] Bloch's views have been countered most recently by Professor Barlow; for his arguments, and further references, see *VER*, pp. xiv, xxv et seq.

[131] *VER*, pp. 44–8.

account of the homage paid Edward by British and foreign rulers,[132] his just administration of the law,[133] his love of hunting,[134] his generosity to the poor[135] and even his celibacy,[136] are all reminiscent of passages in the earlier *Life*, and the description of Edward's personal affability seems to have verbal echoes of it.[137] Like the encomiast, the author may have had an eleventh-century continental model. Helgaud, a monk of Fleury, wrote the *Life of King Robert*, the Pious,[138] of France soon after 1031. But though the works have some resemblance, this should not be overstressed. The *Life of King Robert* does not have introductory verses (Dudo of St Quentin's *History of the Dukes of Normandy* does have rather similar verses).

Hagiography was the strongest influence on the *Life of King Edward*. The hagiographical element occurs in both books. Book I asserts that, before Edward's birth, Beorhtweald a monk of Glastonbury (bishop of Ramsbury from 995 to 1045) had a vision predicting Edward's holiness: he saw St Peter 'mark out for him a life of chastity'.[139] It also has the well-known description of Edward's appearance in old age, based, it seems, on the account of St Omer in the *Life* of the saint; Edward, it writes, 'was a very proper figure of a man, of outstanding height and distinguished by his milk-white hair and beard, full face and rosy cheeks, and thin white hands with long translucent fingers'.[140]

The hagiographical element is even more marked in Book II, which reads like a saint's Life (though there is no section on posthumous miracles such as would be appended to a typical hagiography). Edward's chastity is emphasized and miraculous cures are attributed to him. The author says that Edward had frequently cured people when he was a young man in Normandy.[141] He recounts three cures that were worked through his agency in England: one is the cure of a scrofulous woman by the king's touch, and two are cures of blind men by courtiers who bathed their eyes with water in which Edward had washed his hands.[142] The miraculous cures are all in one part of the book. As some pages are missing from this section of the manuscript, there may originally have been more miracles. In fact three further cures are given by the early twelfth-century writers, Osbert of Clare (in his *Life of Edward the Confessor*) and William Malmesbury (in the *Gesta Regum*), who both used the *Life*. The most recent editor of the *Life*, Pro-

[132] *VER*, pp. 10–12 *passim*: cf. *Asser*, c. 76[21–5].
[133] *VER*, p. 13; cf. *Asser*, cc. 105–6 *passim*.
[134] *VER*, p. 40; cf. *Asser*, cc. 22[15], 76[5].   [135] *VER*, p. 41; cf. *Asser*, c. 76[16].
[136] *VER*, pp. 8–9 (see also ibid., pp. 60, 73); cf. *Asser*, c. 74[44–5], which asserts that Alfred was chaste before marriage.
[137] *VER*, p. 12; 'erat ... continua gravitate iocundus ... gratissime cum quouis affabilitatis'. Cf. *Asser*, c. 76[18–21]; 'ac maxima et incomparabili contra omnes homines affabilitate atque iocunditate ... se iungebat.'
[138] Helgaud of Fleury's *Vita Roberti Regis* is printed in Migne, *PL*, vol. cxli, coll. 910 et seq.
[139] *VER*, p. 9.
[140] *VER*, p. 12 and n. 1. For similar references to Edward's appearance cf. ibid., pp. 3, 80.
[141] *VER*, p. 62.   [142] *VER*, pp. 61–3.

fessor Frank Barlow, accepts these extra miracles as part of the original text and prints them accordingly.[143] However, such textual emendation is inevitably subjective. Professor Barlow himself rejects Edward's Vision of the Seven Sleepers, although it is in the manuscript of the *Life* and in Osbert of Clare and William of Malmesbury.[144] If the Vision was not in the original *Life*, the existing text must have been revised soon after it was written, no doubt because of the growth of the cult of Edward.

The hagiographical tone of much of the *Life* caused Marc Bloch to attack its authenticity. He asserted that the *Life* was forged a generation after Edward's death to foster a cult of Edith at Wilton. Alternatively it could have been forged by the monks of Westminster in honour of their patron. The Westminster monks lacked a saint of the fame of St Alban or St Edmund, whose posthumous reputations made the fortunes of the houses where they were supposed to be buried. So in the twelfth century the monks of Westminster developed the cult of Edward the Confessor to attract pilgrims – and offerings – to his tomb. The cult was sponsored by the Angevin kings to strengthen their hold on the throne (the wives of Henry I and King Stephen descended from the Old English royal line); they tried to secure Edward's canonization (this objective was achieved in 1161).[145]

But such arguments are unnecessary to explain the hagiographical element in the *Life*. As has been seen, the *Life of King Alfred* was influenced by hagiography, though to a lesser extent. Moreover, there were good reasons for the strength of hagiographical influence on the *Life of King Edward*. The cult of Edward probably started in his court before his death, long before the Westminster monks got to work on it, and grew immediately afterwards. Thus it had a court, not a monastic origin.[146] In a similar way the legend of King Alfred had begun to grow already in his lifetime.

The idea of a holy king was fashionable in the eleventh century. The power to cure illness, an adjunct of sainthood, had become in France an adjunct of kingship. Robert the Pious was the first French king reputed to exercise thaumaturgical powers.[147] The idea was probably introduced at Edward's court by his Norman courtiers. And it may be symptomatic of a cynical attitude of some Englishmen to Edward's alleged holiness that Archbishop Stigand scoffed at his death-bed prophecy.[148] Edward's appointment as king by God, the divine favour he enjoyed, his pious life and celibacy also have a continental parallel: Henry II of Germany (1002–24) was supposed to have had a similar character and he too became a confessor of the church.[149]

---

[143] See ibid., pp. xxxviii, 64–6.

[144] Ibid., pp. xxxviii et seq., 66–71. Professor Barlow substantiates the view that the earliest version of the *Life* did not have the Vision of the Seven Sleepers in 'The Vita Ædwardi (Book II); the Seven Sleepers: some further evidence and reflections' in *Speculum*, xl (1965), pp. 385–97.

[145] For the development of the cult see *VER*, pp. 112–33 (Appendix D).

[146] *VER*, pp. lxxiii–lxxiv.   [147] See *VER*, pp. lxxiii–lxxiv, 122 and n. 4.

[148] *VER*, pp. 76–7.   [149] See *VER*, pp. lxxiv, lxxviii.

There were other factors which may have contributed to the dominance of hagiographical elements in the *Life*. Perhaps Edward did possess some saintly qualities. It must be admitted that other authorities do not explicitly confirm the *Life*'s picture of Edward as a near saint. On the contrary the sketch of his character in a poem on him in the Anglo-Saxon Chronicle depicts him as a warrior,[150] and the *Life* itself alleges that he liked hunting. He could act as a ruthless diplomatist, capable of destroying the house of Godwin, and on occasion he treated his mother[151] and wife[152] with uncompromising severity. Nevertheless the distinguishing feature of his career was his ability to rule for twenty-four years, in comparative peace, doing remarkably little; perhaps this indicates a saintly personality. Political factors may also have contributed to the hagiographical tone. The author's insistence that Edward was chosen by God may have been intended to reinforce his legal and hereditary right to the throne which was not beyond question (Edward was not King Ethelred's eldest son, whose heir was still living).[153] The stress on Edward's celibacy may have been to explain his childless marriage.[154]

The preponderance of the hagiographical element in Book II accords with a typical feature of much Anglo-Saxon biography (the relegation of a man's spiritual life to the second part of a biography). But here too the author may have been influenced by politics. If, as seems likely, the *Life* was begun just before the Norman Conquest, the author presumably intended to write the story of a successful, happy reign, of the pious king and queen rewarded by prosperity. But perhaps the Norman Conquest intervened while the author was completing Book I; so events belied his purpose. Therefore he changed his theme. At the end of Book I the king is dying, while the queen weeps, full of foreboding because of the quarrel of Harold and Tostig (the author sees the brothers' quarrel as the cause of the English defeat). And because reality had failed the author, he turned to the life of the spirit, devoting Book II to Edward's spiritual virtues: as he could not prove the reign successful, he would prove the ruler holy. Moved by patriotic feelings, he attributed to Edward almost theocratic powers.[155]

There is the problem of who wrote the *Life*. It is clear from the work that the author was foreign. As he mentions St Omer ('the town named after the famous St. Omer who lies honourably within'[156]), and Baldwin V count of Flanders ('that old friend of the English people'[157]) three times, besides spelling place-names in a Teutonic way,[158] it is generally assumed that he came from Flanders. And he was probably a monk of St Bertin, like the encomiast, or a canon of St Omer. He was in England when he wrote and

---

[150] ASC, *s.a.* 1065.

[151] On his accession Edward deprived Emma of her property; ASC, *s.a.* 1043.

[152] Edward temporarily sent Edith away in disgrace during his quarrel with Earl Godwin; ASC, *s.a.* 1051 (E) and *VER*, p. 23 and n. 4.

[153] See also *VER*, pp. lxix–lxx.

[154] See *VER*, pp. lxxv–lxxviii.

[155] See *VER*, pp. xxvi–xxviii, lxxix.

[156] *VER*, p. 55.

[157] *VER*, pp. 22, 24–6, 54–5.

[158] *VER*, p. xliii and n. 1.

knew well Westminster abbey and the nunnery of Wilton. He also had some connection with Canterbury.[159] The *Life* shows that he was poor, lonely, persecuted as he thought, by 'many', and was befriended by Queen Edith.[160]

There is no further information in the *Life* about the author and the work remains anonymous. However, there are two possible candidates for authorship, both monks of St Bertin. Folcard, who acted as abbot of Thorney from about 1067 to about 1083, was a noted hagiographer of English saints. It is apparent from the prologue of his *Life of St. John of Beverley* that he had quarrelled with his ecclesiastical superiors and owed the restoration of his fortunes to a queen. But so little is known of the chronology of his life that there is no certain evidence supporting his authorship:[161] quarrels and royal favour were not rare in the middle ages.

A stronger case can be made for the authorship of the hagiographer Goscelin.[162] Much can be learnt about him from his saints' Lives, composed between 1078 and 1099, and from the *Liber Confortatorius* which he wrote in about 1080 for Eve, a nun of Wilton who later became a recluse at Angers. Some of the facts correspond with what is known about the author of the *Life*. He joined the household of Herman (died 1078), another monk of St Bertin, when Herman became bishop of Sherborne in 1058. He sailed down the Thames with Herman,[163] attended the dedication of Edward's new church at Westminster,[164] and the dedication by Herman of Queen Edith's new church at Wilton.[165] For a time (starting before 1065)[166] he was a chaplain at Wilton, where Edith stayed periodically from Edward's death until her own in 1075.[167] After Herman's death he quarrelled with Osmund, his successor as bishop, and finally settled at St Augustine's, Canterbury.[168]

The *Life* describes Herman as a distinguished and learned bishop.[169] It gives a remarkable account of the Thames, on the banks of which foreign merchants displayed their wares,[170] which resembles that in Goscelin's *Life of St. Wulsin*.[171] It has a detailed architectural description of Westminster abbey and gives a surely eye-witness account of the dedication of Wilton

[159] See *VER*, p. xliv.

[160] *VER*, pp. 2, 59–60.

[161] Folcard's claim to authorship is urged by Professor Barlow who nevertheless recognizes its limitations; *VER*, pp. li–lix.

[162] His claim is favoured by R. W. Southern, 'The first Life of Edward the Confessor' in *EHR*, lviii (1943), pp. 396–400. The evidence is also discussed in *VER*, pp. xlv–li; the known facts of Goscelin's life are summarized and his works listed in ibid., pp. 91–111 (Appendix C).

[163] *The Liber Confortatorius of Goscelin of St. Bertin*, ed. C. H. Talbot (Studia Anselmiana, fasc. xxxvii, Analecta Monastica, Rome 1955), p. 49.

[164] Ibid., pp. 28–9.

[165] 'La legende de Ste. Edith en prose et vers par le moine Goscelin', ed. A. Wilmart in *An. Boll.*, lvi, fasc. iii and iv (1938), pp. 86–7.

[166] *VER*, p. 94 n. 3.

[167] She witnessed a charter there on 28 February 1072; F. H. Dickinson, 'The sale of Combe' in *Proc. of the Somerset Arch. and Nat. Hist. Soc.*, xxii (1876), pp. 106–13.

[168] See *VER*, pp. 102–4.   [169] *VER*, p. 47.   [170] *VER*, p. 44.

[171] 'The Life of Saint Wulsin of Sherborne by Goscelin', ed. C. H. Talbot in *Revue Bénédictine*, lxix (1959), p. 75 (c. 1). Cf. also Talbot, *Liber Confortatorius*, p. 49.

(with a notice of the fire in the town which preceded it), and an epithalamium of the abbey. It is the only authority for the dispute between the monks of Christ Church, Canterbury, and the king over the election of an archbishop (the monks had elected one of their number, Ælric, while the king had chosen Rodbert).[172] It is also the only authority for the dispute between Earl Godwin and Archbishop Robert over Canterbury lands.

The author of the *Life* describes himself as lonely 'like a pelican in the wilderness':[173] Goscelin similarly describes himself, using the same image, in the *Liber Confortatorius*.[174] There are some stylistic similarities, notably in the use of verse, between the *Life* and Goscelin's *Life of St. Edith* (of Wilton).[175] It seems clear that the author of the *Life* liked women. His remark that Queen Edith endowed Wilton generously because women feel the pinch of poverty worse than men and are less able to remedy it, shows understanding of the feminine predicament.[176] Goscelin's *Liber Confortatorius* suggests that he had a warm affection for Eve and the fact that he wrote Lives of at least four female saints may indicate an interest in and respect for women.[177]

However, there are objections to accepting Goscelin as the author of the *Life*. It has been argued that it is unlikely that Goscelin wrote the *Life* because its statement that in 1051, when Godwin quarrelled with King Edward, Edith was sent to Wilton contradicts the evidence of the Anglo-Saxon Chronicle which records that she went to Wherwell abbey: Goscelin, who had lived at Wilton, would hardly have made such a mistake. However, there is no proof it is a mistake. The author of the *Life* knew both Wilton and Edith, and the statement, if not a scribal error, should carry as much weight as the Chronicle's.[178] Another objection is that Goscelin's known works show no particular reverence for Edward. But as they were written a decade or more later than the *Life*, when Norman rule was established and had been accepted by Goscelin, he might not have liked to hark back on the last of the English dynasty.[179] Alternatively he simply put one *Life* out of his mind when he wrote the next.

---

[172] *VER*, pp. 18–19.

[173] *VER*, p. 58. Cf. Ps. ci. 7–8 (Vulgate).

[174] Talbot, *Liber Confortatorius*, p. 27.

[175] For these similarities, see R. W. Southern, 'The first Life of Edward the Confessor', p. 399. Cf. *VER*, pp. xlix–l. Professor Barlow is more impressed by the differences in style between the *Life* and Goscelin's works than by their similarities.

[176] *VER*, p. 47. The epithalamium addressed to Wilton treats the nunnery on the analogy of a bride about to become a mother. This is a conventional conceit, but nevertheless is vividly done, illustrating the life of an excessively prolific mother. She is to be 'surrounded by a hundred thousand cots, with babes not rending mother's heart with tears. . . . Nor will you fear for lack of milk. . . . Nor do the numbers tire or labours vex: you long indeed for ever-growing brood. . . . Loved by your spouse for your fecundity' etc.; *VER*, pp. 48–9.

[177] See *VER*, pp. 98–9.

[178] It may be noted that in one place at least the *Life* has a correct fact while the Chronicle is in error: it states (*VER*, p. 25) that Tostig's wife Judith was the sister of Baldwin count of Flanders; the Chronicle (D, *s.a.* 1051) states that she was his kinswoman. See Southern, 'The first Life of Edward the Confessor', p. 394.

[179] See *VER*, pp. l–li.

Whoever its author, as the *Life* was almost certainly written more or less concurrently with the Norman Conquest and settlement, it is a valuable historical source. The author was fairer-minded than the encomiast, although he too intended to praise his patroness, her husband and family (in this case the house of Godwin). He did not suppress or distort evidence. He deplored Edward's reliance on Norman courtiers for counsel,[180] and admitted Earl Godwin's bad case in the dispute with Archbishop Robert over lands in Kent.[181] Nor did he entirely exonerate Godwin of the murder of Edward's brother Alfred.[182] His knowledge of events, many of which he dates, was considerable and his historical interpretations deserve attention. He maintained that Edward owed the peace of the kingdom to the efforts of Godwin and his sons,[183] and later was unable to suppress the quarrel of Harold and Tostig because the approaching winter and men's dread of civil war prevented him assembling an effective army.[184]

The author knew more about public events and public figures than the encomiast. He attempted to describe the characters of important people. Not content, as the encomiast had been, to scatter his comments throughout the work, he gives long character sketches, of over a page, of Godwin,[185] Harold[186] and Tostig.[187] He also gave one of Edith but owing to the loss of leaves from the only known manuscript, this is not now extant. Nevertheless something can be gathered about her from the rest of the work and from the works of authors who used the missing section of the *Life*. The author states that she influenced politics,[188] liked reading[189] and sewing,[190] and was kind to women[191] and to the poor.[192] 'She was a woman to be placed before all royal ladies or persons of royal and imperial rank as a model of virtue and integrity, maintaining both the practices of the Christian religion and worldly dignity.'[193]

The *Life* has some apparently intimate touches which suggest that Edith treated her husband with deference and consideration. 'Although by custom and law a royal throne was always prepared for her at the king's side, she preferred, except in church and at the royal table, to sit at his feet, unless he reached out his hand to her, or with a gesture invited or commanded her to sit next to him.'[194] As Edward did not trouble about dress, Edith, the *Life* states, 'kindly arrayed him in his royal finery' on state occasions. Edward 'would not have minded at all if clothes had been provided at far less cost. He was, however, grateful for the queen's solicitude in these matters and with some kindness of feeling used to remark on her zeal most appreciatively to his intimates.'[195]

---

[180] *VER*, pp. 17–19. The author's loyalty was to the English against both Danes and Frenchmen; cf. ibid., pp. 5–7 *passim*.

[181] *VER*, p. 19.   [182] *VER*, pp. 20–8.   [183] *VER*, p. 40.
[184] *VER*, p. 53.   [185] *VER*, pp. 5–7.   [186] *VER*, pp. 31–2.
[187] *VER*, p. 32.   [188] *VER*, pp. 3–4, 54.   [189] *VER*, pp. 14–15.
[190] *VER*, pp. 14–15, 41.   [191] *VER*, p. 47.   [192] *VER*, p. 42.
[193] Ibid.   [194] Ibid.   [195] *VER*, p. 41.

5

Anglo-Saxon Sacred Biography and Local History

In contrast to the tradition of secular biography, that of sacred biography flourished in Anglo-Saxon England and produced some masterpieces. The greatest scholars of the age, Bede, Ælfric and possibly Byrhtferth, besides other less known but on the whole competent authors, contributed to it. The Anglo-Saxons also produced a number of local histories, that is histories of particular monasteries or ecclesiastical sees.

The term 'sacred biography' is here used to mean the Lives of saints and biographies of bishops, abbots and the like. The distinction between hagiographies and biographies is far from clear cut, because most of the saints were ecclesiastical dignitaries, and sainthood at this period had no canonical status: it was not until the mid-twelfth century that papal canonization was formalized.[1]

Hagiography was intended to praise the saint and edify the reader. The writer usually recorded portents heralding the saint's birth, the miracles worked by the saint, and his posthumous manifestations. Some Lives had a liturgical purpose. Thus it has been suggested that the *Life of Gregory the Great* written at Whitby in about 700, which was based on homilies for sermons, was intended to provide lessons to be read on the feast of St Gregory.[2] Adelard's *Life of St. Dunstan*[3] is divided into twelve lessons, as were the post-Conquest Lives of John of Beverley.[4]

The value of saints' Lives to the historian has long been recognized. Those of the Anglo-Saxon period were the sources used by Norman hagiographers – who added little but error and fictional embellishment.[5]

[1] See E. W. Kemp, *Canonization and Authority in the Western Church* (Oxford 1948), pp. 82–106.
[2] B. Colgrave, 'The earliest Life of St. Gregory the Great, written by a Whitby monk' in Chadwick, *Celt and Saxon*, p. 122. For a printed text, see *The Earliest Life of Gregory the Great*, ed. B. Colgrave (Kansas 1968).
[3] Printed in *Memorials SD*, pp. 53–68.
[4] Printed in *Historians of the Church of York*, ed. James Raine (RS, 1879–94), vol. 1, pp. 511–29
[5] This point is well expressed by J. A. Robinson, 'St. Oswald and the church of Worcester' *British Academy Supplemental Papers*, v (London 1919), p. 38, who writes of the post-Conquest historians that they 'have coloured the history of the tenth century according to their later conceptions; but they had little to guide them that we have not before us today, and we need to be constantly on the watch against their misinterpretations and amplifications.' He analyses the pre-Conquest evidence relating to Archbishop Oda and its post-Conquest accretions in ibid., pp. 38–51.

They give a picture of the saints, who were usually important both in the religious life of the time and also in secular affairs. Embedded in the miracles is usually a factual and fairly accurate account of the saint's career written within a decade or two of his death by a contemporary and often a close companion.

Most hagiographers interpreted their subject widely, giving details of the saint's acquaintances, events concerning him, places he visited and churches he built. Some of the later hagiographies give the impression that the author was using the Life as a vehicle for conveying extraneous material which caught his attention or entirely absorbed his interest – a particular subject of attention being the religious house with which the saint was associated. The later saints' Lives are important sources for local history, some virtually giving an account of the foundation and growth of the saint's monastery.

Local history, in the form of histories of particular monasteries and churches, can be discussed with biographies because they are closely related to them. They are linked in two ways. First, the hagiographer, besides being interested in the saint's monastery while the saint was still alive, might extend his interest after the saint's death. The hagiographer often described the saint's posthumous power and cult. From the beginning of monasticism in Northumbria, the association of a saint with the house of his origin survived his death: where his body rested he continued to exercise supernatural gifts. Even if a church could not claim to have a saint's body intact, some part of it, or an object (piece of clothing, a book) which had belonged to the saint, might perform similar service. Thus there developed the cult of relics (Bede mentions that Willibrord took relics of saints on his mission to the Old Saxons[6]). The saint's presence alive or dead constituted the holiness of the place, the foundation-stone of the monastery's tradition. And the hagiographer, in fulfilling his duty of recording the dead saint's acts (and so incidentally of establishing beyond doubt that his body lay in the monastery), was obliged to trace the community's history.

The other link connecting biographies with local histories is the fact that the earliest local histories are a series of biographies of the heads of the institution concerned (the abbots of the monastery, the archbishops of the metropolitan see, and the like). The author made what he chose of the holiness of the subjects of the biographies, but emphasized facts relating to the place's history. The place gained, in varying degrees, dominance over the biographical framework, achieving a personality of its own. And just as the hagiographer wrote primarily to praise a saint, so the local historian's strongest motive was to praise a place. This he did particularly by emphasizing its holiness. But he also recorded its acquisition of earthly goods, property and privilege.

[6] *HE*, v. 11. Pope Gregory sent relics to St Augustine (*HE*, i. 29) and instructed him to use relics to replace heathen idols (*HE*, i. 30). For other references to relics by Bede see *HE*, iii. 6, 26; *Hist. Abb.* § 6.

There were three main periods when biographies were written, each divided from the next by times of war and political upheaval which, by disturbing all monasteries and destroying some, hampered literary creation. The first period was the 'golden age' of Northumbria, from the end of the seventh to the middle of the eighth century. A thin trickle of institutional histories links this period to the next. The second period began with the monastic revival of the late tenth century and lasted until the early eleventh century. The third period was the late eleventh century, when the Lives were written of bishops and abbots who began ruling in Anglo-Saxon times and whose power survived into William I's reign. Thus the biographical tradition bridged the Conquest, to be admired and emulated by the Normans.

Generally speaking each period has distinctive features. The biographies of the first period are the most purely hagiographical. They centre mainly on the saint, although two of them (the Whitby *Life of Gregory the Great* and the *Life of Bishop Wilfrid* of York)[7] show that their authors were also interested in the history of the monasteries where they wrote. The biographies of the second period show that the authors, like the saints, were absorbed in the progress of the monastic revival. Works of the third period demonstrate the authors' anxiety to define the rights and possessions of the saint's (or other ecclesiastic's) see or monastery.

In the first period the one local history (Bede's *History of the Abbots of Wearmouth and Jarrow*),[8] and all except one of the hagiographies, were written in Northumbria. There were three Lives of St Cuthbert (one by an anonymous monk of Lindisfarne, and two, one in prose and one in verse, by Bede),[9] the *Life of Gregory the Great* and the *Life of Bishop Wilfrid*. The non-Northumbrian work was the *Life of St. Guthlac*, a Mercian saint, by an East Anglian called Felix.[10] The Lives of St Cuthbert and the *Life of St. Guthlac* belong to the traditional type of hagiography found in such standard works as Athanasius's *Life of St. Antony*. This kind of Life begins with a preface in which the author usually says that he wrote at the command of a superior and felt inadequate to the task. There follows an account of the saint's life from birth, with numerous miracles and a full description of his pious death.[11]

Of the three Lives of St Cuthbert, the most important was by the monk of Lindisfarne. It is the earliest and was the basis of Bede's prose and metrical Lives. Bede added a few details but most of his additions are verbal and

---

[7] Printed in *The Life of Bishop Wilfrid by Eddius Stephanus*, ed., with an English translation, B. Colgrave (Cambridge 1927).

[8] Printed in Plummer, vol. 1, pp. 364–87.

[9] For printed editions of the Lives of St Cuthbert see p. 15 nn. 14, 21.

[10] The most recent edition is *Felix's Life of St. Guthlac*, ed., with an English translation, B. Colgrave (Cambridge 1956).

[11] For this hagiographical tradition see Colgrave, 'Bede's miracle stories' in Thompson, *Bede*, p. 204.

hagiographical trimmings.[12] The Lindisfarne monk wrote some time between 699 and 705,[13] at the command of Eadfrith bishop of Lindisfarne (698–721) and the community. As a biography of a famous churchman it has considerable value. It gives a picture of a missionary bishop, travelling from place to place, living in a tent, to convert the still largely pagan inhabitants of the most inaccessible regions of Northumbria.[14] The portable altar he must have used on such occasions still survives.[15] The *Life* shows how Cuthbert rivalled the Celtic saints in his austerity and love of isolation: to mortify the flesh, he would stand neck-deep in the sea,[16] and he spent his last two years in great privation on Farne Island. The blend of the hagiography and genuine biography in the *Life* is well illustrated by an incident it describes: Cuthbert had a vision of the defeat of King Egfrith by the Picts at Nectansmere while he was at Carlisle, looking at the wall and well 'formerly built in a wonderful manner by the Romans', conducted by Waga the reeve of the city.[17] This is the first reference to a sight-seeing tour in English literature.

Felix's *Life of St. Guthlac* falls into the same category as the Lives of St Cuthbert. Felix was in fact much influenced by Bede's prose *Life of St. Cuthbert* and borrowed passages from it.[18] He wrote, probably between 730 and 740,[19] at the command of Alfwold king of the East Angles (*c.* 713–749). Exactly why an East Anglian king wanted a hagiography of a Mercian saint is not clear. But perhaps he regarded Crowland, where Guthlac became a hermit in about 699, with close interest because it was on the borders of his kingdom. Moreover, it is possible that Ethelbald king of Mercia (716–57) took refuge in Alfwold's kingdom when he was in exile during the reign of Ceolred who was king of Mercia from 709 to 716.[20] Felix speaks highly of King Ethelbald, describing his visits to St Guthlac and the generous gifts he subsequently gave at his tomb.[21]

Felix's *Life of St. Guthlac* has some interest for the general history of the times. For example, no other authority mentions that Ethelbald went into exile because of the enmity of King Ceolred (Ethelbald, as a grandson of Penda's brother Eowa, was a possible rival of Ceolred).[22] And it gives a picture of a noble (Guthlac was related to the Mercian royal family) who spent his youth fighting the Britons of Wales before becoming a monk of Repton.[23] The *Life* also has value for local history. The very fact that it mentions no monastic community at Crowland strongly suggests that the claim by later medieval writers that St Guthlac founded Crowland abbey is

---

[12] See Colgrave, *Lives*, pp. 13–16.   [13] See ibid., p. 13.
[14] For a reference to St Cuthbert's use of tents see *VSC* (Anon.), iv. 5. For the survival of heathenism see *VSC* (Bede), cc. 3, 9.
[15] See C. A. Raleigh Radford on St Cuthbert's portable altar in *The Relics of Saint Cuthbert*, ed. C. F. Battiscombe (Oxford 1956), pp. 326–35.
[16] *VSC* (Anon.), ii. 3.   [17] *VSC* (Anon.), iv. 8.   [18] See *Felix*, p. 16.
[19] *Felix*, pp. 18–19.   [20] *Felix*, p. 6 and c. 49.   [21] *Felix*, cc. 40, 45, 49, 52.
[22] *Felix*, pp. 5–6 and c. 49.   [23] *Felix*, cc. 2–20 *passim*.

false.[24] And the *Life* gives a good description of the ancient long barrow (either prehistoric or Roman) in which St. Guthlac lived at Crowland: 'Now there was in the island of Crowland a mound built of clods of earth which greedy comers to the waste had dug open, in the hope of finding treasure; in the side of this there was a sort of tank-like cavity, and in this Guthlac the man of blessed memory began to live, having built a hut over it.'[25]

In the Lives of St Cuthbert and in the *Life of St. Guthlac*, the saint occupies a central place throughout the narrative. The authors of the other two works, the *Life of Bishop Wilfrid* and the *Life of Gregory the Great*, did not keep so strictly to their subject – the authors were concerned not only to record the life of the saint, but also the history of the religious house (or houses) with which he was connected.

The *Life of Wilfrid* was written by a monk of Ripon, possibly Eddius Stephanus,[26] within ten years of Wilfrid's death (in 709). The *Life* which contains few miracles, is a valuable historical source because of the important role Wilfrid played in public life. It gives an account, with documents copied in full,[27] of Wilfrid's quarrels as archbishop of York (664–78, 686–91) with Theodore archbishop of Canterbury and the royal court. Bede gives a less full though more accurate account of the same events, using the *Life* as one of his sources. The author's interest in the history of Wilfrid's two monasteries, Ripon and Hexham, caused him to deviate from a narrowly biographical theme. He uses the *Life* to record facts about them. He records the foundation of Ripon – with the exact grant of forty hides given by King Aldfrith to Wilfrid, who was the first abbot, for it.[28] There is an account of the dedication of the church and a description of the building: it was 'a church of dressed stone, supported by various columns and side aisles', and the altar 'with its bases was vested in purple woven with gold'.[29] The author carefully traces the vicissitudes of Ripon during Wilfrid's quarrels with Theodore and the king (when Wilfrid lost his property he was allowed to keep Ripon and Hexham).[30] And he gives a full account of Wilfrid's final leave-taking of the monks of Ripon in 709, and of his subsequent funeral at Ripon, noting that Tatberht succeeded to the abbacy in accordance with Wilfrid's expressed wishes.[31]

The author's interest in Hexham is slightly less close. However, he records the circumstances of the foundation of St Andrew's, on land given by Queen

---

[24] See F. Liebermann, 'Ueber ostenglische Geschichtsquellen des 12, 13, 14 Jahrhunderts besonders den falschen Ingulf' in *Neues Archiv der Gesellschaft für ältere deutsche Geschichtskunde* (Hanover–Leipzig 1892), xviii, pp. 246–7. See also *Felix*, pp. 7–13.

[25] *Felix*, c. 28.

[26] The evidence for Eddius's authorship is weak. See *Eddius*, pp. ix–x.

[27] See ibid., pp. xi–xiii. For copies of documents see ibid., cc. 30–2, 43, 51, 54.

[28] Ibid., c. 8.

[29] Ibid., c. 17. The passage is noticed in H. M. and J. Taylor, *Anglo-Saxon Architecture* (Cambridge 1965, 2 vols), vol. 2, pp. 516–17.

[30] *Eddius*, cc. 47 (p. 96), 51 (p. 106).   [31] Ibid., c. 66. Cf. c. 63.

Ethelthryth,[32] and the arrangement Wilfrid made before his death for the succession of Acca as abbot and bishop of Hexham.[33] And he has a vivid and detailed description of the church itself: it had 'crypts of wonderfully dressed stone, a substantial building above ground with numerous columns and side aisles, and adorned with walls of great length and height, surrounded by various winding passages with spiral stairs leading up and down. . . . We have not heard of any other house on this side of the Alps built on such a scale.'[34] The author also describes the state of the cathedral at York when Wilfrid became archbishop. The stone church built by Paulinus was in a ruinous condition. 'The roof leaked, the birds flew in and out of the unglazed windows, nesting in and defiling the neglected walls.' Wilfrid renewed the roof, covering it with lead, put glass in the windows, washed the walls and richly furnished and endowed the church.[35] By such passages the author shows his interest in Wilfrid's churches in their own right, that is, in local history.

Local history occupies an even more important part in the *Life of Gregory the Great* written by a Whitby monk between 704 and 714.[36] It differs considerably from the other saints' Lives of the period. This was partly no doubt because, being early, it could not be modelled on a native tradition. Moreover, Pope Gregory died at least a century before it was written and had no direct association with Whitby. The author, apparently ill supplied with reference books, knew little about him.[37] However, his account of the conversion of the English is independent of Bede's in the *Ecclesiastical History*: for example his version of the story of how Pope Gregory saw some English youths in Rome differs slightly from the version given by Bede.[38] It is likely that this story and the others he tells about the conversion came from Canterbury, where the memory of St Augustine was still alive. The connection with Canterbury would have been through the abbess of Whitby, Eanfled, the daughter of King Edwin and his Kentish queen Ethelberg. Eanfled herself was born and educated in Canterbury, coming north on her marriage with King Oswy (she took the veil at Whitby after his death).

[32] Ibid., c. 22.

[33] Ibid., c. 65.

[34] Ibid., c. 22. This passage was used in the twelfth century by Richard of Hexham for his account of the church (see p. 288 and n. 149 below). It is noticed in Taylor, *Anglo-Saxon Architecture*, vol. I, p. 297). For a literary reconstruction of Wilfrid's church from archaeological evidence, see ibid., pp. 297–312.

[35] *Eddius*, c. 16.

[36] See *VSG*, p. 48.

[37] The author admits his lack of information: see the printed text in *VSG*, §§ 3, 30 (pp. 77, 129).

[38] See *VSG*, § 9 (pp. 13–14). Cf. Colgrave, 'The earliest Life of St. Gregory', p. 123. For evidence that the *Life of Gregory* is independent of *HE*, see E. C. Butler in 'Chronicle, Hagiographica' in *Journal of Theological Studies*, vii (1906), pp. 312–13, and H. Moretus in *An. Boll.*, xxvi (1907), pp. 66–72. The early date of the *Life* was established by H. Thurston, who, however, argued that it was based on Bede; see H. Thurston, 'The oldest Life of St. Gregory' in the *Month*, civ (1904), pp. 337–53. See also Colgrave, 'The earliest Life of St. Gregory', p. 121, and *VSG*, pp. 56–9.

She was succeeded as abbess of Whitby by her daughter Aelfleda. It seems probable that Eanfled was responsible for introducing the cult of St Gregory at Whitby, and perhaps for the acquisition of a relic of him.[39]

The association of Whitby with the Northumbrian royal house is reflected in the *Life of Gregory*. The author used Gregory's career to provide a setting for St Augustine's mission to the English. He narrowed this subject down to the conversion of Northumbria under King Edwin, whose own conversion had secured the triumph of Christianity in Northumbria, and whose death fighting the heathen gave him some claim to martyrdom. The author blended Edwin's life with St Gregory's, as if it would thus gain reflected glory.[40] The fact that the *Life* records the details of Edwin's burial at Whitby[41] suggests that his cult was fostered there, alongside that of St Gregory. Whitby lacked its own particular famous saint, so it is not improbable that Edwin was chosen to supply the lack, to be to the abbey what Oswald (who also died in a battle against pagans) was to Bamburgh, Lindisfarne and Bardney, and what Cuthbert was to Lindisfarne. As will be seen, the conscious promotion of a cult for the benefit of a monastery became a common feature of Anglo-Saxon hagiography.

Thus hagiographies in this early period could be expanded to include local history. Moreover, the best local history produced by the Anglo-Saxons was written at this time, Bede's *History of the Abbots of Wearmouth and Jarrow*.[42] Bede wrote it, to praise his monastery, between 716 and 731, deriving its form from hagiography. It is a series of biographies of the abbots, Benedict Biscop, Sigfrid and Ceolfrid. Bede used for his account of Ceolfrid an anonymous *Life of Ceolfrid* written at Wearmouth.[43] This *Life* included miracles alleged to have been worked by Ceolfrid. But Bede, although he emphasized Ceolfrid's piety, omitted the miracles, and so dropped the purely hagiographical element.

Bede gave detailed accounts of the abbots' acquisition of lands, papal privileges, books, church ornaments and vestments, and commented on the monastic observance at Wearmouth/Jarrow. For example, he records that Benedict Biscop obtained seventy hides of land from King Egfrith for his foundation.[44] And some of the treasures he brought back from his frequent visits to Rome were exchanged for more lands: two silk cloaks 'of incomparable workmanship' were traded with Ecgfrith for three hides 'on the south bank of the river Wear';[45] and a beautiful volume of the Geographers was exchanged for eight hides.[46] Bede records that both Benedict Biscop and

---

[39] See Colgrave, 'The earliest Life of St. Gregory', pp. 131–2.

[40] For Edwin, see *VSG*, §§ 12, 14–16 (pp. 95–101 *passim*).

[41] *VSG*, §§ 18–19 (pp. 101–5).

[42] For the *History of the Abbots of Wearmouth and Jarrow*, see W. Levison, 'Bede as historian' in Thompson, *Bede*, pp. 129–30.

[43] Printed in Plummer, vol. 1, pp. 388–404, and, in an English translation, *The Life of Ceolfrid Abbot of the Monastery at Wearmouth and Jarrow*, ed. D. S. Boutflower (Sunderland 1912).

[44] *Hist. Abb.* § 4.   [45] Ibid., § 9.   [46] Ibid, § 15.

Ceolfrid obtained papal privileges for the monastery, 'by which it was made safe and secure from any outside interference'.[47]

Bede is particularly full on the books, relics and works of art brought from Rome by Benedict Biscop and given to Wearmouth/Jarrow, including a series of pictures of the Virgin Mary and the twelve apostles and biblical illustrations, some arranged in types and antitypes, as Bede explains.[48] They were to decorate the walls of the churches, 'so that every one who entered, even if they could not read, wherever they looked, might have before them the beloved countenance of Christ and his saints, though it were but a picture, and with their minds thus stirred might reflect on the benefits of our Lord's incarnation, and, with the perils of the last judgement before their eyes, might examine their hearts the more closely.'[49]

Bede records the introduction of Roman chant in the monastery by John, precentor of St Peter's, Rome, who accompanied Benedict Biscop back,[50] and he remarks on the nature of the Rule introduced by Benedict Biscop.[51] And so he adapted biography to the needs of local historiography, and wrote a unique account of the growth of a monastery in dark age England.

The tradition of Bede struggled on in Northumbria in the next two centuries. Three local histories survive from this period, all written under Bede's influence. The writers' deep sense of the holiness of the Northumbrian saints was stimulated particularly by the Lives of St Cuthbert and the *Ecclesiastical History*. It is likely that Bede's metrical *Life of St. Cuthbert* encouraged two of the authors to write in Latin verse. Although none of the authors cites the *History of the Abbots of Wearmouth and Jarrow*, it may have provided the idea of writing institutional histories. All three writers were dominated by the biographical form – from which, however, they were prepared to deviate when their knowledge failed or their interests extended to non-biographical fields.

The earliest of the works was Alcuin's *De Pontificibus et Sanctis Ecclesiae Eboracensis Carmen* (*Song on the Archbishops and Saints of the Church of York*),[52] an account in verse of Northumbria from Roman times to Alcuin's day, with particular laudatory emphasis on the Northumbrian saints and the archbishops of York. Alcuin ends with the death of Archbishop Albert in 780. As he joined Charlemagne's court in 782 Alcuin may have finished the work while at Tours where he remained until his death in 804. The *Carmen* shows the predominant influence of Bede. Much of the early material is derived from the *Ecclesiastical History* and the Lives of St Cuthbert, and

---

[47] Ibid., §§ 6, 15.   [48] Ibid., §§ 6, 9.   [49] Ibid., § 6.   [50] Ibid., § 6.
[51] See ibid., §§ 6, 11, 16.
[52] The standard edition is in *MGH, Poetae Latini aevi Carolini*, vol. 1, ed. E. L. Duemmler (Berlin 1881), pp. 169 et seq. (*MGH, Poetae latini medii aevi*). A useful edition, with English captions in the margin, is in Raine, *Historians of the Church of York*, vol. 1, pp. 349–98. For an account of the *Carmen* see F. J. E. Raby, *A History of Secular Latin Poetry in the Middle Ages* (2nd ed., Oxford 1957, 2 vols), vol. 1, pp. 178–80.

Bede's authority is generously acknowledged.[53] Alcuin gives a eulogistic account of the life and work of this 'distinguished doctor of outstanding merit'.[54] Besides sharing Bede's devotion to Northumbrian saints, he had a similar taste for visions of the afterworld (he not only includes Drythelm's vision but also ends with a similar vision which a boy of York had in Alcuin's time).[55]

Alcuin wrote, as he says, for the instruction of scholars at York. However, it is likely that he also hoped to convince a wider audience that no region in western Europe was holier than Northumbria and no city more cultured than York. The *Carmen* is not a pure institutional history, for the first two-thirds concerns Northumbria in general. This section is of little historical value as it is derivative. Alcuin could not add much to Bede about the early archbishops of York – indeed he admits that everything he writes about John of Beverley was from the *Ecclesiastical History*.[56] Nevertheless he shows a consciousness of York as a place. He starts with a description of the city's site and Roman walls and towers, indicating its strategic and commercial importance in Roman times.[57]

As soon as Alcuin reaches the period within his own memory, the *Carmen* becomes a valuable source. The biographical form reasserts itself and he gives two consecutive lives of the archbishops he had known, Egbert (732 or 734 to 766) and Albert (767–80) and notices Eanbald's succession.[58] Although elsewhere in the work there are a number of visions and miracles, Alciun attributes none to these archbishops. He concentrates on their piety, generosity and learning. He particularly emphasizes Albert's promotion of and teaching in the school at York. Before succeeding as archbishop, Albert, 'a pious and wise doctor and priest', had been master of the York scholars.[59] Perhaps the most interesting section in the *Carmen* is a list of some of the books in Albert's library. The list is unique evidence that York had one of the best libraries in western Europe.[60]

The next local history, written between 803 and 821, was the *Carmen Æthelwulfi (Song of Æthelwulf)*,[61] a metrical history in praise of an unidentified cell of Lindisfarne.[62] It was probably modelled on Alcuin's work,[63] and was influenced by the hagiographical element in Bede's *Ecclesiastical History* and by the Lives of St Cuthbert. The author, Æthelwulf, was an inmate of the cell where he had gone as a boy, and claims he was the author of another work, on pious Englishmen. He wrote the *Carmen* for his

[53] Alcuin, *Carm.*, ll. 743, 1206.   [54] Ibid., ll. 1288–1305.   [55] Ibid., ll. 1601–47.
[56] Ibid., ll. 1206–8.   [57] Ibid., ll. 19–37.   [58] Ibid., l. 1522.
[59] Ibid., ll. 1426–32.
[60] Ibid., ll. 1540–56. See F. M. Stenton, *Anglo-Saxon England* (Oxford 1947), p. 188.
[61] The standard edition is *Æthelwulf De Abbatibus*, ed. A. Campbell (Oxford 1967).
[62] T. Arnold in his edition of Æthelwulf in *SD*, vol. 1, pp. 265–94, attributed the work to the priory of Crayke (see ibid., pp. xxxii–xxxix). But Professor Campbell disproves this view; see *Æthelwulf*, pp. xxv–xxvi.
[63] See ibid., p. xlvi.

community and dedicated it to Egbert 'the priest' (*sacerdos*), presumably Egbert bishop of Lindisfarne from 802 to 821.[64]

The *Carmen Æthelwulfi* throws light on one of the most obscure periods of English history. It has a full account of the foundation of the house.[65] A noble, Eanmund, fell into disfavour with the Northumbrian king Osred, who persecuted the nobles, forcing some, including Eanmund, to become monks. So Eanmund decided to found a monastery and consulted Eadfrith bishop of Lindisfarne (698–721), meeting him on the island itself ('where the waves are eager to curl over the shore with grey water, but rush to lay them bare as they go on their backward course, and the blue depths encircle a sacred land, but afford an easy journey when they lay the shores bare'[66]). He also consulted Egbert, the pious Northumbrian who, as Bede records, studied in Ireland. A site was chosen on a hill, 'with bushes and a winding path'. The community flourished and up to Æthelwulf's time had suffered no attacks (presumably Æthelwulf was here thinking of the Danish sack of Lindisfarne in 793).

Æthelwulf was rather less influenced by the biographical type of literature than Alcuin had been. He gives the succession of the abbots with praise for their piety, abstemiousness and other virtues (he attributes no miracles to them). He claims to have been the constant companion of Wulfsig for six years before the latter became abbot.[67] But Æthelwulf's main interest was in the community. He wanted to preserve the memory of certain monks he admired. He writes about his teacher Hyglac, a monk lector (also mentioned by Bede),[68] Ultan, a famous Irish scribe who joined the community,[69] the generous and pious Frithugils,[70] the monk Cwicwine who was skilled in metalwork,[71] and the priest Wynfrith who had charge of the monks' clothes.[72] In his effort to enhance their reputations he records miracles and visions with which they were associated. Following the Bedan tradition he was especially impressed by visions of the afterworld. He describes one which seems to be modelled on Drythelm's vision.[73]

The institution emerges as an entity distinct from its rulers in the *Historia de Sancto Cuthberto*, a history of St Cuthbert's see from its foundation to 945 (with later additions until King Canute's time).[74] The *Historia* was written by an anonymous monk of St Cuthbert in the mid-tenth century. It begins with St Cuthbert's life, taken from Bede's Lives, then has an account of how the monks of Lindisfarne fled from their monastery and wandered for seven years with St Cuthbert's body until they buried it at Chester-le-Street, and ends with short Lives of the bishops of Chester-le-Street. Into this framework the author fitted meticulous details about the see's acquisition of landed

[64] Ibid., Preface and ll. 13–34.   [65] Ibid., ll. 35 et seq.   [66] Ibid., ll. 95–8.
[67] Ibid., ll. 548–52.   [68] Ibid., ll. 507 et seq., 743–4.   [69] Ibid., ll. 206 et seq.
[70] Ibid., ll. 270 et seq.   [71] Ibid., ll. 278 et seq.   [72] Ibid., ll. 579 et seq.
[73] Ibid., ll. 321–94; cf. pp. xxxii–xxxiii.
[74] Printed in *SD*, vol. 1, pp. 196–214. The value as a historical source of *Hist. SC* is discussed by
    E. Craster, 'The patrimony of St. Cuthbert' in *EHR*, lxix (1954), pp. 177–99.

property. He gives the names of estates and traces their boundaries with such exactness that the Durham writer (who used the *Historia de Sancto Cuthberto* as a source) was able, a century later, to refer to the work as a cartulary (*cartula*).[75]

One reason why the history of the institution itself, not the biographies of the bishops, predominated was obviously the availability of material. The author could discover little about the bishops after St Cuthbert; but he had heard traditions about the peregrinations of St Cuthbert's body and had access to the see's business documents.[76] Another reason for his emphasis on local history was his interest in it. This was due to the insecurity of the times, when society was disrupted by the Danish invasions and by raiders from Scotland. The author thought it necessary to establish beyond doubt that the see still had St Cuthbert's body. He may have been afraid men would think it had been snatched by marauding soldiers, or even that the monks themselves had taken it for safety to Ireland. The monks had planned such a transportation and the author is insistent that divine intervention (a timely storm in the Irish channel) caused them to change their minds.[77] The *Historia* represents St Cuthbert as posthumously defending his see, guarding fugitives to the sanctuary of his church (*patrocinium*)[78] and visiting with death or trouble those violating his rights or trespassing on his property.[79] The author regarded the see as the personification of the saint: gifts are 'to St. Cuthbert' and King Athelstan places his charter to the community at the head of St Cuthbert's uncorrupt corpse.[80]

The author probably hoped, by such hagiographical sword-rattling, to defend St Cuthbert's see from external attacks and encroachments. He had in mind both looters, and also Danish settlers who were given estates in Northumbria.[81] But the author's main line of defence was the careful delimitation of the see's property, with a record of its ancient and indisputable right to its lands. He even falsifies evidence to prove that certain estates had been given by King Oswy during St Cuthbert's lifetime.[82] And so for the first time insecurity and fear of controversy provided as powerful an incentive as piety for the writing of an institutional history.

---

[75] *SD*, vol. i, p. 72. Cf. Craster, op. cit., p. 177.

[76] See Craster, op. cit., *passim*.

[77] *Hist. SC*, § 20.

[78] Edred son of Ricsige fled to St Cuthbert's *patrocinium* because he had killed Eardwulf; *Hist. SC*, § 24. King Guthfrith's grant to St Cuthbert (*c.* 883) of the right of asylum is recorded in *Hist. SC*, § 13.

[79] See the fate of King Aelle, Halfdan king of the Danes, and the Dane Onalafball, who all encroached on St Cuthbert's property; *Hist. SC*, §§ 10, 12, 23. The story that St Cuthbert helped King Alfred against the Danes (*Hist. SC*, pp. 204–7) is probably an insertion *temp.* King Canute; see *SD*, vol. i, p. 207 note a.

[80] *Hist. SC*, § 26.

[81] Ibid., § 23, provides unique early evidence for the size of the shares allocated to a leader in the Scandinavian armies when conquered lands were divided; see F. M. Stenton, *The Danes in England* (Raleigh Lecture on History, British Academy, 1927), p. 4 and n. 1.

[82] *Hist. SC*, § 3 and note a.

Veneration for the founders of a religious movement was the chief motive for writing saints' Lives in the second period of biographical composition. This period began with the revival of Benedictine monasticism in the late tenth century. The monastic revival took place during the political recovery of England after the Viking invasions, and drew its inspiration from the tradition of the early English church and from the reformed houses of France and Flanders, notably from Fleury and St Peter's, Ghent. It was the work of three ecclesiastics: St Dunstan, abbot of Glastonbury and then archbishop of Canterbury (960–88), Ethelwold, bishop of Winchester (963–84), and Oswald, bishop of Worcester (961–92) and, holding the sees concurrently, archbishop of York from 972. They were helped by King Edgar, who took a deep interest in the movement, and by other lay patrons, notably Æthelwine, the noble who gave Oswald the site for Ramsey abbey.

Clearly the monastic revival acted as a powerful incentive to biography. Authors wanted to commemorate the achievements of the reformers and their patrons, and to establish the holiness of England in past times. The principal biographies were of the three leaders of the revival: the *Life of St. Oswald* by an anonymous monk of Ramsey, written between 995 and 1005;[83] two Lives of St Dunstan, one by a Flemish clerk or monk, whose name began with 'B', resident in England, written between 996 and 1004,[84] and the other by Adelard, a monk of St Peter's, Ghent, composed between 1004 and 1011;[85] and two Lives of St Ethelwold, one by Ælfric the grammarian, written in 1005 or 1006,[86] and another by Wulfstan, a monk of Winchester, written soon after Ælfric's work, on which it is mainly based.[87] King Edgar's contribution to the revival is commemorated in a short historical treatise in English on his establishment of monasteries, perhaps by St Ethelwold himself[88] (Ethelwold translated the Rule of St Benedict into English for Edgar[89]).

A number of other hagiographies were written in this period, a few throwing light on monastic origins. The first was probably Abbo of Fleury's work on the martyrdom (in 870) and miracles of St Edmund, king of the East Angles, written while Abbo was at Ramsey, between 986 and 988. This *Passio Sancti Edmundi* has one or two apparently authentic details about

[83] Printed in Raine, *Historians of the Church of York*, vol. 1, pp. 399–475.

[84] Printed in *Memorials SD*, pp. 3–52.   [85] See p. 67 n. 3.

[86] Printed in *Ab.*, vol. 2, pp. 255–66. An English translation is in *English Historical Documents*, vol. 1, *c. 500–1042*, ed. D. Whitelock (London 1955), pp. 832–9.

[87] Printed in J. Mabillon, *Acta Sanctorum ordinis S. Benedicti* (Paris 1668–1701, 9 vols), saec. v, pp. 608–24, and Bollandists, *Acta Sanctorum*, 1 August, pp. 88–98. For the authorship of the biography, see D. J. V. Fisher, 'The early biographers of St. Ethelwold' in *EHR*, lxvii (1952), pp. 381–91. Whitelock, *Documents*, pp. 832–9, notes facts in Wulfstan which are not in Ælfric.

[88] Printed, with a rendering in modern English, in *Leechdoms, Wortcunning and Starcraft of Early England* . . . , (RS, 1864–6, 3 vols), ed. T. O. Cockayne, vol. 3, pp. 432–45. See also Whitelock, *Documents*, pp. 846–9.

[89] The twelfth-century *Liber Eliensis*, ii. 37, records a gift to Ethelwold from King Edgar on condition that he translated the Rule of St Benedict for him (see *LE*, pp. x, 111 and n. 7, 414).

St Edmund's life.[90] The date of two other hagiographies is uncertain, but they probably belong to the monastic revival. One is the *Life of Grimbald*, a monk of St Bertin's whom King Alfred summoned to his court.[91] It has many miracles but shows the author's interest in the New Minster at Winchester. It tells how Grimbald, with the help first of King Alfred and then of Edward the Elder, accomplished the foundation of the New Minster and became its first abbot. The other hagiography, of uncertain date, is the rather similar *Life of St. Ecgwin*. Although predominantly miraculous, it includes details purporting to record the circumstances of the foundation of the abbey of Evesham.[92] The Lives of a number of other English saints were written by Ælfric.

We are primarily concerned here with the biographies of SS. Dunstan, Ethelwold and Oswald.

The authors wrote because of their admiration for the saints concerned and enthusiasm for the monastic revival. They drew on two biographical traditions, the one English and the other continental. There is no doubt that they were emulating the Northumbrian biographers. Like the anonymous *Life of St. Cuthbert* and the *Life of Wilfrid*, two of the present works were written soon after the saints' deaths by men who knew them well – 'B' knew St Dunstan, and Ælfric knew St Ethelwold. Three of the other biographers (Adelard, the biographer of St Oswald, and Wulfstan) had probably at least seen the saint. Even Abbo of Fleury, writing more than a century after St Edmund's death, claimed to have had his information indirectly from Edmund's sword-bearer (who had passed the information to King Athelstan, who told St Dunstan).[93]

Stylistically all the biographies of the tenth-century reformers, except Ælfric's *Life of St. Ethelwold*, resembled the saints' Lives of the earlier period. They are unitary; that is they begin with the saint's birth and give a fairly chronological account of his life. However the *Life of St. Ethelwold* is arranged according to subject-matter. It begins with St Ethelwold's parentage and the portents heralding his birth. It proceeds with his birth, early life and subsequent career. Then it has a few remarks on his character and a collection of miracles connected with him. It notes his death and ends with two posthumous miracles. Such subject division is reminiscent of the arrangement of the *Life of King Alfred*, the *Encomium Emmae Reginae* and the *Life of King Edward*.

---

[90] Printed in *Memorials SE*, vol. 1, pp. 3–25.

[91] This *Life* survives in the thirteenth-century breviary of Hyde abbey. See *The Monastic Breviary of Hyde Abbey, Winchester*, ed. J. B. L. Tolhurst (HBS, lxix–lxxi, lxxvi, lxxviii, lxxx, 1932–42), vol. 4, ff. 287–91. For the probable date of the *Life* see P. Grierson, 'Grimbald of St. Bertins' in *EHR*, lv (1940), pp. 538–41.

[92] The text is in BM MS. Cotton Nero E I, ff. 22–32 (an eleventh-century book from Worcester cathedral priory; see N. R. Ker, *Medieval Libraries of Great Britain* (London 1941), p. 207). It is noticed by Hardy, *Catalogue*, vol. 1, pp. 415–16.

[93] Abbo, p. 4.

The reformers themselves were influenced by the English past. The regulations they drew up in the *Regularis Concordia* quote Pope Gregory the Great's instructions to St Augustine 'to establish suitable customs' in England.[94] The reformers particularly admired the Northumbrian era. St Oswald toured the region that was once ancient Northumbria, salvaged some relics of Northumbrian saints from Hexham and tried (unsuccessfully) to re-found Ripon abbey.[95] A number of the reformers' foundations were in fact re-foundations of monasteries destroyed by the Danes – at Abingdon, Ely, Peterborough, Malmesbury and Winchester. St Ethelwold revived the cult of the English saints; Etheldreda at Ely and Swithun at Winchester.[96] This conscious antiquarianism affected contemporary scholarship. Possibly 'B' had in mind St Cuthbert's gift of tears when he wrote of Dunstan, 'the holy spirit within him flowed out in streams from his eyes' (though Dunstan wept for joy – Cuthbert had wept for the repentance of sinners).[97] Perhaps too 'B' was thinking of St Cuthbert when describing how devils attacked Dunstan.[98]

The influence of Bede can be definitely seen in the works of the Ramsey biographers, Abbo and the author of the *Life of St. Oswald*. This is not surprising as other evidence shows that Byrhtferth, Ramsey's most famous scholar, was an admirer of Bede.[99] It has been suggested that he was the author of the *Life of St. Oswald*, but this is unlikely on stylistic grounds.[100] Abbo drew a conscious parallel with St Cuthbert when he insisted that St Edmund's body was uncorrupt: if the reader finds this hard to believe, he says, he should remember the incorruptibility of St Cuthbert's body.[101] Perhaps he was trying to improve on Bede's statement when he asserted that Oswen, the woman who looked after St Edmund's corpse, had to cut his hair and nails once a year.[102] Bede's influence on the *Life of St. Oswald* is also

94 See *Regularis Concordia*, ed., with an English translation, Thomas Symons (Nelson's Medieval Texts, 1953), p. 3 (cf. ibid., p. 49 and n. 3).

95 *VSO*, p. 462.

96 *VSE* (Ælfric), §§ 17, 18. The pages for the feasts of SS. Swithun and Etheldreda have miniatures and rich decoration in St Ethelwold's Benedictional; see *The Benedictional of St. Ethelwold*, ed. Francis Wormald (London 1959), pp. 11–12 and plates 6, 7.

97 *VSD*, p. 50. Cf. *VSC* (Bede), pp. 212, 348.

98 *VSD*, pp. 27–8, 44–6.

99 On the authenticity of the commentaries attributed to Byrhtferth on Bede's scientific works cf. G. F. Forsey, 'Byrhtferth's *Preface*' in *Speculum*, iii (1928), pp. 505–22. Byrhtferth's *Manual* is based primarily on Bede's treatment of the 'Computus': it is printed in *Byrhtferth's Manual*, ed. S. J. Crawford (EETS, original series, no. 177, 1929), vol. i.

100 Byrhtferth's authorship is postulated by S. J. Crawford, 'Byrhtferth of Ramsey and the anonymous Life of St. Oswald' in *Speculum Religionis, being Essays and Studies ... presented to C. G. Montefiore* (Oxford 1929), pp. 99–111. His conclusion is disputed by J. A. Robinson, 'Byrhtferth and the Life of St. Oswald' in *Journal of Theological Studies*, xxxi (1930), pp. 35–42. The views of Crawford and Robinson are discussed by J. D. V. Fisher, 'The anti-monastic reaction in the reign of Edward the Martyr' in *Cambridge Historical Journal*, x (1952), pp. 257–9, who suggests that the existing *Life* is based on a lost Life by Byrhtferth which was rewritten and interpolated in a Mercian monastery.

101 Abbo, p. 4.

102 Abbo, p. 20.

explicit. The author relates how St Oswald miraculously saved from sinking a boat overloaded with Ramsey monks going to pray in a near-by church on Rogation Sunday: the author compares the miracle with one attributed to St Cuthbert (in the metrical *Life*).[103] Similarities with Bede's *Ecclesiastical History* may perhaps be detected in the author's interest in topography and place-name derivations. He describes York, the capital of the Northumbrians, with its impressive walls, a population of about 30,000 adults, and prosperous trade – especially with the Danes.[104] He suggests derivations of the name 'Ramsey'. Either, he says, it was so called because of the numerous rams there or, because of the many fine trees, it took its name from the Latin for branch (*ramus*).[105] Possibly the author was partly indebted to Bede for his interest, to be discussed below, in general political history.

The author of the *Life of St. Oswald* was also influenced by another type of English literature (itself related to the Norse saga tradition): his account of the battle of Maldon is in the heroic, epic style of *Beowulf* and the verse *Battle of Maldon*. The hero Byrhtnoth (a local East Anglian thegn) is the hero, towering over everyone, striking to right and left, until, surrounded by corpses, he fell fighting for the English cause against the Danes.[106] Continental influence on the biographies is to be expected in view of the strong incentive to the reformers provided by continental monasticism. Possibly the authors knew the *Life of Odo*, abbot of Cluny (927–42), by the monk John, his disciple.[107] However, no clear-cut distinction can be made on stylistic grounds: England shared the common European hagiographical tradition.

The English were obviously short of people capable of writing hagiographies: three of the six authors were foreigners. Abbo was a monk of Fleury who stayed at Ramsey from about 986 to 988. He enjoyed a considerable literary reputation in England, for when the monks of St Augustine's, Canterbury, became dissatisfied with the prose style of 'B''s *Life of St. Dunstan*, they sent a copy to Abbo, who was then in France, so that he could turn it into elegant verse. The identity of 'B' is unknown. Bishop Stubbs, the editor of the *Life of St. Dunstan*, suggests that he was a clerk of Ebracher, archbishop of Liège (959–71).[108] 'B' stayed in England and his work shows that he had a close connection with St Augustine's, Canterbury,

103 *VSO*, p. 448; *VSC* (*met.*), c. viii.

104 *VSO*, p. 454. Cf. Stenton, *Anglo-Saxon England*, p. 534.

105 *VSO*, p. 432. E. Ekwall, *The Concise Oxford Dictionary of English Place-Names* (4th ed., Oxford 1960), p. 380, gives 'wild garlic island' as the derivation of Ramsey.

106 *VSO*, p. 455. For the interest of this passage, which corroborates many details in the poem on the battle of Maldon, see *The Battle of Maldon*, ed. E. V. Gordon (Methuen's Old English Library, 1937, reprinted 1964), pp. 5–6, and George Clark, '*The Battle of Maldon*: a heroic poem' in *Speculum*, xliii (1968), p. 55.

107 Printed in Migne, *PL*, vol. cxxxiii, coll. 43–86.

108 See *Memorials SD*, pp. xii–xxvi. A connection with Ebracher would give a special significance to the comparison of St Dunstan with St Martin (*VSD*, p. 50) as Ebracher promoted the cult of St Martin.

and with Glastonbury, about which he knew and cared much. The other biographer of St Dunstan, Adelard, never, as far as is known, came to England. But he may have met Dunstan when he stayed at St Peter's, Ghent, during his exile from 955 to 957.

The author of the *Life of St. Oswald* shows traces of the influence of Fleury. He gives a paean on Fleury[109] and twice cites the works of Abbo.[110] He is especially interested in St Benedict whose body, according to tradition, had been translated to Fleury in the dark ages. He has citations from Haymo's sermon on St Benedict,[111] and recounts two visions in which St Benedict figures.[112] Ælfric mentions Fleury in passing as the place where Ethelwold wished to study[113] and to which he sent his pupil Osgar.[114]

All the biographies of the reformers are of considerable value to the historian today. This is partly because of the scarcity of other literary sources: there is only one secular biography for the period and no local histories, while the Anglo-Saxon Chronicle is a fairly bald record of events. Sir Frank Stenton pointed out that the Lives are 'of the first importance to history'[115] and Professor Knowles used them as his main sources for the monastic revival.[116] Each of the six works contribute, in varying degrees, to our knowledge of one or more of the following: the saint's character, the monasteries with which he was connected and the monastic revival, and contemporary political history. These aspects will be discussed in turn, with particular reference to the three best-informed Lives, 'B''s *Life of St. Dunstan*, Ælfric's *Life of St. Ethelwold* and the anonymous *Life of St. Oswald*.

'B' had the best pen for character. He portrays Dunstan as mystical, artistic and sensitive. Though hagiographical in tone, the *Life* has an authentic touch. Dunstan's visions appear as inspired dreams rather than supernatural occurrences. And about much of what 'B' says Dunstan can be confirmed from other sources. He describes Dunstan as an accomplished artist.[117] An excellent drawing survives today reputed to be by Dunstan;[118] it is of Christ carrying a sceptre and book with a monk (perhaps by another artist) kneeling before him. Above the monk is a Latin couplet, meaning, 'Oh merciful Christ I ask you to keep me, Dunstan, safe. Do not allow ethereal storms to overwhelm me.' This picture could reasonably be dated to Dunstan's lifetime. In addition 'B', who says Dunstan was a gifted musician,[119] relates two visions showing his love of music[120] and describes a

---

[109] *VSO*, p. 422.   [110] *VSO*, pp. 431–2, 460–1.   [111] *VSO*, p. 418.
[112] *VSO*, pp. 440, 442.   [113] *VSE*, § 7.   [114] *VSE*, § 10.
[115] Stenton, *Anglo-Saxon England*, p. 454.
[116] M. D. Knowles, *The Monastic Order in England* (2nd ed., Cambridge 1963), pp. 31–56 *passim*.
[117] *VSD*, pp. cxi–cxv, 20.
[118] The drawing is in Bodley MS. Auctarium F. 4. 32; see F. Wormald, *English Drawings of the Tenth and Eleventh Centuries* (London 1952), pp. 24–5, 74 (no. 46) and Plate 1.
[119] *VSD*, pp. 20.
[120] *VSD*, pp. 41, 48–9.

miracle which demonstrates that Dunstan was a composer: one day while he was drawing a pattern for a stole, a harp hanging on the wall played an anthem beginning 'Gaudent in caelis'. An anthem with the same *incipit* was written at this time; it is attributed to Dunstan on the evidence of the passage in the *Life*.[121] A twelfth-century Canterbury writer, Eadmer, attributed the famous anthem *Kyrie Rex splendens* to Dunstan: and modern historians see no reason to doubt the attribution.[122]

Although 'B' may have had St Cuthbert in mind when describing Dunstan's gift of tears, Abbo of Fleury confirms that this actually was a characteristic of Dunstan.[123] 'B' also gives a personal detail about Dunstan which sounds authentic. He describes how Dunstan used to take walks in Canterbury, visiting the holy places and singing hymns, in the quiet of the night in order to avoid being mobbed by the crowd and because he was too busy in the daytime.[124] 'B''s account of Dunstan's quarrels with the court suggests a passionate, touchy disposition. Adelard adds little to this picture of Dunstan except hagiographical accretions and some possibly true details about his death.[125]

On the other hand Ælfric does not bring the reader face to face with Ethelwold. His biography is factual rather than personal, giving a detailed and well-balanced narrative of Ethelwold's early life, education, work as a monastic reformer, and an account of his holiness, but no intimate touches. Perhaps this reflects the austere character of a disciplinarian, an impression strengthened by an unattractive story Ælfric tells about Ethelwold. When Ethelwold was abbot of Abingdon he used to tour the domestic offices daily. One day he entered the kitchen to find that the monk responsible for cooking had exceeded his duties – he had washed up and tidied the kitchen as well as prepared the food. So Ethelwold said to the monk who was standing by a boiling pot: 'My brother, you have robbed me of this obedience which you practise without my knowledge; if you are such a soldier of Christ as you show yourself, put your hand in the boiling water and draw out a morsel of food for me from the bottom.' The monk did so – miraculously he felt no pain.[126]

Nor does the author of the *Life of St. Oswald* give a picture of the saint, although his full accounts of two of Oswald's visits to Ramsey suggest that he had at least seen him.[127] There is an impression that the author was more interested in Oswald's times than in his life, and he knows little of Oswald's

---

[121] *VSD*, p. 21. Cf. Knowles, op. cit., p. 556.

[122] See Knowles, op. cit., p. 552.

[123] Abbo, p. 4.

[124] *VSD*, p. 48. He also visited other sacred places 'ob animarum edificationem'; *VSD*, p. 46.

[125] J. A. Robinson, 'The Saxon bishops of Wells: a historical study in the tenth century' in *British Academy Supplemental Papers*, iv (London 1919), pp. 28–40, seeks to establish the truth of the passage in Adelard stating that Dunstan left Glastonbury to join Æthelhelm archbishop of Canterbury (914–23), and that Æthelhelm introduced him to King Athelstan (924–39), whom he had anointed.

[126] *VSE* (Ælfric), § 10. [127] *VSO*, pp. 447, 463–7.

activities in the north. Perhaps the fact that Oswald was not buried at Ramsey (he was buried at Worcester) partly accounts for the author's rather lukewarm attitude to him. Of all the biographers he strays most from his theme. He justifies his digression on the life of Oswald's uncle Oda, archbishop of Canterbury,[128] just as the encomiast of Queen Emma was to justify his excursions into her family history – with a reference to Virgil's *Aeneid*. Abbo knew almost nothing historical about St Edmund – not even the date of his death, which was recorded in the Anglo-Saxon Chronicle; his only piece of credible information is that St Edmund came from Old Saxony. The work demonstrates that legend had already transmuted the record of St Edmund's life from history to hagiography.

Ælfric like Ethelwold was dedicated to the cause of monastic reform. He was a pupil of Ethelwold at Winchester and in 987 was sent to teach in the abbey of Cerne in Dorset, founded by Æthelmar, son of Æthelweard the ealdorman. Æthelmar also founded Eynsham abbey of which Ælfric became abbot in 1005. He wrote a shortened version of the *Regularis Concordia*[129] for the monks of Eynsham. His *Life of St. Ethelwold* is largely concerned with Ethelwold's part in the reform movement. It emphasizes his efforts to enforce the Rule of St Benedict,[130] and records his re-foundations at Abingdon and Ely and new foundations at Peterborough and Thorney.[131] Ælfric does justice to the important part played in the monastic revival by the Anglo-Saxon kings. He describes the initial gift by King Edred of land to Ethelwold for the foundation at Abingdon: the details are so precise that it seems likely that Ælfric was here using a charter as his source.[132] The abbey did not immediately prosper, because though King Edred visited the site to plan the buildings, he and his party spent the time feasting and drinking. Edred died shortly afterwards and the abbey was not constructed until King Edgar's reign. Ælfric records that Edgar agreed to Ethelwold's expulsion of the secular clerks from the Old and New Minsters at Winchester.[133] As an impartial biographer, giving due credit to others who contributed to the monastic revival, Ælfric comments that thus monasteries were founded throughout England with the king's consent, 'partly by the counsel and action of Dunstan and partly by that of Ethelwold ... living according to the Rule'.[134]

The author of the *Life of St. Oswald* shows a similar interest in the monastic revival. He records Oswald's foundations at Westbury, Worcester and Winchcombe and his (attempted) re-foundation at Ripon.[135] He

---

[128] For the historical value of the section in the *Life of St. Oswald* on Archbishop Oda's life, see J. Armitage Robinson, 'St. Oswald and the Church of Worcester', pp. 38–42.

[129] Edited by M. Bateson in *Compotos Rolls of the Obedientiaries of St. Swithin's Priory, Winchester*, ed. G. W. Kitchin (Hampshire Record Society, 1892), pp. 173–98.

[130] *VSE* (Ælfric), c. 19.

[131] Ibid., c. 17.

[132] Ibid., c. 7.

[133] Ibid., c. 16.   [134] Ibid., c. 18.   [135] *VSO*, pp. 424, 435, 462.

describes in detail the origins of Ramsey abbey.[136] He praises the site – an island of meadows and woods, surrounded by marshes and streams full of fish. Like Ælfric he recognized Edgar's contribution to the revival and the importance of secular munificence. He describes the meeting of bishops and others summoned by Edgar to promote monastic reform: it was presumably on this occasion that the *Regularis Concordia* was drawn up.[137] However, the patron of Ramsey abbey itself was not the king, but an ealdorman, Æthelwine, whom Oswald met at a funeral. Having refused a site offered by Edgar as unsuitable, Oswald accepted Æthelwine's offer of one at Ramsey.[138] The author devotes much space to Æthelwine. He describes his close and friendly association with the abbey which he visited every year,[139] on one occasion advising the monks on the election of an abbot,[140] and his burial in the abbey church.[141] He also mentions the affairs of Æthelwine's family, and notes the burial of one of his brothers at Ramsey.[142]

Dunstan's biographer 'B' was interested in the origin of Glastonbury abbey (which is not mentioned in the Anglo-Saxon Chronicle), and his evidence has been partly confirmed by modern archaeology. He describes Glastonbury as a holy place, set in the marshes, and founded by more than human agency, where St Patrick was buried and Irish hermits lived.[143] Excavations have uncovered a Celtic monastery.[144] 'B' was well informed about the history of Glastonbury in Dunstan's time. He describes the stone church built by Dunstan[145] which has recently been excavated. He gives an account of Dunstan's friend Æthelfleda, who lived near the abbey, was its benefactress and was buried in it.[146] He knew about Dunstan's brother Wulfric who was steward of the abbey estates, and has details about his funeral.[147] He had also heard of events near Glastonbury. He tells the famous story of King Edmund's change of heart in regard to Dunstan because of a near fall over a cliff while hunting at Cheddar.[148] Again archaeology seems to corroborate 'B''s general accuracy, for a tenth-century royal palace has been uncovered at Cheddar.[149]

Abbo may have known little about St Edmund but he is a unique source for the origin of St Edmund's abbey. He is the earliest known authority for the existence of a community of secular clerks at Beodricsworth (the later Bury St Edmunds) looking after St Edmund's body, before the foundation of

---

[136] *VSO*, pp. 429–34. The description of the site of Ramsey is partly based on Abbo, p. 7.

[137] *VSO*, pp. 425 et seq. See Knowles, op. cit., p. 42.

[138] *VSO*, pp. 427–8.   [139] *VSO*, p. 447.   [140] *VSO*, p. 468.

[141] *VSO*, p. 475.   [142] *VSO*, pp. 428–9.   [143] *VSD*, pp. 7, 10.

[144] For a summary of the evidence, see J. and H. Taylor, 'Pre-Norman churches of the border' in Chadwick, *Celt and Saxon*, pp. 254–7.

[145] *VSD*, p. 25. For the pre-Conquest churches at Glastonbury, see Taylor, *Anglo-Saxon Architecture*, vol. 1, pp. 250–7.

[146] *VSD*, pp. 16–20.   [147] *VSD*, p. 28.   [148] *VSD*, pp. 23–4.

[149] P. Rahtz, 'The Saxon and Medieval Palaces at Cheddar, Somerset – an interim report of excavations in 1960–62' in *Medieval Archaeology*, vi–vii, 1962–3 (London 1964), pp. 53–66.

the monastery by King Canute in 1020. A story Abbo tells of how some robbers broke into the place shows that this early community had precincts (the robbers entered them) and a sacristan who slept in the church (the robbers woke him).[150]

Of the six biographies, the *Life of St. Oswald* has the most information about and interest in contemporary affairs. It has a detailed account of King Edgar's coronation in which St Oswald, as archbishop of York, participated.[151] The author borrowed material from the coronation *ordo* of King Edgar,[152] and the details he gives of the banquet after the ceremony suggest that he had access to an eye-witness account. The queen, he says, feasted apart from the king with the abbots and abbesses. She was dressed in linen clothes resplendent with jewels and gold, and sat higher up than anyone else. The author digressed to political subjects which have no bearing on Oswald. He gives the earliest account of the murder of King Edgar's successor, Edward the Martyr (in 978 or 979).[153] According to the Anglo-Saxon Chronicle he was murdered at Corfe in Dorset. The *Life of St. Oswald* tells how he went to visit his mother and was met by a party of thegns who stabbed him while he was still on his horse. The account of the battle of Maldon is of value because the author was a contemporary of the hero, Byrhtnoth, and should have been well informed because Byrhtnoth was a neighbour of Ramsey abbey, personally known and respected there.[154]

Ælfric shows no interest in contemporary politics; his interest in the king is incidental to his account of the monastic revival. And 'B' gives rather a confused picture of the political background to Dunstan's career (he was not interested in politics for their own sake). He tries to describe Dunstan's quarrels with the king and court, telling a colourful story of how Dunstan recalled King Edwy to his coronation banquet from the company of two 'loose women'.[155] The king was 'wallowing between the two of them in evil fashion, as if in a sty', while his crown, glittering with gold and silver and gems, was thrown carelessly on the floor. This story is redolent of legend and does not stand up to critical examination: one of the 'loose women' became Edwy's wife – and a respected figure – and the other was her mother. So all that can be concluded is that Dunstan offended the royal family and was consequently exiled.

The biographies, therefore, reflect and record the enthusiasm of the age for the reconstruction of monastic life in England. As a literary achievement

---

[150] Abbo, p. 21.

[151] *VSO*, pp. 436–8. For Edgar's coronation and this account in the *Life* see P. E. Schramm, *A History of the English Coronation*, translated by L. G. Wickham Legg (Oxford 1937), pp. 19–22.

[152] The *ordo* of King Edgar is printed by P. E. Schramm, 'Die Krönung bei dem Westfranken und Angelsachsen von 878 bis um 1000' in *Zeitschrift der Savigny-Stiftung für Rechtsgeschichte*, liv (Kanonistische Abteilung xxiii, Weimar 1934), pp. 222–30.

[153] *VSO*, pp. 449–51. Cf. Stenton, *Anglo-Saxon England*, p. 368.

[154] *VSO*, p. 456. See p. 81 and n. 106 above, and Stenton, *Anglo-Saxon England*, pp. 370–1.

[155] *VSD*, p. 32. Cf. Stenton, *Anglo-Saxon England*, pp. 360–1.

Ælfric's *Life of St. Ethelwold* is the best. But 'B''s *Life of St. Dunstan* has the most vivid character portrait, and the *Life of St. Oswald* has embedded in its rambling, shapeless proportions a store of useful information about the contemporary scene.

Works of the third period of Anglo-Saxon biography were written a decade or so after the Norman Conquest. But they may be treated as part of the Anglo-Saxon tradition because they concern ecclesiastics who began to rule in Anglo-Saxon times. These men came to terms with the Normans and their power continued under the new regime. The biographies, bridging the Conquest, help the historian to determine the nature of the transition. However, of the four Lives to be discussed here, only one is a substantial piece of work. This is the *Life of Wulfstan*, bishop of Worcester (1062–95), written some time between 1095 and 1113 by Coleman, a monk of Worcester (it is in English, the other Lives are in Latin).[156] The next most ambitious biography was of Æthelwig, abbot of Evesham (1059–77), probably written fairly soon after his death.[157] The other two biographies are very short: one was another *Life of Wulfstan* composed shortly after Wulfstan's death by Hemming, a monk of Worcester;[158] the other was an anonymous *Life of Leofric*, bishop of Exeter (1050–72), written soon after 1072.[159] To this group also belongs the first self-contained autobiography written in England – of Giso bishop of Wells (1060–88).[160]

Coleman's *Life of Wulfstan* was much indebted in style and content to the Anglo-Saxon tradition of ecclesiastical biography. But the other, shorter, biographies resemble the earlier Lives far less closely. Though the tradition of writing the Life of a famous ecclesiastic soon after his death was well

---

[156] Printed, from William of Malmesbury's Latin translation (see p. 167 below), *The Vita Wulfstani of William of Malmesbury*, ed. R. R. Darlington (Camden Soc., 3rd series, xl, 1928). An English translation is by J. H. F. Peile, *William of Malmesbury's Life of St. Wulfstan . . .* (Oxford 1934). For a recent account of the *Life*, see D. H. Farmer, 'Two biographies by William of Malmesbury' in *Latin Biography*, ed. T. A. Dorey (London 1967), pp. 165–74. Mr Farmer attributes to William of Malmesbury a greater share in the composition of the *Life* as it exists today than I do.

[157] This Life only survives in the early thirteenth-century *Chronicle of the Abbey of Evesham*; *Eve.*, pp. 87–96. See pp. 89 and n. 171, 90, 111–13 below.

[158] Printed in *Hemingi Chartularium Ecclesiae Wigornensis*, ed. Thomas Hearne (Oxford 1723), pp. 403–8. Hemming's cartulary has other short passages of historical narrative; for the value of some of them see J. A. Robinson, 'St. Oswald and the Church of Worcester', pp. 4–5.

[159] Printed in *The Leofric Missal as used in the Cathedral of Exeter . . . 1050–1072*, ed. F. E. Warren (Oxford 1883) and in *The Exeter Book of Old English Poetry*, ed. R. W. Chambers, M. Förster and R. Flower (London 1933), pp. 8–9, and also in A. W. Haddan and W. Stubbs, *Councils and Ecclesiastical Documents relating to Great Britain and Ireland* (Oxford 1869–71, reprinted 1964, 3 vols), vol. i, pp. 691–2.

[160] The autobiography of Giso only survives because it was copied into a history of the bishopric of Bath and Wells composed in Henry II's reign. It is printed, as part of this later work, with an English translation, in *Ecclesiastical Documents: viz. 1. A Brief History of the Bishoprick of Somerset from its Foundation to the year 1174 . . .*, ed. Joseph Hunter (Camden Soc., 1840), pp. 15–20.

established in Anglo-Saxon times, these short works show the development of a new and powerful literary motive. Controversy, actual or foreseen, not piety, was the authors' chief incentive to composition. The *Historia de Sancto Cuthberto* has been already mentioned as a precocious example of an institutional history partly moulded by fear of controversy over rights and property. Such fears and their actuality grew in the troubles of Edward the Confessor's reign and were accentuated by the Norman Conquest which caused disputes over land tenure and property boundaries. Men's desire to protect themselves by committing immemorial custom to writing led to record-keeping.

These tensions are reflected even in Coleman's traditionally constructed *Life of Wulfstan*. And they permeate the shorter biographies and Giso's autobiography. The short works are monographs rather than full-scale books. In them the hero is identified with some crisis in the institution's history, and his biography (or autobiography) is a record of that crisis. There is no attempt at portraying the man or at a comprehensive account of his life.

Coleman's *Life of Wulfstan* is modelled on Ælfric's *Life of St. Ethelwold*. Wulfstan is depicted as a saint of the same calibre as those of the tenth-century monastic revival. Like Ælfric, Coleman divided his work into three sections and devoted each section to much the same subjects as Ælfric had. The first concerns Wulfstan's early life and education up to his consecration as bishop of Worcester. The second relates to his episcopate, and the third to his character, personal habits, and miracles when alive and dead. The *Life* portrays him as a saintly man in private life, and as a bishop who worked hard at his pastoral duties and contributed to religious life by fostering the monasteries at Great Malvern[161] and Westbury.[162] It shows that he was an able administrator; it records his contribution to the prosperity of Worcester cathedral[163] which since Canute's reign had fallen on hard times financially,[164] and his building activities.[165] Perhaps the author's loyalty to the Anglo-Saxon dynasty accounts for his selective treatment of Wulfstan's political career. He mentions the help Wulfstan gave Harold immediately before the Conquest in repressing the northern revolt,[166] but passes over the fact that he also helped William I put down the 1075 and 1088 revolts, and served him as a judge at least once.[167]

It is likely that Coleman wrote in English as a piece of conscious revivalism, to emphasize the merits of Anglo-Saxon England. The fact that the *Life* was in the vernacular may be the reason why the work was all but lost. The Anglo-Saxon text is no longer known: the *Life* is only preserved in a Latin translation by William of Malmesbury. As the Worcester monks asked William to translate the work because they could not understand it, it does not seem impossible that they allowed the superseded original to be lost or

---

161 *VW*, ii. 2. 162 *VW*, iii. 10. 163 *VW*, i. 5.

164 See *VW*, pp. xxiii–xxiv. 165 *VW*, i. 8, 14. 166 *VW*, i. 16.

167 *VW*, pp. xxvii–xxviii.

destroyed. On the other hand it could have been mislaid when sent to Rome in the early thirteenth century to provide evidence for Wulfstan's sanctity during the canonization process.[168]

Although, like his Anglo-Saxon predecessors, Coleman was writing a hagiography to record the saint's acts, he introduced a change of emphasis. He was concerned not only to erect a pious monument for the edification of the faithful, but also to compile a useful reference book for the monks of Worcester. He narrated in detail the story of Wulfstan's struggle to vindicate the rights and property of his see against the archbishop of York. When Ealdred bishop of Worcester was appointed to the archbishopric of York in 1062, he tried to hold the bishopric of Worcester as well. His attempt was frustrated by Pope Nicholas II, and Wulfstan was elected bishop of Worcester. But Ealdred retained his influence over the see and some of its property. It was not until after the Conquest that Wulfstan emancipated the see from the archbishop of York's control and regained the property. Biographically speaking this was a personal triumph, but Coleman gives it a wider reference, stressing the independence of the see of Worcester from the archbishopric of York and incidentally its subjection to the archbishopric of Canterbury.[169]

Controversy provided an even more powerful incentive to the biographer of Æthelwig abbot of Evesham. The author's primary purpose was to define and substantiate the abbey's titles to real estate. His work no longer survives in its original form and it is impossible to reconstruct its text with certainty. It is embedded in the *Chronicle of the Abbey of Evesham* compiled by Thomas of Marlborough in the early thirteenth century.[170] Marlborough's work itself incorporates an earlier History of the abbey to about 1086 written probably in the late eleventh or early twelfth century (this is discussed on pp. 111–12). The Life of Æthelwig is in this early work. The evidence that the Life was once a work on its own has been discussed by Professor Darlington.[171] It rests mainly on its disproportionate length in comparison with the Lives of the other abbots in the history, and on a passage which says: 'Hitherto we have spoken much of the lord abbot Æthelwig. . . . Now *at the end of this work* [the italics are mine] we will show in order the lands which he acquired for his church.' The list of lands follows and then the author records Æthelwig's death. Moreover, the author writes as if Æthelwig had not been long dead. He gives vivid details of Æthelwig's life and claims that his information came partly from his own observation.[172]

---

[168] See *VW*, pp. viii n. 4, xlvii.　　　　[169] *VW*, pp. xxv–xxvii, xxxi; i. 10–13; ii. 1.
[170] See p. 87 n. 157 above.
[171] I find the arguments of R. R. Darlington, 'Æthelwig, abbot of Evesham' in *EHR*, xlvii (1938), pp. 1–22, 177–98, *passim*, that the Life of Æthelwig once existed as a separate, near contemporary work, convincing. However, M. D. Knowles, op. cit., pp. 704–5, adduces evidence showing that the present text cannot be much earlier than *c.* 1110 – but all the phrases quoted by Professor Knowles to prove this thesis could well be, as he himself admits, interpolations by a reviser.
[172] *Eve.*, p. 94.

The Life is a combination of narrative biography and charter material. The biographical part describes Æthelwig's rule as abbot. Nothing is said of his career before his promotion and no miracles are attributed to him. Prominence is given to his political activities, how he administered the midlands for William I and was regarded as an authority on Anglo-Saxon law.[173] Then comes the land-list:[174] this was probably included because of the controversy between Æthelwig's successor Abbot Walter and Odo of Bayeux over the abbey's title to lands acquired by Æthelwig. It seems that Æthelwig's influence enabled him to hold estates to which he had no permanent title. After his death, local opposition to Walter's attempt to keep the property was so bitter that the king appointed a commission of inquiry under Odo of Bayeux.[175]

The three remaining works commemorate the success of the men who re-established their communities' prosperity after the troubles immediately preceding and following the Norman Conquest. Another feature of these works was the exact definition of the internal distribution of property between the bishops and their chapters. The authors must have hoped by codification to prevent disputes between the communities and their heads. Moreover, they probably intended to prevent royal encroachments on the communities' property during vacancies. (On the death of a bishop his property reverted to the king, as feudal overlord, until the appointment of a successor: therefore, unless the cathedral community's property was clearly defined, the king would obtain that too.) The significance of these works as records is illustrated by Hemming's *Life of Wulfstan*, which is more like an inventory of charters in narrative form than a biography. The general words on Wulfstan's piety quickly give way to an account of his territorial acquisitions, with a careful specification of his allocation of property to the Worcester monks.

The *Life of Leofric*, preserved in the missal Leofric gave to Exeter cathedral, is mainly a record of the transference of the see from Crediton to Exeter in 1050 and Leofric's gifts to the new bishopric. It notices Leofric's consecration briefly and mentions his piety in general terms. It proceeds with a detailed account of the transference of the see, citing in full the letter of Pope Leo ordering King Edward to make the change, and copying passages from the royal charter recording the ceremony: 'I [the king] leading Bishop Leofric by the right arm while my queen Edith led him by the left, placed him on the episcopal throne, in the presence of my great men and relatives, my nobles and chaplains.'[176] The account which follows of Leofric's gifts is almost certainly from a list of his benefactions which still survives today (it is an inventory of lands, church furniture, vestments and books procured by

---

[173] *Eve.*, p. 89. Cf. Darlington, 'Æthelwig', pp. 10–18.   [174] *Eve.*, pp. 96–7.

[175] See Darlington, 'Æthelwig', pp. 21–2.

[176] The full text of the charter is printed in Haddan and Stubbs, op. cit., vol. 1, pp. 693–4. For an English translation of part of the charter see Chambers, Förster and Flower, op. cit., p. 7.

Leofric for Exeter cathedral).[177] Of Leofric's generosity the biographer writes: 'Leofric himself supported the community for a long time out of his own property. He restored and improved the place with great trouble as far as he could. And he increased its lands by giving it three of his own manors.'

Similarly, Giso's autobiography records his contribution to the prosperity of the bishopric of Wells. Giso briefly mentions his consecration as bishop in 1060 and that he was from St Trudo (in Lorraine). His problem at Wells was to restore the bishopric's prosperity after the depredations of various lords, notably Earl Harold. Giso considered excommunicating Harold and used to remonstrate with him ('I sometimes privately and sometimes openly rebuked him for the attacks he made on the church committed to my charge').[178] After the Conquest Giso obtained, as he records, William I's confirmation of the rights and property of the cathedral church.

Giso did not regard the struggle for the restoration of Wells's fortunes as a materialistic one. Increased prosperity meant an increase in the number of canons. More revenues meant that he could construct communal buildings – a cloister, refectory and dormitory, so that the canons could observe proper obedience. Giso records the lands he acquired, specifying those he allocated to the canons.[179] His work had a dual purpose: it was intended both to define the property of the see, so that it could be defended from external attack; and also to distinguish what belonged to the canons from what belonged to the bishop, to prevent future dispute. He planned in the future to compile a more detailed record, to make known 'what belongs peculiarly to the use of the canons, and what to the demesne and disposal of the bishop, and so, posterity being freed of all uncertainty on this subject, one party may not encroach on the rights of the other'.[180]

---

[177] Printed in Chambers, Förster and Flower, op. cit., pp. 18–32.
[178] *Giso*, pp. 17–18.   [179] Ibid., pp. 18–19.   [180] Ibid., p. 20.

6

Historians of the Norman Conquest

There is no satisfactory contemporary narrative of the Norman Conquest and settlement.[1] The historians of the time fall into two groups, the English and the continental. In the English group are the authors of the Anglo-Saxon Chronicle. In the continental group are William of Jumièges, the author of the *Carmen de Hastingae Proelio* (*Song of the Battle of Hastings*), and William of Poitiers. Each group is probably entirely independent of the other, telling a slightly different story, and each has serious faults: the English historians are too brief and unanalytical, and the continental too biased in favour of the Normans.

Two known versions of the Anglo-Saxon Chronicle have accounts of the Norman Conquest and settlement. The northern version (D) continues until 1079 and the Peterborough version (E) to 1154. The version written at Abingdon (C) ends in 1066 just before the Conquest, after describing the battle of Stamford Bridge.[2] Possibly there was another version, at Worcester. The evidence for this is in the chronicle of John of Worcester, which up to 1130 apparently used a version of the Chronicle resembling D in some places and E in others.[3]

The Anglo-Saxon Chronicle reflects the English point of view. There is no hint in any version that Earl Harold promised William duke of Normandy the succession to the English throne on Edward the Confessor's death. As it is fairly certain from other authorities that Harold did make such a promise,[4] it seems likely that the author of the Chronicle suppressed the fact to justify the English resistance to William. All versions of the Chronicle (C, D and E) give a detailed account of Harold's great victory at Stamford Bridge over Tostig and Harold king of Norway. Both E and D agree that Harold was unprepared for William's attack at Hastings but fought bravely.

The fullest account of the Conquest and settlement is in the northern

---

[1] For a useful short survey of the sources for the Conquest see Chibnall, *OV*, vol. 2, pp. 368–70 (Appendix III).

[2] For these versions, see pp. 38–40.

[3] See *The Peterborough Chronicle*, ed. D. Whitelock (Early English Manuscripts in Facsimile, iv, Copenhagen 1954), p. 31.

[4] D. C. Douglas, *William the Conqueror* (London 1964), pp. 175–8.

version (D). The description of the battle of Hastings was probably written very soon after it. The author ends the annal for 1066 with a prayer for better times which suggests that he wrote before the result of the victory was definitely known.[5] His account is very short but he alone records that the battle was fought 'at the hoary apple tree'. He writes in a tone of sadness rather than bitterness, regarding the defeat of the English as God's punishment for their sins. He laments the sufferings of the English after the Conquest but achieves a fair degree of impartiality: he strongly criticizes Archbishop Ealdred and other English leaders for not submitting to William earlier than they did,[6] and it is possible to detect a note of sympathy for the Conqueror in the account of Robert Shorthose's revolt in 1078–9.[7]

In its present form the Peterborough version (E) is not contemporary with the reign of William the Conqueror. It is based on a text which was written in southern England, possibly at Canterbury. This text was rewritten at Peterborough in about 1121.[8] As only the rewritten text is known, it is impossible to be sure what comprised the original: however, clearly the Peterborough version is a revision of the earlier one. As it exists today this version has the same undertones of sadness for the unhappiness of the English as the northern version, and is particularly critical of William's financial impositions.[9] Nevertheless the author was influenced by Norman historiography, thus providing evidence that the English were beginning to accept and assimilate with their conquerors. He incorporated Norman material and had absorbed some Norman ideas. His interest in Norman history is shown by the inclusion of entries (in Latin) relating to Norman affairs from the *Annals of Rouen* for the years from 876 to 1062.[10] Moreover, he inserted the favourable character-sketch of William, mentioning his wisdom, strength, justice, dignity and piety;[11] the original of this portrait was by a courtier, for it records that the author had seen the king 'and lived at his court'.[12] The chronicler's remark on William's impartial severity against everyone who opposed him, even his own brother Odo of Bayeux, is reminiscent of a passage in William of Poitiers.[13] He also, like the Norman historians, comments on the transitory nature of earthly prosperity: he concludes the notice of the

---

[5] See F. M. Stenton, 'The historical background' in *The Bayeux Tapestry, a Comprehensive Survey*, ed. F. M. Stenton (2nd ed., London 1965), p. 20.

[6] 'It was a great piece of folly that they had not [submitted] sooner, since God would not make things better, because of our sins'; *ASC* (D), *s.a.* 1066 (p. 144).

[7] 'We will not write here more of the harm he inflicted on his father': *ASC* (D), *s.a.* 1079 (p.160).

[8] Whitelock, *Peterborough Chronicle*, p. 30; Garmonsway, *ASC*, pp. xxxix–xli.

[9] *ASC* (E), *s.a.* 1086, 1087. Cf. the account of the Domesday inquest *ASC* (E), *s.a.* 1085.

[10] See Whitelock, *Peterborough Chronicle*, p. 27; *The Peterborough Chronicle*, ed. H. A. Rositzke (New York 1951), p. 14. Annals relating to universal history and English church history were also inserted.

[11] See p. 33.

[12] *ASC* (E), *s.a.* 1087 (p. 163).

[13] William of Poitiers commends William the Conqueror for not favouring his relatives, even his uncle Mauger, archbishop of Rouen. William deposed Mauger for his misrule, preferring the laws of God to the ties of blood; *GGDN*, pp. 128 et seq.

Conqueror's death with these words: 'Alas, how deceitful and untrustworthy is this world's prosperity. He who had been a powerful king and lord of many a land, had then of all the land only a seven-foot measure; and he who was once clad in gold and gems, lay then covered with earth.'[14]

Abroad, the plight of the English was watched with sympathetic eyes by one of their countrymen. Ælnoth was a priest at St Alban's church at Odense in Denmark. He had probably accompanied relics of St Alban when they were carried there from St Albans in 1085. In about 1109 he wrote the *Life of St. Canute*, king of Denmark, who was martyred in 1086,[15] inflating it into what is virtually the first history of Denmark. He includes one fact about Anglo-Norman history not recorded elsewhere. He relates that in 1085 the English nobles appealed to King Canute for help in throwing off the Norman yoke; Canute gathered an army for the purpose but had to disband it because of discontent among the troops.

The continental historians, William of Jumièges, the author of the *Carmen de Hastingae Proelio*, and William of Poitiers, are in a different category from the Anglo-Saxon chroniclers. They were literary historians, who wrote their complete works more or less at one sitting. Although they record events roughly in chronological order, they give few, if any, dates. They use the biographical form, expanded to include the history of their people. Moreover, they belong to a class of writers common in medieval France, but rare in England. They were official or semi-official historians. It is not known whether they were strictly speaking official historians writing at King William's command, but they were certainly semi-official ones, for they saw events from the royal point of view. In addition, they were panegyrists – though not all to the same extent.

William of Jumièges was a monk of the abbey there, which had been re-founded by William I duke of Normandy, in about 935. William of Jumièges finished the *Gesta Normannorum Ducum* (*Deeds of the Dukes of the Normans*)[16] soon after 1070 or 1072 (scholars do not agree on the *terminus a quo*).[17] The *Gesta* begins with an account of the origins of Normandy, and proceeds to record the acts of the dukes in chronological order to 1070. William dedicated the work to William the Conqueror, and then he or a successor rededicated it to William Rufus after the latter's accession to the throne, promising to add the acts of Robert Shorthose, duke of Normandy from 1087 to 1106 (but he never did).[18] The *Gesta* borrows from Dudo of St

---

[14] *ASC, s.a.* 1087 (p. 163). For the idea of the transitory nature of earthly prosperity in continental writers see pp. 100, 159–60 below.

[15] Printed in *Scriptores Rerum Danicarum Medii Ævi*, ed. J. Langebek *et al.* (Hafniae 1772–1878, 9 vols), vol. 3, pp. 327–90. For details concerning Ælnoth and the *Life* see Langebek's introduction, ibid., pp. 325–7.

[16] Printed *Guillaume de Jumièges, Gesta Normannorum Ducum*, ed. J. Marx (Société de l'Histoire de Normandie, 1914).

[17] Marx in *GND*, p. xv, favours 1070 or 1071, and Foreville in *GGDN*, pp. xxvii–xxviii, the year 1072.

[18] *GND*, pp. xvi, 143–4.

Quentin[19] to 966, supplemented with material from Jordanes,[20] hagiography and the archives and oral traditions of Jumièges. Thenceforth it apparently uses no known literary authority.[21] The last book (VII) relates to William the Conqueror; roughly the first half concerns his rule in Normandy and the second the conquest and settlement of England.

William of Jumièges praised the Conqueror partly by praising his ancestors and race. He omitted most of the legends in Dudo relating to early Norman history, because he considered them 'pure flattery, and neither honest nor edifying'.[22] But he retained some of them and borrowed much from Jordanes which is equally absurd. To increase their stature, he linked their early history with that of the Greeks and Romans. He asserted that the forebears of the Normans were as wise as the Greeks, that they descended from the Trojans, and were ruled by Antenor after his expulsion from Troy.[23] He also praised William the Conqueror directly. He calls him the wisest and most gracious king, as strong as Samson and as just as Solomon.[24] He records William's victories and testifies to the respect he inspired at home and abroad, the peace he imposed on his subjects, and the justice of all his acts.

William of Jumièges attempted to make William the Conqueror's seizure of the English throne appear legitimate. This caused him to distort historical truth. He was the first historian to defend William's claim to the throne. His principal argument was that Earl Harold when in Normandy had sworn to Duke William 'many oaths with regard to the kingdom'.[25] This statement is generally accepted by historians today as true.[26] But William of Jumièges's embellishments are probably fictitious. There is no trustworthy corroborative evidence for the statement that Edward the Confessor sent first Robert archbishop of Canterbury to William to make William heir to the English throne, and then sent Harold to do fealty for the crown.[27] Equally unconfirmed is the story that Earl Harold was imprisoned by Guy count of Ponthieu, and released by William, who, after the oath-taking, sent him home loaded with presents.[28] The purpose of the story was probably to establish that William had a claim on Harold's gratitude.

But William of Jumièges is far less of a panegyrist than the other two contemporary Norman historians. He is less fulsome in his eulogy and less dishonest in his bias, and admits that he was not the best qualified man to praise

---

[19] See *GND*, pp. xvi–xvii, 2, 68 n. 2.

[20] For Jordanes, see J. W. Thomson, *A History of Historical Writing* (New York 1942, 2 vols), vol. 1, pp. 147–8.

[21] On its relationship to William of Poitiers, see p. 99 and nn. 66, 67 below.

[22] 'animadvertens ea penitus adulatoria, nec speciem honesti vel utilis pretendere'; *GND*, p. 2.

[23] *GND*, p. 8. Cf. p. 204 and n. 172 below.

[24] *GND*, p. 1.

[25] Harold was allowed by William to return to England 'facta fidelitate de regno plurimis sacramentis'; *GND*, p. 133 and n. 1.

[26] See p. 92 and n. 4.

[27] *GND*, p. 132 and n. 2.

[28] *GND*, pp. 132–3.

William the Conqueror because he was not of the court circle.[29] His exposition of the Conqueror's claim to the throne is simplicity itself compared with that of William of Poitiers. Nor does he denigrate Harold beyond blaming him for perjury.[30] And he even records a fact discreditable to his hero – the cruel revenge on the city of Alençon (which is passed over in silence by William of Poitiers).[31]

William of Jumièges has some of the detachment and objective interest in history typical of the best monastic historians. He makes historical observations – for example on the perennial enmity of Normans and Frenchmen.[32] His interest in English history (no doubt stimulated by the Conquest) is demonstrated by notices of eleventh-century events in England. For example he gives the succession of the kings.[33] He pays particular attention to the sons of Queen Emma, daughter of Richard I duke of the Normans. He lists her children by her two marriages,[34] and records the exile in Normandy and careers of her sons by King Ethelred.[35] He wrote not only to praise but, like other monastic historians, to dispel ignorance[36] and to edify his readers[37] (he regarded the defeat of the English at Hastings as God's punishment for the murder of King Ethelred's son Alfred).

The *Gesta Normannorum Ducum* attracted considerable attention from contemporaries and was widely circulated, especially in Normandy. About fifteen years after it was completed, William of Jumièges, or a successor, made two slight additions to the text,[38] and it was further interpolated in a number of Benedictine houses. The most recent editor[39] lists ten medieval manuscripts with the text more or less as William wrote it, two with the additions made early in the twelfth century at St Stephen's, Caen,[40] seven with the interpolations made at St Évroul by Orderic Vitalis,[41] and twelve with those made at Mont-St-Michel by Robert of Torigni in the mid-twelfth century.[42] The chronological arrangement of the work made interpolation easy, and the fact that it was by a Benedictine no doubt facilitated its wide dispersal among houses of the order. Copies came to England: a twelfth-century text, with the St Stephen's additions, was in the cathedral library at Durham,[43] an early fourteenth-century one with Robert of Torigni's inter-

---

[29] *GND*, p. 143 (epilogue). [30] *GND*, p. 133. [31] *GND*, p. 126.

[32] 'exquo Normanni arva Neustriae ceperunt incolere, mos fuit Francis semper eis invidere, concitantes reges adversus illos insurgere, terras quas possident suis majoribus violenter eos surripuisse asserentes'; *GND*, p. 129.

[33] *GND*, pp. 109–10. [34] *GND*, pp. 82, 83.

[35] *GND*, pp. 121–2. William clearly regarded his excursions into English history as digressions, for he ends two (ibid., pp. 83, 122) with the remark that now he will return to his main theme.

[36] e.g. William states that he has inserted the issue of Emma 'ut Edwardi regis ortum ignorantibus monstraremus'; *GND*, p. 83.

[37] William states in the epilogue (*GND*, p. 143) that he recorded the Conqueror's acts as 'an exhortation for good men'.

[38] See *GND*, pp. xvi, 128, 142–4. [39] For a list of the manuscripts see *GND*, pp. xxix–lx.

[40] See below. [41] See p. 159 n. 178. [42] See pp. 199–200 and n. 133.

[43] BM MS. Harley 491; *GND*, p. xxxi. For the possibility of use of William of Jumièges's work by the author of the *Historia Regum* at Durham see p. 149 n. 88 below.

polations was at St Mary's, York,[44] and a fragment (probably fourteenth century) survives from Holy Trinity at Norwich.[45] Moreover, in the second quarter of the twelfth century William of Malmesbury used a version for the *Gesta Regum*. His adoption of the biographical form for the *Gesta* must have been partly due to William of Jumièges's influence.[46] And it is likely that the Durham monk who wrote the *Historia Regum* in the early twelfth century[47] and Henry of Huntingdon[48] both used William of Jumièges.

Unlike William of Jumièges, the two other continental writers of the period had a limited circulation. The *Carmen de Hastingae Proelio*[49] is extant in only one (incomplete) medieval manuscript and no citations from it have been identified in the works of contemporary historians in England. No manuscript of William of Poitiers's *Gesta Guillelmi Ducis Normannorum et Regis Anglorum* is known today (the only copy known to have survived to modern times was burnt in the fire of 1731 in the Cottonian library).[50] The failure of the *Carmen* and William of Poitiers's work to be widely disseminated was no doubt partly due to the fact that the authors were not monks, but clerics. Both writers were of noble parentage and were men of the world who spent part of their lives at the royal court.

The authorship of the *Carmen* is not beyond dispute. The Norman historian Orderic Vitalis, writing two generations after the Conquest, records that Guy bishop of Amiens (1058–76) composed a poem 'in which he described the battle of Senlac [that is Hastings] . . . attacking and condemning Harold, and praising and glorifying William'.[51] Orderic also records that Guy accompanied Matilda as her chaplain to England in 1067 when he had already completed his poem.[52] Pertz[53] discovered the *Carmen* in a twelfth-century manuscript in the Royal Library in Brussels.[54] It has no indication of

---

[44] Corpus Christi College, Cambridge, MS. 181; Marx (*GND*, p. xxxviii) does not mention its provenance. It is attributed to St Mary's, York, by N. R. Ker, *Medieval Libraries of Great Britain* (2nd ed., Royal Historical Soc., 1964), p. 217. For its probable use by Richard of Hexham see p. 216 and nn. 277–8 below.

[45] Corpus Christi College, Cambridge, MS. 138; Marx (*GND*, p. xl) does not mention its provenance, for which see Ker, op. cit., p. 137.

[46] See WM, *GR*, vol. 1, p. cvii. Godfrey of Jumièges was abbot of Malmesbury from ?1090 to 1105 or 1106 (see *VCH*, *Wilts.*, vol. 3, p. 215) and it is possible that he brought a copy of William of Jumièges to Malmesbury.

[47] See *SD*, vol. 2, p. xxi.   [48] See *HH*, p. lviii.

[49] Printed in *Scriptores Rerum Gestarum Willelmi Conquestoris*, ed. J. A. Giles (London 1845), pp. 27–51. Cf. n. 55 below.

[50] The most recent edition of William of Poitiers is *Guillaume de Poitiers, Histoire de Guillaume le Conquérant*, ed., with a French translation, Raymonde Foreville (les Classiques de l'Histoire de France au Moyen Age, xxiii, Paris 1952). For the manuscript, see ibid., pp. l et seq. For a recent account of William of Poitiers and the *Gesta* see T. A. Dorey, 'William of Poitiers: "Gesta Guillelmi Ducis"' in *Latin Biography*, ed. T. A. Dorey (London 1967), pp. 139–55.

[51] *OV*, iii. 15 (vol. 2, p. 158).

[52] *OV*, iv. 4 (vol. 2, p. 181).

[53] See H. Petrie, *Monumenta Historica Britannica* (only vol. 1 published, London 1848), p. 96.

[54] MS. 10615–10729, ff. 227ᵛ–230ᵛ in the Royal Library in Brussels. This is a composite manuscript and the items containing works of classical authors are noticed in Paul Thomas, *Catalogue des Manuscrits de classiques latins de la Bibliothèque Royale de Bruxelles* (Université de

authorship beyond a dedication from 'W' to 'L' – which could be interpreted as from 'Wido' to 'Lanfranc'. It seems likely that the *Carmen* is to be identified with Guy's work. However, there is a doubt, especially as the contents of the *Carmen* do not exactly correspond to Guy's poem as described by Orderic. And if Guy was not the author of the *Carmen* it could have been written at any time between the battle of Hastings and the early twelfth century (the date of the manuscript), and would not be an authoritative source.[55]

On the other hand if Guy was the author, the *Carmen* would be an important source for the battle of Hastings. For Guy was an intimate of the court circle and, although not actually at the battle, wrote within three years of it, that is before either William of Jumièges or William of Poitiers. In this case the passages in William of Poitiers's work, reminiscent of some in the *Carmen*, may have been derived from the *Carmen*.[56] Moreover, the information found only in the *Carmen* and not in the other two authorities would be worthy of credence: for example the *Carmen* is the only one to record that a minstrel called Incisor Ferri (Taillefer in French) walked in front of the Norman army, juggling until he was killed.[57] It gives some indication of the identity of one of the four men who mutilated King Harold's body – William of Poitiers names three. The *Carmen* calls the fourth 'the heir of Ponthieu': this could refer either to Count Guy, who was Guy of Amiens's uncle, or to one of his sons. There is no other evidence for the presence of 'the heir of Ponthieu' at Hastings.[58]

Gand, Recueil de Travaux publiés par la Faculté de Philosophie et Lettres, 18me fascicule, Ghent 1896), nos 207, 208. A thirteenth-century fragment of the *Carmen* is in the same library in MS. 9799–9809, f. 142ᵛ; noticed in J. van den Gheyn *et al.*, *Catalogue des Manuscrits de la Bibliothèque Royale de Belgique* (Brussels 1901–48, 13 vols, in progress), vol. 2, p. 277, no. 1327, (the classical contents of the volume are noticed in Thomas, op. cit., no. 130).

[55] For a full discussion of the evidence, with further references, see G. H. White in GEC, *Peerage*, vol. 12, pt 1, Appendix I, pp. 36–8, who points out that the *Carmen* does not correspond to Orderic Vitalis's account of Guy's work, because it does not condemn Harold. He asserts that it is based on William of Poitiers's work, written between 1071 and 1076, and so could not be by Guy and is not authoritative. D. C. Douglas, *William the Conqueror* (London 1964), p. 200 n. 2, concedes that in view of G. H. White's arguments the *Carmen* must be treated with caution (previously Professor Douglas accepted the *Carmen* as by Guy and as authoritative; see D. C. Douglas, 'The companions of the Conqueror' in *History*, xxviii, 1943, p. 138). However the opposite view, that the *Carmen* was by Guy and was used as a source by William of Poitiers, has been plausibly, but not conclusively, argued recently by F. Barlow, 'The Carmen de Hastingae Proelio' in *Studies in International History*, ed. K. Bourne and D. C. Watt (London 1967), pp. 35–67. Since the above account of and note on the *Carmen* were written, and the typescript prepared for the press, the edition by Catherine Morton and Hope Muntz, *The 'Carmen de Hastingae Proelio' of Guy Bishop of Amiens*, has been published (Oxford 1972). The editors accept Guy of Amiens's authorship and claim that the poem was completed before 11 May 1068, or at latest by 1070.

[56] Douglas, *William the Conqueror*, p. 200 n. 2, suggests this possibility. The latest editor of William of Poitiers states without reservation that William was indebted to the *Carmen*: see *GGDN*, pp. xxxv et seq. Cf. the previous note.

[57] See Douglas, 'Companions', p. 139 (Taillefer is also mentioned by Henry of Huntingdon and Gaimar).

[58] Ibid., p. 139.

As a panegyric the *Carmen* in some respects resembles William of Jumièges. The Conqueror is 'the fount of justice and peace, the enemy of enemies, the guardian of the church'.[59] But it is more eulogistic than William of Jumièges — more space is devoted to praises of the Conqueror, and the terms are more fulsome. The *Carmen* depicts the king as excelling his prototypes: he is 'wiser than Solomon, more expeditious and generous than Charlemagne'.[60] William of Poitiers elaborated the same idea. The *Carmen* also introduces the comparison of King William with Julius Caesar, conqueror of the Britons.[61] This too was a theme developed in detail by William of Poitiers. And in proportion as King William is raised to the rank of an epic hero, King Harold is degraded to the role of villain. He is not only condemned as a perjurer, but compared with Cain because he fought and killed his brother.[62] William of Poitiers blackened his character beyond recognition.

William of Poitiers was born in about 1020 of noble parentage at Préaux in Normandy, where his sister became a nun of St Leger's.[63] In his youth, before taking orders, he fought for Duke William. He studied at Poitiers from about 1045 to 1050. The schools at Poitiers were an offshoot of those of Chartres and a centre of humanism. William returned to Duke William's service, this time as his chaplain, and subsequently became archdeacon of Lisieux, and probably wrote the *Gesta Guillelmi Ducis Normannorum et Regis Anglorum* (*Deeds of William Duke of the Normans and King of the English*) between 1073 and 1074.[64]

In its present state the text of the *Gesta Guillelmi* is damaged, so that it is incomplete at the beginning and end. It begins with Duke William's early youth, not his childhood, and ends in 1067, although originally it probably extended at least to 1071.[65] The first half concerns William's Norman wars, and the second the Conquest and settlement of England. The *Gesta Guillelmi* has some undetermined relationship to both William of Jumièges's work and the *Carmen*, for it has some passages reminiscent of each. The latest editor of the *Gesta Guillelmi* argues persuasively (but not conclusively) that the *Gesta Guillelmi* borrowed from them both.[66] But the possibility remains that William of Jumièges used the *Gesta Guillelmi*. The author of the *Carmen* could have done so if he was not Guy of Amiens and wrote after 1071. Some similarities could be due to the use by all three authors of common oral traditions, and perhaps they also plundered a common literary source, or sources, now lost.[67]

---

[59] Justitiae cultor, patriae pax, hostibus hostis,/Tutor et ecclesiae . . . ; *Carmen de HP*, p. 28.

[60] '. . . sapientior et Salomone;/Promptior est Magno, largior et Carolo'; ibid., p. 48.

[61] Ibid., pp. 28, 37. Cf. *GGDN*, pp. 247–55.   [62] *Carmen de HP*, p. 31.

[63] For his life see *GGDN*, pp. vii et seq.

[64] On the date of its composition see *GGD N*, pp. xvii–xix.

[65] See *OV*, iv. 7 (vol. 2, p. 217 and n. 1).

[66] *GGDN*, pp. xxiii–xxxvii *passim*.

[67] The complex problem of the interrelation of the Norman historians and of the Bayeux Tapestry (pp. 103–4 below) is discussed at length by Sten Körner, *The Battle of Hastings, England, and Europe 1035–1066* (Lund 1964), pp. 75 et seq., and by F. Barlow, op. cit., pp. 35–67 *passim*.

William of Poitiers was well equipped to write the *Gesta Guillelmi*. He was 'in the know' at court and had access to official documents. He was himself present at some of the Norman campaigns he describes. His connection with Préaux gave him intimate knowledge of one famous Norman family, the Beaumonts, who were patrons of the abbey. The authority of statements in the *Gesta Guillelmi* which are also in William of Jumièges and the *Carmen* is not seriously impaired by the likelihood that William of Poitiers used those works. He himself was so well informed that his repetitions of their statements could fairly be regarded as confirmatory.

William of Poitiers had considerable ability as a historian. He grasped that the primary duty of a historian is to be truthful,[68] and that truth should never be distorted in the interest of literary style. He made clever use of documentary sources, working evidence from William the Conqueror's laws into his account of the Norman settlement.[69] He was capable of graphic descriptions and his training in the classics made him an excellent latinist. Under the influence of the Roman historians, Livy, Caesar, Sallust, Tacitus and Suetonius,[70] he could write history in the grand manner. And emulating the themes of the poets Virgil and Statius he could even give his narrative an epic ring.[71]

Nevertheless, despite the influence of the classics, William of Poitiers wrote in the tradition of the Christian historians. He emphasized the moral purpose of history. Like William of Jumièges, he considered that the course of history should edify the reader.[72] But he is more specific than William of Jumièges. He regarded as particularly edifying the spectacle of the transitory nature of earthly prosperity (he illustrates this with a reference to the death of Geoffrey Martel 'amidst his ill-gotten gains'[73]). Here he anticipated Orderic Vitalis, who developed and exhaustively used the idea. Aided by the study of Cicero and St Augustine, William of Poitiers came near to the concept of natural law (which exists apart from man by divine sanction). All authority came from God: a prince only exercised legitimate power if he observed Christian precepts, and a tyrant had no right to rule, because of his iniquity.[74]

---

[68] Parturire suo pectore bella quae calamo ederentur, poetis licebat, atque amplificare utcumque cognita per campos figmentorum divagando. Nos ducem sive regem, cui nunquam impure quid fuit pulchrum, pure laudabimus; nusquam a veritatis limite passu uno delirantes [*sic* for declinantes?]; *GGDN*, i. 20 (p. 44).

[69] *GGDN*, ii. 33 (pp. 232 and n. 2, 234 and n. 3).

[70] For the influence of classical models on William of Poitiers, see *GGDN*, pp. xxxviii–xliii. For the influence of Sallust on William of Malmesbury, see B. Smalley, 'Sallust in the middle ages' in *Classical Influences on European Culture A.D. 500–1500*, ed. R. R. Bolgar (Cambridge 1971), pp. 171, 173–5.

[71] For a comparison of William the Conqueror's prowess as a warrior with that of Achilles and Aeneas, see p. 102 and n. 92 below.

[72] On the historian's obligation to record the good acts of a man so that they can be imitated, see *GGDN*, i. 36, 58 (pp. 84, 86, 136).

[73] *GGDN*, i. 35 (p. 84). For Orderic, see pp. 159–60 below.

[74] See *GGDN*, p. xli and references, and, with regard to William the Conqueror and Harold, pp. 101–2 nn. 80–5 below.

But William of Poitiers to a certain extent abused his erudition, talents and opportunities. He was a panegyrist, subordinating everything to the praise of the Conqueror. Where he thought necessary he suppressed, distorted and probably invented facts, and tediously elaborated his hero's praises, sometimes avowedly at the expense of authentic details.[75] His intention was to demonstrate that King William had a legitimate claim to the English throne. He expanded with obviously fictitious embellishments William of Jumièges's brief statement that Harold swore to Duke William 'many oaths with regard to the kingdom': he asserted that Harold promised to keep a garrison for William at Dover and other places throughout England.[76] He adds the statement that William had a hereditary right to the throne[77] to a long account of Edward the Confessor's designation of William as his successor.

In order to depict the Conqueror as a perfect Christian prince, William of Poitiers gives a false impression of his character in some respects. Although other authorities confirm that he was brave and pious, they do not confirm that he was merciful to the English. William of Poitiers suppresses any mention of his brutality in England and Normandy (he does not mention his sack of the town of Alençon). His assertion that William offered to fight Harold in judicial combat in order to save the English from slaughter,[78] and that the English, because of William's virtues, wished him to be their king,[79] are without historical foundation. Just as William of Poitiers sought to establish that the Conqueror had a right to rule partly because he was good,[80] so he tried to prove that Harold had no authority because he was bad.[81] He suppressed all mention of Harold's victory at Stamford Bridge. He accused Harold of ingratitude to Duke William for his kindness to Harold when Harold was in Normandy.[82] Harold was a usurper (since the throne was rightly William's),[83] and a tyrant (because he 'enslaved' his subjects).[84]

[75] He omits details of the preparations for the invasion of England as 'superfluous' (*GGDN*, ii. 2, p. 150), and omits those concerning individual heroism at the battle of Hastings (*GGDN*, ii. 19, p. 192) in order 'to complete the praises of Duke William'. He also for the sake of brevity omits details of the treasures King William gave to St Stephen's, Caen; *GGDN*, ii. 42 (p. 256).

[76] *GGDN*, i. 42 (p. 104).

[77] William of Poitiers asserted that this right derived from the fact that Edward the Confessor's mother Emma was the daughter of Richard I duke of Normandy; *GGDN*, ii. 30 (p. 222).

[78] *GGDN*, ii. 12 (p. 178).

[79] *GGDN*, ii. 30 (p. 221).

[80] William of Poitiers asserts that God supported Duke William's invasion of England partly because his cause was just and partly because his purpose was the reform of the church rather than personal aggrandizement and enrichment; *GGDN*, ii. 5 (p. 158). He also asserts that Edward the Confessor had chosen William as being the most worthy and suitable man to rule England (*GGDN*, ii. 12, p. 174) and that his counsellors held the same view after the Conquest (*GGDN*, ii. 29, p. 218).

[81] *GGDN*, ii. 8, 32 (pp. 166 and n. 5, 230). William of Poitiers uses the same argument to help justify Duke William's seizure of Maine, asserting that Geoffrey Martel's intolerably oppressive rule was replaced by the just rule of Duke William; *GGDN*, i. 37 (pp. 86, 88).

[82] *GGDN*, i. 46 (p. 114).

[83] *GGDN*, ii. 13 (p. 180).

[84] *GGDN*, ii. 32 (p. 230). William of Poitiers asserts that Harold was justly killed because he was a tyrant; *GGDN*, ii. 25, 31, 32 (pp. 204, 224, 230).

Above all he was a perjuror,[85] and perjury was a black sin in the eyes of the church.

Thus William of Poitiers, by turning his learning to the service of William the Conqueror, produced a biased, unreliable account of events, and unrealistic portraits of the two principal protagonists. He explicitly states that he has omitted circumstantial details in order to return to the praise of King William.[86] He devotes long pages to personal panegyric of the Conqueror. His favourite method is to compare and contrast his hero with the heroes of classical antiquity. His judgment was invariably in favour of William. Agamemnon's fleet was smaller than William's, and while Xerxes only united two towns, William united two countries.[87] William conquered the English more quickly and completely than Caesar (despite his larger army) conquered the Britons.[88] William was more circumspect than Caesar[89] and braver than Marius or Pompey.[90] His case for claiming the English throne would have convinced even Cicero.[91] Although his deeds would not, in William of Poitiers's view, make a more heroic epic than those of Achilles or Aeneas, they would make a more edifying and truthful one.[92] On the other hand Harold is equated with Hector and Turnus.[93]

Nevertheless, despite his shortcoming, William of Poitiers was so well informed that the *Gesta* cannot be dismissed as worthless. Most of the panegyrical passages are easy to isolate, and there remains much material that William had no interest in misrepresenting. He places Earl Harold's oath-swearing to William at Bonneville-sur-Touques, and he may well be right.[94] There is no reason to doubt the truth of his account of the battle of Hastings (which is in substance much the same as that in the *Carmen*). He makes it quite clear that the English put up a valiant resistance and that the decisive blow, the death of Harold and his brothers, only fell at the end of the day.[95] No doubt William was just in his praise of the bravery of Robert de Beaumont.[96] He is far more lavish with personal names than William of Jumièges or the *Carmen*, and it is to him that scholars owe the identity of twelve of William the Conqueror's companions at Hastings.[97] He agrees with the *Carmen* in his account of the resistance of London to the Conqueror. Moreover, he makes a number of incidental references to England which are of interest. He mentions the wealth of England (a bait to the Normans),[98] and the skill of English women in needlework, and of men in other crafts.[99] He describes the site of London and its importance as a centre of trade,[100] and the position of Dover.[101]

[85] *GGDN*, ii. 1, 14 (pp. 146, 182).   [86] See p. 101 n. 75.   [87] *GGDN*, ii. 7 (p. 162).
[88] *GGDN*, ii. 39 (pp. 246, 248).   [89] *GGDN*, ii. 40 (p. 252).
[90] *GGDN*, ii. 9 (p. 168).   [91] *GGDN*, ii. 12 (p. 178).
[92] *GGDN*, ii. 7, 22 (pp. 164, 198, 200).   [93] *GGDN*, ii. 22 (p. 198).
[94] *GGDN*, i. 42 (p. 102 and n. 3).   [95] *GGDN*, ii. 23 (p. 200).
[96] *GGDN*, ii. 43 (p. 260).   [97] Douglas, 'Companions', pp. 134 et seq.
[98] *GGDN*, ii. 31 (pp. 222, 224).   [99] *GGDN*, ii. 42 (pp. 256, 258).
[100] *GGDN*, ii. 28 (p. 214).   [101] *GGDN*, ii. 27 (p. 210).

Thus there are few literary accounts of the Norman Conquest written at the time, and no unbiased ones. This gives additional importance to another source of evidence, the Bayeux tapestry.[102] The tapestry gives a picture narrative in embroidery, with brief written captions. It is 230 feet long and was once longer, for it is now ragged and incomplete at the end. The first event depicted is Harold being sent by Edward the Confessor to Normandy. There he is shown taking an oath to Duke William by which he promises him the succession to the English throne. The last sequence is the defeat of the English at Hastings.

It is likely that the tapestry was commissioned by Odo of Bayeux (who died in 1097), for display either in one of his palaces[103] or at the dedication of Bayeux cathedral.[104] Study of the design and embroidery proves fairly conclusively that it was of English workmanship and, as Odo was in charge of Kent from 1067 to 1082, it seems likely that it was executed at Canterbury.[105] Its technical and artistic quality would corroborate William of Poitiers's praise of the skill of English needlewomen. The Anglo-Saxons had used tapestries to decorate their palaces from the earliest times. Beowulf describes how ' on the walls shone woven hangings, gleaming with gold, and much that was wonderful to see for all men who gaze on such things '.[106] And it is known that Æthelflaed, the widow of Byrhtnoth (the hero of the battle of Maldon) gave to Ely abbey a tapestry depicting the deeds of her husband.[107] Such hangings were also in vogue on the continent. For example a poem by Baudri, abbot of Bourgueil (1079–1130) describes the rich pictorial embroideries which decorated the walls of the palace of the Conqueror's daughter Adela (who married Stephen count of Blois).[108]

In general the Bayeux tapestry gives an account of the Conquest similar to that of William of Poitiers's *Gesta Guillelmi* from which it may have derived some of its information.[109] It justifies the Norman Conquest by making Harold's oath to Duke William and his perjury the principal theme. The climax is the oath, and the cause of Harold's downfall his perjury. But there are differences from the *Gesta Guillelmi*. The tapestry emphasizes the part played in events by Odo. And it places Harold's oath-taking at Bayeux, not at Bonneville-sur-Touques. As William of Poitiers, not the tapestry, is pro-

---

[102] The most recent edition is *The Bayeux Tapestry, a Comprehensive Survey*, ed. F. M. Stenton (2nd ed., London 1965).

[103] This is the view expressed by C. R. Dodwell, 'The Bayeux tapestry and the French secular epic' in *Burlington Magazine*, cviii (1966), pp. 549–60.

[104] See Stenton in *Bayeux Tapestry*, p. 11.

[105] This view is expressed by Stenton and Professor Francis Wormald in ibid., pp. 11, 34.

[106] *Beowulf*, ll. 994–6.

[107] See *LE*, ii. 63 (p. 136). For this and evidence of the skill of the English in embroidery, and of the existence of other tapestries in England and on the continent, see F. Wormald and G. Wingfield Digby in *Bayeux Tapestry*, pp. 29, 46–7, respectively.

[108] See P. Lauer, 'La Poème de Baudri de Bourgueil adressée à Adèle . . . et la date de la tapisserie de Bayeux' in *Mélanges d'histoire offerts à M. Charles Bémont* (Paris 1913), pp. 43–58.

[109] See Körner, op. cit., pp. 100–5.

bably right on this point, it is likely that the tapestry here reflects its connection with Bayeux.[110] Moreover, it shows sympathy for the English: there is a picture of a mother leading her son from a house which two Norman soldiers are setting on fire. It makes no attempt to denigrate Harold, but depicts him as a great man who suffered a terrible punishment because of his perjury:[111] there is a touch of classical tragedy in this interpretation of his downfall.

[110] See Stenton in *Bayeux Tapestry*, p. 9.
[111] See ibid., p. 15.

7

Anglo-Norman Sacred Biography and Local History

In the generation after the Norman Conquest the Anglo-Saxon saints and their relics were on trial. The problem was to decide which saints of the Anglo-Saxon period should have their feasts observed. Claims to sanctity rested on tradition and there were many saints with merely local reputations whose legends rested on dubious evidence. Lanfranc questioned their right to liturgical commemoration. His dilemma is well illustrated by two stories. Apparently at his instigation the Norman abbot at Evesham, Walter (1077–1104), submitted the abbey's relics to the test of fire: only those which were not consumed by the flames were to be regarded as genuine.[1]

The other story is told by Eadmer in the *Life of St. Anselm* (archbishop of Canterbury 1093–1109). Eadmer relates that one day Archbishop Lanfranc said to Anselm (then abbot at Bec): 'These Englishmen among whom we are living have set up for themselves certain saints whom they revere. But sometimes when I turn over in my mind their own accounts of who they were, I cannot help having doubts about the quality of their sanctity.' He went on to discuss with Anselm the claim to sainthood of Elphege, the archbishop of Canterbury murdered by the Danes in 1012. Lanfranc pointed out that he was not killed for confessing Christ but for refusing tribute to the Danes. Anselm argued in Elphege's defence that he had died for love of justice, to defend his Christian flock against its pagan persecutors. Eadmer remarks that Lanfranc was at that time still ill informed about English customs and asserts that it was essential to approach the matter historically.[2]

Lanfranc revised the liturgical calendar of Christ Church, Canterbury, striking off the feasts of many English saints: only SS. Augustine and Elphege survived the purge. But in the course of the twelfth century many of the English saints were reinstated.[3] This reversal of Lanfranc's policy was partly the result of the work of the late eleventh-century hagiographers at Christ Church.

---

[1] *Eve.*, p. 323.
[2] *The Life of St. Anselm Archbishop of Canterbury by Eadmer*, ed., with an English translation, R. W. Southern (Nelson's Medieval Texts, 1962), pp. 50–3.
[3] For the changes made by Lanfranc in the Christ Church calendar, see F. A. Gasquet and E. Bishop, *The Bosworth Psalter* (London 1908), pp. 27–39.

Lanfranc's scepticism was symptomatic of the age. The Norman Conquest created a threat to continuity. There were direct attacks on existing institutions and traditions, and everywhere was the fear of such attacks.[4] The monasteries responded by writing down the lives of the saints associated with them. These works were much more than edificatory hagiographies. To some extent they were local histories. The hagiographer tried to discover the origin of the monastery of which his saint was patron. He tried to trace the monastery's history through the saint's cult. And his passion for relics made him try to account for antiquities surviving in his own day. Thus hagiography resulted in historical research and the historical interpretation of evidence.

In this way the Anglo-Saxon hagiographical tradition was used to establish continuity with the pre-Conquest period. Another method would have been to write an institutional history as a series of biographies, like Bede's *History of the Abbots of Wearmouth and Jarrow*. But this method was used only once – at Evesham. More important was the application of the biographical form to contemporary figures. To this time belong two first-rate contemporary biographies, of St Anselm of Canterbury and Archbishop Thurstan of York. The authors' preoccupation with the defence of established privilege differentiated these biographies from their Anglo-Saxon precursors. Contentious material almost eclipsed the biographical element in some works (for example in the *De Obsessione Dunelmi*). And a few tracts are written which are purely *pièces justificatives* – fighting weapons intended to be useful in controversy: such was the tract written at Norwich to disprove the claim of the abbey of Bury St Edmunds that it had never been an episcopal see.

Many of the hagiographies of the Anglo-Saxon saints were by professional hagiographers. (The best known was Goscelin of St Bertin.) The rest were written in the religious houses with which the saints were connected. Individual monasteries also produced contemporary biographies and historical tracts. Certain areas were particularly productive of these types of literature. The principal centres[5] were Evesham and Worcester,[6] in the Severn valley; in the north country, Durham and York; in East Anglia, Bury St Edmunds and Norwich; and Canterbury. As will be seen, the literary

---

[4] Cf. p. 88 above.

[5] Interest in local history was also shown by the monks of Ely and Westminster. At Ely the abbey's early history was included in a *Life of St. Etheldreda* (which was perhaps based on an Anglo-Saxon archetype); see *LE*, pp. xxx et seq. Between 1109 and 1131 a monk, at the order of Bishop Hervey, translated from Anglo-Saxon into Latin a short work on St Ethelwold and the tenth-century re-foundation of Ely: this work forms Book II, up to the end of c. 49, of the *Liber Eliensis* (for which see p. 273 below); see *LE*, pp. ix–x, xxxiv, li–liii, 395–9. The account of the foundation of Westminster abbey written by the monk Sulchard between 1072 and 1081 appears to be purely legendary; see *The History of Westminster Abbey by John Flete*, ed. J. A. Robinson (Cambridge 1909), pp. 3–5, 40–3. Goscelin included a similar mythical account of the foundation in his *Life of St. Mellitus*; see ibid., pp. 5–7, 38–40.

[6] For biographical writing at Worcester, treated as a direct continuation of the Anglo-Saxon tradition, see pp. 88–9 above. For the influence of Worcester historians on historiography at Christ Church, see pp. 129–30 below.

traditions of Evesham and Durham were connected, and Worcester influenced Canterbury. It is noteworthy that three of the monasteries listed
(Canterbury, Worcester and Durham) had a historiographical tradition in
Anglo-Saxon times. And these three houses became important centres of
national historiography in the Anglo-Norman period: from this it may be
inferred that interest in local history fostered an interest in wider historical
issues.

I have used the term 'professional hagiographers' to denote men commissioned to write a hagiography for a community to which they were not
attached. These professionals seem generally to have been foreigners (which
suggests that there was a shortage of competent Englishmen). For example
Folcard, abbot of Thorney from about 1067 to 1083 and previously a monk
of St Bertin's, wrote the *Life of St. John of Beverley* for Ealdred, archbishop
of York (1061–9), and the *Life of St. Botulf* for Walkelin, bishop of Winchester (1070–98).[7] The community of St Gregory at Canterbury employed
a German called Bertram to prove that the mortal remains of St Mildred
rested in their church.[8] Eadmer wrote disapprovingly about such foreign
professionals to the monks of Glastonbury in about 1120; he said that if they
had wanted to prove that they had the body of St Dunstan (which was in fact
at Canterbury), 'why didn't you consult some foreigner? ... who would
have invented some likely lie which you could have bought?'[9]

But the foreign hagiographers did not deserve indiscriminate condemnation. The most notable was Goscelin, the former monk of St Bertin who
may have written the *Life of King Edward*. He was remarkable because he
was the first prolific hagiographer since Bede whose interest in English
saints was not confined to those in one locality. He wrote Lives of about
twenty saints associated with monasteries throughout England.

Unlike Bede he did not wait for his material to come to him: he went to it.
He is the first man known to have studied English local history on the spot,
travelling the land and staying in monasteries to write the lives of their
saints. He was the forerunner of William of Malmesbury who admired and
borrowed from his work. William wrote of him: 'He did research over a
long period on many bishoprics and abbeys, and gave to many places
monuments of his outstanding learning. He was second only to Bede in his
praise of the saints of England. ... In addition, he improved the Lives of
innumerable saints by bringing their literary style up to date.'[10]

Little is known of Goscelin's activities during his early years with Bishop

---

[7] For Folcard see *VER*, pp. lii et seq. The *Life of St. John of Beverley* is printed *Historians of
the Church of York*, ed. James Raine (RS, 1879–94), vol. 1, pp. 239–91. The *Life of St. Botulf*
is printed by the Bollandists, *Acta Sanctorum*, 3 June, p. 402.

[8] BM MS. Cotton Vespasian B XX, f. 265. Cf. pp. 110–11 below.

[9] *Memorials SD*, p. 415. Cf. R. W. Southern, *Saint Anselm and his Biographer* (Cambridge 1963),
p. 232.

[10] WM, *GR*, vol. 2, p. 389.

Herman, but between 1077 and 1079 he wrote his first known *Life* – that of St Wulfsige of Sherborne.[11] In about 1080 he wrote the *Life of St. Edith* of Wilton (probably written while he was chaplain to the nuns of Wilton). Soon afterwards he may have visited Winchester,[12] and then he went to East Anglia. Perhaps he went to Peterborough; certainly he went to Ely where he wrote on St Etheldreda,[13] and to Ramsey where he wrote the *Life of St. Ives*, dedicating it to Herbert Losinga, who was abbot of Ramsey from 1087 to 1091 before becoming bishop of Norwich (1091–1119). Goscelin may also have visited Chester and written the *Life of St. Werburg*. Some time in the 1090s he went to St Augustine's, Canterbury, making it his home until his death early in the twelfth century. There he wrote his Canterbury hagiographies under the patronage successively of Archbishops Lanfranc and Anselm. Possibly in about 1101 he visited Much Wenlock in Shropshire to write the *Life of St. Milburg*.[14]

Wherever possible Goscelin took Bede as his starting point. Those of Goscelin's hagiographies, for example the Canterbury Lives, which merely recapitulate and elaborate Bede, are of course of little value to the historian today. But Goscelin did more than rely on literary sources. He questioned men whose memories reached back before the Norman Conquest, and he studied original documents. Some of his works have unique information about early monastic history. For example the *Life of St. Wulfsige* has details about the monastery at Sherborne, the *Life of St. Edith* throws light on the history of Wilton abbey and the *Life of St. Wulfhild* on Barking abbey. The *Life of St. Milburg*, which may be by Goscelin, is an important source for the origins of the abbey of Much Wenlock.

As the companion of Bishop Herman Goscelin must have had access to information about the bishopric of Sherborne. He probably asked the monks for facts: when he wrote a very old man might have remembered St Wulfsige, bishop from 992 to 1001–2. Goscelin includes in the *Life of St. Wulfsige*[15] the history of the see to Herman's time. He gives the succession of the bishops and some details about their episcopates. He describes the community at Sherborne before it was given abbatial status in 1022, naming three of its deans.[16] He describes how King Canute and Queen Emma visited the abbey, and how Emma, seeing that the roof of the church was in bad condition, paid for its repair.[17]

---

[11] For Goscelin's career, and a list of his works, see *VER*, Appendix C, pp. 91–111. Cf. pp. 64–5 above.

[12] See *VER*, p. 99. It has been suggested that the *Life of Grimbald* (for which see p. 79 and n. 91 above) was by Goscelin, but the attribution is very doubtful; see P. Grierson, 'Grimbald of St. Bertin's' in *EHR*, lv (1940), pp. 539–40.

[13] He wrote a prose Life of St Etheldreda; see *LE*, p. 215 and n. 1.   [14] See pp. 109–10.

[15] Printed and discussed by C. H. Talbot, 'The Life of St. Wulsin of Sherborne by Goscelin' in *Revue Bénédictine*, lxix (1959), pp. 68–85.

[16] i.e. Agelward, ibid., c. xvii (p. 82): Wulfric, ibid., c. vii (p. 78); c. xxiv (p. 85); Ælfric, ibid., c. xxi (p. 84).

[17] Ibid., c. xiii (p. 81).

In the *Life of St. Edith*[18] Goscelin describes the dedication performed by St Dunstan of the new church at Wilton.[19] He describes St Edith's position at Wilton: she was not, as has been assumed, the abbess, but was under the tutelage of her mother, the Abbess Wulfthryth.[20] The *Life* provides evidence that Edith's influence spread beyond Wilton: it records that Bishop Ethelwold 'consecrated' her to St Mary's, Winchester, and to Barking abbey. It also names two of Wulftrude's successors to the abbacy.[21]

Goscelin's *Life of St. Wulfhild* relates that King Edgar gave Barking to Wulfhild,[22] who became its abbess, after he had failed to seduce her.[23] Goscelin specifies the estates King Edgar gave to the foundation.[24] He intimates that Wulfhild was not a popular abbess, for she was eventually expelled by the nuns with the support of Edgar's third wife, Queen Ælfthryth,[25] only returning after twenty years' absence. She died at Barking, and Goscelin records that she was succeeded by Lifledis.[26]

Documentary evidence was used for the *Life of St. Milburg*,[27] patron saint of Much Wenlock, founded in about 680. There is no proof that this *Life* was by Goscelin, but it is generally ascribed to him on stylistic grounds.[28] Moreover, St Milburg was the sister of St Mildred who was buried at St Augustine's, Canterbury; therefore it is not unlikely that Goscelin would have written her Life while living at St Augustine's. The community of Much Wenlock dispersed soon after the Norman Conquest, and the abbey was re-founded by Roger of Montgomery, earl of Shrewsbury, for Cluniacs from La Charité-sur-Loire. The efforts of the new community to revive the traditions of the old one culminated in 1101, when the monks claimed to discover the body of St Milburg. The *Life of St. Milburg* was written at about this time. It includes a document called St Milburg's Testament.[29] This is composed of five charters specifying the lands acquired by St Milburg for the original foundation. The Testament may be authentic, but possibly it was concocted to substantiate the ancient traditions of the monastery.

[18] Printed and discussed by A. Wilmart, 'La Légende de Saint Édith en prose et vers par le moine Goscelin' in *An. Boll.*, lvi (1938), pp. 5–101, 265–307.

[19] Ibid., pp. 87 et seq.

[20] Ibid., p. 95 n. 4.

[21] The *Life* (ibid., p. 100) records that Brihtgyva was the third abbess after Wulfthryth, and (ibid., p. 36) that Godyva was ruling when Goscelin wrote.

[22] Printed and discussed by M. Esposito, 'La Vie de Sainte Vulfhilde par Goscelin de Cantorbéry' in *An. Boll.*, xxxii (1913), pp. 10–26.

[23] Osbern also records a scandal between King Edgar and a nun of Wilton; see pp. 128–9 below.

[24] Ibid., c. iv (p. 17).

[25] Ibid., c. ix (pp. 21–2).

[26] Ibid., c. xiii (p. 24).

[27] For the text, which is unprinted, see *VER*, p. 111. The *Life of St. Milburg* is discussed in some detail by H. P. R. Finberg, *The Early Charters of the West Midlands* (Leicester 1961), pp. 197 et seq.; cf. Finberg, *Lucerna* (London 1964), p. 70.

[28] See *VER*, p. 111 n. 1.

[29] Printed, with an English translation, by Finberg, *The Early Charters of the West Midlands*, pp. 201–6. Professor Finberg defends the authenticity of the Testament.

However, whether authentic or not, its inclusion in the *Life* suggests that the author was as much concerned with the origin of the abbey as with St Milburg.

In general, these Lives show that Goscelin was a conscientious antiquarian. Moreover, when involved in controversy, he could think as a critical historian. A good example of his historical ability is the tract called *Libellus contra inanes usurpatores Sanctae Mildrethae* (*Tract against the inane Trespassers against St Mildred*),[30] written towards the end of the eleventh century as a result of the dispute between the monks of St Augustine's and the canons of the hospital of St Gregory at Canterbury. The subject of the dispute was the whereabouts of the body of St Mildred of Thanet: the monks of St Augustine's said it lay in their church, and the canons of St Gregory claimed that it lay in theirs. Goscelin puts both cases in the tract, arguing strongly in favour of St Augustine's. Briefly, this is what he says: a little before 1085 Archbishop Lanfranc founded the hospital of St Gregory, putting a community of canons in charge of it. He transferred some relics, the contents of two tombs, from Lyminge in Kent to the church of St Gregory. One tomb was said to contain the remains of Ethelburga, daughter of Ethelbert king of Kent, who married Edwin king of Northumbria in 625. She returned to Kent in 631 and (reputedly) founded a monastery at Lyminge. At first the canons of St Gregory did not identify the occupant of the other tomb. Then they said it was St Mildred of Thanet. In order to substantiate this claim they had to dispose of the long-established contention of the monks of St Augustine's that St Mildred rested with them. According to the tradition of St Augustine's, St Mildred died on Thanet where she had been abbess early in the eighth century, and was buried in the monastic church. There she stayed, until in 1030 she was translated by Abbot Ælfstan to St Augustine's, at the instigation of King Canute and Queen Emma.

Somehow the Gregorians had to account for the presence of St Mildred's body at Lyminge. This they did by inventing a story. Their argument rested on the identification of Ethelburga the founder of Lyminge with St Eadburga, Mildred's successor as abbess of Thanet. They strengthened the connection between Mildred and Eadburga by saying that Mildred was a direct descendant of Eadburga. According to their story Eadburga fled from Thanet to Lyminge, presumably with St Mildred's body, when the Danes attacked the monastery.

Goscelin tried to demolish this tale with various arguments. He relied partly on miracles attesting that St Mildred was buried at St Augustine's; he relates that St Mildred appeared to the sacrist of St Augustine's in the time

---

[30] BM MS. Cotton Vespasian B XX, ff. 261–76. I am grateful to the late Francis Wormald for calling my attention to this tract. The manuscript was written at St Augustine's between about 1100 and 1130 according to C. R. Dodwell, *The Canterbury School of Illumination* (Cambridge 1954), p. 123.

of Abbot Scotland (1070–87)[31] and slapped the face of a man who slept through a service celebrated in her honour. But he also used historical arguments. He pointed out that Ethelburga could not possibly be the same person as St Eadburga, because the chief events of Ethelburga's life were well known from 'both histories and chronicles',[32] whereas St Eadburga of Thanet belonged to a later age[33] – this made equally absurd the Gregorians' claim that St Eadburga was a forebear of St Mildred. Goscelin had no objection to the Gregorians' claim that they had found the tomb of Ethelburga at Lyminge, but denied that the other tomb had St Mildred's name on it. As evidence he said that in the time of Wido abbot of St Augustine's (1087–99) Ralph, parish priest of Lyminge, swore on oath before the abbot, sacrist and others that Mildred's name was not engraved on the tomb.[34]

As has been seen, Bede's influence on Goscelin was strong. It was also strong in the abbeys of Evesham and Winchcombe, which from 1059 to 1077 were ruled jointly by Abbot Æthelwig. Study of the *Ecclesiastical History* inspired the monks to send a mission to revive monastic life in the north.[35] Aldwin, a monk of Winchcombe, wished to visit the holy places of ancient Northumbria and emulate the asceticism of the Bedan saints. He set out in 1073 or 1074 with two monks from Evesham. Walcher bishop of Durham persuaded them to go to Jarrow, where they built a hut by Bede's ruined church. They were joined by other monks from the south and in 1078 a group settled at Wearmouth. Walcher's successor as bishop, William of St Carilef, was also a student of Bede.[36] In 1083, inspired by the *Life of St. Cuthbert*, he instituted a monastic community in Durham cathedral with monks from Wearmouth.

Both Evesham and Durham produced abbatial histories. The History of the Abbey of Evesham to some extent resembles, and the *History of the Church of Durham* specifically refers to, Bede's *History of the Abbots of Wearmouth and Jarrow*.[37] The History of the Abbey of Evesham has already been mentioned in connection with the biography of Abbot Æthelwig which it incorporates.[38] It is only known from the early thirteenth-century

---

[31] Vesp. B XX, f. 264ᵛ.

[32] Ibid., ff. 262, 262ᵛ, 266. See Bede, *HE*, ii. 9, 11, 14, 20.

[33] St Eadburga, otherwise called Bugga, reputedly died in 751. She was the daughter of Centwine, king of the West Saxons (676–85), and abbess of the minster on the Isle of Thanet. Some of St Boniface's letters to her have survived. For a summary of her life see *DNB*, vol. 6, p. 305. For a poem by St Aldhelm on the church she built see R. Ehwald, *Aldhelmi Opera* in *MGH*, *Auctorum Antiquissimorum*, xv (Berlin 1919), pp. 14–18.

[34] Vesp. B XX, ff. 263, 268ᵛ, 269.

[35] For the post-Conquest monastic revival in the north see M. D. Knowles, *The Monastic Order in England* (2nd ed., Cambridge 1963), pp. 166 et seq. and *Libellus de exordio atque procursu Dunelmensis Ecclesiae* (for which see pp. 114–21 below) in *SD*, vol. 1, pp. 7–11, 108 et seq.

[36] See *SD*, vol. 1, pp. 120–1. William of St Carilef's copy of Bede's *HE* is still preserved, together with at least fifteen of his other books, in the chapter library at Durham (B II. 35); R. A. B. Mynors, *Durham Cathedral MSS. to the End of the Twelfth Century* (limited edition, Oxford 1939), p. 41. For William's library see ibid., pp. 32 et seq.

[37] *SD*, vol. 1, p. 29.   [38] See pp. 89–90 above.

chronicle of Thomas of Marlborough (it forms the first part of Book III). Thomas wrote the *Chronicle of the Abbey of Evesham* in order to prove the abbey's exemption from the authority of the bishops of Worcester. It is very likely that he interpolated passages into the earlier History and tampered with the original text in order to strengthen the case against Worcester.[39] Apparently the original History covered the period from the traditional date of the foundation of the abbey in 714 to the rule of Abbot Walter (1077–1104); as his death is not recorded, presumably he was still alive at the time of writing. The evidence for the inclusion by Thomas of Marlborough of such a pre-existing History is stylistic. To 1077 the sections on each abbot begin with some such phrase as 'Anno igitur', 'Deinde vero', or 'Qua de re'. Thereafter until Marlborough's time the abbots are introduced by 'Huic (*or* Isti) successit'. The account of the abbots before 1077 is much more detailed than that of the subsequent abbots until Marlborough's own day. Stylistically the section on Abbot Æthelwig belongs to the History. For example it records that he suffered from a complaint (gout) 'quem Greci podagra appellant'.[40] It is noted of the previous abbot that he was incapacitated by an infirmity 'quam Greci paralysin appellant'.[41] This stylistic uniformity is probably due to the revision of Æthelwig's biography by the author of the History.

Like Bede in the *History of the Abbots of Wearmouth and Jarrow*, the author does not attribute miracles to the abbots. He was even capable of criticizing his own community. He blamed the Evesham monks for refusing to allow Ælfweard, bishop of London (1035–44), a former abbot of Evesham, to enter the monastery when he was mortally ill.[42] The monks' refusal was not only unkind – it was also unwise. For Ælfweard went to Ramsey abbey instead and gave it the books and the other valuables he had with him. The author gives a judicious account of the Norman abbot Walter. He praises his learning and energy, but criticizes the rash way he involved the abbey in disputes with its tenants over land.

But the similarity to Bede's work of the Evesham History should not be exaggerated. The History reflects the contemporary passion for relics. It records that King Canute gave the Evesham monks the relics of St Wistan,[43] and that Bishop Ælfweard gave them the relics of St Odulf.[44] It relates how the relics of St Ecgwin were stolen by two Evesham monks and given to a lady called Aldith, and how they were recovered for the abbey.[45]

This preoccupation with relics is very apparent in the works of Dominic,

---

[39] For anti-Worcester passages probably inserted by Thomas of Marlborough, see Appendix B below (p. 519).

[40] *Eve.*, p. 95.   [41] *Eve.*, p. 87.

[42] *Eve.*, p. 85. Cf. the account of the incident in Florence of Worcester; see *FW*, vol. 1, pp. 198–9, s.a. 1044. The chronicle of Ramsey states that Ælfweard was a leper; *Chronicon Abbatiae Ramseiensis*, ed. W. D. Macray (RS, 1886), p. 157. For the significance of the notice in the Anglo-Saxon Chronicle, s.a. 1044, see *ASC*, p. 108 n. 3.

[43] *Eve.*, p. 83.   [44] *Eve.*, p. 83.   [45] *Eve.*, pp. 93–4.

prior of Evesham, who wrote hagiographies probably in the first quarter of the twelfth century. By his time the influence of Bede seems to have declined at Evesham. Instead his works resemble the saint's Lives of the late tenth and early eleventh centuries. His hagiographies are inflated to carry the local history of Evesham abbey. The *Life and Miracles of St. Ecgwin* is arranged in twelve lessons to be read on St Ecgwin's feast day.[46] It is followed by the charter founding the abbey which St Ecgwin was supposed to have written.[47] Then there are miracles of St Ecgwin arranged in twelve lessons for the feast of his translation, and a historical account of the translation. Finally Dominic added a book of miracles. This composite work on St Ecgwin was copied by Thomas of Marlborough into the *Chronicle of the Abbey of Evesham* as Books I and II.

Dominic also wrote a tract on notable monks of Evesham, and the *Translation and Miracles of St. Odulf* and *Life of St. Wistan*, who were both buried there.[48] It has been argued that Dominic was the author of the Evesham History.[49] But differences in the account of the abbey's affairs given in his known works, from that in the History, make this unlikely (however, certainty is impossible in the present state of the evidence, as the variants could be due to the fact that Thomas of Marlborough revised the History but did not apparently revise Dominic's hagiographies). For example the story of the theft of St Ecgwin's relics has slight variants. The *Life* describes the thieves as two boys of Evesham; the History describes them as two monks. The *Life* mentions the punishment of one of them; the History says that both were punished. The *Life* says that Aldith promised to return the relics and give the manor of Swell to the monastery; the History makes no mention of Swell in this context. The *Life* relates that on Aldith's death the relics reached Worcester cathedral, from which Abbot Æthelwig recovered them by process of law; the History asserts that Æthelwig regained them from 'a certain powerful man' to whom Aldith's son had given them.[50] Moreover the History supplies the name (Godric) of the master craftsman who worked on the tomb of St Ecgwin; Dominic merely calls him 'the father of the monk Clement who later became prior'. The History adds that Godric himself subsequently became a monk of Evesham and lived 'a good life for many years' until his death.[51]

[46] Printed in *Eve.*, pp. 1–17. For a *Life of St. Ecgwin* written in Anglo-Saxon times see p. 79 and n. 92 above.

[47] *Eve.*, pp. 17–20. P. H. Sawyer, *Anglo-Saxon Charters* (Royal Historical Soc., 1968), no. 1251.

[48] These three works are printed in *Eve.*, pp. 313–37.

[49] See *VCH*, *Worcester*, vol. 2, p. 113. Knowles, *Monastic Order*, Appendix viii, pp. 704–5. Professor Knowles dates the account of Æthelwig in the history of the first quarter of the twelfth century (considerably later than Professor Darlington dates it), because, for example, it calls Serlo abbot of Gloucester (d. 1104) 'of venerable memory'. But such a phrase could be the result of Thomas of Marlborough's revision (cf. p. 519 below).

[50] *Eve.*, pp. 45–6, 93–4. Possibly the omission in the History of all mention of Worcester in this context was the result of Thomas of Marlborough's revision.

[51] *Eve.*, pp. 86–7. Cf. p. 44.

Similarly there is a small variation between the *Translation and Miracles of St. Odulf* and the History: the former records that Bishop Ælfweard paid £100 for St Odulf's relics; the History say 100 marks.[52] And the *Life of St. Wistan* records that King Canute gave the manor of Broadwell to Evesham, while the History says that Abbot Æthelwig redeemed it for 6 marks.[53]

Dominic supplements the information about the abbey in the History. Thus, whereas the latter briefly notes Abbot Walter's building activities (he built the crypt and choir and began a new tower),[54] Dominic, in the *Life and Miracles of St. Ecgwin*, specifies problems encountered by Walter and demonstrates the practical value of relics in their solution. Deploring the destruction of the Anglo-Saxon church ('one of the most beautiful in England'),[55] he records how Walter, 'lacking the means of work, was in great straits. He was short of everything – now stone, now wood, now the greatest of all human necessities, money'. Walter therefore sent two monks carrying the relics of St Ecgwin on tour to collect funds (the method was to put the relics on view to the people; then one of the monks preached a sermon and a collection was made). They visited Oxford, London, Winchester and Dover with considerable success. Walter also planned to send St Odulf's body to Winchcombe abbey for the same purpose, but the saint objected to removal:[56] the reliquary became so heavy that the monks turned back – on the return journey it was miraculously light. On another occasion St Odulf frustrated a desire of Queen Edith to take some of his relics. The queen ordered that relics from many monasteries should be taken to her at Gloucester. But when she demanded that St Odulf's reliquary should be opened she was struck blind; her sight was only restored when she swore not to disturb his relics.[57]

The *Life of St. Wistan* shows a more creditable aspect of life at Evesham. It claims that monks of Evesham first introduced monasticism in Denmark by founding the abbey at Odense.[58] This is an example of the use of a saint's Life as a vehicle for institutional history, for the statement has no apparent connection with St Wistan.

Of the north country centres of historiography, York and Durham, the latter was the most prolific. Four historical works were written there. In two of them the influence of Bede is very marked. Both of these are histories of the see of St Cuthbert from its foundation by Aidan in 635. One goes up to

[52] *Eve.*, pp. 83, 314. [53] *Eve.*, pp. 83, 325. [54] *Eve.*, p. 97.
[55] *Eve.*, p. 55. [56] *Eve.*, pp. 318–19. [57] *Eve.*, p. 317.
[58] *Eve.*, p. 325. Cf. Knowles, *Monastic Order*, p. 164 and n. 1, who suggests that the foundation took place in 1095–6, and more especially, for the settlement of Odense cathedral priory by monks of Evesham, Peter King, 'The cathedral priory of Odense in the middle ages' in *Saga-Book of the Viking Society*, xvi (1962–5), pp. 194–5 and *passim*. The church of the new monastery was dedicated to St Canute: for the church dedicated to St Alban, where Ælnoth of Canterbury had been a priest, see p. 94 above.

1072[59] and the other to 1096.[60] The latter is now known as the *Historia Dunelmensis Ecclesiae* (*History of the Church of Durham*), but in the middle ages was called *Libellus de exordio atque procursu istius, hoc est Dunelmensis Ecclesiae* (*Tract on the Origin and Progress of the Church of Durham*).[61] The other two Durham works are tracts produced as a result of controversy, the so-called *De Obsessione Dunelmi* (*The Siege of Durham*)[62] and the *De Injusta Vexatione Willelmi Episcopi* (*The Unjust Persecution of Bishop William*).[63]

The two histories are modelled partly on Bede's *History of the Abbots of Wearmouth and Jarrow* and *Life of St. Cuthbert*. But they also show traces of other influences. They represent a continuation of the Northumbrian tradition manifested in the tenth-century *Historia de Sancto Cuthberto*. Moreover they reflect the trouble of the writers' own times. The unrest of the north under Norman rule created political bias in its historians. Such bias is apparent both in the two narrative histories, and also in the two tracts.

In the histories the emphasis is on continuity and normality: the authors tried to prove that the see had an unbroken history which no political event had disrupted. The History of the see to 1072 was probably the earlier work of the two, and a copy may originally have been in a Gospel book chained to the cathedral altar, presumably for the information of the monks and pilgrims.[64] This History gives a favourable account of Æthelric bishop of Durham from 1042 to 1056 (unlike the *Libellus* and other authorities). He was a monk of Peterborough whose rule aroused such opposition among the cathedral canons that he was forced to return to his abbey. Æthelric, it says, was unable to resist 'the violence of evil minded men', and left his bishopric 'rather than lose the liberty and peace of his church'.[65] The History also stresses that William the Conqueror was well disposed towards the see. It relates that the wisest men of the church told him about St Cuthbert and the bishopric's long history from the time of Aidan. As a result, King William confirmed its liberties and granted it estates: the grants are specified in charters appended to the work.

The *Libellus*, which ends with the death of William of St Carilef, is a longer and more ambitious work. It is generally ascribed to Symeon, a monk of Durham and the putative author of the *Historia Regum*. There is evidence connecting Symeon with historical productions – though none connecting him directly with the *Libellus*. A monk Symeon attended the

[59] Printed in E. Craster, 'The Red Book of Durham' in *EHR*, xl (1925), pp. 523–9.
[60] Printed in *SD*, vol. 1, pp. 3–135. For historical writing at Durham in the middle ages see H. S. Offler, *Medieval Historians of Durham* (Inaugural Lecture, printed for the University of Durham, 1958).
[61] Offler, op. cit., p. 6.
[62] Printed in *SD*, vol. 1, pp. 215–20.
[63] Printed in ibid., pp. 170–95.
[64] Craster, op. cit., pp. 520–1.
[65] Craster, op. cit., p. 528.

translation of St Cuthbert in 1104. Someone wrote a detailed account of the ceremony: this work has been attributed to Symeon.[66] 'Symeon, the humble servant of the servants of St. Cuthbert', wrote an account of the archbishops of York in a letter to Hugh, dean of York (either Hugh the dean from 1090 to 1109, or another Hugh who was dean from 1130 to 1132).[67] There is also a letter of 1126, or soon after, addressed to the monk Symeon by Sigar, parish priest of Newbald in the East Riding, recounting a vision experienced by one of his parishioners called Orm: the letter would suggest that Symeon was recognized as the rightful recipient of local news.[68]

The evidence that Symeon wrote the *Libellus* is inconclusive. There is only one manuscript naming him as author. This was written in the late twelfth century and belonged to the Cistercian house of Sawley in Yorkshire.[69] The early partly autograph text owned by Durham cathedral bears no ascription to Symeon.[70] The *Libellus* is therefore, strictly speaking, an anonymous work. It states in the preface that the author wrote at the order of his superiors. One of them was presumably Turgot, prior of Durham from 1087 to 1109 (to whom a biography of St Margaret of Scotland is attributed[71]). Thus it is likely that the author's point of view was the official Durham one.

The climax of the *Libellus* is the reintroduction of monks in St Cuthbert's cathedral. This theme is outlined in the preface and expanded in the course of the work which leads up to the momentous event.[72] The beginning is linked with the end, for, as the author says, William of St Carilef 'did not institute a new monastic order but restored an ancient one'.[73] The last few

---

[66] The authority for Symeon's presence at the 1104 translation is Reginald of Coldingham, *Reginaldi Monachi Dunelmensis Libellus de admirandis Beati Cuthberti Virtutibus*, ed. J. Raine (Surtees Soc., vol. 1, 1835), p. 84. The account of the 1104 translation is in the last section of a history of St Cuthbert's translations and miracles (printed in *SD*, vol. 1, pp. 247–61; vol. 2, pp. 333–62, and in *Symeonis Dunelmensis Opera et Collectanea*, ed. H. Hinde (Surtees Soc., li, 1868), vol. 1, pp. 158–201). On the attribution of this section to Symeon see *SD*, vol. 1, pp. xii–xiii, xxxi–xxxii and n. 1, and *SD*, ed. Hinde, p. xlv.

[67] Printed in *SD*, vol. 1, pp. 222–8 (see p. 226 note c.).

[68] H. Farmer, 'The vision of Orm' in *An. Boll.*, lxxv (1957), pp. 72–82. Cf. pp. 148–9 below.

[69] Cambridge University Library MS. Ff. 1. 27. See P. H. Blair, 'Some observations on the *Historia Regum* attributed to Symeon of Durham' in Chadwick, *Celt and Saxon*, pp. 73 et seq. Cf. *SD*, vol. 1, xxiii.

[70] Durham MS. Cosins V. ii. 6. See *SD*, vol. 1, p. xv.

[71] Printed in *SD*, ed. Hinde, vol. 1, pp. 234–54. The attribution to Turgot, which rests on the fact that the author gives his initial as 'T' (ibid., p. 234), was apparently first made by the fourteenth-century chronicler John of Fordun (see his *Chronica Gentis Scotorum*, ed. W. F. Skene (Edinburgh 1871, 1872, 2 vols; vol. 2 is an English translation), vol. 1, p. 216; cf. ibid., pp. 217, 218). This attribution is accepted by Knowles, *Monastic Order*, p. 170; Professor Knowles points out that if Turgot was the author he must have known St Margaret well, and this intimacy with the Scottish royal family would explain why King Alexander I gave him the bishopric of St Andrews. However, Turgot's authorship is unproved and was doubted by Hinde; see *SD*, ed. Hinde, pp. lviii–lx. It has also been suggested that Turgot wrote the section of the work on the translations of St Cuthbert (see n. 66 above) up to the account of the 1104 translation; see *SD*, ed. Hinde, p. xlv.

[72] *SD*, vol. 1, pp. 119 et seq.   [73] Ibid., p. 11.

chapters show how the community strengthened the foundations of its prosperity. The author used as sources Bede's *Ecclesiastical History*, his *History of the Abbots of Wearmouth and Jarrow*, his *Life of St. Cuthbert*, the Northumbrian annals, the *Historia de Sancto Cuthberto*[74] and probably the History of St Cuthbert's church to 1072.[75] He also apparently used documents which are now lost and oral traditions surviving in the cathedral community.

At Durham the past was the inspiration of the present. The author of the *Libellus* tried to demonstrate that St Cuthbert's power had always protected, and always would protect, his community. Just as in the tenth century St Cuthbert had confounded the enemies of his community, so in the eleventh he inflicted temporary insanity on a plunderer of his shrine. When William the Conqueror tried to tax St Cuthbert's tenants, the angry saint appeared to the tax-collector in his sleep, who at once fell ill and only recovered on leaving St Cuthbert's territory.[76]

The *Libellus* makes it seem that Bede was almost a living presence at Durham. The author had apparently visited the chapel dedicated to Bede at Jarrow and the stone cottage (*mansiuncula*) where it was said Bede used 'to sit, meditate, read, dictate and write, free from all disturbance'.[77] The author gives a full account of Bede's life and an assessment of his work. He tells how the monks of Durham obtained Bede's mortal remains. Alured, great-grandfather of Ailred of Rievaulx[78] and sacrist of Durham in the first quarter of the eleventh century, was an unscrupulous relic-hunter. He used to go to Jarrow every year for the anniversary of Bede's death. On one occasion he left very early in the morning without a word to anyone. He never went there again 'as though he had achieved what he had planned'. Henceforth if asked he said no one knew better than he where the relics of Bede were, for 'the same tomb which contains the most holy body of father Cuthbert also has the bones of the venerable doctor and monk, Bede'.[79]

The *Libellus* rather strangely describes Alured as 'honest and very religious'. Compelled 'by a vision' he scoured the sites of the ancient Northumbrian churches and monasteries for the bones of the saints whose acts were recorded in the *Ecclesiastical History*. He showed the relics to the people (presumably collecting money for St Cuthbert's) and took a portion of each saint home. Among those he salvaged were the relics of Boisil abbot of Melrose.

The *Libellus* appeals to Boisil's career as a precedent for an action taken by Bishop William of St Carilef. William appointed the prior of Durham, Turgot, as archdeacon in the bishopric. The *Libellus* remarks: 'He did not do this without authority or example. For it is read in the *Life of St. Cuthbert*

[74] Cf. pp. 76-7 above.   [75] Craster, loc. cit., p. 530.   [76] *SD*, vol. 1, p. 107.
[77] Ibid., p. 43.   [78] See p. 213 below.   [79] *SD*, vol. 1, pp. 88-9.

that the blessed Boisil when he was "praepositus" of the monastery [of Lindisfarne] used often to go and preach to the people. . . . Now he who is prior was called "praepositus" by the blessed Benedict.'[80] There is evidence that this strong Bedan influence was not confined to the Durham monks. The vision of Orm is very like Drythelm's vision of the afterworld which Bede describes in the *Ecclesiastical History*.[81] The *Libellus* itself records a similar vision experienced by Eadulf, a man who lived near Durham, explicitly comparing it to the one described by Bede.[82]

But unlike Bede the author of the *Libellus* had to try to reconstruct the distant, not the immediate past. And he had to try to bridge a dark period of English history – the period of the Danish invasions. There may therefore have been an element of wishful thinking in his attempt to clothe objects at Durham with early associations. It is quite credible that the statues of St Mary and John the Baptist in the cathedral were given, as the *Libellus* states, by Tostig's wife Judith before the Norman Conquest.[83] But the assertion that the stone cross in St Cuthbert's cemetery had belonged to Ethelwold bishop of Lindisfarne (d. 740), that the crack through it was acquired when the Danes raided Lindisfarne and that it had accompanied St Cuthbert's body during its wanderings, can at best rest only on tradition.[84] At worst it could have been invented to add sanctity to the sights of Durham for the benefit of pilgrims.

The account in the *Libellus* of the Lindisfarne Gospels should be treated with the same caution. The tenth-century authority, the *Historia de Sancto Cuthberto*, makes no mention of any Gospel-book associated with St Cuthbert. But the *Libellus* does. It asserts that one was taken with St Cuthbert's body from Lindisfarne.[85] It was a beautiful book decorated inside with letters and illuminations of outstanding excellence, and outside with gold and gems. As the party bearing St Cuthbert's body tried to embark at the mouth of the Derwent for Ireland, a storm blew up and the Gospels were swept overboard and lost. Later they were miraculously recovered from the beach at Whithorn. This story cannot be true, for Whithorn is thirty miles from the mouth of the Derwent.[86] Legends of the miraculous recovery of books of Gospels and the like from water are not uncommon in Celtic lore. The *Life of St. Margaret of Scotland* attributed to Turgot has a similar story concerning her Gospel lectionary.[87] This lectionary has survived and contains an eleventh or twelfth century inscription about the alleged accident.[88]

---

[80] Ibid., p. 129.
[82] *SD*, vol. 1, pp. 114–16.
[84] Ibid., p. 39.
[81] See pp. 28 n. 116, 116 above.
[83] Ibid., p. 95; Cf. p. 101.
[85] Ibid., pp. 64–8.
[86] See T. J. Brown, 'The lives of the authors and the later history of the MS' in *Codex Lindisfarnensis*, ed. T. D. Kendrick, T. J. Brown and others (Oltun and Lausanne 1960), pp. 21–3.
[87] See the *Life of St. Margaret*, printed in *SD*, ed. Hinde, vol. 1, p. 250 (and see next note).
[88] Brown, loc. cit., p. 23 and n. 2. The inscription is printed in *The Gospel Book of St. Margaret*, a facsimile edition by W. Forbes-Leith (limited edition, Edinburgh 1896), p. 11.

The *Libellus* identifies the Gospel-book with one preserved at Durham in his day. The book, he records, was written by Bishop Eadfrith, bound by Bishop Ethelwold, and decorated with metalwork by the anchorite Bilfrid.[89] This passage and the account of the book leaves no doubt that the author was speaking of the Lindisfarne Gospels now preserved in the British Museum. The volume has stains made by water at the top of some pages. The stains were not made by sea water and may have been caused by a jar of water spilling on the book while on its shelf. Similar marks occur in other early Durham books.[90] Therefore it seems likely that the story in the *Libellus* was an attempt to provide a miraculous explanation for a slight blemish on one of the cathedral's greatest treasures. Nevertheless there is no need to suppose that the Lindisfarne Gospels did not originally accompany St Cuthbert's body. It would be hard to explain in any other way the presence in the Durham library of this and a number of other early Northumbrian books. One, the Stonyhurst Gospels, was actually found in St Cuthbert's tomb when it was opened in 1104.[91]

The attempt of the *Libellus* to establish continuity between the pre- and post-Conquest periods led to wishful thinking: the attempt at proving that St Cuthbert's see had a past of unbroken glory led to dishonest bias. The author fashioned his evidence to fit his theories. He claimed, for example, that the descendants of the very men who had carried St Cuthbert's body from Lindisfarne were in his day members of the community of Durham cathedral priory.[92]

The author of the *Libellus* was faced with a problem in regard to the nature of the community which the coffin-bearers established at Chester-le-Street. The bearers had been accompanied by laymen and by women and children, and the community they founded did not observe a monastic Rule. Its members were what in a later period would have been called 'secular canons'. By the time the *Libellus* was written the distinction between secular canons and monks was clearly defined, and antagonism had developed between these two categories. The monks' monopoly of the bishoprics was being challenged by the secular clergy. In response the monks emphasized the discipline of the monastic observance. Moreover, both the religious and the seculars were influenced by the Hildebrandine reform movement with its emphasis on clerical celibacy and its consequent anti-feminist tendencies.

The *Libellus* glosses over the secular nature of St Cuthbert's community after the flight from Lindisfarne. It asserts that though its members were not, strictly speaking, monks, they lived like monks, preserving the ancient monastic tradition of their see as far as possible.[93] The *Libellus* also attributed to the patron, St Cuthbert, an anti-feminism which he never felt. It is well

[89] *SD*, vol. 1, pp. 67–8.   [90] Brown, op. cit., p. 22.

[91] See R. A. B. Mynors, 'The Stonyhurst gospel' in *The Relics of St. Cuthbert*, ed. C. F. Battiscombe (Oxford 1956), pp. 357–8.

[92] *SD*, vol. 1, pp. 79–80.   [93] Ibid., pp. 57–8.

established in Bede's *Life of St. Cuthbert* that he was friendly with a number of women whom he frequently visited. But the *Libellus* claims that he rigorously excluded all women from his church (the reason being, according to the *Libellus*, that St Cuthbert deplored the immorality, recorded by Bede, in the mixed monastery of Coldingham).[94] The *Libellus* represents St Cuthbert posthumously as even more opposed to women: he allowed no woman near his shrine[95] or in the cemetery of his church,[96] inflicting terrible vengeance on female trespassers.[97] The *Libellus* was clearly trying to provide historical precedents for contemporary attitudes.

With regard to the history of the community at Durham, the *Libellus* is strongly biased. It achieves a calculated impression, not by the invention of evidence, but by the suppression of some facts and the overemphasis of others. It minimizes the political troubles which involved St Cuthbert's church, reducing them to domestic proportions. This is seen in the treatment of the fates of the two brothers, successively bishops of Durham, Æthelric (1042–56) and Æthelwine (1056–71). They had both previously been monks of Peterborough. It asserts that before Æthelric resigned his bishopric in 1056, he had dug up a hoard of money at Chester-le-Street.[98] When Æthelric returned to Peterborough he took the treasure with him for building roads and churches. After the Norman Conquest he was accused in the king's court of robbing the church of Durham. He was imprisoned and died in captivity. But other Anglo-Norman historians do not give the impression that Æthelric's crime was merely against Durham. They imply that he was implicated in treasonable plots against the king.[99]

The *Libellus* apparently suppresses a similar charge against Bishop Æthelwine. Æthelwine was deprived of his bishopric in 1071 and tried to leave England, taking (according to the *Libellus*) part of the Durham treasure. But his ship was wrecked on the coast of Scotland and he was taken to the king at Ely. He was accused of stealing the church treasure, which he adamantly denied, and was imprisoned at Abingdon. There he died of a broken heart.[100] Again the other authorities give his downfall a wider, political significance. They state that he had joined Earl Morcar and Siward Bearn in an insurrection against the king.[101]

The same desire to play down the political troubles in the north is apparent in the treatment in the *Libellus* of the murder of Bishop Walcher. It merely says that Walcher was murdered because of the hostility provoked by the

---

[94] Ibid., p. 59. [95] Ibid., p. 58. [96] Ibid., p. 60.
[97] Ibid., pp. 60–1, 95 [98] Ibid., pp. 91–2.
[99] ASC (D and E), *s.a.* 1069, records that 'Bishop Æthelric in Peterborough had an accusation brought against him, and was sent to Westminster, and his brother Æthelwine was outlawed.' The Chronicle is more explicit concerning Æthelwine's treachery; see below and n. 101.
[100] *SD*, vol. 1, p. 105.
[101] ASC (D and E), *s.a.* 1071, Cf. Geffrei Gaimar, *L'Estoire des Engleis*, ed. Alexander Bell (Anglo-Norman Text Soc., xiv–xvi, Oxford 1960), ll. 5457–63, and *FW*, vol. 2, p. 9 (*s.a.* 1071).

high-handed behaviour of his followers. His death is given a religious touch: the *Libellus* states that Eadulf had prophesied his death.[102] It stresses that the people of Durham bravely resisted the party responsible for the murder, and asserts that many innocent suffered when King William ravaged the north in revenge for Walcher's death.[103] Other authorities give a fuller account of the motives for the murder.[104] Similarly, motives for the quarrel between William of St Carilef and William Rufus are suppressed, the quarrel being attributed rather cryptically to 'the machinations of certain people'.[105] But other authorities attribute it to Bishop William's participation in a plot with Odo of Bayeux against Rufus in favour of Duke Robert.[106]

And so by the judicious suppression of some facts and the emphasis of others the *Libellus* built a bridge over the Conquest, and preserved, as a living tradition, the long history of St Cuthbert's church. It could write triumphantly of William the Conqueror: 'He confirmed by his consent and authority the laws and customs of the saint just as they had been established formerly by the authority of kings.'[107]

The *Libellus* is not only concerned with the spiritual glory of the bishopric. It is also concerned with its material prosperity. Preoccupation with St Cuthbert's possessions is evident in the careful record (derived partly from the *Historia de Sancto Cuthberto*) of the acquisition of property, and in the allegation that Æthelric and Æthelwine robbed the Durham treasury[108] – the *Libellus* points out that William of St Carilef 'never took anything from the church'.[109] Evidently the author did not think that the bishopric was adequately endowed after the Conquest despite the efforts of William of St Carilef and the generosity of William the Conqueror.[110]

As the *Libellus* was about the distant past as well as contemporary times, the author could not always use the strictly biographical method adopted by Bede in the *History of the Abbots of Wearmouth and Jarrow*. After the end of the seventh century, lack of information forced him to abandon the biographical form until his own time. Then he returned to the biographical method, writing the history of St Cuthbert's church as a series of the Lives of the bishops. The biographical method also dominates the two tracts written at Durham, the *De Obsessione Dunelmi* and the *De Injusta Vexatione Willelmi*. Both are hybrid works; the biography encloses the principal theme. The theme of the first tract was the right of Durham to certain estates; the theme of the second was William of St Carilef's relations with William Rufus.

---

[102] *SD*, vol. 1, pp. 115–17.   [103] Ibid., p. 118.

[104] *FW*, vol. 2, p. 16 (*s.a.* 1080). Cf. the account based on Florence of Worcester in the *Historia Regum* attributed to Symeon; *SD*, vol. 2, p. 24.

[105] *SD*, vol. 1, p. 128.

[106] See *FW*, vol. 2, pp. 21–2; and *HH*, p. 214; WM, *GP*, iii. 133 (p. 273).

[107] *SD*, vol. 1, p. 108.

[108] Ibid., pp. 91–2, 105. The *Libellus* also records that Durham was despoiled in 1069 (ibid., p. 101), and by Odo of Bayeux (ibid., p. 118).

[109] William 'nihil unquam de ecclesia auferebat'; ibid., p. 125.   [110] Ibid., p. 124.

The biography in the *De Obsessione Dunelmi* is of Uhtred, earl of Northumbria, a benefactor of St Cuthbert's. He helped Bishop Ealdhun to clear the site for the new church at Durham[111] and subsequently married Ealdhun's daughter Ecfrida. The tract begins with an account of how Uhtred assisted Ealdhun in the defence of Durham against Malcolm king of Scotland (1005–34). There follows an account of Uhtred's career until his murder in 1016. Then there is a brief history of his successors to the earldom of Northumbria, with notices of the marriages of his daughters, to the time of Earl Waltheof (whom the Conqueror executed in 1076).

The *De Obsessione Dunelmi* is the first known attempt to record the history of an English earldom (it can be compared with another history of the earls of Northumbria written, probably also at Durham, in the reign of Henry I[112]). The history of the earldom is used as a pretext for tracing the descent of certain estates of St Cuthbert's. When Uhtred married Ecfrida, he received six manors belonging to the bishopric as dowry. He was to hold them as long as he was married to her. In due course Uhtred repudiated Ecfrida and she, on becoming a nun, returned the estates to the bishop. Nevertheless Uhtred's and Ecfrida's descendants continued to claim the estates: the *De Obsessione* records their struggle with the bishops of Durham for possession.

The biography of William of St Carilef constitutes the framework for the principal theme of the *De Injusta Vexatione Willelmi*. After a brief résumé of the events of William of St Carilef's episcopate to the death of William the Conqueror, there is a detailed account of his quarrel with William Rufus in 1088. This is followed by a short concluding section on his life from his reconciliation with William Rufus until his death in 1096.

The account in the *De Injusta Vexatione Willelmi* of the quarrel between William of St Carilef and Rufus is a remarkable piece of contemporary reportage.[113] In the spring of 1088 Rufus seized the bishop's lands. Like the *Libellus*, the *De Injusta Vexatione Willelmi* offers no explanation beyond saying that the bishop 'was surrounded by plots'. It gives copies of the

---

[111] Ibid., p. 81.

[112] The account of the earls of Northumbria is copied into the *Historia Regum* attributed to Symeon of Durham; *SD*, vol. 2, pp. 196–9. See also GEC, *Peerage*, vol. 9, p. 705 n. 6.

[113] This is not the view expressed by H. S. Offler, 'The Tractate "De Iniusta Vexatione Willelmi Episcopi Primi"' in *EHR*, lxvi (1951), pp. 321–41, who believes that the work was produced in the second quarter of the twelfth century at Durham. But I agree with Professor Southern, *St. Anselm and his Biographer* (Cambridge 1963), p. 148 n. 1, that Professor Offler's arguments are unconvincing, as there is no adequate motive known for such a forgery. Nor do I agree with Professor Offler (op. cit., pp. 322–3) that the biographical sections must have been added to the work later; the biographical framework is in accordance with the literary fashions of the eleventh century. Previously scholars have accepted the tract as a genuine, contemporary work: see Knowles, *Monastic Order*, p. 169 n. 1; G. B. Adams, *Council and Courts in Anglo-Norman England* (New Haven, Yale Historical Publications, vol. 5, 1926), pp. 46–65 *passim*; C. W. David, *Robert Curthose* (Cambridge, Mass. 1920), Appendix B, pp. 211–16 (reprinted with slight revision from *EHR*, xxxii (1917), pp. 382–7); F. Liebermann, *Historische Aufsätze dem Andenken an Georg Waitz gewidmet* (Hanover 1888), p. 159 n. 10.

bishop's self-justificatory letters to the king. There follows a description, written from the bishop's point of view, of his trial in the king's court, complete with *verbatim* reports of what the parties said. The whole work is lively and circumstantial, and sympathetic to William of St Carilef. It is the earliest known account of the proceedings in the king's court, and was probably written by one of the bishop's party.

The only well-known piece of historiography written at York in the Anglo-Norman period was Hugh the Chantor's *History of the Church of York*, for the years from 1066 to 1127.[114] Like the *De Injusta Vexatione Willelmi*, it concerns events which took place in the author's own time. Hugh became a canon of York probably as early as 1100 and later in life was the precentor. He was an intimate of Thurstan archbishop of York (1114–40), accompanying him in exile from 1117 to 1121, and to Rome in 1123. He probably died in 1139. In form Hugh's work resembles Bede's *History of the Abbots of Wearmouth and Jarrow* and (though in prose) Alcuin's *De Pontificibus et Sanctis Ecclesiae Eboracensis Carmen*: it is virtually a series of biographies of the archbishops from Thomas I to Thurstan.

Hugh's work has characteristics of the biographical type of local history – it is partly a laudatory record of the archbishops' achievements. For example the account of Thomas I ends with a general appreciation of him ('none was more generous or less severe, or more agreeable in company whether on serious business or in good fun')[115] and with his epitaph. There is also a businesslike record of prebends established in the cathedral by Thomas II[116] and a eulogy of Thurstan.[117] Hugh is particularly full on Thurstan. Like Eadmer he emphasizes his hero's popularity[118] and influence abroad – in France and at the papal court. He asserts that Thurstan's advice was the determining factor in a number of important decisions. It was due mainly to his mediation that peace was made between the king of England and the king of France in 1120.[119] And it was due to him that the pope granted William of Corbeil, the elect of Canterbury, the pallium in 1123 despite doubts about the canonical validity of his election.[120] Above all, Hugh attributes to Thurstan's influence the appointment of Archbishop William of Corbeil as papal legate in England in 1125.[121] William of Corbeil's appointment temporarily resolved the deadlock between the archbishops of Canterbury and York over the primacy of England. For it was a compromise giving *de facto* supremacy to the archbishop of Canterbury and which nevertheless did not humiliate the archbishop of York.

Hugh was deeply interested in the controversy between the metropolitans. His obsession with it transformed the traditional structure of his work. The

---

[114] The most recent edition is *Hugh the Chantor, The History of the Church of York 1066–1127*, ed., with an English translation, Charles Johnson (Nelson's Medieval Texts, 1961). For Hugh's life see ibid., pp. vii–ix.

[115] *Hugh the Chantor*, pp. 11–12. [116] Ibid., p. 32. [117] Ibid., p. 34.

[118] See ibid., pp. 81–2, 91. [119] Ibid., p. 97. [120] Ibid., pp. 113–14.

[121] Ibid., p. 126.

latter is (with insignificant digressions) a *pièce justificative* to prove that archbishops of York should be free from subjection to Canterbury. He based his thesis simply on Gregory the Great's letter to St Augustine establishing two equal metropolitans in England.[122] But he has little further concern for past history. He tries to show that in his own time the archbishops had made a creditable stand against the claims of Canterbury. Though Thomas II had through weakness (he was too portly and fat for sustained effort[123]) and ignorance professed obedience to the archbishop of Canterbury,[124] Thurstan had remedied Thomas's lapse by devoting his life to the contest. In the course of describing York's struggle against Archbishop Ralph and then William of Corbeil, Hugh tells the famous story of how the forged charters produced by the Canterbury monks to support their archbishop's claim to the primacy were laughed out of court in Rome in 1123.[125] Hugh's account, fortified with transcripts of numerous documents, is the counterpart to Eadmer's narrative (told from the Canterbury point of view) in the *Historia Novorum in Anglia*.[126]

Though Hugh was writing as a direct result of controversy, he had many of the qualities of an excellent historian. He understood the political significance of events: for example he saw that the papal solution to the investiture contest had in fact very little effect in England on the power of the king over the appointment of bishops.[127] Moreover, Hugh's understanding of contemporary politics enabled him to fit the controversy between Canterbury and York into its national context. Thus he suggests that William the Conqueror favoured the primacy of Canterbury because he thought that it would contribute to the subjugation of the north.[128] Hugh shows a clear understanding of the king's relationship with his ecclesiastics: they could not visit Rome[129] or receive papal letters without the king's consent.[130] He grasped the difference between acts done by the king formally, with the consent of the magnates, and those done by his will alone (Thomas II's profession to the archbishop of Canterbury was not to the prejudice of the church of York because it was merely done at the king's will and not as a result of a formal judgment).[131] Hugh even recognized that Henry I supported the Canterbury party because he was trying to maintain the customs observed in his father's time,[132] while the York party was clinging to a theoretical right established by Gregory the Great and reinforced by subsequent popes. And sometimes Hugh suppressed his personal predilections in favour of the interests of the church in general. Thus though he disliked

---

[122] See e.g. ibid., pp. 31, 34, 35, 39, 42 etc.   [123] Ibid., p. 29.
[124] Ibid., pp. 27–30.
[125] Ibid., pp. 114–15. For this occasion, see R. L. Poole, *Lectures on the History of the Papal Chancery* (Cambridge 1915), pp. 143–6. For other references to the Canterbury forgeries see *Hugh the Chantor*, pp. 5, 105.
[126] See p. 141 below.   [127] *Hugh the Chantor*, pp. 13–14.   [128] Ibid., p. 3.
[129] Ibid., pp. 47, 53, 57.   [130] Ibid., p. 108.   [131] Ibid., pp. 29–30.
[132] Ibid., pp. 26, 78–9.

monks and was well disposed to the secular clergy,[133] he defends the right of the monks of Canterbury freely to elect their archbishop.[134]

The genesis of local history at Bury St Edmunds resembles that at Durham in some respects. Piety and controversy both contributed to it. As at Durham the cult of the patron saint constituted an essential element in the record of the abbey's history. The incentive of controversy was provided by the conflict with the bishop of the East Anglian see of Elmham. On the other hand, unlike the Durham monks, those of St Edmund's abbey were on good terms with the Norman kings. The impact of the Conquest was minimized by the fact that Abbot Baldwin, who ruled from 1065 to 1097, was a Norman. He had been Edward the Confessor's physician and became William the Conqueror's.

The first man known to have done research into the abbey's history was Hermann, a monk of Bury St Edmunds who had previously been a clerk of Herfast, bishop of Thetford. He wrote the *De Miraculis Sancti Edmundi*[135] at the order of Abbot Baldwin,[136] some time after 1095.[137] He had two objects: to record the abbey's ancient holiness, and to vindicate its exemption from the authority of the bishop of Elmham. Unlike the Durham historians he did not write under the influence of Bede. He used the Anglo-Saxon Chronicle, drew on hagiographical tradition, examined the abbey's records and listened to local gossip.

Hermann begins with St Edmund's martyrdom in 870 (he gets the date from the Anglo-Saxon Chronicle) and his burial at Sutton. He admits that nothing is known of St Edmund's cult until the saint's translation to Beodricsworth in the reign of Athelstan. Then Hermann describes the secular community which looked after the shrine, and the removal of the saint's body to London to avoid the Danish attacks early in the eleventh century. He is the earliest literary authority for King Canute's foundation of the abbey to replace the secular community in 1020. He reconstructs the history of the abbey until the Conquest from the charters granted to it by the eleventh-century kings. He continues the abbey's history into the reign of William the Conqueror, bringing it to a climax with the dedication in 1094 of Abbot Baldwin's new church. Its 'carved vaults rivalled the style of the temple of Solomon; those who see or have seen it say they have never beheld anything more spacious.'[138]

This history is set against the political background of the times and decorated with descriptions of St Edmund's miraculous manifestations. Hermann is the first writer to record the legend that St Edmund's ghost slew

---

[133] See ibid., pp. 43, 70.　　　　[134] Ibid., p. 109.
[135] Printed in *Memorials SE*, vol. 1, pp. 26–92.　　[136] See ibid., p. 27.
[137] The work is incomplete at the end; the latest date it mentions is 1095; *Memorials SE*, p. 92.
[138] Ibid., p. 85.

King Sweyn when he tried to tax Beodricsworth.[139] He mentions other occasions when St Edmund was supposed to have protected his community,[140] and describes numerous cures worked at his tomb.

Into this history is fitted a detailed account of the abbey's struggle with Herfast bishop of Elmham (1070–2; in 1072 Herfast moved the East Anglian see to Thetford and died in about 1085). Between 1070 and 1072 Herfast tried to establish his see at Bury St Edmunds. This would have brought the abbey under his authority. Hermann claimed to know the circumstances well, for he had written Herfast's correspondence on the matter.[141] Herfast appealed to precedent, saying that his predecessors had exercised episcopal functions in the abbey; Baldwin also appealed to precedent. According to Hermann, Baldwin claimed that the abbots of St Edmund's had been blessed by various bishops, not exclusively by those of Elmham (as they would have been if subject to the bishops of Elmham). Here Baldwin seems to have been guilty of some special pleading. He asserted that Uvius had been blessed by the bishop of London,[142] but Hermann does not mention this in his account of Uvius.[143] Baldwin also said that Abbot Leofstan was blessed by the bishop of Winchester[144]; again Hermann does not record this in his account of Leofstan.[145] The case was argued before king and pope, and eventually Baldwin obtained a papal privilege of exemption from episcopal control.

Although Hermann records these legal technicalities, he does not abandon the edificatory tone of the work. He was not primarily writing a controversial pamphlet. He relates a story to explain how Herfast was defeated by Abbot Baldwin. One day Herfast was out riding and had an accident because St Edmund was angry with him. His eyes were hurt by a branch and he was persuaded to go to Abbot Baldwin for treatment. But Baldwin would not apply the necessary poultices until Herfast had promised not to persist in the attempt to move the see to Bury St Edmunds. Hermann remarks that Baldwin saved Herfast's eye but that it remained scarred to his dying day.[146]

The struggle between St Edmund's abbey and the East Anglian bishop was renewed in the early twelfth century by Bishop Herbert de Losinga (1090/1–1119) who had his see at Thetford until 1094 or 1095 and then at Norwich. Losinga challenged the abbey's right of exemption from episcopal control and tried to fix his see there. This dispute gave rise to a pamphlet of a purely controversial kind, written between 1103 and 1119 by an anonymous monk of Norwich. The purpose of the tract was to prove that Losinga's claim was justified on historical grounds.[147] The Norwich monk suppressed the existence of St Edmund and stated that the abbey grew from the secular

---

[139] Ibid., p. 37. [140] See *Memorials SE*, pp. 54–6. [141] Ibid., p. 62.
[142] Ibid., p. 66. [143] Ibid., p. 48. Uvius was the first abbot of Bury St Edmunds.
[144] Ibid., p. 66. [145] Ibid., pp. 51–6 *passim*. [146] Ibid., pp. 62–4.
[147] Printed and discussed by V. H. Galbraith, 'The East Anglian see and the Abbey of Bury St. Edmunds' in *EHR*, xl (1925), pp. 222–8.

cathedral founded by Felix bishop of East Anglia (c. 630–47) as his see. This cathedral was dedicated to St Mary. King Canute made this secular community into a cathedral priory, at the instance of Ælfric bishop of Elmham, and Harold Harefoot elevated it into an abbey, appointing the prior as abbot.

Professor Galbraith has described this narrative as an 'unconvincing perversion of the facts as far as these are known'.[148] To accept it as true it would be necessary to discard not only Hermann's history, but also the evidence of Bede (who ascribes no see to Felix and does not mention Beodricsworth at all), and of the charters granted by Canute and Harthacanute to St Edmunds. Nevertheless the Norwich case could contain a grain of truth: Professor Galbraith himself admits that the history of Beodricsworth in the late ninth and early tenth century is obscure. But it is known to have been an important centre and if it were briefly an episcopal see, this would explain why St Edmund was translated there. Moreover the Norwich writer had the perspicacity to isolate a problem in the abbey's account of its origins. Why should Ælfric bishop of Elmham have been so active a participant in the foundation of an abbey exempt from the control of his own bishopric?

The monks of Christ Church, Canterbury, showed considerable interest in their community's past, although they produced no consecutive, institutional history. Instead two monks, Osbern and Eadmer, wrote separate Lives of the archbishops which include local history.

Osbern was an Englishman by birth who found it hard to adapt to Norman rule at Christ Church. Lanfranc sent him to Bec for two years to help him make the readjustment.[149] On his return he wrote a *Life of St. Elphege*, at Lanfranc's command,[150] and a *Life of St. Oda*, archbishop from 942 to 958 (the only known text of this work was destroyed in the Cottonian fire of 1731).[151] Osbern also wrote a *Life of St. Dunstan* and the *Miracles of St. Dunstan*, using as sources the Lives by 'B' and Adelard.[152] He supplemented the information on St Dunstan given by his sources with legend and, in one instance, with personal observation. His most vivid piece of writing is a first-hand description of Dunstan's cell at Glastonbury:[153]

> Adjoining the church [St Dunstan] built a cell with his own hands; it is a lean-to or a sort of den, or perhaps it should be called by

---

[148] Ibid., p. 222.
[149] For Osbern's career, see Southern, *St. Anselm and his Biographer*, pp. 248–52.
[150] Printed in Wharton, *Anglia Sacra*, pt 2, 122–42. This *Life* is purely hagiographical. It formed the basis of Eadmer's *Life of St. Elphege*.
[151] WM, *GP*, pp. 24–5, quotes Osbern's *Life of St. Oda*.
[152] For Osbern's *Life of St. Dunstan* see *Memorials SD*, pp. xxxi et seq. It is printed in ibid., pp. 69–128. His *Miracles of St. Dunstan* are printed in ibid., pp. 129–61.
[153] Ibid., pp. 83–4.

some other name, for I cannot think of an accurate one, as it is more like a tomb than a human dwelling. Let me record what I myself saw, that (as far as I can judge) the length of his cell is not more than five feet and its breadth two and half feet. Moreover the height equals the stature of a man if he were to stand in the dug-out earth; otherwise it would not reach even to his chest. Thus, as I have said, it seems more like a tomb for the dead than a habitation for the living. So it is clear that he never lay down to sleep and always stood to pray. What was a door to him who entered, became a wall to him who had entered. For indeed in such a small building it was impossible for a door to be made except of the whole side. There is a small window in the middle of the little door through which light shone on the labourer.

But though Osbern had visited Glastonbury his work shows a marked tendency to belittle the traditions of that abbey. He calls Dunstan the first abbot of Glastonbury[154] and minimizes the importance of the community there before Dunstan's time, explicitly denying that it was a monastic one.[155] On the other hand he glorifies Canterbury. He adds to Adelard's *Life* that Dunstan had an especial veneration for St Oda who was buried in the cathedral.[156] Dunstan himself emerges as a national prophet. Osbern asserts that Dunstan prophesied the disasters that subsequently overtook England and which 'are seen in our times'.[157] This seems to be a veiled reference to the Norman Conquest as well as to the Danish invasions. Osbern's attitude to the Conquest was ambivalent. He regarded it as a punishment for the sins of King Ethelred and his family and counsellors, particularly for the murder of Edward the Martyr. And yet to him Lanfranc was 'the most saintly and wise man of our age'.[158]

Osbern was not a man of great gifts. His Latin is verbose and contorted, and his critical faculty negligible. The *Life of St. Dunstan* contains factual errors. Osbern states that Worcester cathedral in Dunstan's time was dedicated to St Mary – but it was dedicated to St Peter. He alleges that King Edgar founded the nunnery at Shaftesbury; it was King Alfred's foundation. He states that Edward the Martyr was conceived in sin by a nun. In fact his

---

[154] Ibid., p. 92.

[155] Ibid., p. 74. Osbern regarded Dunstan as the motive force in the tenth century monastic revival; ibid., pp. 110–11.

[156] Ibid., p. 109.

[157] Ibid., p. 117. Professor Southern, in *St. Anselm and his Biographer*, pp. 311, 312 n. 1, states that Osbern was here referring only to the Danish invasions and not to the Norman Conquest. However, Osbern concludes his account of Dunstan's prophecy with the words: 'Quae omnia ita contigisse in annalibus legere, et *nostris temporibus est videre*' (the italics are mine). Therefore Eadmer's account (see p. 137 and n. 7 below) is based on, and is not a development of, Osbern's. Osbern gives a more limited application to the prophecy in *Memorials SD*, pp. 115, 127.

[158] Ibid., p. 143.

mother was King Edgar's first wife Æthelflaed. Nevertheless his choice of subjects and his ideas were an inspiration, and his faults and mistakes a challenge to a greater historian, Eadmer.

Eadmer is best known for his two main works, the *Life of St. Anselm*[159] and the *Historia Novorum*, a history of contemporary events,[160] both written between 1093 and 1125. But in the same period he also wrote a number of minor works, all hagiographies. The principal ones were a *Life of St. Dunstan*,[161] a *Life of St. Breguwine* (archbishop of Canterbury from 761 to 764),[162] a *Life of St. Oda*,[163] a *Life of St. Oswald* (of Worcester)[164] and a *Life of St. Wilfrid* (of York).[165]

These minor works are of interest because they demonstrate how hagiography provided Eadmer with his historical training.[166] They also throw light on Eadmer's ideas and attitudes, and on the tradition influencing him. They particularly show the strength of the influence exerted by Worcester, a centre of Anglo-Saxon historiography and biography. As has been seen, the Worcester tradition had undergone a remarkable revival after the Norman Conquest. Eadmer's contact with the cathedral priory was due partly to the interchange of personnel between Worcester and Christ Church which resulted in a lively correspondence between the houses. This contact was reinforced by a shared concern for the primacy of Canterbury: Bishop Wulfstan relied on Canterbury's archiepiscopal support in his struggle against the archbishop of York.

Eadmer's close connection with Worcester is illustrated by the fact that he wrote the *Life of St. Oswald* at the request of the Worcester monks.[167] Moreover a letter from Eadmer to the Worcester monks survives, advising them to elect a monk as bishop.[168] The historiographical help Eadmer obtained from Worcester appears in his *Life of St. Dunstan*. He based the *Life* mainly on Osbern's (he also used the *Lives* by 'B' and Adelard), but the Worcester monks enabled him to correct two of Osbern's mistakes. One of Eadmer's informants was a monk called Ethelred who, having been subprior and precentor of Christ Church, became a monk of Worcester in Bishop Wulfstan's time.[169] Another informant was Nicholas, prior of Worcester. Thus, as a result of competent historical research, Eadmer was able to give a

[159] For the standard printed edition see p. 105 n. 2 above.
[160] Printed in *Eadmeri Historia Novorum in Anglia*, ed. M. Rule (RS, 1884). An English translation of Books I to IV is by G. Bosanquet, with a foreword by R. W. Southern, *Eadmer's History of Recent Events in England* (London 1964).
[161] Printed in *Memorials SD*, pp. 162–249.
[162] Printed in Wharton, *Anglia Sacra*, pt 2, pp. 184–90.
[163] Printed in ibid., pp. 78–87.
[164] Printed in Raine, *Historians of the Church of York*, vol. 2, pp. 1–40.
[165] Printed in ibid., vol. 1, pp. 161–266. For a sermon Eadmer preached on St Wilfrid, see ibid., vol. 1, pp. 227–37 (cf. Southern, *St. Anselm and his Biographer*, p. 367).
[166] This is the view expressed by Professor Southern in *St. Anselm and his Biographer*, p. 277.
[167] Southern, ibid., p. 283 n. 2, suggests that it was written between 1113 and 1115.
[168] Printed in Wharton, *Anglia Sacra*, pt ii, p. 238. Cf. Southern, *St. Anselm*, p. 286.
[169] *Memorials SD*, p. 163.

correct account of the dedication of the cathedral church at Worcester: it was dedicated to St Peter during Dunstan's episcopate, but to St Mary under Oswald. Eadmer explains that Oswald found on his accession that the community of secular clerks attached to the cathedral were 'unwilling to turn from their depravity' and were irremovable 'because they were powerful and of noble birth'. Therefore Oswald 'built next to that church, a church of the blessed Mary Mother of God, in which he served God with his monks'. As the monks grew in popularity with the people their numbers increased, while the reputation of the clerks dwindled. Some of the clerks became monks and in due course the church of St Mary became the bishop's cathedral.[170] Prior Nicholas helped him correct Osbern's error about Edward the Martyr's parentage, sending him a résumé of King Edgar's career and marriages. Nicholas states explicitly that Edward the Martyr was the son of Edgar's first wife, Æthelflaed who, though legitimately married, was never crowned.[171]

Eadmer's minor works reflect his passionate loyalty to Christ Church and to its past glory. Although he tried (in the Lives of St Breguwine and of St Oda) to trace its history back beyond St Dunstan's day, he realized that its distant past was irrevocably lost and so virtually he began its history with St Dunstan. St Dunstan personified the cathedral community's golden age. The subsequent catastrophies which had overtaken the Anglo-Saxons were in accordance with St Dunstan's prophecy and a punishment for their sins.[172] Eadmer regarded Christ Church as a microcosm of England. Its tribulations culminated in the fire which in 1067 burnt down the church and conventual building, as a punishment for the luxurious living of the monks.[173] Eadmer asserts that before Lanfranc's reforms the monks of Christ Church lived like earls rather than monks 'in all worldly glory, with gold and silver, with

---

[170] Ibid., p. 197. J. Armitage Robinson, 'St. Oswald and the church of Worcester' in *British Academy Supplemental Papers*, v (1919), pp. 3–4, ignores Eadmer's explanation of the change of the dedication of Worcester cathedral, and cites the similar explanation given by William of Malmesbury in his *Life of St. Dunstan* (*Memorials SD*, p. 303), who adds that Oswald acted 'by holy guile' ('sancto ingenio'). Although Stubbs (ibid., p. lxix) remarks on the similarities between Eadmer's and William of Malmesbury's *Lives* of St Dunstan, he reserves judgment on whether William used Eadmer's *Life*, because William never acknowledged it. Nevertheless it is beyond reasonable doubt that this and other passages in Eadmer (see pp. 176 and n. 82, 177 n. 83 below) were used by William. The reason for the change in the Worcester dedication is also given in Hemming's cartulary (see p. 143 below) which, however, says that Oswald built the new cathedral dedicated to St Mary because St Peter's was too small (the presence of recalcitrant canons in St Peter's is not mentioned); see Robinson, op. cit., pp. 4–5.

[171] Printed in *Memorials SD*, pp. 422–4; cf. p. lxvii. Nicholas was elected prior in 1113. He also wrote to Eadmer stating the case against the claims of the archbishopric of York to equality with Canterbury; printed in Wharton, *Anglia Sacra*, pt 2, pp. 234–6.

[172] *Life of St. Dunstan* in *Memorials SD*, p. 222, and *HN*, p. 3. For Eadmer's debt to Osbern see p. 128 n. 157 above.

[173] Eadmer (following Osbern, *Memorials SD*, pp. 141–2) asserts that St Dunstan caused the church to be burnt to punish the monks for burying King Harold's unchristened son in it; ibid., pp. 230–1.

changes of fine clothes and delicate food, not to speak of the various kinds of musical instruments in which they delighted, nor of the horses, dogs and hawks with which they sometimes took exercise.'[174]

William of Malmesbury based his strictures on life at Christ Church on this passage by Eadmer.[175] There is no doubt that Eadmer exaggerated the depravity at Christ Church. The reason he did so was probably his sincere adherence to the Benedictine ideal. St Dunstan had reintroduced the Benedictine Rule into England and Lanfranc revived its strict observance, especially at Christ Church. Therefore Eadmer, like Osbern, held Lanfranc in the highest respect. 'There was nobody at that time who excelled Lanfranc in authority and breadth of learning.'[176] Eadmer was not only concerned with the internal integrity of Christ Church, he was also concerned for its external relations, notably its authority over the province of York. All Eadmer's views are epitomized in his attitude to Anselm – who represented, as it were, the re-embodiment of St Dunstan and was the protagonist of Canterbury's claims against York.

Eadmer wrote the Lives from the standpoint of his own day, stressing the primacy of Canterbury and the fame of Christ Church. For example he used past history to support Canterbury's present claims in the *Life of St. Oswald*: he uses it to demonstrate Canterbury's primacy in Oswald's time – he stresses the initiative of the archbishop in church affairs and suppresses King Edgar's powerful influence. Similarly in the *Life of St. Wilfrid* he accompanied his account of the struggle between Wilfrid and Theodore with a firm statement of Canterbury's metropolitan rights at that date.

He wrote the *Life of St. Wilfrid* partly because Wilfrid's relics reputedly rested at Christ Church, a gift from Oda.[177] The monks of Christ Church, like those of Evesham and Durham, were indefatigable collectors of relics, an occupation Eadmer shared (he tells how he himself acquired a relic of St Prisca).[178] He habitually emphasizes the wealth of relics owned by Christ Church. One of his most eloquent pieces of writing is a letter to the monks of Glastonbury refuting their ('absurd') claim to have stolen the body of St Dunstan from Christ Church during the Danish invasions.[179] His *Life of St. Breguwine* is mainly an account of the burial places of the archbishops in the eighth century baptistry (Eadmer knew practically nothing about Breguwine). Interest in relics led to an interest in the location of tombs, and that resulted in architectural interests. Thus Eadmer's tract on the relics of St Ouen[180] contains an account of the old church which was burnt down in 1067, written from information supplied by monks who could remember it.

[174] Ibid., pp. 237–8. See Southern, *St. Anselm*, p. 247.
[175] See p. 176 and n. 82 below.
[176] *VSA*, p. 50.
[177] Southern, *St. Anselm*, p. 278 and n. 1.
[178] *VSA*, p. 132; *HN*, pp. 162–3.
[179] Printed in *Memorials SD*, pp. 412–22.
[180] Printed in A. Wilmart, 'Edmeri Cantuariensis cantoris nova opuscula de sanctorum veneratione et obsecratione' in *Revue des Sciences religieuses*, xv (1935), pp. 362–70. Cf. Southern, *St. Anselm*, pp. 262, 370–1. For an English translation of the section on the relics of saints in

Therefore Eadmer's minor works show how hagiography equipped him as a historian. And they show the great importance he attached to Christ Church. Both his acquired techniques and his formed opinions had a profound effect on his two masterpieces, the *Life of St. Anselm* and the *Historia Novorum in Anglia*. These works were conceived as one. The *Life of St. Anselm* concerned Anselm's private life. The *Historia Novorum* concerned his public life. Each was intended to be complete in itself and complementary to the other.[181] The *Life* has references to the *Historia* (the latter gives details and documentation of public affairs only briefly mentioned in the *Life*). The value of the *Life* to the historian today is mainly biographical, although it has much information about Christ Church. The *Historia*, which will be considered in the next chapter, mainly concerns the relations of church and state under William Rufus and Henry I.

Eadmer drew on at least two literary traditions. One was the Anglo-Saxon biographical tradition. Presumably it was from this that Eadmer derived the idea of treating Anselm's life in two parts, public and private. Coleman's *Life of St. Wulfstan* contains the division between public and private life in a rudimentary form (to 1066 the *Life* is mainly devoted to Wulfstan's public career; after 1066 it mainly concerns his miracles and private life[182]). Eadmer may also have developed the idea of a bipartite biography under the influence of the secular biographical tradition. The latter, derived from Suetonius and transmitted in the *Life of King Alfred*, the *Encomium Emmae Reginae* and the *Life of King Edward*, had evolved such an arrangement.[183]

It was a common practice among the Anglo-Saxons for someone who knew a bishop well to write his Life soon after his death. This practice may have influenced Eadmer. But he may also have been influenced by the tradition of biography at the abbey of Bec, itself derived ultimately from Cluny. Archbishop Anselm, once a monks of Bec, was a close friend of another former Bec monk, Gilbert Crispin, abbot of Westminster from 1085 to 1117. Some time after 1093 Gilbert had written a *Life of Herluin*, the first abbot of Bec (1040-77).[184] This biography is the principal authority not only for Herluin's life but also for the foundation of Bec and for Lanfranc's work as prior there. At least in Normandy Eadmer's *Life of St. Anselm* may have been regarded as a continuation of Gilbert Crispin's *Life of Herluin*: in one early manuscript in the library at Bec the *Life of St. Anselm* immediately followed

---

the cathedral and their location, including architectural descriptions, see Robert Willis, *The Architectural History of Canterbury Cathedral* (London 1845), pp. 1-19. Cf. pp. 255-6 below.

[181] Eadmer states this explicitly in the preface to his *Life of St. Anselm*; *VSA*, pp. 1-2.

[182] See Southern, *St. Anselm and his Biographer*, p. 314 n.

[183] Dr Southern, ibid., p. 236, denies that secular biographies had any influence on Eadmer, but the reasons for this view are not evident.

[184] Printed and fully discussed by J. A. Robinson, *Gilbert Crispin Abbot of Westminster* (Cambridge 1911). That the *Life* was written after 1093 appears from the reference to Anselm as archbishop of Canterbury; ibid., p. 103.

the *Life of Herluin*.[185] Gundulf, bishop of Rochester (1077–1108), a close friend of Anselm, was another former monk of Bec: his biography was also written soon after his death.[186]

But Eadmer's work does not closely resemble either the Anglo-Saxon or the Bec biographies. Eadmer wrote less to emulate past biographers than to express his personal loyalty to and affection for Anselm. He wrote the *Life* and the *Historia* in their earliest form while Anselm was still alive (he revised them later). Eadmer was Anselm's constant companion. He was a member of his household: his official position was keeper of the archbishop's chapel and relics. From about 1093 to 1100, Eadmer made notes for the biography. He tells in the *Life* how Anselm discovered this occupation.[187] At first Anselm was interested and corrected the draft. Then he decided that the production of such a biography was incompatible with his own struggle for humility, so he ordered Eadmer to destroy it. In fact Eadmer made a copy before destroying the original. After Anselm's death in 1109, Eadmer revised and completed the work. Soon before 1114 he added two chapters to the end of the *Life* describing two posthumous miracles attributed to Anselm. And soon after 1122 he appended to the *Life* a book on Anselm's miracles. This, together with a thorough revision of the text, completed the work.[188] At about the same time Eadmer added to the *Historia* an account of the see of Canterbury to 1122. It is the section of the *Life* and *Historia* to 1100, the probable date when Anselm forbade Eadmer to continue the biography, which was written strictly contemporarily with events.

The novelty of the work to 1100 derived from this contemporaneity. Eadmer was the first man since Bede to treat his subject intimately. Although he wrote to edify his readers with a portrait of a saintly man, Anselm does to some extent come alive in his pages. Eadmer describes his character vividly. He describes his abstemiousness and preference for edificatory talk to food. 'He ate indeed while he talked, but sparingly, so that you would sometimes wonder how he supported life. He himself confessed, and we know that it was true, that when he was engaged in a lengthy argument he was more than usually careless about his food, and we who sat nearest to him sometimes kept secretly plying him with bread.'[189]

Anselm's love of conversation is reflected in Eadmer's *Life*, for he records much of his talk. Previous writers had put edificatory or heroic phrases into their subjects' mouths, but there is no evidence that such talk was real. Eadmer is the first Englishman who apparently recorded actual conversations.

---

[185] See ibid., p. 60 n. 1. The earliest recension of the *Life of St. Anselm* is only found in continental manuscripts; see *VSA*, pp. xiii et seq.

[186] Printed in Wharton, *Anglia Sacra*, pt ii, pp. 273 et seq. For Anselm's friendship with Gundulf see *VSA*, pp. 66, 86; cf. ibid., p. 49 n. 1, and Southern, *St. Anselm and his Biographer*, pp. 69–70.

[187] *VSA*, pp. 150–1.

[188] For the stages in the growth of the *Life*, see *VSA*, pp. xiii–xxiii.

[189] *VSA*, p. 78; cf. p. 14. For realistic passages in Eadmer's *Historia Novorum* see p. 139 below.

The talk he records sounds genuine and is in keeping with what is known of Anselm's character.[190] Eadmer's principal reason for recording Anselm's talk was no doubt admiration for his conversational powers. But he may also have been influenced by the *Lives of the Desert Fathers*,[191] which records conversations, by the bible and perhaps by records of legal proceedings.[192]

Most of the sayings Eadmer recorded are similes with an edificatory purpose. For example, he records Anselm's conversation with an abbot on the education of the boys brought up in a monastery.[193] The abbot asked, '"What is to be done with them? They are incorrigible ruffians. We never give over beating them day and night, and they only get worse." Anselm replied with astonishment: "You never give over beating them? And what are they like when they grow up?" "Stupid brutes," said the abbot. To which Anselm retorted, "You have spent your energies in rearing them to good purpose! from men you have reared beasts."' He then proceeded to prove that a judicious amount of freedom is needed in bringing up a boy, just as space and light are needed for the healthy growth of a young tree.

Eadmer describes Anselm's dislike of business. When others were arguing some legal point, 'he would discourse with those who would listen about the Gospel or some other part of the bible, or at least some subject tending to edification. And often if there was no one to listen to such talk, he would compose himself, in the sweet quietness of a pure heart, to sleep.'[194] Arguments on business matters made him depressed and even ill, and he committed the administration of his household to Baldwin, a monk from Bec.[195]

This avoidance of secular affairs led to trouble. Many of the monks of Christ Church thought that Anselm neglected their interests and stayed away on his manors too much. The opposition to him was particularly bitter during his exiles from England from 1097 to 1100 and from 1103 to 1106. This faced Eadmer with a dilemma. His love of Anselm was only equalled by his love of Christ Church. For the first time an English biographer could not identify his saint with the fortunes of his monastery. Eadmer tried to justify Anselm in relation to Christ Church. He said that his absences from the community to stay on his manors were inevitable, in accordance with tradition, and to the benefit of his tenants.[196] He also stressed Anselm's generosity to Christ Church.[197]

But Eadmer's principal defence of Anselm was the picture he gave of his sanctity. Anselm disliked business because he loved tranquillity. His sometimes excessive leniency to others should be weighed against his

---

[190] See Southern, *St. Anselm*, pp. 219–20. Other people besides Eadmer collected Anselm's sayings and sermons; see ibid., pp. 220 et seq.
[191] Southern, *St. Anselm*, p. 327.
[192] See for example the tract *De Injusta Vexatione Willelmi Episcopi*, mentioned on pp. 122–3.
[193] *VSA*, p. 37.   [194] *VSA*, p. 46.
[195] *VSA*, pp. 80–1.   [196] *VSA*, p. 71.
[197] *HN*, p. 75. Eadmer also asserts that as archbishop-elect Anselm struggled to keep Christ Church's property out of the king's hands; *HN*, pp. 40–1.

severity to himself.[198] He was a worthy successor to St Dunstan, who had also suffered exile.[199] In one way Eadmer infers that Anselm excelled Dunstan; Anselm (unlike Dunstan) had a continental reputation. When he was at the siege of Capua he was honoured by the pope, by rich and poor, Christians and infidels.[200] And he was treated with the greatest respect at the council of Bari[201] and during exile at Lyons.[202]

The growth of criticism of Anselm was probably the reason why Eadmer soon after 1122 gave the *Life* an even more hagiographical tone, by the addition of the miracles. In its earliest form the *Life* was essentially personal, the product of personal loyalty and friendship. Then Eadmer felt compelled to give greater emphasis to Anselm's sanctity in order to answer his critics. This meant that the *Life*, which was conceived as a biography fairly free from the miraculous element, was revised to bring it into line with conventional hagiographies.

---

[198] *VSA*, pp. 59–60.
[199] A parallel with St Dunstan is implied in the miracle of the well at Liberi; *VSA*, p. 109 and n. 1. Moreover, Eadmer asserts that a Canterbury monk had a vision of St Dunstan appearing to St Anselm; *VSA*, pp. 154–5.
[200] *VSA*, pp. 110–12.   [201] *VSA*, pp. 112–14.   [202] *VSA*, pp. 116–17.

8

Anglo-Norman Historians

After a generation of silence a number of Anglo-Normans wrote histories of England.[1] At Christ Church, Canterbury, Eadmer wrote a compendious biography of Archbishop Anselm, including much national history. The Anglo-Saxon Chronicle was continued at Peterborough, while Latin annals were written at Worcester. Historical collections, including a good contemporary history, were made at Durham. Abroad, an Englishman, Orderic Vitalis, who had become a monk of St Évroul in Normandy, wrote a long *Historia Ecclesiastica (Ecclesiastical History)* of England and Normandy. He was the most gifted of all the Anglo-Norman historians, with the exception of William of Malmesbury who will be discussed in the next chapter. The authors wrote primarily in the Anglo-Saxon tradition. They were influenced by the Anglo-Saxon biographies and chronicles, and by Bede. These influences were reinforced by continental historiography, notably by the universal history of Marianus Scotus.

Eadmer was the first Anglo-Norman to write contemporary history. The *Historia Novorum in Anglia*, which he wrote between about 1095 and 1123,[2] was (as has been explained above) the second part of a bipartite biography of Anselm constructed on the Anglo-Saxon model. It was the account of Anselm's public acts (the *Life of St. Anselm* concerned his character and private life). The *Historia Novorum* deserves to be treated as a history and not only as a biography, for two reasons. First, Anselm was a public figure. Second, it starts before and goes beyond the chronological limits of Anselm's life.

Eadmer states his purpose in writing. It was to record how Anselm was made archbishop, why he was so long in exile, and what was the outcome of his dispute with the monarchy.[3] The result of such a broad treatment of Anselm's life was that Eadmer wrote the history of church/state relations in England. In order to show how the confrontation between Anselm and

---

[1] For a useful concise survey of the Anglo-Norman historians see R. R. Darlington, *Anglo-Norman Historians* (Inaugural Lecture, Birkbeck College, London University, in 1947).

[2] A full account of the composition of the *Historia Novorum* is in R. W. Southern, *St. Anselm and his Biographer* (Cambridge 1963), pp. 298–309. The complete text of the *Historia* is in *Eadmeri Historia Novorum in Anglia*, ed. M. Rule (RS, 1884). An English translation of Books I–IV is by G. Bosanquet, with a foreword by R. W. Southern, *Eadmer's History of Recent Events in England* (London 1964).

[3] Eadmer, *HN*, p. 1.

William Rufus arose, and what were the long-term effects of Anselm's struggle, it was necessary to begin before Anselm's lifetime and to end several years after his death. Therefore Eadmer begins with Dunstan's prophecy that disaster would overtake the English as a result of King Ethelred's sins.[4] Having described the political history of England (with a passing mention of the martyrdom of Elphege archbishop of Canterbury) from the late tenth century to the Norman Conquest, Eadmer deals with Lanfranc at some length.

Eadmer set the stage for Anselm's archiepiscopate. He describes on the one hand how William the Conqueror built up royal power in the church (he forbade ecclesiastics to recognize the pope or excommunicate tenants-in-chief without royal assent).[5] He describes on the other hand Lanfranc's success as archbishop (Lanfranc restored monastic life at Christ Church and upheld the dignity of Canterbury).[6] Eadmer emphasizes that as long as Lanfranc lived there was harmony between king and archbishop, and that William Rufus was responsible for the subsequent discord. After Anselm's death Eadmer tried to prove that his achievements were lasting: he claims that the primacy of Canterbury, for which Anselm had fought, was partially established, and that the decrees which he had issued for the reform of the secular clergy were enforced.

But this enlargement of the biography cannot be entirely explained as an attempt to place Anselm's life in its historical perspective. It was also due to the fact that Eadmer was using the biography as a vehicle for history in the typical Anglo-Saxon way. He was writing the history of the relations of church and state in his day, with particular emphasis on the primacy of Canterbury. He was also propounding a view of English history: he saw the Danish invasions and Norman Conquest as the fulfilments of Dunstan's prophecy.[7] Moreover, he implies that the Norman Conquest was justified not only because Harold was a perjuror, but also because of the decayed state of English monasticism, which he attributes to the Danish invasions.[8] By enabling Lanfranc to reform the monasteries, William the Conqueror was pleasing God and turning his seizure of power to the benefit of England.[9] Despite his denial that he was concerned with secular affairs,[10] Eadmer in-

---

[4] HN, p. 3.   [5] HN, pp. 9–10.   [6] HN, pp. 12–14.

[7] Eadmer writes that he has mentioned England's sufferings from the Danish invasions 'non historiam texens, sed quam veridico vaticinio pater Dunstanus mala Angliae ventura praedixerit scire volentium intellectui pandens'; HN, p. 5. Since he says that the fulfilment of the prophecy is still to be seen 'in nostris tribulationibus' (HN, p. 3), he presumably regarded the Norman Conquest as part of it. See Southern, St. Anselm, pp. 311–12.

[8] HN, pp. 4–5. Cf. p. 158 n. 172 below for reference to a similar passage in Eadmer's Life of St. Dunstan. Orderic Vitalis and William of Malmesbury express the same view (see p. 158 and nn. 174–6 below). For the possibility of a relationship between the works of these three writers see pp. 157–8 and nn. below.

[9] For Lanfranc's reforms at Christ Church, Canterbury, St Albans and Rochester see HN, pp. 13–15. For his co-operation with William I, see HN, p. 12.

[10] Eadmer refrains from noticing William I's secular ordinances because 'nihil ea nostri officii scribere refert'; HN, p. 10.

cludes notices of them: for example he records William Rufus's victory in Wales,[11] Henry I's taxation of the country in 1105,[12] Henry's reform of the coinage in 1108,[13] and the wreck of the White Ship.

Although Eadmer adopted the Anglo-Saxon biographical form, he adapted it to the conditions of the age. The tone of the work is not like a biography of the Anglo-Saxon period. It reflects the tensions and conflicts of Eadmer's day. Eadmer himself was not a happy man. As an Englishman by birth, he resented the Norman invaders. He writes that he will refrain from describing how William the Conqueror treated the English nobility.[14] He refers to Wulfstan ('of blessed memory') as 'the one sole survivor of the venerable fathers of the English people, a man eminent in all religious life and unrivalled in his knowledge of the ancient customs of England'.[15] And, after Anselm's death, Eadmer deplores the fact that Henry I appointed only foreigners to abbacies, while Englishmen, however suitable, had no chance of promotion.[16]

A biographer in Anglo-Saxon times was able to harmonize the life of his hero with the history of the monastery with which he was associated, the saint becoming the personification of the institution. This was because there was no conflict between the saint and his monastery. But Eadmer could not identify Anselm with Christ Church, because as time passed the monks grew more and more critical of Anselm's prolonged absences and neglect of business matters. So Eadmer was forced to justify Anselm. He records his generosity to Christ Church[17] and his attempts at defending its interests.[18] He argues that he could not avoid staying in exile from 1103 to 1106 because the pope had not removed the prohibition against lay investiture.[19] Eadmer accuses Henry I of delaying papal withdrawal of the prohibition by failing to send a representative to Rome.[20] He tries to prove that Anselm was in every way a worthy successor to Lanfranc. He emphasizes the fruitful co-operation of Henry I and Anselm which followed their reconciliation,[21] implicitly comparing their co-operation with that of William the Conqueror and Lanfranc.[22]

Criticism of Anselm grew after his death. Just as it had caused Eadmer to add the book of miracles to the *Life of St. Anselm*, so it made him add two final Books (V and VI) to the *Historia Novorum*. Eadmer did this although he had intended to end with Anselm's death and considered himself unqualified

---

[11] *HN*, p. 77. [12] *HN*, pp. 171–2. [13] *HN*, p. 193.

[14] *HN*, p. 9. [15] *HN*, pp. 45–6. [16] *HN*, p. 224.

[17] *HN*, p. 75. Eadmer records Anselm's gift of a manor for seven years to the convent, in exchange for 200 marks he had taken to help the king; he concludes 'Haec ex gestae rei veritate proponimus, ut ora obloquentium qui usque hodie Anselmo depraedatae ecclesiae crimen intentant, si fieri potest, obturemus'.

[18] See *HN*, p. 39, for Anselm's attempt to recover Christ Church lands from William Rufus.

[19] *HN*, pp. 134–6, 149–51, 162, 168.

[20] *HN*, pp. 170–1.

[21] *HN*, pp. 191 et seq.

[22] For Lanfranc and William I, see *HN*, pp. 12, 22.

to write more.[23] For in 1119 when he began the continuation he no longer had access to first-hand information. In that year he had left the household of Anselm's successor Ralph d'Éscures, whom he had accompanied abroad in 1116, and returned to Christ Church. He begins the continuation by trying to prove that Anselm had been a success as head of Christ Church: Anselm had found it heavily in debt, had enriched it with his generosity and, like Lanfranc, had defended its interests.

As a historian Eadmer had considerable merits. He succeeded in building an excellent contemporary history around Anselm's life. He had all the advantages of an eye-witness and cultivated a good memory ('from childhood it has always been my way to observe carefully and to impress on my memory any new things which I happened to meet with, particularly if connected with the church'[24]). As has been seen,[25] Eadmer described Anselm fairly realistically in the *Life of St. Anselm*. He also has some vivid descriptive passages in the *Historia Novorum*. For example he describes how, at the Council of Rockingham, Anselm 'leaned back against the wall and slept peacefully while his enemies carried on their little conclaves for quite a long time'.[26] He relates that when Anselm arrived at Dover in 1197 before going into exile, the king's clerk, William Warelwast, 'would not let him cross until he displayed to him one by one every single item which he was taking with him. So the bags and chests were brought before him and opened, and all Anselm's household chattels were overturned and ransacked in the hope of finding money, while a huge crowd of people standing round watched this disgraceful work, astonished at its novelty, and cursed it as they watched.'[27] There is a particularly graphic account of the Council of Bari. Eadmer notes the clatter as the people changed their seats in order to give Anselm a more honourable place.[28]

Eadmer fully understood the value of a document quoted *verbatim*. He had access to Anselm's correspondence and official documents concerning the archbishopric because he was keeper of Anselm's chapel: the archives were probably stored for safe-keeping with the relics kept in the chapel.[29] Eadmer made use of his opportunities and quoted numerous documents. The greatest number of documents is cited after 1100. In this section documents take up an increasing proportion of the text and the narrative account dwindles. This has led to the suggestion that it was in 1100 that Anselm discovered Eadmer writing the biography and forbade him to continue:[30] perhaps it was only after Anselm's death that Eadmer was able to complete the work, and, not

---

[23] *HN*, p. 217. At the same time Eadmer added the last two pages of Book IV. See Southern, *St. Anselm*, p. 307.

[24] *HN*, p. 107.   [25] See pp. 133–4.

[26] *HN*, p. 58.   [27] *HN*, p. 88.   [28] *HN*, p. 105.

[29] *HN*, p. 181. For the use in the eleventh century of the royal chapel as a place for keeping official documents, see V. H. Galbraith, *Studies in the Public Records* (London 1948), pp. 40–1. Cf. Southern, *St. Anselm*, p. 198.

[30] Southern, *St. Anselm*, pp. 300–1, 315. Cf. p. 133 above.

having contemporary notes, was forced to rely mainly on documentary evidence.

On the other hand Eadmer valued documents for their own sake. He explicitly justifies the copying of documents *in extenso* on a number of grounds: they provide precedents ('in future they may be of use as precedents' if such wrongs continue to be perpetrated in England[31]), they amplify his information, and they give weight to his arguments. He expresses the hope that 'our readers or hearers shall not be incensed because we are so much taken up with letters. For this is a part, and an important part, of the task which we have in hand; the whole cannot be known of any matter when parts of it are unknown.'[32] He quotes Anselm's correspondence in order to prove that Anselm was not responsible for his long delay in returning to England in 1105.[33] He emphasizes the force of the written word against hearsay; he implies that Anselm was right to rely on a papal letter (which he quotes) confirming the prohibition against lay investiture, rather than defer to a rumour which alleged that the pope had changed his mind.[34] It sometimes seems as if Eadmer cites letters in order to publish criticism of Anselm without having to identify himself with it. He gives copies of letters to Anselm bitterly criticizing him for not coming home.[35] These letters assert that the reasons for Anselm's absence were not good enough to justify the hardships it inflicted on Canterbury and the church in England.

But Eadmer has faults as a general historian. He tends to exaggerate Anselm's influence. For example he says that in 1101 King Henry would have lost his throne to Duke Robert had not Anselm won over the magnates to the king's side. But probably it was Henry's diplomacy, not Anselm's, which achieved this result.[36] Moreover, little engaged Eadmer's interest which did not directly concern Anselm and Canterbury. He relied for information on what he saw and on Anselm's mail-bag. His curiosity rarely ranged further afield, and when he did digress from his main theme, his digressions show an ingrowing tendency. His interests become more particular, the horizon narrower, when he departs from the thread of his narrative. He digressed on Christ Church, Canterbury, and as he was keeper of Anselm's relics as well as his chapel, his ruminations often concern relics. Such digressions interrupt the narrative without illuminating it. For example he appends to his account of the Council of Bari three pages concerning the cope which the archbishop of Benevento wore. He relates how the bishop had obtained

---

[31] *HN*, p. 175; 'Quae scripta eo quo missa sunt ordine subter annotanda putavi, ratus ea futuris temporibus exempli gratia profutura, si altiori consilio Deus non sedaverit in regno Anglorum quae sub oculis eius hodie fiunt maxima mala.' Cf. *HN*, p. 191, where, after a papal letter on lay investiture, Eadmer writes: 'Hanc epistolam iccirco placuit huic operi admiscere, ut ea teste monstraremus, quae de investituris ecclesiarum diximus rata esse.' For a similar example of a letter quoted *in extenso* as a precedent, see *HN*, pp. 136–7.

[32] *HN*, p. 175.   [33] *HN*, pp. 134–7.   [34] *HN*, pp. 137–8.

[35] *HN*, pp. 160–2, 167–8, 173–4.

[36] *HN*, pp. 126–8. See J. O. Prestwich in *EHR*, lxxxi (1966), p. 106.

this cope from the monks of Christ Church in exchange for an arm of St Bartholomew. A similar digression impairs the literary quality of the work. Book IV deals with the investiture controversy. The narrative seems to be building up to a climax – the compromise achieved by Pope Paschal II, Henry I and Anselm. Eadmer cites Paschal's letter absolving Anselm from the duty of excommunicating clergy who were invested by laymen, or laymen who invested anyone. But instead of pointing out the importance of this compromise, Eadmer tells a long story about how Anselm acquired a precious relic – some hair of the Virgin Mary.[37]

It was Eadmer's love of Canterbury which led him to commit his worst sin as a historian. This occurs in his treatment of the controversy between Canterbury and York over the primacy. The dispute broke out again before the death of Anselm who had insisted that Gerard, archbishop-elect of York, should make a profession of obedience to him before his consecration. The quarrel outlasted Anselm's life, and both Ralph d'Éscures and Thurstan archbishop of York appealed to the pope in 1116–17. Eadmer, who became increasingly obsessed with the dispute, records the events and arguments in the two final books which he added to the *Historia Novorum*. He supported Canterbury's case by historical arguments, that is by the tradition of the primacy of Canterbury which had been started by St Augustine.[38] But Eadmer also documented his argument by inserting a number of papal bulls which the Christ Church monks had forged to prove Canterbury's right.[39] Eadmer related how these 'ancient' bulls were discovered in an old Gospel book, and that many of them were illegible because of their age or indecipherable because of their archaic handwriting.[40] Probably Eadmer did not forge the documents himself,[41] but he must have known that he was copying forgeries into what had virtually become an official history of Canterbury.

One reason for Eadmer's progressively narrowing interests, and for his willingness to become an accessory to forgery, was that he wrote primarily to please and instruct the monks at Christ Church.[42] In fact the *Historia*

---

[37] *HN*, pp. 179–81. For the passage on the relic of St Bartholomew, which Eadmer admits is a digression, see *HN*, pp. 107–10.

[38] *HN*, pp. 276–9. Eadmer's personal commitment to the cause of the primacy of Canterbury was shown by his behaviour when elected bishop of St Andrews in 1120: he insisted on being consecrated by the archbishop of Canterbury and on consulting him on the difficulties he encountered as a result of the election; *HN*, pp. 282 et seq. Cf. Southern, *St. Anselm*, p. 236.

[39] *HN*, pp. 261–76. For a detailed discussion of these forgeries see R. W. Southern, 'The Canterbury forgeries' in *EHR*, lxxiii (1958), pp. 193–226. Professor Southern argues convincingly that the bulls were forged between 1121 and 1123, and not, as previously thought, in 1072.

[40] *HN*, pp. 261, 276.   [41] Southern, 'The Canterbury forgeries', p. 226.

[42] Eadmer says in the preface (*HN*, p. 1) that he wrote to comply with the wishes of his friends, and ends Book IV with the hope that the monks of Christ Church will not consider his work wasted labour (*HN*, p. 215). His wish to amuse is shown by the statement that he must be brief in order not to bore his readers; see *HN*, pp. 61, 67.

Novorum had a wider appeal (it was used by the chroniclers at Worcester and Durham, and by William of Malmesbury[43]), but as a type of historiography it was not influential. It was part of the last bipartite biography to be written in England, and it was the last biography to be used, in the Anglo-Saxon way, as a means of recording history. The future lay with the annalistic type of historiography exemplified by the Anglo-Saxon Chronicle. Although the jejune record of events in the Chronicle and its derivatives is inferior in literary quality to Eadmer's narrative, it was easier for later writers to alter and add to. Therefore this form of historiography survived, to become the basis of the monastic chronicle of medieval England.

The Anglo-Saxon Chronicle, which was being continued at Peterborough, recorded national events and was informative about Scottish, Welsh and Norman affairs. But during Henry I's reign the annals become shorter (from 1132 to 1134 the chronicler has no news to record except notices relating to the domestic affairs of Peterborough). The Chronicle continues the Anglo-Saxon tradition of objectivity in relation to national affairs and is inclined to be critical of the monarchy.

The financial exactions of William Rufus won the inexorable enmity of the chronicler. He writes, under 1100, that Rufus 'was very strong and fierce to his country and to his men and to all his neighbours, and very terrible . . . and because of his avarice, he was always harassing this nation with military service and excessive taxes, for in his days all justice was in abeyance'. Rufus's policy of keeping bishoprics and abbeys vacant so that he could draw the revenues particularly angered the chronicler. He had greater hopes of Henry I because he married Matilda, one 'of the true royal family of England', and promised law and justice.[44] The chronicler supported Henry I and not Duke Robert in 1101 because the latter 'set out to carry war into this country'. Fear of civil wars and love of peace are very evident in the Chronicle,[45] particularly in the account of the reign of King Stephen. The chronicler criticizes Stephen for squandering his treasure 'like a fool' and for not exacting 'the full penalties of the law', so that traitors 'perpetrated every enormity'. But he calls him 'a mild man, gentle and good'.[46] The chronicler ends with Henry Plantagenet's accession, on a hopeful note. Before Henry's arrival from Normandy no one dared do wrong because 'they were in such great awe of him'.

Such criticism of the monarchy was not due to nascent liberalism but to the predominance of local loyalty in the Chronicle. As the years pass, its

---

[43] See pp. 144, 149, 170–1 below. Only two medieval manuscripts of the *Historia Novorum* survive: one (Corpus Christi College, Cambridge, MS. 452) is a copy, of the first half of the twelfth century, from Christ Church, Canterbury; *HN*, pp. ix–xv.

[44] See *ASC*, pp. 176, 177; *s.a.* 1100.

[45] See *ASC*, the end of the annal for 1096, and *s.a.* 1135, 1140.

[46] *ASC*, pp. 198–9; *s.a.* 1137.

interests become increasingly provincial. More and more space is devoted to the affairs of Peterborough. National history becomes merely the context into which local history is fitted. The views expressed are less political attitudes than the grumbles typical of farmers in all ages. Taxes are perpetually unpopular, and the chronicler repeatedly complains about bad weather and crop failure: in 1095 the weather was so unseasonable that the crops hardly ripened, in 1098 the rains were so heavy that nearly all cultivation was destroyed on the marshland, and in 1103 the wind did more damage to the crops than anyone could remember. And in 1131 the worst plague in living memory decimated cattle, pigs and hens throughout England, so that there was a shortage of meat, cheese and butter.

The monks of Peterborough resented any interference from the outside world. They were particularly bitter when Henry I foisted a Norman abbot, Henry of Poitou, on them in 1127. The only external contact they liked was with other Benedictine houses. The chronicler was well informed about other monasteries of the order, and there was still some sharing of the Anglo-Saxon Chronicle between them. Peterborough was not the only house to have an up-to-date copy. A fragment of unknown provenance survives which includes the annal for 1114.[47] William of Malmesbury used a now lost version up to about 1120 and the Worcester chronicler used one up to 1130.[48]

Worcester was a centre of historical writing in the revived Anglo-Saxon manner. As has been seen, Coleman, a monk of Worcester, wrote a biography in Anglo-Saxon of Bishop Wulfstan, and Worcester monks provided Eadmer with information about Anglo-Saxon history – and with the literary model for his biography of Anselm. Wulfstan himself knew a lot about Anglo-Saxon history[49] and commissioned the monk Hemming to compile a cartulary with historical notes, using the cathedral archives. Moreover, he ordered a Worcester monk to write a history of England. So a Latin chronicle was begun at Worcester some time before Wulfstan's death in 1095. As it survives today this Worcester chronicle begins with the Creation of the world and ends in 1140.[50]

It used to be generally assumed that the name of the monk who wrote the Worcester chronicle, the *Chronicon ex Chronicis* (*Chronicle of Chronicles*) to

---

[47] See *ASC*, p. xvii, and *s.a.*

[48] *ASC*, p. xx, and pp. 145, 172 and n. 46 below.

[49] Eadmer records that Anselm asked Wulfstan what the customs were concerning the archbishop of Canterbury's right to dedicate churches on his estates; *HN*, pp. 46–7.

[50] At present the standard edition of the chronicle is *Florentii Wigorniensis Monachi Chronicon ex Chronicis*, ed. Benjamin Thorpe (English Historical Society, 1848, 1849, 2 vols) which has serious shortcomings. A good edition of the section from 1118 to the end is *The Chronicle of John of Worcester 1118–1140*, ed. J. R. H. Weaver (Anecdota Oxoniensia, 1908), which has a useful account of the manuscripts and a critique (p. 4) of Thorpe's editorial methods. For the shortcomings of Thorpe's edition see also *The Chronicle of Bury St. Edmunds 1212–1301*, ed. A. Gransden (Nelson's Medieval Texts, 1964), p. xvii.

1118 was Florence.[51] The reason for this view was a passage in the chronicle in the annal for 1118. It reads: 'On the nones of July died Dom. Florence monk of Worcester; this chronicle of chronicles excels all others because of his deep knowledge and studious application.'[52] However, there are two objections to the attribution of the chronicle to 1118 to Florence. In the first place there is evidence pointing to a monk named John as author. In the second place the chronicle shows no break at 1118. When Orderic Vitalis visited Worcester shortly before Florence's death, he found, he records, a monk called John writing a chronicle which he had begun at Wulfstan's command.[53] And under 1138 the chronicle itself, in a verse apostrophizing the reader, asks for corrections to be made 'if John has offended in any way'.[54]

The only independent evidence that there was a change of authorship in 1118 is the fact that the Durham chronicle, the *Historia Regum* (*History of the Kings*), used a version to 1118. On the other hand the Worcester chronicle has a stylistic unity before and after 1118 (the same distinctive phrases occur throughout[55]), and there is a sustained interest in chronology.[56] As will be seen, the early manuscript of the chronicle has nothing to support the view that there was a break at 1118. Moreover, in its present form, the Worcester chronicle from 1095 was written after about 1124 – that is after Florence's death. This is proved by the fact that the author used Eadmer's *Historia Novorum*, which was not available in its final form until some time between 1121 and 1124.[57] Therefore in order to accept that Florence wrote the Worcester chronicle to 1118, it would be necessary to assume that Orderic wrote 'John' by mistake for 'Florence' and that the text was revised soon after Florence's death (to insert the material from the *Historia Novorum*). The most likely interpretation of the evidence is that the extant Worcester chronicle is the work of John, writing from about 1124 to 1140, and that he used material collected by the assiduous Florence.[58]

The chronicle has some information about the author's life. Under 1132 it records that he was standing next to Uhtred, precentor of Worcester,

[51] For a discussion of the problems connected with this view, see *VW*, pp. xv–xviii.

[52] *JW*, p. 13; 'Non. Iulii obiit Domnus Florentius Wigornensis monachus. Huius subtili scientia et studiosi laboris industria, preeminet cunctis haec chronicarum chronica.'

[53] *OV*, vol. 2, p. 161.   [54] *JW*, p. 49.

[55] See for example the many notices of fires in towns and elsewhere. The phrase 'incendio conflagravit' or 'conflagravit incendio' is used *s.a.* 1092 (*FW*, vol. 2, p. 30), 1101 (ibid., p. 48), 1122 (*JW*, p. 17), 1130 (ibid., p. 30), 1133 (ibid., p. 38), and 1137 (ibid., p. 43). Phrases such as 'igne cremata est', 'igne combusta est' occur *s.a.* 1113 (*FW*, vol. 2, p. 66), 1133 (*JW*, p. 37) and 1137 (ibid., p. 43). However, as these phrases are fairly usual ones, not too much weight should be attached to their occurrence before and after 1118.

[56] For passages containing detailed chronological information see *s.a.* 1095 (*FW*, vol. 2, p. 36), 1131 (*JW*, p. 34) and 1138 (ibid., p. 53). See also p. 145 n. 63 below.

[57] These objections to Florence's authorship of the chronicle to 1118 are expressed by R. R. Darlington (*VW*, pp. xvi–xviii and nn.) who also suggests that the Worcester chronicle used William of Malmesbury's *Gesta Regum* and *Gesta Pontificum*; if this were so it would date the original compilation to not earlier than 1125.

[58] This is the view expressed by R. R. Darlington, *Anglo-Norman Historians*, p. 14.

during mass when Uhtred, who died soon afterwards, was suddenly taken ill. The author was much distressed because Uhtred had 'loved me like a foster-father'.[59] Later the author was an exile at Winchcombe where he met Henry I's physician Grimbald who told him some anecdotes about the king.[60] By 1139 he must have been back at Worcester for he was at lauds in the cathedral when a hostile force arrived from Gloucester.[61]

The Worcester chronicler borrowed the annalistic arrangement of his work from the Anglo-Saxon Chronicle. He drew most of his information for the pre-Conquest period from a now lost version of the Anglo-Saxon Chronicle which reached to 1130.[62] As this lost version had additions to, and variations from the surviving texts, the Worcester chronicler's Latin translation is of value to the present-day historian. Whether the chronicler himself turned it into Latin or used some existing translation is not known. (Already in Anglo-Saxon times parts of the Chronicle had been translated into Latin by Asser and Æthelweard.)

Other works besides the Anglo-Saxon Chronicle encouraged the Worcester chronicler's predilection for annals. He had studied Bede's *De Temporibus* (which includes a chronicle of the world)[63] and used the chronological summary to the *Ecclesiastical History*.[64] Particularly important was the influence of the universal chronicle by Marianus Scotus, an Irish monk who lived as a recluse at Fulda.[65] His chronicle, covering the period from the Creation to 1082, was brought to England at the instigation of Robert de Losinga, the learned bishop of Hereford (1079–95),[66] and soon attracted attention. It may have been brought to Worcester by Losinga, who was a close friend of Wulfstan.[67] The Worcester chronicler used it to supplement the Anglo-Saxon Chronicle on continental affairs. Moreover, he borrowed a chronological peculiarity from Marianus, who had a distinctive method of dating. He believed that the accepted date of the Incarnation was twenty-two years too late (William of Malmesbury thought that

[59] *JW*, p. 36.
[60] *JW*, pp. 33. It appears from the passage that he was at Winchcombe before Henry I's death. H. W. C. Davis, quoted in a note in Weaver's preface (*JW*, p. 10), dates his exile about 1134.
[61] *JW*, p. 57.
[62] The surviving D text of the Anglo-Saxon Chronicle, which ends in 1079, may have been written at Worcester; see p. 39 above.
[63] For passages discussing the views Bede expressed on chronology in *De Temporibus*, see *s.a.* 703 and 725 (*FW*, vol. 1, p. 45).
[64] The Worcester chronicler claims that he is continuing Bede's *HE* (see *s.a.* 734, *FW*, vol. 1, p. 53). He records, *s.a.* 707, the starting of *HE* (ibid., p. 46). His annal for 540 (ibid., p. 5) seems to be copied from Bede's chronological summary.
[65] For Marianus's life see *s.a.* 1028, 1056, 1058 and 1069 (*FW*, vol. 1, 184, 215, 217; vol. 2, p. 3).
[66] Robert wrote a work based on excerpts from Marianus's chronicle. This was known to William of Malmesbury who records that Robert first had Marianus's chronicle brought to England (WM, *GP*, p. 301; *GR*, iii. 292 (vol. 2, p. 345)). For Robert's tract see W. H. Stevenson, 'A contemporary description of the Domesday survey' in *EHR*, xxii (1907), pp. 72–84, and p. 176 n. 81 below.
[67] See the Worcester chronicle, *s.a.* 1095 (*FW*, vol. 2, p. 37), and Stevenson, op. cit., p. 73.

Marianus's views on chronology had much to recommend them[68]). Therefore the Worcester chronicle gives two dates for each year, one according to
the normal Dionysian calculation and one according to Marianus's system.

To 1121 the Worcester chronicle is mainly a compilation from well-
known authorities (besides the sources mentioned, it has citations from
Asser's *Life of King Alfred*). But it has some passages of unknown derivation. From the early twelfth century the number of entries which are independent of known sources increases. And from 1121, apart from some slight
use of the Anglo-Saxon Chronicle, the author used no known history or
biography. He was writing an account of events fairly soon after they
took place, deriving his information from documents and hearsay.

A manuscript of the Worcester chronicle survives which is an early draft
from 1110 – perhaps the author's autograph.[69] It confirms the view that
from the early twelfth century the chronicle becomes a first-hand, contemporary account of events written up at intervals. The entries, having been
neatly copied in one hand to 1110, thereafter are written in various hands and
shades of ink and have numerous corrections (erased and rewritten words,
and words written between the lines). The changes of handwriting and ink
suggest either that the author was writing sporadically or that he employed
a number of copyists.

The manuscript and the contents of the chronicle show that as it survives
today the chronicle from 1128 to the accession of King Stephen was revised
after Henry I's death. The passage concerning the Council of London in
1128, where the nobles swore fealty to the Empress Matilda, is on an erasure
and begins with the rubric 'Concerning the oath already changed into
perjury, to the peril of many': this rubric was obviously written after the
death of Henry I. Moreover, there is evidence that originally the entry was
placed in the annal for 1130, immediately before the account of Henry I's
three visions and a story concerning a German noble.[70] Under 1130 the
author refers to King Stephen as 'now ruling', and under 1134 to Henry of
Winchester as 'now papal legate': since Henry was appointed legate in
1139 the annal must have reached its present form after that date.

It is likely that the author intended to end the chronicle in 1130. He subsequently added the account of the Council of London (presumably the
information did not reach him in time for insertion in its appropriate place).
He also added Henry I's three visions, which are lavishly illustrated
with tinted drawings in the manuscript,[71] and the story about the German
nobleman. Then during Stephen's reign he put the account of the
Council of London into its proper place and added annals from 1131,

---

[68] *GP*, p. 300. See Stevenson, op. cit., p. 73 n. 3.
[69] Corpus Christi College, Oxford, MS. 157. For a description of this MS. and a discussion of its
claim to be the author's autograph see *JW*, pp. 7–9.
[70] See *JW*, pp. 26 nn. 1 and 3, 31 nn. 3 and 5.
[71] Reproduced here as Plate VI and as the frontispiece in *JW*.

using contemporary notes (this is suggested by the number of exact dates).

The Worcester chronicle, therefore, revived the Anglo-Saxon tradition of contemporary historiography. The content of the chronicle to some extent resembles the Peterborough chronicle. It has a similar blend of national with local history. Examples of entries relating particularly to Worcester are the account of a trial by ordeal held in the cathedral church in 1130 and the notice of the death of the precentor Uhtred in 1132. However, it is noticeable that up to the early twelfth century the focus is kept pretty well on national events (there is not an undue amount of material relating to St Wulfstan – perhaps because Coleman had already described his life in full).

Like the Peterborough chronicle, the Worcester one has a pro-English bias, although not so markedly. It describes Waltheof's execution in 1076 as 'wrong and cruel', and claims that he was truly penitent when in prison for his acts. 'Men wish to bury his memory, but it is truly believed that he rejoices with the angels in heaven. This is attested by Lanfranc to whom he made confession and who accepted his penitence.'[72] The chronicle contrasts William Rufus unfavourably with the Anglo-Saxon kings. The latter had endowed the church, but Rufus robbed it.[73] The Worcester chronicler is not obsessed, like the Peterborough one, with the weather or the harvest, but likes to record the destruction of buildings by fire[74] (which reflects his urban, not rural, outlook).

The Worcester chronicle differs from the Peterborough chronicle in other respects. Although both were written primarily to record events, their methods are not quite the same. Unlike the Peterborough chronicler, the Worcester one was archive-conscious. He realized the value of a document cited *verbatim* to substantiate his record. Here he may have been influenced by Bede. But Wulfstan himself had fostered the care of archives at Worcester, and Eadmer provided a contemporary example of the inclusion of documents in a historical work. The Worcester chronicler gives the texts of the decrees of the ecclesiastical councils held in London in 1125 and 1127.

The Worcester chronicle does not read as smoothly as the Peterborough one. This is partly because of the insertion of these documents. But it is also because the chronicler includes blocks of other types of record, that is lists of obits and ecclesiastical preferments; these are often grouped together at the end of annals. But the object of the Worcester chronicler was not only to record events. It was also to edify and amuse. Therefore he interrupted the record of events with an account of Henry I's visions and the three stories relating to Germany (including the one about the German nobleman),[75]

---

[72] *FW*, vol. 2, p. 12. [73] Ibid., p. 45. [74] See p. 144 n. 55 above.

[75] William of Malmesbury also included stories of German derivation. See pp. 171 and n. 35, 172 below. For the popularity among the Anglo-Normans of stories about the marvellous and the collections they made of them (particularly of legends of the Virgin Mary) see R. W. Southern, 'The place of England in the twelfth-century renaissance' in *History*, xlv (1960), pp. 211–13. Such collections come from Canterbury, Evesham, Malmesbury and Bury St Edmunds, all centres of the Anglo-Saxon revival. See *JW*, pp. 34–6, 45–8.

which reflect contemporary taste for the marvellous. It is only in the reign of Stephen that the chronicle gives a detailed, continuous history.

Like the Anglo-Saxon Chronicle in earlier days, the Worcester chronicle is important partly because it formed the basis of the chronicles of a number of monasteries. Soon after 1130, copies of the chronicle to the end of 1130 were made for the abbeys of Abingdon,[76] Bury St Edmunds,[77] Peterborough[78] and Gloucester.[79] In each case the chronicle was edited to suit the needs of its new home, by cutting out some of the material specifically relating to Worcester, and/or inserting material mostly relating to the editor's own house. For example the Gloucester version leaves out the notices of the trial by ordeal at Worcester and the death of the precentor Uhtred, and adds notice of the death of Roger de Berkeley, a benefactor of St Peter's, Gloucester.[80] The Gloucester copy is the only one to which were subsequently added the annals in the Worcester chronicle from 1131 to 1140. These annals also show the work of a Gloucester editor: he not only intruded passages about Gloucester, but also about general political events, and continued the chronicle at least to 1141 and possibly later.

A copy of the Worcester chronicle reached Durham and there formed the basis of the *Historia Regum* for the years from 848 to 1118. The *Historia Regum*, a history of England from the early seventh century until 1129, is commonly attributed to Symeon of Durham, the precentor of St Cuthbert's, Durham, to whom is also ascribed the *Libellus de exordio atque procursu . . . Dunelmensis Ecclesiae*.[81] But the evidence that he wrote the *Historia Regum* is weak (Symeon's claims to be a historian have been examined above[82]).

[76] Lambeth MS. 42. See *JW*, p. 9; Weaver collated the Abingdon text.

[77] Bodley MS. 297 (see pp. 380–1 and n. 2 below). The so-called *Annals of St. Neots*, which have extracts from the Worcester chronicle, were probably compiled early in the twelfth century (as they survive today they end incomplete at 914). They are printed in *Asser*, pp. 117–45. Stevenson suggested (*Asser*, pp. 99–102) the likelihood that the *Annals* were written at Bury St Edmunds. His view is corroborated by Mr T. A. M. Bishop who attributes the manuscript containing them (Trinity College, Cambridge, MS. 770, pp. 1–74) to Bury St Edmunds and dates it to the second quarter of the twelfth century; *Asser*, p. cxli n. 3.

[78] Corpus Christi College, Cambridge, MS. 92. See *JW*, p. 9 and p. 403 n. 152 below.

[79] Trinity College, Dublin, MS. 503. E.6.4. To 1123 this MS. has short annals abstracted from the Worcester chronicle and was written at Worcester. Then it has the chronicle from 1123 to 1140 in a thirteenth-century hand; this section contains numerous additions relating to Gloucester and was obviously written there. It is described in *JW*, pp. 6–7, where the Gloucester omissions and additions are discussed; they are printed in *FW*.

[80] Roger de Berkeley (junior) was buried in St Peter's (see *JW*, p. 25 n. 3). He was probably the son of Roger de Berkeley (senior) who became a monk of St Peter's before his death in 1093; GEC, *Peerage*, vol. 2, p. 124.

[81] See pp. 115–16 above. The *Historia Regum* is printed in *SD*, vol. 2, pp. 3–283, the text cited here, and in *SD*, ed. Hinde, pp. 1–131. Mr Hunter Blair gives a detailed analysis of the contents of the *Historia* in 'Some observations on the *Historia Regum* attributed to Symeon of Durham' in Chadwick, *Celt and Saxon*, pp. 63–118 *passim*. Some of his views are critically examined by H. S. Offler, 'Hexham and the *Historia Regum*' in *Transactions of the Architectural and Archaeological Society of Durham and Northumberland*, ii (1971), pp. 51–62.

[82] See p. 116.

It is true that the only known text of the *Historia* ascribes the work to Symeon.[83] But this text was written two generations after Symeon's time, in the late twelfth century (it is noteworthy that the manuscript belonged to the abbey of Sawley in Yorkshire, which also owned the earliest known text of the *Libellus* explicitly ascribed to Symeon[84]). Moreover, even if Symeon wrote either the *Historia* or the *Libellus*, it is unlikely that he wrote both since internal evidence suggests that they were by different authors.[85]

Besides the question of *who* wrote the *Historia Regum*, there is the problem of *what* he wrote. For the *Historia Regum* is a collection of historical miscellanea rather than a unitary history. It is made up of the following sections: (1) Kentish legends relating to the seventh and eighth centuries; (2) an account of the kings of Northumbria from the mid-sixth century until 737; (3) material from the *Ecclesiastical History* mainly relating to Bede; (4) annals from 732 to 802 from a lost Northumbrian source;[86] (5) annals from 849 to 887, mainly from Asser's *Life of King Alfred*; (6) annals from 888 to 957 which in their present form are later than 1042;[87] (7) extracts from the *Gesta Regum* of William of Malmesbury; (8) annals from 848 to 1118, based mainly on the Worcester chronicle but also partly derived from the *Libellus*, Eadmer's *Historia Novorum*, Dudo of St Quentin and William of Jumièges;[88] (9) annals from 1119 to 1129.

Only the last section is original in the sense that it is not derived from an earlier source but was written fairly close to the events it records. This section could be the work of Symeon. Moreover, it is possible that he collected together the rest of the material and edited it. However, some of the earlier material, items (1) to (5), may have been already assembled by the early tenth century.[89] As it survives today, the *Historia Regum* is not in the form that the Durham monk (whether Symeon or not) left it: some time after its completion someone with an interest in Hexham inserted additional Hexham material.[90] Then, between 1161 and 1175, the still surviving copy was made for Sawley which has further modifications.[91]

[83] See *SD*, vol. 2, pp. x, 3, 283; H. S. Offler, *Medieval Historians of Durham* (Durham 1958), p. 9 and n. 14; Blair, 'Observations', pp. 74–6.

[84] See p. 116 and n. 69.

[85] See Offler, *Medieval Historians*, p. 9. Hinde, in *SD*, ed. Hinde, pp. xxvii et seq., points out discrepancies between the *Historia Regum* and the *Libellus*; the variants either indicate that both works were not by the same man, or that the *Historia Regum* was heavily revised at Hexham.

[86] See p. 31.   [87] See p. 32, and Blair, 'Observations,'p. 106.

[88] Arnold states (*SD*, vol. 2, p. xxi) that the *Historia Regum* 'uses Dudo and William of Jumièges as sources of information on affairs of Normandy and France'. The passages Arnold cites are so brief that it is impossible to be sure that they derive even in part from these works: some of them have no close parallels in Dudo or William of Jumièges, but one (ibid., p. 155) does resemble a passage in William (*GND*, p. 83). A twelfth-century copy of William's work was at Durham; see p. 96 above.

[89] See Blair, 'Observations', pp. 117–18.

[90] Ibid., pp. 70–1, 87–90, 115, 117. For the additions to the *Historia Regum* made at Hexham, see Offler, 'Hexham and the *Historia Regum*', pp. 53–5.

[91] Blair, 'Observations', pp. 78, 110–11. The view that the Sawley copy of *Historia Regum*, printed by Arnold, does not represent the text as first written, but has later additions and modi-

Therefore, the *Historia Regum* up to 1119 is a historical collection, the value of which to the present-day historian depends on its sources. In fact items (4) and (6), being copied from lost annals, are valuable. Moreover, item (5) may derive from a lost version of Asser, which may have been written in about 900.[92] The compiler made no attempt at producing a continuous, cohesive history. He included, without correlation, whatever interested him. Items (5), (6) and (8) triplicate the record for the years from 849 to 887. Item (5) contains an early version of Asser, while item (8) has material from the passages in the Worcester chronicle derived from Asser, or from item (5) itself.

The strongest incentive to the production of this collection was the desire to preserve the records of St Cuthbert's church. This developed into a wider historical perspective – the desire to preserve the religious tradition which had been disturbed by the Norman Conquest. From local history, the compiler turned to the history of the whole area, and of the kingdom. The main inspiration was Bede. The work was conceived as a continuation of the *Ecclesiastical History*,[93] from which there are many citations. The stories about saints at the beginning of the work recall Bede's love of hagiography. There are few digressions into the history of St Cuthbert's church, presumably because this had been fully dealt with in the *Libellus*: this relegation of local history to a separate book corresponds to Bede's method.[94] But it was the annalistic, not the narrative type of history which the author adopted for the non-derivative section from 1119 to 1129. Here he was influenced not only by Bede's chronological summary to the *Ecclesiastical History*,[95] but also by the Northumbrian annals, the Anglo-Saxon Chronicle and the Worcester chronicle.

This original part of the *Historia Regum* has a contemporary account of events. In general the author's approach is factual. Like the Worcester chronicler his main intention was to record facts. For this reason he copies a number of documents in full.[96] His account of the ecclesiastical council at Westminster in 1126, which includes a copy of the decrees issued, is almost

---

fications, has been corroborated and amplified by the researches of Mr Todd and Professor Offler on a twelfth-century historical collection preserved in Bibliothèque Nationale MS. nouv. acq. Cat. 692; see J. M. Todd and H. S. Offler, 'A medieval chronicle from Scotland' in *Scottish Historical Review*, xlvii (1968), pp. 153–4, and Offler, 'Hexham and the *Historia Regum*', *passim*. Cf. p. 261 n. 104 below.

[92] See p. 48 n. 42.

[93] *SD*, vol. 2, pp. 27–8.

[94] For citations from the *History of the Abbots of Wearmouth and Jarrow* see ibid., pp. 15–23 *passim*. There are citations from *HE* (ibid., pp. 28–30) and of one of Bede's poems (ibid., pp. 23–7).

[95] There are citations from the continuation to Bede's chronological summary (*SD*, pp. 30–1). The author also refers (ibid., p. 23) to a work of Bede which he calls 'de annalibus, hoc est, de rebus singulorum annorum'. Perhaps this is a reference to the universal chronicle in *De Temporum Ratione*; see Blair, 'Observations', p. 86.

[96] He writes (ibid., p. 270) at the head of the decrees of the Council of Rome in 1123, 'quorum capitula scire volentibus subscripta inveniuntur'.

identical with that given by the Worcester chronicler:[97] this suggests that both writers used some official hand-out. Nevertheless, despite the Durham chronicler's factual method, he could write moving prose. For example there is the account of Henry I's grief at the loss of his eldest son William who went down on the White Ship. The king heard 'of the death from a sad messenger. Henry was at first overcome by this sudden catastrophe, as though weak-spirited, but soon, hiding his grief from disdain of fortune, he recovered his regal dignity.'[98] The chronicler also had strong prejudices. Like Eadmer, he became increasingly obsessed with the controversy between Canterbury and York over the primacy. He presented the case from the point of view of York and devoted a disproportionate amount of space to it.

The Anglo-Norman histories so far discussed show a renewed interest in recording events. And they show the preponderant influence of the Anglo-Saxon historiographical tradition founded by Bede and developed by the Anglo-Saxon biographers and chroniclers. But none of these Anglo-Norman writers tried to reproduce narrative history on the grand scale of Bede: that was left to Orderic Vitalis.

Orderic Vitalis, although he lived in Normandy, deserves to be considered with the Anglo-Norman historians.[99] He was born in England, at Atcham, near Shrewsbury, in 1075. His father was Odelerius d'Orléans who had come to England between 1066 and 1068 with Roger de Montgomery earl of Shrewsbury (1074–94). His mother was probably English, as Orderic refers to himself as *angligena*.[100] Odelerius sent Orderic at the age of five to study in Shrewsbury and to serve in the church of the monastery which he had founded there. When Orderic was ten, Odelerius sent him to Normandy to become a monk. His purpose was pious, to give Orderic a better chance of salvation by removing him from the ties of family affection.[101] Orderic became a monk of St Évroul. Perhaps he went to this abbey because Roger de Montgomery was one of its patrons. Although Orderic never saw his father

---

[97] Ibid., pp. 278–81.

[98] Ibid., p. 259.

[99] The standard edition of Orderic is still *Orderici Vitalis Historiae Ecclesiasticae Libri Tredecim*, ed. A. Le Prévost and L. Delisle (Société de l'Histoire de France, Paris 1838–55, 5 vols; reprinted 1965). A new edition of Books III–VI has now appeared, *The Ecclesiastical History of Orderic Vitalis*, ed., with an English translation, Marjorie Chibnall (Oxford 1969, 1972, vols 2 and 3; the rest of the work is to be published in due course, vol. 1 last). Dr Chibnall's edition is definitive and anything I have said about Orderic may have to be modified in the light of her further published researches. As Le Prévost's is still the complete edition I have given references to it (Dr Chibnall gives marginal references to his pagination). For a detailed account of Orderic's life, work and times see L. Delisle in *OV*, vol. 5, pp. i–cvi, and H. Wolter, *Orderic Vitalis, ein Beitrag zur Kluniazensischen Geschichts-schreibung* (Wiesbaden 1955); Wolter emphasizes the influence of Cluny on Orderic and, in my view, underestimates the influence of English writers. For a short account of Orderic's life and works see Chibnall, *OV*, vol. 2, pp. xiii–xvi.

[100] See Chibnall, *OV*, vol. 2, p. xiii.

[101] *OV*, xiii. 44 (vol. 5, p. 134).

again, he retained his love of England and thought of himself as an exile.[102] He visited England in about 1115, spending five weeks at Crowland abbey, and later visited Thorney and Worcester.

St Évroul had an important place in the eleventh-century monastic revival in Normandy. Its foundation in 1050 marked the beginning of the second wave of new foundations (many of which emanated from St Évroul). St Évroul, like Bec, exercised a strong influence on English monasticism. Its monks became abbots of Crowland,[103] Thorney,[104] St Benet of Hulme[105] and Bury St Edmunds.[106] It also had contacts with Tewkesbury abbey, which was founded by a Norman magnate, Robert fitz Hamo.[107] The English connection was the closer because St Évroul owned lands in England[108] and founded a priory there.[109] Thus, by birth and background, Orderic had close associations with England. This affected his historical writing. He saw England and Normandy not only as a political entity in his time, but also as culturally united. He had a strong interest in English affairs and sympathy for the English and he was influenced by English writers.

Orderic's life's work was the *Ecclesiastical History of England and Normandy*. He began it at the order of Roger of le Sap, abbot of St Évroul from 1091 to 1123,[110] and dedicated it to Roger's successor, Guérin des Essarts (1123–37).[111] The work is in thirteen books which Orderic wrote between 1114 or 1115[112] and 1141. He wrote Books III to VI and VIII to XIII consecutively, but the other books were written out of order: he wrote Books I and II (and added the prologue to Book III) in 1136, when he was working on Book XI, and he wrote Book VII some time after 1135. He revised at least part of the work (including Books I, II and VI) in 1141.

Roughly speaking, the work as it was first conceived (that is Books III to VI and VIII to XIII) is a history of Normandy to the middle of the eleventh century, of the Conquest of England and of the reigns of William I, William II and Henry I in England and Normandy. Orderic added the first two books and Book VII to turn the work into a universal history, putting it in its European context. (Book I has a Life of Christ and a universal history from the creation of the world to 1141; Book II has Lives of the apostles and popes; Book VII is mainly a résumé of French, Norman and English history from 688 to 1087.[113]) Orderic devotes a fair amount of space to English

---

[102] *OV*, v. 1, 14 (vol. 2, pp. 302, 423); xiii. 44 (vol. 5, pp. 134–5).

[103] Geoffrey d'Orléans, abbot of Crowland 1109–24.

[104] Robert de Prunelai, abbot of Thorney 1113/14–51. Guérin des Essarts, abbot of St Évroul 1123–37, visited Thorney; *OV*, vi. 10 (vol. 3, p. 123).

[105] William Basset, abbot of St Benet of Hulme 1127–34.

[106] Robert, abbot of Bury St Edmunds 1100–02.   [107] *OV*, vi. 4 (vol. 3, p. 14).

[108] See D. J. A. Matthew, *The Norman Monasteries and their English Possessions* (Oxford 1962), pp. 29 n. 1, 31–2, 65.

[109] For the priory at Ware, Herts, see ibid., p. 57 and *OV*, vi. 5 (vol. 3, p. 23 and n.).

[110] See *OV*, i. prologue (vol. 1, p. 2); v. 1 (vol. 2, p. 300).

[111] *OV*, i, prologue (vol. 1, p. 3); v. 1 (vol. 2, p. 300).   [112] See Chibnall, *OV*, vol. 2, p. xv.

[113] For the construction of the *Ecclesiastical History* see L. Delisle in *OV*, vol. 5, pp. xliii–li.

ecclesiastical and political affairs (see especially Book III, chapter 14, Book IV and Book XIII, chapters 37–42). He inserted one section at the express request of Englishmen: the abbot and monks of Crowland asked him to include the Life of their patron saint, Guthlac, and the account of their lay patron, Earl Waltheof.[114]

His sympathy for the English appears in his account of the Norman Conquest. He praised Earl Waltheof as a fine and pious man,[115] and admired the Anglo-Saxon saints.[116] He was sorry for the sufferings of the English[117] under Norman rule. He deplored the oppression of English monks by tyrannical Norman abbots such as Thurstan at Glastonbury.[118] Orderic scorned Norman ecclesiastics who ingratiated themselves at court in order to gain preferment in England[119] and was warm in his admiration of one Norman monk, Guitmund of La-Croix-Saint-Leufroi, for refusing preferment in England. Guitmund wrote to William the Conqueror saying that he did not want to rule foreigners – unhappy men reduced to slavery who would be unwilling to accept him: the religious should have no part in robbery.[120] Orderic even gives a rather unflattering character-sketch of the Norman people: 'The Normans are a warlike race, and unless restrained by firm rule, are always ready to make trouble. In all societies wherever they are found, they struggle for mastery, and disregarding all sanctions of truth and good faith are always moved by fierce ambition.'[121]

But inevitably Orderic's divided loyalties resulted in an ambivalent attitude to the English. He had to justify the Norman Conquest. He did this partly by arguing that the condition of the church and the level of morality had seriously declined (due to the Danish invasions[122]) before the Conquest. The English were a rough and almost illiterate people, drunken, gluttonous, lustful and effeminate,[123] and the north country people were particularly barbarous.[124] It was the Norman Conquest which rectified the situation, because William the Conqueror and Lanfranc co-operated in reform.[125]

Of English writers, Bede had the greatest influence on Orderic. A number of Bede's scriptural commentaries[126] were in the library at St Évroul and Orderic himself made a copy of the *Ecclesiastical History*.[127] He borrowed

---

[114] *OV*, iv. 15 (vol. 2, p. 268). For the value of the *Ecclesiastical History* for the history of Crowland see Chibnall, *OV*, pp. xxiv–xxix.

[115] *OV*, iv. 14 (vol. 2, p. 266).

[116] *OV*, iv. 15 (vol. 2, p. 268).

[117] *OV*, iv. 3, 8 (vol. 2, pp. 17 1, 224).

[118] *OV*, iv, 8 (vol. 2, p. 226).

[119] *OV*, iv. 8 (vol. 2, p. 225).

[120] *OV*, iv. 8 (vol. 2, pp. 226 et seq.).

[121] *OV*, ix. 3 (vol. 3, p. 474). For a similar characterization of them by William of Malmesbury see pp. 158 n. 177, 173 below.

[122] *OV*, iv. 6 (vol. 2, pp. 206–8). For the possibility that this passage is related to passages by Eadmer and William of Malmesbury see p. 158 and nn. 172, 175, 176 below.

[123] *OV*, iv. 6 (vol. 2, p. 208). For the possibility that this passage is related to one in William of Malmesbury see p. 158 and n. 176 below.

[124] *OV*, iv. 4 (vol. 2, p. 184). See p. 174 and n. 58 below.

[125] *OV*, iv. 6 (vol. 2, pp. 208 et seq.).

[126] See Chibnall, *OV*, vol. 2, p. 246 n. 2.

[127] Ibid., p. xvii and n. 4.

from both the *Ecclesiastical History*[128] and the universal chronicle in *De Temporum Ratione*[129] – but was mainly influenced by the former. He gave his work the same title and adopted some features of Bede's method. He expressed the hope that Abbot Guérin, to whom he dedicated the work, would correct any errors:[130] Bede dedicated his *Ecclesiastical History* to King Ceolwulf, asking him to correct it. Like Bede he gives very full accounts of his literary sources. Most of the works he used are described near the beginning of Book III – originally Book I[131] (Bede describes his sources in the preface). Both Orderic and Bede close their histories with short autobiographies.[132]

Orderic's method of citing documents *in extenso* and the way he uses verbal information are also reminiscent of Bede's technique. But here it is not possible to assume that Orderic was only influenced by Bede, because such methods were fairly common (Eadmer, for example, used them). Orderic copies letters, charters and decrees of councils. And he had a taste for epitaphs. Bede inserted Gregory the Great's epitaph in the *Ecclesiastical History*: Orderic included many epitaphs. They are mainly of Norman magnates and ecclesiastics and Orderic had seen most of them himself.[133] Epitaphs had a great vogue at this time; Orderic records that a competition was held for the best epitaph on the death of William abbot of Fécamp in 1108. The winning verses were inscribed in gold on the tomb, and were so moving that they made readers weep.[134]

Possibly Bede's influence was one reason why Orderic wrote history in the grand manner of Christian historiography. Like Bede he stressed the Orosian concept: history was the manifestation of God's will on earth. He wrote partly for the edification of his readers, trying to improve their prospects of salvation by showing how God punishes the sinful. Orderic ex-

---

[128] For references to Bede's *Ecclesiastical History* see *OV*, x. 15 (vol. 4, p. 96); xii. 47 (vol. 4, p. 487). For general references to Bede as a historian see *OV*, i. prologue (vol. 1, p. 2); iv. 6 (vol. 2, p. 207); v. 9 (vol. 2, p. 350).

[129] For references to the chronicle (*De Sex Ætatibus Mundi*) in *De Temporum Ratione*, see *OV*, i. 22, 24 (vol. 1, pp. 95 and n. 1, 152–3 and n.). Orderic erroneously asserts that he is citing *De Temporibus* and that *De Sex Ætatibus Mundi* ends in 734 (it only goes to 725; the chronological summary in Bede's *HE* was continued to 734: see p. 29 above).

[130] *OV*, i, prologue (vol. 1, p. 4). Cf. Bede's preface to *HE*.

[131] *OV*, iii. 15 (vol. 2, pp. 157–61).

[132] *OV*, xiii. 44 (vol. 5, pp. 133–6). For a reference to Bede's summary of his life see *OV*, v. 9 (vol. 2, pp. 350–1).

[133] Orderic in many cases describes the type of tomb and its exact location in the church, chapterhouse or elsewhere, in such detail as to make it almost certain that he had read the epitaph *in situ*. See for example his accounts of epitaphs in the cathedral and elsewhere at Rouen, *OV*, v. 4 (vol. 2, p. 313); viii. 25 (vol. 3, p. 432); xi. 4 (vol. 4, p. 185); xi. 40 (vol. 4, p. 300): at Cluny, xii. 30 (vol. 4, p. 424): at Troarn, viii. 6 (vol. 3, p. 304): at Préaux, viii. 25 (vol. 3, p. 429); at Fécamp, xi. 30 (vol. 4, pp. 270–1); and at Longueville, xi. 4 (vol. 4, pp. 183–4). He had presumably seen that at Thorney; *OV*, xi. 33 (vol. 4, p. 282). But there is no indication that he had seen those at Lewes or Thetford; *OV*, viii. 9 (vol. 3, p. 318); xi. 32 (vol. 4, p. 277). He himself wrote an epitaph for Avicia, the wife of one of the benefactors of St Évroul, who was buried in the cloisters there; *OV*, vi. 8 (vol. 3, pp. 45–6).

[134] *OV*, xi. 30 (vol. 4, pp. 270–1).

cluded pagan history (that of the Greeks and Romans) because it was irrelevant to his edificatory purpose.[135] He would have preferred also to exclude secular history, but he found this impossible because the times were so degenerate that there were not enough saints and miracles to fill a volume. He therefore decided to include secular history as an object lesson for Christians.[136]

Orderic attributes a number of catastrophes to God's intervention in men's affairs. For example he believed that the death of William Rufus and the fall of Ranulf Flambard were punishments for their oppression of the church.[137] He intimates that the sinking of the White Ship was God's revenge for the victims' sins. But like Bede he does not let the divine cause exclude the rational one. For example he explains that the White Ship was wrecked on a rock, because of the drunkenness of the crew.[138] Moreover, Orderic resembles Bede in his use of saints' Lives to edify readers. He gives the legends of St Évroul,[139] St Taurinus (first bishop of Évreux),[140] St Judoc,[141] St Martial,[142] St William[143] and St Guthlac.[144] He makes many passing references to saints, especially those connected with Normandy (St Ouen,[145] St Philibert[146] and St Wandrille[147]), and gives accounts of saints' relics preserved in Normandy and near by.[148]

Orderic's addition of two extra books on world history to the beginning of his work probably owes something to English influence. He borrowed much of his material for them from Bede's *De Sex Ætatibus Mundi* (in *De Temporum Ratione*). Moreover, when he visited Worcester he met the chronicler John, whose chronicle includes the universal chronicle of Marianus. It is likely that Orderic regarded John's attempt at a world history as well worth emulating (he also knew the universal chronicle of Sigebert of Gembloux, covering the years from 381 to 1112[149]). He writes that John was 'a monk of venerable character and learning [who] in his continuation

[135] *OV*, i, prologue (vol. 1, p. 3).
[136] *OV*, xi, prologue (vol. 4, p. 159). For Orderic's views on the degeneracy of his own times see also *OV*, v. 1 (vol. 2, pp. 302–3); vi. 1 (vol. 3, p. 3). He comments on the decreased number of miracles in England; *OV*, vi. 10 (vol. 3, p. 133).
[137] *OV*, x. 14, 18 (vol. 4, pp. 86, 108).
[138] *OV*, xii. 25 (vol. 4, p. 416 and n.). God also punished sin by fires, floods and pirates; *OV*, xiii. 16 (vol. 5, pp. 41–2).
[139] *OV*, vi. 11 (vol. 3, pp. 50–83).
[140] *OV*, v. 7 (vol. 2, pp. 325–32).
[141] *OV*, iii. 13 (vol. 2, pp. 134–43).
[142] *OV*, ii. 16 (vol. 1, pp. 360–82).
[143] *OV*, vi. 3 (vol. 3, pp. 5–12).
[144] *OV*, iv. 16 (vol. 2, pp. 268–79).
[145] *OV*, iii. 1; v. 9 (vol. 2, pp. 4, 347).
[146] *OV*, iii. 1; v. 9 (vol. 2, pp. 5, 347).
[147] *OV*, v. 9 (vol. 2, p. 347).
[148] e.g. for relics of SS. Évroul and Wandrille, see *OV*, vi. 10 (vol. 3, p. 104); for relics of the B.V.M., see *OV*, ix. 15 (vol. 3, p. 609); for the translation of the relics of St Nicholas of Myra, see *OV*, vii. 12–13 (vol. 3, pp. 205 et seq.).
[149] See p. 162 below.

of the chronicle of Marianus Scotus gives a faithful account of King William and of the events which took place in his reign and in those of his sons William Rufus and King Henry to the present day.'[150]

Orderic shared the attitude of John of Worcester and other contemporary English historians to the monarchy and royal court. Unlike the native-born Norman historians, Orderic treats secular rulers fairly objectively. He criticizes the Norman historians as sycophantic time-servers, calling Dudo of St Quentin a panegyrist[151] and accusing William of Jumièges and William of Poitiers of writing in order to secure the king's favour.[152] He describes the Conqueror's reign 'without flattery, seeking favour neither with the vanquished nor the victors'.[153] He was bitterly critical of William Rufus (like both Eadmer and John of Worcester), hating him mainly because of his ill-treatment of the church. On the other hand Orderic gives on the whole a favourable account of Henry I. He approved of him because he kept the peace and administered justice,[154] which enabled the church to prosper and the peasantry to cultivate the land.[155] He praises his skill in negotiating with the magnates.[156] No doubt Henry's visit to St Évroul contributed to Orderic's partiality for him: Henry gave the monks sixty salted hogs and ten bushels of wheat, and confirmed the abbey's title to its properties.[157] Nevertheless Orderic could tell a story to Henry's discredit.[158] He also had an ambivalent attitude to King Stephen. Like the Peterborough chronicler he blames him for weakness, but he states that the clergy, monks and ordinary people were filled with grief because of Stephen's defeat at Lincoln in 1141; 'he was kind and courteous to those who were good and peaceful, and if his treacherous nobles had allowed it, he would have put an end to their wicked schemes and been a generous protector and benevolent friend of the country'.[159]

---

[150] *OV*, iii. 15 (vol. 2, p. 159).

[151] *OV*, iii, prologue (vol. 2, p. 2).

[152] *OV*, iii. 5 (vol. 2, p. 72); 'de gestis Normannorum studiose scripserunt, et Willelmo iam regi Anglorum favere cupientes praesentaverunt.'

[153] *OV*, iii. 15 (vol. 2, p. 161); 'In sequentibus vero latius de rege Guillermo disseram, miserasque mutationes Anglorum et Normannorum sine adulatione referam, nullius remunerationis a victoribus seu victis expetens honorificentiam.'

[154] *OV*, x. 15 (vol. 4, pp. 91–3); xi. 2 (vol. 4, pp. 163–7); xii. 23 (vol. 4, pp. 236–9).

[155] Orderic shows deep sympathy for the sufferings of the peasantry in the internecine Norman wars. See *OV*, ix. 3 (vol. 3, p. 476); 'Sic Normannia suis in se filius furentibus miserabiliter turbata est, et plebs inermis sine patrono desolata est': *OV*, xiii. 30 (vol. 5, p. 85); 'tranquillitas pacis, opitulante Deo, Normanniam refovit. Inermis plebs, quae dispersa fuerat, sua tuguria repetiit, et aliquandiu post nimias tumultuum tempestates in egestate magna siluit, et aliquantulum securior quievit': and *OV*, xiii. 38 (vol. 5, p. 117); 'Plebs invalida Normanniae moesta trepidabat, et rectore carens Altissimi auxilium invocabat.' For the detrimental effect of wars on ecclesiastical order and monastic discipline, see *OV*, viii. 18 (vol. 3, p. 384); xii. 7 (vol. 4, p. 331).

[156] For Henry's skill in negotiating with Duke Robert in 1101, see *OV*, x. 18 (vol. 4, p. 114). For his pacificatory nature in general, see *OV*, xii. 46 (vol. 4, p. 484).

[157] *OV*, xi. 43 (vol. 4, pp. 301–3).

[158] The story relates that Henry allowed the eyes of two of his grand-daughters to be put out and their noses cut off; *OV*, xii. 10 (vol. 4, pp. 336–9).

[159] *OV*, xiii. 43 (vol. 5, p. 129).

Orderic was a bitter critic of the court circle and courtiers – men who made their fortunes by ingratiating themselves with the king. He hated Ranulf Flambard who typified what he disliked in a court *parvenu*: Flambard had risen to power from humble origins (Orderic tells a wild story that his mother was a witch[160]), in defiance of the accepted order of society, by means of ambition, flattery and intrigue.[161] Orderic hated the oppressive (though often efficient) administrative measures of such new men.[162]

Orderic's invectives against court manners have a homiletic ring. Here his writing may well have been influenced by Cistercian sermons.[163] He criticized life at Henry I's court because homosexuality and dandyism were rife.[164] He vividly describes the fashions popular among the nobility. The men

> insert their toes, the extremities of their bodies, into things similar to serpent's tails, which look like scorpions. Sweeping the dusty ground with the prodigious trains of their robes and mantles, they cover their hands with gloves too wide and long for useful employment, and encumbered with these superfluities, lose the use of their limbs. Their brows are bare like rogues, while at the back of their heads they cultivate long hair like whores.... Their locks are curled with hot irons, and instead of wearing caps, they bind their heads with fillets.[165]

Orderic attributes the introduction under William Rufus of pulley-shoes to the fact that Fulk count of Anjou had bunions and, to disguise the deformity had special shoes made with long, pointed toes.[166]

Both Eadmer and William of Malmesbury had, like Orderic, close connections with the historiographical tradition at Worcester. It seems likely that Worcester served as a clearing-house for the works of all three authors.[167] Orderic may have used Eadmer's *Historia Novorum* (he certainly knew the *Life of St. Anselm*[168]). This is suggested by the fact that

---

[160] *OV*, x. 18 (vol. 4, p. 109).

[161] *OV*, viii. 8 (vol. 3, pp. 310 et seq.); x. 18 (vol. 4, pp. 107–10).

[162] For Orderic's knowledge of, and attitude to Flambard, see R. W. Southern ,'Ranulf Flambard and early Anglo-Norman administration' in *TRHS*, 4th series, xvi (1933), pp. 99–100, 106–10. Cf. H. S. Offler, 'Rannulf Flambard as Bishop of Durham' in *Durham University Journal*, lxiv (1971), pp. 14–25 *passim*.

[163] See the sermon which Orderic records that the bishop of Séez preached before Henry I condemning court fashions; *OV*, xi. 11 (vol. 4, pp. 207–10).

[164] *OV*, viii. 10 (vol. 3, pp. 323–6).   [165] *OV*, viii. 10 (vol. 3, pp. 324–5).

[166] *OV*, viii. 10 (vol. 3, p. 323).

[167] Professor David Knowles, *The Monastic Order in England* (2nd ed., Cambridge 1963), p. 80, notes that the passages in Orderic quoted on p. 158 and nn. 170–3 below resemble passages by Eadmer and William of Malmesbury. Dr Chibnall, *OV*, vol. 2, pp. xxiv–xxv, comments that Orderic and William of Malmesbury treat a number of themes 'in a similar way', but concludes that on the present evidence no direct borrowing by either author can be proved, though they obviously used common sources.

[168] See Chibnall, *OV*, vol. 2, p. xvii.

Orderic justifies the Norman Conquest in the same way as Eadmer, by emphasizing the reformation which it brought about in the church.[169] There is also one similarity in detail: Orderic asserts that the English monks before the Conquest could hardly be distinguished from seculars;[170] and Eadmer claims that Lanfranc raised the monks of Christ Church, Canterbury, 'from the secular life in which he found them too much engrossed'.[171] Orderic may have known Eadmer's *Life of St. Dunstan* which makes this point with even more force[172] (the same statement, with a wider reference to include all English monks, is in William of Malmesbury's *Gesta Pontificum*[173]).

A number of passages by Orderic resemble parts of William of Malmesbury's *Gesta Regum*. Orderic could have used both the *Gesta Regum* and the *Gesta Pontificum*: William wrote them in 1125, and Orderic wrote the relevant sections of the *Ecclesiastical History*, that is Books IV and IX (where the passages occur), in 1125 and 1135 respectively. But there is no proof of direct borrowing, for though the gist of the passages is the same in both authors, the words are not. Therefore Orderic and William may have drawn on the same source which is now unknown. The passages concerned relate to Harold's oath to Duke William,[174] to the decayed state of monasticism in England before the Norman Conquest and its revival afterwards,[175] to the degenerate morals of pre-Conquest Englishmen,[176] and to the warlike character of the Normans.[177] Some of these passages, and others,

[169] This is the argument in *OV*, iv. 6 (vol. 2, p. 208 et seq.). For Eadmer see p. 137 above.

[170] *OV*, iv. 6 (vol. 2, p. 208); 'Per longum itaque retro tempus transmarinorum monachatus deciderat, et parum a saecularitate conversatio monachorum differebat.'

[171] Eadmer, *HN*, p. 12; 'a saeculari vita, in qua illos invenit plus aequo versari.'

[172] *Memorials SD*, p. 236; the monks of Christ Church 'Quos a tempore Danorum qui beatum Ælfegum occiderunt, cessante disciplina, in saeculari videbat conversatione ultra quam debebant jacere': ibid., pp. 237–8; they 'more comitum potius quam monachorum vitam agebant'. Cf. pp. 130–1 above.

[173] WM, *GP*, i. 44 (p. 70); 'Monachi Cantuarienses, sicut omnes tunc temporis in Anglia, secularibus haud absimiles erant, nisi quod pudicitiam non facile proderent.'

[174] *OV*, iii. 11 (vol. 2, p. 117); Cf. WM, *GR*, ii. 228 (vol. 1, pp. 279–80); iii. 238 (vol. 1, p. 298).

[175] *OV*, iv. 6 (vol. 2, p. 208); 'Destructis monasteriis monastica religio debilitata est, et canonicus rigor usque ad Normannorum tempora reparatus non est. Per longum [see n. 170 above] . . . differebat. Habitu fallebant ac professionis vocabulo, dediti ganeae, peculiis innumeris, foedisque praevaricationibus. Hic itaque ordo Guillelmi regis instinctu ad instituta regularia corrigebatur, ac ad consuetudines beatificas perductas valde honorabatur.' Cf. WM, *GR*, iii. 245 (vol. 2, pp. 304–6 *passim*); 'Monachi, subtilibus indumentis et indifferenti genere ciborum, regulam ludificabant . . . religionis normam, usquequaque in Anglia amortuam, adventu suo [Normanni] suscitarunt'.

[176] *OV*, iv. 6 (vol. 2, p. 208); Danish attacks weakened government in England and therefore: 'Huiuscemodi dissolutio clericos et laicos relaxaverat, et utrumque sexum ad omnem lasciviam inclinaverat. Abundantia cibi et potus luxuriem nutriebat, levitas et mollities gentis in flagitium quemquam facile impellebat.' Cf. *GR*, iii. 245–6 (vol. 2, p. 305); 'Optimates, gulae et veneri dediti, ecclesiam more Christiano mane non adibant; sed in cubiculo, et inter uxorios amplexus, matutinarum sollempnia et missarum a festinante presbytero auribus tantum libabant. . . . Illud erat a natura abhorrens, quod multi ancillas suas ex se gravidas, ubi libidini satisfecissent, aut ad publicum prostibulum aut ad externum obsequium venditabant. Potabatur in commune ab omnibus, in hoc studio noctes perinde ut dies perpetuantibus.'

[177] *OV*, ix. 3 (vol. 3, p. 474); 'Indomita gens Normannorum est, et, nisi rigido rectore coerceatur, ad facinus promptissima est. In omnibus collegiis, ubicumque fuerint, dominari appetunt, et

have parallels in the *Historia Anglorum* of Henry of Huntingdon (these will be discussed on pp. 198–9). Moreover, there are parallels between Orderic and William of Malmesbury's *Historia Novella*; these, too, will be dealt with later (pp. 198–9 and nn. 124, 125).

Orderic was also influenced by the Norman historians,[178] particularly by William of Poitiers.[179] His literary style is far more polished than that of his English contemporaries. He has many allusions to the classics[180] and himself wrote verse.[181] Like William of Poitiers he tries to enhance the glory of the Norman race by connecting its origins with classical antiquity.[182] He gives Roman derivations to Norman place-names: for example he claims that Rouen was so called from 'Rodomus' which meant (he asserts) 'house of the Romans'.[183]

Orderic's reiterations of the theme that all earthly achievements are ephemeral is also reminiscent of William of Poitiers.[184] He uses it to reinforce the edificatory purpose of the work, asserting that the human spirit is guided to virtue by the study of past and contemporary events (which is sometimes the only way of understanding the present).[185] He draws the moral from the death of William the Conqueror: he who had once been so powerful and successful lay naked in death, robbed and deserted by those whom he had fed and enriched, his rotting corpse a witness to the end of his worldly glory.[186] Sometimes Orderic uses a simile to illustrate his point: both records of the past and its physical remains are destroyed by political vicissitudes 'like hail and snows in the waters of a rapid river';[187] divine justice teaches men by misfortune and when they are cleansed it rewards them 'just as the weather becomes fair after a storm'.[188] He also mentions

---

veritatis fideique tenorem praevaricantes, ambitionis aestu, multoties effecti sunt.' Cf. *GR*, iii. 246 (vol. 2, p. 306); 'Porro Normanni ... gens militiae assueta, et sine bello pene vivere nescia; in hostem impigre procurrere, et ubi vires non successissent, non minus dolo et pecunia currumpere ... paribus invidere, superiores praetergredi velle, subjectos sibi vellicantes ab alienis tutari; dominis fideles, moxque levi offensa infideles.' Both writers comment, in different ways, on the warlike and barbaric nature of the north-country people; *OV*, iv. 4 (vol. 2, p. 184), and *GP*, iii, prologue (p. 209).

[178] Orderic interpolated a copy of the chronicle of William of Jumièges; see *GND*, pp. xi–xii, xxxiii–xxxv. The manuscript with Orderic's autograph additions is reproduced by Madame Lair, *Matériaux pour l'édition de Guillaume de Jumièges préparée par Jules Lair avec une préface et des notes par Léopold Delisle. Manuscrits autographes d'Orderic Vital. Manuscrit original de Robert de Torigni* (Paris 1910). For Orderic's autograph of the *Ecclesiastical History*, see p. 165 and n. 243 below.

[179] See Chibnall, *OV*, vol. 2, pp. xviii, xx–xxi, xxiii, xxxii, xxxiv.

[180] See Delisle in *OV*, vol. 5, p. xxxix.

[181] See *OV*, vi. 8; viii. 3 (vol. 3, pp. 46, 287–9).

[182] *OV*, iv. 8 (vol. 2, p. 229); ix. 3 (vol. 3, p. 474).

[183] *OV*, v. 6 (vol. 2, p. 324). For a similar derivation for Illebone see *OV*, xii. 23 (vol. 4, pp. 396–7).

[184] See e.g. *OV*, ix. 1 (vol. 3, p. 457). Cf. p. 100 above.

[185] *OV*, vi. 1 (vol. 3, pp. 1–2).

[186] *OV*, vii. 16 (vol. 3, pp. 249–50). Cf. pp. 93–4 above.

[187] *OV*, vi. 9 (vol. 3, p. 68).

[188] *OV*, viii. 24 (vol. 3, p. 420).

the wheel of fortune – 'fickle fortune is daily rotated'.[189] Such earthly vicissitudes are ordained by God to teach mankind.[190] Nothing remains of men's efforts except sometimes written records of them.[191] Orderic gives this orthodox medieval view a particular application. He says that the Norman nobility were wise to endow monasteries because they could take nothing with them beyond the grave. Their souls would benefit from the good act, and also from the prayers of the monks.[192]

But Orderic's work cannot be wholly interpreted in terms of the influences which helped to shape it. Orderic was a scholar with a lively, original mind, and he produced a very individual book. His personality is reflected in his work. He was a man of strong feelings, retaining his affection for his family though he lived abroad.[193] He was devout and wrote primarily for the glory of God.[194] He did not find writing easy (he complains of the labour, the cold and the lack of scribes[195]), but did not stop until, 'worn out by age and infirmity, he was in the sixty-seventh year of a life spent in the service of Christ'.[196]

The *Ecclesiastical History* shows that Orderic was very learned, well read in the literary sources of history. He used about fifty literary sources,[197] besides documentary and oral evidence. He acquired some of his material at St Évroul, using the library and archives there and questioning visitors. He was particularly helped by the abbey's contacts with other Benedictine houses. For example English monks came to stay at St Évroul (Orderic obtained a Life of St William from a monk, Anthony, from Winchester[198]). St Évroul had close connections with Sta Eufemia, an abbey in southern Italy founded by Robert Guiscard and colonized by monks from St Évroul: Orderic derived much of his information about the Normans in south Italy from this source.[199]

[189] *OV*, viii. 24 (vol. 3, p. 416); 'En volubilis fortuna quotidie rotatur, et mundi status variabiliter agitatur.' For parallels in William of Malmesbury and Henry of Huntingdon, see pp. 183, 199 below.

[190] *OV*, ix. 1 (vol. 3, p. 457); xiii. 27 (vol. 5, pp. 77–8).

[191] *OV*, xiii. 27 (vol. 5, pp. 77–8).   [192] *OV*, vi. 8 (vol. 3, pp. 48–50).

[193] For references to his father and family, see *OV*, iv. 7; v. 14 (vol. 2, pp. 220, 416–22 *passim*); xiii. 44 (vol. 5, p. 134). The strength of Orderic's family feeling is perhaps indicated by a comment he makes on the wreck of the White Ship: he says that he inserts a list of the dead from feelings of piety alone 'quoniam tetra vorago neminem absorbuit de mea consanguinitate, cui lacrymas affectu sanguinis effundam, nisi ex sola pietate'; *OV*, xii. 25 (vol. 4, p. 419).

[194] *OV*, i, prologue (vol. 1, p. 5). Cf. vi. 10 (vol. 3, p. 83); 'Ecce vitam sancti patris Ebrulfi veraciter descripsi, eamque . . . idcirco huic opusculo diligenter inserui, ut legentibus prosit tanti notitia patroni, Dominoque Deo placeat meus labor et affectus, qui satago propalare nutritoris mei gloriosos actus, ad laudem illius in quo vivimus, movemur et sumus.'

[195] On the labour of writing, see *OV*, vi. 10 (vol. 3, p. 134); ix. 1 (vol. 3, pp. 459–60); ix. 18 (vol. 3, p. 624): on the cold, see *OV*, iv. 19 (vol. 2, p. 298); on the shortage of scribes see *OV*, ix. 1 (vol. 3, p. 460).

[196] *OV*, xiii. 44 (vol. 5, p. 133).   [197] See Delisle in *OV*, vol. 5, pp. lxiii–xciii.

[198] *OV*, vi. 3 (vol. 3, p. 5).

[199] See Chibnall, *OV*, vol. 2, p. xxii. For Orderic on the Normans in Sicily, see E. Jamison, 'The Sicilian Norman kingdom in the mind of Anglo-Norman contemporaries' in *Proceedings of the British Academy*, xxiv (1938), pp. 242–7. Cf. p. 163 and n. 225 below.

But (unlike Bede) Orderic did not work only at his desk. He liked travelling. He travelled in Normandy[200] and visited England. He went to France in 1105,[201] in 1119 attended the papal council at Rheims[202] and in 1132 was at a gathering of monks at Cluny.[203] At some unknown date he also visited Cambrai.[204] And wherever Orderic went he accumulated material for his book. He often meticulously specifies the sources of his oral information. For example he writes that he heard the circumstances of the wreck of the White Ship from the sole survivor, 'Berold, a butcher of Rouen . . . the poorest of them all . . . who related all the particulars of the sad event to the crowd of anxious enquirers, and lived afterwards for twenty years in good health.'[205] And he reports the fire in the abbey church at Cluny partly on the evidence of a boy of twelve who saved himself by climbing on the roof.[206]

As a writer, Orderic's most notable characteristics are his untiring interest in and sensitive response to the events of his times. His interests dominate the structure of his work. He did not learn from the English writers how to arrange his material according to subject-matter or in chronological order. Rather he let his interests pursue their bent. He interrupts subjects, repeats himself and digresses. His work has been described as being in 'prodigious confusion'.[207] The result is a very long book, full of vivid detail and unique information but hard to use for reference.

The *Ecclesiastical History* gains cohesion because it reflects Orderic's reasons for writing and his interests. He began the work for the benefit of the novices and monks of St Évroul.[208] But as he proceeded he aimed at a wider audience. At the beginning of Book V he states that he is writing of Norman affairs for the benefit of the people of Normandy.[209] His attack on 'scurrilous critics', who discourage historians so much that they stop writing (to the impoverishment of civilization),[210] presupposes the attention of the literary world. Moreover, he claims that he is writing for posterity.[211]

Therefore the *Ecclesiastical History* has information on St Évroul to please and instruct the community there; it has information on the ecclesiastical and secular history of Normandy for the benefit of all Normans; and it has material to edify and amuse any reader. These aspects will be discussed in turn.

---

[200] See p. 154 and n. 133 above. In 1134 he visited Merleraud, near St Évroul; *OV*, xiii. 16 (vol. 5, pp. 39–40).

[201] *OV*, xi. 15 (vol. 4, p. 215).

[202] Orderic gives a very detailed account of the council; *OV*, xii. 21 (vol. 4, pp. 372–93).

[203] *OV*, xiii. 13 (vol. 5, pp. 29–30).   [204] *OV*, iii. 15 (vol. 2, p. 161).

[205] *OV*, xii. 25 (vol. 4, pp. 414–15).

[206] *OV*, xiii. 16 (vol. 5, p. 42). Nevertheless it is sometimes hard to be certain whether Orderic is using written or oral information; see Chibnall, *OV*, vol. 2, pp. xxii–xxiii.

[207] See Delisle in *OV*, vol. 5, p. xliv.

[208] *OV*, v. 13 (vol. 2, p. 400); cf. v. 14 (vol. 2, p. 423).

[209] *OV*, v. 1 (vol. 2, p. 301).   [210] *OV*, vi. 1 (vol. 3, p. 2).

[211] e.g. *OV*, i, prologue (vol. 1, pp. 2–3).

Orderic hoped to improve the *esprit de corps* of the inmates of St Évroul by telling them about the abbey. Much of the material relating to St Évroul is in Book III (originally Book I). Orderic records its history to his own times. He has information about relics and other treasure preserved in the abbey. He mentions, for example, the great illuminated psalter kept in the choir and still in use in his day,[212] and, to add to its interest, he says where it came from. It was given by Queen Emma when wife of King Ethelred to her brother Robert archbishop of Rouen. His son William stole it and gave it to his wife Hawise, the mother of Robert II de Grentemésnil. The latter, who (as will be seen) became abbot of St Évroul, presented the book to the abbey.

Orderic uses his work partly to encourage the monks' labour in the scriptorium. As an object-lesson of an industrious scribe he quotes the example of a monk of St Évroul called William Gregory who was an outstanding scribe and illuminator and 'whose works are still used for reading and chanting'.[213] He describes the contribution which Abbot Thierry (1050–7) made to the enlargement of the library. Thierry not only acquired books but also transcribed them: the abbey's gradual and antiphonary and a book of collects were his work.[214] Thierry ordered monks to copy books and used to tell a story to discourage laziness. He related how there was a sinful monk who was nevertheless an industrious scribe and copied a large volume of canon law. When he died and appeared before God for judgment, his sins were weighed one by one against every letter he had written. The letters just outweighed the sins, so his soul was saved.[215]

To some extent Orderic hoped his book would serve as a useful compendium of knowledge and a guide to study. His detailed descriptions of his sources gave the work a bibliographical value. Orderic draws his readers' attention to two new books, John of Worcester's continuation of Marianus Scotus (which he had seen at Worcester), and Sigebert of Gembloux's chronicle (which he had seen at St Sepulchre's, Cambrai). 'These chronicles', he writes, 'are not yet generally known.'[216] He also copies a legend (concerning the translation of St Nicholas of Myra) from a book by John archdeacon of Bari 'for the information of students who have not yet seen John's book'.[217] This desire to make facts readily available for readers partly accounts for the encyclopaedic quality of the *Ecclesiastical History*.

The record which Orderic preserved of the endowments of St Évroul had a liturgical purpose. He wanted to ensure that the monks prayed for their benefactors. He writes that he enumerated the endowments 'so that the

---

[212] *OV*, iii. 2 (vol. 2, pp. 41–2). For this psalter see Chibnall, *OV*, vol. 2, p. 42 n. 1.

[213] *OV*, iii. 5 (vol. 2, pp. 77–8).   [214] *OV*, iii. 3 (vol. 2, pp. 47–8).

[215] *OV*, iii. 3 (vol. 2, pp. 48–50).

[216] *OV*, iii. 15 (vol. 2, pp. 160–1); 'Haec ideo huic chartae gratis indidi, ut istos codices avidi lectores inquirant sibi, quia magnum sapientiae fructum ferunt et vix inveniri possunt. A modernis enim editi sunt, et adhuc passim per orbem diffusi non sunt.'

[217] *OV*, vii. 12 (vol. 3, p. 205). Orderic also inserts the prophecies of Merlin for those who did not yet know about them; see p. 165 and n. 242 below.

piously given alms should be known to the novices – that they should know who gave the things which they use, and when they were given and their value.'[218] Orderic justifies the detailed account he gives of the abbey's benefactors because 'it is my wish, by means of the written word, to fix firmly in the memory of posterity the history of our founders and their benevolent fellow labourers, so that the children of the church may be mindful before God, in the presence of the angels, of those by whose endowments subsistence is provided for them.'[219] The monks expressed their gratitude by praying for the souls of the benefactors. Orderic calls the readers' attention to the day (26 June) set apart for prayers for them. On that day the mortuary roll was spread out and the names read. This roll also contained the names of the monks' parents and relatives for whom prayers were also said.[220]

Orderic's concern for the benefactors of St Évroul was one reason for the widening of his interests.[221] This was because important members of the Norman nobility were closely associated with the abbey. A co-founder, Robert II de Grentemésnil, became a monk there and was abbot from 1059 to 1061.[222] He was one of the Norman family of Giroie, a number of whose other members endowed St Évroul.[223] Orderic follows the fortunes of the Giroies, sometimes tracing their careers outside Normandy. He describes, for example, the Welsh campaigns of Robert of Rhuddlan, a Giroie by birth and a benefactor of St Évroul.[224] In his account of the Norman conquests in Sicily, Orderic gives prominence to the part played by William of Montreuil, cousin of Robert II de Grentemésnil and a benefactor of St Évroul.[225] He had information which is independent of known literary authorities about Richard I, prince of Capua, presumably because William of Montreuil married Richard's daughter.

The Montgomerys were also benefactors of St Évroul. Orderic's interest in Hugh de Montgomery, earl of Shrewsbury (1094–8), was no doubt reinforced by Odelerius's association with Hugh's father Roger de Montgomery.

---

[218] *OV*, v. 13 (vol. 2, p. 400); 'Possessiones Uticensis ecclesiae volo hic breviter annotare, ut eleemosynae fideliter datae pateant novitiorum notitiae, ut utentes eis sciant a quibus vel quo tempore datae sint vel pretio comparatae.'

[219] *OV*, vi. 8 (vol. 3, p. 47); 'Opto equidem fundatores et benivolos cooperatores eorum scripto commendare tenaci memoriae posterorum, ut filii Ecclesiae coram Deo in conspectu angelorum memores sint eorum, quorum beneficiis in hac mortali vita sustentantur, ad peragendam servitutem conditoris universorum.'

[220] *OV*, iii. 7 (vol. 2, pp. 100–1).

[221] For the progressive expansion of Orderic's theme in Books III and IV see Chibnall, *OV*, vol. 2, pp. xv–xvi.

[222] *OV*, iii. 2, 5 (vol. 2, pp. 40, 68).

[223] For a family tree of the Giroie-Grentemésnils see Wolter, op. cit. (n. 99), at the end of the volume.

[224] *OV*, viii. 3 (vol. 3, pp. 283–7).

[225] William de Montreuil (son of William Giroie) was accompanied by a monk of St Évroul on the Sicilian campaign; *OV*, iii. 3 (vol. 2, pp. 56–7). For Orderic's information on the Normans in Sicily see Chibnall, *OV*, vol. 2, pp. xxii–xxiii, xxx–xxxii. Cf. p. 160 and n. 199 above.

Orderic records Hugh's death in 1098 during an attack by Magnus III of Norway on Anglesey – he uses this as an excuse for a digression on Norwegian history.[226] Interest in the Montgomerys strengthened Orderic's interest in the neighbouring Norman abbeys, for Roger de Montgomery not only endowed St Évroul, but also founded the abbeys of Troarn,[227] St Martin's at Séez,[228] and the nunnery of Almenèches.[229] But it was not only the friends of the abbey of St Évroul who engaged Orderic's attention. He was also interested in its enemies. He records with unwavering hatred the career and ultimate downfall of Robert of Bellême, the pillager and incendiary of the Norman monasteries (including the neighbouring Almenèches[230]).

In this way Orderic's interests radiated from St Évroul. But the expansion of his horizon was not only due to interest in the activities of the benefactors. It was also due to his interest in the Benedictine order, particularly in its revival under Cluniac influence in eleventh-century Normandy and in England after the Norman Conquest. Orderic himself was a convinced Benedictine. He preferred Benedictine moderation to the enthusiasm of the new Orders. Although he admired the Cistercians, he criticized them for preferring their new rules to the traditions of the past.[231] He praised the Cluniacs, but deplored the disorders which followed the deposition of Abbot Pons in 1122[232] and thought their rule became too strict under Abbot Peter.[233] He particularly valued the Benedictine contribution to learning. He records in detail how Abbot Thierry built up a good library at St Évroul,[234] and expresses great admiration for Bec and its eminent monks, notably Lanfranc and Anselm.[235] Orderic's Benedictine outlook coloured his views of England. He bitterly resented the appointment in 1123 of an Augustinian canon (William of Corbeil) to the see of Canterbury. He mentions monastic sees as a distinctive feature of the English church and describes the English as very much attached to monks from the earliest times: he claims that only three archbishops of Canterbury (all of whom were affected by special circumstances) had not been monks.[236] 'But now customs and laws are changed so that monks are oppressed and trodden on, and clerks are honoured.'[237]

Orderic's desire to entertain all his readers is evident throughout the *Ecclesiastical History*.[238] This wish appears in his excellent descriptive

---

[226] *OV*, x. 6 (vol. 4, pp. 26–32).
[227] See e.g. *OV*, iii. 2 (vol. 2, pp. 21–2).
[228] See e.g. *OV*, iii. 3 (vol. 2, pp. 46–7).
[229] Wolter, op. cit., p. 22.
[230] The abbess and some of the nuns took refuge at St Évroul; *OV*, xi. 3 (vol. 4, pp. 179–83).
[231] *OV*, viii. 27 (vol. 3, p. 451).
[232] *OV*, xii. 30 (vol. 4, pp. 423 et seq.).
[233] *OV*, xiii. 13 (vol. 5, pp. 29–30).
[234] See p. 162 above.
[235] *OV*, iv. 6, 10 (vol. 2, pp. 210 et seq., 244 et seq.).
[236] *OV*, xii. 31 (vol. 4, pp. 431–2).
[237] *OV*, xii. 31 (vol. 4, p. 432); 'Nunc autem mores et leges mutatae sunt, et clerici, ut monachos confutent et conculcent, clericos extollunt.'
[238] Orderic often cuts short a subject for fear of boring his readers; see e.g. *OV*, vi. 10 (vol. 3, p. 85); viii. 8 (vol. 3, p. 310); ix. 18 (vol. 3, p. 623).

passages (for example the description cited of court fashion[239]). As a raconteur, few chroniclers equalled him: a particularly good example is the account of the sinking of the White Ship.[240] And he shared with his contemporaries a love of the marvellous. He tells how a pregnant cow was cut open at Ely (at the order of Bishop Hervey) and three piglets found in it: a pilgrim prophesied from this the death of three great people in that year and terrible subsequent catastrophes.[241] Moreover, having read Geoffrey of Monmouth, Orderic inserted the prophecies of Merlin.[242]

If Orderic hoped to be widely read, his hope was frustrated. Only two early manuscripts of the *Ecclesiastical History* are known to have survived. The first is the copy from the library of St Évroul, which was written under Orderic's supervision and is partly in his own handwriting.[243] It has the signs of an early draft. There are corrections affecting the subject-matter, spaces left for additions, passages on erasures and marginal additions. The other medieval copy is from St Stephen's, Caen, and was probably copied from the St Évroul manuscript. It is likely that the later manuscripts of the work, dating from the fifteenth to the eighteenth centuries, all descend from the St Évroul text. The impression that the work was little known outside St Évroul in the middle ages is confirmed by the fact that it was used by only one chronicler of note.[244]

Although Orderic did not become a best-seller, he ranks high as a historian. His work lacks the clear chronological framework of the Worcester chronicle (he gives too few dates). But he has a concept of history, a breadth of vision and a narrative power which the Worcester chronicler cannot equal. Eadmer's *Historia Novorum* is better arranged than Orderic's work, and has the advantage of being a first-hand account. But Eadmer's interests were much narrower and grew progressively more so, while Orderic's vision expanded as time passed. Of Anglo-Norman historians, only William of Malmesbury bears comparison with him.

---

[239] See p. 157 above.   [240] *OV*, xii. 26 (vol. 4, pp. 411–19).

[241] *OV*, xii. 1 (vol. 4, pp. 312–13).

[242] *OV*, xii. 47 (vol. 4, pp. 486–94). The mid-twelfth century catalogue of books in the St Évroul library does not list a copy of Geoffrey of Monmouth's *Historia Regum Britanniae* (for this catalogue see Delisle in *OV*, vol. 5, pp. vii–xi). There was a copy at Bec which was used by Robert of Torigni and Henry of Huntingdon (see p. 200 below. For Geoffrey, see pp. 201 et seq. below, and for Orderic's use of his work see J. S. P. Tatlock, *The Legendary History of Britain* . . . (Berkeley and Los Angeles 1950), pp. 418–21).

[243] This manuscript of the *Ecclesiastical History* is now in the Bibliothèque Nationale: Anciens fonds latins no. 4207 D (Colbert 3761) containing the prologue and Books I and II; Anciens fonds latins no. 4702 E (Colbert 3762) containing Books III–VI; Supplément latin no. 1135 containing Book VII (beginning only) and Books IX–XIII. For a reproduction of a page in Orderic's hand see Plate IV. For a reference to another autograph of Orderic see p. 159 n. 178 above. The annals of St Évroul are also partly in his hand; they are described by Delisle in *OV*, vol. 5, pp. lxviii–lxx. For Orderic's autographs see also Chibnall, *OV*, vol. 2, pp. xxxix–xl. The other medieval manuscript of the *Ecclesiastical History* is Vatican MS. fonds de la reine de Suède no. 703; see Delisle in *OV*, vol. 5, p. xciii et seq.

[244] Robert of Torigni derived some of his additions to Sigebert of Gembloux from Orderic; see *OV*, vol. 5, p. lix.

9

William of Malmesbury

The abbey of Malmesbury in Wiltshire had an undistinguished history except for a brief period of fame, roughly the first half of the twelfth century, during which the romanesque church (with its remarkable sculptured friezes of biblical history and of the apostles in the south porch) was built, and William of Malmesbury was a monk there. Before that time the level of culture was low, and after it the monks relapsed into mediocrity, scarcely remembering the work of their greatest brother.[1]

According to tradition, the abbey was founded by an Irish monk, Meildub, and St Aldhelm in the seventh century.[2] During the Danish invasions the community became secularized and was not revived as a monastery until the tenth century when St Dunstan replaced the secular clerks with monks. The 'renaissance' at Malmesbury was started by Abbot Godfrey who ruled 1087 × 91–?1105 and was the founder of the monastic library. William of Malmesbury, born in 1095 or a little earlier, of prosperous parents, one Norman and the other English,[3] became an oblate early in life. As a child he helped Abbot Godfrey in the library and later as librarian he continued the abbot's work with enthusiasm and success.[4] The library was the basis of his learning. Like Bede, William was a polymath, a student of the scriptures, hagiography, theology, the classics, and civil and canon law.[5]

But it was as a historian that William became famous. He started to write

---

[1] The *Eulogium Historiarum* written at Malmesbury in about 1367 is to 1356 a compilation of various well-known authorities, including William of Malmesbury; see *Eulogium Historiarum sive Temporis*, ed. F. S. Haydon (RS, 1858–63, 3 vols), vol. 1, p. xliv.

[2] For the history of Malmesbury abbey see Dom Aelred Watkin in *VCH, Wilts.*, vol. 3, pp. 210–31. One of the sculptures in the south porch is reproduced in A. W. Clapham, *English Romanesque Architecture* (Oxford 1930, 1934, 2 vols), vol. 2, plate 33.

[3] See WM, *GR*, prologue to Book III (vol. 2, p. 283). For an account of William of Malmesbury's life see ibid., vol. 1, pp. xi et seq.

[4] See WM, *GP*, v. 271 (p. 431).

[5] For a list of William's known works see WM, *GR*, vol. 1, pp. cxv et seq. A useful survey of William's various studies is H. Farmer, 'William of Malmesbury's life and work' in *Journal of Ecclesiastical History*, xiii (1962), pp. 39–54. Eight manuscripts on a wide variety of subjects, including his own *Gesta Pontificum* (Vegetius's *De re militari*, Martianus Capella, John Scotus's *De divisione naturae*, the Gospels of St Luke, the works of St Anselm, Bede, canons of the councils, computistical works, etc.), are known which are written in William of Malmesbury's hand. See N. R. Ker, *Medieval Libraries of Great Britain* (2nd ed., Royal Historical Soc., 1964), p. 128 and n. 9; five of the manuscripts are described in detail in N. R. Ker, 'William of Malmesbury's handwriting' in *EHR*, lix (1944), pp. 371–6. See also p. 175 and n. 66 below.

history from personal choice, though possibly under the influence of a tenuous tradition of historical writing at Malmesbury. Before he began work, historical notes covering the years from 1064 to 1139 were entered on a decemnovenalian table in the abbey.[6] Moreover, he may well have been inspired by the historiographical tradition of Evesham abbey,[7] thirty-six miles away, and more especially by that of Worcester, forty-four miles away (his acquaintance with historical activity at Worcester is shown by the fact that he translated Coleman's *Life of Wulfstan*).[8] William's historical works were the *Gesta Regum Anglorum* (*Deeds of the Kings of the English*),[9] a history of England from the coming of the Saxons to 1120; the *Gesta Pontificum Anglorum* (*Deeds of the Archbishops and Bishops of the English*),[10] an ecclesiastical history of England from the Conversion to 1125; the *Historia Novella* (*Recent History*),[11] a history of England from 1128 to 1142; and an institutional history, the *De Antiquitate Glastoniensis Ecclesiae* (*On the Antiquity of the Church of Glastonbury*).[12] One of William's hagiographies, the *Life of St. Dunstan*,[13] also contains historical material.

As a historian William deserves his reputation for two reasons: he occupies an important place in the development of historical method, and his works are repositories of information and views of value to the historian today. William was the first man since Bede to produce a corpus of historical works. He absorbed both the Anglo-Saxon and the Anglo-Norman traditions of historiography, adding his own individual genius. From the resultant amalgam he produced the second secular national history, as distinct from an ecclesiastical history, to be written in England in literary form (Æthelweard's chronicle was the first). And he was the first historian in England to make extensive use of topography and ancient monuments as historical sources. To the historian today William is important because some of the sources he

---

[6] MS. Auct. F. 3. 14 (treatises on the calendar) in the Bodleian Library, Oxford, ff. 120 b^r to 120 c^v. The historical notes are printed, and collated with corresponding passages in the *Gesta Regum* and the *Gesta Pontificum*, by W. H. Stevenson, 'A contemporary description of the Domesday survey' in *EHR*, xxii (1907), pp. 81–2. At least one note, a record of the length of Henry I's reign at the foot of f. 120 b^v, is probably in William's handwriting; see Ker, 'William of Malmesbury's handwriting', p. 375.

[7] William used a collection of stories on the miracles of the Virgin Mary by Dominic of Evesham for his own *Miracles of the Virgin*; see Farmer, 'William of Malmesbury', p. 51. Cf. p. 171 n. 35 below.

[8] See p. 87 and n. 156.

[9] The standard edition is *Willelmi Malmesbiriensis Monachi de Gestis Regum Anglorum Libri Quinque*, ed. W. Stubbs (RS, 1887–9, 2 vols). For an English translation see J. A. Giles, *William of Malmesbury's Chronicle of the Kings of England* (Bohn's Antiquarian Library, London 1866).

[10] The standard edition is *Willelmi Malmesbiriensis Monachi de Gestis Pontificum Anglorum Libri Quinque*, ed. N. E. S. A. Hamilton (RS, 1870).

[11] The most recent edition is *The Historia Novella by William of Malmesbury*, ed., with an English translation, K. R. Potter (Nelson's Medieval Texts, 1955).

[12] Printed in *Adami de Domerham Historia de Rebus Gestis Glastoniensibus*, ed. T. Hearne (Oxford 1727, 2 vols), vol. i, pp. 1–122.

[13] Printed in *Memorials SD*, pp. 250–324.

used for the Anglo-Saxon period are now lost, and particularly because he wrote a first-rate contemporary account of the early years of King Stephen's reign. William increased the popularity of historical studies in the monasteries. His works were widely read by monks, and much copied. The fact that they survive in a comparatively great number of early copies has had an important result. Collation of the manuscripts has made it possible to trace William's development as a historian. For the first time an English historian can be seen at work, revising his writings as his views changed.

William was on the whole conscientious. He had weighed carefully the historian's duty: it was, as he saw it, to record the truth, as far as it could be discovered, about important people and events,[14] without fear or favour, clothing it in literary form,[15] for the edification[16] and amusement of his audience.[17] As will be seen, he showed considerable critical acumen. However, William had shortcomings. He was a product of his age, and when discussing monastic origins could fall far short of his scholarly ideals. He felt obliged to 'prove' the great antiquity of Malmesbury and Glastonbury: to do this he sometimes made uncritical use of legend and he copied forged charters.

William's career as a historian divides into two phases, separated from each other by about ten years which he spent on other studies. Each has distinctive features. The first was William's most creative period. It was short, lasting about a year, 1125, and to it belong his most ambitious works on past history, the *Gesta Regum* and the *Gesta Pontificum*. William's second historiographical period was longer, lasting from 1135 to 1143, the year of his death. It seems that the creative urge had left him, for revision, short monographs and contemporary reportage are the distinguishing features of this phase. He revised the *Gesta Regum* twice and the *Gesta Pontificum* once, to embody the alterations in his opinions worked by the passing years. And he wrote the *De Antiquitate Glastoniensis Ecclesiae* and the *Life of St. Dunstan*. Three years before he died, he started his one important excursion into contemporary history, writing the *Historia Novella* probably until his last illness – he left the work unfinished.

The historical works will be considered from two points of view. First,

---

[14] For emphasis on the necessity of truth see especially *GR*, i. 49 (vol. 1, 53); prologue to Book IV (vol. 2, pp. 357–8); v. 445 (vol. 2, p. 518). Cf. *HN*, prologue (p. 1); 524 (p. 77). William cites documents *verbatim* to keep near the truth: see *GR*, i. 29; ii. 173 (vol. 1, pp. 30, 203); *GP*, i. 28 (p. 44). For his dislike of panegyric when it distorted the truth see his attack on David the Scot's (now lost) history of the struggle between Henry V and the papacy; *GR*, iv. 420, 426 (vol. 2, pp. 498–9, 502).

[15] For the importance William attached to literary style see p. 175 and nn. 73–5 below. He praises the elegant style of Goscelin and Eadmer: *GR*, iv. 342 (vol. 2, p. 389); *GP*, i. 45 (p. 74), respectively.

[16] For the intention to edify see *GR*, i. 71 (vol. 1, p. 74); prologue to Book II (vol. 1, p. 103); prologue to Book IV (vol. 2, p. 358). Cf. *GP*, prologue to Book I (p. 4) and *HN*, prologue (p. 1).

[17] For the intention to amuse, see *GR*, vol. 2, pp. xc–xci, and *GP*, prologue to Book I (p. 4). William often expresses the fear that he may bore his readers: *GR*, i. 47 (vol. 1, p. 47); *GP*, i. 40 (p. 62); v. 187 (p. 331). Cf. *HN*, prologue (p. 1).

the specific literary influences which helped to shape William's work will be dealt with. Second, William's own individual contribution to the development of historical writing and the value of his works as sources to the historian today will be discussed in two sections corresponding with his two periods of historiographical activity.

William was the self-appointed successor to Bede, aiming to fill the gap in literary historiography left after Bede's death until his own day. He recognized Bede as the only 'professional' historian of Anglo-Saxon times.[18] The influence of Bede on him is very evident. Together the *Gesta Regum* and *Gesta Pontificum* are similar in scope to the *Ecclesiastical History*, and like it they are arranged according to provincial divisions, not strictly chronologically. Especially the *Gesta Pontificum* shows a similar devotion to commemorating the acts of native saints; and the history of Malmesbury abbey incorporated in Book V has some parallel in the *History of the Abbots of Wearmouth and Jarrow*. William's treatment of his sources resembles Bede's: he begins the *Gesta Regum* with a review of them reminiscent of the preface to the *Ecclesiastical History*, and elsewhere he weighs the merits of literary authorities.[19] He was, like Bede, tireless in the search for evidence. He used the works of nearly all the historians, biographers and hagiographers of the Anglo-Saxon period, and many of those of his own generation written both in England and on the continent.[20] And like Bede he searched for archive material.

William was also strongly influenced by the Anglo-Saxon biographical tradition. He used Asser's *Life of King Alfred* (either directly or indirectly[21]), the now lost Life of King Athelstan and the *Life of King Edward* (but not the *Encomium Emmae*). He used the Lives of the tenth-century monastic reformers, and he knew the works of the Anglo-Norman hagiographers of his own time – Goscelin, Coleman, Osbern and Eadmer. The influence of the hagiographers is plainly seen in the numerous Lives of saints he included in the *Gesta Pontificum* and in his own hagiographies.[22] The Life of St Aldhelm, co-founder of Malmesbury abbey, which William wrote as Book V (the last book) of the *Gesta Pontificum*, is reminiscent of hagiographies written in

---

[18] *GR*, prologue to Book I (vol. 1, p. 2).

[19] e.g. he praises the learning and wisdom of Bede and Alcuin, and estimates the relative value of Bede and Eddius as authorities of Wilfrid's life: prologue to Book I (vol. 1, p. 1); i. 57, 66 (vol. 1, pp. 61–2, 68–9); *GP*, prologue to Book III (p. 210).

[20] For a list of his sources see *GR*, vol. 1, pp. xx–xxi. Stubbs does not here list William of Poitiers, but see p. 170 and n. 26 below.

[21] It has been thought that William of Malmesbury only knew the *Life of King Alfred* through the extracts in 'Florence of Worcester'. However, Professor Whitelock suggests that he knew the work itself, or at least an abbreviated version of it; see D. Whitelock, 'William of Malmesbury on the works of King Alfred' in *Medieval Literature and Civilization: Studies in Memory of G. N. Garmonsway* (London 1969), pp. 91–3.

[22] For William's hagiographies of saints connected with Glastonbury see *GR*, vol. 1, pp. cxvii–cxx.

the Anglo-Saxon tradition – William used the Life as a vehicle for the abbey's history.

It is likely that the influence on William of the Anglo-Saxon biographical tradition extended even further. It may have given him the idea of dividing the historical work of his first period into secular and ecclesiastical history. As has been seen, some Anglo-Saxon biographers were familiar with the technique of arranging their books according to subject-matter.[23] A king's public acts were discussed in one section, his character in another; a saint's youth was described in one part, his later life in another, and his miracles in a third section. Eadmer's work on St Anselm was the most perfect example of such a division according to subject: here the two parts were entirely separate, forming two distinct books. Such an arrangement could well have suggested to William the advantages of treating secular history distinct from ecclesiastical history (though in fact the *Gesta Regum* overlaps the *Gesta Pontificum* to some extent, having much information on church affairs).

However, William's main incentive to writing secular narrative history came from the continent. He was interested in the history of Europe as a whole, asserting that it would be wrong to neglect the affairs of England's continental neighbours, because England was a part of Europe.[24] He was therefore receptive of continental influence and absorbed the continental tradition of courtly historiography. He was well acquainted with the works of William of Jumièges and William of Poitiers. He was probably following their example when he adopted the title *Gesta* and built his history of England from the last half of the eleventh century around biographies of the kings. Like William of Jumièges[25] and William of Poitiers[26] he tended to eulogize the principal characters (though he could also be bitterly critical – especially of William Rufus). He attributed piety and chastity to the Conqueror.[27] Despite his subsequent dislike of Rufus, he begins the account of the reign with a eulogy on his prowess in arms.[28] And he asserts that divine portents heralded the death of both the Conqueror and Rufus.[29]

The influence of Suetonius on William of Malmesbury was strong. This reached him directly, through reading the *Lives of the Caesars*, and indirectly, through his use of William of Poitiers (who was indebted to Suetonius[30]) and of the English secular biographies, Asser and the *Life of King Edward* – and perhaps through his use of the ecclesiastical biographies by Coleman and

---

[23] See pp. 51–2, 56, 60, 132 above.
[24] See *GR*, i. 67 (vol. 1, p. 69), and the dedicatory letter to Robert earl of Gloucester at the end of Book III (vol. 2, p. 356).
[25] For William's use of William of Jumièges see *GR*, vol. 1, p. xxi.
[26] For William's use of William of Poitiers see *GR*, vol. 2, p. cxi.
[27] *GR*, iii. 267, 273 (vol. 2, pp. 326, 331).
[28] *GR*, iv. 305 (vol. 2, p. 359). For an adverse estimate of his character see *GR*, iv. 312 et seq. (vol. 2, pp. 366 et seq.).
[29] *GR*, iii. 272 (vol. 2, p. 331); iv. 332–3 (vol. 2, pp. 377–8).
[30] See p. 100 above. For William of Malmesbury's debt to Suetonius see Marie Schütt, 'The literary form of William of Malmesbury's "Gesta Regum"' in *EHR*, xlvi (1931), pp. 255–60.

Eadmer. William compares the Conqueror with Julius Caesar[31] and adopts the Suetonian technique of illustrating facets of character with trivial anecdotes. For example he tells a story to illustrate William Rufus's extravagance and lack of business sense. The king severely reprimanded his chamberlain for buying him a pair of boots at a low price – 'Three shillings,' he exclaimed angrily. 'You son of a whore, since when has the king worn such a cheap pair of boots? Go and bring me a pair worth a silver mark.'[32]

Like Suetonius, William gives detailed character-sketches of the ruler towards the end of the account of the reign.[33] Here the secular biographers of the Anglo-Saxon period were his precursors. He also gives concrete, vivid descriptions of the kings' physical appearances. The author of the *Life of King Edward* had described the appearance of Edward the Confessor, but William's model for his pen-portraits was Suetonius. His descriptions are in the Suetonian style and have verbal echoes of the descriptions of the Caesars. Like Suetonius, William treated the subject of his description objectively and so was unflattering where apposite. He writes of the Conqueror: 'he was of noble height, immensely fat, and his forehead bare of hair'; Rufus was 'squarely built, had a florid complexion and yellow hair, an open countenance and different-coloured eyes, varied with glittering specks; he was of astonishing strength, though not very tall, and had a protruding stomach'; Henry I was of 'medium stature, taller than a short man but shorter than a tall one. He had black hair, receding at the forehead, mild, bright eyes, a brawny chest and a fat body.'[34]

Suetonius wrote to amuse, not to edify, and though William wrote partly to edify he also tried to please. His desire to entertain was encouraged by contemporary foreign influences, which help to account for the secular, in places gay, almost frivolous, tone of the *Gesta Regum*. This is particularly apparent in the good stories William copied from some now lost German source. Most of the stories relate to Gerbert and to the Emperor Henry III.[35] They were obviously intended to entertain the reader: Bishop Stubbs suggests that William included them in order to float the heavier portions of his narrative.[36] It is hard to account for their presence otherwise, as some are hardly edifying. Two stories tend to demonstrate the rewards of immorality:

---

[31] See *GR*, iii. 254 (vol. 2, p. 312); iv. 320 (vol. 2, p. 374). For a reference to Caesar's *Gallic War* see *GR*, iii. 239 (vol. 2, p. 301).

[32] *GR*, iv. 313 (vol. 2, p. 368).

[33] For William the Conqueror see *GR*, iii. 279–80 (vol. 2, pp. 335–6); for William Rufus see *GR*, iv. 312–21 *passim* (vol. 2, pp. 366–74 *passim*); the character-sketch of Henry I comes before the end of the reign; *GR*, v. 411–12 (vol. 2, pp. 486–8).

[34] *GR*, iii. 279; iv. 321; v. 412 (vol. 2, pp. 335, 374, 488). For descriptions of two churchmen by William in the same style see that of Wulfstan bishop of Worcester in *VW*, p. 46, and of Thomas I archbishop of York in *GP*, ii. 116 (p. 257). Cf. R. W. Southern, *St. Anselm and his Biographer* (Cambridge 1963), p. 327 n. 1.

[35] For these legends see *GR*, vol. 2, pp. lxvi–xci. For the collection of stories on the Virgin Mary which William made late in life see R. W. Southern, 'The place of England in the twelfth-century renaissance' in *History*, xlv (1960), pp. 211–12. Cf. p. 147 above.

[36] See *GR*, vol. 2, pp. xc–xci.

a German clerk who becomes the lover of a princess is given a bishopric to lead him back to virtue;[37] another German clerk is rewarded with a bishopric because he refuses to celebrate mass after a night with his mistress.[38] Some of the stories lack even a distorted moral purpose; for example, there is the tale of a German noble being devoured by mice.[39] Lust, bastardy and gluttony are the favourite themes – William's humour almost anticipates Rabelais.

During his first historiographical period, William was not impressed by the Anglo-Saxon Chronicle. He apparently regarded it as a crude sort of record, hardly deserving to be called history.[40] He was conscious of the problems inherent in writing such contemporary history – the mass of undigested material and the danger of offending living people.[41] He admits that owing to his isolation from centres of affairs he lacked complete information on current events and could not see them, or the personalities of his time, in perspective. And because rumours spread news, he was afraid of boring people by telling them what they already knew. So he decided to select information, trying to fill gaps in common knowledge.

Therefore the *Gesta Regum* and *Gesta Pontificum* are about past history and William made little attempt to bring them up to date. Their literary form made it difficult to add recent news – there was no chronological framework into which to fit it. He partially kept the episcopal succession in the *Gesta Pontificum* up to date by adding names of recently appointed bishops in the margins.[42] His hesitant attitude to contemporary history helps to explain the disappointingly slight account of Henry I's reign in the *Gesta Regum*.[43] And he never continued the latter beyond 1120 although he intended to: he asked readers to send him additional information, promising to insert it in the margins,[44] and later claimed to have continued the work to 1128.[45]

Despite the fact that William borrowed annals from the Anglo-Saxon Chronicle for the *Gesta Regum*,[46] the Chronicle's annalistic type of contemporary historiography had no influence on him at this time. But in his second historiographical period the case was different. Then he turned to contemporary history and wrote it up in annalistic form. He recorded the events of Henry I's reign in 'three little books which I have called chronicles':[47] this work is now lost. He wrote a short account of Henry I's reign

---

[37] *GR*, ii. 190 (vol. 1, pp. 231–2).   [38] *GR*, ii. 191 (vol. 1, pp. 232–3).
[39] *GR*, iii. 290 (vol. 2, p. 344).   [40] See *GR*, prologue to Book I (vol. 1, p. 1).
[41] For William's views on contemporary history see *GR*, prologue to Book V (vol. 2, pp. 465–6).
[42] For marginal notices of the succession of bishops see *GP*, iv. 169 (pp. 304 and n. 2, 305); iv. 174 (pp. 310 and n. 8, 311). The death of Thurstan archbishop of York, on 6 February 1140, is also noticed in the margin; *GP*, iii. 125 (p. 266 and n. 2).
[43] For William's failure as a historian of Henry I's reign see Stubbs's comments; *GR*, vol. 2, pp. cxxxv–cxxxvi.
[44] See *GR*, prologue to Book II (vol. 1, p. 104).
[45] *GR*, v. 446 (vol. 2, p. 518 and n. 4).
[46] See *GR*, vol. 1, p. xx.   [47] See *HN*, prologue (p. 1).

from 1126, and a detailed account of Stephen's reign to 1142 in the *Historia Novella*, which like the Anglo-Saxon Chronicle comprises factual entries in strictly chronological order.

One result of the mixture of English and continental influences on William's historiography was an ambivalent attitude to the Anglo-Saxons. In general he considered them unwarlike, accusing them of effeminacy, lust, gluttony, drunkenness, laxity in religious observance, and meanness in their dwellings.[48] He contrasted them with the Normans, outstanding for their military skill and bravery, notable for their pride and ambition, and the inhabitants of magnificent buildings.[49] The English defeat at Hastings was due, William writes, to the Anglo-Saxons' lack of military ability, combined with their impetuous rashness.[50] And yet a few pages earlier he had praised the heroic resistance of the far outnumbered English soldiers and extolled the stand made by Harold and his brothers, only defeated by death.[51]

The main purpose of the *Gesta Pontificum* was to commemorate the Anglo-Saxon saints. This was partly because William, as a successor of Bede, wanted to remedy the lack of English hagiographies for the saints living after Bede's day: Bede had recorded the lives of the early saints; William intended to record the lives of the later ones. Like Bede he thought that saints had a universal and eternal right to reverence. And like both Gildas and Bede he found the theme of the good old days useful for exhorting men to mend their ways.[52] But he was not prepared to disparage the Normans of his own day by contrasting their paucity of saints with the Anglo-Saxons' plenty. Therefore he claimed that the Normans had famous saints too – though his account of them is meagre beside his account of the Anglo-Saxon ones.[53]

William of Malmesbury's historiography cannot be interpreted solely in terms of the literary influences on it. He was a gifted writer and a highly intelligent historian, responsive to the problems of his own times, with views and methods of his own.

His ambivalent attitude to the Anglo-Saxons was not only due to the fact that he used both English and Norman sources. No doubt it was also partly due to his own mixed parentage, half English and half Norman, which must have divided his loyalties. Moreover, his historical objectives were hard to reconcile. On the one hand he wanted to establish the continuity of English church history and to prove that the Anglo-Normans had worthy predecessors in England. On the other he wanted to justify the Norman Conquest by demonstrating the Anglo-Saxons' deficiencies. One justifica-

---

[48] *GR*, iii. 245 (vol. 2, p. 305). For a similar comparison of the two peoples see *GR*, ii. 198 (vol. 1, p. 240).
[49] *GR*, iii. 246 (vol. 2, p. 306).   [50] *GR*, iii. 245 (vol. 2, p. 305).
[51] *GR*, ii. 228 (vol. 1, p. 282); iii. 242–3 (vol. 2, p. 303).
[52] See *GP*, ii. 84, 91 (pp. 185, 196). Cf. *GR*, iii. 278 (vol. 2, p. 334).
[53] *GR*, iv. 342 (vol. 2, pp. 389–90).

tion for the Norman Conquest was the reform of the allegedly corrupt Anglo-Saxon church by William I and Lanfranc.

The merits and demerits of William of Malmesbury as a historian are well illustrated in the *Gesta Regum* and *Gesta Pontificum*, the products of his first period of historical writing. One of his great merits was his recognition of the value of visual evidence. Unlike Bede,[54] William apparently travelled widely in England, turning the fruits of his tireless sightseeing to historical purposes. He understood that what a historian sees may be as significant as what he reads (the story of the rule of Julius Caesar, William writes, is to be read in annals and seen in the ruins of ancient buildings[55]). As a sightseer and interpreter of geographical, architectural and archaeological evidence, William of Malmesbury had no rival among his predecessors and was a forerunner of William of Worcester. Many of his descriptions of ancient monuments are invaluable to the historian today because the objects themselves have been destroyed.[56]

The *Gesta Pontificum* is virtually a gazetteer of ecclesiastical England.[57] The section on every bishopric begins with a description of the see, its site and buildings; and the religious houses, noticed at the end of each section, are also topographically described. Places north of the Humber receive equal attention to those nearer home. William's comments on the broad dialect and rough manners of the northerners suggest that he went north himself.[58] Such a view receives some support from his exact copy of the inscription on the façade of a Roman vaulted hall in Carlisle,[59] and the account of Wilfrid's magnificent monastery, with turrets and spiral stairs, at Hexham.[60]

In the south, William seems to have visited most important places. He gives, for example, what appears to be first-hand descriptions of Wulfstan's tomb at Worcester,[61] the site of Rochester and the stained glass in the cathedral,[62] and the isolated location of Athelney and the round church

[54] Although Bede did not travel in search of visual information, he had a developed sense of geography; see pp. 23–4 and nn. William of Malmesbury's use of visual evidence is more fully discussed in A. Gransden, 'Realistic observation in twelfth-century England' in *Speculum*, xlvii (1972), pp. 33–6.

[55] *GR*, i. 1 (vol. 1, p. 5).

[56] For descriptions by William of churches which have since vanished see G. Baldwin Brown, *The Arts in Early England* (London 1903–37, 6 vols; new ed. of vol. 2, *Anglo-Saxon Architecture*, London 1925), vol. 2, p. 187 (a round church at St Albans) and pp. 174–5 and n. 63 below (a round church at Athelney). William has valuable information about the Saxon church at Bradford-on-Avon; see Baldwin Brown, op. cit., vol. 2, pp. 17, 160, 297, 302.

[57] William even sometimes gives the mileage between places; see e.g. *GP*, prologue to Book I (p. 3); ii. 73, 94 (pp. 140, 200); iii. 117 (p. 255).

[58] *GP*, prologue to Book III (p. 209).

[59] *GP*, prologue to Book III (pp. 208–9). William's transcription (which is not apparently quite accurate) is noticed in R. G. Collingwood and R. P. Wright, *The Roman Inscriptions of Britain* (vol. 1, *Inscriptions on Stone*, Oxford 1965), pp. 316–17, n. 950.

[60] *GP*, iii. 117 (p. 255). William could of course have obtained his information from travellers: Baldwin Brown, op. cit., pp. 175–6, does not regard his account of Hexham as an important source for Hexham's architectural history.

[61] *GP*, iv. 148 (p. 288).   [62] *GP*, i. 72 (pp. 133, 138).

there.[63] He also mentions the fruitful plains of Gloucestershire (with an account of the Severn bore).[64] Perhaps William's enthusiastic notices of monastic hospitality, for example at Tewkesbury and Reading, were a form of thanks for a visit.[65] The very copy of the *Gesta Pontificum* which William took with him on his travels probably still survives. For the autograph manuscript of the *Gesta Pontificum* is pocket-size, suitable for such journeys. It was obviously written piecemeal (this is shown by the many changes in the shade of ink) and William's alterations can be seen in the text itself, and additions are crowded in the margins.[66]

His accumulation of evidence of various types, literary, oral and visual, shows his industry: his handling of it shows some critical sense. He seems to regard the Arthurian legends with some reservation[67] and suspends judgment on the tradition that Bede visited Rome,[68] and on Queen Edith's virginity.[69] He cautiously states that with regard to past history, it is not he himself but the authors he uses who vouch for the truth of the record.[70] He speaks of oral tradition with equal circumspection. Deploring that the Anglo-Saxons had not written down the acts of most of their saints, he turned his attention to sifting legends; but, he asserted, he would rather omit a saint's life altogether than expose the saint to ridicule by relying on untrustworthy witnesses.[71]

He knew how to treat literary sources intelligently. He was capable of collating texts (he points out that some of St Oswald's miracles were only recorded in certain manuscripts of Bede's *Ecclesiastical History*[72]). He was not misled by the literary style of authors: he could distinguish between the form of a work and the value of its content. He admitted that Osbern's literary style was excellent although he disapproved of him on other grounds.[73] He condemned the Latin, as bombastic and unnecessarily complex, of Æthelweard and the author of the (now lost) Life of King Athelstan, but he recognized the historical value of their works[74] (he even admitted that the Latin of Aldhelm, Malmesbury's patron saint, whose style these two writers imitated, left much to be desired[75]).

---

[63] *GP*, ii. 92 (p. 199). See Baldwin Brown, op. cit., pp. 182, 196, 372, 375.

[64] *GP*, iv. 153 (pp. 292–3).   [65] *GP*, ii. 89 (p. 193); iv. 157 (p. 295).

[66] Magdalen College, Oxford, MS. 172. A page is reproduced on Plate V. See also p. 180 and n. 125 below. Hamilton reproduces five pages of the MS. in facsimile at the beginning of his edition of *GP*, and gives in his footnotes a conscientious account of William's alterations etc. to the manuscript. I am grateful to Mr N. R. Ker and Dr G. L. Harriss, successively librarians of Magdalen College, for allowing me to examine the MS.

[67] *GR*, i. 8 (vol. 1, p. 11); iii. 287 (vol. 2, p. 342).

[68] *GR*, i. 57 (vol. 1, p. 62). Cf. Bede's *HE*, i. xvi–xvii.   [69] *GR*, ii. 197 (vol. 1, p. 239).

[70] *GR*, prologue to Book I (vol. 1, p. 3); cf. i. 53 (vol. 1, p. 58).

[71] *GP*, iv. 186 (p. 328); prologue to Book V (p. 331).

[72] *GR*, ii. 208 (vol. I, p. 260 and n. 6); vol. 2, p. xciii and n. 4.

[73] *GR*, ii. 149 (vol. 1, p. 166). For William's disapproval of the content of Osbern's *Life of St. Dunstan* see p. 184 and n. 153 below.

[74] *GR*, prologue to Book I (vol. 1, p. 1); ii. 132 (vol. 1, p. 144).

[75] *GR*, i. 31 (vol. 1, p. 31).

Generally speaking, William was a rational historian, capable of deducing a reasonable effect from a given cause. For example he argued that the tradition that St Aldhelm was King Ine's nephew was unlikely to be true because, as the chronicles record, Ine's only brother died before Aldhelm's time.[76] And he argued that the tower of the conventual church at Malmesbury could not have been built by Abbot Ælfric, as King Athelstan, who died over thirty years before Ælfric's succession, was buried under it.[77] As will be seen, William's rational faculty was even more in evidence in his second historiographical period.

But William had faults as a historian: he made mistakes and he was sometimes excessively biased. These faults appear both in the *Gesta Regum* and in the *Gesta Pontificum*, and include the confusion of John Scotus with John the Old Saxon,[78] and Gerbert with Pope John XV.[79] Despite his interest in chronology he gave some wrong dates[80] and accepted the eccentric chronological system of Marianus Scotus – which misled few of William's contemporaries.[81] He had a great gift of imagination, which appears in his numerous excellent stories (besides those he copied from the lost German source). But sometimes this led him to extremes. One slender fact or unauthenticated rumour could rouse the story-teller in him. For example it has recently been shown that his graphic account in the *Gesta Pontificum* of the degeneracy of the monks of Christ Church, Canterbury, at the time of Lanfranc's succession is merely an imaginative interpretation of a short, dry paragraph in Eadmer's *Life of St. Dunstan*.[82]

In his first period of historical writing, William showed two kinds of bias. First, he had a strong prejudice against a number of magnates in the kingdom, both bishops and laymen, in fact any great man who had ever offended the monastic order. Second, he had regional bias: he favoured Canterbury in the controversy between the metropolitans of Canterbury and York, and he favoured Malmesbury abbey and its patron saint, Aldhelm. The history of the Canterbury/York controversy and of Malmesbury take up a considerable amount of space in the *Gesta Pontificum* and a number of pages in the *Gesta Regum*. William argued the case for Canterbury as a partisan, not as a dispassionate judge, and tried to strengthen Canterbury's claim by citing *in extenso* a number of charters, without apparently realizing that they

---

76 *GR*, vol. 1, p. 35 n. 1.

77 *GP*, v. 246 (p. 397).

78 *GR*, ii. 122 (vol. 1, p. 131); *GP*, v. 240 (p. 393). For some of William's other mistakes see *GR*, vol. 2, pp. xxiii–xxv, xxxii–xxxiv. For Abbot Ælfric see p. 177 n. 88 below.

79 *GR*, vol. 1, p. 193 n. 3.

80 See e.g. *GR*, vol. 1, p. xlvi; ii. 106 (vol. 1, p. 106 and n. 1); vol. 2, p. xxiii.

81 William records that Marianus's chronicle was brought to England by Robert de Losinga, bishop of Hereford (1079–95); see p. 145 n. 66 above. Robert's abridgment of it is in a manuscript (Auct. F. 3. 14 in the Bodleian Library) which William of Malmesbury knew; see W. H. Stevenson, 'A contemporary description of the Domesday survey' in *EHR*, xxii (1907), pp. 72 et seq., and N. R. Ker, 'William of Malmesbury's handwriting', p. 374.

82 *GP*, i. 44 (pp. 70–1). See Southern, *St. Anselm*, p. 247 n. 1. Cf. the next note.

were forgeries.[83] However, only modified blame attaches to William for including the notorious Canterbury forgeries. He himself had no hand in manufacturing them, and a twelfth-century monk with little knowledge of diplomatic would find it almost impossible to distinguish a genuine charter from a spurious one.

William's purpose in regard to Malmesbury abbey was to establish its antiquity and venerability. He lived in the golden age of trade in relics, and although he ostensibly condemned the relics race[84] he was more than an indifferent spectator: he had money on the horses and chalked up the winners. While William could doubt that Bamburgh still had St Oswald's arms,[85] he had no hesitation in believing that St Aldhelm still rested in his abbey church,[86] or that the ancient chasuble preserved there had belonged to the saint.[87]

The history of Malmesbury abbey during the Danish invasions is obscure, but there is no undisputable evidence suggesting that a monastic community survived. William apparently recognized that the first reliable reference to the post-Bedan monastery was by Abbo of Fleury, who mentions that an abbot of Malmesbury met St Dunstan.[88] Nevertheless he tried to fill the hiatus in the abbey's history. He sought to authenticate his account (in Book V of the *Gesta Pontificum*) with a series of charters copied *verbatim* purporting to record grants to the abbey, mainly from the kings of England.[89] These allegedly date from the late seventh to the tenth century. Modern scholarship has shown that, though a few are genuine, a number are spurious and others are of doubtful authenticity, at least in their present form. William himself may well have had a hand in concocting the forgeries[90] and it is hard to exonerate him from the charge of knowingly including forged

---

[83] *GP*, i. 25–39 (pp. 39–62); *GR*, iii. 294–9 (vol. 2, pp. 346–52). William's account of Lanfranc's speech at the Council of Winchester in 1072 (*GP*, i. 41, pp. 63–5) is apparently an elaboration of the account given by Eadmer in the *Historia Novorum*, and William copied the forged charters either from Eadmer or from some Canterbury collection of documents; see R. W. Southern, 'The Canterbury forgeries' in *EHR*, lxxiii (1958), pp. 213 n. 1, 219–20.

[84] *GP*, v. 263 (p. 419).   [85] *GR*, i. 49 (vol. 1, p. 53).

[86] *GP*, v. 217 (p. 364); Cf. v. 231 (p. 385).

[87] *GP*, v. 218 (p. 365): William describes the chasuble as being of fine scarlet silk with peacocks enclosed in black roundels embroidered on it. Mr Donald King, Keeper of Textiles at the Victoria and Albert Museum, informs me that this peacock motif was popular from the seventh century or earlier until the thirteenth century.

[88] *GP*, v. 253 (pp. 405–6). Cf. Abbo of Fleury in *Memorials SE*, vol. 1, p. 3. William identified the abbot of Malmesbury who met St Dunstan as Ælfric (Ælfric became abbot of Malmesbury c. 965 and bishop of Crediton in 977; M. D. Knowles, C. N. L. Brooke and V. C. M. London, *The Heads of Religious Houses, England and Wales, 940–1216* (Cambridge 1972), p. 54. His ignorance of the early history of Malmesbury is shown by his confusion of Abbot Ælfric with Ælfric the grammarian; see *GP*, p. 406 n. 3. Moreover, it is not certain that the abbot whom St Dunstan met was Ælfric; see *Memorials SE*, vol. 1, p. 3 n. b.

[89] For the charters cited in *GP*, Book V *passim*, with the estimates of modern scholars on their authenticity, see P. W. Sawyer, *Anglo-Saxon Charters* (Royal Historical Soc., 1968), nos 149, 243, 256, 260, 305, 306, 320, 356, 363, 436, 841, 1169. 1205.

[90] See Sawyer, op. cit., no. 436.

material in the history. However, in his defence it should be remembered that attitudes to forgery in the twelfth century were different from those today.[91] The twelfth-century monastic forger saw himself as providing documentary proof of his house's right to privilege, and title to property, which the monastery had undoubtedly held beyond living memory. He was merely answering a need. And he often used a genuine charter or charters as the basis of his forgery. It is unlikely, therefore, that William's primary object was to deceive: it was to corroborate Malmesbury abbey's right to property which William sincerely believed it held.

William promoted the cult of St Aldhelm to increase the prestige of Malmesbury. He tried to associate local features with St Aldhelm. He stated that the stones near Malmesbury marked the places where the bearers of his body had rested[92] (he died at Doulting in Somerset and had to be carried back to Malmesbury). St Aldhelm, William asserted, had built the chapel at Wareham in Dorset which gave miraculous shelter to shepherds and worked cures.[93] William explained a crack in the altar at Bruton with a reference to St Aldhelm. The altar was given, according to William, by Pope Sergius to St Aldhelm and was cracked during the journey over the Alps because the animal (possibly, he says, a camel) fell while carrying it.[94]

It remains to assess William's achievement in the *Gesta Regum* and *Gesta Pontificum*. The reader is impressed by the emphasis on style; William aimed at writing a polished literary work. To a certain extent he succeeded. His Latin is excellent and some of his anecdotes and stories have a timeless wit and humour. But the *Gesta Regum* is cumbersome in construction, with many excursions from the main theme. And the *Gesta Pontificum*, though better arranged, is overloaded with material relating to the Canterbury/York controversy and to St Aldhelm and Malmesbury.

As a source for the historian today the usefulness of the *Gesta Regum* is limited by the fact that most of William's sources still survive: notable exceptions are the Life of King Athelstan,[95] a lost version of the Anglo-Saxon Chronicle[96] and some books of German stories.[97] As has been seen, the strictly contemporary part of the work is disappointing. The *Gesta Pontificum* relied less on written sources because these were scarce. For the period from the late eighth to the tenth centuries William could find practically no information about many episcopal sees (often he merely lists the bishops).

Nevertheless from one point of view these works were successful. William had intended to entertain his readers. And the comparatively great number

---

[91] For twelfth-century forgery see V. H. Galbraith, *Studies in the Public Records* (London 1948), pp. 49–50.

[92] *GP*, v. 230 (pp. 383–4).   [93] *GP*, v. 217 (p. 363).

[94] *GP*, v. 222 (p. 373).   [95] See pp. 53–5 above.

[96] It is not certain which version or versions of the Anglo-Saxon Chronicle were used by William; see *GR*, vol. 2, p. cxxviii. For passages from the Chronicle see *GR*, iii. 282 (vol. 2, p. 337); iv. 322–31 (vol. 2, pp. 374–6); *GP*, v. 277 (pp. 442–3).

[97] See pp. 171–2 above.

of manuscripts which survives of both works shows that here he succeeded. The latest editor of the *Gesta Regum* lists twenty-five medieval copies (and has evidence for the previous existence of more).[98] The latest edition of the *Gesta Pontificum* lists nineteen medieval copies.[99]

Copies of the *Gesta Regum* reached the Benedictine abbeys of Gloucester,[100] Glastonbury,[101] St Albans,[102] Bury St Edmunds,[103] Rochester,[104] Battle,[105] Faversham[106] and Reading,[107] and the priory of St Martin's at Dover.[108] The work was popular with the Augustinian canons;[109] copies were at Kirkham in Yorkshire, Newark in Surrey, and at Holy Trinity, London, and possibly at Carlisle and Llanthony. Perhaps William's kind words about the Cistercians[110] may be one reason why a particularly fine copy was at Margam in Glamorganshire.[111] Another copy was in the Cistercian abbey of Merevale in Warwickshire.[112] The Augustinian friars[113] and the canons of St Paul's in London[114] also had copies. Moreover, the *Gesta Regum* was widely cited and plundered by William's contemporaries and by later medieval chroniclers in England and even on the continent.[115] Bishop Stubbs pointed out that its medieval plunderers often copied the good stories (particularly popular were the stories of the statue and the ring, and of the witch of Berkley), and suggested that these accounted for William's widespread fame.[116] Like most successful authors, William rightly gauged the tastes of his readers.

Manuscripts of the *Gesta Pontificum* are known to have been at Bury St Edmunds, Rochester and St Albans, and with the Augustinian canons of Bridlington and Thornton.[117] A fourteenth-century copy was at York minster.[118] One Malmesbury copy appears to have been lent around: fourteenth- and fifteenth-century notes in it record its loan to the bishop of.

---

[98] *GR*, vol. 1, pp. lxvi–xci.   [99] *GP*, pp. xx–xxv.   [100] See *GR*, vol. 1, p. lxxxvi.

[101] See Ker, *Medieval Libraries*, pp. 90–1.   [102] *GR*, vol. 1, pp. lxxxiii–lxxxiv.

[103] *GR*, p. lxxvii.   [104] *GR*, pp. xlix, lxxiv–lxxv.   [105] *GR*, pp. xlix, lxxiii.

[106] *GR*, p. xci.

[107] Ker, *Medieval Libraries*, p. 156. Stubbs, *GR*, vol. 1, p. lxxxviii, notices the volume, Lambeth MS. 371, but does not mention its provenance.

[108] *GR*, p. xci.

[109] For these copies owned by the Augustinian canons see *GR*, vol. 1, pp. lxxviii, xci, and, for the Newark copy, Ker, *Medieval Libraries*, p. 133 (the provenance of this volume, Laud MS. Misc. 548 in the Bodleian Library, was not recognized by Stubbs; *GR*, vol. 1, pp. lxviii–lxix).

[110] For William's favourable account of the Cistercians see *GR*, iv. 334–7 (vol. 2, pp. 380–5). He also admired the Cluniacs; *GP*, ii. 89 (p. 193).

[111] *GR*, vol. 1, p. lxxxi.

[112] Ker, *Medieval Libraries*, p. 130; Stubbs, *GR*, vol. 1, pp. lxxxiv–lxxxv, describes the Merevale volume (All Souls, Oxford, MS. 33), but does not mention its provenance.

[113] *GR*, vol. 1, p. xci.

[114] Ibid.

[115] See *GR*, vol. 1, pp. xcii–xciii. For continental MSS. containing extracts from *GR*, see pp. xcix–cviii.

[116] *GR*, vol. 2, pp. xc–xci; cf. vol. 1, p. ciii.

[117] For the manuscripts of *GP* surviving from these houses see *GP*, pp. xx–xxiv.

[118] Rawlinson B 199 in the Bodleian Library; noticed in *GP*, p. xxi. Its provenance is given in Ker, *Medieval Libraries*, p. 216.

Exeter, to the prior of Pilton (in Devon) and to the abbot of Glastonbury.[119] Sometimes the *Gesta Regum* and the *Gesta Pontificum* were adapted to the needs of individual houses. The Bury copy of the *Gesta Regum* curtails the material relating to the history of Glastonbury,[120] the Gloucester copy inserts a Gloucester charter.[121] The two Bridlington copies of the *Gesta Pontificum* omit the history of Malmesbury and all but a brief outline of the Life of St Aldhelm.[122]

In the ten-year pause before his second historiographical period (from 1125 to 1135), William became a sadder and a wiser – perhaps a disillusioned – man. His commentary on the Lamentations of Jeremiah, written in this interval, mentions that his fortunes had changed for the worse.[123] His former self-confidence, bordering on conceit,[124] gave way to self-criticism. When revising the *Gesta Pontificum* he wrote in bold dark letters across half a page of erasure, 'Fateor imbecillitatem meam; nollo spe pugnare' (roughly 'I confess my weakness – I despair of remedying it'):[125] the passage erased was a bitter attack on the prevalence of simony in the church and on the general corruption of the times.

External factors probably contributed to this depressive mood. Malmesbury was effected by the civil war which followed Henry I's death. The castle of King Stephen's supporter, Roger bishop of Salisbury, loomed over the abbey, an ever present reminder of political strife and of the estrangement of the monks from the secular clergy. Roger was on very bad terms with the monks because he usurped the abbey's liberties from 1118 until his death in 1139. William took the opposite side to Roger in politics: his sympathies were with the empress Matilda. He dedicated the *Historia Novella* to Matilda's half-brother and principal supporter, Robert earl of Gloucester (to some extent the *Historia* is a panegyric on Robert), and when William revised the *Gesta Regum* he dedicated that too to the earl.[126] William may have had another more personal reason for despondency at this time. There are indications that his histories had met with criticism[127] and that he suffered some estrangement from his own community, possibly being passed

---

[119] See the description of Trinity College, Cambridge, MS. 727 (R. 5. 36) in *GP*, pp. xxiii–xxiv.
[120] *GR*, vol. 1, p. 167 n. 5.   [121] *GR*, vol. 2, p. 521 note on § 397.
[122] See *GP*, pp. xx–xxi.
[123] The prologue to the commentary on Lamentations, containing this statement, is printed in *GR*, vol. 1, pp. cxxii–cxxiii, and (with an English translation) by Hugh Farmer, 'William of Malmesbury's commentary on Lamentations' in *Studia Monastica*, iv (1962), p. 288 and n. 17.
[124] e.g. William points out that he is the first or only continuator of Bede and that any successor will owe him a debt; *GR*, v. 445 (vol. 2, p. 518); he refers to his literary reputation; *GP*, v. 186 (p. 331); and he congratulates himself on his achievements as librarian of Malmesbury; *GP*, v. 271 (p. 431).
[125] Magdalen College, Oxford, MS. 172, f. 39ᵛ; *GP*, p. 121 n. 1.
[126] Although the first recension of the *Gesta Regum* is not formally dedicated to the earl it has an epilogue addressed to him; *GR*, vol. 1, pp. lvi–lviii; v. 446–9 (vol. 2, pp. 518–21).
[127] See *GR*, prologue to Book IV (vol. 2, p. 357).

over for the abbacy in 1140.[128] William's troubles at Malmesbury may account for his declining interest in the fortunes of the house. Instead he turned his attention to Glastonbury abbey, writing the *De Antiquitate Glastoniensis Ecclesiae* to prove that its history went back to the earliest Christian period in Britain.

But William's change of mood and outlook had more profound effects on his historical writing. The works of his second historiographical period show a more rational and cautious approach than those of the first period. He declares in the *Life of St. Dunstan* that as death approaches he will redouble his attempt at accuracy,[129] and concentrate on careful reportage rather than on imaginative, amusing stories and elegant style. Above all he is more moderate in his judgments, as a result of intellectual maturity, and possibly also because he was afraid of provoking fresh criticism and of offending the great. William revised the *Gesta Regum* between 1135 and 1140, modifying the censure of William I and William II and of the secular clergy.[130] At the same time he revised the *Gesta Pontificum* even more drastically, toning down or suppressing full-blooded criticism and scurrilous stories about the great men of his day.

The course of these revisions can be fairly accurately traced because of the excellent manuscript tradition. The manuscripts of the *Gesta Regum* divide into three recensions: the first recension belongs to William's first historiographical period; the second and third recensions to the second period. By comparing the texts in these groups, it is possible to see which passages William rewrote in a milder tone. For example the Conqueror's avarice is condemned in the first recension but justified in the two later ones ('because he could not rule a new kingdom without a lot of money').[131] He modified his censure of William Rufus and his court: the approving laugh with which Rufus acknowledged Flambard's services is attributed in the second recension to the courtiers;[132] the passage referring to the court as a sink of iniquity is suppressed, and another, anticipating Henry I's reforms, is substituted.[133] William also modified his attacks on bishops: in 1125 he had described John of Bath as silly and unstable; in 1140 he merely said he began his reforms too rigorously.[134]

Some of the revisions of the *Gesta Regum* show William suppressing unlikely, gossipy explanations of events. In the first recension he ascribed the death of Robert of Normandy's wife to evil medical advice given to her in childbed by a rival; in the second version the advice is attributed to an ignorant midwife.[135] The first recension states that many people thought that the tower of St Swithun's fell because the wicked Rufus was buried

---

[128] See *GR*, vol. 1, pp. xxxviii–xl.
[129] *Memorials SD*, p. 324.
[130] For details of the revision see *GR*, vol. 1, pp. xxxiii et seq., xlvii.
[131] *GR*, iii. 280 (vol. 2, p. 335).
[132] *GR*, iv. 314 (p. 369 and n. 2).
[133] *GR*, iv. 314 (p. 370 and n. 1).
[134] *GR*, iv. 340 (p. 388 and n. 4).
[135] *GR*, iv. 389 (p. 461 and n. 3).

beneath it. But William later dismissed this notion as absurd, pointing out that the fall was due to a crack in the fabric.[136]

The revision of the *Gesta Pontificum* can be clearly seen in William's autograph manuscript, written in 1125.[137] Almost as soon as this text was completed it was copied by other scribes. William then revised the autograph manuscript, adding material in the margins, erasing passages and cutting out leaves. By comparing the revised autograph with the early copies, it is possible to see exactly what alterations the revision entailed. Many of the major alterations are similar to those in the *Gesta Regum*: they are suppressions and modifications by an author who had grown more level-headed and cautious. For example William rewrote two passages bitterly criticizing William Rufus for his treatment of Lanfranc and the church ('he did nothing that was not bad, nothing that he had promised, and aggravated present calamities with threats of worse . . .'), substituting milder, and in one case excusatory, words.[138] He entirely suppressed his eloquent invectives against Ranulf Flambard ('the plunderer of the rich, the destroyer of the poor, the confiscator of inheritances'[139]), Robert Bloet, bishop of Lincoln ('wicked from wantonness . . . who never hesitated at the guilt or infamy of any form of lust[140]), and Samson, canon of Bayeux, the brother of Thomas I archbishop of York ('a self-indulgent glutton . . . a veritable sink of eatables'[141]).

William's most important work in his second historiographical period was the *Historia Novella*. In it he emerges as a contemporary historian of the first rank. His previous prejudice against writing annals had apparently vanished. Perhaps his fear of offending the ruling classes was less acute after the death in 1139 of Roger bishop of Salisbury. The *Historia* is a fairly factual account of events, without the literary embellishments characteristic of William's

---

[136] *GR*, iv. 333 (p. 379 and n. 1). Here William seems to regard the rational cause of the event as an *alternative* to divine causation (Bede treats divine and rational causation as complementary; see pp. 21 and n. 68, 22 above). Similarly William states that Thomas I, archbishop of York, died *either* because he was too fat *or* because of a divine punishment for breaking open St Oswald's tomb at Gloucester; *GP*, p. 263 n. 2.

[137] See p. 175 and n. 66 above.

[138] See Plate V and *GP*, p. 73 and nn. 1, 3. Having noted that Rufus before his accession promised to help Lanfranc, William of Malmesbury originally wrote: 'Sed potestate potitus nichil fuit malum quod non ageret, nichil quod non promitteret; praesentes provintialium calamitates minis perjorum acerbans. Super quos fallacis sponsionis ab archiepiscopo ammonitus . . .'; for this he substituted:'Sed potestate potitus, multisque pro defectione principum pene omnium angoribus conflictatus, promissa negligebat. Quapropter sponsionis ab archiepiscopo ammonitus'. The other passage originally read: 'Rex abjecto respectu omnis boni, omnia aeclesiastica in fiscum redegit. Juvenili calore et regio fastu praefervidus, humana divinaque juxta ponderans et sui juris estimans. Sed de ejus moribus alias locuti sumus, in hoc quoque pontificum opere, cum se causa dederit, dicemus.' William substituted: 'Rex enim malorum susurronum consiliis plus justo credulus, omnes sibi redditus annumerabat. Sed de talibus alias dixi, multum, ut decet, regiae majestati deferens.'

[139] *GP*, p. 274 n. 5. For this and the two following examples see *GP*, pp. xv, xvi, and Hugh Farmer, 'William of Malmesbury's life and work' (see n. 5 above), pp. 45–6.

[140] *GP*, p. 313 n. 4. [141] *GP*, p. 289 n. 3.

earlier works. From about 1140 he wrote within a year or two of the events described,[142] and apparently only his death prevented him adding another book, as he had promised.[143] In the course of writing, William added 'stop-press' news arriving too late for inclusion in the original text. No autograph of the *Historia* is known but the late news can be isolated by collating the manuscripts of the first recension with those of the second; the late news is only in the second recension. There are about six such additions, including a notice of Earl Robert's capture of Harptree, Sudeley and South Cerney,[144] and Geoffrey de Mandeville's change of sides.[145]

Although the *Historia* is heavily biased in favour of Earl Robert and Matilda, it is a valuable historical record. William was at the Council of Winchester and witnessed other events he notices.[146] He does justice to King Stephen's virtues (his courage, energy, good nature and courtesy) as well as deploring his shortcomings. He shows remarkable fairness to Roger bishop of Salisbury, expressing sorrow at his complete disgrace and miserable end, pointing him out as an example of the mutability of fortune. William's loyalty to Earl Robert was not without justification for the earl deserved praise.

The two remaining works written at this period are of less value to the historian today. They show that William still had a strong tendency to bias when dealing with a monastery which interested him. Now the object of his favour was Glastonbury abbey, not Malmesbury. The reason for his interest in Glastonbury is not clear. He certainly wrote one of the works, the *De Antiquitate Glastoniensis Ecclesiae*, to please Henry of Blois, bishop of Winchester, for he dedicated it to him: and Henry had a close connection with Glastonbury, ruling it together with his see from 1126 until his death in 1171.[147] William had visited Glastonbury but it is not known what further association he had with the abbey. Perhaps he stayed there during his troubles at Malmesbury.

William wrote the *De Antiquitate Glastoniensis Ecclesiae* some time between 1129 and 1139,[148] to disprove the assertion by Osbern in his *Life of St. Dunstan* that Dunstan was the first abbot of Glastonbury.[149] William claimed that the abbey had existed before Dunstan's time and that Glastonbury had been a holy place for many centuries. To substantiate his arguments he stated that the bodies of Aidan, Ceolfrid and Hild (and others)

---

[142] The account of the eclipse *s.a.* 1140 seems to be contemporary; *HN*, 484 (p. 43).

[143] *HN*, 524 (p. 77).

[144] *HN*, 483 (p. 42). For this and other late additions see *HN*, pp. xli–xlii.

[145] *HN*, 499 (p. 59).

[146] See *HN*, 457, 469, 485, 492 (pp. 12, 26, 43, 52), and *GR*, vol. 1, pp. xl–xlii.

[147] See J. Armitage Robinson, 'William of Malmesbury "On the Antiquity of Glastonbury"' in his *Somerset Historical Essays* (Oxford 1921), pp. 3, 4.

[148] On the date of *De Ant. Glast.* see *GR*, vol. 1, pp. xxvii–xxviii.

[149] See Osbern's *Life of St. Dunstan* in *Memorials SD*, p. 92. Cf. *De Ant. Glast.*, p. 71.

rested there,[150] and inserted one or two forged charters.[151] William's *Life of St. Dunstan* was also written as a reply to Osbern's work.[152] William pours scorn on Osbern's inaccuracy and lack of information, specifically criticizing him for reporting *verbatim* what Dunstan said to some demons – Osbern, William says, was not here relying on the oldest authorities.[153]

The reputations of both the *De Antiquitate Glastoniensis Ecclesiae* and William's *Life of St. Dunstan* have suffered because their texts were tampered with by the Glastonbury monks. The latter gave these works a final furbishing after the fire which destroyed the monastery in 1185. They inserted legendary material, including the legend of Joseph of Arimathea's visit to Glastonbury, and spurious charters.[154] It is this Glastonbury text of the *De Antiquitate* which survives today as a separate work.[155] But William had included much of his original text in the second recension of the *Gesta Regum* (but, presumably for the sake of balance, he omitted most of it from the third recension).[156] Therefore by comparing the passages in the *Gesta Regum* with the extant Glastonbury version, a rough idea can be obtained of what the Glastonbury monks added. Exactly what the revision by the monks of Glastonbury of the *Life of St. Dunstan* entailed is not known. But it certainly suffered at their hands. Bishop Stubbs suggested that its account of the (alleged) translation of St Dunstan's body to Glastonbury was one of the monks' interpolations.[157]

Therefore, though the *De Antiquitate* and the *Life of St. Dunstan* show bias, bordering on dishonesty, they did not in their original forms have as much fictitious matter as they do today. And both works illustrate some of William's merits as a historian. For the *Life of St. Dunstan* William recognized the value of 'B''s *Life*, today accepted as the best source[158] (although he mainly used Osbern's *Life*). Nevertheless William casts doubt on the story 'B' tells of how St Dunstan found King Edwy in bed with two loose women during his coronation feast: Sir Frank Stenton shared William's

---

[150] *De Ant. Glast.*, p. 29.

[151] The text of *De Ant. Glast.* as it exists today has a number of spurious charters and charters of doubtful authenticity (see Sawyer, *Anglo-Saxon Charters*, nos 152, 246, 250, 257, 499, 783, 966). But I have here accepted the conclusion of Armitage Robinson (see below and n. 155) that all of these were probably forged by the Glastonbury monks after 1185 and only those also in the second recension of the *Gesta Regum* (see Sawyer, *Anglo-Saxon Charters*, nos 257, 499, 783) were in William's text of *De Ant. Glast.*

[152] William's *Life of St. Dunstan* is fully discussed by H. Farmer, 'Two biographies by William of Malmesbury' in *Latin Biography*, ed. T. A. Dorey (London 1967), pp. 161–5.

[153] *Memorials SD*, pp. 287–8, and see p. 175 and n. 73 above. Similarly, William states in his translation of Coleman's *Life of Wulfstan* that he will avoid direct speech because it jeopardizes truth; *VW*, p. 2.

[154] See n. 151 above.

[155] The view expressed here, that William was not responsible for the largely fictitious *De Ant. Glast.* as it survives today, is that elaborated by J. Armitage Robinson, 'Glastonbury', pp. 1–25 *passim*.

[156] See *GR*, vol. 1, pp. lviii–lxi.   [157] *Memorials SD*, pp. xxxiii–xxxvii.

[158] William's *Life of St. Dunstan* in *Memorials SD*, pp. 252 and n. 4, 258 and n. 1, 263 and n. 1, 265 and n. 1.

scepticism.[159] William's account of the history of Glastonbury in the *De Antiquitate* has been corroborated in its general outline by recent archaeology. A Celtic monastery and a series of ancient churches, the earliest dating back to the seventh century, have been excavated.[160] William is at his best touring the abbey's antiquities. He describes the two early Anglo-Saxon free-standing crosses (he calls them pyramids) in the cemetery. The tallest, he records, was twenty-six feet high and had five panels on which were carvings of people with their names. The other cross was eighteen feet tall and had four panels carved with names. Although the names were almost indecipherable from age, William managed to transcribe some of them.[161]

Despite his faults – his bias, inconsistencies, mistakes and omissions – William was a notable historian. He was learned and original, and was a good writer. He wrote many sorts of history, past history in literary form, contemporary history in annalistic form, local history and biography, and thought about the problems of historiography. He is the first historian since Bede whose character emerges clearly from his works. He was not apparently spiritually minded but his avid interest in men's achievements and his wit make him an attractive writer. But above all he is an important landmark in historiography because he can be seen at work: it is the first time we have anything near a comprehensive view of a historian's method, or even a limited view of the effect of personal development on historical writing.

---

[159] Ibid., p. 283. Cf. p. 86 and n. 155 above.

[160] For a summary of the findings of recent excavations at Glastonbury see J. and H. Taylor, 'Pre-Norman churches of the border' in Chadwick, *Celt and Saxon*, pp. 256–7.

[161] *De Ant. Glast.*, pp. 44–5. For William's account of the 'pyramids', an attempt to identify some of the names he transcribed, and the subsequent history of the 'pyramids', see Ælred Watkin, 'The Glastonbury "Pyramids" and St. Patrick's "companions"' in *Downside Review*, lxiii (1945), pp. 30–41.

Historians of King Stephen's Reign

The reign of King Stephen was rich in historical and quasi-historical productions. A characteristic of the period was the emergence of secular clerks as authors, and of laymen as a public who liked listening to readings from history books. Only three notable authorities were Benedictine monks: William of Malmesbury's *Historia Novella* is one of the most important sources of evidence, but the chronicle of John of Worcester ends in 1140,[1] and the Peterborough copy of the Anglo-Saxon Chronicle is disappointingly brief and provincial in outlook.[2] By contrast a number of histories were written by secular clerks (Henry of Huntingdon, Geoffrey of Monmouth, Gaimar and Alfred of Beverley). The *Gesta Stephani* (*Deeds of Stephen*) was also probably by a secular clerk. Moreover, in the north an Augustinian canon (Richard of Hexham) and a Cistercian (Ailred of Rievaulx) wrote histories. The works by the seculars reflect the rising importance in cultural life of the secular clergy; and the works by Richard of Hexham and Ailred reflect the intellectual revival achieved in the north by the new religious orders.

The most significant historiographical trend was the increasing influence of romance literature.[3] It is hard to define the precise meaning of romance: romance literature has many facets and its determining feature is the tone of a work rather than its specific content. A romance writer, whose object was to entertain, not to record or edify, loved warfare for its own sake. He loved to describe battles and heroism. Twelfth-century literary romance was typified by *chansons de geste*, long poems in French about the military exploits of legendary heroes. Romance literature subsumed the epic tradition: the epic hero was a more sombre and serious figure, battling for his people, than the hero of romance. The latter was depicted in individualistic, almost psychological terms (he might love a beautiful woman and commit adultery by means of a clever ruse). Romance was a product of the courts of kings and nobles, and often showed the strong influence of courtly culture.

---

[1] See p. 144. For a brief account of the chronicle sources for King Stephen's reign see R. H. C. Davis, *King Stephen 1135–1154* (London 1967), pp. 146–50.

[2] See pp. 142–3.

[3] For a detailed survey of the subject see W. P. Ker, *Epic and Romance* (2nd ed., London 1908, reprinted 1931).

Romance sometimes had a profound influence on historiography and sometimes merely a superficial one. The popularity of the genre received a strong stimulus by the publication in about 1136 of Geoffrey of Monmouth's *Historia Regum Britanniae* (*History of the Kings of Britain*), a prose work on the legendary British past written with romance values. Under the influence of the *Historia* and of contemporary *chansons de geste*, Gaimar wrote a history of the English, interpreted in accordance with the canons of romance literature: *L'Estoire des Engleis*, in Anglo-Norman, has a historical basis but loses value as a historical source because of the literary conventions it adopts. However, the effect of romance on the other English historians was less pervasive. An occasional passage has a romance tone, and the tradition promoted the love of warfare, leading to the extensive use of literary rhetoric – fictitious speeches of heroes and dramatic descriptions of martial exploits. And it encouraged the contemporary penchant for legends and anecdotes, particularly clever ruses, a taste already evinced by William of Malmesbury and the Worcester chronicler. Therefore in general the influence of romance literature altered the tone rather than transformed the character of historiography. The older traditions survived and flourished, particularly in the north. And only Geoffrey of Monmouth abandoned the Christian intention of historical writing: the other authors followed the medieval tradition that history should fortify the Christian ethic.

One good effect of romance was that it prompted historians to try to make their works acceptable to people who read or liked to have books read to them. The authors' wish to amuse resulted in the inclusion both of dramatic battle scenes, and also of prodigies and portents, miracles and the marvellous, which encroached on, but by no means obliterated, the record aspect of their histories. Those authors who wished to amuse had considerable success. It is true that the works of the north-country historians had a limited appeal, but not only Geoffrey of Monmouth's *Historia Regum Britanniae* soon became a best-seller; Henry of Huntingdon's *Historia Anglorum* was remarkably popular. Historians wrote for a receptive public – the very number of histories written is symptomatic of a fairly widespread interest in history.

An added inducement to writing entertainingly was the authors' desire to please their patrons. At this period patrons played an important part in historiographical development. It has been seen that William of Malmesbury dedicated his last history, the *Historia Novella*, to a patron, Robert earl of Gloucester.[4] Geoffrey of Monmouth also dedicated his work to Robert of Gloucester (among others). A great ecclesiastical patron was Alexander, the prince-like bishop of Lincoln (1123–48). He was another of Geoffrey's dedicatees, and the patron of Henry of Huntingdon. Patronage of history was not confined to the greatest magnates. Walter Espec, lord of Helmsley in Yorkshire (he died in 1153) was Ailred's patron. He loved reading history

---

[4] See p. 180.

and hearing *chansons de geste*,[5] and it was he who borrowed Geoffrey of Monmouth's *Historia* from Robert earl of Gloucester, to lend to a lesser noble, Ralph Fitz Gilbert who lent it to his wife Constance.[6] 'Patronage' can have various meanings in this context. Sometimes it may mean, as in the case of Henry of Huntingdon, that the patron commissioned the writing of the history. Sometimes it may mean that the author hoped for his patron's help and protection – no doubt Geoffrey of Monmouth hoped to enlist Bishop Alexander's favour. Sometimes it indicates friendship and admiration: Ailred was a friend of Water Espec. Sometimes it may merely represent the author's wish to associate a famous name with his publication. But the result was always the same: if ever the patron crossed the author's pages he was sure to be eulogized.

It is not known whether King Stephen himself was interested in history. He may have been, for Geoffrey of Monmouth dedicated some copies of the *Historia Regum Britanniae* to him. There were historical interests in court circles. Henry I, Stephen's uncle, enquired about the origins of the French monarchy when he invaded France in 1128.[7] Stephen's mother Adela and his cousin and rival the Empress Matilda both had histories dedicated to them by Hugh of Fleury.[8] The family of Matilda's second husband, Geoffrey count of Anjou, had its own official history, the *Gesta Consulum Andegavorum* (*Deeds of the Counts of Anjou*), which was started in 1107 and continued throughout the twelfth century.[9] This work gives a laudatory account of the acts, particularly the military exploits, of the counts of Anjou. A somewhat similar work was written about King Stephen, the *Gesta Stephani*.[10] This describes the events of Stephen's reign from the king's point of view and eulogizes Stephen to 1148. Then it sides with Henry Plantagenet, praising him until his accession when the work ends.

The *Gesta Stephani* gives a vivid, detailed and fairly accurate account of events and is independent of all known literary authorities.[11] This seems to indicate that the information was collected soon after the events took place. But in its present form the *Gesta* was written up in two stages, not strictly contemporarily.[12] First in about 1148 an account was written of Stephen's reign to 1147. That this section was written down at one time, after the events, is suggested by the references it has to information recorded later in the work.

---

[5] See Ailred, *Relatio*, p. 185.   [6] See p. 209 and n. 215.   [7] *HH*, pp. 248–9.

[8] Hugh's *Historia Ecclesiastica* was dedicated to Adela, and his *Modernorum Regum Francorum Actus* to Matilda; printed *MGH, Scriptores*, ix, 349–64, and 376–95, respectively. For Hugh see G. Waitz in ibid., ix, 337–49.

[9] Printed in *Chroniques des Comtes d'Anjou*, ed. P. Marchegay and A. Salmon, with an introduction by E. Mabille (Société de l'Histoire de France, Chroniques d'Anjou, Paris 1856, 1871, 2 vols), vol. 1, pp. 32–157. For the evolution of the *Gesta* see ibid., pp. ii et seq.

[10] Printed in *Gesta Stephani*, ed., with an English translation, K. R. Potter, with contributions to the introduction by R. A. B. Mynors and A. L. Poole (Nelson's Medieval Texts, 1955).

[11] On its value as a historical source see Poole in *GS*, pp. xv–xxix.

[12] For the dates when the *Gesta* was written, see R. H. C. Davis, 'The authorship of the *Gesta Stephani*' in *EHR*, lxxvii (1962), p. 212.

Thus in describing the loyal support given by Henry de Tracy to Stephen (in 1139), the author promises to enlarge on the subject later. This he does in his account of the events of 1143 and 1147.[13] The second part of the work was written after 1153. Here again there seems to be a forward reference (an apparent mention in the events of 1148/9 of the succession of a bishop which took place in 1153). Although the work is arranged chronologically, it does not date events. This may confirm that it was written up after events from contemporary notes.[14]

There is no conclusive evidence of the authorship of the *Gesta Stephani*, or even whether the author was English or French (the only surviving medieval manuscript is from the Premonstratensian abbey of Vicoigne in the diocese of Arras).[15] But it is fairly certain that he was a secular clerk, not a monk. He shows none of the characteristics of a monastic writer such as pre-occupation with his religious house in particular and his order in general: on the contrary his sympathies are with the secular clergy.[16] It has been suggested that the author was a clerk of Stephen's brother, Henry of Blois, bishop of Winchester.[17] But this is unlikely as he does not praise Henry without reserve[18] and gives an erroneous piece of information about him.[19] Neither is it likely that he was a clerk in Stephen's household, for he does not mention Stephen's serious illness in 1142.[20] Moreover, his character portrait of Stephen is conventional rather than intimate and he gives no account of his physical appearance.

Professor Davis thinks that the author was Robert of Lewes, bishop of Bath from 1136 to 1166. To support this view he produces various pieces of circumstantial evidence.[21] For example the author of the *Gesta* is interested in and well informed about Bath, Robert's see, and its neighbourhood. He hates Bristol, the Empress Matilda's stronghold: this would have been Robert's attitude because he was an enthusiastic supporter of Stephen. Also we know that the author of the *Gesta* changed loyalties between 1148 and

---

[13] *GS*, pp. 55, 99, 140, respectively. For other examples of such forward references see: p. 64 (a reference from an event in 1139 to one in 1141; cf. p. 75); p. 67 (a reference from an event in 1140 to one in 1143–4; cf. p. 109 and *Chronicon Abbatiae Rameseiensis*, ed. W. D. Macray (RS, 1886), pp. 329 et seq.); p. 72 (a reference from an event in 1140 to one in 1141; cf. p. 77).

[14] This point is made by K. R. Potter, *GS*, pp. xxxi–xxxii, who does not, however, mention the forward references.

[15] This manuscript (MS. 793 in the Municipal Library of Valenciennes), discovered by Sir Roger Mynors, is of the first half of the fourteenth century. It is probably a copy of the text, now lost, which was in the episcopal library at Laon and which A. Duchesne used for his edition in *Historiae Normannorum Scriptores Antiqui* (Paris 1619); see Mynors in *GS*, pp. xi–xiv.

[16] For example he approves of the appointment of the secular William of Corbeil to the archbishopric of Canterbury: *GS*, p. 6. For examples of the author's favourable attitude to the episcopal office (for which see Davis, op. cit., p. 223), see *GS*, pp. 40, 50–1, 68, 103, 105, 125, 141.

[17] See *Chrons. Stephen, Henry II and Richard I*, ed. Howlett, vol. 3, pp. viii–xii.

[18] See *GS*, p. 104, for criticism of Henry.

[19] See the mistake over the name of Henry's nephew; *GS*, p. 142 and n. 1.

[20] See *GS*, pp. xxx–xxxi, 91 n. 1.

[21] Davis, 'Authorship', pp. 209–32 *passim*.

some time after 1153:[22] Robert joined Henry Plantagenet's party between 1148 and April 1153.[23] The *Gesta* has much detailed, first-hand information about people and places in the west country, the area where Robert lived and travelled.[24] However, these and the other arguments of Professor Davis are not conclusive. There remains the possibility that the author was a Frenchman: this would satisfactorily account for the careful explanation of some English place-names (for example Bath *quod ex Anglicae linguae proprietate trahens vocabulum, Balneum interpretatur*[25]), which Professor Davis rather unconvincingly attributes to the author's artificial, pseudo-classical style.

The chief features of the *Gesta* are the eulogy of Stephen and Henry Plantagenet, the graphic accounts of warfare (especially the sieges of castles), its excellent topographical descriptions, and its strongly edificatory tone. It describes Stephen as 'generous and courteous, bold and brave, judicious and patient'.[26] Stephen was, the author asserts, incorruptible: he neither sold benefices nor justice.[27] The author praises Stephen for his skill as a soldier[28] and for not losing heart during the anarchy.[29] He justifies some of his failures. For example he attributes a temporary reverse in battle against the earl of Chester to Stephen's weakness from a wound.[30] He emphasizes the magnitude of Stephen's troubles. No sooner, he asserts, had Stephen solved one problem than another appeared, like the heads of Hercules's hydra, and his enemies were stronger than Alexander's.[31] The author's main contention in defence of Stephen was that he always took advice. Sometimes Stephen was ill advised and did wrong as a result. For example he yielded to bad advice when he imprisoned and dispossessed Roger bishop of Salisbury, Alexander bishop of Lincoln and Nigel bishop of Ely.[32] But in such cases the counsellors

---

[22] Ibid., pp. 211–12.   [23] Ibid., p. 225.

[24] However, the author's preoccupation with the west-country should not be exaggerated: see for example his topographical description of Ely (cited p. 191 below) where there is no evidence Robert ever was, as Davis admits (ibid., p. 225).

[25] *GS*, p. 39; cf. ibid., p. 138 for a similar explanation of Woodchester. See Davis, 'Authorship', p. 220 Davis similarly argues that the author's use of classical words for English officials indicates that the *Gesta* is by a highly educated ecclesiastic (ibid.): but equally it could be due to a foreigner's unfamiliarity with English usage. Moreover Davis argues (ibid., p. 222) that the author's disgust over the sufferings of the poorer classes during the anarchy suggests the compassion of a bishop with pastoral care. But a similar compassion is also a feature of Orderic Vitalis (see p. 153 above), a monk – and one who wrote abroad.

[26] *GS*, p. 3.

[27] *GS*, p. 14. However, the author notices that Stephen gave the abbey of Ramsey to a monk for money; ibid., p. 66 and n. 1.

[28] *GS*, p. 32.   [29] *GS*, p. 58.

[30] *GS*, p. 132. The author also justifies Stephen's seizure of the treasure of Roger bishop of Salisbury when he died: he asserts that the canons offered him the money voluntarily and that he used it for good works; ibid., p. 65.

[31] *GS*, pp. 46–7.

[32] See *GS*, p. 50; 'in hoc nimirum stultissimo, immo et insano deuictus et impulsus consilio'. The author also asserts that Stephen broke his promises to the church partly on account of bad counsellors 'qui bonum quandoque peruertunt animum'; ibid., p. 18. For other examples of Stephen taking counsel see ibid., pp. 27, 28, 61.

were to blame; Stephen was right to follow advice. The author emphasizes the importance of advice to legitimate rule. He makes this point in his account of the accession of Stephen, when Stephen's supporters were trying to persuade the archbishop, William of Corbeil, to anoint him. William said that the matter should be carefully debated, everyone should ratify the accession of the man who was to rule all, and everyone should agree on 'what was to be enacted and what rejected'.[33] Conversely the author asserts that Matilda, who disregarded the advice of her counsellors, ruled by arbitrary will.[34] The author considered Stephen the legitimate king because he had been chosen by the magnates, and they had done homage to him.[35] Stephen wanted peace and the maintenance of law and order.[36] But the magnates made this impossible by extending their power at the expense of the king's,[37] and by behaving tyrannously.[38]

There are numerous descriptions of warfare. Sometimes the author indulges in literary rhetoric. For example, he puts a speech into the king's mouth before the capture of Coventry castle,[39] and has a moving account of the plea for mercy by the wife of Baldwin de Redvers ('barefoot, her hair loose on her shoulders, and shedding floods of tears').[40] But more often the descriptions, particularly of sieges, are more remarkable for their factual, realistic elements. The author describes how besiegers built mounds for attacking castles, tunnelled under their walls[41] and threw blazing torches into them,[42] showered the garrisons with arrows and stones,[43] erected engines to pelt them with missiles,[44] and how the besieged suffered from drought.[45] The author must have had first-hand information about contemporary campaigns, for he correlates his accounts of military exploits with topographical descriptions. For example, in describing how Stephen took the Isle of Ely, he says that it was 'an agreeable island, large, thickly inhabited, rich in land that is fertile and fit for pasture, impenetrably surrounded on all sides by meres and fens, accessible only in one place'. Stephen was advised to 'collect a quantity of boats at a place where the water surrounding the island seemed to be less wide, place them broadside on, and build a bridge over them to the shores of the island with a foundation of hurdles laid lengthwise'. This Stephen did and so took the Isle.[46]

---

[33] 'parique consensu quid statuendum, quidue respuendum sit, ab omnibus prouideatur'; *GS*, p. 6.

[34] In 1141 Matilda was no longer relying on her supporters' advice; 'iamiamque non illorum consiliis, ut decebat et ut eis promiserat, inniti, sed suo quaeque prouisu, suae et dispositionis praesumptu, cuncta ordinare'; *GS*, pp. 79–80.

[35] *GS*, p. 75.

[36] Stephen preferred 'in pacis et concordiae amore cuncta componere, quam scisma dissensionis quoquomodo enutrire'; *GS*, p. 23. Stephen made peace with Henry Plantagenet in order to end the war; ibid., p. 158.

[37] *GS*, pp. 128–9.

[38] For barons and bishops acting tyrannously see *GS*, pp. 82, 125, 131.

[39] *GS*, pp. 133–4.   [40] *GS*, p. 27.   [41] *GS*, p. 22–3.   [42] *GS*, p. 55.

[43] *GS*, pp. 22, 121.   [44] *GS*, p. 121.   [45] *GS*, pp. 25–9 *passim*.

[46] *GS*, p. 66.

The description of Ely is one of a number of topographical descriptions. There are also descriptions, with particular reference to their castles, of Exeter, the Isle of Wight, Bedford, Bristol, Bath, Oxford, Cricklade and Faringdon.[47] The account of Exeter is characteristic of those of towns and castles: 'Exeter is a large town, with very ancient walls built by the Roman emperors, the fourth place, they say, in England, abundantly supplied with fish from the sea, and meat as well, with a flourishing shipping trade. There is a castle in it raised on a very high mound surrounded by an impregnable wall and fortified with towers of hewn limestone constructed by the emperors.' If William of Malmesbury wrote a guide to holy England, the author of the *Gesta Stephani* was well on his way to writing a guide to English towns and castles.

Despite the author's interest in and knowledge of warfare, military architecture and urban England, the tone of the *Gesta* is not predominantly secular. The author had a close interest in church affairs, and the edificatory theme is all pervasive. He devotes space to the condition of the church. Though he deplores Stephen's attack on Roger of Salisbury, Alexander of Lincoln and Nigel of Ely, he bitterly criticizes their wealth and magnificence,[48] and he blames Henry of Winchester for acting more like a robber than a bishop.[49] He criticizes some (unnamed) bishops for not taking sterner spiritual measures against the barons during the anarchy, and others for fortifying themselves in castles and plundering the countryside.[50] Of all the iniquities perpetrated in the anarchy, he objects most to the robbing and burning of churches, monasteries and nunneries, and particularly to their use as fortifications.[51]

The *Gesta* (to 1148) represents Stephen's reign as the king's punishment for sin and his retribution.[52] Divine portents herald King David's attack on Northumberland in 1138[53] and Stephen's defeat at Lincoln in 1141.[54] 'The supreme architect of the universe, though invisible, yet condescends kindly to our ignorance and instructs us visibly about the future.' The author compares such contemporary heavenly portents with two recorded in the Old Testament, by which men 'surely recognized coming evil'.[55] References to the bible frequently reinforce the moral purpose of the *Gesta*. People are compared with biblical characters[56] and the argument is strengthened with

---

[47] *GS*, pp. 22, 29, 32, 37–8, 38–9, 92, 113, 120, respectively. For a short description of Scotland see ibid., p. 36.

[48] *GS*, pp. 48, 64–5. [49] *GS*, p. 104.

[50] *GS*, pp. 103–4.

[51] See *GS*, pp. 102–3, for attacks on church property in general. The nunneries of Wherwell (p. 87) and Wilton (p. 97) were sacked, and Hereford cathedral (p. 72) and Ramsey abbey (p. 109) were used as forts.

[52] See Davis, 'Authorship', pp. 210, 223.

[53] *GS*, pp. 33–4.

[54] *GS*, p. 74. This is also mentioned by Henry of Huntingdon; *HH*, p. 271.

[55] *GS*, p. 34.

[56] e.g. *GS*, pp. 39, 42.

biblical quotations: for example the contention that Stephen's troubles were particularly grievous because his enemies were his own people is corroborated by a quotation from John xiii. 18: 'A man's foes shall they be of his own household.'[57]

The author's edificatory purpose affects his attitude to historical causation. Events are ascribed to the will of God. It was God's wish that Stephen should be captured at the battle of Lincoln 'so that his elevation afterwards should be loftier and more unexpected'.[58] The author sometimes explicitly prefers a divine to a rational cause. He asserts that the springs of water in Exeter castle dried up because God willed them to. The author admits that some say that the sun dried up the wells. But, he reiterates, 'for my part I do not ascribe it to the heat of the sun or to any accident, but loudly proclaim that the divine power was concerned in the drying up of the wells.' He points out that when the castle had surrendered to the king there was again a good supply of water which had always previously been inexhaustible.[59] The author also uses the idea of changeable fortune to emphasize the instability of earthly achievement. Like William of Malmesbury, in the *Historia Novella*, he mentions the wheel of fortune.[60] He regards the changes of fortune as being in God's disposition.[61] But he gives rational explanations for some events. Although he describes Matilda's escape from Oxford as a miracle (because she crossed the river without getting wet and passed through the king's pickets without being heard) he gives a reasonable explanation: the water was covered with thick ice and the pickets were blowing trumpets and shouting.[62]

The *Gesta Stephani* was concerned only with contemporary history. The most ambitious work of the period, including both past and present history, was Henry of Huntingdon's *Historia Anglorum (History of the English)*.[63] Henry was probably born in Cambridgeshire or Huntingdonshire;[64] his father was a clerk called Nicholas, and Henry may have had some association with Ramsey abbey since he refers to Abbot Aldwin as 'dominus meus'. As a young boy he entered the household of Robert Bloet, bishop of Lincoln from 1093 to 1123, and became archdeacon of Huntingdon. On Robert's death Henry served his successor Alexander of Blois, who was bishop from 1123 to 1148. Alexander was the nephew of Roger bishop of Salisbury,

---

[57] *GS*, p. 47. [58] *GS*, p. 76.

[59] *GS*, pp. 25–6.

[60] 'nunc Fortuna secula nostra rotans istum ad summa sustollit, et mox eundem ad inferiora deicit'; *GS*, p. 62. Cf. p. 125 for a similar reference. See p. 183 above for William of Malmesbury's use of the concept of fortune.

[61] *GS*, p. 117. [62] *GS*, pp. 94–5.

[63] The most recent edition is *Henrici Archidiaconi Huntendunensis Historia Anglorum*, ed. Thomas Arnold (RS, 1879). For an English translation see *The Chronicle of Henry of Huntingdon*, ed. and translated by T. Forester (London 1853).

[64] For his life see *HH*, pp. xxxi–xxxiv.

the supporter of King Stephen, and was famous for the magnificence of his court. He was a friend of St Bernard,[65] and a patron both of the Cistercians and the Augustinian canons. It was he who commissioned Henry to write a history of the English from the earliest times to the present day.[66]

Henry began writing soon before 1133, bringing the history down to 1129. Writing at various dates between 1129 and 1154, he continued the history to Henry II's accession, intending to add a book on Henry II's reign, but apparently he died before he could do so.[67] As Henry extended the work, he also recast it. In 1135 he added a prologue and put the existing epilogue after the continuation which he had added for the years from 1130 to 1135. In 1145 he increased the number of books into which the history was divided from seven to eight and incorporated two more books. These two additional books do not belong to the historical narrative of the work. One, the De Summitatibus (On Exalted Subjects), comprises three letters which Henry had written for publication rather than for the addressee in particular. The first was written between 1131 and 1135 and addressed to Henry I, concerning the succession of kings and emperors of various kingdoms in the world;[68] the second letter was to Warin 'a Briton' and gave a brief account of the British kings from Brutus to Cadwallader, taken from Geoffrey of Monmouth;[69] and the third was to 'Walter' (possibly an archdeacon of Leicester)[70] who was dead by the time Henry had completed the letter,[71] and was about 'contempt of the world' (De Contemptu Mundi).[72] The other additional book was the De Miraculis and related to the miracles of English saints.[73] Henry inserted these two new books (as Books VIII and IX) after Book VII of the history, which went down to the death of Henry I, and renumbered the original Book VIII (which covered the years from 1135 onwards) as Book X.[74]

Henry's work had immediate success. Twenty-five medieval copies are known to be extant, five, and possibly three more, being of the twelfth century.[75] The provenance of eight of these manuscripts is known. It is

[65] Epistola, no. 64; Migne, PL, vol. clxxxii, coll. 169–70.

[66] HH, p. 3.

[67] For the growth of the Historia Anglorum see HH, pp. xi–xvi. Arnold's arguments concerning the successive editions of Henry's work are not clear or convincing.

[68] This is not printed, but is noticed, by Arnold; see HH, pp. xiv, xix–xx.

[69] Noticed by Arnold in HH; pp. xx–xxi. Printed in Migne, PL, vol. clx, coll. 423–4 and in RT, vol. i, pp. 97–111. Cf. p. 200 below.

[70] For a brief notice of Walter, archdeacon of Leicester, 'vir omnino laudandus', see HH, p. 302.

[71] For his death and an elegy on it see the end of De Contemptu Mundi; HH, pp. 319–20.

[72] Printed in HH, pp. 297–320. Cf. p. 197 below.

[73] Described and extracts printed in HH, pp. xxiv–xxx.

[74] See HH, p. xv.

[75] For a list of MSS. see HH, pp. xxxvi–xlii. The 'Savile' MS., which Arnold numbers 2 (HH, p. xxxvii) and was unable to trace, is now BM MS. Egerton 3668. Incidentally Arnold (HH, p. xxxvii n. 1) mis-dates the sale 1862, and misquotes the sale catalogue (which is Sotheby, 6 February 1861, lot 10). This MS. was previously Phillipps MS. 25151, so the 'Savile' MS.

noteworthy that only two copies are known to have belonged to English Benedictine houses: there is a twelfth-century copy from Durham cathedral priory,[76] and a thirteenth-century one from Gloucester abbey.[77] The other copies of known provenance come from houses of the Augustinian canons (a twelfth-century copy from Merton, in Surrey,[78] a twelfth- or thirteenth-century copy from Southwick in Hampshire,[79] and a fourteenth-century copy from Llanthony in Gloucestershire),[80] from the Arrouaisians of Bourne in Lincolnshire (a twelfth- or thirteenth-century copy),[81] and from the Dominican convent in Lincoln itself (a fourteenth-century copy).[82] One early copy may be from the Cistercian abbey of Kirkstall.[83] A northern historian, Alfred of Beverley,[84] and probably Ailred of Rievaulx,[85] both writing before 1150, had access to the *Historia*. Henry's influence was not confined to England. Before the middle of the twelfth century a copy was at Bec,[86] and soon after one was at Mont-Saint-Michel,[87] and there was a twelfth- or thirteenth-century copy at Jumièges.[88]

As a monastic chronicler would have done, Henry shows a strong affection for his home, Lincoln. He relates how in 1085 Bishop Remigius, on removing his see from Dorchester to Lincoln, 'built a strong and beautiful church to the virgin of virgins, on a strong and beautiful site on the steep slopes of that city, next to the castle crowned with mighty towers'.[89] When Bishop Alexander had to rebuild the cathedral, owing to destruction by fire, he did this 'in so wonderful a style that it was more beautiful than when first built

---

cannot be, as Arnold suggested, identified with Phillipps MS. 8079 (*HH*, p. xliii, n. 31); the British Museum has no record of the whereabouts of Phillipps MS. 8079. A twelfth-century copy of the *Hist. Angl.*, not recorded by Arnold, is in Ushaw College, Co. Durham; see W. Levison, 'A combined MS. of Geoffrey of Monmouth and Henry of Huntingdon' in *EHR*, lviii (1943), pp. 41–51.

[76] BM MS. Egerton 3668. This manuscript belonged to Durham cathedral priory until the fifteenth century, when it came into the possession of the Carmelites of Lincoln. I owe this information to Mr J. P. Hudson of the Department of Manuscripts in the British Museum.

[77] Lambeth MS. 179; *HH*, p. xl. For its provenance see N. R. Ker, *Medieval Libraries of Great Britain* (London 1941), p. 92.

[78] Lambeth MS. 118; *HH*, p. xxxviii. For its provenance see Ker, op. cit., p. 131.

[79] BM MS. Arundel 48; *HH*, p. xxxviii. For its provenance see ibid., p. xxxviii n. 2 and Ker, op. cit., p. 181. For a reference to a picture in it, see p. 364 and n. 59 below.

[80] BM MS. Additional 24061; *HH*, p. xl. For its provenance see Ker, op. cit., p. 108.

[81] Lambeth MS. 327; *HH*, p. xxxviii. For its provenance see Ker, op. cit., p. 11.

[82] BM MS. Royal 13 B VI; *HH*, p. xl. For its provenance see Ker, op. cit., p. 119.

[83] Levison, op. cit., p. 46.

[84] See p. 212.

[85] See pp. 215 and n. 268, 216 and nn. 279–80, 217 below.

[86] This copy is now lost. It probably reached to 1147 and was the exemplar of the surviving copy from Mont-Saint-Michel (see the next note and *Chronique de Robert de Torigni*, ed. L. Delisle (Soc. de l'Histoire de Normandie, 1872, 1873, 2 vols), vol I, pp. lix–lxi).

[87] Bibl. Nat. MS. Lat. 6042; *HH*, p. xxxvii and n. 1. Robert of Torigni, abbot of Mont-Saint-Michel, 1154–86, had a copy of the *Historia Anglorum* to 1135 (see p. 200 below) and later had a copy of it to 1147, of which Bibl. Nat. MS. Lat. 6042 may be a transcript: see Delisle, op. cit., pp. lv–lxi.

[88] Bibl. Pub. Rouen; *HH*, p. xxxviii and n. 1.

[89] *HH*, p. 212.

and was excelled by none in all England'.[90] Henry managed to include quite a lot of material relating to the see of Lincoln. Most of this is in the letter *De Contemptu Mundi*. Under pretext of illustrating the fact that all men die, he gives an account of the clerks (now dead) whom Remigius introduced into his new cathedral.[91] Henry writes partly from memory and partly from what he had heard.[92] He then describes their successors, some of whom were still living. For example the nephew of the earliest treasurer, Rayner, held the office in Henry's day.[93] Henry names the three archdeacons appointed by Remigius, and gives a list of their successors until his own time. The bishops of Lincoln are eulogized, especially in the historical books of the *Historia*. Remigius himself is praised: he was 'small in stature but large of heart, dark in complexion but enlightened in his works'.[94] There is an element of eulogy in the description of Bishop Robert Bloet (although Henry does intimate that he loved worldly splendour too much[95]), which contrasts sharply with the account given by William of Malmesbury.[96] In Henry's view he 'excelled everyone in grace of person, beauty of mind and gentleness of address',[97] he was 'kind and humble, he raised many men up and crushed none, he was the father of orphans and the beloved of those nearest him'.[98] The eulogy of Henry's dedicatee, Bishop Alexander, is even more fulsome. There is a panegyrical verse on him,[99] and he is described as 'always courteous, just, good-humoured and cheerful'.[100] Henry enlarges on his magnificent style of living and his great generosity. But in a section written after Alexander's death, Henry criticizes him for having spent beyond his means.[101]

Henry probably allowed himself some reservations in his eulogy of the bishops of Lincoln partly because of his desire to edify his readers – he used the bishops' lives to illustrate moral precepts. Henry's edificatory intention permeates the *Historia*. In the traditional way, God is represented as punishing sin. Thus God punished the sins of the English with plagues and invasions,[102] He punished Duke Robert with perpetual imprisonment for refusing the kingdom of Jerusalem,[103] He inflicted capture and a miserable death on Roger bishop of Salisbury because he broke his oath to the Empress Matilda,[104] and He avenged with death the sacrilege of Geoffrey de Mandeville.[105] But this does not mean that Henry was always an irrational historian. He sometimes reconciled rational with divine causation. For example he attributed the failure of the crusaders in 1148 to God's displeasure with them for their sins; as a result they first suffered from famine, were then betrayed, and were finally defeated in battle.[106]

[90] *HH*, pp. 278–9.   [91] *HH*, pp. 301–3.
[92] 'Sed non loquimur nisi de auditis et visis'; *HH*, p. 301.   [93] *HH*, p. 301.
[94] *HH*, p. 212. Cf. William of Malmesbury, *GP*, iv. 177 (p. 313) for a similar remark.
[95] *De Contemptu Mundi* in *HH*, p. 299.   [96] *GP*, iv. 177 (p. 313 and n. 4).
[97] *HH*, p. 216.   [98] *De Contemptu Mundi* in *HH*, p. 300.   [99] *HH*, pp. 246–7.
[100] *HH*, p. 278.   [101] *HH*, p. 280.   [102] *HH*, p. 139.   [103] *HH*, p. 236.
[104] *HH*, p. 256.   [105] *HH*, p. 277.   [106] *HH*, p. 280.

Henry stresses the transitory nature of worldly prosperity. He omits an account of the Roman emperors 'because they have no glory now'. They 'for whose power and majesty scarcely the whole world sufficed ... are nothing now'.[107] The moral is that only heavenly glory lasts. The same point is made in reference to the deaths of Ranulf Flambard[108] and Henry I.[109] The theme is elaborated in the letter to Walter, *De Contemptu Mundi*, which is virtually a sermon.[110] Examples from history are used to demonstrate the wisdom of contempt for the world. The greatest men, both good and bad, kings such as Henry I, bishops such as Robert Bloet, nobles like Robert count of Meulan, all die, some after misfortune and unhappiness. The argument is reinforced with biblical precepts. For example, the misfortunes of Bishop Bloet show that 'Cursed be the man that trusteth in man, and maketh flesh his arm' (Jeremiah xvii. 5),[111] and the fall of Robert count of Meulan and others illustrate the precept that 'the wisdom of this world is foolishness with God' (I Corinthians iii. 19).[112]

Henry loved a good story, but he used stories, as a preacher would, to point a moral. The famous story, for which he is the earliest authority, that Henry I died from eating a surfeit of lampreys, is told to illustrate Ovid's adage that 'men strive against rules and seek forbidden things'.[113] There is no reason to disbelieve this account, but some of Henry's tales are purely legendary. He wrote the well-known one about King Canute and the tide to demonstrate that earthly power is nothing compared with God's. Canute, with all his regal authority, ordered his throne to be put on the sea shore when the tide was coming in. He said to the rising waters: 'You are subject to my rule, and the land on which I sit is mine – there is no one who can resist my authority with impunity. I order you therefore not to rise on to my land, nor to presume to wet either the clothes or the feet of your ruler.' But the sea, rising in its usual manner, wet the king's feet and legs without respect. The king therefore got up and said, 'May all the inhabitants of the world know that the power of kings is vain and frivolous, and no king is worthy of the name except Him, at whose nod land and sea obey eternal laws.'[114]

Finally, Henry's desire to edify appears in Book IX of the *De Miraculis*. The rest of the *Historia* does not have hagiographical miracles. These are grouped together in this one book. Much of the information is derived from

---

[107] See *HH*, pp. 37–8. Cf. p. 66 (the end of Book II).

[108] *HH*, p. 244.

[109] *HH*, p. 257. Cf. the account of William the Conqueror's death in the Anglo-Saxon Chronicle (p. 94 above) and in Orderic (p. 159 above).

[110] Henry, having said that he will now describe great men who have fallen from power and are forgotten, addresses Walter: 'Audi igitur, Waltere consors charissime, sermocinationem de viris illustribus, sed tamen in audiendo taediosum, licet eos oculis nostris inspeximus'; *HH*, p. 314.

[111] *HH*, p. 300.   [112] *HH*, p. 306.

[113] Ovid, *Amor.*, iii. 4. 17. See *HH*, p. 254.

[114] *HH*, pp. 188–9. The same story is told by Geoffrey Gaimar; see p. 210 and n. 230 below.

Bede,[115] but some is added concerning more recent English saints. Henry advises those readers who want to know more about these saints to visit their churches themselves.[116] For St Swithun the reader should go to Winchester, for St Aldhelm to Sherborne, for St Milburg to Wenlock, and so on. Henry seems to have meant his readers to look at the shrines and read the saints' Lives and books of miracles kept in the church.[117] He was doing on a small scale what William of Malmesbury did at length in the *Gesta Pontificum* (to which Henry's work may be related[118]) – providing a guidebook for pilgrims.

This admonition to study saints 'on the spot' is reminiscent of Goscelin's and William of Malmesbury's method. But the interest in hagiography goes back to Bede. Henry's debt to Bede as a historian was considerable. On the advice of Bishop Alexander he made the *Ecclesiastical History* the basis of the early part of his work, starting, as Bede did, with a geographical description of Britain.[119] Like Bede, Henry appreciated the value of history as a record. He copied documents in full and apparently intended (foreshadowing Matthew Paris) to put decrees of councils and other documents in a separate book, instead of in the text of the *Historia*, in order to keep the historical narrative in scale.[120] Henry was also indebted to the Anglo-Saxon Chronicle. When Bede stopped, the Chronicle became Henry's principal source until his own time. He continued to make sporadic use of it until 1121[121] and probably, like William of Malmesbury, got the idea of writing continuous contemporary history from the Chronicle.

Henry drew on the tradition of the Anglo-Norman historians. There is no evidence of direct borrowing from either William of Malmesbury or Orderic Vitalis. But there are such strong similarities between some aspects of their works as to suggest that they may have used a common source. However, the parallels could be the result of no more than a common intellectual background. All three authors mention Harold's oath to Duke William, promising him the succession to the English throne.[122] They all give a similar description of the warlike character of the Normans, though Henry goes farther than the other two, asserting that God chose the Normans on account of their brutality to punish the English.[123] The three authors all criticize King Stephen for being too lenient and easily led.[124] They all

---

[115] *HH*, p. xxiv. [116] *HH*, pp. xxv–xxvi. [117] *HH*, p. xxvi and n. 1.
[118] See below. [119] *HH*, p. 3.
[120] Henry states that the decrees of Archbishop Theodore, issued at the Council of Hertford (673) 'in ultimo librorum ponentur'; *HH*, p. 101 and n. b. Henry says that he omits St Augustine's questions to Gregory the Great and the replies 'quia prolixa sunt' and adds 'in decretis vel canonibus lector quaerat et inveniet'. There is no evidence supporting Arnold's conjecture that this is a reference to Henry's projected book; ibid., p. 69 and n. a.
[121] See *ASC*, p. xix.
[122] Cf. *HH*, p. 197; *OV*, iii. 11 (vol. 2, 117); WM, *GR*, ii. 228 (vol. 1, pp. 279–80). Cf. p. 158 above.
[123] 'Elegerat enim Deus Normannos ad Anglorum gentem exterminandam, quia praerogativa saevitiae singularis omnibus populis viderat eos praeminere. Natura siquidem eorum est ut,

emphasize the effect of the vagaries of fortune on the destinies of man, and mention, at least by implication, the wheel of fortune.[125] In one place Henry's work has a parallel in one of William's (the *Gesta Pontificum*) but not in Orderic's: this is the account of the miracle of St Werburg in *De Miraculis*.[126] In other places the *Historia* resembles Orderic's work but not William's. Henry gives a short account of St Bricstan (Orderic gives a long one).[127] They both comment on the lack of miracles in their time.[128] To stress the transitory nature of all earthly achievement, and even of historical records of them, Henry and Orderic use a rather similar image, derived from Psalm lviii. 6. Henry says that everything comes to nothing 'like running water'; Orderic says that memorials of the past vanish 'like hail or snow melt inexorably into the waves of a fast flowing river'.[129] Sometimes Henry pushes an argument farther than Orderic does. Orderic implied that the wreck of the White Ship was due to God's vengeance for immorality: Henry explicitly states that it was the result of homosexuality at court.[130] Orderic alleges that Henry I allowed his grand-daughters' eyes to be put out, while, according to Henry of Huntingdon, he actually gave the order for this to be done.[131]

Although it is hardly possible that there was any direct relationship between Henry's and Orderic's work, Henry did have contact with another Norman historian. In 1139 he accompanied Theobald archbishop of Canterbury to Rome, and on the way they stayed at Bec.[132] There he met the historian Robert of Torigni (otherwise called Robert de Monte). Robert was at this time a monk of Bec and had just started his historical studies – interpolating and continuing (to 1135) William of Jumièges's *Gesta Normannorum*

---

cum hostes suos adeo depresserint, ut adjicere non possint, ipsi se deprimant, et se terrasque suas in pauperiem et vastitatem redigant; semperque Normannorum domini, cum hostes contriverint, cum crudeliter non agere nequeant, suos etiam hostiliter conterunt'; *HH*, p. 208. Cf. pp. 158 n. 177, 173 above for the parallel in Orderic and William.

[124] Cf. *HH*, p. 259 (for Stephen's being led by bad counsel cf. *HH*, p. 266); *WM, HN*, p. 16; *OV*, xiii. 41 (vol. 5, 121).

[125] 'Nullus igitur de felicitatis assiduitate confidat; nullus de fortunae stabilitate praesumat; nullus in rota volubili sedem confixam diu superesse contendat'; *HH*, p. 267. For the parallels in Orderic see p. 160 and n. 189 above and in William see p. 183 above.

[126] *HH*, p. xxviii; *WM, GP*, iv. 172 (p. 308).

[127] *HH*, p. xxv; *OV*, vi. 10 (vol. 3, pp. 123–33).

[128] *HH*, pp. xxviii–xxix; *OV*, vi. 1 (vol. 3, p. 2); and cf. v. 1 (vol. 2, p. 302), vi. 10 (vol. 3, p. 133).

[129] 'Nunc enim fere nemo eorum recordatur. Omnis memoria eorum interire incepit; mox nulla erit; ad nihilum devenient tanquam aqua decurrens'; *HH*, p. 314 (*De Contemptu Mundi*). 'Codicibus autem perditis, antiquorum res gestae oblivioni traditae sunt; quae a modernis qualibet arte recuperari non possunt, quia veterum monimenta cum mundo praetereunte a memoria praesentium deficiunt, quasi grando vel nix in undis cum rapide flumine irremeabiliter fluente defluunt'; *OV*, vi. 9 (vol. 3, pp. 67–8). Psalm lviii. 6 reads, 'Omnes morimur, et tanquam aquae dilabimur, quae non revertuntur'. For the destructability of historical records see also *HH*, p. 317 (*De Contemptu Mundi*); 'Sed et pellis ovina, in qua depinguntur eorum nomina, perdita videtur omnino, nec invenimus oculos, qui eam perlegere velint.'

[130] *HH*, p. 242; *OV*, xii. 25 (vol. 4, p. 416).

[131] *HH*, p. 311 (*De Contemptu Mundi*); *OV*, xii. 10 (vol. 4, p. 337).

[132] See Henry's letter to Warin the Briton; see p. 194 and n. 69 above.

Ducum.[133] Later, in 1154, Robert became abbot of Mont-Saint-Michel which he ruled until his death in 1186.[134] There he wrote his chronicle, a continuation of Sigebert of Gembloux covering the years from 1112 to 1186, composed in various stages. He borrowed much of his information about English history before 1147 from Henry of Huntingdon's *Historia*. As has been seen, a copy of the *Historia* to 1147 from Mont-Saint-Michel still survives, probably a transcript of the original copy used by Robert.[135] Previously he had a copy to 1135 at Bec, which presumably Henry gave him on his visit,[136] and must subsequently have obtained the extended version. Robert in his turn influenced Henry, by showing him a copy of Geoffrey of Monmouth's *Historia Regum Brittaniae*.[137] Henry was delighted with, and amazed at, this largely legendary history of the British kings which had been written only three years before and was still almost unknown in England. He summarized some of its contents in his letter to 'Warin the Briton'[138] and when he next revised his own history he inserted a few passages from Geoffrey's work.[139]

Henry liked Geoffrey's work partly because he found it amusing. As a writer, even before he read Geoffrey, he had some features in common with him. Part of his own object was to amuse his readers, and he, like Geoffrey, catered for the contemporary love of good stories (two of Henry's famous stories have already been mentioned) and romance history. The Canute story not only in itself, but also in its context, shows Henry's taste for legend. For it is part of a triad, a characteristic mythopoeic feature. Canute's attempt to command the tide was, according to Henry, one of three 'gracious and splendid things' done by the king.[140] Henry's predilection for the magic digit three also appears in his attribution to Henry I of three divine gifts, three virtues and three vices,[141] and the division into three of the royal dynasties of France.[142]

Like Geoffrey of Monmouth, Henry was interested in King Arthur, giving

---

[133] His interpolations and continuation are printed in William of Jumièges, *GND*, pp. 199–334.

[134] For Robert's life and works see *RT*, vol. 2, pp. i–xix, and pp. 261–3 below.

[135] See p. 195 nn. 86, 87.

[136] For Robert's references to Henry's work see *RT*, vol. 1, pp. 94 n. 1, 96–7.

[137] Robert mentions Henry's visit to Bec and that he lent him a copy of Geoffrey of Monmouth, asking him to make excerpts from it; *RT*, vol. 1, p. 96. Professor Brooke has pointed out that as Henry of Huntingdon was archdeacon in the diocese where Geoffrey of Monmouth lived, the latter must quite deliberately have concealed the existence of his book from Henry, who had to go to Normandy before seeing a copy; C. N. L. Brooke, 'The archbishops of St. David's, Llandaff and Caerleon-on-Usk' in *Studies in the Early British Church*, ed. N. K. Chadwick (Cambridge 1958), p. 231 and n. 2.

[138] See p. 194 and n. 69 above.

[139] Henry may have got the identification of Kaerperis as Porchester and the name of King Liud (Lud), from Geoffrey; *HH*, pp. 7, 17. Cf. J. S. P. Tatlock, *The Legendary History of Britain* (University of California Press, 1950), pp. 31 n. 121, 49.

[140] See p. 197 and n. 114 above.

[141] *HH*, pp. 236, 255. Cf. ibid., pp. 301–2.

[142] *HH*, pp. 248–9.

an account of his battles (derived from Nennius).[143] And like Geoffrey he was interested in a nation's mythical ancestors belonging to classical times: he traces the ancestry of the French kings back to Antenor, an exile from the fall of Troy.[144] Such mythical royal genealogies are a feature of romance literature. The influence of the latter, with its penchant for dramatic descriptions of martial heroism, can perhaps be seen in Henry's account of King Stephen's prowess at the battle of Lincoln:[145]

> No respite, no breathing time, was given to the royal army except where the bravest of kings stood, where the enemy were terrified by the unmatched force of his blows. When the earl of Chester saw this, envying the king his glory, he rushed at him with all the weight of his soldiers. Then the king's huge axe gleamed like lightning, driving back some, felling others. At length it was shattered by the rain of blows. The king drew his sword with which he wrought wonders, until that too was broken.

Geoffrey of Monmouth did not create the appetite in his contemporaries for romance history: he fed and sharpened an existing appetite. There is little definite information about Geoffrey's life. He calls himself 'of Monmouth' and there is no reason to doubt that he had some early connection with Monmouth. He also shows a close interest in Caerleon-on-Usk which has led to the suggestion that he was a Welshman. However, as he disliked the Welsh and expressed approval of the Bretons perhaps he was a Breton by birth. By 1129 Geoffrey was settled in Oxford. He became bishop of St Asaph's in 1152 and probably died in 1154.[146]

Geoffrey probably wrote the *Historia Regum Britanniae* in 1136.[147] It is a legendary history of the Britons from prehistoric times until the late seventh century A.D. It was very popular in the middle ages, both in England and abroad. Nearly two hundred medieval manuscripts are known to have survived (more than of Bede's *Ecclesiastical History*), about fifty dating from the twelfth century, and over one-third of the total are in continental

---

[143] *HH*, pp. 48–9.

[144] *HH*, p. 248.

[145] *HH*, p. 274.

[146] For Geoffrey's life see J. E. Lloyd, 'Geoffrey of Monmouth' in *EHR*, lvii (1942), pp. 460–8, and H. E. Salter, 'Geoffrey of Monmouth and Oxford' in *EHR*, xxxiv (1919), pp. 382–5. For a useful résumé of the evidence, with further references, see Geoffrey of Monmouth, *The History of the Kings of Britain*, translated with an introduction by Lewis Thorpe (Penguin Classics, 1966), pp. 10–14.

[147] The standard edition (of the Welsh as well as the Latin version) is *The Historia Regum Britanniae of Geoffrey of Monmouth*, ed. Acton Griscom (London 1929). A good modern translation is by Lewis Thorpe (see previous note). The *Historia* was certainly written before 1139 (as Henry of Huntingdon saw a copy at Bec in that year), but how long before is uncertain. Griscom, op. cit., pp. 42–98, dates it to April 1136; Tatlock, op. cit., p. 437, dates it between 1130 and 1138.

Europe.[148] Geoffrey's influence on subsequent historians was great.[149] From the late twelfth century to the sixteenth his history of the ancient Britons was the generally (but not universally) accepted authority.[150] Furthermore, it was paraphrased in prose and verse, and translated into Welsh, Old English and Anglo-Norman.[151] The vernacular versions were the stock from which grew numerous chronicles. The *Brut* chronicles (so called from the Brutus story), are continuations of the vernacular versions.[152] The *Historia* became popular because it was (according to the tastes of the age) entertaining, because it was patriotic and because there was little genuine information available on the subject.

Geoffrey was a romance writer masquerading as a historian. No historian today would object to him if he had avowedly written a historical novel (like Sir Walter Scott) or a romance-epic (like Malory). But on the contrary he pretended to be writing history. He begins, like Bede and William of Malmesbury whose works he knew, by stating his 'authorities'. He claims that he used oral tradition, and 'a certain very old book written in the British language' which had been given him by Walter archdeacon of Oxford.[153] He later says that Walter brought the book 'from Brittany' ('ex Britannia').[154] He claims that this book, 'attractively composed to form a consecutive and orderly narrative, set out all the deeds of these men, from Brutus, the first king of the Britons, down to Cadwallader, the son of Cadwallo. At Walter's

---

[148] For lists of the manuscripts see *HRB*, pp. 551–77, and Jacob Hammer, 'Some additional manuscripts of Geoffrey of Monmouth's *Historia Regum Britanniae*' in *Modern Language Quarterly*, iii (1942), pp. 235–42. See also p. 194 n. 75 above. For variant versions of the *Historia* see Hywel D. Emanuel, 'Geoffrey of Monmouth's *Historia Regum Britanniae*: a second variant version' in *Medium Ævum*, xxxv (1966), pp. 103–10 (and further references therein).

[149] For the influence of the *Historia* on chroniclers in England see Laura Keeler, 'The *Historia Regum Britanniae* and four mediaeval chroniclers' in *Speculum*, xxi (1946), pp. 24–37. The influence of the *Historia* spread far afield: see Jacob Hammer, 'Remarks on the sources and textual history of Geoffrey of Monmouth's *Historia Regum Britanniae*, with an excursus on the *Chronica Polonorum* by Wincenty Kadłubek (Magister Vincentius)' in *Bulletin of the Polish Institute of Arts and Sciences in America*, ii (1934–44), pp. 501–64, and Margaret Schlauch, 'Geoffrey of Monmouth and early Polish historiography: a supplement' in *Speculum*, xliv (1969), pp. 258–63.

[150] For the triumph of Geoffrey's *Historia* and the ultimate decline of its reputation in the sixteenth century see T. D. Kendrick, *British Antiquity* (London 1950), especially chapters I, V, VI.

[151] For the vernacular versions see Tatlock, op. cit., pp. 451–531 and next note. See also, for the Welsh versions, Acton Griscom's introduction to *HRB, passim*.

[152] For the *Brut* chronicles see Legge, *A-N Lit.*, p. 280 and nn. (and her index for further references); F. W. D. Brie, *Geschichte und Quellen der mittelenglischen Prosachronik 'The Brute of England'* (Marburg 1905); *The Brut or the Chronicles of England*, ed. F. W. D. Brie (EETS, cxxxi, 1906, cxxxvi, 1908, 2 vols); W. J. Keith, 'Laȝamon's *Brut*: the literary differences between the two texts' in *Medium Ævum*, xxix (1960), pp. 161–72; and Alexander Bell, 'The Royal Brut interpolation' in *Medium Ævum*, xxxii (1963), pp. 190–202.

[153] *HRB*, i. 1 (p. 219).

[154] *HRB*, p. 536. Tatlock, op. cit., p. 423, states that 'there can be no question at all that *ex Britannia* can only mean from Brittany.' But this view is not accepted by all scholars; see Thorpe, op. cit., p. 284 n. 1 and cf. p. 39 n. 4) who translates it as 'from Wales'.

request I have taken the trouble to translate the book into Latin.'[155] Whether or not this 'very old' book ever existed has been much debated by scholars.[156] Certainly no definite trace of it has been found. On the whole it seems most likely that Geoffrey invented its existence. He probably did no more than borrow from Gildas, Nennius, Bede, William of Malmesbury (the *Gesta Regum* and *Gesta Pontificum*) and the earliest recension of Henry of Huntingdon,[157] supplementing these authorities partly from oral tradition but mainly from his imagination.

The way Geoffrey treats his known sources corroborates the view that he was capable of intellectual dishonesty. He cites Gildas seven times as his authority. But three statements he alleges that he derived from Gildas are not from him,[158] and twice the reference to Gildas is only accurate in a very general sense – Geoffrey exaggerates his debt.[159] He tries to give his work the appearance of historicity by asserting that he will not quote the 'sayings of the Eagle' because 'they are not true': but later he does cite them.[160] Nor is there good evidence that Geoffrey drew to any appreciable extent on oral tradition. He gives the earliest known version of the legend of King Lear. Scholars have failed to prove that the Lear legend existed before Geoffrey wrote.[161] He gives a long account of King Arthur and his exploits. Here, though there were already some legendary tales about Arthur,[162] Geoffrey was the first man to write an elaborate Arthurian legend.[163] Moreover, the prophecies of Merlin seem to have been worked up by Geoffrey from the 'Ambrose' legend in Nennius.[164]

---

[155] *HRB*, i. 1 (p. 219). I have followed Professor Thorpe's translation for this and the following quotations.

[156] e.g. see Tatlock, op. cit., pp. 423 et seq.; Kendrick, op. cit., p. 5.

[157] Geoffrey explicitly mentions William of Malmesbury and Henry of Huntingdon at the end of his work, advising them to be silent about the British kings as they know nothing about them; *HRB*, p. 536. This explicit reference does not occur in all the manuscripts. For references relating to Geoffrey's debt to William and Henry see the index to Tatlock, op. cit., under 'Henry of Huntingdon' and 'William of Malmesbury'.

[158] *HRB*, i. 17 (p. 252); ii. 17 (p. 275); iii. 5 (p. 282). Nor are these statements in Nennius whom Geoffrey may, like other early writers, refer to as 'Gildas' (see *HRB*, i. 1 (p. 219) and Tatlock, op. cit., p. 4).

[159] These are the references to Gildas as the authority for the lives of the early British saints (here the references may be to Nennius); *HRB*, iv. 20 (p. 330); vi. 13 (p. 372). For a correct reference see *HRB*, xii. 6 (p. 520) and the general reference at the beginning, i. 1 (p. 219). Cf. Tatlock, op. cit., pp. 201, 235, 279, 285.

[160] *HRB*, ii. 10 (p. 261); xii. 18 (p. 534). Cf. Thorpe, op. cit., p. 23.

[161] *HRB*, ii. 10–14 (pp. 262–70). For a discussion of the Lear story, with references to other modern works, see Tatlock, op. cit., pp. 381–3.

[162] e.g. see Nennius, *HB*, c. 56; WM, *GR*, i. 8 (vol. 2, p. 11); iii. 287 (vol. 2, p. 342). For pre-Galfredian Arthurian legends see T. Jones, 'The early evolution of Arthur' in *Nottingham Mediaeval Studies*, viii (1964), pp. 3–21 (i.e. a translation by G. Morgan from the Welsh of Professor Jones's article which was first published in the *Bulletin of the Board of Celtic Studies*, xvii (1958), pp. 237–52).

[163] For a discussion of the Arthurian legends in *HRB*, with references to other modern works, see Tatlock, op. cit., pp. 178–229.

[164] *HB*, cc. 40–2. For a discussion of the prophecies of Merlin, with references to other modern works, see Tatlock, op. cit., pp. 403–21.

Possibly sometimes Geoffrey incorporated a shred of true history, derived from folklore, in his fantastic stories. For example he states that the stones of Stonehenge were brought from Ireland. Modern science has shown that they come from the Prescelly mountains in Pembrokeshire. At least here Geoffrey apparently preserves the tradition that the stone was not local.[165] Again he tells how the Britons decapitated a Roman legion by the Walbrook river in London. Modern archaeologists have dug up a number of human skulls from the Walbrook. Possibly Geoffrey here too incorporated an ancient tradition of slaughter.[166] But on the whole it seems most likely that Geoffrey's 'oral tradition' did not amount to much: his legends were the products of his imagination, helped in some cases by short notices in earlier written authorities and/or embryonic folk-tales.

Geoffrey dedicated his work to various people. Some copies he dedicated to Robert earl of Gloucester and Waleran de Beaumont count of Meulan (1104 to 1166),[167] others to Robert and to King Stephen, some to Robert alone, and one to Stephen alone.[168] He dedicated the Prophecies of Merlin to Alexander[169] bishop of Lincoln and then to Alexander's successor, Robert de Chesney (bishop from 1148 to 1166).[170] Probably Geoffrey hoped to interest all these people in his career. The multiplicity of dedicatees, all great men, shows a general desire to please the powers-that-were. Geoffrey tried to please by providing the Anglo-Normans with famous predecessors in Britain, by writing a 'tract for the times', and by telling romantic stories. Unlike the reputable historians of the day he had no moral, edificatory purpose, and no interest in recording historical facts.

In his attempt to give Britain a glorious past Geoffrey was trying to bring British history into line with continental histories. There was a dearth of information about the early Britons. After Virgil wrote the *Aeneid*, the Romans had claimed descent from Aeneas, an exile from the fall of Troy, and since the seventh century the French kings had claimed descent from another Trojan exile, Antenor.[171] Dudo of St Quentin asserted that the Normans also were ultimately descended from Antenor.[172] Now Geoffrey

---

[165] *HRB*, viii. 10–12 (p. 410–14). See also Stuart Piggott, 'The sources of Geoffrey of Monmouth' in *Antiquity*, xv (1941), pp. 305–19 ('The Stonehenge Story'). Piggott also postulates (op. cit., pp. 269–86, 'The "pre-Roman" king-list') that Geoffrey used Welsh dark age king-lists.

[166] *HRB*, v. 4 (p. 336). Griscom, *HRB*, pp. 211–14, supports the view that here Geoffrey incorporated a genuine tradition, but Tatlock, op. cit., pp. 31–3, does not agree.

[167] *HRB*, i. 1 (pp. 219–20).

[168] For these various dedications see Tatlock, op. cit., pp. 436–7.

[169] *HRB*, vii. 2 (p. 384).

[170] For the dedication to Bishop Alexander and Bishop Robert de Chesney, see Tatlock, op. cit., p. 444.

[171] The earliest reference to the Trojan origin of the Franks is in the chronicle of Fredegar (ii. 4–8; iii. 2), written in the seventh century; ed. Bruno Krusch in *MGH, Scriptores Rerum Merovingicarum*, vol. 2, 1888), pp. 45–7, 93. The legend was known at Henry I's court; see *HH*, pp. 248–9 (cf. pp. 95, 201 above).

[172] Dudo, *De Moribus et Actis Primorum Normanniae Ducum*, ed. J. Lair (Mémoires de la Société des Antiquaires de Normandie, 3rd series, vol. 3, 1865), pp. 32–4; i. 1 (p. 130).

tells how Brutus, yet another exile from Troy, after many adventures, settled in Britain with his followers, becoming its first inhabitant. This leads Geoffrey to his first false etymology (like those employed by some continental historians[173]): Britain, he asserts, was so called after Brutus.[174] Others follow – Billingsgate and London were named after the legendary British kings Belinus[175] and Lud[176] (such etymologies compare unfavourably with the sensible ones given by Bede and Asser). In this way Geoffrey provided classical ancestors for the British kings and ancient associations for some British towns.

Geoffrey attributed heroic qualities to the British kings, particularly to his three principal heroes, Brutus, Belinus and Arthur. And he asserts that the Britons defeated the Romans and sacked Rome.[177] He denies that Britain was ever truly subject to Rome – its subjection was voluntary[178] – and distorts the history of the Anglo-Saxon settlements to make it appear that the Britons more than held their own. Geoffrey was of course faced with the undeniable fact that the Anglo-Saxons did eventually defeat the Britons in England. So in order to protect the glorious reputation of the Britons he makes Arthur retire wounded to Avalon,[179] leaving the Britons to await his return as their saviour in accordance with the prophecy of Merlin.[180] Geoffrey emphasized that the present-day Welsh did not inherit the tradition of the ancient Britons. They were effete:[181] it was the Bretons who were the heirs of British heroism.[182] Such an argument, combining the glorification of the Britons with the denigration of the Anglo-Saxons and the contemporary Welsh, was bound to please the Anglo-Normans. They wanted Britain to have a glorious past, but they partly justified the Norman Conquest by the deficiencies of the Anglo-Saxons, and the hostile Welsh were one of their problems on the borders of England and Wales. Geoffrey pandered to the race-consciousness of his contemporaries. This 'racialism' appears in the works of William of Malmesbury, Henry of Huntingdon and Orderic Vitalis, in their sketches of the characteristics of the Normans.[183] As will be seen, the north-country writers – Ailred of Rievaulx and Richard of Hexham – had no doubt about the racial inferiority of the Picts: they regarded them as hardly human.[184] Geoffrey emphasizes that the Britons kept their blood pure. He asserts that they refused to intermarry with the Picts,[185] and tells how a shipload of women was sent to join those Britons who had gone to settle in Brittany, so that there would be no intermixture with Gallic blood.[186]

---

[173] e.g. see Orderic Vitalis, *Historia Ecclesiastica*, cited p. 159 and n. 183 above.
[174] *HRB*, i. 16 (p. 249).   [175] *HRB*, iii. 10 (p. 291).   [176] *HRB*, iii. 20 (p. 301).
[177] *HRB*, iii. 9 (pp. 287–90).   [178] *HRB*, iv. 11 (p. 320).   [179] *HRB*, xi. 2 (p. 501).
[180] *HRB*, vii. 3 (p. 388); xii. 17 (p. 533).   [181] *HRB*, xii. 19 (p. 535).
[182] For the migration of most of the Britons to Brittany see *HRB*, xii. 4–6 (pp. 516–21).
[183] See pp. 153, 158 n. 177, 173, 198 and n. 123 above.
[184] See pp. 215–17 and n. 284 below.   [185] *HRB*, iv. 17 (p. 327).
[186] *HRB*, v. 15 (p. 350).

The value Geoffrey's work has as a historical source is as a mirror of his own times, not as a record of the past. It reflects contemporary ideas and institutions. Geoffrey as a protégé of Robert of Gloucester, was a supporter of the Empress Matilda. So he praises women rulers, giving examples of successful British queens such as Marcia who (so he says) issued a law code from which the Mercian laws used by King Alfred took their name.[187] Geoffrey also abuses perjurors (Stephen had taken an oath to Henry I to support Matilda's claim to the throne) and describes the horrible fates that overtook them.[188] He gives examples of the calamities resulting from disputes among relatives for the right to the British throne.[189] Succession to the throne was by inheritance – Geoffrey does not mention any elective element. His idea of monarchy is typical of his times. King Arthur gave generous gifts to his followers[190] and could call on a feudal host.[191] The description of King Arthur's crown-wearing at Whitsun at Caerleon, and the council with his magnates which followed, is based on Anglo-Norman custom.[192] Geoffrey describes the feast held on this occasion, when the queen and her attendants dined alone 'as was the custom of Troy': actually this was an arrangement which went back to Anglo-Saxon times.[193] Geoffrey also reflected the imperial aspirations of the Anglo-Norman kings. Arthur's conquests in Europe and Scotland echo William the Conqueror's struggle to spread his power from Normandy into Maine and Brittany, and from England into Scotland.[194]

Geoffrey thought that there were three hallmarks of good kingship: law-making, the construction of fine buildings and the making and protection of roads. Geoffrey's emphasis on law-making reflects the legislative activity of the Anglo-Norman kings, especially of Henry I. Besides Marcia, he particularly mentions Dunvallo Molmutius as a famous British law-giver, whose laws 'are still famous today among the English',[195] and were (so Geoffrey asserts) translated from Welsh into Latin by Gildas, and into Anglo-Saxon by King Alfred.[196] One of these laws 'decreed that the temples of the gods and the cities should be so privileged that anyone who escaped to them as a fugitive or when accused of some crime must be pardoned by his accuser

---

[187] *HRB*, iii. 13 (pp. 293–4).

[188] See the account of Modred, *HRB*, xi. 1–2 (pp. 496–501).

[189] e.g. see the quarrel of Brennius and Belinus, sons of Dunvallo Molmutius; *HRB*, iii. 1–7 (pp. 276–86). Tatlock, op. cit., pp. 355–6, points out that Brennius's career was an analogue of that of Robert duke of Normandy, while Modred's treason to King Arthur, *HRB*, x. 13; xi. 1 (pp. 496–8) was intended as an analogue of King Stephen's behaviour; Tatlock, op. cit. pp. 426–7.

[190] *HRB*, ix. 12 (p. 455); ix. 14 (p. 458).

[191] *HRB*, ix. 19 (pp. 465–6).

[192] *HRB*, ix. 12 et seq. (pp. 451 et seq.).

[193] *HRB*, ix. 13 (pp. 456–7). For the Anglo-Saxon custom see the account of King Edgar's coronation feast in the *Vita S. Oswaldi*; *VSO*, p. 438.

[194] See Tatlock, op. cit., pp. 308 et seq.   [195] *HRB*, ii. 17 (p. 275).

[196] *HRB*, iii. 5 (p. 282).

when he came out.'[197] The idea of sanctuary in cities probably comes from Mosaic law, but sanctuary in churches was well established already in Anglo-Saxon times, and was incorporated in the so-called *Laws of Edward the Confessor* (compiled between 1115 and 1150)[198] and in the *Leis Willelme* (compiled between about 1090 and 1135).[199] The ancient Britons were, according to Geoffrey, great builders. Here again he implies a parallel with the Anglo-Normans. Belinus had built in London 'a gateway of extraordinary workmanship. . . . On top of it he built a tower which rose to a remarkable height; and down below at its foot he added a water-gate which was convenient for those going on board their ships.'[200] Geoffrey was of course thinking of the Tower of London built by William the Conqueror. Moreover, Belinus was a road-builder. He had built four trunk-roads, two running north–south and two east–west, besides other roads between towns. He then confirmed the Molmutine Laws relating to the protection of the highways: anyone committing an act of violence on the roads was to be punished.[201] Geoffrey borrowed his account of the four great roads from Henry of Huntingdon.[202] All of them are referred to in the *Leis Willelme*[203] and in the *Laws of Edward the Confessor*[204] which mention that they are protected by the king's peace. Some of the contemporary touches in Geoffrey's work relate to folk history. For example he is the earliest authority for an old drinking custom. Hengist's daughter Ronwen greets Vortigern on her bent knee saying 'wassheil'. She then drinks, and he says 'drincheil', and drinks himself, from the same cup.[205]

Geoffrey's principal object was to amuse. To do this he turned to the literary conventions of courtly romance with tales of heroism and love. Geoffrey does mention church affairs in passing, but the tone of his work is predominantly secular. He even converts a hagiographical legend into a secular one. The story of the shipping of British women to Brittany derives from the *Life of St. Ursula*.[206] St Ursula, the daughter of a British king, was sent with eleven thousand and ten virgins to marry a pagan continental tyrant, and was martyred with her companions for refusing to marry him. Geoffrey's women, sent to prevent the Britons from marrying into another race, were also killed before they could marry – but by shipwreck. Geoffrey shows a bias against monks: he asserts that the British king Constans, a puppet of Vortigern, was weak because he had been a monk and 'what he

---

[197] *HRB*, ii. 17 (p. 275).

[198] F. Liebermann, *Die Gesetze der Angelsachsen* (Halle 1903–16, 3 vols), vol. 1, p. 630. For the date, cf. ibid., p. 627 n.a.

[199] Ibid., p. 493.

[200] *HRB*, iii. 10 (p. 291). Cf. Tatlock, op. cit., p. 106. WM, *GR*, iii. 246 (vol. 2, p. 306), praises the Normans as great builders.

[201] *HRB*, ii. 17 (p. 275); iii. 5 (pp. 281–2).   [202] *HH*, p. 12.

[203] Liebermann, op. cit., pp. 510–11.   [204] Ibid., p. 637.

[205] *HRB*, vi. 12 (pp. 370–1). Cf. Tatlock, op. cit., p. 370.

[206] *HRB*, v. 15, 16 (pp. 350–1). Cf. Tatlock, op. cit., pp. 236 et seq.

had learned in the cloister had nothing to do with how to rule a kingdom'.[207] Geoffrey preferred war to peace (he thought that peace made men indolent, lazy and corrupt).[208] Nor does he show any sympathy for the sufferings of the peasantry in wartime. Rather he despises the peasants, who were 'slow-witted . . . and useless in battle'. 'It is easier for a kite to be made to act like a sparrow-hawk than for a wise man to be fashioned at short notice from a peasant.'[209]

Geoffrey gives vivid descriptions of battles, such as his detailed account of Arthur's campaign in Gaul, with imaginary speeches and the disposition of the army described in full. Of Arthur's personal combat he writes:[210]

> Arthur dashed straight at the enemy. He flung them to the ground and cut them to pieces. Whoever came his way he either killed himself or killed his horse under him at a single blow. They ran away from him as sheep from a fierce lion whom raging hunger compels to devour all that chance throws in his way. Their armour offered them no protection capable of preventing Caliburn, when wielded in the right hand of this mighty king, from forcing them to vomit forth their souls with their life blood.

There is an element of sadism in Geoffrey's work. This appears not only in the accounts of battles but also in the deeds of monsters. For example he describes how the monster living on top of Mont-Saint-Michel carried off a small girl and an old woman, her nurse. The child died with fright in the monster's embrace. The monster buried her and raped the old woman.[211] Women play an important part in the *Historia*, not only as successful British rulers but also as the objects of men's love. Geoffrey describes a number as being exceptionally beautiful, and the power of their beauty leads men to illicit passion. Thus Modred committed adultery with Queen Guinevere[212] and King Uther managed to go to bed with Ygerna, wife of Gorlois duke of Cornwall, by persuading the magician Merlin to make him look like Gorlois.[213]

Geoffrey no doubt hoped that his patrons, pleased with his book, would help to disseminate it by telling friends about it, and even lending or giving away copies. And there is evidence that at least one of his patrons, Robert earl of Gloucester, did contribute to the dissemination of the work. A twelfth-century copy of the *Historia* was at Margam, a Cistercian foundation of Robert of Gloucester:[214] possibly he gave it to the abbey. Earl Robert

---

[207] *HRB*, vi. 7 (p. 361). [208] *HRB*, ix. 15 (p. 461). [209] *HRB*, vi. 3 (p. 356).
[210] *HRB*, x. 11 (p. 493). [211] *HRB*, x. 3 (pp. 469–70). [212] *HRB*, x. 13 (p. 496).
[213] *HRB*, viii. 19 (pp. 423–6).
[214] BM MS. Royal 13 D II. Attributed to Margam by Ker, *Medieval Libraries*, p. 129. Mr Ker also attributes a twelfth century copy (Royal 14 C XI, ff. 222–48ᵛ) to Battle abbey (ibid., p. 8), and a twelfth-thirteenth century copy (Magdalen College, Oxford, MS. 170) to the Benedictine priory of Eye in Suffolk (ibid., p. 86).

certainly gave a copy to Walter Espec who had it at his castle at Helmsley in Yorkshire and lent it to Ralph Fitz Gilbert. Ralph's wife Constance passed it on to Geoffrey Gaimar, asking him to translate it into Norman French.[215]

Little is known about Gaimar who wrote *L'Estoire des Engleis* shortly before 1140;[216] he was probably a secular clerk of Norman extraction. He had some connection with Walter Espec, for besides indirectly obtaining Geoffrey of Monmouth's work from him, he referred to Walter's brother-in-law or nephew, Nicholas de Trailli, in the *Estoire*, asking him to vouch for his use of the sources he lists.[217] Walter, who died in 1153, was the founder of the Cistercian abbey of Rievaulx and the Augustinian priory of Kirkham, both in Yorkshire, and of the Cistercian abbey of Wardon in Bedfordshire, thus having contacts with both north and south England. Gaimar's patron, Ralph Fitz Gilbert, also had widespread connections.[218] He was a member of an old Lincolnshire family, founder of the Augustinian priory at Markby and a benefactor of the Cistercian abbey of Kirkstead. He held land in Hampshire, where he was a benefactor of the Augustinian priory at Southwick, and in the north country. Gaimar's work shows particular interest in and knowledge of affairs in Hampshire, Lincolnshire and the north. [219]

Gaimar's *Estoire* is the first known romance history in vernacular verse (it is in octosyllabic rhymed couplets) written in England. It was probably primarily intended to be read aloud. Its popular success was small: the most recent editor lists only four medieval copies of the thirteenth and fourteenth centuries.[220] In its present form it covers the period from the Anglo-Saxon settlements to the death of William Rufus. Therefore, although Gaimar refers to his use of Geoffrey of Monmouth's *Historia*, obviously regarding it as a work of first-rate interest and importance,[221] the *Estoire* starts just about where the *Historia* stops. The reason for this is that the original beginning of the *Estoire* is now lost. Gaimar probably began with the fall of Troy or Jason's quest for the Golden Fleece; then, using Geoffrey of Monmouth's works and some others, he continued to the point where his work now starts.

---

[215] This is stated by Gaimar, *L'Estoire des Engleis*, ed. A. Bell (Anglo-Norman Text Society, xiv–xvi, 1960), ll. 6430–1, 6447–52. Dr Bell's is the standard edition, with a detailed introduction and is used below. An English translation is in vol. 2 of *Lestorie des Engles solum la Translacion Maistre Geffrei Gaimar*, ed. T. Duffus Hardy and C. Trice Martin (RS, 1888, 1889, 2 vols). I refer to Dr Bell's line-numbers which do not exactly correspond to those in the Rolls Series edition as Dr Bell printed from a different MS. (the line-numbers in his edition ante-number those in the Rolls Series edition by a few lines).

[216] For the few facts known about Gaimar see Bell, op. cit., pp. ix–x; for the date of *L'Estoire* see ibid., p. lii; for the content and literary importance of *L'Estoire*, see Legge, *A–N Lit.* pp. 27–36.

[217] Gaimar, l. 6476 and n.

[218] For Ralph Fitz Gilbert see Gaimar, p. ix, and Legge, op. cit., p. 28.

[219] For his interest in these areas see p. 210 and nn. 226, 227, 229 below.

[220] Gaimar, pp. xv–xviii.   [221] Gaimar, ll. 6453–60.

But this section was replaced by Wace's verse history of this period in Norman French.[222] Wace wrote about 1155 and his romance work became very popular. The practice of stringing together the works of various men to form a continuous history was very common in the twelfth century.

But Gaimar's *Estoire* still has echoes of the *Historia*. Besides mentioning Arthur (to set the stage for Hengist)[223] and Belinus (to compare him with William Rufus),[224] the tone of the *Estoire* is similar to that of the *Historia*. Although the backbone of the work is a Norman-French translation of the Anglo-Saxon Chronicle,[225] it is filled out with legends, with the obvious intention of entertaining the nobility. It presents Anglo-Saxon history seen through the eyes of romance. There is the story of the heroism of Haveloc, a legendary king of Lindsey.[226] There is the story of the adultery of Osbert, king of Northumbria from 848 to 867, with the wife of his noble, Buern.[227] There is a legend of King Edgar's desire, frustrated by the trickery of Ethelwold, to marry the beautiful Ælfthryth[228] who died a penitent at Wherwell abbey in Hampshire[229] (the Anglo-Saxon Chronicle, under 965, briefly notes that Edgar married Ælfthryth). Such a love of fables was shared by other contemporary historians – William of Malmesbury and Henry of Huntingdon (like Henry, Gaimar has the story of King Canute and the tide[230]). Gaimar probably collected the legends from local oral traditions[231] (the numerous stories concerning Danes must have been of Danish origin).

Gaimar shows no bias against the English, although he disapproves of Godwin who murdered the half-Norman Alfred. He gives the legend of the gallant resistance of Hereward, 'who was right brave',[232] to William the Conqueror. On the other hand he praises William the Conqueror, 'the good king'.[233] More significant of his desire to praise the Anglo-Norman kings is his eulogy of William Rufus. All the other historians of the time give an adverse account of Rufus, but according to Gaimar he was 'a wise and courteous man':[234]

> Never was a king so well loved,
> Nor honoured by his folk.[235]

---

[222] For this lost section see Gaimar, pp. xi–xiii. Cf. Tatlock, op. cit., pp. 455–6.

[223] Gaimar, ll. 33, 43 et al. Cf. p. 211 and n. 238 below.

[224] Gaimar, l. 5968. Cf. ll. 4370–6. Cf. p. 211 below.

[225] For Gaimar's use of the Anglo-Saxon Chronicle see *ASC*, p. xix.

[226] Gaimar, ll. 99–816. The *Lay of Haveloc*, for which Gaimar is the earliest authority, originated in Lincolnshire; see A. Bell, *Le Lai d'Haveloc* (Manchester 1925), pp. 68–9.

[227] Gaimar, ll. 2601–720. The legend of Buern originated in the north; see Gaimar, pp. lviii–lix.

[228] Gaimar, ll. 3607–968.

[229] Gaimar, ll. 4081–8. For the possibility that Gaimar derived this legend from Wherwell abbey see Gaimar, pp. lxxi–lxxii.

[230] Gaimar, ll. 4693–722.

[231] As in the *Carmen* attributed to Guy of Amiens, he mentions the juggler Taillefer who preceded the troops at the battle of Hastings, throwing first his lance, and then his sword, three times in the air; Gaimar, ll. 5265–300.

[232] Gaimar, l. 5494.   [233] Gaimar, l. 5415.   [234] Gaimar, l. 5844.

[235] Gaimar, ll. 5917–18.

And again,

> ... he reigned for a long time
> And pacified the country well,
> And kept such justice and right
> That no inhabitant lost anything through wrong.[236]

Gaimar compares Rufus with the ancient British heroes:[237]

> On account of his great nobleness
> All his neighbours were subject to him.
> And if he could have reigned longer
> He would have gone to Rome to claim
> The ancient right of that country
> Which Brennius and Belinus had.

The description of Rufus's court seems to imply a comparison with King Arthur's. Rufus had a 'marvellous company of barons' and three hundred ushers dressed in 'vair or gris, or rich cloth from foreign lands', to whom he gave livery, liberal pay and great honour.[238] Gaimar even distorts the circumstances of Rufus's death to make them more flattering to the king. Other authorities imply that when Rufus was shot with Walter Tirel's arrow he died unabsolved.[239] William of Malmesbury adds that his body was robbed and desecrated by his companions, and carried by some country people in a farm-cart to Winchester.[240] Orderic Vitalis gives a similar account.[241] But according to Gaimar, a hunter gave Rufus some herbs as the last sacrament, and he died in a state of grace. His barons were overcome with grief – one fainted – and took great trouble making a bier, which they carried on foot, weeping, to Winchester, where he was buried with great honour.[242] This reads like a conscious refutation of contemporary accounts.

Gaimar ends with Rufus's death because, he says, the reign of Henry I had already been dealt with by 'David'. This work, now lost, was, according to Gaimar, written at the command of Henry I's wife Adela of Louvain (who married Henry in 1121 and died in 1151). It was set to music by David, and Constance Fitz Gilbert bought a copy, which she often read, for one silver mark. From Gaimar's descriptions, it appears to have been a panegyric in verse, but lacking the romance element: Gaimar advises David to add some jokes, some stories about hunting and life at court, and a love interest.[243]

---

[236] Gaimar, ll. 6205–8.   [237] Gaimar, ll. 5963–8.

[238] Gaimar, ll. 5972 et seq. Cf. Arthur's Whitsun court at Caerleon, mentioned on p. 206 and nn. 192–3 above.

[239] According to the Anglo-Saxon Chronicle, *s.a.* 1100, Rufus died unrepentant.

[240] *GR*, iv. 333 (vol. 2, pp. 378–9).   [241] *HE*, x. 14 (iv. 87–90).

[242] Gaimar, ll. 6322–427.

[243] Gaimar, ll. 6477–520. It has been suggested that this David was the bishop of Bangor (1120–?1139) who, according to WM, *GP*, v. 420, 426 (pp. 498–9, 502), wrote a Life of the Emperor Henry V; see Gaimar, p. xi.

Gaimar himself united the Norman tradition of royal panegyric with the nascent tradition of courtly romance. The value of his work as a historical source is small. Though he used a lost version of the Anglo-Saxon Chronicle, very little of his additional material can have derived from that version. And even when not led astray by his love of legends and eulogy, he is an inaccurate writer. Therefore when he asserts that King Alfred ordered a copy of the Anglo-Saxon Chronicle to be chained in all the important churches, he may have merely been thinking about Alfred's instructions for the distribution of his translation of Gregory's *Pastoral Care*.[244] But historians today do put some reliance on a few of his statements. For example some weight is attached to his information about the treachery of Æthelwine bishop of Durham in 1071,[245] and also to his intimation that William Rufus was not killed by accident, but was murdered by Walter Tirel as a result of a conspiracy.[246]

It has been seen that by 1139 a copy of Geoffrey of Monmouth's *Historia* was at Mont-Saint-Michel,[247] and that at about that time Walter Espec had a copy at Helmsley.[248] It has also been seen that Robert of Torigni, Henry of Huntingdon and Gaimar liked the *Historia*. Probably by 1143 a copy was in the hands of another would-be-historian – Alfred, treasurer and sacrist of Beverley minster in Yorkshire. He wrote a history of England from the British period to 1129.[249] He states in the preface that he wrote during a period of enforced idleness: his church had stopped divine services because so many people were excommunicated. He may have been referring to the result of the decrees of the legatine council held by Henry of Blois, bishop of Winchester, in 1143 which, to meet the exigencies of the anarchy, declared excommunicate all who did violence to the clergy. Alfred's work is a compilation from well-known sources, among them Bede, 'Symeon of Durham', Henry of Huntingdon and Geoffrey of Monmouth. But it has some significance, besides exemplifying the contemporary interest in history; it shows the quick spread of Geoffrey's popularity: Alfred, who follows Geoffrey, often *verbatim*, almost exclusively for nearly half his book, asserts that the *Historia* was being widely read, enjoyed and talked about. Even more remarkable is the fact that, despite the use he made of the *Historia*, Alfred distrusted its veracity and only selected those passages which seemed to him credible.[250]

Already at this early stage Geoffrey probably had another critic, Ailred of Rievaulx. Ailred, abbot of Rievaulx from 1147 to 1167, was a close friend of

---

[244] Gaimar, ll. 2327–36. Cf. *ASC*, pp. xix–xx.

[245] Gaimar, ll. 5451–6. Cf. *ASC*, p. 154 n. 4.

[246] Gaimar, ll. 6259–304. Cf. A. L. Poole, *From Domesday Book to Magna Carta* (Oxford 1951), pp. 113–14.

[247] See p. 199.   [248] See p. 209.

[249] Printed in *Aluredi Beverlacensis Annales*, ed. T. Hearne (Oxford 1716).

[250] Ibid., pp. 2–3.

Walter Espec, the abbey's founder.[251] It is quite likely, therefore, that Ailred saw Walter's copy of Geoffrey's *Historia*. In this case the references in Ailred's *Speculum Caritatis* (*Mirror of Charity*), written in 1142–3,[252] to the Arthurian legends are references to Geoffrey's account of them. Ailred asserts in the *Speculum* that novices weep more readily over 'fictitious tales of someone (I don't know who) called Arthur' than over pious books. He brands such stories as 'fables and lies'.[253] If Ailred was criticizing the *Historia* (and not some pre-Galfredian Arthurian legends), he was a fore-runner of another north-countryman, William of Newburgh, who regarded the *Historia* with great scepticism.[254]

Ailred himself wrote a history (probably between 1155 and 1157[255]), the *Relatio de Standardo* (*Story of the Standard*), an account of the Battle of the Standard fought in 1138 by the Anglo-Normans of the north against the Scots led by King David. Ailred and the other important north-country historian, Richard of Hexham, were more old fashioned in their historio-graphy than Henry of Huntingdon, Geoffrey of Monmouth and Gaimar, all writing further south. Although they were not uninfluenced by modern literary trends, their work was chiefly moulded by the Benedictine his-toriographical tradition which had survived and been developed at Durham. They were members of religious orders, and were more serious and pious, less gossipy and worldly, than the three seculars mentioned. They wrote to record and edify, not to amuse, and avoided legends. And they wrote for their own religious communities, not for the wider public of clerks and educated laymen.

Ailred was deeply imbued with the Northumbrian past. His father, Eilaf, was the hereditary priest of Hexham[256] (Wilfrid's monastery had ceased to exist during the Danish invasions and at least by the eleventh century the church was served by a secular priest). He held the office until 1113 when Thomas II archbishop of York introduced a community of regular canons, which he replaced a few years later by Augustinian canons. Ailred's great-grandfather was Alured son of Westou, sacrist of St Cuthbert's, Durham, and the pirate of Northumbrian relics. The Augustinian canons of Hexham maintained the Bedan tradition, translating the relics of the saints in 1155 (Ailred wrote a hagiographical piece on the occasion[257]). Ailred himself became canon of Kirkham and subsequently, in about 1134, a Cistercian at

[251] An excellent account of Ailred's life, works and background is by F. M. Powicke in his edition of Walter Daniel's *Life of Ailred of Rievaulx* (Nelson's Medieval Classics, 1950).

[252] For the date of the *Speculum Caritatis* see *VAAR*, pp. lvi, xci. The *Speculum* is printed in Migne, *PL*, vol. cxcv, coll. 505–620.

[253] 'Nam et in fabulis, quae vulgo de nescio quo finguntur Arcturo, memini me nonnunquam usque ad effusionem lacrymarum fuisse permotum'; ibid., vol. cxcv, col. 565.

[254] See pp. 264–5 and n. 137 below.

[255] On its date see *VAAR*, pp. xcvii, xcix.

[256] For Ailred's family see Raine, *Hexham*, pp. li et seq. and p. 289 below.

[257] *VAAR*, pp. xxxviii–xxxix. The work on the Hexham saints is edited by Raine, *Hexham*, pp. 173–203. For a further discussion of this work see p. 289 below.

Rievaulx. Although the Cistercian order was a foreign one, it did nothing to lessen Ailred's devotion to the Anglo-Saxon past. On the contrary, Cistercian piety and austerity seem to have strengthened Ailred's sympathy for the Northumbrian saints.

The idea of Northumbria as an entity still had some reality in Ailred's day, for the boundary between England and Scotland remained unfixed. It was fought over by David of Scotland and by the Anglo-Normans. Ailred's loyalties straddled the wavering boundary, and he appears to have loved the memory of ancient Northumbria more than either the Scots or the Anglo-Normans of his own day. As a Cistercian he recognized no boundary, for Rievaulx had daughter houses in Scotland – at Melrose in Roxburghshire and Dundrennan in Galloway. In addition, Ailred had close connections with the Scottish royal family, for he had been educated at the Scottish court.[258] He admired King David and was a friend of his son Henry. The royal family appealed to his piety (David's mother Margaret and his stepson Waldef both became saints) and to his English patriotism (Margaret, the daughter of Edward the Etheling, belonged to the English royal house).

Ailred's divided loyalties are reflected in his writings. The *Relatio de Standardo* was his only historical work,[259] his other works were religious and hagiographical. In form it is not unlike the *De Obsessione Dunelmense*[260] and the *De Injusta Vexatione Willelmi Episcopi*,[261] both written at Durham. Like them it combines biography with a *pièce justificative*, a tract for the times. The biographical material relates to Walter Espec. It describes what he looked like: 'he was very tall, with arms and legs of great size, so that no one exceeded or equalled him in height. He had black hair, a profuse beard, and an open, bold brow, large, penetrating eyes, a full but drawn face, and a voice like a trumpet, uniting eloquence (which came easily to him) with a certain majesty of sound.'[262] It lists the religious houses Walter endowed, Rievaulx and Wardon for the Cistercians, and Kirkham for the Augustinian canons.[263] And it describes the part he took in the Battle of the Standard.[264] The argument of Ailred's tract is the desirability of peace and harmony between the English and the Scots. He puts into the mouth of Robert Bruce ('a worthy old man . . . belonging by law to the king of England but from youth an adherent of the king of Scots')[265] a speech addressed to King David trying to avert the combat: he points out that in the past the English and the Normans had helped David hold his throne against his enemies. David's real

---

[258] *VAAR*, pp. xxxix–xliii.

[259] Printed in *Chrons. Stephen, Henry II, and Richard I*, vol. 3, pp. 181–99.

[260] The only MS. of the *Relatio* is in Corpus Christi College, Cambridge, MS. 139, which also has the unique copies of the *De Obsessione* and of the *Historia Regum* attributed to Symeon of Durham. See P. H. Blair, 'Some observations on the *Historia Regum* attributed to Symeon of Durham' in Chadwick, *Celt and Saxon*, p. 68.

[261] See p. 122.   [262] *Relatio*, p. 183.   [263] Ibid., pp. 183–4.

[264] Ibid., pp. 185–9, 198.   [265] Ibid., p. 192.

enemies, Bruce argues, are the men (i.e. the Picts) of Galloway on whom David was relying for the first time.[266] Ailred also gives a particular slant to the account of the battle, in order to keep this idea of the underlying friendship between England and Scotland. He often refers to the principal combatants as Galwegians and Frenchmen (*Galli*),[267] not as Scots and English, thus obscuring the fact that the Scots were fighting the Anglo-Normans.

But the *Relatio* contains new elements as well as old. It was probably based on the account of the Battle of the Standard in Richard of Hexham's chronicle which will be discussed next. Ailred seems also to have known Henry of Huntingdon's *Historia Anglorum*.[268] The graphic account of the battle, together with the speeches of important people, are in accordance with the contemporary taste for martial *gestes*. Moreover there are eulogistic passages reminiscent of such works as the *Gesta Stephani*. The account of Walter Espec is panegyrical. He is described as 'far more noble in Christian piety than in appearance', and an undue prominence is given to his part in the battle. It is known from other sources that he did take part in the fighting, but there is no confirmatory evidence that he delivered a long harangue from the standard just before the combat (according to Henry of Huntingdon the speech was given by Ralph, bishop of Orkney). Nor is there any reason to suppose that after the battle the victorious English crowded round Walter 'whom they revered as the leader and father of that place',[269] to give thanks to God. Ailred also eulogized King David and his son. He mentions David's bravery and piety, and asserts that he listened sympathetically to Robert Bruce's speech, only persisting in the war because his nephew persuaded him.

As Ailred praised Walter Espec it is unlikely that his work was intended to please King David. And as he praised David it is unlikely he meant to entertain Walter Espec. In fact it is most probable that, like most other monastic historians, he wrote primarily for his own community and those connected with it. There is a traditionalist element in Ailred's work. He recorded the acts of his abbey's patron and other information which would have interested a Cistercian. He not only listed Walter's foundations, he also recorded the expansion of the Cistercian order, mentioning the foundations at Fountains and Waverley.[270] Moreover he emphasizes the religious aspect of the Scottish war, how the relics and banners of saints were taken from the Northumbrian churches to accompany the English army, how Archbishop

---

[266] Ibid., pp. 192–5.   [267] Ibid., pp. 187–90 *passim*.

[268] The address Ailred puts in Walter Espec's mouth resembles in some respects the speech Henry of Huntingdon attributes to the bishop of Orkney. Cf. ibid., p. 186 and *HH*, p. 262. Compare also *Relatio*, p. 186, 'Quis Apuliam, Siciliam, Calabriam nisi vester Normannus edomuit?' with the assessment of the Norman character in *HH*, p. 208, 'Quod scilicet in Normannia et Anglia, Apulia, Calabria, Sicilia, et Antiochia, terris quas eis Deus subjicit, magis magisque apparet.'

[269] *Relatio*, pp. 198–9.   [270] Ibid., pp. 183–4.

Thurstan exhorted the people to resist the invaders,[271] and how the bishop of Orkney blessed and absolved the soldiers before the battle.[272]

The other north-country historian at this period was Richard, canon, then prior (1141 to some time between 1155 and 1167[273]) of Hexham. Ailred may have known him through his close connections with Hexham (he probably attended the translation of the relics in 1155[274]) and may have drawn on Richard's chronicle for the *Relatio*. Richard's chronicle, *De Gestis Regis Stephani et de Bello Standardii* (*The Deeds of King Stephen and concerning the Battle of the Standard*) covers the years from 1135 to 1139.[275] Like Ailred, Richard wrote for his own community. Stylistically his chronicle divides into two parts. First there is a summary of Henry I's achievements, followed by an account of events in chronological order to 1139. His assessment of Henry I was influenced by contemporary historiography. In places it is panegyrical: Henry is praised for keeping law and order, and there is a list of his virtues ('he was a man of counsel and foresight, sagacity and prudence' and the like).[276] Some features, for example the notice of Henry's marriages[277] and religious foundations[278] suggest a relationship with Robert of Torigni's continuation of William of Jumièges. The unflattering mention of Henry's lust and avarice,[279] and the story of his death from eating lampreys[280] suggest that Richard knew Henry of Huntingdon's *Historia Anglorum*. If so, this would explain a passage in Richard's work. He refers the reader for further information about King Henry to 'the chronicles about the acts of the English'.[281] He may have been thinking of the *Historia*, for one version goes down to 1135. He may also have been thinking of the *Historia Regum* attributed to Symeon of Durham, though it only goes down to 1130.

The second section of the chronicle, to 1139, was written fairly soon after the events described. Its main purpose was to record and edify, not amuse. There are no legends and the style is factual and more or less uninfluenced by contemporary historiography. Like the author of the *Historia Regum* and

---

[271] Ibid., p. 182.

[272] Ibid., pp. 195–6.

[273] See Raine, *Hexham*, p. 193 n. 1.

[274] *VAAR*, p. xxxviii.

[275] Printed in *Chrons. Stephen, Henry II and Richard I*, vol. 3, pp. 139–78 (the edition cited below), and in Raine, *Hexham*, pp. 63–106. Compare the accounts in the two works of Thurstan's exhorting the English (*Ric. H.*, pp. 159–60; *Relatio*, p. 182), of Robert Bruce as peacemaker (*Ric. H.*, pp. 161–2; *Relatio*, pp. 192–5), of the bishop of Orkney absolving the soldiers (*Ric. H.*, p. 162; *Relatio*, pp. 195–6), and of the part played by the Galwegians in the battle (*Ric. H.*, pp. 163–4; *Relatio*, pp. 190–1, 196–7).

[276] *Ric. H.*, p. 140.

[277] Compare *Ric. H.*, p. 141, with Robert of Torigni's continuation of William of Jumièges in Guillaume de Jumièges, *GND*, p. 305 (cf. pp. 279–80, 300).

[278] Compare *Ric. H.*, p. 141, with *GND*, pp. 310–11. Robert (*GND*, p. 314) also dates Henry's death in a similar way to Richard, p. 139, and like Richard eulogizes him (see *GND*, pp. 267, 315).

[279] Compare *Ric. H.*, p. 142, with *HH*, pp. 255–6.

[280] Compare *Ric. H.*, p. 142, with *HH*, p. 254.

[281] *Ric. H.*, p. 144.

earlier Northumbrian historians, Richard cites letters and documents in full. Unlike Ailred, although he describes the Battle of the Standard he does not put speeches in the mouths of the leaders. He is as much concerned as Ailred with Anglo-Scottish relations and his chronicle ends with details of the treaty between King Stephen and King David. But he treats the subject more objectively than Ailred. He has no lay patron whom he wishes to praise. Walter Espec is briefly mentioned[282] and King David is not praised – he is criticized for his cruelty and obstinate refusal to make peace with the English.[283] Richard's main concern is with the sufferings of Hexham and of the Northumbrian people from the depredations of the Scots. He particularly deplores the barbarity of the Picts of Galloway whom he regards as scarcely human.[284] His work is strongly edificatory in tone. He gives quotations from the bible and regarded events as determined by the divine will. The Scots' defeat and massacre at the Battle of the Standard was God's vengeance for their depredations.[285] The account of the Battle of the Standard gives it the appearance of a holy war. Richard records that the standard itself, an old ship's mast, had a silver pyx with the Host on top of it and was surrounded by the banners of the patron saints of Northumbria.[286] Archbishop Thurstan and the army fasted for three days before the battle and Thurstan would have accompanied the army himself, but was dissuaded because he was too old. He promised that the parish priests with their crosses and parishioners should go to the battle and sent the bishop of Orkney who absolved the soldiers.[287] Richard particularly emphasizes the power of the Hexham saints in protecting property. He records how Hexham gave asylum to people running away from the marauding Scots, and how two Picts who plundered an oratory in the church went mad, due to God's vengeance.[288]

If there are heroes in Richard's account of Anglo-Scottish relations, they are ecclesiastics, not laymen. Richard stresses that Thurstan rallied the English, making them forget their quarrels.[289] After the Battle of the Standard the initiative is attributed to the papal legate, Alberic, who arrived in England in 1138 to reform the church. Richard, having given a brief résumé of Alberic's life and virtues,[290] describes his peacemaking activities in the north. Alberic persuaded King David to indemnify the church of Hexham for the damage the Scots had done,[291] and to make the Picts of Galloway return the English women they had captured.[292] Alberic started the peace negotiations between King David and King Stephen, only leaving

---

[282] *Ric. H.*, p. 159.　　　　[283] *Ric. H.*, pp. 155, 162.

[284] He describes them as 'bestiales homines' who acted 'more brutorum animalium' and sold English women 'aliis barbaris'; *Ric. H.*, p. 157.

[285] *Ric. H.*, p. 164.　　　　[286] *Ric. H.*, p. 163.　　　　[287] *Ric. H.*, pp. 160–2.

[288] *Ric. H.*, pp. 153–4.　　　　[289] *Ric. H.*, pp. 159–60.　　　　[290] *Ric. H.*, p. 167.

[291] *Ric. H.*, p. 171.

[292] *Ric. H.*, p. 171. Alberic also released William Cumin from prison; *Ric. H.*, p. 169.

for home when they were well begun.[293] The terms of the treaty which end the book were the culmination of his diplomacy.

Thus the reign of King Stephen produced a number of historical works, remarkable both for their quality and variety. The period may have been one of anarchy, but in it lived such great ecclesiastics as Roger of Salisbury and Alexander of Lincoln, the lay nobility flourished, and the new religious orders rapidly expanded.[294] These phenomena were reflected in historical writing. In the south, under the aegis of ecclesiastical and lay patrons, a new type of history, influenced in varying degrees by romance literature, was written. In the north the new orders adopted and continued the tradition of Benedictine historiography, adapting it to the needs of the age.

[293] *Ric. H.*, p. 176.
[294] On the remarkable expansion of the Cistercian order, 1135–53, see M. D. Knowles, *The Monastic Order in England* (2nd ed., Cambridge 1963), pp. 246 et seq.

Historians of the Reigns of Henry II and Richard I: the 'Seculars'

In the first half of Henry II's reign few people wrote history. There were John of Hexham, John of Salisbury, and Wace. Only John of Hexham wrote a national history in chronicle form. As he was a member of a religious order he will be considered in the next chapter. John of Salisbury's *Historia Pontificalis* (*Memoirs of the Papal Court*), probably written in about 1164, is a papal history (from 1148 to 1152), only touching on English affairs where relevant.[1] Between 1160 and 1170 Wace, a clerk of Caen, wrote a verse romance, the *Roman de Rou*, at Henry II's command.[2] But this is of little value for English history. It gives an account of the Norman dukes and Anglo-Norman kings (derived mainly from Dudo of St Quentin, William of Jumièges and William of Poitiers) until the death of Henry I: its few additions to its sources are not to be relied on.

In the course of the 1170s historical writing revived, and the 1180s and 1190s are remarkable for the number of well-known historians, both secular clerks and members of religious orders, who wrote then. Among them are such names as William of Newburgh, Richard of Devizes and Gervase of Canterbury (all members of religious orders), and the seculars Ralph Diceto and Roger of Howden. If we can speak of a golden age of historiography in England it was probably the last twenty years of the twelfth century. This revival owed much to the influence of the royal court. Henry II commissioned Wace and then Benoît de Sainte-Maure[3] to write their historical romances, and he was a patron of Gerald of Wales and Walter Map whose works, though not primarily historical, contain historical material. As far as is known, Richard I did not actually commission a history but he was the hero of two extant works written in his reign, *L'Estoire de la*

---

[1] The most recent edition is *Ioannis Saresberiensis Historia Pontificalis*, ed., with an English translation, Marjorie Chibnall (Nelson's Medieval Texts, 1956) (*Hist. Pont.*).

[2] The standard edition is *Maistre Wace's Roman de Rou et des Ducs de Normandie*, ed. H. Andresen (Heilbronn 1877, 1879, 2 vols). For Wace as a historical source see D. C. Douglas, *William the Conqueror* (London 1964), pp. 50, 68, 184, 199 n. 5, 409.

[3] The standard edition is *Chronique des Ducs de Normandie par Benoit*, ed. Carin Fahlin (Lund 1951–67, 3 vols).

Guerre Sainte (*History of the Holy War*) by Ambroise[4] and the *Itinerarium Peregrinorum et Gesta Regis Ricardi* (*Itinerary of the Pilgrims and the Deeds of King Richard*).[5]

The principal histories started in Henry II's reign were the chronicle which goes under the name of Benedict of Peterborough (covering the years from 1169 to 1192),[6] the chronicle of Roger of Howden (for the period from the death of Bede to 1201),[7] and the chronicle of Ralph Diceto (from the Creation to 1200).[8] These works have a common characteristic, a strong interest in the country's administration (their interest in politics is limited: the one great political issue of the day, the Becket controversy, happened before the revival in historical writing and these historians looked back at it in the light of Becket's martyrdom). They show the same desire to record information as the earlier chroniclers, but have a greater concern for and knowledge of legal and constitutional affairs. The Worcester chronicler and Henry of Huntingdon had usually recorded where the king spent the great annual feasts; the chroniclers of the revival often recorded exact royal itineraries, that is, the king's whereabouts from day to day. This had become a matter of public interest: Walter Map remarks that Henry II always informed his subjects where he would be on a particular day.[9] Itineraries relating to other important people also occur in these histories.

Interest in the administration, and the development of the record-aspect of historiography, were undoubtedly a result of Henry II's judicial reforms which had promoted a preoccupation with precedents. The machinery of government was multiplying archives, and officials were becoming increasingly record-conscious. The desire to codify unwritten custom is shown by the account of common law known as *Glanvill* (probably compiled between 1187 and 1189[10]) and by Richard Fitz Neal's account of the

---

[4] The standard edition is *L'Estoire de la Guerre Sainte: Histoire en vers de la Troisième Croisade (1190–1192) par Ambroise*, ed. Gaston Paris (Paris 1897). For an English translation see M. J. Hubert, *The Crusade of Richard Lionheart*, with notes etc. by J. L. La Monte (Columbia University Records of Civilization, 34, New York 1941).

[5] The standard edition is in *Chrons. and Mems. Ric. I*, vol. 1. For an English translation see Kenneth Fenwick, *The Third Crusade. An Eye Witness Account of the Campaigns of Richard Coeur-de-Lion in Cyprus and the Holy Land* (London 1958).

[6] The standard edition is still *The Chronicle of the Reigns of Henry II and Richard I, A.D. 1169–1192, known commonly under the name of Benedict of Peterborough*, ed. W. Stubbs (RS, 1867, 2 vols).

[7] The standard edition is still *Chronica Magistri Rogeri de Houdene*, ed. W. Stubbs (RS, 1868–71, 4 vols). An English translation is by H. T. Riley, *The Annals of Roger de Hoveden* (London 1853, 2 vols).

[8] The standard edition is *The Historical Works of Master Ralph de Diceto*, ed. W. Stubbs (RS, 1876, 2 vols).

[9] *Walter Map, De Nugis Curialium*, ed. M. R. James (Anecdota Oxoniensia, Medieval and Modern Series, 1914), v. 6 (p. 235). For an English translation see *Walter Map's 'De Nugis Curialium'*, translated by M. R. James with historical notes by J. E. Lloyd (*Cymmrodorion Record Series*, no. ix, 1923). For a summary of the facts known about Walter's life see the preface to the edition by T. Wright (Camden Soc., old series, 1850).

[10] See *Glanvill*, ed. G. D. G. Hall (Nelson's Medieval Texts, 1965), p. xxxi.

Exchequer. Fitz Neal, bishop of London (1189–98) and treasurer of England from about 1158 to 1196, wrote the *Dialogue of the Exchequer* between 1174 and 1183.[11] The same desire to record customs encouraged historical writing. Fitz Neal himself wrote a history, the Tricolumnis, which is now lost. He says in the *Dialogue* that as a young man he wrote a work on Henry II. It was arranged in three columns (as the title indicates): one relating to the affairs of the English church, one to Henry's noble deeds 'which are beyond human belief', and one to various matters of public and private interest and to 'judgments of the king's court'.[12] The desire to record precedents is explicitly stated by John of Salisbury in the preface to the *Historia Pontificalis*: 'the records of chronicles are valuable for establishing or abolishing customs, for strengthening or destroying privileges.'[13]

In Richard I's reign interest centred on the king and the crusade rather than on the governmental machine. The 'administrative' histories were continued, but more remarkable was the development of the romance tradition of historiography. Wace and Jordan Fantosme had fostered this tradition under Henry II, but it emerged with new vitality and in a more polished form in *L'Estoire de la Guerre Sainte* and in the *Itinerarium Peregrinorum et Gesta Regis Ricardi*, both long accounts, one in verse and one in prose, of the Third Crusade, figuring Richard I as a hero of romance. They show how romance literary conventions could be adapted to the narration of what was, in general, authentic history. Romance literature itself reached its zenith in France in the late twelfth century. Its tone had changed from that of the earlier period. Though it maintained its love of warfare, giving dramatic descriptions of battles and personal combat, it had been progressively modified by the environment of royal and noble courts, acquiring chivalric elements – an aristocratic flavour and respect for the conventions of court life.[14]

Besides the administrative and the romance historians, there were the two clerks, Walter Map and Gerald of Wales, who were not historians but whose works reflect historiographical trends. Walter was a court satirist and Gerald a professional *littérateur*, and both were products of the twelfth century classical renaissance. They used history mainly to provide ammunition for their arguments. Their treatment of historical material often illustrates the contemporary taste for historical reconstruction. That is, they treated evidence creatively, blending oral and literary sources together to produce a literary narrative, and did not copy sources almost word for word in turn, as their predecessors tended to do. They also underline another new historiographical feature, a heightened perception of reality. They give realistic

---

[11] See *Dialogus de Scaccario*, ed. C. Johnson (Nelson's Medieval Classics, 1950), pp. xx–xxii.
[12] See ibid., pp. 27, 77. Stubbs suggested that 'Benedict' incorporated the Tricolumnis; see n. 17 below.
[13] *Hist. Pont.*, ed. Chibnall, p. 3.
[14] See S. Painter, *French Chivalry* (New York 1957), *passim*.

character-sketches of people and graphic descriptions of places. Moreover they, like the historians of the day, had an appetite for anecdotes and good stories, many with a pagan, not a Christian, tone: there are earthy stories about people and fantastic ones about ghosts and marvels. Finally the fact that Walter and Gerald made extensive use of history exemplifies the contemporary taste for history. Some clerks wrote history simply because they liked it: in this category are John Pike, master of the school of St Martin le Grand in London,[15] and Ralph Niger, who had studied in the schools in Paris, was a correspondent of John of Salisbury and entered the service of Henry II's son Henry.[16] As they were both mainly compilers and not original writers they will not be discussed below.

The writers of this revival will be considered in three groups. First, the 'administrative' historians; second, the romance historians; and third, the satirists. In the first group are the chronicle which goes under the name of Benedict of Peterborough, that of Roger of Howden and Ralph Diceto's works. In the second are the metrical chronicle of Jordan of Fantosme, the *Itinerarium Ricardi* and Ambroise's *L'Estoire de la Guerre Sainte*. In the third are Walter Map's *De Nugis Curialium* (*On the Trivialities of Courtiers*) and the works of Gerald of Wales.

The chronicle which is known under the name of Benedict of Peterborough seems to have been written fairly contemporarily with the events it records from about 1171 to 1177. From 1177 to 1180 it is very brief, and from 1180 to the end in 1192 it seems to contain contemporary notes but was revised in or after 1192.[17] The chronicle is associated with Benedict, abbot of Peterborough (1177–93) because a very early copy (of *c.* 1177) has the heading 'Gesta Henrici II Benedicti Abbatis' ('Abbot Benedict's Deeds of Henry II'). But this heading is in a late thirteenth-century hand and can only mean

---

[15] For the historical works of John Pike see Hardy, *Catalogue*, vol. 2, p. 124; vol. 3, pp. 12, 376. For his copy of the chronicle of Robert of Torigni (BM MS. Royal 13 C XI) see *RT*, vol. 1, p. xxiii, and the *Catalogue of Western MSS. in the Old Royal and King's Collection* (printed for the Trustees of the British Museum, 1921, 3 vols), vol. 2, pp. 106–7.

[16] Ralph Niger wrote two chronicles. They are printed in *The Chronicles of Ralph Niger*, ed. R. Anstruther (Caxton Soc., 1851). Ralph was a partisan of Thomas Becket and was exiled by Henry II. He expresses his bitterness in a virulent character-sketch of King Henry (the most original passage in the longer of his chronicles); ibid., pp. 167–9. For a revision, made in the early thirteenth century, of Ralph Niger's estimate of Henry, see p. 331 n. 92 below. Ralph was a prolific writer. Most of his works were on scriptural and theological topics. His two chronicles are written late in life, probably at the end of the twelfth century. His career is fully described, and his works described and listed, in G. B. Flahiff, 'Ralph Niger: an introduction to his life and works' in *Mediaeval Studies*, ii (1940), pp. 104–26. In one of his works, *De Re militari et tribus Viis Jerosolymitanae Peregrinationis*, Ralph put forward detailed arguments against the Third Crusade; see ibid., pp. 119–20 and Flahiff, '*Deus non vult*: a critic of the Third Crusade' in ibid., ix (1947), pp. 162–88.

[17] *BP*, vol. 1, pp. xliv–xlvi. Stubbs suggests that there was a change of authorship in 1180, and that to 1177 the work is an edited version of Richard Fitz Neal's Tricolumnis; ibid., p. lviii.

that the volume belonged to Abbot Benedict or was copied at his order.[18] Whoever wrote the chronicle, it was not Abbot Benedict. The only possible evidence there is that the chronicle had an East Anglian connection is the fact that the author obtained some information about Norway from Augustine archbishop of Nidaros who stayed at Bury St Edmunds from 1181 to 1182.[19] In fact the chronicle is remarkably free from any local attachments (this makes it unlikely that it was a monastic production).

The author's centre of interest is the king and the governmental machine. He has a tendency to praise both Henry II and Richard I. Henry is praised for his generosity,[20] his forgiveness of his sons,[21] and his position as an arbiter of Europe.[22] But the author has reservations concerning the oppression of the poor by Henry's justices,[23] and regards Richard's accession as a new dawn.[24] Richard, the author hoped, would continue Henry's work but rectify its shortcomings. Soon the author begins to deplore the extortionate methods of Richard's deputy, the justiciar William Longchamp, when the king was on the crusade.[25] The author had a fairly intimate knowledge of the affairs of the court and administration. He remarks on Henry's dilatory method of doing business. The negotiations for the marriage of his niece with the king of Hungary in 1186 came to nothing, because Henry put off answering the envoys 'from day to day, as was his custom'.[26] The author gives details of the appointment in 1177 of an almoner of the royal household.[27] Henry chose him 'with the counsel of his bishops and other wise men', and ordered him to hear the claims of the poor: he was to receive for the poor one-tenth of all food and drink consumed in the royal household.

The author's interest in the central government is shown in a number of well-informed passages. Under 1178 he records that Henry, in order to save his subjects from the oppression of too many judges, reduced their number from eighteen to five. The judges were not to leave the *curia regis*, where they were to hear all suits, referring those which they could not settle to the king himself.[28] In the following year the author records that Henry made another attempt at reforming the administration of justice, by dividing England into four parts and assigning judges to each: the chronicle gives the names of the (twenty-one) judges and the counties in their areas.[29] Under 1190 the author

---

[18] *BP*, vol. 1, pp. xxi–xxiii. The manuscript is BM MS. Cotton Julius A XI: it has the text to 1177. It is presumably identical with the volume catalogued as 'Gesta regis Henrici secundi et genealogia eius' with Abbot Benedict's other books by Robert of Swaffham (died *c*. 1273) in his history of Peterborough abbey: see Joseph Sparke, *Historiae Anglicanae Scriptores Varii* (London 1723), p. 99.

[19] *BP*, vol. 1, pp. xlvii, 266–9.

[20] For his generosity see the notice of his appointment of an almoner; ibid., p. 169 (cf. below and n. 27).

[21] See *BP*, vol. 1, p. 301.   [22] See *BP*, vol. 1, pp. 285, 287. Cf. pp. 138–43.

[23] *BP*, vol. 1, p. 207. Cf. his strictures on the forest law; ibid., pp. 94, 99, 105.

[24] *BP*, vol. 2, pp. 75–6.   [25] *BP*, vol. 2, p. 106.   [26] *BP*, vol. 1, p. 346.

[27] *BP*, vol. 1, p. 169.   [28] *BP*, vol. 1, pp. 207–8.   [29] *BP*, vol. 1, pp. 238–9.

records that Richard I appointed justices for the crusading fleet and gives a full tariff of the punishments they should inflict.[30] Under 1184 is a detail about taxation: Ranulf de Glanville advised Henry against allowing the papal envoys to levy a tax, because it would be a bad precedent.[31]

Interest in the central government is also shown by the number of official documents in the chronicle. The inclusion of such material was an old practice, but the author developed it to such an extent that towards the end the chronicle reads more like a register than a literary work. There are not only royal letters,[32] but also the texts of the assize of Clarendon, the assize of arms and that of the forests, besides the regulations for the justices of the fleet, and a copy of the Compromise of Avranches.[33] There are also various diplomatic documents, notably the text of the renewal of the treaty made at Ivry in 1180,[34] and letters from the pope and others, most relating to the Third Crusade and many written for publication (for example the letter of Pope Alexander on the misfortunes of Palestine, 1181[35]). And there is a copy of the marriage settlement for Henry II's daughter Joanna on her marriage with William II king of Sicily, complete with a realistic picture of William's *rota*.[36] Furthermore, the record aspect of the chronicle is reflected in the royal itineraries. For example under 1177 the author writes: 'After Easter the king went to London, and then he went on pilgrimage to St Edmund, king and martyr, arriving on the following Sunday. And on the next day he went from there to the city of Ely on pilgrimage to St Etheldreda the virgin. From there he went to Geddington where many Welshmen came and swore fealty to him.'[37] The most remarkable itinerary (which will be discussed more fully below) is that which traces Richard I's progress from 7 August 1190, when he sailed from Marseilles, to 7 September 1191, when he left the Holy Land for home.[38] Besides giving these royal itineraries,

---

[30] *BP*, vol. 2, pp. 110–11.   [31] *BP*, vol. 1, p. 311.

[32] e.g. *BP*, vol. 2, pp. 38–9, 136–8.

[33] *BP*, vol. 1, pp. 108–11, 278–80, 323–4; vol. 2, pp. 110–11; vol. 1, p. 33, respectively. Since I wrote the above section on 'Benedict' and Roger of Howden, an article by J. C. Holt, 'The assizes of Henry II: the texts', has appeared in *The Study of Medieval Records: Essays in Honour of Kathleen Major*, ed. D. A. Bullough and R. L. Storey (Oxford 1971), pp. 85–106, which includes consideration of both chronicles. Professor Holt accepts without reservation that Howden wrote 'Benedict' (my view, expressed below, is more cautious). His researches emphasize the very great value of the texts of Henry II's assizes, which he discusses in detail, preserved in 'Benedict' and Howden.

[34] *BP*, vol. 1, pp. 247–9.   [35] *BP*, vol. 1, pp. 272–4.

[36] The text of the settlement is printed from the copy in Roger of Howden (*RH*, vol. 2, pp. 95–7) in *Foedera*, vol. 1, pp. 35–6. For the picture of the *rota* see *BP*, vol. 1, p. 172 n. 4 and *RH*, vol. 2, p. 98 and n. 1. An example of this *rota* ('une superbe *rota* et *signaculum*, de couleur rouge vermillion') preserved at Monreale (tav. vi c.) is noticed in A. Engel, *Recherches sur la numismatique et la sigillographie des Normands de Sicile et d'Italie* (Paris 1882), p. 87. For the *rotas* of the Sicilian kings, including references to this one, see K. A. Kehr, *Urkunden der Normannisch-Sizilischen Könige* (Aalen 1962), pp. 164–72.

[37] *BP*, vol. 1, p. 159. Cf. pp. 180, 182, 280.

[38] *BP*, vol. 2, pp. 112–91 passim. See p. 227 below.

the chronicler begins each annal with a notice of where the king spent Christmas and who was with him, and records where he was at Easter and Whitsun.

But the chronicle is more than a record of the central government. It is a national record. Facts of national importance, the promotions of ecclesiastics and deaths of important men, are noticed. Moreover, the author was interested in European affairs. It is true that usually his interest in European events derives from his interest in the king: for example he records in detail the wars and treaties between England and France, and the affairs of Henry II's son-in-law, Henry the Lion of Saxony. But he was also interested in continental affairs for their own sake, describing, for example, the campaigns of Henry VI of Germany.

The author not only records facts in the course of each annal, but from 1186 to 1189 he groups some together at the end of the annals, thus making brief summaries of the year. For example at the end of 1187 he has such entries as, 'In the same year there was a serious plague among men and animals, and murrain among cattle. In the same year the countess of Brittany, after the death of her husband Geoffrey, the king of England's son, married Ranulf the younger, earl of Chester, by gift of King Henry.'[39] Such brief entries are in the tradition of the Anglo-Saxon Chronicle. As some (at the end of 1186, 1188) are merely summaries of information that the author had already given in full earlier in the annal, they were probably intended to enable the reader to gain a quick impression of the year. But a few were added after the completion of the rest of the annal and show that the author expanded the chronicle when he revised it. For example at the end of the annal for 1186 there are notices referring to Hubert Walter which were added after his election to the archbishopric in 1193.[40] In order to make the addition of such entries possible, a page or two was left blank at the end of every year, the annal for the next year beginning on a new page.[41] Similar blank spaces were left for names which were not known at the time of writing.[42]

As has been said, the chronicle was revised in or after 1190. This was done with the aid of what the reviser referred to as 'a new book'.[43] This 'new book' was the chronicle of Roger of Howden. Before discussing in detail its relationship to 'Benedict' it must be briefly described.[44] To 1148 it was compiled from well-known sources, principally the *Historia post Obitum Bedae* (*History after the Death of Bede*), a mid-twelfth century compilation from Durham, made up of extracts from the *Historia Regum* attributed

[39] *BP*, vol. 2, p. 29.　　　　[40] *BP*, vol. 1, p. 360 and n. 1.
[41] The earliest text, Julius A XI (see n. 18 above), which is very near the author's first draft, has these blank leaves at the end of annals: *BP*, vol. 1, p. xxi.
[42] See *BP*, vol. 1, p. xxii.　　　　[43] *BP*, vol. 1, p. 9 n. 2. Cf. ibid., p. xxvii.
[44] For the remarks below on the composition of the chronicle, see *RH*, vol. 1, pp. xxv–lxxi *passim*.

to Symeon of Durham and from Henry of Huntingdon. From 1148 to 1169 Roger is independent of all known chronicles except that of Melrose abbey (or its source).[45] For the Becket contest he relied on letters and seems to have constructed the narrative himself. From 1170 to 1192 he copied 'Benedict', adding material and altering some passages. From 1192 to 1201 he is original, writing a contemporary account of events. The evidence that Roger of Howden wrote the chronicle is good: it is in an early manuscript of the chronicle. There are two early manuscripts: one, having what appears to be notes by the author, has pages missing at the beginning,[46] the other is an exact copy of the above, made before the loss of the early leaves and having the title 'Incipiunt Chronica Magistri Rogeri de Houedene'.[47] But though it is certain Roger wrote the chronicle, it is not certain exactly who he was. The name Roger was very common. The minster of Howden in Yorkshire was as large and famous as Beverley (the church belonged to the prior and convent of Durham and the manor to the bishop). So one would expect the combination 'Roger of Howden' to occur quite frequently. However, a Roger of Howden became vicar of Howden between 1173 and 1176.[48] This Roger was at the siege of Acre in 1191 and died between 1191[49] and 1202.[50] A Roger of Howden was also a royal clerk. In 1174 he went on a diplomatic mission for Henry II to Galloway. In 1175 he held an enquiry for the king concerning vacant abbeys. In 1185 he was an itinerant justice of the forests, and acted as an itinerant justice again in 1187, 1189 and 1190.[51]

The problem is whether Roger the chronicler was also the parson and the royal clerk.[52] There is little difficulty in identifying the chronicler with the royal clerk. Like 'Benedict', Roger's chronicle is a quasi-official record of the central government. Roger, following 'Benedict', gives the texts of Henry II's assizes, and adds a copy of *Glanvill*[53] and of the Laws of England.[54] He copies numerous documents in full, gives royal itineraries and

[45] It has been suggested that Roger of Howden used the same Scottish annals, now lost, as the Melrose chronicle; see *The Chronicle of Melrose*, facsimile, ed. A. O. and M. O. Anderson (limited edition, London 1936), pp. xii–xiv.

[46] BM MS. Royal 14 C II: see *RH*, vol. 1, p. 3 n. 1. This manuscript has the chronicle to 1180; its sister volume, with the chronicle from 1181 to 1201, is in the Bodleian Library, Laud Misc. 582: see *RH*, vol. 1, pp. lxxiv–lxxx. Professor J. C. Holt (see n. 33 above) accepts that the marginal additions and corrections in these manuscripts are in Howden's hand. See also pp. 228–9 and n. 70 below.

[47] BM MS. Arundel 69; see *RH*, vol. 1, p. lxxx. A similar title is in the early thirteenth-century copy in BM MS. Arundel 150 (see *RH*, vol. 1, p. lxxxii) and the Hatfield MS. (ibid., p. lxxxiii).

[48] See F. Barlow, 'Roger of Howden' in *EHR*, lxv (1950), p. 354.

[49] See D. M. Stenton, 'Roger of Howden and Benedict' in *EHR*, lxviii (1953), pp. 576–7.

[50] Barlow, op. cit., p. 356.

[51] For Roger the royal clerk's career see *RH*, vol. 1, pp. xvii–xxii *passim* and Barlow, op. cit., pp. 356–7.

[52] Professor Barlow (op. cit., pp. 352–60) postulates that parson, royal clerk and chronicler were the same man.

[53] The copy of *Glanvill* is in BM MS. Royal 14 C II (see *RH*, vol. 1, pp. lxxv–lxxvii; vol. 2, p. xlviii). For its textual value see *Glanvill*, ed. G. D. G. Hall, pp. xxxi, lv–lvi, lxvi.

[54] *RH*, vol. 2, pp. 215–52.

regularly notices where the king spent Christmas. He records appointments to bishoprics and abbeys, which closely concerned the king. The evidence in favour of the view that this was the work of Roger, the royal clerk, outweighs two possible objections. One is that though 'Benedict' mentions Roger of Howden by name as the royal emissary in the negotiations with Galloway, Roger's chronicle does not, though it notices the transaction[55] (but the tradition of anonymity was so strong among chroniclers that it would not be surprising if Roger cut his own name out). The other is that the chronicle criticizes the oppressive practices of the royal justices[56] (however, there is no reason to suppose that because he had been a justice he was indifferent to abuse).

The identification of the chronicler with the parson is not so easy. It is true, as will be seen below, that the chronicle of Roger of Howden shows a strong north-country interest. But anyone with the name 'of Howden' would presumably have had close Yorkshire connections. Moreover, the chronicle shows no particular concern for the minster of Howden itself, which one would expect the parson to have.[57] Another objection is that when Roger the parson acquired the living, he was described as 'a clerk of the church'.[58] If this meant that he was serving in the church it is hard to see how he could also have been a royal official.

It has been suggested that there is an important piece of evidence corroborating the theory that Roger the chronicler was the same man as the parson.[59] This is the detailed itinerary of Richard I during the Third Crusade. The itinerary gives Richard's exact movements from day to day, both dates and places. Obviously this itinerary is from the journal of someone who accompanied Richard. As Roger the parson was at the siege of Acre it could be his own journal.[60] But this argument is only valid if one accepts an important corollary: Roger of Howden must also be the author of 'Benedict', for Roger copied the itinerary from 'Benedict'.[61] And this hypothesis involves difficulties. A comparison of 'Benedict''s version of the itinerary with Roger's shows a difference. 'Benedict''s version is quite arid and has no personal touches at all. But Roger adds two graphic details. One concerns Richard's attempt to protect his ships from worm. Richard had his ships

[55] Cf. *BP*, vol. 1, p. 80 and *RH*, vol. 2, p. 69.
[56] *RH*, vol. 4, p. 62.
[57] For references to Howden, see ibid., vol. 2, p. 71; vol. 3, pp. 35, 179, 284–5; vol. 4, pp. 77, 117.
[58] Professor Barlow (op. cit., p. 359) regards this phrase as a euphemism for the son of the former parson.
[59] Lady Stenton, op. cit., pp. 574–82 *passim*.
[60] The evidence that Roger parson of Howden was at the siege of Acre has only recently come to light (ibid., pp. 576–7) but previously Hardy (*Catalogue*, vol. 2, p. 494) suggested that the itinerary was the author's own journal.
[61] Stubbs (*BP*, vol. 1, pp. liii–liv) considered but rejected the supposition that Roger wrote 'Benedict'. Lady Stenton believes that the new evidence proving that Roger parson of Howden was at the siege of Acre, makes it virtually certain (1) that Roger the parson was the chronicler, and (2) that he wrote 'Benedict'. I think that the evidence on both points is inconclusive (see below).

taken ashore at Messina 'because many of them had been damaged by the ravages of worms. For in the river Del Far[62] there are thin worms called in that language "brom" whose food is every kind of wood. When they attach themselves to any wood they never leave go, unless forced to, until they have perforated it.'[63] The other detail is about the flying-fish off Sardinia and Corsica; 'these fish are like cuttle-fish, which leaving the sea fly through the air, and after they have flown about a furlong, descend again into the sea. There are many falcons there pursuing these fish in order to eat them. Someone who saw this testified to it, and what he said was true, for when he was sitting at table, on the high ship, one of these flying fish fell in front of him on the table.'[64] If 'Benedict' preserves the original journal Roger (the parson and chronicler) wrote on the crusade, it is hard to see why in his earlier chronicle he left out these two vivid touches, but inserted them in his final chronicle.[65] On the whole it seems most likely that 'Benedict' acquired this journal from some crusader (such journals were not uncommon),[66] copying it into his chronicle,[67] and that Roger copied it from 'Benedict' (or from the original journal), inserting additional information. Therefore the occurrence of this journal in 'Benedict' and Howden does little to support the view that Roger the chronicler was the parson of Howden or that he wrote 'Benedict'. Both questions remain open.

In some respects Roger's chronicle differs from 'Benedict'. In the sections copied from 'Benedict' Roger makes mistakes which are not in 'Benedict',[68] and sometimes gives a different account of the same event.[69] There are differences in historical method between the two works. Roger, like 'Benedict' allowed for later additions to the annals by leaving a page or more blank

[62] 'The river Del Far' was probably the narrowest part of the straits of Messina, the Puerta di Faro.

[63] *RH*, vol. 3, pp. 71–2. This description is probably of the ship-worm (*Teredo norvegicus*, a bivalve mollusc which is common in the Mediterranean and bores holes in wood).

[64] *RH*, vol. 3, p. 53.

[65] Lady Stenton (op. cit., p. 580) not only argues that Roger (parson and chronicler) accompanied Richard I on the crusade and wrote the journal of his itinerary, but also accompanied Philip II home again, writing the itinerary which is in *BP*, vol. 2, pp. 192–206 *passim* and *RH*, vol. 3, pp. 155–66 *passim*. But this hypothesis neglects the fact that on stylistic grounds it is unlikely that Philip's itinerary is by the same author as Richard's: unlike Richard's it is a purely *geographical* itinerary, saying where Philip went and describing the places, but giving no dates. For example it reads: 'He next came to the city of Myra, of which St. Nicholas held the bishopric and which the Greeks call Stamire. After that he reached a good harbour, one safe from all winds and storms, called Kekov'; *RH*, vol. 3, p. 158. (Stubbs cited evidence suggesting that it was extracted from some lost work; ibid., p. 159 n. 2, and cf. *BP*, vol. 2, p. 203 and n. 2.) Therefore, though Roger the parson of Howden could have written one of the itineraries, it seems most unlikely that he wrote both.

[66] For a similar journal, recording the journey of John of Oxford, bishop of Norwich, to Sicily in 1176, see *RD*, vol. 1, pp. 416–17.

[67] This was Stubbs's view: *BP*, vol. 1, p. liii. Elsewhere Stubbs suggests that this journal was by Richard I's biographer, Milo: *Chrons. and Mems. Ric. I*, vol. 1, pp. xxxviii–xl.

[68] See *RH*, vol. 1, pp. lviii–lix; for an example see vol. 2, p. 195 n. 2.

[69] Stubbs (*RH*, vol. 2, p. lii) notices that Roger (ibid., pp. 199–201) gives a different account of Henry the Lion from 'Benedict'.

at the end of each year (some of the blank pages were in fact used for such additions),[70] but he did not develop 'Benedict''s practice of ending annals with a summary of the year. On the other hand he adopted other expedients to make his long chronicle less unwieldy. He collected into one paragraph information on one subject which he found scattered over a number of years in 'Benedict',[71] and he abbreviated some of 'Benedict''s material.[72] Possibly it was this desire to keep his chronicle on a manageable scale which caused him to omit some of 'Benedict''s information concerning the administration: he omits the passage under 1178 about the *curia regis*, and shortens the one under 1179 about the division of England into judicial circuits (he also leaves out the detail on Henry II's dilatory business habits and the notice of Henry's appointment of an almoner).[73] Both Roger and 'Benedict' were slightly influenced by romance historiography (they include imaginary conversations and apostrophize the reader), but Roger is more fascinated by the marvellous than 'Benedict'[74] and more interested in people's characters (he gives quite long character-sketches of Thomas Becket, Geoffrey archbishop of York and of Richard I).[75]

Particularly remarkable is the strong north-country interest shown by Roger. 'Benedict' includes north-country material, but not apparently more than the importance of the subject warrants.[76] Roger, however, inserts additional north-country material into 'Benedict'. For example he adds a notice of the grant of Sadberge to Durham in 1189 and of the subsequent dispute with the king over it,[77] and a graphic account of the quarrel between the archbishop of York and his chapter.[78] In his continuation to 'Benedict' he keeps his north-country interest: he records, for instance, the death of Hugh du Puiset bishop of Durham at Howden,[79] and, under 1201, that King John dug for treasure at Corbridge ('but nothing was found except stones marked with bronze, lead and iron').[80] Moreover, as has been mentioned, Roger used north-country sources for the early part of the chronicle (the *Historia post Obitum Bedae* and the *Melrose Chronicle*).

[70] Laud Misc. 582 (see n. 46 above). This manuscript is the work of two or more scribes but it is very near to the author's own draft. Additions have been written on the blank pages at the end of the annals for 1198 and 1200 (the blank pages at the end of the other annals have not been used, though ruled for writing). From 1195 the writing of the text is irregular and the hand changes frequently.

[71] See for example *RH*, vol. 2, pp. 94 n. 2, 118 nn. 2, 3.

[72] For example he abridges 'Benedict's' account of the Council of Westminster in 1176; see ibid., p. 92 n. 1. He also gives a careful abridgment of the acts of the Council of Lombers; see ibid., p. 106 n. 1.

[73] See pp. 223 et seq. and nn. above.

[74] See e.g. ibid., pp. 132–3, 302–3; vol. 4, pp. 170–2 (cf. ibid., vol. 4, p. xiv).

[75] Ibid., vol. 2, pp. 11–12; vol. 3, pp. 287–8, 289–90, respectively.

[76] This is Stubbs's view; *BP*, vol. 1, p. lvi.

[77] *RH*, vol. 3, pp. 13–14, 38, 261.

[78] Ibid., pp. 31–2.

[79] *RH*, vol. 3, pp. 284–5.

[80] *RH*, vol. 4, p. 157.

It cannot be argued that the differences between Roger's chronicle and 'Benedict' make it impossible to accept that Roger wrote 'Benedict'. They could represent Roger's intellectual development and his carelessness. Moreover the especial concern shown in Roger's chronicle for affairs in the north could be due to a change of residence: Roger of Howden could have written 'Benedict' to about 1190 while in the king's service, and subsequently returned to his home in the north where he completed 'Benedict' to 1192, and wrote the new, long chronicle.[81] If one accepts that Roger the chronicler was the parson of Howden, this view can be corroborated with another piece of evidence. Both 'Benedict' and Roger are sketchy and inaccurate on English history during the Third Crusade, which could be explained by the absence of Roger parson of Howden on the crusade.[82] However, this evidence, like the rest, is purely circumstantial: the works could be by different authors both of whom went on crusade; or the defects in both accounts of English history from 1190 to 1191 could be coincidental.

On the whole it seems safest to accept 'Benedict' as an anonymous compilation, and Roger the chronicler as the royal clerk, but not necessarily the parson. The most important point about both chronicles in the study of historiography is that the interests of their author, or authors, centred primarily on the royal government. The other administrative historian, though he fits less well into the class, was Ralph Diceto. His connection with the government was due less to his occasional employment in the king's service than to his place of residence, St Paul's, in London. Ralph Diceto was born some time between about 1120 and 1130 (the derivation of his name is uncertain: it may be from Diss in Norfolk).[83] He became a canon of St Paul's and visited Paris in the 1140s, perhaps to study at the university. In 1152/3 he was appointed archdeacon of Middlesex and in 1180/1 became dean of St Paul's, holding office probably until he died or resigned before May 1201.[84]

Ralph led an active public life. He may have attended the baptism of Prince Henry in 1155. In 1162 he was employed in the negotiations for the translation of Gilbert Foliot from the see of Hereford to London, and took an active part on Gilbert's behalf in the Becket controversy. From 1162 he was known to Henry II and was sometimes at court, and he attended the coronation of Richard I. Life at St Paul's kept him in close touch with national events. In 1191 the magnates held a council in the cathedral,[85] and in 1194 Richard I was solemnly received there.[86] But most of the visitors

---

[81] This is Lady Stenton's argument; op. cit., pp. 581–2.

[82] See Lady Stenton, op. cit., p. 578.

[83] For Diceto's life, etc. see *RD*, vol. 1, pp. ix et seq.

[84] *John Le Neve, Fasti Ecclesiae Anglicanae 1066–1300, 1, St. Paul's, London*, compiled by D. E. Greenway (London 1968), pp. 5–6, 15–16, and more particularly D. E. Greenway, 'The succession to Ralph de Diceto, Dean of St. Paul's' in *BIHR*, xxxix (1966), pp. 86–95 (cf. p. 231 n. 101 below).

[85] *RD*, vol. 2, p. 99.   [86] Ibid., p. 114.

were ecclesiastics: Richard of Dover archbishop of Canterbury, visited St Paul's in 1183,[87] the archbishop of Cologne in 1184;[88] Baldwin archbishop of Canterbury in 1187;[89] Walter of Coutances archbishop of Rouen in 1194;[90] and the papal legate John of Salerno in 1200,[91] among others.

Ralph numbered among his friends important public figures, men such as Hubert Walter, archbishop of Canterbury, justiciar from 1193 to 1198,[92] William Longchamp, bishop of Ely, chancellor from 1189 to 1197, and Walter of Coutances, archbishop of Rouen, who was in charge of the Great Seal from 1173 to 1189 and was justiciar in 1191. Ralph also knew well Gilbert Foliot, bishop of London from 1163 to 1187, his successor Richard Fitz Neal, and Arnulf bishop of Lisieux. Ralph obtained information from William Longchamp[93] and useful correspondence from Walter of Coutances,[94] Gilbert Foliot[95] and from Fitz Neal.[96] Possibly Ralph used Fitz Neal's lost Tricolumnis[97] and may have been influenced by his historiography. And it is likely that through Fitz Neal Ralph became acquainted with Thomas Brown, Fitz Neal's close associate at, and a high official of the Exchequer. Ralph could have obtained his information about Sicily from Brown who had previously served King Roger.[98] At least some of his information about Normandy came from Walter of Coutances. The *Ymagines Historiarum* (*Images of History*), Ralph's chronicle covering the period from 1148 to 1200, has a full account, mainly derived from Walter's letters, of Walter's troubles with Richard I and the transactions over Les Andelys in 1196.[99] It is likely that the friendship of Arnulf of Lisieux was a factor in developing Ralph's interest in France and the Angevin empire.[100]

Ralph's two principal historical works were the *Abbreviationes Chronicorum* (*Epitome of Chronicles*), covering the period from the Creation of the world to A.D. 1148, and the already mentioned *Ymagines Historiarum*.[101] He also wrote a number of short historical works (*opuscula*).[102] Ralph probably began writing towards the end of the 1180s and from 1188 he gives a contemporary account of events. The *Abbreviationes* is a series of brief annals,

---

[87] Ibid., p. 21.　　　　[88] Ibid., p. 31.　　　　[89] Ibid., p. 47.　　　　[90] Ibid., p. 115.

[91] Ibid., p. 173.

[92] Ralph dedicated his work on the archbishops of Canterbury to Hubert. See ibid., p. lxi.

[93] RD, vol. 1, p. lxxiv; vol. 2, pp. 127–8. Diceto wrote a letter full of historical allusions to congratulate Longchamp on his appointment as justiciar; RD, vol. 2, pp. 177–9.

[94] See RD, vol. 1, p. lxxv.

[95] RD, vol. 2, pp. 77–8, 107–8.　　　　　　　　　　[96] See RD vol. 1, p. lxxxv.

[97] See RD, vol. 2, pp. xxx–xxxi. Cf. p. 234 below.

[98] See ibid., p. xxxii. For Thomas Brown's career see R. L. Poole, *The Exchequer in the Twelfth Century* (Oxford 1912), pp. 67, 116, 118 et seq., 122.

[99] RD, vol. 2, pp. 111–13, 122, 135–42, 144, 148–58, 160–2.

[100] See RD, vol. 1, pp. xxxi–xxxii, and pp. 234–6 below.

[101] Printed in ibid., pp. 3–263, 267–440; vol. 2, pp. 3–174. D. E. Greenway, 'Ralph de Diceto', pp. 94–5, points out that if Diceto died in November 1199 or November 1200 he cannot have written the last section of the *Ymagines* which, in that case, must have ended with King John's coronation on 27 May 1199, the point at which two of the manuscripts end.

[102] Printed in RD, vol. 2, pp. 177–285.

interspersed with good stories, almost all borrowed from well-known authorities. Towards the end it has some original material (most relating to St Paul's). The *Ymagines* has material taken from the chronicle of Robert de Torigni until 1171 (perhaps until 1183),[103] but is otherwise independent of all known literary sources.

Ralph makes his connection with the royal court evident. He praises Henry II 'who governed peacefully so wide a realm, having subdued the Scots and the Welsh'.[104] He depicts Henry as a good father, always generous and forgiving his sons.[105] The Becket controversy and the martyrdom presented Ralph with a problem: he could not defend Henry's behaviour. He therefore gives a clear and almost impartial account of events (partly drawn from the correspondence of Gilbert Foliot), and ultimately exonerates Henry by describing his deep grief at the murder: Ralph believed that God accepted Henry's penitence and that the capture of the king of Scotland in 1174 was a token of divine forgiveness.[106] Ralph begins his account of the controversy with a statement of the problem of the criminous clerks. He understood the importance of Henry's legal reforms and gives a classic exposition of the change made in judicial organization in 1179.[107] The king, 'seeking to benefit those least able to help themselves . . . and most assiduous in meting out justice to every man', had tried various classes of people as justices but found them all corrupt. He therefore appointed the bishops of Winchester, Ely and Norwich to be chief justiciars, hoping that they 'would turn neither to left hand nor to right, neither oppress the poor in their judgments nor favour the cause of the rich by taking bribes'.

This account of the 1179 reorganization is accompanied by a paean on bishops. Henry, in his search for reliable justices eventually 'raised his eyes to heaven and borrowed help from the spiritual order. Thus he took care to provide for men's needs by setting apart from the generality of mankind those who, although they live among men and watch over them, yet possess qualities of insight and courage superior to those of an ordinary man.' Ralph was biased in favour of the secular clergy and against the Black Monks[108] (he had less objection to the Cistercians and none to the Augustinian canons). He saw with satisfaction the growing importance of the secular clergy in the episcopate. One purpose of his work was to record the history of and eulogize the church in England. Of the total thirty-two appointments made to bishoprics between 1173 and 1200, he records twenty-seven, giving details of the bishops' elections and consecrations.[109]

---

[103] See ibid., p. x. For Robert of Torigni see pp. 261–3 below.
[104] Ibid., p. 8.
[105] *RD*, vol. 1, pp. 394, 404.
[106] Ibid., pp. 383–4.
[107] Ibid., pp. 434–7. Translated in *English Historical Documents*, vol. 2, *1042–1189*, ed. D. C. Douglas and G. W. Greenaway (London 1953), pp. 481–2.
[108] For his anti-monastic bias see *RD*, vol. 1, p. 389 n. 1.
[109] For his interest in episcopal vacancies see *RD*, vol. 1, pp. 366–8 *passim*.

PLATE I A page with a miniature, probably of St Gregory, from the copy of Bede's *Historia Ecclesiastica* written at Wearmouth/Jarrow in 746. The 'Augustinus' written on the halo is a later addition; see P. Meyvaert, *Bede and Gregory the Great* (Jarrow 1964), pp. 3-4. (MS. Q. v. 1. 18 in the Leningrad Public Library, f. 26ᵛ, for which see chapter 2, n. 30.)

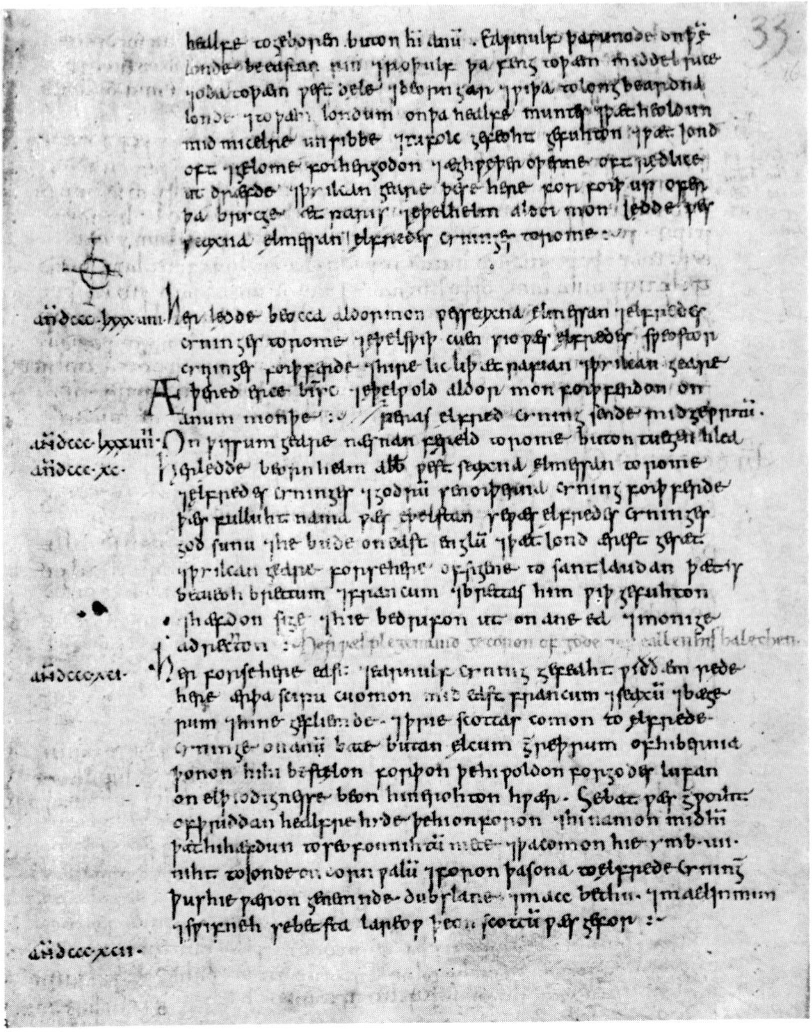

PLATE II The Anglo-Saxon Chronicle: the annals for 887–92 in the A version, in a late ninth or very early tenth century hand. (Corpus Christi College, Cambridge, MS. 173, f. 16.)

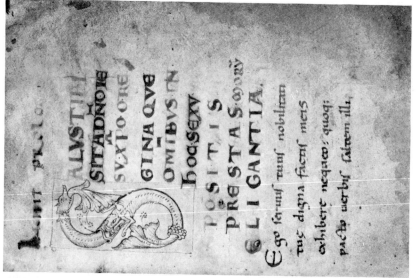

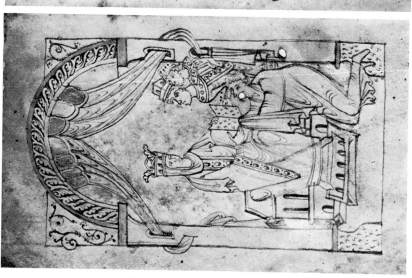

PLATE III The copy of the *Encomium Emmae Reginae* probably written especially for Queen Emma, *c.* 1040. (BM MS. Additional 33241, ff. 1ᵛ, 2.) (*a*) The frontispiece; Queen Emma, with Harthacanute and Edward, being presented with the *Encomium* by the author. (*b*) The first page of the text.

willmo duci normannorṗ pͥmo p roꝺbͧ cantuari-
orṗ ſummū pontıficē · poſtea p eundē heraldū inte-
grā angı̈cı regnı mandauerac conceſſione · ıpſūq̇
concedentıbs anglıſ fecerac toɵıuſ ıurıſ ſuı heređe·

Denıq̇ ıpſe heralꝺ apud rotomagū willmo ducı
corā optımatıbs normannıe ſacmentū fecerac · &
homo eı facͭ oͥa q̇ abıllo rẽqſıca fuerant ſup ſcıſſi-
maſ relıgıaſ ıurauerac. Tunc q̇ dux eundē heraldū
ın expedıtıone ſecū cͭ conanū comıtē brıtonum
duxerac · armıſq̇ fulgentıbs & equıſ alııſq̇ ınſıgnıſ
cū comılıtonıbs ſuıſ ſpectabılıc ornauerac. Erat eñ
ıdē angı̈uſ magnıtudıne & elegantıa uırıbuſq̇ cor-
porıſ · anımıq̇ audacıa & lıngue facundıa multıſq̇
facetııſ & pͤbıtatıbs admırabılıſ. Sed qd eı tanta
dona ſıne fıde q̇ bonorṗ omnıū fundamentū ͭ con-
tulerͭ · In patrıā nempe ſuam ut regreſſuſ ē p
cupıdıtate regnı dño ſuo fıdē mentıc eſt. Nā regem
eduardū q̇ morbo ınguelcente ıā mortı prımus
erat cırcuuenıc · eıq̇ cͤlſfretatıonıſ ſue & pͤfectı-
onıſ ın normannıā ac legatıonıſ ſerıem retulıc.

Deınde fraudulentıſ aſſertıonıbs adıecıc · quod
willmͤ normannıe ſıbı fılıā ſuā ın conıugıum
dedıc · & totıuſ anglıcı regnı ıuſ utpote genero
ſuo cceſſerıc. Quod audıenſ egrotuſ prınceps
mıratͧ ē · tͤ credıdıc & cceſſıc qd uafer tıranñ
comentatͧ ē. P oſt alıquot tͤpıſ pıe memorıe
rex eduardus xxrıııí anno regnı ſuı nonaſ ıanuarıı luna
ı̈ne defuncͭ eſt & ın nouo monaſ terno q̇ ıpſe ın occıdentalı parte urbıſ
condıɵ & tͤ precedentı ſeptımana dedıcarı fecerac ꝗ̇pe altare ꝗ̇ beatı petrıſ apl̃ı
tͤpe melltı epı ſepulͭ ē. Tunc herald ıpſo tumulatıonıſ dıe dū
cū oſtenſıone Plebſ ın exeqıſ dılectı regıſ adhuc maderet flecıbſ ·
ſıgnorṗ con a ſolo ſtıgando archıepo que romanͥ papa ſulpen-
ſecrauerac dat a dıuınıſ officııſ p ꝗ̇buſdā crımınıbſ · ſıne cͤ
munı cͤnſu alıorṗ preſulū & comıtū pcerūq̇

(a)

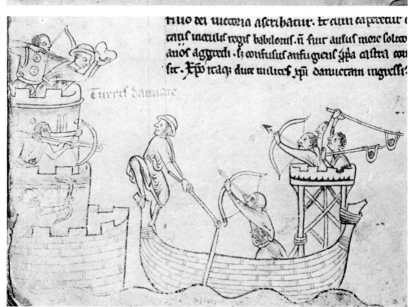

(b)

(b)

(a)

PLATE XI Possible examples of revision of chronicles because of political circumstances. (*a*) The last paragraph (1265) of John de Taxter's chronicle, showing the erasure of the sentence stating that Simon de Montfort worked miracles posthumously. (BM MS. Cotton Julius A I, f. 43ᵛ.) The letters c.b.a. after the text are the Dominical letters of the three following years. (*b*) The Chronicle of London, showing the word 'insane' (before 'Parlamentum'), to describe the Parliament of Oxford (1258), written on an erasure. (*Liber de Antiquis Legibus* in the Corporation of London Record Office, f. 75ᵛ.)

(b)

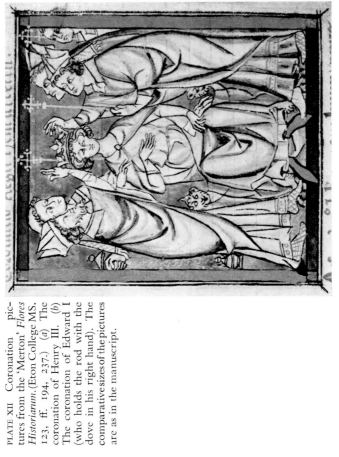

(a)

PLATE XII Coronation pictures from the 'Merton' *Flores
Historiarum*. (Eton College MS.
123, ff. 194, 237.) (*a*) The
coronation of Henry III. (*b*)
The coronation of Edward I
(who holds the rod with the
dove in his right hand). The
comparative sizes of the pictures
are as in the manuscript.

He also records such matters as Archbishop Hubert's legation from the pope.[110] Ralph's interest in English church history includes the domestic history of St Paul's. Details about St Paul's begin in 1136 and range from important material relating to the election of a bishop of London,[111] to comparatively trivial information like the expenses incurred by the dean and canons on a journey to Normandy,[112] and there is even an entry recording that a whale was stranded ashore at the Naze, a manor of St Paul's (Ralph points out that the whale belonged to the canons and not to the king).[113]

As an archdeacon Ralph was well informed about canon law (he quotes from the *Digest*).[114] In his accounts of episcopal appointments he is careful to point out that the process laid down by canon law was observed and to note any deviations or peculiarities. Thus he makes it clear that the pope had issued a dispensation to Richard of Dover so that he could become archbishop of Canterbury despite his illegitimate birth.[115] Symptomatic of Ralph's legalistic outlook are his frequent appeals to precedent. He justifies the translation of William of Champagne from one archbishopric to another (from Sens to Rheims) with a series of historical precedents.[116] He is especially anxious to justify the employment of ecclesiastics in secular affairs, and does this by citing precedents. He asserts that there would have been nothing wrong in Henry II employing Thomas Becket when archbishop as chancellor because the archbishop of Mainz and the archbishop of Cologne were similarly employed by the king of Germany and the emperor.[117] He wrote to his friend William Longchamp, bishop of Ely and justiciar of England, saying that Longchamp was to Richard I what Alcuin had been to Charlemagne: a king needed scholars, even more than soldiers.[118] He also pointed out that Gregory VI had delegated his pastoral duties in order to devote himself to the chancery,[119] and that Roger of Salisbury provided a precedent for the secular employment of bishops.[120] Similarly he used historical precedents to prove the subjection of St Augustine's, Canterbury, to the archbishop's jurisdiction.[121]

Ralph was therefore writing a record of church and state. This record aspect of his work is emphasized by the way he handled his material. He was not the first English historian to try to make the information he had collected readily accessible to his readers. 'Benedict' had appended summaries at the end of some annals. Roger of Howden often collected together in one paragraph material relating to one subject. And it is known that Richard Fitz

---

[110] *RD*, vol. 2, pp. 125–6.   [111] Ibid., p. 62.   [112] Ibid., pp. 69–70.

[113] Ibid., pp. 121–2.   [114] Ibid., p. 12 and n. 3.

[115] *RD*, vol. 1, pp. 387–9. Cf. the detailed account of the election to Rouen in 1184 (*RD*, vol. 2, p. 21), and the king's letter about the Durham election in 1195 (ibid., pp. 128–9).

[116] *RD*, vol. 1, pp. 412–13.   [117] Ibid., p. 308.   [118] *RD*, vol. 2, p. 178.

[119] Ibid., p. 179.   [120] *RD*, vol. 1, p. 435; vol. 2, p. 77.

[121] *RD*, vol. 1, p. 428.

Neal had adopted an arrangement for easy reference in his Tricolumnis. Nevertheless Ralph went much further than these writers. He must have realized that the mass of information and documents available had made historical writing unwieldy and the purely annalistic arrangement inadequate. Therefore, for easy reference, he made summaries and abstracts. The *Abbreviationes Chronicorum* is virtually a summary of events from the Creation to 1148, taken from a variety of sources. Similarly the *Ymagines* begins with a summary of its contents, the *Capitula Ymaginum Historiarum* (*Headings from the Images of History*). He abstracted from his two principal works in order to produce his short tracts, the *opuscula*. These are on various subjects: for example he abstracted lists of popes, bishops, church councils, and the like, and accounts of the archbishops of Canterbury, of the Becket controversy, of the coronations of the kings of England, and a history of the counts of Anjou.[122]

Ralph owed his interest in the organization of historical material partly to his experience with the archives of St Paul's. While he was dean he was responsible for making a survey of churches owned by St Paul's, for a record of chapter acts, and for the drawing up of various other business documents.[123] Moreover, he may well have been influenced by the methods of the royal Exchequer about which he probably learnt from Richard Fitz Neal and/or from Fitz Neal's associates, men such as Thomas Brown. Ralph's most original experiment in historiographical technique was his use of signs to call attention to specific topics – he used the same system in his work on the archives at St Paul's.[124] He begins the *Abbreviationes* with a list of the twelve signs which he had inserted in the margins of the *Abbreviationes* and *Ymagines* to enable the reader to find passages on particular subjects.[125] Six of the subjects thus designated relate to the church: they are the persecutions of the church, schisms, councils, the privileges of the church of Canterbury, the elections of the archbishops of Canterbury, and the controversies between church and state. One of the other subjects concerns the anointing of kings. Four relate to the dukes of Normandy and counts of Anjou and their contacts with the kings of England, and one to Henry II's

---

[122] See p. 231 and n. 102 above.

[123] For Diceto's work on the records at St Paul's see ibid., pp. lv–lxi. His survey is printed, from the manuscript written in Diceto's own day (now Rawlinson MS. 372 in the Bodleian) in W. H. Hale, *The Domesday of St. Paul's of the Year 1222* (Camden Soc., 1858), pp. 109–17.

[124] Diceto's survey begins with a list of contents: one of the headings reads 'De cartis per ordinem positis vel notatis tali signo ✠'; Hale, op. cit., p. 110. This proves that already at this period charters at St Paul's were marked, according to subject-matter, with distinctive signs and stored as thus categorized (it is known that at least from the late thirteenth century clerks of the royal Exchequer used a similar system of *signa* to arrange documents; see p. 364 n. 56 below). There is abundant evidence for the use of the system at St Paul's in the fifteenth century: see the *signa* in the headings in the calendar compiled by Dean Thomas Lisieux in 1440; St Paul's Cathedral Library MS. W. D. 11, ff. 53–67ᵛ.

[125] See Plate VII. For Matthew Paris's use of *signa* see p. 364 and n. 56 below.

quarrel with his sons (five of these subjects reappear in the prologue to the *Abbreviationes* where Ralph writes that his work will be particularly concerned with them). Possibly Ralph had more than the reader's immediate convenience in mind when he marked these passages; he may have intended to prepare the works for abstracting (in fact four of Ralph's *opuscula* correspond to these special subjects).

Ralph wanted to make wide sweeps of history comprehensible to the reader. He provided a compendium of historical knowledge for the period before his own time, making a far more ambitious attempt at world history than any previous Englishman. He was very learned and conscious of the authority of earlier writers. He begins the *Abbreviationes* with a survey of his sources, listing the names of forty-seven historians from Trogus Pompeius to Robert of Torigni. In the course of his work he notes where each authority ends. He uses earlier writers not only to reconstruct the sequence of past events, but also to enliven his work with amusing anecdotes and to provide parallels with contemporary events (in the same way as he drew legal precedents from the past). He used such parallels to point a moral or illustrate a statement. For example he follows his account of Prince Henry's treachery to Henry II with a series of stories about the fate of disobedient sons taken from the bible and late classical and medieval writers.[126] In order to illustrate the equal footing on which Prince Henry and Philip II stood in 1179 he compared them with Offa and Charlemagne.[127] Unfortunately Ralph is not critical in his use of sources. He accepts Geoffrey of Monmouth's statements without hesitation (he made an abstract of the *Historia Regum Britanniae*[128]) and regarded many events as fulfilments of Merlin's prophecies.[129]

Ralph was, therefore, a more original and erudite historian than 'Benedict' or Roger of Howden. Although they shared his general interest in European history, he had closer contacts than they with France and the Angevin empire and had a particular interest in Anjou and Aquitaine. The *Abbreviationes* and *Ymagines* have much information about the counts of Anjou which Ralph abstracted for one of his *opuscula*.[130] A version of this abstract was apparently made for circulation in France and a manuscript of it was in the middle ages at St Victor's in Paris, a house which had close associations with Ralph's friend, Arnulf of Lisieux.[131] Ralph borrowed most of the

---

[126] *RD*, vol. 1, pp. 355–66. Diceto's addiction to biblical parallels was no doubt due to his study of the bible, for which see ibid., p. lv.

[127] Ibid., p. 439.

[128] *RD*, vol. 2, pp. 222–31.

[129] See *RD*, vol. 1, pp. 296–7; vol. 2, pp. 64, 67, 163, 202.

[130] *RD*, vol. 2, pp. 267–8. For passages relating to the counts of Anjou in his main works see *RD*, vol. 1, pp. 135–6, 154–6, 243, and the next two notes.

[131] For the authorship of this work, entitled 'De Origine Comitum Andegavorum', which is printed in *Chroniques des Comtes d'Anjou*, ed. P. Marchegay and A. Salmon, with an introduction by E. Mabille (Société de l'Histoire de France, 1856, 1871), see *RD*, vol. 2, pp. xxiv–xxix *passim*.

material relating to Anjou from the *Gesta Consulum Andegavorum*.[132] But some of the passages are not derived from the *Gesta* or from any known authority, and therefore may be by Ralph himself.

Particularly remarkable is the vivid description of the city of Angers.[133] It describes the topography of Angers and then the river Loire. It continues: '[the Loire], in order to allow free thoroughfare to the citizens, has workshops in little houses (of earth, wood and stones) built over its waters, placed opposite each other and arranged under one almost uniform roof so that they make the bridge (which is mainly wooden in the middle) like a proper street, always open to passers-by but sheltered from the sun.' There follows an equally vivid account of Aquitaine, first its name and topography, and then the customs of its inhabitants. This includes a description of their cookery. It says that 'the men of Poitou love beef as an ordinary food. When the pepper and garlic have been mixed up together in a mortar, the fresh meat needs as a condiment either the juice of wild apples or that of young vine shoots or of grapes.' It next describes how they cook ducks. These details are more realistic and everyday than anything else in Ralph's works. If he did write them he must have visited or been born in Anjou or Aquitaine.[134]

Cultural intercourse between England and the Angevin empire had an important effect on historical writing. The tradition of the romance historians was strong in Normandy. Gaimar, who had written the history of England from the earliest times to the death of William Rufus in Anglo-Norman verse, was probably a Norman by birth. Wace, whom Henry II commissioned to write the *Roman de Rou*, was a clerk of Caen. And Benoît, who succeeded Wace as Henry's official romance historian, came from Sainte-Maure in Gascony. Gaimar, Wace and Benoît took their material mainly from well-known works: their original contributions were small. But authors such as Jordan Fantosme and Ambroise were genuine historians, using real information about contemporary events, some from personal observation. They merely adapted their material to conform to some of the conventions of romance literature: their primary aim was to amuse readers and listeners; they told the story, embellished with imaginary conversations and speeches (but with few, if any, dates), built around a hero or heroes, whose bravery and generosity they exaggerated.

Jordan Fantosme, who was probably born in England, studied under Gilbert de la Porrée, the chancellor of the schools at Chartres.[135] He himself

---

[132] *RD*, vol. 2, p. xxiv. For the *Gesta* see p. 188 and n. 9 above.

[133] *RD*, vol. 1, pp. 291–2. This passage is also in Marchegay and Salmon, op. cit., pp. 336–8.

[134] *RD*, vol. 1, pp. 293–4. This passage is not in Marchegay and Salmon, op. cit., but Stubbs suggests (*RD*, vol. 1, p. 293 n. 1) that it was probably by the same author ('whether Ralph Diceto or not') as the description of Angers.

[135] For Jordan's life see M. D. Legge, *A–N Lit.*, pp. 75–7, and *Chrons. Stephen, Henry II, and Richard I*, vol. 3, pp. lxi–lxii.

became chancellor of the schools at Winchester, and a clerk of Bishop Henry of Blois (1129–71). Therefore he was a product of the educational system of the twelfth-century renaissance, which undoubtedly influenced his historical work. In 1175 (or perhaps late in 1174), after the death of his patron, Jordan wrote a chronicle (the *Chronique de la Guerre entre les Anglois et les Ecossois*), in Anglo-Norman verse on the war between the English and the Scots from 1173 to 1174, and on the rebellion of the earl of Leicester.[136]

Stylistically the chronicle resembles the *chansons de geste* and has romance features. However, as Henry II was in Normandy during this war, Jordan could not make him the romantic hero of the poem (nevertheless, he calls him 'the best king that ever lived',[137] compares him with Moses and Charlemagne, and claims that no one in history or fiction was braver than he[138]). Jordan therefore concentrates mainly on the prowess of a number of heroes. There is for example a description of the brave knight who defended the castle of Brough-under-Stainmore against the Scots:[139]

> Now hear of his deeds, and of his great strength:
> When his companions had all surrendered,
> He remained in the tower and seized two shields,
> He hung them on the battlements, stayed there a long time,
> And hurled at the Scots three sharp javelins:
> With each of the javelins he struck a man dead.
> When those ran short, then he took sharp stakes
> And hurled them at the Scots; so he killed some of them:
> And ever he goes on shouting: 'soon shall you all be vanquished'.
> Never by a single vassal was a fight better maintained.

The influence of Jordan's classical education is discernible in the chronicle. Its theme is a tragedy brought about by pride.[140] It relates how fortune first favoured Henry II's eldest son, Prince Henry, and his allies King William of Scotland and Earl David. But, because of their shortcomings and misdeeds, fortune turned against them. The end of the story has a typical medieval touch: King Henry triumphed because, as a result of his sincere penitence for the murder of Becket, God took his side. This artificial, literary arrangement makes the chronicle unique in English historiography. It may partly explain why such favourable accounts are given of King William and Earl David (heroes of the tragedy). Jordan says of 'gentle' King William that 'a nobler man never governed a kingdom',[141] and that he was a brave soldier.[142] William, according to Jordan, only fought the English because he was misled by bad counsel,[143] and it was not he, but his French and

---

[136] The standard edition, with a parallel English translation, is in ibid., pp. 202–377.
[137] JF, l. 2. [138] JF, ll. 113–17. [139] JF, ll. 1500–9.
[140] See Legge, *A-N Lit.*, pp. 78–9. [141] JF, l. 673. [142] JF, l. 1772.
[143] JF, ll. 640, 678, 1139.

Flemish mercenaries, who ravaged Northumberland.[144] An even more favourable portrait is given of David.[145]

But the influence of classical tragedy may not be the only reason for Jordan's approval of King William and Earl David. His approval may reflect a survival of the pro-Scottish attitude shown by Ailred of Rievaulx in the *Relatio de Standardo*.[146] Loyalty in the border country was still divided: an important man like the bishop of Durham could remain neutral during the war,[147] and an Augustinian canon could visit the Scottish court to ask for peace.[148] This same Augustinian canon was one of Jordan's informants. Jordan claimed to base his chronicle on his own observation and on first-hand information. Despite its literary embellishments the chronicle is a valuable historical source. Jordan gives graphic passages containing authentic history. For example there is an eye-witness account of the capture of King William.[149] He describes how, at the battle of Alnwick, King William's horse was killed and rolled on him when it fell so that the king could not get up. He surrendered to Ranulf de Glanville and was taken on a palfrey to Newcastle.[150] Jordan ends the chronicle with an equally vivid account of how William's capture was announced to King Henry. The king had gone to bed depressed with the situation in the north, when a messenger from Ranulf de Glanville forced his way into his room with the news, despite the remonstrances of the chamberlain, who said the king should not be disturbed.[151] But Jordan is not only interested in dramatic incidents. He has an appreciation of politics. He gives a clear account of Prince Henry's treachery to his father. Prince Henry allied with Philip II of France and promised Northumberland and Huntingdon to King William of Scotland and Earl David in exchange for their support.[152] Jordan also gives information about the state of England, mentioning Northumberland's past prosperity, Norfolk's present wealth,[153] and the reputation of Bury St Edmunds for hospitality and of its knights for bravery.[154] And he shows some critical judgment: despite his wish to praise King Henry, he hints at his guilt over the murder of Thomas Becket.[155]

The other metrical chronicle of this period is *L'Estoire de la Guerre Sainte*, an account of the Third Crusade, by a poet called Ambroise. Richard I is its hero. He was an ideal subject for a romance history. His life inspired

[144] e.g. JF, ll. 1729–30.   [145] JF, ll. 1102–5, 1137, 1141–4.
[146] See p. 214 above.   [147] JF, ll. 534–5.
[148] JF, l. 712 (for a suggestion, apparently based on slender evidence, that the poem from line 645 to 765 was an insertion, see ibid., p. 259 n.). Jordan also claims to have been informed about King William's attack on Bamborough from a baron he 'knew well'; ibid., l. 1159.
[149] 'I do not relate a fable as one who has heard it,
    But as one who was there; I myself saw it'; JF, ll. 1774–5.
[150] JF, ll. 1780–1829.   [151] JF, ll. 1950 et seq.
[152] JF, ll. 1107–12, noticed by A. L. Poole, *From Domesday Book to Magna Carta* (Oxford 1951), p. 276.
[153] JF, ll. 772–4, 908–11.   [154] JF, ll. 1005, 1014.
[155] JF, ll. 1606, 1920.

men to write about it in romantic terms (the biography of him, now lost, written by his chaplain Anselm and his almoner Milo abbot of Le Pin may well have been in the same style[156]). The *Estoire* itself is so closely related to another work, the *Itinerarium Peregrinorum et Gesta Regis Ricardi*, that it is best discussed in conjunction with it. The *Itinerarium* was a compilation made between 1216 and 1222 by Richard, a canon of the Augustinian priory of Holy Trinity in London.[157] This Richard may have been a chaplain to Stephen Langton, and later he may have been the same Richard who was prior of Holy Trinity from 1222 to 1250.[158] The *Itinerarium* is in Latin prose and divided into six books. Scholars agree that Richard's work was derivative, but disagree as to his sources. However, the evidence suggests that Richard's two main sources were both by men who had actually been on the crusade. His first authority, providing material for Book I, was probably a chronicle called the *Itinerarium Peregrinorum* which was written between 1191 and 1192 by a chaplain of the Templars.[159] This chronicle gives an account of the affairs of the Holy Land from 1187 to 1190. It was by an eyewitness who wrote 'in the din of battle'.[160] He was obviously sensitive to new impressions and a keen observer. He gives a detailed topographical description of Acre[161] and describes the Negroes in the sultan's army: they were 'of enormous height and terrible ferocity, wore red turbans on their heads instead of helmets, and brandished clubs bristling with iron teeth, the blows of which neither helmet nor shield could withstand'.[162]

[156] This Life was mentioned by John of Peterborough; *Chronicon Angliae Petroburgense*, ed. J. A. Giles (Caxton Soc., 1845), p. 111. Milo and Anselm are both mentioned by Ralph of Coggeshall who perhaps used their work for his chronicle; see Stubbs, *Chrons. and Mems. Ric. I*, vol. 1, pp. xxxiii–xxxvi. Ralph learnt the details of Richard I's capture by the duke of Austria from Anselm's own mouth – Anselm was with Richard at the time; see p. 330 below.

[157] The case for his authorship is put by W. Stubbs in *Chrons. and Mems. Ric. I*, vol. 1, pp. xli–lviii *passim*. The ascription rests on two pieces of medieval evidence: (1) the *Libellus de expugnatione sanctae terrae* (wrongly attributed to Ralph of Coggeshall) ends with an extract from the *Itinerarium* and states that if anyone wishes to know about the crusade of Richard and Philip 'legat librum quem dominus prior Sanctae Trinitatis de Londoniis ex Gallica lingua in Latinum tam eleganti quam veraci stilo transferri fecit' (see *RC*, p. 257); (2) Nicholas Trevet quotes from the *Itinerarium* attributing it to Richard, canon of Holy Trinity, London – 'qui itinerarium eiusdem regis [Ricardi] prosa et metro scripsit' (see *NT*, p. 116). The metrical work referred to was probably a poem on the crusade which is now lost but was still extant in the sixteenth century; see J. G. Edwards, 'The *Itinerarium Regis Ricardi* and the *Estoire de la Guerre Sainte*' in *Historical Essays in Honour of James Tait*, ed. J. G. Edwards, V. H. Galbraith and E. F. Jacob (Manchester 1933), p. 71 n. 3.

[158] This identification of Richard is given in *Das Itinerarium Peregrinorum. Eine zeitgenössische englische Chronik zum dritten Kreuzzug in ursprünglicher Gestalt*, ed., with a critical introduction, H. E. Mayer (Schriften der Monumenta Germaniae Historica, 18, Stuttgart 1962), pp. 96–102. Cf. *Chrons. and Mems. Ric. I*, p. lxvii.

[159] This is the work, designated *IP¹*, edited by Mayer, op. cit., with a full collation of the manuscripts. It is substantially the same as Book I in Stubbs's edition of Richard's *Itinerarium* (*IP²*), so the references below to the chapters in *IP¹* are applicable both to Mayer's edition and to Book I of Stubbs's edition of *IP²*. Cf. p. 240 n. 166 below.

[160] *IP¹*, prologue.   [161] *IP¹*, c. 32.

[162] *IP¹*, c. 35. However, this account of the Negro soldiers may be romantic rather than realistic

His loyalty was to the crusade. He calls the fallen crusaders martyrs[163] and blames the failure of the crusade on the disunity of the leaders.[164] He shows no particular attachment to King Richard and the chronicle in no way centres on him: on the contrary if it has a hero it is the Emperor Frederick Barbarossa, for the author incorporates a chronicle (presumably of German derivation) recording Frederick's acts.[165]

Richard, having probably used the *Itinerarium Peregrinorum* as his main authority for Book I, may have derived the next five books from the *Estoire*.[166] Alternatively, if, as is possible, Ambroise himself relied on some earlier source now lost, Richard may have also used that source and not the *Estoire* itself.[167] The possibility that Richard used a common source and not the *Estoire* direct is suggested by differences between Richard's *Itinerarium* and the *Estoire*. These could either represent Richard's addition of new material and his mistakes in rendering the Norman French of the *Estoire* into Latin, or they could indicate that he was using a common source. The section of Richard's *Itinerarium* related to the *Estoire* (i.e. Books II–VI) describes King Richard's journey to the Holy Land, *via* Messina and Cyprus. There follows a flash-back of events since Richard's accession and then there is an account of the crusade until Richard left for home and a brief notice of his capture and imprisonment. Finally there is an account of his acts after he returned to England, which is not in the *Estoire*. Like the earlier *Itinerarium Peregrinorum*, the *Estoire* or its source was the work of an eye-witness. Either Ambroise himself or the author of his lost source was probably a Norman clerk from the region of Évreux (the *Estoire* gives many names connected with Évreux and its *environs*).[168] He says he was one of the pilgrims who visited Jerusalem in 1192,[169] and he wrote after his return home, probably between 1195 and 1196.[170] In the account of Books II–VI below, references are to Richard's *Itinerarium* (with supplementary references in the footnotes to the *Estoire* where possible), and the term 'author' used of the man (whether Ambroise or not) who wrote Richard's source and not to Richard himself.

The author, depicting King Richard as a romance hero, says he was as

---

(but such a distinction may have meant little to medieval writers), for medieval romance literature has a number of references to the blackness of Negroes. See e.g. *King Horn*, ed. G. H. McNight (EETS, original series, no. 14 (1866)), l. 1415, usually dated to the twelfth century which speaks of 'Sarazyns lodlike and blake' ('Sarazins blake' in another version). I owe this reference to Professor G. K. Hunter: see also his 'Othello and colour prejudice' (*Proceedings of the British Academy*, 1967) p. 142 and *passim*.

[163] *IP¹*, c. 31.   [164] *IP¹*, c. 64.
[165] See *IP¹*, cc. 18–24. Cf. Mayer, op. cit., p. 81.
[166] Mayer, op. cit., *passim*, designates Books II–VI of the *Itinerarium IP²*.
[167] For a summary of the views of various scholars on the problem of a possible common archetype behind the *Estoire* and *IP²* see Mayer, op. cit., pp. 107–51.
[168] See Edwards, op. cit., p. 68.
[169] *IP²*, vi. 33 (p. 435) and *Estoire*, ed. G. Paris, ll. 12013 et seq.
[170] This is the date given by Gaston Paris; *Estoire*, p. 1.

brave as Hector, as magnanimous as Alexander, as eloquent as Nestor, and as wise as Ulysses:[171] he was exceptionally handsome and athletic,[172] and dressed richly on state occasions.[173] There are descriptions of the magnificence of the royal court:[174] when Richard feasted, everything he used was valuable: the dishes and cups were all of gold or silver, wonderfully decorated with human figures and animals, in bas-relief or engraved, and studded with precious stones.[175] He was generous to his followers, paying them more than King Philip did,[176] and was kind to the sick.[177] Above all, he was brave, 'the flower of manhood, the crown of chivalry'.[178] The author gives numerous stories of Richard's heroism. For example there is the story of his single combat with a wild boar, 'of immense size and terrifying appearance'. Eventually, having broken his lance in the boar's breast, Richard struck off its head with his sword.[179] In contrast King Philip is vilified; he did not observe the pomp proper to kings, and was mean and cowardly.[180]

Despite his romantic style, the author is a good historian. He does not hide Richard's faults. He shows the king's quick temper, sulkiness and obstinacy,[181] and his refusal to take advice.[182] The author's primary loyalty is to the crusade. He praises King Richard for preferring the crusade to the government of England,[183] and deplores the half-heartedness of the crusaders of his day.[184] He wrote partly to promote enthusiasm for the recapture of Jerusalem. Moreover, like the author of the *Itinerarium Peregrinorum*, he was observant and his writing reflects the impact of the crusade and the Near-East on an ordinary western mind. He was amazed, for example, at the safe arrival of King Richard's horses in Cyprus: he describes how they were disembarked, exhausted by the month at sea (during which they had had to stand continuously).[185] He mentions the problems of an army on the move: a deluge of rain made 'the salted meat, commonly called bacon', go bad,[186] and the soldiers were bitten by mosquitoes.[187] The Turks made a deep

---

[171] *IP²*, ii. 5 (p. 143); vi. 23 (p. 421); vi. 37 (p. 447).

[172] *IP²*, ii. 5 (p. 144).   [173] *IP²*, ii. 36 (p. 197).

[174] *IP²*, ii. 13 (p. 155) and *Estoire*, ll. 559 et seq.

[175] *IP²*, ii. 24 (p. 173) and *Estoire*, ll. 1087 et seq.

[176] *IP²*, iii. 4 (pp. 213–14) and *Estoire*, ll. 4569 et seq. Cf. *IP²*, v. 6 (p. 317) and *Estoire*, ll. 8075 et seq.

[177] *IP²*, v. 2 (p. 310) and *Estoire*, ll. 7837 et seq.

[178] *IP²*, vi. 4 (p. 389). Cf. *IP²*, vi. 22 (pp. 416–19) and *Estoire*, ll. 11470 et seq.

[179] *IP²*, v. 31 (p. 345).

[180] *IP²*, ii. 13, 16 (pp. 156, 160–1) and *Estoire*, ll. 573 et seq.; iii. 21 (pp. 236–7) and *Estoire*, ll. 5245 et seq.

[181] For example he describes how Richard took to his bed in anger because the other army commanders did not agree with his plans; *IP²*, v. 43 (p. 360) and cf. *Estoire*, ll. 9502 et seq.

[182] For Richard's refusal to take advice see *IP²*, ii. 33 (p. 192) and *Estoire*, ll. 1608 et seq.; iv. 28 (p. 288) and *Estoire*, ll. 7166 et seq.; v. 42 (p. 359) and cf. *Estoire*, ll. 9433 (p. 288) et seq.

[183] *IP²*, v. 46–7 (pp. 365–6) and cf. *Estoire*, ll. 9681 et seq.

[184] *IP²*, v. 21 (p. 332).

[185] *IP²*, ii. 33 (p. 192) and *Estoire*, ll. 1565 et seq.

[186] *IP²*, iv. 34 (p. 304) and *Estoire*, ll. 7641 et seq.

[187] *IP²*, v. 44 (p. 361) and *Estoire*, ll. 9525 et seq.

impression on him. He describes their battle tactics: they were much more lightly armed than the crusaders, carrying only a bow and arrows, a club, sword and knife. They relied on their horses, 'the fastest and most agile in the world', to flee from their opponents until their pursuers stopped, then they stopped too, attacking once more until again pursued, and so on until the enemy was exhausted.[188] There are signs that the author had some sympathy for the Turks. He remarks on their bravery[189] and mentions the two fine horses Safadin gave King Richard, saying that Safadin would have been one of the best men had he only been a Christian.[190] He even gives the Turkish word for king.[191]

Books II–VI, therefore, of the *Itinerarium* are an excellent eye-witness account of the crusade told in the romance style with King Richard as the hero. But there are passages in it (which are not in *Estoire*) which show that the author was also interested in the royal administration and knew the value of documentary evidence. He notes that when the king's seal-bearer was drowned at sea, the great seal itself was saved.[192] And having recorded King Richard's return to England after his captivity he gives a long account, derived from official documents, of Richard's regulations concerning weights and measures.[193]

King, court and administration interested the remaining two writers, the satirist Walter Map and the professional *littérateur* Gerald of Wales. They were friends and their lives have many points in common.[194] They were born in the western regions, Walter in Gloucestershire or Herefordshire and Gerald in south Wales (at Maenor Pyr in Pembrokeshire). They became clerics and archdeacons: Gerald became archdeacon of Brecknock in 1175, and Walter became archdeacon of Oxford in 1196. And they were both unsuccessful candidates for the bishopric of St David's. They studied in Paris and had connections with Oxford: Walter was archdeacon of Oxford and Gerald read one of his works to the university students. They also had connections with Lincoln: Walter Map became precentor of Lincoln some time before 1186; Gerald retired to Lincoln to study theology and write in 1196. Most important was the connection of each with the royal court. Walter's connection with it began soon after 1160. In 1173 he was an itinerant justice in Gloucestershire (Gerald says that Walter was often an

---

[188] *IP²*, iv. 8 (p. 247) and *Estoire*, ll. 5649 et seq.

[189] *IP²*, iii. 15, 18 (pp. 228, 233) and *Estoire*, ll. 5067 et seq.

[190] *IP²*, vi. 22 (p. 419) and *Estoire*, ll. 11550 et seq.

[191] *IP²*, iv. 28 (p. 287) and *Estoire*, l. 7124.

[192] *IP²*, ii. 30 (p. 184).

[193] *IP²*, vi. 37 (pp. 448–9).

[194] For an account of Walter Map's life see *Gualteri Mapes De Nugis Curialium*, ed. T. Wright (Camden Soc., old series, 1850), pp. v–viii. For Gerald of Wales there is a good summary by H. R. Luard in the *DNB*. See also *The Autobiography of Giraldus Cambrensis*, ed. and translated by H. E. Butler, with an introductory chapter by C. H. Williams (London 1937): this autobiography is compiled from extracts from Gerald's works.

itinerant justice), and in the same year he was with Henry II at Limoges. He went on a mission to the court of King Louis VII and probably attended the Lateran Council in 1179 as Henry II's representative. Some time after 1186 Walter was with King Henry in Anjou, and he also served the king's eldest surviving son, Henry, until the prince's death in 1183. He died some time between 1208 and 1210. Gerald probably entered Henry II's service in 1184 and was sent to Ireland with Prince John. He was at Henry's negotiations with Richard count of Poitou in 1189. He served Richard I, apparently carrying letters for him until he left the court and went to live in Lincoln. He died in about 1220. Gerald's attitude to the royal family seems to have gradually soured owing to his failure to obtain the bishopric of St David's in 1176, 1192 and finally in 1214. The works of neither Walter nor Gerald are primarily historical. But those of both are essential for understanding the period and reflect contemporary trends in historiography.

Walter Map's *De Nugis Curialium*[195] was written in stages between about 1181 and 1192. Its main characteristic is the strong influence it shows of the classics, notably Horace and Juvenal, who are among the numerous classical authors Walter cites. The *De Nugis* is a collection mainly of court gossip and satirical jibes, 'a little book I have jotted down by snatches at the court of King Henry'.[196] Its arrangement is desultory: he compares it with 'a forest or a timber yard'.[197] One theme of the book, typical of classical satire, is to show that the worries, backbiting and frivolity of court life make it impossible to write good literature.[198] And yet Walter, as a courtier dependent on his patron for his livelihood, praises Henry for the generosity of his hospitality at court: 'No one but an idiot was poor in those days. Food and drink were supplied more lavishly than they used to be. Whoever made it his object to live at the expense of others was everywhere so kindly maintained that in no place need he blush for his mean state.'[199]

In accordance with the satirical tradition, Walter used anecdotes to expose human folly and frailty and the corruption of the age. Some of these anecdotes throw light on Walter's contemporaries, men such as Thomas Becket[200] and King Henry's son Geoffrey.[201] The historiographical interest of the *De Nugis* is increased by the last section which is an attempt at creative historical writing, based, not on the slavish copying of earlier sources, but on Walter's own impressions formed after a study of written and oral information. In this section Walter intended to preserve the memory of great men, as 'Lucan had done of Caesar, Virgil of Aeneas, and Homer of Achilles'.[202] So Walter

---

[195] The standard edition is by M. R. James (see n. 9 above), who lists in the introduction (pp. xxi–xxix) the classical writers cited by Map, and discusses the date and arrangement of the work.

[196] *Walter Map, De Nugis Curialium*, ed. M. R. James, iv. 2 (p. 140).

[197] Map, ii. 32 (p. 103). [198] Map, iv. 2, 13 (pp. 140–1, 187).

[199] Map, v. 6 (pp. 235–6). [200] Map, i. 24 (p. 38).

[201] Map, v. 6 (pp. 246–7). There is also a character-sketch of Prince Henry; Map, iv. 1 (pp. 139–40).

[202] Map, v. 1 (pp. 203–4).

describes King Canute, Earl Godwin, William Rufus and Henry I. He ends with an account of Henry II, giving a long and apparently unbiased character-sketch of him[203] which is of considerable value to the historian today. Walter comments on Henry's learning and legal ability: 'he had discretion in the making of laws and the ordering of all his government, and was a clever deviser of decisions in unusual and dark cases.'[204] But like 'Benedict', he blames him for being dilatory, especially in settling legal disputes.[205] Moreover he is scathing about the corrupt administration of justice which he attributed to the king's ignorance of what was going on. Money, he says, is the source of all pardons.[206] However, he excludes the Exchequer from his condemnation: 'There is one place in which money can do no miracles, for the glance of the king seems ever fresh there. I heard a judgment there given in favour of a poor man against a rich one.'[207]

Gerald of Wales was a much more voluminous writer than Walter.[208] He hoped one day to write a great work,[209] but meanwhile he was content to write 'best-sellers' aimed at amusing readers and, by gaining the favour of great men, at helping Gerald's promotion in his clerical career.[210] To ensure attention he dedicated one work to Henry II,[211] another to Richard count of Poitou,[212] and another to King John,[213] and he dedicated two works to Hugh bishop of Lincoln[214] and two to Stephen Langton archbishop of Canterbury.[215] Gerald succeeded in his desire to please: his works survive in numerous copies and he republished them in a number of different versions.[216] Five of Gerald's works (excluding biographies and works on local history which will be discussed below[217]) have a substantial amount of historical material. They are the *Topographia Hibernica* (*Topography of Ireland*) and the *Expugnatio Hibernica* (*Conquest of Ireland*), both written in about 1187, the *Itinerarium Kambriae* (*Itinerary of Wales*) and the *Descriptio Kambriae* (*Description of Wales*), both written after Gerald returned from his

---

[203] Map, v. 6 (pp. 234–8, 241–2).   [204] Map, v. 6 (p. 237).   [205] Map, v. 6 (p. 241).

[206] Map, v. 7 (pp. 252–3).   [207] Map, v. 7 (p. 253).

[208] The standard edition of his works is *Giraldi Cambrensis Opera*, ed. J. S. Brewer and others (RS, 1861–91, 8 vols). An English translation of many of them is by T. Wright, *The Historical Works of Giraldus Cambrensis* (London 1905). For Gerald's biographical works see pp. 310–11 below. For one of his local histories, *De jure et statu Menevensis Ecclesiae*, see H. E. Butler, 'Some new pages of Giraldus Cambrensis' in *Medium Ævum*, iv (1935), pp. 143–52.

[209] See the original preface to the *De Principis Instructione* in *GW*, vol. 8, p. lxvii.

[210] See the preface to the second edition of *Expugnatio Hibernica* (*GW*, vol. 5, pp. 410–11), for Walter Map's comment on Gerald's failure to win promotion by writing.

[211] *Topographia Hibernica* is dedicated to Henry II; ibid., p. 20.

[212] *Expugnatio Hibernica* is dedicated to Richard; ibid., p. 222.

[213] He dedicated the second edition of the *Expugnatio Hibernica* to King John; ibid., p. 405.

[214] He dedicated the second edition of *Itinerarium Kambriae* and the first edition of the *Descriptio Kambriae* to Hugh bishop of Lincoln; *GW*, vol. 6, pp. xi, xxii.

[215] He dedicated the third edition of *Itin. Kambriae* and the second edition of *Descriptio Kambriae* to Langton; ibid., pp. xxxviii, xli, 3, 7, 13, 155.

[216] The various editions are discussed in the introductions to Brewer's volumes.

[217] See pp. 310–11 below.

tour of Wales with Archbishop Baldwin who was preaching the crusade, and the *De Principis Instructione* (*On the Instruction of a Prince*), begun before 1192, but the final version was not completed until after King John's death. Gerald's historical material shows two general features: his interest in the court and government, and his acute powers of observation. He gives long character-sketches of Henry II[218] and his sons[219] and of other important public figures.[220] Moreover, he wrote partly to instruct rulers. He gives advice on how Ireland and Wales could best be administered.[221] The *De Principis Instructione* in three books, begins with a book on how a prince should behave. Its last two books (added after Gerald was disillusioned with royalty because he had failed to obtain the see of St David's) are virtually a homily on the fate which overtakes a sinful king. These sections tell the history of Henry II's reign as a tragedy: Henry's success and prosperity rise high, on the wheel of fortune, but then, because of the murder of Becket, they decline, until he dies a lonely and a broken man.[222]

Gerald's acute perception of the world around him gives his works on Ireland and Wales considerable value to the student of social history. He concentrated on Ireland and Wales because he thought that historians had neglected them in favour of England.[223] He records the popular customs, antiquities and phenomena of natural history which he observed on his travels. For example he gives a famous description of the native Welsh. He describes how they live and what they eat, even remarking on their care of their teeth: 'Both sexes exceed any other nation in attention to their teeth, which they make like ivory by often rubbing them with green hazel and wiping them with a woollen cloth.'[224] He describes the ruins of Roman Caerleon, including the system of heating by hypocausts.[225] He describes with great admiration an old Irish Gospel-book which may have been the Book of Kells.[226] And there are a number of descriptions of animals, for

---

[218] There is a character-sketch of Henry II, including an account of his physical appearance, in *Exp. Hib.*, i. 46 (*GW*, vol. 5, pp. 301–6; also printed in translation in Douglas and Greenaway, *Documents*, pp. 386–8). A eulogy of him is in *Top. Hib.*, iii. 48 (*GW*, vol. 5, pp. 190–3).

[219] For the characters of Henry II's sons see *Top. Hib.*, iii. 49 (ibid., pp. 193–201).

[220] See for example the scurrilous character-sketch of William Longchamp in Gerald's *Life of Geoffrey Archbishop of York*; *GW*, vol. 4, pp. 399 et seq. For Gerald's biased accounts of some of the Angevin nobility in Ireland see *GW*, vol. 5, pp. lxviii–lxix.

[221] For advice on how to administer Ireland see *Exp. Hib.*, ii. 36 (ibid., pp. 388–94), and Wales see *Desc. Kambriae*, ii. 9 (*GW*, vol. 6, pp. 222–3).

[222] This theme is reminiscent of Henry of Huntingdon's in *De Contemptu Mundi* (see p. 197 above). It seems likely that when at Lincoln Gerald read Henry's work.

[223] See *Top. Hib.*, first preface (*GW*, vol. 5, p. 6) and *Itin. Kambriae*, first preface (*GW*, vol. 6, pp. 157–8). Gerald of Wales's powers of observation are discussed at greater length in A. Gransden, 'Realistic observation in twelfth-century England' in *Speculum*, xlvii (1972), pp. 48–51.

[224] *Desc. Kambriae*, i. 11 (*GW*, vol. 6, p. 185). Gerald of Wales's interest in social anthropology is well illustrated by the marginal pictures in an early copy of *Top. Hib.* (from St Augustine's, Canterbury); see Plate VIII.

[225] *Itin. Kambriae*, i. 5 (*GW*, vol. 6, pp. 55–6).

[226] *Top. Hib.*, ii. 38 (*GW*, vol. 5, pp. 123–4).

example of the beaver which still survived in Wales.[227] Gerald combined this record of first-hand observations with folk-lore. He seems to have been very superstitious and credulous, though some of the fantastic stories may have been intended to amuse his readers, not to record facts. This mixture of perception with superstition is typified by Gerald's attitude to Geoffrey of Monmouth: in two places he expresses doubts on Geoffrey's veracity[228] but he frequently borrows statements from the *Historia Regum Britanniae*, treating it as authentic history.[229]

[227] *Itin. Kambriae*, ii. 3 (*GW*, vol. 6, pp. 114–17).
[228] See *Itin. Kambriae*, i. 5 (ibid., p. 58) and *Desc. Kambriae*, i. 7 (ibid., p. 179).
[229] See for example the account of Stonehenge: *Top. Hib.*, ii. 18 (*GW*, vol. 5, pp. 100–1). There are a number of references to the prophecies of Merlin (e.g. *Exp. Hib.*, ii. 28; ibid., p. 366).

12

Historians of the Reigns of Henry II and Richard I: the 'Religious'

Five members of religious orders wrote well-known histories under Henry II and Richard I. The Augustinian canons are here grouped with the monks though their order was not, by strict definition, monastic. But at this period their historiography was much influenced by the Benedictine historians, and their background and outlook closely resembled those of the monks.

Robert of Torigni began writing his chronicle in 1154 and continued until 1186 (he is called 'de Torigni' because he was born at Torigni in Normandy, but is sometimes called 'de Monte' because he was abbot of Mont-Saint-Michel, also in Normandy).[1] John of Hexham, who became prior of Hexham in about 1160, probably also wrote under Henry II: his chronicle covers the years from 1130 to 1154.[2] Gervase of Canterbury began his corpus of historical works in about 1185 and continued writing until the early years of the thirteenth century.[3] Richard of Devizes, a monk of St Swithun's, Winchester, wrote an account of the early years of Richard I (to 1192) between 1192 and 1198.[4] And between 1196 and 1198 William of Newburgh, a canon of the Augustinian priory of Newburgh, wrote a chronicle of England from the Norman Conquest to 1197.[5]

Some general features distinguish the writings of these monks and regular canons from those of the secular clergy. To a greater or lesser degree (some writers more, some less) the religious were dominated by loyalty to their own house, being deeply concerned with its fortunes and friends. This pre-

---

[1] The standard edition is *Chronique de Robert de Torigni*, ed. Léopold Delisle (Société de l'Histoire de Normandie, 1872–3, 2 vols).

[2] The chronicle of John of Hexham is printed in *SD*, vol. 2, pp. 284–332, and in Raine, *Hexham*, vol. 1, pp. 107–72 (the latter edition is cited below). An English translation is in Joseph Stevenson, *The Church Historians of England* (London 1853–8), vol. 4, pt 1, pp. 3–58.

[3] The standard edition of Gervase's historical works is *The Historical Works of Gervase of Canterbury*, ed. W. Stubbs (RS, 1879–80, 2 vols).

[4] The most recent edition is *The Chronicle of Richard of Devizes of the Time of King Richard the First*, ed., with an English translation, J. T. Appleby (Nelson's Medieval Texts, 1963).

[5] The standard edition of William of Newburgh's *Historia Rerum Anglicarum* is in *Chrons. Stephen, Henry II, and Richard I*, vol. 1, pp. 3–408; vol. 2, pp. 411–583. An English translation is in Stevenson, op. cit., vol. 4, pt 2, pp. 397–672.

occupation frequently influenced, even distorted, their view of events: Gervase of Canterbury was so obsessed with local history that he only just merits consideration with the general historians. However, the religious had some advantages as historians over the seculars: they could draw on their community's archives and library, and profited by news brought by visitors to the guest-house. And all except William of Newburgh benefited from established historiographical traditions in their houses, which trained them in the handling of historical material. In general the 'religious' historians were far less influenced than the seculars by romance literature and courtly satire.

Nevertheless the distinction between 'religious' and 'secular' historians is far from clear cut. On the one hand some secular historians had strong local attachments (the best example is Ralph Diceto who was dedicated to the interests of St Paul's). On the other hand some monastic historians were so influenced by the seculars as to be almost indistinguishable from them. Richard of Devizes in his *Cronicon de Tempore Regis Richardi Primi (Chronicle of the Time of Richard I)* is one extreme example of a monk writing almost in the style of a secular clerk. Like the author of the *Itinerarium Ricardi*, Richard wrote in the romance literary tradition, while his taste for satire and amusing anecdotes, and his scathing attitude to the country's *de facto* rulers, show affinity with the court satirist Walter Map and the professional *littérateur* Gerald of Wales.

The influence of romance literature on Richard of Devizes appears in his treatment of the principal characters in the chronicle, and of their times. Richard of Devizes depicts King Richard as the romantic hero and King Philip as the villain. He loves to describe battles and his writing has a chivalric tone (his interest in court life appears, for example, in his remarks on women). King Richard is described as a just ruler and fearless warrior. Richard of Devizes refers to him (inaccurately) as Henry II's favourite son: King Henry 'like a phoenix, has risen again a thousand times better in his son'.[6] Richard, 'that fearful lion',[7] struck the first blow in battle, and the fall of Acre should be ascribed to his energy alone.[8] His soldiers declared that 'they would all wade through blood to the Pillars of Hercules, if he so desired.'[9] Richard who 'flew to avenge Christ's injuries'[10] was the moving force behind the Third Crusade. He is contrasted with King Philip of France, depicted like the villain in a literary romance: Richard was more just[11] and generous to his soldiers than Philip.[12] The mean, cowardly Philip was responsible for the failure of the crusade: encumbered with him, Richard was 'like a cat with a hammer tied to its tail'.[13] In accordance with the romance tradition Richard does not belittle his hero's enemies. Like the author of the *Itinerarium Ricardi*, he shows some admiration for the Turks. He not only

[6] *R. Dev.*, p. 76.   [7] Ibid., p. 20.   [8] Ibid., pp. 37–8, 43–4.
[9] Ibid., p. 21.   [10] Ibid., p. 5.   [11] Ibid., pp. 16–17.
[12] Ibid., p. 42–3.   [13] Ibid., p. 78.

puts the praise of King Richard into the mouth of Saladin's brother, Safadin,[14] he also contrasts the abstemiousness and toughness of the infidel soldiers with the gluttony and drunkenness of the crusaders.[15]

The tone of Richard of Devizes is bellicose, not pacific. He loves war, not peace. He has vivid descriptions of armies and battle scenes. King Richard's soldiers march with 'clashing, glittering armour' to the sound of trumpets and clarions;[16] at a siege 'the sky was hidden by the violent rain of arrows, a thousand darts pierced the shields extended along the ramparts, and the walls were left without guards, for no one could look out without at once getting an arrow in his eye.'[17]

The dramatic effect of Richard's chronicle is heightened, as in romance literature, by the florid style which owed much to classical literary rhetoric; there are numerous allusions to such classical authors as Virgil, Horace, Juvenal, Lucan and Ovid.[18] Imaginary speeches are put into people's mouths, petitioners weep copiously,[19] the irate roll on the ground foaming at the mouth,[20] the shocked grow ashy pale and collapse in a faint.[21] Sometimes Richard's love of dramatic effect makes him distort historical fact. Presumably it was for the sake of drama that Richard said that Saladin's brother, Safadin, was sent as the emissary to negotiate a truce with the crusaders; in fact, on this occasion not Safadin but the emir Badr-al-Din was the sultan's ambassador.[22]

The aristocratic flavour appears, for example, in Richard of Devizes' lack of sympathy for the populace. Describing the welcome the Londoners gave Count John, he writes, 'nothing was lacking in the salutations of the fawning populace except the parrot-cry "chere Basileos"',[23] and, when the Londoners gained self-government, he defines, with clumsy alliteration, such a municipal commune as 'the tumult of the people, the terror of the realm, and the tepidity of the priesthood'.[24]

Richard sometimes gives women a romantic role: Queen Eleanor was 'an incomparable woman, beautiful yet virtuous, powerful yet gentle, humble yet keen-witted'.[25] And he even mentions an Amazon-type woman, another favourite figure in romance literature, saying that the countess of Aumale was more like a man than a woman.[26] Nor was Richard without an interest in court gossip. He remarks, for example, that when Berengaria ('more prudent than pretty') reached Cyprus with King Richard's crusaders she may still have been a virgin,[27] and he hints at the (allegedly) scandalous relations between Queen Eleanor and her uncle Raymond prince of Antioch.[28]

Richard of Devizes had some rudimentary interest in psychological

[14] Ibid., pp. 75–8. [15] Ibid., pp. 73–4. [16] Ibid., p. 16.
[17] Ibid., p. 24; cf. pp. 43–4.
[18] For a good example of a speech packed with classical tags see ibid., pp. 63–4 and nn.
[19] Ibid., p. 59. [20] Ibid., p. 49. [21] Ibid., pp. 50, 63.
[22] Ibid., p. 79 n. [23] Ibid., p. 46. [24] Ibid., p. 49.
[25] Ibid., p. 25. [26] Ibid., p. 10. [27] Ibid., pp. 25, 35.
[28] Ibid., pp. 25–6.

motivation, and this may well have derived from romance literature. He was interested in patterns of human behaviour, especially when they influenced the course of events. For example he says that William Longchamp, bishop of Ely (who ruled England when King Richard was on crusade), expelled Hugh du Puiset from control of the Exchequer 'because all power always has been, still is, and always will be jealous of anyone sharing it'.[29] Again, he says that Queen Eleanor failed to achieve a permanent reconciliation between Longchamp and Walter of Coutances archbishop of Rouen in 1191 because 'the habits of thought contracted through a long hatred could not be changed'.[30]

The satirical aspect of the chronicle, demonstrating Richard's affinity with Walter Map, appears in his prologue. Richard wrote for a friend, Robert, formerly prior of Winchester, who had become a Carthusian monk of Witham (founded by Henry II in 1178–9). Richard makes witty remarks about Robert's desertion of the Benedictine order for the Carthusians. He asks 'by how much is the Carthusian cell loftier and nearer to heaven than is the cloister at Winchester?' He particularly implies an incongruity between the strict, enclosed life of the Carthusian monks and their appetite for news of the outside world. It was to satisfy Robert's desire for such news that Richard wrote. The story of the sins of the world would, Richard hoped, increase Robert's appreciation of his own 'cloistered heaven'.

Other passages in the chronicle are also satirical. Richard uses satire to attack the secular canons, in his day the rivals of the Benedictines,[31] in much the same way as Map used it to attack the monks. The immediate cause of a bitter invective against secular canons was the substitution by Hugh of Nonant bishop of Coventry of a secular chapter for a monastic one in his see at Coventry. Richard accuses the canons of Coventry of being non-resident, spending their prebendal income on themselves, and of under-paying the vicars they appointed to hold the cathedral services. 'These irregular clerks regular', he writes, of that 'glorious order of secular clerks', build themselves 'large splendid lodgings around the church, perhaps for their own use, in case any occasion should arise, even once in their lives, for visiting the place'. Meanwhile if a poor man knocks at the gate of such a canon, the impoverished vicar would say, 'Go away and beg for food somewhere else, for the lord of this house is not at home.'

Perhaps the satirical tradition augmented the scorn which Richard poured on the men who ruled England when the king was on crusade. Richard has hardly a good word for the powers-that-were. Count John was a 'light-minded youth', who 'slept in clover' while his brother fought the infidel.[32] He and his brother Geoffrey were of an 'innate perversity'[33] and Geoffrey stirred up trouble against William Longchamp, the chancellor.[34] The latter,

[29] Ibid., p. 10. [30] Ibid., p. 60. [31] Ibid., pp. 70–1.
[32] Ibid., pp. 60, 77. [33] Ibid., p. 40. [34] Ibid., p. 46.

'a man with three titles and three heads',[35] in addition to his various iniquities, made a fool of himself by escaping from England in a woman's clothes.[36] And Walter of Coutances, 'cowardly and timid', shamelessly abandoned the crusade.[37] Richard's love of anecdotes is also reminiscent of Walter Map. (For example, he tells how Archbishop Geoffrey, when imprisoned by Longchamp, spat out the food which his warder had prepared for him.[38])

Thus Richard of Devizes was strongly influenced by the romance and satirical literary traditions. Moreover, he shared with two secular writers an interest in cities and urban life. Ralph Diceto described Angers[39] and William Fitz Stephen wrote the famous account of London.[40] Richard mentions in a satirical manner the characteristics of a number of English towns but is most eloquent on Winchester, to him the most favoured place in England. He puts his panegyric rather strangely into the mouth of a French Jew, in his advice to a Gentile boy about to look for work in England.[41] Richard's choice of a Jew as the vehicle for the panegyric is curious and seems to reflect pro-Jewish sentiments. He was obviously interested in the Jewish community in Winchester – he praised the citizens of Winchester for tolerating and protecting the Jews in the city when elsewhere in England Jewish lives and property were the object of violent attack.[42] The Jew starts by telling the boy to avoid certain English cities and towns – Bath because it is 'placed or rather dumped in the midst of valleys, in exceedingly heavy air and sulphurous vapour', and Bristol because 'there is no one there who is not or has not been a soap-maker, and every Frenchman loves soap-makers as he does a dung-heap.' Then he describes Winchester:

> that city is a school for those who want to live and fare well. There they breed men; there you can have plenty of bread and wine for nothing. Monks are there of such mercifulness and gentleness, clerks of such wisdom and frankness, citizens of such courteousness and good faith, women of such beauty and modesty, that for a little I would go there myself and be a Christian among such Christians.

Nevertheless, though Richard of Devizes was influenced by secular literary traditions, his writing has features typical of monastic historiography, and he was a passionate champion of Benedictinism. The drift of the prologue is that Carthusian austerity compares badly with Benedictine moderation. Contrasting the secular canons with the monks who preceded them in the cathedral chapter at Coventry, Richard gives a paean on the monks; 'they

---

[35] Ibid., p. 13.   [36] Ibid., p. 53.   [37] Ibid., p. 27.
[38] Ibid., p. 42.   [39] See p. 236 above.   [40] See pp. 307–8 below.
[41] R. Dev., pp. 64–7.   [42] Ibid., pp. 4, 64.

praised the Lord with their own mouth, not through a vicar, and lived and walked in the Lord's house in harmony all the days of their lives, caring for nothing of this world beyond their bare food and clothing; their bread was ready for the poor and their door stood open at all times for the traveller.'[43]

Like other monastic chroniclers, Richard of Devizes wrote partly to record events. And as a record his chronicle has considerable value. For example it gives a detailed and fairly accurate account of the negotiations resulting in the Treaty of Winchester (1191), containing information recorded by no other authority.[44] Richard intended the chronicle to grow as more information reached him. His own autograph manuscript survives[45] showing how he left wide margins for additions – many passages in the chronicle are in fact marginalia.

This method of adding news in the margins was characteristic of monastic annals. It was used, for example, in the Winchester annals[46] which cover the period from the Creation to 1202 and were partly compiled in Richard of Devizes' day. It has been suggested that Richard himself wrote the sections from the beginning to 1066, and from 1196 to 1210.[47] Possible evidence for his authorship of these sections is provided by stylistic similarities between them and Richard's chronicle.[48] However, as the annals are, by their nature, merely brief chronological notes for each year, and as Richard's chronicle is for the most part (it has a few annalistic passages) a full narrative history, it is hard to compare the two works, and therefore impossible to be certain that Richard had a hand in the annals. Moreover, no comparison between the contents of the annals and those of his chronicle can be made because the entries in the annals for the years from 1190 to 1196 (which include the years covered by Richard's chronicle) are missing, owing to loss of leaves from the only known manuscript.[49] But it is worth noting as possible evidence against Richard's part-authorship of the annals that the latter give, under 1197, a

---

[43] Ibid., p. 71.

[44] Ibid., pp. 33–5. For a comparison of Richard's account of these events, which led up to the Treaty of Winchester, with the accounts in the other authorities, see Appendix F in ibid., pp. 90–8.

[45] For a description of this manuscript (Corpus Christi College, Cambridge, MS. 339) see ibid., pp. xviii–xxiv *passim*. For a reproduction of one page, see ibid., opposite p. xvi.

[46] The Annals of Winchester are printed in *Annales Monastici*, ed. H. R. Luard, vol. 2, pp. 3–79. The *Annales* survive in two manuscripts, both of which have wide margins used for additions; see ibid., p. xii.

[47] See J. T. Appleby, 'Richard of Devizes and the Annals of Winchester' in *BIHR*, xxxvi (1963), 70–5 *passim*. See also *R. Dev.*, pp. xxiv–xxvi. One of the manuscripts of the Annals is in the same volume as the autograph of Richard of Devizes' chronicle (CCC MS. 339) and is in the same hand. This text (known as A) of the Annals only goes down to 1139. The other text (known as B) is in BM MS. Cotton Domitian A XIII; this text is the same as A to 1066, has different annals from 1066 to 1139 and then continues to 1202. Luard, op. cit., prints A to 1066 and then B to the end. Extracts from the annals in A from 1066 to 1139 are printed by Appleby, 'Richard of Devizes and the Annals of Winchester', pp. 75–7.

[48] For the stylistic similarities see Appleby, op. cit., pp. 72–5.

[49] See *Ann. Mon.*, vol. 2, p. 64.

very favourable portrait of William Longchamp for whom Richard's chronicle had not a good word.

The best example of a chronicler writing in the monastic traditions, and only slightly influenced by secular literary traditions, was Gervase of Canterbury. His thought was dominated by loyalty to his house, Christ Church, Canterbury. His devotion to Christ Church moulded his historiography, and he profited from the cathedral's historiographical tradition, archives and library. Gervase became a monk of Christ Church in 1163, probably at the age of about eighteen. By 1193 he was the sacrist, holding office until some time before 1197. He died in or soon after 1210.[50] He lived through the most momentous years in Christ Church's history, the murder of Thomas Becket in 1170 and the fire which destroyed the choir of the cathedral in 1174.

Both events had a traumatic effect on the convent, which is reflected in Gervase's historical works. Becket's martyrdom gave Christ Church one of England's most popular saints; the fire made necessary the building of the new choir, which not only drained the priory's resources but also, while building was in progress, absorbed the monks' attention for nearly a decade. Moreover, to the years from 1178 to 1183 belongs the bitter quarrel between Archbishop Baldwin and St Augustine's, Canterbury, concerning the archbishop's jurisdiction over the abbey. And in 1185 began Christ Church's prolonged dispute with Archbishop Baldwin because the latter tried to control the convent's administration and also to found a college of secular canons in one of the convent's churches.

Archbishop Baldwin's disputes with St Augustine's and Christ Church were the immediate cause why Gervase, at the request of his community, began studying and writing history.[51] In about 1185 he wrote a tract on the archbishop's dispute with St Augustine's. This tract was not historical in form: it argued the archbishop's case and then it argued the abbey's case. The arguments, however, are based on historical precedents. The history of St Augustine's and its relations with the archbishop are traced from the conversion period to Gervase's own day. The purpose of the tract was no doubt to record precedents, but the fact that the abbey's case is given as well as the archbishop's shows that it was a literary exercise rather than a business document. Gervase's next known work, concerning the cathedral priory's struggle with Archbishop Baldwin, is similar in form to the previous one.

Gervase's more ambitious works developed from these two tracts. In or soon after 1188 he began the *Chronica*,[52] first prefixing copies of the tracts,

[50] For Gervase's life see *GC*, vol. 1, pp. xi et seq.

[51] See ibid., pp. xvii–xix. His early tracts, the *Imaginationes*, are printed in ibid., pp. 29–83.

[52] For the date when Gervase started the *Chronica* see ibid., pp. xx–xxi. The *Chronica* is printed in ibid., vol. 1. For one aspect of the struggle between Archbishop Baldwin and Christ Church, as recorded by Gervase, see A. Gransden, 'Childhood and youth in medieval England' in *Nottingham Mediaeval Studies*, xvi (1972), pp. 13–14.

and then writing a history of Christ Church, set against a background of general history, from the time of St Augustine until 1199 (Gervase planned to continue it into King John's reign, but never did so).[53] The *Chronica* formed the basis of Gervase's next historical work, the *Gesta Regum*. The latter is partly an abstract of the *Chronica*: Gervase omitted much of the Canterbury material and added many other passages, to produce a political history of England from the earliest times.[54] The *Gesta* continued to 1210 though it is not quite certain that Gervase rather than some other contemporary Canterbury monk wrote the section from 1199 to 1210.[55] Gervase was certainly the author of the Lives of the Archbishops of Canterbury (to 1205)[56] and the *Mappa Mundi*, a list of the monasteries of England.[57]

The fact that local loyalty provided the initial stimulus which prompted Gervase to turn his attention to history affected his historiography both favourably and adversely. An advantageous result was that controversy involving Christ Church forced him to undertake genuine historical research. It led him to examine the cathedral's past in order to justify its disputed claims. He recorded the progress of quarrels, copying documents in full, so that the *Chronica* would be a book of reference in case of future disputes.[58] Gervase himself became the recognized authority on Canterbury customs. As he himself states, he settled a dispute in 1193 as to whether the archbishop should carry his cross before he had received the pallium; Gervase told him what the customs were and put the details in the *Chronica*.[59]

A good example of how controversy heightened historical perception is provided by the twelfth-century forgery cases. Litigation resulted in the earliest attempts at testing the authenticity of charters. Gervase records how a forgery was detected in court in 1181. The monks of St Augustine's, in order to fortify their claim to exemption from obedience to the archbishop, produced what purported to be a papal diploma granted to St Augustine of Canterbury. But though, as Gervase points out, the parchment was old (it

---

[53] For the projected book on King John's reign see ibid., pp. xxvii, 594; vol. 2, pp. xiii–xv.

[54] For the *Gesta* see ibid., vol. 1, pp. xviii, xxx–xxxi; vol. 2, pp. viii–xvi. It is printed in ibid., vol. 2, pp. 3–106.

[55] Stubbs considers it likely that Gervase wrote the section from 1199 to 1210 (printed in ibid., vol. 2, pp. 92–106); see ibid., vol. 1, pp. xxx–xxxii; vol. 2, p. xiii.

[56] For the Lives of the Archbishops of Canterbury (*Actus Pontificum Cantuariensis Ecclesiae*) see ibid., vol. 1, pp. xxvii–xxx; vol. 2, pp. xl–xlii. They are printed in ibid., vol. 2, pp. 325–414.

[57] For the *Mappa Mundi* see ibid., vol. 1, pp. xxvii–xxix; vol. 2, pp. xlii–xliii: and for a full discussion of its contents and historical value see M. D. Knowles, 'The Mappa Mundi of Gervase of Canterbury' in *Downside Review*, xlviii (1930), pp. 237–47. It is printed in *GC*, vol. 2, pp. 414–49.

[58] Gervase states that he described in detail the election of Archbishop Baldwin in 1184 'ad cautelam illorum, qui futuris temporibus electioni Cantuariensis archiepiscopi debent interesse'; *GC*, vol. 1, p. 325. Similarly he described how the cross was delivered to a newly elected archbishop 'ut sciant posteri quomodo fieri debeat'; ibid., p. 521.

[59] Ibid., p. 521.

was a re-used piece), the handwriting, style and the leaden bull were not sufficiently ancient.[60]

Gervase's concern for Christ Church fostered his visual sense – he loved the actual structure of the cathedral. His account of the cathedral is the most vivid and precise architectural description yet written in England.[61] He clearly appreciated the value of visual evidence, for he advised his readers not only to read his book, but, better still, to go and look at the cathedral for themselves.[62] It seems possible that Gervase was personally involved in the rebuilding of the cathedral. The master-builder, William of Sens, injured his back by falling from the scaffolding and had to direct the work from his bed. Perhaps Gervase was the 'industrious and ingenious' young monk whom William appointed (despite the envy of the other monks) to supervise the builders.[63]

Gervase undertook in the *Chronica* both to describe the new church and also to record the appearance of the two earlier ones, the pre-Conquest church and that built by Archbishops Lanfranc and Anselm. His purpose was, he says, to prevent the two previous churches (both destroyed by fire) ever being forgotten.[64] To describe the pre-Conquest church he relied on the architectural account in Eadmer's work on the relics of St Ouen.[65] Undoubtedly Gervase's predilection for architectural descriptions was partly due to Eadmer's influence. Eadmer had written primarily to explain exactly where the relics and altars of the saints were: Gervase showed the same interest in the location of the relics and also of the archbishops' tombs. One of his objectives must have been to prove that no relics had been lost but that all were duly removed to the new choir. To Gervase the crowning event in the reconstruction of the choir was the placing of the tomb of Thomas

[60] Ibid., pp. 296–7. For the controversy see M. D. Knowles, 'Essays in monastic history, 1066–1216; IV. The growth of exemption' in *Downside Review*, l (1932), pp. 411–15. For examples (excluding this one) of the detection of forgery in the twelfth century see R. L. Poole, *Lectures on the History of the Papal Chancery* (Cambridge 1915), pp. 145–9. For later examples see V. H. Galbraith, *Studies in the Public Records* (London–New York 1948), pp. 48–52.

[61] For the account of the destruction and rebuilding of the cathedral see *GC*, vol. 1, pp. 3–29. This account is discussed and translated in Robert Willis, *The Architectural History of Canterbury Cathedral* (London 1845), pp. xiv–xvi, 32–62. The plan of the waterworks at Canterbury, perhaps drawn by, or under the direction of, the engineer Wibert, preserved in the Eadwine Psalter, belongs to much the same period (the plan is to be dated *c.* 1167) as Gervase's architectural description of the cathedral, and reflects a similar desire to record Christ Church's physical appearance; the plan is reproduced in *The Canterbury Psalter*, ed. M. R. James (London 1935), at the end of the volume, and described in ibid., pp. 53–6.

[62] Comparing the new with the old choir Gervase writes 'Quae omnia visu melius quam auditu intelligere volenti patebunt' (*GC*, vol. 1, p. 27), and again 'Haec omnia clarius et delectabilius oculis possunt videri quam dictis vel scriptis edoceri' (ibid., p. 28).

[63] Gervase records that William 'cuidam monacho industrio et ingenioso qui cementariis praefuit opus consummandum commendavit, unde multa invidia et exercitatio malitiae habita est, eo quod ipse, cum esset juvenis, potentioribus et ditioribus prudentior videretur'; ibid., p. 20.

[64] See ibid., pp. 11 (bottom of page), 27 (top of page).

[65] Ibid., pp. 7–9. See pp. 131 and n. 180, 132 above.

Becket in it: the tomb worked miracles whose fame 'spread all over Europe, abolishing incredulity'.[66]

The choir burnt down in 1174 was the one built by Prior Conrad under Archbishop Anselm, itself replacing Lanfranc's choir. Lanfranc's nave still stood in Gervase's day (it was pulled down and rebuilt in the late fourteenth century) and was spared by the fire. Gervase admits that as he never saw Lanfranc's choir he cannot describe it.[67] But he describes Conrad's choir as far as he could remember it. Next he describes the progress of the rebuilding during the nine years following the fire, and how it was held up by accident, rain and lack of money. He ends with a brilliant comparison between the style of Conrad's choir and that of the new one. He points out that the new columns were nearly twelve feet higher than the old ones, and, unlike the latter, had carved capitals. Rib-vaults had replaced the previous plain stone vaults and painted wooden roofs. He notices that the new choir had two triforia instead of one, was higher and lighter than the earlier building, and had more marble and carving. He ends with an explanation why the new choir was narrow towards the end (one reason was because the architect decided to leave the two old towers standing, thus restricting the available space).

In his enthusiasm for architectural descriptions and architectural history Gervase was a precursor of Matthew Paris.[68] His interest shows a strongly antiquarian trend in his thought. This antiquarianism also appears in the *Mappa Mundi*. In his prologue[69] he says that he wants to preserve the memory of the Britain of his day, remarking that nothing now remained of the land described by the 'ancients' (he is here referring obliquely to Geoffrey of Monmouth), which makes it important to record the face of contemporary Britain so that it also will not be forgotten. He concentrated on monastic Britain, arranging his information under counties. He drew three columns, writing in the first column 'archbishopric', 'bishopric', 'abbey' or 'priory' – whichever was relevant. In the second column he gave the name of the place and the patron saint, and in the third column he put the order to which the foundation belonged. He ended the entry for each county with a list of the hospitals and castles in it, and a note as to its source of fresh and salt water. Gervase's work has some affinities with William of Malmesbury's *Gesta Pontificum*, which perhaps inspired Gervase to make such a monastic survey. On the other hand the tabulated arrangement may have derived from the episcopal lists of such writers as Florence of Worcester. But no one except Gervase attempted a survey of monasteries until Sir William Dugdale in the seventeenth century compiled

---

[66] Ibid., p. 18. [67] Ibid., p. 12.

[68] For Gervase of Canterbury's antiquarian interests and architectural descriptions see A. Gransden, 'Realistic observations in twelfth century England' in *Speculum*, xlvii (1972), pp. 39–40. For Matthew Paris's visual sense, see pp. 362 et seq. below.

[69] *GC*, vol. 2, pp. 414–15.

the *Monasticon Anglicanum*. A modern work resembling Gervase's is M. D. Knowles's and R. N. Hadcock's *Medieval Religious Houses of England and Wales*.

It has been seen that Gervase's antiquarian interests originated in his love of Christ Church. Perhaps it was due to this same affection that he became interested in chronology, for there was a chronological problem connected with the martyrdom of Thomas Becket. He was martyred on 29 December in 1170, according to present-day reckoning. But in the middle ages such a date led to chronological complications. Some chroniclers began the year on Christmas day, some on the feast of the Circumcision (1 January), some on the feast of the Annunciation (25 March), and some on Passion Sunday (the fifth Sunday in Lent). Therefore Becket's martyrdom could have been in 1170 or 1171 according to the reckoning adopted. Gervase recognized the problem. Though he began the year at Christmas, he made an exception for the date of the martyrdom, placing it in 1170 because this was the generally accepted date.[70] But to justify this year-date he has a page discussing the different dates adopted as the first day of the year. He was the first chronicler to discuss this problem which has sometimes caused chronological confusion among medievalists to the present day.

It can therefore be seen how Gervase's interest in local history, generated by his love of Canterbury, could make him take a wider view of historical problems. And as a historian of national events, his local attachments had one marked advantage: they enabled him to take an objective view of the king and government. He had not the same temptation to eulogize the king as the romance historians had. Neither did he try to satirize the king and magnates – his attitude to both was detached so long as they did not interfere with Christ Church: when they did interfere he liked them if they helped the cathedral, and disliked them if they harmed it. Though on the whole Bishop Stubbs's opinion that Gervase had no political attitude seems true,[71] there are indications in his last years that he evolved rudimentary 'constitutional' views similar to those later developed by the St Albans chroniclers.

Gervase began to dislike Henry II, Richard I and John because they offended Christ Church. Henry II was not only the cause of Becket's murder, but also failed to give the convent firm support when the monks tried to assert their right to choose an archbishop in 1184.[72] Gervase says that Richard I lost his temper in the chapter at Christ Church when trying to settle the monks' quarrel with Archbishop Baldwin.[73] The convent's com-

---

[70] On the date of Thomas Becket's murder see *GC*, vol. 1, pp. 90–1; cf. ibid., pp. 229 n. 1, 231 and n. 3, 232. For Gervase's discussion on different eras and other chronological problems see ibid., 88–90; for a notice of this passage in Gervase see *Handbook of Dates for Students of English History*, ed. C. R. Cheney (*Royal Historical Soc.*, 1948), p. 3.

[71] *GC*, vol. 1, p. xlvii.

[72] Ibid., p. 319. See also the account of Henry's death; ibid., p. 449.

[73] Ibid., p. 471.

plaints against King John were more serious. In 1205 there was the dispute between king and convent over the latter's election of Stephen Langton to the archbishopric.[74] And during the Interdict John drove the monks from Christ Church, leaving them penniless.[75]

The question is how far Gervase's personal dislike of the king (representing the corporate dislike felt by the convent) was transmuted into a constitutional, political attitude. There are some indications that ideas of limitation of authority by the community were generated in the convent at Christ Church itself. Gervase remarks, when recapitulating the early history of the relationship of Christ Church to the archbishops, that the division of the cathedral's property between the convent and archbishop should only be altered 'by common counsel, and not by presumption or tyranny'.[76] He also notes with satisfaction that in 1149 Archbishop Theobald appointed a prior of Christ Church with the consent of the convent,[77] and he emphasizes that the convent clung to its charters to secure the monks' rights against the archbishop.[78]

A parallel pattern of thought occurs in the political sections of the *Chronica* and *Gesta Regum*. Gervase says in the *Chronica* that Thomas Becket scorned *aulici*,[79] and is insistent that both Richard I and John were led astray by bad counsellors.[80] Either Gervase or his continuator (if Gervase was not responsible for the section of the *Gesta Regum* from 1199 to 1210[81]) express other views prophetic of those later held by the St Albans chroniclers. Thus the *Gesta* states that in 1204 preparations for the defence of England against French invasion were made 'with the assent of the king and of all the magnates'.[82] It also asserts that in 1205 'all the magnates being assembled at Oxford, King [John] was compelled to swear that he would preserve unharmed the laws of the realm of England with their counsel.'[83] Perhaps this early attempt at checking John's power was really made.[84] In any case, the language is like that used by the St Albans chroniclers about twenty years later. Moreover the *Gesta*, like the St Albans chronicles, has almost hysterical abuse of John. It accuses him of such deceit that his word could never be trusted,[85] and expatiates on England's sufferings under his rule.[86] And it inveighs against the king's financial impositions[87] and the greed of the Roman curia,[88] favourite themes of the later chroniclers.[89]

Gervase's works have value for general history (for example they have an important text of the Inquest of Sheriffs in 1170,[90] and a unique account of

---

[74] *GC*, vol. 2. pp. 98–101. [75] Ibid., p. 101. [76] *GC*, vol. 1, p. 43.

[77] Ibid., pp. 48, 141. [78] Ibid., pp. 467, 470–1. [79] Ibid., p. 160.

[80] Ibid., pp. 458, 461, 593. [81] See p. 254 above and n. 55. [82] *GC*, vol. 2, p. 96.

[83] Ibid., pp. 97–8.

[84] See J. C. Holt, *Magna Carta* (Cambridge 1965), p. 103.

[85] *GC*, vol. 2, p. 106. Cf. p. 369 below.

[86] Ibid., p. 102. [87] Ibid., pp. 101, 105. [88] See *GC*, vol. 1, p. 303.

[89] See e.g. p. 368 below.

[90] Ibid., pp. 217–19. See Stubbs, *Charters*, pp. 174–8.

the second coronation of Richard I in 1194 at Winchester[91]). But there is no doubt that though Gervase's obsessive love of Christ Church provided the motive for his historical writing, it also in general proved a severe limitation. Eadmer's view of history had narrowed as he grew older and found Christ Church increasingly harassed with difficulties. Gervase's view started narrow and remained narrow. He was unable to concentrate on, or appreciate the importance of, national and foreign events. For example in describing one quarrel between Archbishop Baldwin and Christ Church he compares Baldwin with Saladin, and his 'capture' of the convent with the fall of Jerusalem. And he calls the monks who died in Italy (where they went to appeal to the pope against Baldwin) martyrs.[92] Under 1189 Gervase notes that Ranulf de Glanville came to England to collect forces for the crusade: but he immediately reverts to the quarrel between Christ Church and Baldwin, recording how Glanville visited the convent in an attempt to mediate (he quotes Glanville's speech in the conventual chapter).[93]

On the whole, therefore, it is true to say that Gervase's attitude to historical events can only be understood in relation to his loyalty to Christ Church. Moreover, his historical method was profoundly influenced, for better and for worse by the fact that he was a monk of Christ Church. He benefited from the cathedral archives and library just as Ralph Diceto had benefited from those of St Paul's; but his access to so many books had, as will be seen, disadvantages.

From the archives Gervase had access to such records as charters, and the rolls recording the consecration of bishops. Perhaps his acquaintance with business methods and the organization of documents gave him the idea of differentiating historical material according to its subject. Like Diceto (though Gervase added more new material[94]), he abstracted from one work to form another on a different subject. He plundered the *Chronica* in order to write a national history, the *Gesta Regum*, and again, for the Lives of the Archbishops of Canterbury.

Gervase made considerable use of the library and was a learned man, well read in the works of earlier historians. The latter no doubt contributed to his interest in chronology – he discusses the relative merits of the systems used by Marianus Scotus and Dionysius Exiguus.[95] Moreover, his studies gave him an interest in historiography. As far as is known, he was the first man in England to distinguish chronicles from history. The object of both, he says, is the same – to record the truth – but the method varies.[96] The

---

[91] *GC*, vol. 1, pp. 524–7. Cited by P. E. Schramm, *A History of the English Coronation*, translated by L. G. Wickham Legg (Oxford 1937), p. 59.

[92] *GC*, vol. 1, pp. 430–1.   [93] Ibid., p. 447.   [94] See p. 254 above.

[95] Ibid., p. 89.

[96] Ibid., pp. 87–8. This passage is cited in V. H. Galbraith, *Historical Research in Medieval England* (London 1951), p. 2. For the possibility that Gervase was here influenced by Cicero's *De Oratore*, II, 51–64, where Cicero distinguishes between the early annalists and the later rhetorical historians, see *Latin Historians*, ed. T. A. Dorey (London 1966), pp. xii–xiii.

historian's style is elegant and diffuse, using flowery and resounding words, while the chronicler's style is simple and brief. And he criticizes some chroniclers for trying to ape historians. But he does not mean by chronicler what we mean today. He was not thinking of a man who added contemporary news year by year, as it arrived, to a growing body of annals, as the Anglo-Saxon chroniclers had done. He was thinking of a compiler, someone who borrowed one passage from one author, another from the next writer and so on, and fitted his extracts together in chronological order.

Gervase ranks himself among the chroniclers. And though this shows a laudable humility, it also reflects a sad truth. For the very wealth of literature in the Christ Church library was in one respect his undoing. He was an uncritical copyist of other people's works, producing a patchwork of secondary authorities even for the period which he could remember.[97] For example his account of the Becket controversy is taken almost entirely from the standard Lives of Becket,[98] although Gervase knew the archbishop and was at Christ Church during his archiepiscopate. To some extent Gervase aimed to provide a useful compendium of accepted authorities, a sort of 'reader's digest'.[99] Indeed Gervase had little critical sense. He accepted the veracity of Geoffrey of Monmouth without hesitation, asserting (in the *Mappa Mundi*) that if the ancient British buildings had survived they would have proved the truth of the *Historia*.[100]

For his own day, when Gervase could find no literary source to plunder, he did not adopt the annalistic method, but wrote literary narrative in the romance style. His account of the reign of Richard I in the *Chronica*[101] and of the archiepiscopate of Hubert Walter (1193–1205) in the Lives of the Archbishops of Canterbury[102] are highly dramatized, with imaginary speeches attributed to the principal characters. However, they contain some information useful to the historian today, and interesting character-sketches. And the *Gesta Regum* has an additional importance: it became the starting-point of monastic annals (as will be seen, the anonymous monastic chronicles of Christ Church and of St Martin's, Dover, were appended to the *Gesta* and continued nearly to the end of the thirteenth century[103]).

---

[97] For Gervase's sources, which include Florence of Worcester and Henry of Huntingdon, see *GC*, vol. 1, pp. xliii et seq. For his use of a set of annals, now apparently lost, also used by the Winchcombe annalist, see 'The Winchcombe annals 1049–1181', ed. R. R. Darlington in *A Medieval Miscellany for Doris Mary Stenton*, ed. P. M. Barnes and C. F. Slade (Publication of the Pipe Roll Soc., new series, xxxvi, 1960), pp. 112–13. For the Winchcombe annals from 1182 to 1232 see p. 405 n. 13 below.

[98] See *GC*, vol. 1, pp. xii–xiii, 169 n. 2. For Gervase's contacts with Becket, to whom he professed as a monk, see ibid., p. 231.

[99] Sometimes Gervase refers the reader for further information on a subject to other authorities; see ibid., p. 230; vol. 2, pp. 23, 325, 396, 415.

[100] Ibid., vol. 2, p. 414. Geoffrey of Monmouth is the main source for the early part of the *Gesta Regum*; ibid., pp. 5 et seq.

[101] The account of John's reign to 1210 in the *Gesta Regum* has similar features; ibid., pp. 92–106.

[102] Ibid., pp. 406–13.   [103] See pp. 422 et seq. below.

The two monastic writers of this group most influenced by the annalistic tradition are John of Hexham and Robert of Torigni. The chronicles of both are fairly dry, accurate catalogues of events. And both were deeply indebted to the historiographical traditions they inherited. John, who became prior of Hexham in about 1160 and ruled to some time before 1209,[104] wrote his chronicle as a continuation of the *Gesta Regum* attributed to Symeon of Durham. To 1138 he borrowed from Richard of Hexham's chronicle, and he also used John of Worcester[105] and Henry of Huntingdon.[106] His chronicle, arranged in strictly annalistic form, has detailed information about north-country affairs (for example it is very full on the disputes at York over the election of a successor to Archbishop Thurstan who died in 1140[107]). Like Ailred of Rievaulx, John has an ambivalent attitude to the Scottish royal house. Although King David was Henry II's enemy, John praises him as a saintly man.[108] John wrote in the pious style of the north-country historians and makes clear his love of peace.[109]

Robert of Torigni was a much more ambitious historian than John, and the value of his work is further enhanced because, unlike John, he lived in a centre of affairs. He became a monk of Bec in 1128, and was appointed prior in 1149.[110] He was elected abbot of Mont-Saint-Michel in 1154, ruling until his death in 1186. During his abbacy he travelled on business to Guernsey (in 1156) and to England (in 1157 and 1175). A number of important people visited Mont-Saint-Michel, including Henry II who was on very friendly terms with the abbey; he came twice in 1158 (once with Louis VII of France), and once in 1166. Robert had begun writing history by 1139 when Henry of Huntingdon, visiting Bec in the retinue of Archbishop Theobald, discussed historical topics with him.[111] He wrote a corpus of works, all in the

---

[104] For John's life see Raine, *Hexham*, vol. 1, pp. clii–cliv. John did not complete his chronicle (which ends in 1154) until after May 1162; see J. M. Todd and H. S. Offler, 'A medieval chronicle from Scotland' in *Scottish Historical Review*, xlvii (1968) p. 153 and n. 2. The text printed by Arnold is from the Sawley manuscript which also contains the *Historia Regum* attributed to Symeon of Durham. It probably does not represent the chronicle exactly as John wrote it but has later additions and alterations; see ibid., pp. 153–4, and p. 149 and nn. 85, 90 above.

[105] See the notices of the fire in London and the eclipse of the sun under 1133, which are also in John of Worcester; *JH*, pp. 110–11. I find no convincing evidence that John used the works of William of Malmesbury, or the *Gesta Stephani*, though Raine, *Hexham*, vol. 1, p. cliv, states that he did.

[106] Compare John of Hexham's account of Stephen allowing Matilda to go to Bristol (*JH*, pp. 125–6), of Matilda's pride alienating her followers (ibid., p. 137) and of her escape from Oxford in white clothes (ibid., p. 148), with *HH*, pp. 266, 275, 276, respectively.

[107] John is an important authority for the controversy at York; see M. D. Knowles, 'The case of St. William of York' in *Cambridge Historical Journal*, v, no. 2 (1936), pp. 162–77, 212–14 *passim*.

[108] See the character-sketch of King David; *JH*, pp. 168–70.

[109] John remarks that the agreement reached between King Stephen and Duke Henry restored 'peace and justice'; ibid., pp. 170–1.

[110] For the life of Robert of Torigni see *RT*, vol. 2, pp. i–xiii.

[111] See ibid., vol. 1, pp. 96, 97–111; vol. 2, pp. ii–iii; and p. 199 and n. 132 above.

tradition of Norman historiography. He contributed to the brief annals already being compiled at Mont-Saint-Michel,[112] and added to the Lives of the abbots of Bec begun by Gilbert Crispin and continued by Milo Crispin.[113] In about 1149 he interpolated and continued the chronicle of William of Jumièges.[114] He also wrote a tract on the monastic orders and the Norman abbeys.[115] But his most important work was the chronicle of the world from the Creation to 1186.[116]

Robert of Torigni's chronicle is copied to 1112 from the chronicle of Sigebert of Gembloux which Robert interpolated with material mainly about Norman history. His method shows a veneration for authority reminiscent of Gervase of Canterbury (this is illustrated by his decision not to interpolate the section of Sigebert's chronicle which was copied from Eusebius and Jerome, because it would be wrong to tamper with such famous, accepted texts).[117] His interpolations derived from various sources, notably from the annals of Rouen. He used Henry of Huntingdon for English affairs until 1147, but from 1147 his chronicle is original, comprising annals compiled fairly contemporaneously with the events recorded. Robert worked on the chronicle from 1150 until his death.

Robert's chronicle was very popular in Normandy, France and England. It survives in at least eighteen manuscripts, including Robert's autograph.[118] Copies are known to have existed in the middle ages at Bec, Jumièges, Fécamp, Bayeux, Le Valasse and St Wandrille (in Normandy), and at Liré (Maine-et-Loire) and St Victor's, Paris.[119] In England it was almost equally popular. A copy was owned in the late twelfth century by the schoolmaster of St Martin's-le-Grand in London, John Pike (himself a would-be historian).[120] And it was plundered by numerous English chroniclers, including Ralph Diceto, Roger of Wendover, Matthew Paris, Nicholas Trevet, Thomas Wykes and the annalists of Waverley and Osney.[121]

Robert of Torigni was a factual and on the whole accurate historian. His chronicle is particularly useful to the historian today because of its detailed information about Henry II's continental campaigns and politics, and his quarrels with his sons. Robert was interested in diplomatic history, using

---

[112] The annals of Mont-Saint-Michel are described and printed in ibid., vol. 2, pp. 207–36. For Robert's contribution to the annals see ibid., pp. xvi, 207–8.
[113] See ibid., p. xvi. Cf. p. 132 and n. 184 above.
[114] See ibid., p. xiii. For Robert's continuation of William of Jumièges see pp. 199–200 and n. 133 above.
[115] Described and printed in RT, vol. 2, pp. xv, 184–206.
[116] Described and printed in ibid., vol. 1, pp. i–iii, 1–369; vol. 2, pp. 1–136. Another edition is in Chrons. Stephen, Henry II, and Richard I, vol. 4, pp. 3–315. An English translation is in Stevenson, Church Historians, vol. 4, pt ii, pp. 675–813.
[117] RT, vol. 1, pp. 95–6.
[118] For Robert's autograph see ibid., pp. xlv–liii.
[119] See ibid., vol. 2, p. xv, and the list of manuscripts in ibid., vol. 1, pp. iii–liii.
[120] Ibid., vol. 1, p. xxiii. See p. 222 and n. 15 above.   [121] See ibid., vol. 2, p. xiv.

treaties as evidence[122] and trying to analyse the origins of disputes and alliances between rulers.[123] Because Henry II was a benefactor of Mont-Saint-Michel and because Robert was influenced by Norman historiography, he tended to eulogize the king. Henry, he says, was universally loved and feared, and was generous and liberal, energetic and brave.[124] Robert glosses over the murder of Becket, emphasizing Henry's penance for the act: he even draws a parallel between Henry's penitence and Christ's repentance for mankind.[125]

Though Robert was a dedicated historian and assiduous collector of material, he had little critical judgment. He liked to write about relics and portents. His connection with Henry of Huntingdon is particularly revealing in this respect. When Henry came to Bec, Robert showed him a copy of Geoffrey of Monmouth's *Historia Regum Britanniae*. Henry made an abstract of the *Historia* and gave it to Warin the Briton.[126] Apparently Robert never questioned the truthfulness of the *Historia*, for he appended a copy of Henry's abstract to the prologue of his own chronicle.

The one historian to criticize Geoffrey of Monmouth at this period was William of Newburgh. Little definite is known about William's life. He was born in 1135 or 1136, was educated in the Augustinian priory of New-burgh,[127] where he subsequently became a canon,[128] and wrote a chronicle, some sermons and a commentary on the Canticles.[129] He began his chronicle, the *Historia Rerum Anglicarum (History of English Affairs)*, in or just before 1196, writing at the request of Ernald abbot of Rievaulx.[130] Ernald, a pupil of Ailred, was interested in history but would not allow one of his monks to write a chronicle because of the Cistercian regulation forbidding literary undertakings.[131] As William's chronicle ends abruptly in 1198, he probably died in that year.

[122] For example Robert gives the terms of the treaties between: Henry II and the count of Blois in 1158 (ibid., vol. 1, pp. 314–15); Henry II and Count Raymond in 1159 (ibid., p. 317); Henry II and William king of Scotland in 1175 (ibid., vol. 2, pp. 56–7); and of the marriage settlement between Prince Philip and Isabella daughter of Baldwin count of Hainault in 1181 (ibid., pp. 94–5).

[123] See for example the historical account of why Count Raymond had a right to Barcelona and why Queen Eleanor had a right to Toulouse; ibid., vol. 1, pp. 317–20 *passim*.

[124] For complimentary notices of Henry II, see for example ibid., pp. 287–8, 312, 359; vol. 2, p. 4.

[125] Ibid., vol. 2, p. 51.   [126] See pp. 194 and n. 69, 199 and n. 132 above.

[127] 'Neuburgensi[s] ecclesia . . . me in Christo a puero aluit'; WN, vol. 1, p. 51. For the chronicler's life see ibid., pp. xvii–xxii.

[128] Ibid., p. 19.

[129] The commentary is printed *William of Newburgh's Explanatio Sacri Epithalamii in Matrem Sponsi*, ed. J. C. Gorman, in *Spicilegium Friburgense*, ed. C. Meersseman and A. Hänggi, vol. 6 (Fribourg 1960).

[130] See ibid., pp. 3–4.

[131] 'Nulli liceat abbati nec monacho nec novitio libros facere nisi forte cuiquam in generali abbatum capitulo concessum fuerit'; *Consuetudines*, c. lviii, printed in P. Guignard, *Les Monuments primitifs de la Règle cistercienne* (Dijon 1878), p. 266. See also M. D. Knowles, *The Monastic Order in England* (2nd ed., Cambridge 1963), pp. 643–4 and n. 6.

An attempt has been made to identify the chronicler with the 'William canon of Newburgh' who appears in a charter of this period, where he is described as the son of Ellis and brother of Bernard prior of Newburgh.[132] This William had married an Emma de Peri between about 1160 and 1165, held property in Oxfordshire and had connections in Yorkshire. He became a canon of the priory late in life (in his fifties), some time before 1185, after an active secular career. But William was a common name and the identification of this William with the chronicler and biblical commentator seems unlikely. In view of the latter's erudition and excellent Latin it is probable that he had been a canon throughout his adult life.[133]

William, starting his chronicle at the Norman Conquest, used a number of literary sources (the *Historia Regum* ascribed to Symeon of Durham, Henry of Huntingdon, Jordan Fantosme, the *Itinerarium Ricardi* and Anselm's biography of Richard[134]). He paraphrased his sources, adding his own observations and a considerable amount of information. The work is of value today partly because it used the biography of Richard I which is now lost,[135] partly because of the original material it contains, and partly because it reflects William's mind. As a historian William had considerable gifts. He was a man of outstanding ability and his chronicle is the most unusual and interesting produced in this period. Though he was indebted to both secular and monastic historiography, to some extent he transcended their limitations: he was superstitious, but had critical acumen and was capable of objective judgment; he was religious,[136] but not dogmatically intolerant; he was interested in local history, but never allowed his local attachments to distort his view or circumscribe his horizon. And he was an excellent descriptive writer and raconteur.

William's critical capacity is best shown in the remarkable passage on Geoffrey of Monmouth. William had the perspicacity to realize that Geoffrey's *Historia* was fiction, not fact. The grounds for his conclusion show that he had mastered the principles of historical criticism.[137] He compared Geoffrey's statements with Bede's *Ecclesiastical History*: if King Arthur had

---

[132] This identification is suggested by H. E. Salter, 'William of Newburgh' in *EHR*, xxii (1907), pp. 510–14. For Prior Bernard see *Early Yorkshire Charters*, ix, ed. C. T. Clay (Yorkshire Archaeological Society, Record series, extra series, vii, 1952), pp. 248–9.

[133] See the criticism of Salter's suggestion by Rudolf Jahncke, *Guilelmus Neubrigensis, ein pragmatischer Geschichtsschreiber des zwölften Jahrhunderts* (Bonn 1912), pp. 135–9. Jahncke's criticisms are sustained by C. N. L. Brooke in a review of Gorman, op. cit., in *EHR*, lxxvii (1962), p. 554 (Gorman also questions Salter's suggestion).

[134] For William of Newburgh's sources see WN, vol. 1, pp. xxv et seq. Possibly William knew Ailred's historical work (for which see pp. 213–16 above); like William, Ailred was sceptical about the Arthurian legends (see p. 213 and n. 253 above).

[135] See p. 239 and n. 156 above.

[136] William attributes some events to divine interference and regards others as divine portents and, like Henry of Huntingdon, thought that history showed that fortune is unpredictable and earthly honours vain; see e.g., ibid., pp. 90, 169.

[137] For William's views on Geoffrey see ibid., pp. 11–18, 166.

really existed, William affirms, Bede would have mentioned him. Moreover, he detected that Bede based his account of the Britons on Gildas, a very early authority. William also attacked Geoffrey with another line of argument: Geoffrey, he points out, mentions that there were three British archbishops at King Arthur's feast. But this was impossible, as the Britons had no archbishops. And he accuses Geoffrey of attributing to Arthur conquests of more kingdoms than existed at that time. Geoffrey wrote, William thought, either to indulge in the luxury of unlicensed lying, or because he wanted to please the Britons by providing them with a long and glorious past. William believed that it was in response to British superstition that Geoffrey made Arthur retire from the active scene rather than die.

Another example of William's rational approach to history and his power of dispassionate judgment is his account of the attacks on the Jews in various English cities in 1190, following Richard I's coronation.[138] His humanity towards the Jews has some parallel in the attitude of Richard of Devizes, but contrasts sharply with the dogmatic intolerance of most of his contemporaries. Here his views foreshadow those of a later historian of the Augustinian order, Thomas Wykes.[139]

William gives a particularly full account of the massacre of the Jews of York in the castle where they had taken refuge. He attributed the attacks not only to the rise of crusading zeal, but also to men's desire to loot Jewish houses and burn the bonds binding debtors to Jewish money-lenders.[140] William deplored the massacres on humanitarian grounds: though he regarded them as God's punishment of the Jews for their prosperity and pride under Henry II, he emphasized that nothing excused the cruelty of the attacks which offended every Christian scruple and all sense of humanity.[141] He mentions one Jew, murdered at Lynn, in favourable terms: 'he was an eminent, humble physician, a worthy man and a friend of Christians.'[142] Another reason for William's indignation was that the riots violated law and order. The royal officials were unable to control the lawlessness and no one was brought to justice; this, he asserted, especially angered the king. William believed that the Jews should be allowed to live at peace with the Christians, in a subservient position, being useful and acting as perpetual reminders of the Crucifixion.[143]

Moreover, William's judicious impartiality appears in his treatment of the conflict between Thomas Becket and Henry II. While deploring Becket's murder, he thought that the criminous clerks were too leniently dealt with by the church,[144] and that during the controversy Becket behaved obstinately, without tact or moderation[145] – for instance in excommunicating the

---

[138] Ibid., pp. 294–9, 308–22. For the attacks on the Jews in 1190 see Cecil Roth, *A History of the Jews in England* (Oxford 1964), pp. 20 et seq.

[139] See pp. 466–7 below.   [140] WN, vol. 1, pp. 308, 312–13, 322.   [141] Ibid., pp. 313, 322.

[142] Ibid., p. 310.   [143] Ibid., pp. 316–17.   [144] Ibid., pp. 140–1.

[145] Ibid., pp. 142–3.

bishops of London and Salisbury after Prince Henry's coronation.[146] And in the controversy between the archbishops of York and Canterbury, William considered that both parties in this 'pointless conflict' showed 'equal obstinacy and pride'.[147]

William rivalled his contemporary Gerald of Wales in his ability to sketch characters and describe places. He gives long character-sketches of important figures, usually as an obituary.[148] He also suggests motives for men's acts, remarking, for example, that Henry II treated the rebels of Galloway leniently in 1184 because he was delighted with the conquest of Ireland.[149] And he resembles Gerald in his taste for generalizations about national characteristics. He describes the French, Welsh and Irish:[150] of the latter he writes, 'they are uncivilized and barbarous in their behaviour, almost totally ignorant of law and order, lazy over agriculture and therefore living on milk rather than corn'. A good example of William's gift for topographical description is his graphic account of Scarborough:[151]

> A huge rock, almost inaccessible on account of precipices on all sides, drives back the sea which surrounds it, except for a narrow ascent on the west. On its summit is a beautiful grassy plain, more than sixty acres in area, with a spring of fresh water issuing from a rock. At the entrance, which is difficult of access, there is a royal castle, and below the incline begins the town which spreads to the south and north but faces west, defended on this side by its own wall, on the east by the castle rock, while both sides are washed by the sea.

But William was more influenced by the monastic than the secular historiographical traditions. Although he obviously admired Richard I for his military prowess, he was on the whole antagonistic to the central government. He has a bitter diatribe against the rule of William Longchamp, 'an unbearable tyrant', who combined papal with royal authority to oppress clergy and laity alike, and who lived like an oriental prince attended by at least a thousand esquires.[152] William also attacks the abbot of Caen for attempting to reform the Exchequer and increase its revenues.[153]

As a historical source William's chronicle has particular value for north-country affairs. He gives detailed accounts of the foundation not only of Newburgh but also of Fountains, Rievaulx and Byland, and has detailed

---

[146] Ibid., p. 161. [147] Ibid., pp. 203–4, 371–2; vol. 2, p. 444.

[148] See e.g. the character-sketches of: Henry II (ibid., vol. 1, pp. 280–3); Richard I (ibid., p. 306); Roger archbishop of York (ibid., pp. 225–6); Henry 'III' (ibid., p. 233); Hugh du Puiset bishop of Durham (ibid., vol. 2, pp. 436–8); William Longchamp (ibid., pp. 489–90). See also p. 267 n. 155 below.

[149] WN, vol. 1, p. 237. [150] Ibid., pp. 174, 107, 166, respectively.

[151] Ibid., p. 104. For topographical descriptions of Wales and Ireland, and Rouen, see ibid., pp. 107, 165–6, 190, respectively.

[152] Ibid., pp. 332–4. [153] WN, vol. 2, pp. 464–5.

information about the archbishops of York and the bishops of Durham.[154] Like other north-country historians, William was interested in Scotland, and respected the Scottish kings.[155] Sometimes he names north-country people who gave him information and to whom he had talked. Thus he learned about the exploits of the rebel Scot, Wimund, from Wimund himself, who became a monk of Byland,[156] and he had spoken to Godric of Finchale on his death-bed.[157] Perhaps it was from a northern source that William got his vivid account of how the news of the capture of William the Lion was delivered to Henry II.[158]

Nevertheless regional loyalties are not dominant in the chronicle. Nor does William show any marked interest in his own priory. On the contrary his concern for, and knowledge of, other parts of England and further afield were remarkable.[159] And Yorkshire was not a remote region in the twelfth century. Its contacts with East Anglia and London were close, and it had commercial and cultural connections with Scandinavia. Scandinavian influence was increased by the fact that from the ninth century Yorkshire had numerous Scandinavian settlers. And Newburgh itself was far from isolated; as an Augustinian foundation it was in touch with other houses of the order.

William's often detailed knowledge of affairs in London may well have derived from the Augustinian priory of Holy Trinity in London. He claimed to have heard from an eye-witness of the revolt in 1194 instigated by William Fitz Osbert, a demagogue who roused the populace to resist taxation.[160] William asserts that Fitz Osbert was well read and an eloquent speaker – he quotes some of his polemics. Moreover, William may have obtained from Holy Trinity a copy of the *Itinerarium Ricardi*, one of his principal sources for the Third Crusade.

William's knowledge of London is equalled by his knowledge of East Anglia. Perhaps his information may have reached him from the Augustinian priory of Thetford in Norfolk, within fifteen miles of Bury St Edmunds with which his East Anglian news is especially connected. He tells a story (which he hesitates to believe) about some 'green children' who were found at Woolpit, near Bury St Edmunds[161] (the same story is told by Ralph of Coggeshall[162]). It also seems likely that William's detailed synopsis of contemporary Norwegian history, ending with a notice of the exile of the archbishop of Nidaros,[163] originated at Bury, for the archbishop stayed in the abbey during his exile.[164]

---

[154] See e.g., WN, vol. 1, pp. 78–82, 95, 225; vol. 2, pp. 436–9.
[155] See for example his character-sketches of King David and King Malcolm; WN, vol. 1, pp. 70–2, 76–7.
[156] Ibid., pp. 73–6.   [157] Ibid., pp. 149–50.
[158] Ibid., pp. 189–90. This story is very like that given by Jordan Fantosme; see ibid., p. 190 n. 4, and p. 238 above.
[159] For notices about French and papal history see, e.g., ibid., pp. 92–4, 143–5.
[160] WN, vol. 2, pp. 466–71.   [161] WN, vol. 1, pp. 82–4.
[162] See p. 330–1 below.   [163] Ibid., pp. 228–32.   [164] Ibid., p. 232 n. 1.

William's powers as a raconteur are illustrated by the true stories he tells and by the fables. A well-told true story relates to an accident which over-took the Augustinian canons of Malton in Yorkshire.[165] They had a lime-kiln and William describes how when firing the kiln as usual one evening, a canon fell into the pit. As he did not re-emerge, the man in charge sent another canon down to see what had happened and, as he disappeared too, the man in charge sent a bystander down. Finally, a third canon was sent who was rescued just in time, though he was ill for several days afterwards. William did not know the cause of death (gas poisoning), but he gave a description of the corpses (they were unblemished 'except for the left eyes which looked bloodshot and bruised').

Typical of William's fables are the numerous ghost-stories he relates. These stories are reminiscent of tales in Icelandic literature.[166] William wrote especially of 'zombies', that is of the dead who rose from their graves to haunt the living. A good example is the story of the corpse of a great rogue which emerged from its tomb at night and 'was borne hither and thither, pursued by a pack of hounds baying loudly', terrifying the neigh-bourhood. So some brave young men dug up the body and burnt it.[167] Perhaps William acquired his taste for such stories of the supernatural from the Scandinavian element in Yorkshire culture.

[165] WN, vol. 2, pp. 497–8.

[166] For William's ghost-stories and their Icelandic parallels see Bruce Dickins, 'A Yorkshire chronicler (William of Newburgh)' in *Transactions of the Yorkshire Dialect Society*, vol. v, pt xxxv (1934), pp. 15–26 *passim*.

[167] WN, vol. 2, pp. 476–7. Cited in Dickins, op. cit., p. 23.

13

Local History from the Reign of King Stephen to John

Local history flourished in the period from King Stephen's reign to King John's. Like general history it had its golden age in Henry II's last years. Interest in it appeared, as has been seen, in the national chronicles. Local loyalty distorted Gervase of Canterbury's perception of general history. Even histories orientated to national affairs had passages on local history. Thus Richard of Devizes betrays his love of Winchester, while the interpolators of Florence of Worcester at Bury St Edmunds incorporated the abbey's history into their chronicle.[1] Furthermore, local loyalty gave rise to works entirely devoted to local history. Some of these are lost (for example the history of the abbots of St Albans written by Bartholomew in the last half of the twelfth century).[2] But many have survived. The best show that the authors were capable of painstaking research and talented creative writing.

Very generally speaking, these local histories divide into two groups, those written in southern England and those written in the north. Each group has its own characteristics. The first group is the largest and comprises the chronicles of two types of monastery. First, there are the local histories of pre-Conquest foundations, both monastic and secular. Second, there are the chronicles of the post-Conquest foundations. Nearly all these chronicles, with the exception of the Walden chronicle and possibly of the Abingdon one, were written in the middle years of Henry II's reign (the period when eight of the biographies of Thomas Becket were written). All show an obsession with controversy, actual or foreseen. They are symptomatic of an age which committed to writing previously unwritten law and customs, the age of *Glanvill* and of the *Dialogue of the Exchequer*. In the local sphere two factors stimulated the move towards the codification of rights and privileges. One was the anarchy of Stephen's reign, the other the judicial reforms of Henry II: the lawlessness of the nobility and the expanding claims of the crown threatened and challenged vested interests. The local historian hoped that by recording past history he would establish his community's reputation more firmly and define its privileges and property more clearly,

---

[1] See pp. 148 and n. 77, 380–1 and n. 2.
[2] See p. 375 and n. 148.

so enabling it to withstand better the encroachments of neighbours and royal officials. He also hoped to reduce internal conflict, thus strengthening the community, by defining the respective spheres of abbot and convent, bishop and chapter.

The second group of local histories, written in the north of England, also had its distinguishing features. The north-country local histories should be associated with the other historical productions of the region, with Ailred of Rievaulx's *Battle of the Standard*, and with William of Newburgh's history of England. Moreover, it will be seen that north-country writers were responsible for hagiographies at this period: Walter Daniel wrote Ailred's *Life* and three monks of Durham wrote separate Lives of St Godric (who died in 1170). This north-country literary tradition was shared by Benedictines, Augustinian canons and Cistercians. It was the two latter orders which produced the local histories. Towards the middle of the century Richard, prior of Hexham, wrote a history of his house. Ailred of Rievaulx also wrote on Hexham's past, but other Cistercians concentrated on the origins of their own houses, producing a remarkable series of foundation histories. On the whole this group of local histories is less concerned with controversy and more pious in tone than the southern group. The two groups of local histories, the southern and the northern, will be discussed in turn.

The histories in the first group are as follows, beginning with the chronicles of the pre-Conquest foundations. There is the Abingdon chronicle, completed before 1164, covering the period from the abbey's first foundation to 1154.[3] To the Norman Conquest the chronicle is mainly composed of copies of charters and documents, with passages of narrative interspersed. But after the Conquest it gives narrative biographies of the abbots which gradually increase in length until they dominate the work. There is the chronicle of Ramsey abbey, begun in about 1170.[4] This has numerous documents, but also some good narrative up to the reign of Stephen. Then it gives a detailed biography of Abbot Walter (1133–60). There is the history of Ely abbey, completed some time between 1169 and 1174. This is the longest of all the local histories.[5] It has many documents (charters, royal and papal letters, inventories and the like) and long sections of narrative, some of which, especially those relating to Bishop Nigel (1133–69) are valuable for general history. But the whole lacks unity and has errors and confusing repetitions.[6]

---

[3] The only edition is *Chronicon Monasterii de Abingdon*, ed. Joseph Stevenson (RS, 1858, 2 vols). For Stevenson's text (which is based on two late, revised manuscripts) and the date of the chronicle, see F. M. Stenton, *The Early History of the Abbey of Abingdon* (Reading 1913), pp. 1 et seq. For thirteenth century interpolations in the version printed by Stevenson, see Appendix XIX ('The alleged dietary of St. Ethelwold at Abingdon') in M. D. Knowles, *The Monastic Order in England* (2nd ed., Cambridge 1963), pp. 716–17.

[4] The only edition is *Chronicon Abbatiae Rameseiensis*, ed. W. D. Macray (RS, 1886).

[5] The standard edition is *Liber Eliensis*, ed. E. O. Blake (Camden Soc., 3rd series, xcii, 1962).

[6] See e.g. *LE*, pp. 252 n. 1, 318 n. 2.

There are the chronicle of Peterborough abbey written soon after 1175, containing both documents and narrative and forming a comprehensible whole,[7] the chronicle of the collegiate church of Waltham (founded by Harold before the Conquest),[8] and the history of the see of Bath and Wells from its foundation to 1174, which has some documents but is mainly narrative.[9]

Finally in this southern group are the chronicles of the post-Conquest foundations. There is the chronicle of Battle abbey from its foundation to 1183:[10] this includes some documents but is mainly a good narrative chronicle by someone with a more sophisticated mind than any of the other local historians. And there is the Walden chronicle[11] for the period from the foundation of Walden in about 1140 to 1200 (Walden became an abbey in 1190), which is not only valuable for the house's history but also for that of its patrons, the de Mandevilles and, because it traces the affairs of its founder, Geoffrey de Mandeville, for general history.

All these works are anonymous with the exception of the Peterborough chronicle and perhaps of the history of Ely. The Peterborough chronicle was by Hugh Candidus who entered Peterborough as a child, became a monk there and was sub-prior under Abbots Martin de Bec (1132–55) and William de Waterville (1155–75).[12] The date of his death is unrecorded. The Ely history may be by the monk Richard, probably to be identified with the Richard who was the sub-prior of Ely and then the prior (from 1177 to sometime between 1189 and 1194), the known author of two short historical tracts on the abbey.[13] Although the name of the man who wrote the Waltham chronicle is unknown, the chronicle has some information about him.[14] He was born in 1119, started his education at Waltham in 1124 under the learned Master Peter, became a censing chorister, and between 1141 and 1144 he became a canon. In 1177 the secular canons were expelled, for 'careless and secular lives', and replaced by Augustinian canons: the author wrote, without bitterness, after his enforced retirement. All that is known of the Abingdon chronicler is that he was a monk of the abbey by at least 1117.[15]

[7] The standard edition is *The Chronicle of Hugh Candidus*, ed. W. T. Mellows (Oxford 1949).
[8] The only edition is *The Foundation of Waltham Abbey*, ed. William Stubbs (Oxford and London 1861). The full title of the tract is *De Inventione Sanctae Crucis nostrae in Monte Acuto et de ductione eiusdem apud Waltham*.
[9] Printed, with an English translation, in *Ecclesiastical Documents: viz. i. A Brief History of the Bishoprick of Somerset from its Foundation to the Year 1174* ... ed. Joseph Hunter (Camden Soc., 1840), pp. 9–28.
[10] The only edition is *Chronicon Monasterii de Bello*, ed. J. S. Brewer (Anglia Christiana, London 1846). There is an English translation by M. A. Lower, *The Chronicle of Battel Abbey from 1066 to 1176* (London 1851).
[11] Sixteenth-century copies of this chronicle are in BM MSS. Vespasian E VI, ff. 25–71[v] and Arundel 29 (see Hardy, *Catalogue*, vol. 3, p. 268). It has never been printed in its entirety but extracts are printed in *Mon. Angl.*, vol. 4, pp. 141–8 and the chapter-heads in ibid., pp. 137–8. It was used by J. H. Round, *Geoffrey de Mandeville* (London 1892; reissued Burt Franklin, New York 1963), pp. 38, 45, 203, 205, 210.
[12] These facts of Hugh's life are in his chronicle; see *HC*, pp. xv–xvi.
[13] See *LE*, pp. xlvi–xlix, 284, 345.   [14] See Stubbs, *FWA*, pp. xxii–xxvii.
[15] *Ab.*, vol. 2, pp. 48–9. See Stenton, *Abingdon*, pp. 4–5.

The anonymity or partial anonymity of all these chronicles, except the Peterborough one, is not of great importance. Only the Battle chronicle shows marked individuality of style and thought. The others reflect the author's personality and opinions far less than the corporate views of the community. They are, as it were, command histories: one, the Ely history, specifically states that it was written at the request of some members of the community.[16] Moreover, some of the chronicles are not by one man, but are composite works. The chronicles of Ramsey and Battle are each probably by two men. There is apparently a change of authorship in the Ramsey chronicle in 1135, with the succession of Abbot Walter,[17] and the first section of the Battle chronicle, on the foundation of the abbey, is by a different man than the subsequent part.[18] Other chronicles, such as the Ely history and the history of the see of Bath and Wells, are composite at least in the sense that they incorporate earlier works more or less intact.

A few general remarks apply, in varying degrees, to most of these histories. They were influenced by some of the same trends as influenced general chronicles. Like the general historians the local ones tried wherever possible to emphasize continuity of past and present, and sought to push the past back as far as possible into antiquity, glorifying it even at the expense of historical accuracy. They also tended to be very archive-conscious, quoting documents *verbatim* to substantiate their arguments and taking an interest in the authenticity, preservation and arrangement of documents: the history of Ely and much of the Abingdon and Ramsey chronicles are little more than inflated cartularies.[19] Moreover, contact with the central government led to an interest in and knowledge of its workings.

Nor was local history uninfluenced by contemporary romance literature. The house itself could become a personification not only, as in the past, of its patron saint, but also of a conceptualized romance hero.[20] It valiantly resists the onslaughts of its enemies, guards its honour with untiring vigilance, and remains pure and generous in a generally corrupt world. The Battle chronicle even uses a military metaphor to illustrate a point.[21] As will be seen the influence of romance could lead to the attributing of mythical origins to an institution. It was also probably from the romance literary tradition that these historians derived their love of a dramatically told story, full of imaginary speeches and talk. Another feature of contemporary general history, the idea of the mutability of the world typified by the wheel of fortune, had little impact on the local historians. It did not suit their purpose which was to prove the ultimate success of their houses. However, the

[16] *LE*, p. 63 (Bk II, prologue).   [17] *Ram.*, p. 325.   [18] *Battle*, pp. 1–21.
[19] Such 'chronicle-cartularies' are mentioned by G. R. C. Davis, *Medieval Cartularies of Great Britain* (London 1958), p. xiii, who lists the Abingdon and Ely ones (nos 3–4, 366–8).
[20] M. D. Legge, *Anglo-Norman in the Cloisters* (Edinburgh 1950), p. 45, makes the point that the Anglo-Norman verse translation of Hugh Candidus's chronicle, made probably early in the fourteenth century (printed in *HC*, pp. 180–99), treats the foundation as the hero.
[21] *Battle*, p. 67.

Ramsey chronicle does show traces of this concept: it begins with a lament on the ephemeral nature of all earthly things, later reverting to the idea[22] and using the image of the wheel of fortune.[23]

The local histories produced by pre-Conquest institutions were particularly concerned with continuity. All these chronicles were interested in the circumstances of the first foundation of the house. Ely and Peterborough had their antiquity attested by Bede. But the Abingdon chronicler, while insisting that Ethelwold did not found but re-found the abbey in the tenth century,[24] had to rely on legend for his house's early history.[25] And here he glossed Geoffrey of Monmouth. He begins by describing how Christianity was introduced into Britain by Faganus and Duvianus (two characters from the *Historia Regum Britanniae*[26]). Then he says that the Irish monk Abbennus arrived, to whom the king of the Britons gave a large part of Berkshire: there Abbennus founded a monastery, on the Mount of Abbennus, from which Abingdon took its name (an eponym worthy of Geoffrey). The historian of the see of Bath and Wells attributed similar legendary origins to the bishopric.[27] He told a romantic courtship-story of King Ine and Æthelburh: their marriage was performed by Bishop Daniel who had his see at Congresbury; as a result of Queen Æthelburh's mediation the see was transferred to Wells. Legend also has an important part in the account of the foundation of Waltham abbey, though in it hagiography rather than romance is predominant. The story goes that a certain Tovi, standard bearer of King Canute, found on his estate in Somerset, at Montacute, a piece of the true cross, as a result of a vision. He transported this in a cart which miraculously stopped at Waltham, also part of his property. There he built a church to house the relic which thenceforth worked miracles. Harold chose this church as the site of his new collegiate foundation.[28]

Interest in past origins led to one more admirable result, genuine historical research. The chroniclers of the pre-Conquest foundations are remarkable for the way they ransacked their houses, libraries and archives for pre-Conquest material. The Abingdon chronicler used Ælfric's *Life of St. Ethelwold*, and the Ramsey one the anonymous *Life of St. Oswald*. The Ely chronicler copied *in extenso* the 'libellus' which Ethelwold had drawn up to record the abbey's property.[29] And the historian of the see of Bath and Wells incorporated Bishop Giso's autobiography.[30] This study of pre-Conquest sources shows that some monks still knew Old English. The Anglo-Saxon

---

[22] *Ram.*, pp. 3, 56, 85, 109 etc.

[23] *Ram.*, p. 118: 'Sed quoniam ex infida rotatione fortunae...'.   [24] *Ab.*, vol. 1, pp. 343–8.

[25] Ibid., pp. xii, 1–3. Abingdon's foundation legend, which probably contains some elements of truth, is fully discussed by the late Gabrielle Lambrick, 'The foundation traditions of the abbey', in M. Biddle, Mrs H. T. Lambrick and J. N. L. Myres, 'The early history of Abingdon, Berkshire, and its abbey' in *Medieval Archaeology*, xii (1969), pp. 26–34. See also Stenton, *Abingdon*, pp. 2–3, 7.

[26] *HRB*, iv. 19 (pp. 328–9).   [27] Hunter, *Ecclesiastical Documents*, pp. 10–14.

[28] Stubbs, *FWA*, pp. viii, 1–10.   [29] *LE*, pp. xxvii, xxviii–ix, 72–117, 395–9.

[30] See p. 91.

Chronicle was drawn on by the historians of Abingdon, Ely, Peterborough and Ramsey. As was said above,[31] Peterborough was the home of the version of the Anglo-Saxon Chronicle which was continued the longest (until 1154) and has numerous additions about the abbey's history. It seems clear that Hugh Candidus did not use the Peterborough version which survives today.[32] He used some lost version which itself may have been the source of the surviving text of the Anglo-Saxon Chronicle. The Ely historian also used pre-Conquest narrative material, notably some lost epic on the deeds of Earl Byrhtnoth, one of the abbey's patrons and the hero of the battle of Maldon (991).[33] Most remarkable is the use by the Abingdon,[34] Ely[35] and Ramsey[36] chroniclers of Anglo-Saxon charters, writs and wills, which they translated into Latin. These are most numerous in the Ramsey chronicle. The Ramsey chronicler obviously took the search for and translation of such documents very seriously. He describes how, to record gifts to the abbey of King Edgar's time, he has examined 'very ancient schedules' of charters and cyrographs which were 'nearly all in English, so we have translated them into Latin, copied them in order into this little book, with rubricated headings to help readers'.[37] Later he says that he translated such documents 'which we found in our archives written in barbarous English, not without difficulty and labour', and comments on the bad condition of some of the documents, 'disintegrating with age'.[38]

Such scholars of pre-Conquest history did not only copy and extract literary works and documents word for word. They also, with varying degrees of success, distilled historical information from them. The historian of the see of Bath and Wells probably used Anglo-Saxon material to produce his inaccurate and inadequate list of the early bishops.[39] Hugh Candidus was more successful in his treatment of the early history of Peterborough. He used charters to construct a list of the pre-Conquest abbots[40] which, though not entirely accurate, has been described by Professor Stenton as 'a conscientious piece of work'.[41] Moreover, in describing how Peterborough was the centre from which a number of cells were founded, he gives information, no doubt derived from charters, not found elsewhere (for example that Peterborough had satellites at Brixworth, Breedon-on-the-Hill and Bermondsey[42]).

[31] See pp. 142–3.

[32] The relationship of Hugh Candidus to the surviving text of the ASC is discussed by Mellows, *HC*, pp. xxi–xxix.

[33] *LE*, pp. 133–6. A version of the legend is also in the Ramsey chronicle; *Ram.*, pp. 116–17. On the legend in *LE* see C. E. Wright, *The Cultivation of Saga in Anglo-Saxon England* (Edinburgh and London 1939), pp. 241–2, and E. V. Gordon, *The Battle of Maldon* (London 1937), pp. 7–9.

[34] See e.g. *Ab.*, vol. 1, pp. 464–5.   [35] See e.g. *LE*, pp. 140, 164–5.

[36] See e.g. *Ram.*, pp. 57 et seq.   [37] *Ram.*, p. 65.   [38] *Ram.*, pp. 65, 176–7.

[39] Hunter, op. cit., pp. 14–15.   [40] *HC*, pp. 22–3.

[41] F. M. Stenton, 'Medeshamstede', p. 325.

[42] *HC*, pp. 15, 20 and see Stenton, 'Medeshamstede', pp. 314–26 *passim*.

These historians did not only rely on written sources for the pre-Conquest period: they also drew on the oral traditions preserved in their communities. A number of stories in the Ramsey chronicle read as if they came from folk-memory. Most relate to the affairs of the abbey. Thus there is the story, belonging to the mid-eleventh century, of how four noble youths who were at school at Ramsey, were sent out by their master to play. They climbed up among the bells and cracked one. The monks were very angry and would have expelled the boys if Abbot Eadnoth (993–1006) had not said it was an accident and forgiven them.[43] Then there is the story of the murder of Abbot Æthelstan by a disgruntled Irish servant, and a detailed account of the unpopular rule of Abbot Wythman (1016–20), who like Bishop Giso was a reformer from Germany.[44] A few of these stories have a more general interest. Two tell how the abbey acquired lands which King Canute had taken from English landowners to give to his followers. One estate was given to Ramsey by Thurkill, a Dane, in recompense for perjuring himself in court (to defend his wife from the charge of murdering her stepson, of which crime she was afterwards convicted).[45] The other estate was given by Bishop Æthelric (who had been one of the boys responsible for cracking the bell at Ramsey). Æthelric got the Danish landowner drunk and then accepted a bet that he would not raise the (nominal) purchase money of fifty marks by morning.[46] By means of hard riding and a royal loan (to get which he interrupted the king at a game of chess), he raised the sum. These stories about the Danish settlers show the strong Scandinavian influence in East Anglia. It is also reflected in the Ely history which has a number of stories reminiscent of Scandinavian sagas. Thus there is the story of King Canute's visit to Ely when he stood up and sang an Anglo-Saxon song to the monks,[47] and there is the story of Hereward the Wake, which may have been handed down orally[48] (it is possible that the material about Byrhtnoth also represents an oral tradition[49]).

Nevertheless, the achievements of these early students of Anglo-Saxon history were not wholly praiseworthy. As has been seen two attributed romantic origins to their foundations, and all had a tendency to decorate the bare narrative of their written sources with purely imaginative details. For example, though the Ramsey chronicle relied mainly for the abbey's early history on the anonymous *Life of St. Oswald*, it inflated the account of the dedication of the church, inserting long speeches by Oswald himself and by the patron Æthelwine.[50] Moreover, in order to substantiate claims to property and privilege some of the chroniclers included forged charters. In their

---

[43] *Ram.*, pp. 112–13.

[44] *Ram.*, pp. 121–4. For this trouble at Ramsey see F. Barlow, *The English Church 1000–1066* (London 1963), p. 103 n. 1.

[45] *Ram.*, pp. 129–34.   [46] *Ram.*, pp. 135–8.

[47] *LE*, p. 153. See Wright, *The Cultivation of Saga*, pp. 36–8.

[48] *LE*, pp. xxxiv–xxxvi, 173–6, 179–88, 191–3. See Wright, op. cit., p. 38.

[49] See Wright, op. cit., p. 49.   [50] *Ram.*, pp. 92–101.

defence it may be argued that they saw themselves as merely replacing charters which had been lost in the course of time.[51] But at least in their present
form some of the charters are not authentic (for example the charters of
King Edgar and King Eadred and the confirmation of Edward the Confessor
in the Ely history,[52] and the charters of Kings Edgar and Edward the Confessor in the Ramsey chronicle).[53] But forgery itself encouraged the study
of archives. The Ramsey chronicler appreciated the importance of having
charters sealed with the royal seal,[54] and comments on the fact that in earlier
days only the king and a few magnates had seals, not people of lesser importance[55] (the same point is made in the Battle chronicle[56]).

The chronicles of Ely, Ramsey and Battle show some interest in and
knowledge of the central government. The Ely history has a passage about
the royal chancery in Anglo-Saxon times, which, if true, is one of the
earliest pieces of information about it. The chronicler says[57] that King
Edgar

> ordained and granted that the church of Ely henceforth and for
> ever should exercise the office of chancellor in the king's court (an
> office also conceded to other churches, that is St. Augustine's and
> Glastonbury), together with the administration of the sanctuaries
> and the rest of the ornaments of the altar. The abbots of these
> houses were to divide the year into three parts, taking over in turn
> at the appointed times. The abbot of Ely always entered upon his
> period of administration on the day of the Purification, at the
> beginning of February, and the abbot himself or whichever of the
> brethren he chose, for the period of the four months allocated to
> him, that is a third of the year, fulfilled this office reverently and
> diligently. Then the others, whom we named, completed the rest of
> the year at the time assigned to them.

The Ramsey chronicle mentions how the decrees of the Council of Rheims
(1049) were carefully preserved in the royal treasury 'by Hugolinus the
chamberlain',[58] and how one part of a triple indenture was kept with the
relics in the royal chapel (the other two parts being kept by Ramsey abbey,
the grantee, and Ralph earl of Hereford, the grantor): the practice of
keeping charters with the royal relics dates back to the tenth century.[59]

[51] For forgery after the Conquest see V. H. Galbraith, *Studies in the Public Records* (London and
New York 1948), pp. 48–50.
[52] See *LE*, pp. l, 414–18 *passim*.
[53] *Ram.*, pp. 181–9, 162–3, respectively. See P. H. Sawyer, *Anglo-Saxon Charters* (Royal Historical
Soc., London 1968), nos 798, 1109.
[54] *Ram.*, p. 69.   [55] *Ram.*, p. 65.   [56] *Battle*, p. 108.
[57] *LE*, pp. 146–7. See Galbraith, *Studies*, pp. 39–40.
[58] For Hugelin/Hugo/Hugolin the Chamberlain see F. Barlow, op. cit., pp. 120 n. 3, 122–3, 192,
302.
[59] *Ram.*, p. 172. See Galbraith, *Studies*, p. 40.

But of all the chronicles that of Battle (I refer to the second main section of it, as the preliminary chapter is by another man) shows the strongest court influence. The fact that Abbot Walter who ruled from 1139 to 1171, was the brother of Richard de Lucy, chief justiciar under Henry II until 1178/9, brought the abbey into close contact with the central government. Richard de Lucy constantly championed the abbey's cause at court and intervened in its legal disputes to see that it got a favourable judgment. Richard's legal reputation was considerable: he is quoted as an authority on judicial matters in the law-book *Glanvill*.[60] The Battle chronicler is distinguished by his thorough knowledge of legal matters and clear exposition of them.[61] He gives a detailed account of the case between the bishop of Chichester and the abbot of Ramsey, over the latter's claim to exemption from obedience to the bishop, which was tried before the king's court in 1157 at Bury St Edmunds.[62] He gives the speeches of Thomas Becket, who, as chancellor, heard the case, of Richard de Lucy who opened it for the abbot, and of the king who interrupted the proceedings. There are also full details of a case heard in the king's court at Clarendon, relating to the abbot's claim to the manor of Barnham.[63] It was in this suit that Richard de Lucy, defending the authenticity of one of the abbot of Ramsey's unsealed charters, pointed out that in the old days 'not every little knight had his own seal, but only kings and really important people'.[64]

The author of the Battle chronicle deals with specific legal matters. He records the earliest known occasion when a distinction was made between a royal proclamation and a law. A ship was wrecked and washed up on the estate of Battle at Dengemarsh (in Kent).[65] The men of Dengemarsh seized the wreck in accordance with an ancient custom that a wreck, if not soon repaired and claimed by the crew, belonged to the lord of the soil on which it was washed up. But, the chronicler states, Henry I issued a proclamation (which is not recorded elsewhere) that a wreck should belong to any survivor or survivors from its crew. As its proclamation had never been confirmed by the common consent of the barons of the realm, the abbot of Battle successfully argued that it had lost its validity on Henry I's death and that the wreck belonged to him. The Battle chronicler's interest in and knowledge of legal matters is similarly illustrated by his explanation of how Henry II, confirming the charter of privileges granted to Battle abbey by William I, altered the normal form of confirmation.[66] Instead of the usual clause specifying the previous grants of liberties to the house (the chronicler quotes a sample phrase), Henry had a general clause inserted, without

---

[60] See *Glanvill*, ed. G. D. G. Hall (Nelson's Medieval Texts, 1965), pp. xxxiii n. 2, xliii n. 4, xliv–xlvi, 78 n. *b*.

[61] For the value of the Battle chronicle for legal history see H. W. C. Davis, 'The chronicle of Battle abbey' in *EHR*, xxix (1914), pp. 426–34.

[62] *Battle*, pp. 84–104.

[63] *Battle*, pp. 105–9.

[64] *Battle*, p. 108: see Davis, op. cit., p. 432.

[65] *Battle*, p. 66: see Davis, op. cit., p. 434.

[66] *Battle*, pp. 165–6: see Davis, op. cit., p. 434.

details. The author puts the explanation into Henry's own mouth: the new charter could now, as it made no specific mention of precedents, supersede all previous ones, thus vitiating the risk of trouble if they were lost. The author concludes that the abbot wisely obtained three sealed copies of the confirmation so that one could always remain in the abbey if copies were required elsewhere.

Battle abbey had a powerful friend in Richard de Lucy. Walden too had powerful friends, for its founder and patron was Geoffrey de Mandeville, and his successors maintained the connection with the house. Abingdon abbey could boast of the friendship of Robert d'Oilli and Ralph Basset.[67] But in general after the Norman Conquest the large, rich monasteries of the old orders had more enemies than allies, and found themselves in a largely hostile world. The crown oppressed them with feudal exactions, the nobility encroached on their property, and the bishops challenged their claims to exemption. Moreover, the new orders, the Cistercians and Premonstratensians, attracted endowments from king and nobility, at the expense of the old foundations. Therefore the local historians gave a picture of the abbeys' struggles to achieve and maintain prosperity, and intended their works to help in those struggles, by recording precedents. As the Battle chronicler, recording in detail the litigation between the bishop of Chichester and the abbot of Battle, wrote:[68]

> It seems right to insert a record of the proceedings. For it will be entertaining to people now and be useful to them in the future, and will be a memorial to the dignity of the church of St Martin of Battle and, as a lasting record, it will be an impregnable shield against the machinations of jealous enemies.

Most of the chroniclers set their histories against a general background, wherever relevant. They interpreted national developments and events in a remarkably uniform way. The tenth-century monastic revival is regarded as a golden age and the Danish invasions as a momentous disaster, the first serious inroad on monastic prosperity. Hugh Candidus writes: 'The Danes came like wild dogs, leaping from ships, attacking unsuspecting people, burning towns, vills and monasteries, killing boys and old men, and raping women.'[69] He adds that even in his day many monasteries remained in ruins.[70] Nevertheless, the Danish kings of England were regarded as favourably as the Anglo-Saxon ones. Canute was, in the words of the Ramsey chronicler, 'inferior to none of his predecessors in virtue and military skill'.[71] On the whole these historians are pro-Anglo-Saxon. The Ramsey chronicler describes Edward the Confessor as a 'simple, upright man, energetic in the things of God, a man who because of his innate goodness hardly

---

[67] *Ab.*, vol. 2, pp. 12–15, 170–1. [68] *Battle*, p. 67. [69] *HC*, p. 23.
[70] *HC*, pp. 23–4, 27. [71] *Ram.*, pp. 125–6.

knew how to be angry even in the face of injuries. Therefore, because without a sharp tongue a king can exercise no proper authority, many considered that on account of his mildness and innocence he was unsuitable for dealing with the business of government. But God, directing his labours, made his rule and majesty feared and adored by all.'[72]

The Norman Conquest is considered a calamity by all the chroniclers of the pre-Conquest houses (obviously the chronicler of William I's own foundation of Battle took the opposite view). Hugh Candidus relates how Peterborough which was once rich became poor, so that its property was hardly worth £50 while formerly it had been valued at £1,500, owing to the depredations of the Norman abbot Turold.[73] Both the Ramsey and the Abingdon chroniclers explain in detail one reason why their abbeys lost property at the Conquest. Previously the abbots had leased out land for a period of years to various Englishmen. These English landholders had lost their estates at the Conquest, together with those they held on lease.[74] Therefore the abbeys lost lands which would otherwise have reverted to them on the expiry of the leases. The Abingdon chronicler was particularly interested in the feudalization of the abbey, giving details of the military fees and of the abbot's arrangements for the subinfeudation of tenancies.[75]

The next blow to the prosperity of the old foundations was the anarchy of Stephen's reign. The chroniclers agree on its serious consequences and some give good accounts of political events. It was because of the anarchy that the Ramsey historian undertook his work.[76]

> In those dark and gloomy days, when King Stephen occupied the throne of England and Abbot Walter, in the malice and turbulent atmosphere of those times, ruled our church, misfortune struck this same church, both from the attacks of enemies and on account of the [abbey's] numerous domestic disputes, as what follows will show the reader. At the end of these troubles, which had resulted in the loss of almost everything, we decided that somehow or other what remained should be preserved when, by the kindness of God, the darkness and gloom had been changed into tranquillity. So we collected together in one volume our cyrographs and the charters of our privileges (documents saved from the destruc-

---

[72] *Ram.*, p. 155.   [73] *HC*, pp. 84–5: cf. *Ab.*, vol. 1, pp. 482–94.

[74] *Ram.*, pp. 145–6; *Ab.*, vol. 1, p. 484.

[75] *Ab.*, vol. 2, pp. 17–22, 25–40 *passim*. For the value of this information and for a more elaborate version of the relevant passages than that printed in the Rolls Series edition see D. C. Douglas, 'Some early surveys from the abbey of Abingdon' in *EHR*, xliv (1929), pp. 618–25. See also J. H. Round, *Feudal England* (London 1895; reissued 1964), p. 306, and C. W. Hollister, *The Military Organization of Norman England* (Oxford 1965), pp. 25–6, 54–5.

[76] *Ram.*, p. 4.

tion of time . . .), as a warning for future ages and to instruct readers.

The chroniclers give vivid accounts of their houses' tribulations during the anarchy. On the Ely estates a bad harvest combined with rapine to produce famine. People died by hundreds and thousands and their corpses lay unburied, a prey to animals and carrion birds. For twenty or thirty miles there was neither ox nor plough to be seen and the smallest bushel of grain cost at least two hundred pence. And the land was filled with cruelty: people of all classes, including women and the aged, were captured, tortured and held to ransom.[77] The Abingdon chronicler notes that the abbey was plundered to pay King Stephen's army,[78] and the Battle chronicler records that when Abbot Walter succeeded in 1139, the house was suffering from the ill effects of the anarchy: it had lost most of its property so that the monks had scarcely enough to live on.[79] The chronicler also explains how the abbey lost the patronage of certain churches because the new lords to whom King Stephen granted the estates on which the churches were situated unjustly claimed the patronage.[80] At Ramsey, internal troubles aggravated the situation. A monk called Daniel plotted to gain the abbacy from Abbot Walter with the connivance of King Stephen, by whom he was installed. Geoffrey de Mandeville, perhaps in support of Daniel, seized the monastery, dispersed the monks, took the house's treasure, and used the church to stable his horses and the vill to quarter his men.[81]

Some of the chroniclers, by following the fortunes of their houses' friends and enemies, were led from local to general history. The affairs of Nigel, bishop of Ely, a prominent supporter of the Empress Matilda, are related at length by the Ely historian: the chronicler gives a detailed account of Stephen's struggle with the bishop over the occupation of the Isle of Ely,[82] and of the battle of Lincoln,[83] after which victory the empress helped Nigel recover the Isle. The doings of Geoffrey de Mandeville figure largely in the Walden chronicle. It makes clear how a faction of the nobility stirred up King Stephen against Geoffrey[84] and complains of the circumstances of his arrest in 1143.[85] It also provides evidence that Geoffrey occupied Ramsey abbey with the approval of the monk Daniel.[86] Those chronicles which express an opinion on Stephen are favourable to him: Hugh Candidus calls him gentle and humble,[87] while the Ely chronicler makes it evident that the

---

[77] *LE*, p. 328. This passage is cited by Round, *Geoffrey de Mandeville*, pp. 218–19.
[78] *Ab.*, vol. 2, p. 210.   [79] *Battle*, p. 135.   [80] *Battle*, pp. 128–9.
[81] *Ram.*, pp. 325–30. The disturbance is described by Round, *Geoffrey de Mandeville*, pp. 210–18 passim .
[82] *LE*, pp. 314–20 passim.   [83] *LE*, pp. lvii, 320–1.
[84] *Mon. Angl.*, vol. 4. p. 142. See Round, *Geoffrey de Mandeville*, p. 203 and n. 6.
[85] *Mon. Angl.*, vol. 4, p. 142. See Round, op. cit., p. 205 and n. 3.
[86] *Mon. Angl.*, vol. 4, p. 142. See Round, op. cit., p. 210 and n. 1.
[87] *HC*, p. 104 (*mitis et humilis*). The author of the *History of the Bishopric of Somerset* was also a supporter of Stephen; see Hunter, *Ecclesiastical Documents*, pp. 5, 39 n. 34.

monks supported the king against Bishop Nigel's military activities.[88] The accession of Henry II was regarded by the chroniclers as a propitious event. The Ely chronicler praised him for his victories,[89] the Abingdon one praised him for restoring peace,[90] and the chronicler of Battle abbey approved of his enforcement of law and order.[91]

Thus these local historians not only have affinities with the general historians, but also throw light on national events. Nevertheless they have characteristics, deriving from local attachments, which are peculiarly their own. They try to inflate the reputation of their houses, to provide records and guidebooks, as it were, for the inmates, and, in some cases, to reduce the possibility of internal discord by codifying customs. They also show some genuine antiquarian interest in their houses' past. Eulogy of the house permeates all the works. The Peterborough, Ely and Ramsey historians begin with a glowing description of the abbey's site (and the etymology of its name).[92] Hugh Candidus describes the advantages of an island in the marsh, how it provides unlimited wood and reeds for burning, and hay to feed animals and thatch houses, while the marsh itself was rich in birds and fish, with streams for transport. And of all marshy sites Peterborough, the 'Golden Borough',[93] had the best, possessing the most pastures and having the benefit of the river Nene.

Wherever possible the chroniclers stress their houses' connections with royalty. Hugh Candidus writes of the patronage of the house of Penda,[94] and the Abingdon chronicler alleges the importance of the Mercian kings in Abingdon's early history.[95] The historian of the see of Bath and Wells emphasizes the part played by King Ine of Wessex in the foundation of the see,[96] while the Battle chronicler eulogizes William the Conqueror.[97] The chroniclers also represent their houses as exempt from external control, often describing how their freedom was won. For example, the Battle chronicler records how the abbey freed itself of any subjection to its mother house of Marmoutier,[98] and to its diocesan, the bishop of Chichester.[99] Moreover,

---

[88] See, e.g. the account of Nigel's defence of the Isle of Ely: 'Primum igitur huius mali exordium cepit in Anglia Baldewinus de Riveris, et post episcopus Nigellus, malignorum instinctu, monachis obnixe dissaudentibus, contra regem munitionem in Ely ex lapido et cemento statuerat firmissimum, quod virtute sancta Æðelðrede crebra dissolvebatur. . . . Episcopus [Nigellus] vero nocte ante discesserat . . . ad dominam imperatricem, que tunc Glowecestrie morabatur, iter arripuit sicque illesus evasit. Monachi autem hoc timentes vehementer plangebant, intendunt esse causam inmensi discriminis et dampni continui ecclesie'; LE, pp. 314–15.

[89] LE, p. 372.   [90] Ab., vol. 2, p. 210.   [91] Battle, p. 72.

[92] HC, pp. 4–6; LE, pp. 2–5; Ram., pp. 7–11; cf. Ab., vol. 1, pp. 6–7 (for a brief description of the site of Abingdon abbey).

[93] Peterborough deserved to be called 'Gildineburch, hoc est aurea civitas', because of the treasures in the church: HC, p. 66.

[94] HC, pp. 7–11 passim.   [95] Ab., vol. 1, pp. 18–32.   [96] Hunter, op. cit., p. 10–14.

[97] For a list of William I's virtues see Battle, p. 6.   [98] Battle, p. 27.

[99] Battle, pp. 83–103. For Battle's claim to exemption from episcopal control see M. D. Knowles, 'Essays in monastic history, 1066–1216: IV. The growth of exemption' in Downside Review, l (1932), pp. 218–25.

the historians of the pre-Conquest foundations underline their abbeys' importance in the monastic world, notably by recording the existence of satellite houses. Just as Hugh Candidus lists Peterborough's colonies,[100] so the chroniclers of Ramsey and Ely mention the daughter houses at Winchcombe[101] and Bury St Edmunds.[102]

Hagiography, especially where there was a patron saint, played an important part in the glorification of the institution. This is particularly marked at Ely, which was defended by the Anglo-Saxon saint, Etheldreda.[103] The chronicler begins his history with a pre-existing *Life of St. Etheldreda*, similar in style to the saints' Lives written by the hagiographer Goscelin (who visited Ely).[104] The Ramsey chronicler borrowed from one of Goscelin's works, the *Life of St. Ives*.[105] Relics also figure largely in most of the histories, especially in those of the pre-Conquest foundations. The Abingdon chronicler includes a list of relics in the abbey drawn up by Abbot Faricius (1100–1117).[106] The miracles the relics worked are recorded, partly no doubt to impress pilgrims with the saints' power (for example, Hugh Candidus relates that the water in which one of Peterborough's relics, the arm of St Oswald, had been washed, was carried to London, where, in the crypt of St Paul's, it worked many miracles[107]). Each chronicler is particularly anxious to prove that the relics of the patron saint are in fact preserved in his house. This preoccupation resulted in the recording of inter-monastic disputes over the possession of relics. Hugh Candidus, having admitted the loss of some Peterborough relics to Ramsey during the Danish attacks, tells how the relics showed unwillingness to stay and so were brought home.[108] Rivalry over relics was acute between Ramsey and Ely. The Ramsey chronicler relates that the monks of Ely retained the body of Eadnoth bishop of Dorchester (1006–16) when it was on its way for burial at Ramsey.[109] And he records how the monks of Ramsey only just managed to acquire the relics of St Felix: while the Ramsey monks were transporting the relics by water to the abbey, a flotilla of small boats from Ely pursued them and they only succeeded in slipping away to safety because God sent a marsh mist.[110]

---

[100] See p. 274 and n. 42. See also *HC*, pp. 66–7.

[101] *Ram.*, p. 73.   [102] *LE*, p. 155.

[103] For examples of St Etheldreda posthumously helping and defending her church, see *LE*, pp. 212–17, 296–9, 338–41, 363–4, 366–71.

[104] For a reference to Goscelin (for whom see pp. 64–5, 107–11) at Ely see *LE*, p. 215 and n. 1, and cf. *VER*, p. 102 and n. 1.

[105] See *Ram.*, pp. xxxi–xxxiii, 114–15. Cf. *VER*, p. 102 n. 2.

[106] *Ab.*, vol. 2, pp. 155–8. The list is headed: 'Haec fecit abbas Faritius et haec scribere iussit, ne posteri se de ignorantia excusent; constringens et eos maledictione perpetua qui ea arroganter vel fraudulenter aboleverint. Nomina sanctorum subscripta sunt in Abbendonensi ecclesia, perscrutarum a piae memoriae Faritio abbate, una cum senioribus eiusdem ecclesie sub anno Incarnationis Christi MCXVI.'

[107] *HC*, p. 108.   [108] *HC*, pp. 50–1, 83.

[109] *Ram.*, pp. 118–19.   [110] *Ram.*, pp. 127–8.

In this way the Anglo-Saxon idea that the saints posthumously protected a religious house survived. But it survived in an attenuated form, increasingly overshadowed by the concept of the abbot as the house's primary champion and protector. In the course of the twelfth century, biographies of the abbots gradually began to dominate local histories. The chroniclers tended to eulogize the abbots: for example, the Abingdon chronicler praised Abbot Faricius for his acquisition of relics, ornaments and lands for the abbey and for his building activities,[111] and Hugh Candidus even attributed miracles to some of the pre-Conquest abbots.[112] This eulogistic tendency is particularly marked in the Battle chronicle, notably in its long abbatial character-sketches. Abbot Ralph (1107–24) is described as a pattern of good works, both a Martha and a Mary: he was a prudent husbandman, as abstemious as Daniel, and he suffered like Job; he was a very Noah in his tolerance, putting up with Ham and blessing Shem and Japheth.[113] Abbot Walter de Lucy is praised not only for his unremittent defence of his house's liberties, his generosity to the abbey and his building achievements, but also for his kindness to lepers and victims of elephantiasis whom he 'kissed with love and piety'.[114] Then there was Abbot Odo (1175–1200) who was a fine preacher and, despite a chronic bowel complaint, insisted on following the hard life of the cloister.[115]

But this tendency to write panegyrics on the abbots did not entirely prevent the chroniclers from criticizing them. They wrote from the point of view of communities to which they belonged. By this period an abbot's property and many of his activities were separate from those of his community. Therefore in some cases the chroniclers reflect the community's ability to assess the abbot's achievements objectively. Thus the Ramsey chronicler says that Abbot Wulfsige (1006–16) had no virtue except meanness and criticizes him for refusing to victual Earl Byrhtnoth's troops.[116] And Hugh Candidus charges Abbot Ernulf (1107–14) with excessive stupidity in a land transaction.[117] Even the Battle chronicler finds a fault in Abbot Walter: he asserts that by failing to create vicarages in the abbey's churches (instead he arranged to receive annual 'rent' from the parsons), he deprived the abbey of a lucrative source of revenue.[118]

Besides being propaganda, as it were, for the glory of the house, aimed at its inmates and friends, a local history was a business record. Even where the chronicler does not actually cite a charter *verbatim*, he gives the weight of authority to his narrative, for the post-Conquest period as for Anglo-Saxon times, by using charters as evidence. A chronicle, therefore, was a useful record of land transactions. The Ely and Ramsey chronicles are par-

---

[111] *Ab.*, vol. 2, pp. 44–9. [112] *HC*, pp. 23, 75. [113] *Battle*, pp. 58–9.
[114] *Battle*, pp. 128, 135–6. [115] *Battle*, pp. 162–3. [116] *Ram.*, p. 116.
[117] *HC*, p. 65.
[118] *Battle*, pp. 129–30. For the importance of this passage as evidence on the creation of vicarages see M. D. Knowles, 'Essays in monastic history, 1066–1216: VI. Parish organisation' in *Downside Review*, li (1933), pp. 508–9.

ticularly concerned with the acquisition of land. And the Ely historian has copies of three inventories of the abbey's goods.[119] Moreover, the Peterborough, Ely and Ramsey chroniclers meticulously record the names of people who gave property to the abbey, sometimes with details of their lives:[120] a benefactor could expect not only a grave within the precincts and a commemoration on the anniversary of his death, but also a place in the abbey's chronicle. Similarly, acts of the abbots may be noted (the Abingdon chronicler records the arrangements Abbot Faricius made for his own anniversary).[121]

Such a record could serve a useful purpose, not only as a precedent book in case of disputes with the outside world, but also when there were conflicts within the community. The possibility of such conflicts existed because there were potentially rival authorities, the abbot and his convent, the bishop and his monastic or his secular chapter. The presence of a bishop made the danger particularly acute. Thus the history of the see of Bath and Wells records, by reproducing Bishop Giso's autobiography, the terms of the pre-Conquest division of property between the bishop and chapter, and after the Conquest it traces the course of the canons' struggle against the hereditary claims of the archdeacons. At Ely the problem arose when the bishopric was created in 1109. The monks fought to establish that the cathedral priory was the heir to the rights and property of the ancient abbey. The Ely historian records Bishop Hervey's allocation of separate revenues for the monks' maintenance, commenting that his allocation was extremely mean, sufficient for little over half the actual number of monks.[122] He then gives copies of the charters of separation granted by Bishop Hervey and Bishop Nigel.[123] Perhaps it was as a warning to future abbots against oppressing the convent that the Ramsey and Abingdon chroniclers cite instances of abbatial oppression. At Ramsey the chronicler records how Abbot Wythman's strict enforcement of the Rule led to episcopal interference and to Wythman's resignation.[124]

The function of the local history as a record shades into its function as a kind of guidebook, to satisfy curiosity. It is likely that the chroniclers had in mind the pilgrim trade, hoping to make the monks better able to inform visitors about the abbey's past history. This may well account for the mention of the churches' ornaments and other objects which the pilgrim might see. The Ely historian describes a precious altar cloth made by Queen

---

[119] *LE*, pp. 196–7, 223–4, 288–94.

[120] For lists of benefactors see e.g. *LE*, pp. 130–44 (with biographical details); *HC*, pp. 67–72; *Ram.*, pp. 47 et seq.

[121] *Ab.*, vol. 2, p. 153.

[122] For Bishop Hervey's separation of episcopal from monastic property see *LE*, pp. 261–2. For a discussion of the division of the abbey lands see *LE*, pp. l, 407–8.

[123] *LE*, pp. 262–3; cf. pp. 203–5, 381–3, for more documents relating to the separation of property.

[124] *Ram.*, pp. 120–4.

Emma: the part hanging down in front of the altar was of a beautiful green decorated with gold thread, and on top it was of blood-coloured satin with ends, trimmed with gold fringe, hanging down to the ground. The chronicler records that Emma made Ely some other wonderful fabrics, without comparison the richest in the vicinity, of purple colour decorated with gold thread and gems and edged with gold fringe.[125] The Ramsey chronicler records that the patron Æthelwine provided the church with decoration for the front of the altar, of wood covered with plates of silver studded with various coloured jewels, and he paid £30 for building the organ which on feast days 'at a great breath of the bellows emitted a beautiful melody and prolonged, resounding noise'.[126] The construction of such ear-splitting organs is also noted by the Abingdon chronicler.[127] Moreover, the latter describes an illuminated Gospel-book given to the abbey by William II.[128] The Ramsey chronicler specifically mentions one volume in his monastic library, a book of verse by Oswald who as a boy broke the abbey bell.[129]

Some of the most vivid passages in these histories concern the monastic buildings. All the chroniclers record the stages in which their houses were built and rebuilt. The most detail is given by the Abingdon and Ramsey chroniclers, who each, for example, give a graphic account of the fall of the tower of the abbey church. At Abingdon it fell in 1091, apparently because of disturbance caused by the laying of the foundations of the new choir. The monks were at matins, which 'by divine instinct', the prior had allowed them to celebrate in the chapter-house. When the dust from the fall cleared it was found that miraculously no one was hurt.[130] In St Oswald's time the tower of Ramsey fell because of poor construction or bad foundations.[131] The fact that the Ramsey chronicler was interested in a building of which no trace remained in his own day indicates that here he was not writing for sightseers, but primarily as an antiquarian. In this capacity he describes the earliest stone church at Ramsey, which was in the Carolingian style: 'two towers overshadowed the roofs; the smaller one, at the west end, at the front of the church, presented a beautiful spectacle from a distance to those entering the island; the larger one, in the centre of the quadripartite structure, was supported by four columns, each attached to the next by spreading arches, to stop them falling apart. According to the architectural style of that distant age, this was a fine enough building.'[132] Similarly the chronicler calls attention to the existence of ruins at Ramsey, the interest of which must have been purely antiquarian as they did not add to the abbey's glory. He writes that in the cemetery can be seen the ruins of a crypt, as 'witness and evidence'[133] of the nunnery which King Canute and Bishop Æthelric had

---

[125] *LE*, p. 149.
[128] Ibid., p. 41.
[131] *Ram.*, pp. 85-7.
[133] 'eiusdem aedificii testis et index'; *Ram.*, p. 126.

[126] *Ram.*, p. 90.
[129] *Ram.*, p. 160.
[132] *Ram.*, p. 41.

[127] *Ab.*, vol. 2, p. 208.
[130] *Ab.*, vol. 2, pp. 23-4.

planned to found: by divine providence (it would not have been good, the chronicler remarks, to have the sexes in such close proximity) they never fulfilled their plan. In the same way, antiquarian interests may well have caused the Ely chronicler to follow in such detail the conflict between the abbey and the bishop of Lincoln, a conflict which had no relevance to the period after the creation of the bishopric of Ely in 1109.[134] Antiquarianism may also have been a contributary cause (nostalgia for past greatness was obviously another reason) for the inclusion in the Ramsey and Ely histories of numerous notices of the acquisition and possession of lands and church ornaments which, as the chroniclers note,[135] were subsequently lost for ever.

Thus, it can be seen that these local historians in the south of England reflected the conditions of their age. Their houses were on the defensive against secular and ecclesiastical authorities. They aimed at writing records to serve as precedent-books in case of future conflict. The involvement of the monasteries in contemporary politics meant that the chroniclers could not ignore political history. And a chronicler, in order to strengthen his house in its struggles with the outside world, tried to augment its reputation. In doing so he bore in mind the pilgrim trade, a lucrative source of revenue. In the course of providing information about his church, he allowed traces of antiquarianism to enter his thought.

In the north of England the attitudes of the local historians, comprising our second group, were different in some respects from those of the southern authors. Some of these chroniclers did not feel it necessary to hide their identity: they not only on occasion, like Bede, included autobiographical material but one, Ailred of Rievaulx, even gives information about his family history. The tone of their works is generally speaking more pious than those of the southern writers, and less defensive towards the outside world. This was partly because their houses were differently circumstanced. The main enemies were raiders from Scotland: in general, notwithstanding some friction (Byland abbey was involved in litigation over land with its lay neighbours, and quarrelled with the abbey of Calder when the latter claimed its obedience), the ecclesiastics and nobles were on friendly terms with the monks.

But the most important factor contributing to the difference of outlook was that religious feeling seems to have been stronger in the north; this was

---

[134] For the struggle between the abbey and the bishops of Lincoln, of which the author gives an account biased in favour of the abbey see *LE*, pp. 137 (and n. 2) to 138, 161 (and n. 1) to 164, 237, 402–3 (Appendix C), 417–18 (Appendix D). See also Knowles, 'The growth of exemption' in *Downside Review*, l (1932), pp. 420–1.

[135] The Ramsey chronicler justifies the inclusion of a list of lands given to the abbey by Æthelric, bishop of Dorchester (1016–34), but subsequently lost, in this way: 'ad commendandum tamen exuberantem in nos viri benevolentiam, catalogo ceterarum duximus inserendas'; p. 144. Cf. *Ram.*, pp. 153, 172, and *LE*, pp. 152, 324–5, 338–9.

primarily due to the Cistercian order and the powerful influence of St Bernard. It caused a group of monks, wanting to observe the Rule of St Benedict in the strict, literal way of the Cistercians, to leave the abbey of St Mary's, York, and settle at Fountains, and a number of other Cistercian abbeys to be founded with Fountains as their mother house. Cistercian religious enthusiasm reinforced the surviving Bedan tradition.[136] These two sources of religious feeling, the new and the old, interacted on each other: the Cistercians absorbed the Bedan tradition, while the Augustinian canons of Hexham, who had an especially revivalist attitude to ancient Northumbria, had close connections with the Cistercians.

Local historians in the north of England were a product of this hybrid culture. In the mid-twelfth century Hexham was a centre of local historiography, to which the Cistercian Ailred of Rievaulx contributed. But after his day until the end of the century no north-country Cistercian is known to have written history: this was because the Cistercians observed the prohibition on creative writing, without special licence, by the general chapter.[137] Then, in the late twelfth and early thirteenth century, the history of the Cistercian settlement in the north was recorded in a series of foundation accounts. These accounts of the origins of the north-country Cistercian abbeys are remarkable for their authors' narrative powers, and for the vivid picture they give of Cistercian expansion. The histories are of Byland abbey,[138] of Byland's daughter house Jervaulx,[139] of St Mary at Fountains,[140] and of its daughter house, Kirkstall.[141]

Hexham priory, as was mentioned above,[142] was a centre for the writing of general histories: where the *Historia Regum* attributed to Symeon of Durham left off, Richard of Hexham and John of Hexham took up the story (though both concentrated primarily on local events, they set them in the context of national history). The same Richard, who became prior in 1141, also wrote a history of Hexham, from the foundation of the earliest church by Wilfrid to about 1138.[143] He wrote in the tradition of Bede, starting with a geographical description of Northumbria (comparable with Bede's description of England) and deriving most of his early material from the

---

[136] For the Bedan tradition in the north country in the twelfth century, see pp. 213, 308.

[137] See p. 263 and n. 131.

[138] Printed in *Mon. Angl.*, vol. 5, pp. 349–54. This chronicle is discussed by C. T. Clay, 'The early abbots of the Yorkshire Cistercian houses' in *Yorkshire Archaeological Journal*, xxxviii (1952), p. 9 and n. 2.

[139] Printed in *Mon. Angl.*, vol. 5, pp. 568–74.

[140] Printed in *Memorials of the Abbey of St. Mary of Fountains*, ed. J. R. Walbran (Surtees Soc., xlii, 1863), pp. 1–129. For the authorship of the chronicle see ibid., pp. vii–x. The chronicle is noticed by Clay, op. cit., p. 15.

[141] Printed, with an English translation, and discussed by E. K. Clark, 'The foundation of Kirkstall abbey' in *Miscellanea* (Thoresby Soc., iv, 1895), pp. 169–208. An incomplete text is printed in *Mon. Angl.*, vol. 5, pp. 530–2. Cf. Clay, op. cit., p. 24 and n. 2.

[142] See pp. 216, 261.

[143] Printed in Raine, *Hexham*, vol. 1, pp. 1–62. For Richard's and John's general histories see pp. 216–18, 261 above.

Ecclesiastical History and from the *Life of St. Cuthbert* (he also used Eddius Stephanus's *Life of Wilfrid*). Moreover, he was influenced by the Durham historians, using the *Libellus* on the history of the church of Durham as a source and stylistic model.[144]

Richard's principal object was to augment the reputation of Hexham as a holy place and to present its history in the way most acceptable to its inmates. In dealing with the Northumbrian period, when the monastery was an episcopal see, he emphasized the prestige of Acca, bishop of Hexham (pointing out that Bede wrote the commentary on Mark and Luke at his request).[145] In order to prove that there was continuity from Bedan times to his own, he was prepared to distort facts. Actually the monastic see was obliterated by the Danish invasions, but Richard asserted that it was transferred to Chester-le-Street and from there to Durham, reinforcing his statement with a reference to the *Libellus*, though the latter clearly and correctly states that the see established at Chester-le-Street was St Cuthbert's see of Lindisfarne.[146] Richard then remarks that because of its former status and prerogatives the church of Hexham was free from any subjection to the bishop of Durham (which was not strictly speaking true).[147] On the other hand he stresses the close ties between Hexham and the see of York: the priory was established in 1113 as a house of Augustinian canons through the influence of Archbishop Thomas. Richard regards Thomas as the patron, praises him and lists his benefactions.[148]

By emphasizing that the priory of canons was a revival of the Bedan abbey, rather than a new foundation, Richard gave the priory an ancient history. Perhaps desire to prove continuity with the past was one reason why he described in such detail Wilfrid's church at Hexham, much of which was still standing in his day. Another reason was his pride in Hexham, for the church had been in its time 'the most beautiful this side of the Alps'. He describes its high walls, its numerous defensive turrets and winding stairs, and extensive underground passages and crypts. Many of these towers, Richard said, still loomed over the priory,[149] and sheltered people of the neighbourhood when Scottish raiders came.[150] Richard stresses the power of Hexham to protect people in time of trouble. Emphasizing the efficacy of the church as a refuge, he claims that it had had the right of sanctuary from the earliest days. In order to define the privilege he gives extracts from a charter of Henry I.[151]

---

[144] Raine, *Hexham*, vol. 1, p. cxlv and *passim*.

[145] Ibid., p. 33.

[146] Ibid., pp. 43 (and n. r) to 45.

[147] Ibid., p. 47 and n. z.

[148] Ibid., pp. 51–8 *passim*.

[149] Ibid., pp. 13–14. Richard uses Eddius's description (see p. 72 above) but slightly expands it. For a comparison of Eddius's with Richard's description see G. Baldwin Brown, *The Arts in Early England* (London 1903–37, 6 vols); new ed. of vol. 2, *Anglo-Saxon Architecture* (London 1925), pp. 151–4.

[150] See Raine, *Hexham*, vol. 1, p. 12 n. q.

[151] Ibid., pp. 60–2. In fact the charter he abstracts from was granted by Henry I to York cathedral: see ibid., p. 61 n. e.

Hexham owed its holiness to association with saints of the Northumbrian period. Richard intended to write a work on the Hexham saints, but he never did so.[152] It was left to Ailred of Rievaulx to fulfil such a plan, with a tract on the relics preserved at Hexham.[153] He wrote at the request of the canons to commemorate the translation of the relics to the priory in 1154,[154] and read his work out aloud at the ceremony. The climax of the work is the account of the translation of the relics to the new shrine. They were placed in three boxes which were put near the altar, on a richly carved and painted table supported by three pillars[155] (details follow about the relics, lives and miracles of the saints). This climax is prefaced by a historical introduction, sketching the history of Hexham from the time of Bede. The pretext for this preliminary section is that it serves to demonstrate the power of the Hexham relics to protect their church.

Ailred did not apparently use Richard's history and gives a slightly different account of the foundation of Hexham as a priory of Augustinian canons. Here he emphasizes the part played by his own family rather than that taken by the archbishop of York. In fact love of his ancestors led him to include family history. He describes how, after the destruction of Hexham by the Danes, his great-grandfather Alured, son of Westou, salvaged the Hexham relics and took them to Durham. When William of St Carilef restored monastic life at Durham, Alured's son Eilaf refused to become a monk and instead obtained the church of Hexham from Thomas archbishop of York, moving there as its priest. Subsequently his son Eilaf, his successor as priest of Hexham and Ailred's father, asked Archbishop Thomas for permission to introduce Augustinian canons into his church.[156] Richard of Hexham makes no mention at all of Alured son of Westou and gives the archbishop of York, not Eilaf, chief credit for the foundation.

Ailred's interest in the foundation of Hexham was no doubt partly the result of his Cistercian education. For the early history of Cîteaux was fully told in the *Exordium Cisterciensis Cenobii* (*The Beginning of the Cistercian Convent*),[157] and there were foundation histories of Clairvaux and other houses in the *Exordium Magnum Ordinis Cisterciensis* (*Great Beginning of the Cistercian Order*).[158] These works, and the earliest *Life of St. Bernard*,[159] influenced the authors of the remarkable series of foundation histories of the

---

[152] 'Virtutes autem, et miracula, quae per eum et per alios fideles servos suos, quorum reliquae ibidem continentur, Deus crebro operatur, hic supersedemus, alibi dicturi, prout Ipse nobis dederit'; ibid., p. 36.

[153] The full title is *De Sanctis Ecclesiae Haugustaldensis, et eorum Miraculis Libellus*. Printed in ibid., pp. 172–203.

[154] See the prologue: ibid., p. 172.   [155] Ibid., pp. lxxiii, 200.

[156] Ibid., pp. 191–2. For a discussion of this piece of family history see ibid., pp. li–lvii.

[157] Printed in P. Guignard, *Les Monuments primitifs de la Règle cistercienne* (Dijon 1878), pp. 61–75. Cf. Knowles, *Monastic Order*, p. 208 n. 1.

[158] The *Exordium Magnum* was written c. 1180. Printed in Migne, *PL*, vol. clxxxv, coll. 995 et seq.

[159] Printed in ibid., vol. clxxxv, coll. 225 et seq.

Cistercian houses in the north of England. Another possible model for them was the account of the foundation of St Mary's, York, probably by its first abbot, Stephen.[160]

The earliest foundation history of an English Cistercian house was, as far as is known, by Philip abbot of Byland (formerly abbot of Lannoy in the diocese of Beauvais).[161] In 1197 he wrote a very detailed and circumstantial account of the foundation and early history of Byland. He obtained his information from his predecessor as abbot, Roger (who ruled from 1142 until his resignation in 1196) and 'from many others'.[162] Moreover, the fact that the work includes a number of precise dates and also one document copied in full (Ailred's arbitration award between Byland and Calder[163]) shows that Philip used the abbey's archives. It is possible that Philip was stimulated to write history by the example of Ailred, who took an active interest in the affairs of Byland abbey.[164] And he could have been influenced by his contemporary the chronicler William of Newburgh, for Byland had close connections with Newburgh priory.[165] Like Ailred and William of Newburgh, Philip wrote partly for the edification of his readers. He wanted the monks of his community to know how 'their predecessors sustained tribulations and oppressions, want and labour, for the hope of eternal glory'.[166] He emphasized the abbey's close relations with St Bernard, noting, for example, how Abbot Roger frequently went to the general chapter at Cîteaux to ask St Bernard for permission to retire from the abbey.[167]

But Philip's work has two principal themes which were not edificatory in intention: one was the abbey's debt and close connection with its lay patrons; the other was its relations with the abbey of Calder. Originally Byland belonged to the order of Savigny, only becoming a member of the

---

[160] The foundation history of St Mary's, York, is printed in *Mon. Angl.*, vol. 3, pp. 544–6, and *Cartularium Abbathiae de Whiteby*, ed. J. C. Atkinson (Surtees Soc., lxix, lxxii, 1879, 1881, 2 vols), vol. 1, pp. xxxiv–xxxvii. The authenticity of this work has been challenged, but it is accepted as genuine by D. Bethell, 'The foundation of Fountains abbey and the state of St. Mary's York in 1132' in *Journal of Ecclesiastical History*, xvii (1966), p. 19, and by A. Hamilton Thompson, 'The monastic settlement at Hackness' in *Yorkshire Archaeological Journal*, xxvii (1924), pp. 390 et seq.

[161] See Clay, op. cit., p. 11 n. 12.

[162] Philip says he writes 'prout ab antiquioribus frequenter audivimus qui a piae recordationis viro domino Rogero praedecessore nostro et pluribus aliis qui de Caldra venerunt, sufficienter fuerunt instructi'; *Mon. Angl.*, vol. 5, p. 349.

[163] See p. 291 and n. 173.

[164] Ailred was an arbiter in the dispute between the abbey of Savigny and the abbey of Furness for the right to the obedience of Byland; see *Mon. Angl.*, vol. 5, p. 352, p. 291 and n. 173 below, and *VAAR*, pp. xii n. 1, lxiii, xcii.

[165] Philip mentions that a relative of Roger de Mowbray, Byland's patron, became a canon of Newburgh (i.e. Samson de Albaneio; see *Mon. Angl.*, vol. 5, p. 351), and when the monks settled at Old Byland they gave their previous site at Hood and other properties to the canons of Bridlington who later moved to Newburgh (ibid., p. 351). Moreover, the prior of Newburgh was a witness to Ailred's arbitration award (see p. 291 and n. 173 below).

Mon. Angl., vol. 5, p. 354.   [167] Ibid.

Cistercian order when the Savigniacs accepted the authority of Cîteaux in 1147.[168] Philip describes how in 1134 a group of monks from the Savigniac abbey of Furness settled on land at Calder, in Coupland, given them 'by a certain local magnate'.[169] But they were defeated by poverty, and tried to return to Furness which would not receive them. So they came under the protection of Gundreda, widow of Nigel de Albini and mother of Roger de Mowbray who was still a ward of King Stephen. From then on the fortunes of the community depended on the Mowbray family. First the monks lived at Hood where a relative of Gundreda, Robert de Alneto, was a hermit. To alleviate their poverty Roger de Mowbray granted them a tithe of the food eaten by his household: a lay brother was detailed to follow his court in order to collect the tithe. But, as Philip explains, the endowment had disadvantages. When Roger de Mowbray's household was a long way from Hood the tithe of food had to be sold and the money sent to the community. Moreover, Roger's guests might consume more than was expected, thus diminishing what the household could spare.[170] Therefore, when in 1143 Roger came of age, he granted the monks a site at Old Byland, acting on the advice of his mother and of Thurstan archbishop of York. Roger continued his patronage of the community. The site of Old Byland proving unsuitable, he gave them first a new one at Stocking near Coxwold, and finally, in 1177, the site in the parish of Byland, and at the same time had his benefactions confirmed by the archbishop of York.[171] He also helped Abbot Roger in a legal dispute. When in 1147 Abbot Roger became involved in a lawsuit with his neighbours over some property, he appealed to Mowbray, who was in Normandy. Mowbray wrote to John the Marshal and William de Warenne to postpone the case until his return, and then came and settled the matter.[172]

One purpose of Philip's chronicle was undoubtedly to record Byland's independence of the abbey of Calder. When the first colony at Calder of monks from Furness left for the new site at Old Byland, Furness sent another group to settle at Calder.[173] This community claimed to be the mother house of Byland abbey. The abbot of Calder asserted that he, not the abbot of Savigny, had authority over Byland. The case, Philip records, was referred to the general chapter at Cîteaux in 1150, which referred it to the arbitration of Ailred of Rievaulx who decided in favour of Byland and Savigny. In a similar way Philip is careful to record the dependence of the abbey of Jervaulx on Byland (he mentions the foundation of Jervaulx with monks from Byland on a site given to Byland by Abbot Serlo of Savigny[174]).

---

[168] For an outline of the early history of Byland and Jervaulx see Knowles, *Monastic Order*, pp. 249–52.
[169] *Mon. Angl.*, vol. 5, p. 349.   [170] Ibid., p. 350.   [171] Ibid., p. 353.
[172] Ibid., pp. 352–3.
[173] Ibid., p. 350. For the dispute and Ailred's arbitration award see ibid., pp. 352–3.
[174] Ibid., p. 352.

The Jervaulx chronicle, also written at Byland,[175] has a similar pattern, except that it includes a number of charters. Like Byland, Jervaulx started as a Savigniac house. The author aims at recording the abbey's difficult beginnings, its debt to lay patrons, and its subjection to Byland. And he ends, for the edification of readers, with a vision a monk of Byland had of the foundation of Jervaulx.[176] The earliest community was of monks from Savigny who settled at Fors. The site at Fors was, the author records, given by 'a generous knight, Akarias son of Bardolf, a great landowner in York-shire'.[177] The chronicler admits that he does not know how these Savigniacs came to England: some people, he says, believe that they came in the house-hold of Alan count of Brittany. Alan became the community's principal patron, and attended the laying of the foundation stone at Fors in 1145.[178] The chronicler states that this abbey was placed by Savigny under the authority of Byland in 1150, which sent an abbot and twelve monks to join the monastery.[179] But the site at Fors proved unpropitious and in 1156 Count Alan's successor Conan moved the monks, with the permission of Hervey the son of their original founder Akarias, to a new site which he had granted to them.[180] This new abbey was called Jervaulx. The chronicler gives copies of the charters of Conan and other magnates granting lands to it, and he records in detail official recognition of Jervaulx by the general chapter at Cîteaux.[181]

Both the Byland and the Jervaulx chronicles relate principally to the abbey's foundations. There is no attempt at a narrative history up to the authors' own time: the subject is the origins rather than the development of the houses. The *Narratio de Fundatione Fontanis Monasterii* (*Account of the Foundation of the Monastery of Fountains*) is more comprehensive: it was written in the early thirteenth century[182] by Hugh, a monk of Kirkstall abbey (a daughter house of Fountains), at the request of John abbot of Fountains. Although its best prose is limited to the foundation of Fountains in 1132, Hugh continued the abbey's history and the history of its daughter houses up to the time of writing. To 1190 (when Abbot William died) he states that he relied on the oral narrative of Serlo, a fellow monk who was a centenarian.[183] However, Hugh undoubtedly added material of his own, and after 1190 he claims to have been the sole author.[184] He was much influenced by the first *Life of St. Bernard*[185] and by the *Exordium Cister-*

---

[175] The text of the Jervaulx chronicle makes it clear that it was written at Byland for it refers to Byland as 'domus nostra' and to Roger abbot of Byland as 'abbas noster'. See e.g. ibid., pp. 570, 571.

[176] Ibid., pp. 573–4. [177] Ibid., p. 568. [178] Ibid., p. 569.

[179] Ibid., p. 571. [180] Ibid., p. 573. [181] Ibid., p. 571.

[182] The exact date is in dispute; see *MF*, p. xiii, and L. G. D. Baker, 'The foundation of Fountains abbey' in *Northern History*, iv (1969), p. 33. The foundation history of Fountains is discussed in ibid., pp. 29–33 and by Bethell, op. cit., pp. 13–14.

[183] *MF*, pp. 116–17.

[184] For Serlo's and Hugh's respective contributions see especially Baker, 'Foundation', pp. 31–2.

[185] See Bethell, op. cit., p. 13 and n. 5.

ciensis Cenobii.[186] In addition, he inserted seven letters into the narrative, six from St Bernard[187] and one from Thurstan, archbishop of York, to William of Corbeil, archbishop of Canterbury.[188] Thurstan's letter itself provided much of the information in the *Narratio* on the events leading up to the migration from St Mary's, York.[189] Thus it is impossible to be sure how much Serlo himself contributed, though he was undoubtedly responsible for the first-hand account of Abbot Richard II.

Serlo and Hugh both give a number of autobiographical details. Serlo says: 'It is now the sixty-ninth year of my conversion' and that he was thirty years old when he went to Fountains. 'So,' he continues, 'I know what happened because I was with the monks when they left York and knew them from my boyhood: I was born in their country, was related to many of them, and was brought up among them. So I relate what I remember and have heard from old men concerning the origins of Fountains.'[190] He next mentions that he was one of the monks sent from Fountains in 1147 to colonize a monastery at Mount St Mary in Barnoldswick. This daughter house failed and the monks moved to Kirkstall where Serlo spent the rest of his life. Hugh himself professed there between 1181 and 1190.[191]

Serlo therefore was an eye-witness for events narrated in the first part of the work, the actual foundation of Fountains and its history to 1147 (after that he depended on what he heard from other people). The early part of the book is one of the best pieces of narrative local history written in this period, capturing the initial enthusiasm of the Cistercians in the north of England.[192] It begins with an account of life at St Mary's, York:[193] 'There the religious trod in the footsteps of their forefathers, observing without argument the institutions accepted by their seniors. They lived according to the manner and custom of their predecessors' traditions, honestly under the authority of the Rule and of the abbot, but nevertheless far from the spirit of the Rule, from their oath of profession, far from the perfection of the Cistercian discipline.' It describes how a group of monks, whom he names, 'longed for the desert, for labour with their hands, for the pottage of the prophets,[194] for the spirit not the flesh', and loved the simplicity and poverty of the

---

[186] See p. 289 and n. 157.

[187] Epistolae nos 94–6, 313, 320–1 (Migne, *PL*, vol. clxxxii, coll. 226–9, 518–19, 526); *MF*, pp. 36–45, 81–3.

[188] For Thurstan's letter, which has been the subject of controversy, see Baker, 'Foundation', pp. 34–5; Bethell, op. cit., pp. 14–16; and Donald Nicholl, *Thurstan, Archbishop of York, 1114–1140* (York 1964), pp. 251–8 (Appendix II).

[189] See Baker, 'Foundation', p. 31.

[190] *MF*, p. 93–3. For a notice of when Serlo took the habit see *MF*, p. 57.

[191] See *MF*, p. x and n. 1.

[192] The element of apologetic in the *Narratio* detracts from its reliability as a historical source. Thurstan's letter gives a fuller and less biased account of the circumstances attending the migration of monks from St Mary's, York, see Bethell, op. cit., *passim*, and Baker, 'Foundation', *passim*.

[193] *MF*, p. 5.

[194] 'Tota aviditate suspiratur ... ad ollas Prophetarum'; ibid., p. 6. Cf. 2 Kings 4. 38–41.

Cistercian order.[195] So they left York: the details of their controversy with the authorities at St Mary's are given in the letter of Thurstan to the archbishop of Canterbury, which Hugh inserted.[196]

Though the later part of the *Narratio* lacks the power of the first section, the emphasis on the virtues of the Cistercian order is maintained. Fountains appears as the mother house of eight daughters.[197] The date of Fountains' own foundation is used as the era from which to date the settlement of the colonies. Each new daughter house is noted in chronological order, its lay or ecclesiastical patron is named, the location given, and the first abbot mentioned, particular notice being given if he happened to be one of the original monks from St Mary's.[198] Similarly the foundation of Fountains' grand-daughters is recorded: thus Newminster, 'the first sprig our vineyard put forth', itself 'conceived and gave birth to three daughters, Pipewell, Sawley and Roche'.[199] One of the colonies from Fountains was in Norway, at Lyse, near Bergen.[200] Such a foundation was characteristic of the international aspect of the Cistercian order. Nowhere is there any trace of the incipient patriotism which occurs in some other chronicles of the period. The Cistercians of northern England were under the direct guidance of St Bernard. The letters of St Bernard, inserted by Hugh into the chronicle, were of exhortation and advice, two addressed to the abbot of St Mary's, one to Archbishop Thurstan and one to Richard abbot of Fountains, all written at the time of the secession from York and of the first settlement.[201] Later St Bernard appointed the abbots of Fountains,[202] and its continued close connection with the central organization of the order is shown by Serlo's and Hugh's mention of visits by English Cistercians to Clairvaux.[203]

The *Narratio* was intended to concentrate on the religious aspects of Cistercian history: it gives few records of acquisition of lands by the abbeys[204] and none of the abbots' building activities.[205] But by the end of the century the Cistercians' original enthusiasm had died down. The *Narratio* mentions, without explanation, opposition among the monks at Fountains to the rule of Abbot Richard III (1150–70).[206] Later, Hugh of Kirkstall, who knew

---

[195] *MF*, p. 7.   [196] *MF*, pp. 11–29.

[197] 'Et haec novissima [*i.e.* Melsa] filiarum quas peperit mater nostra; et cessavit, iterum, parere. Itaque hae sunt cognationes populi nostri; haec soboles matris nostrae. Septem genuit filias; quinque nepotes suscepit ex eis; videns filios filiarum, suarum usque in quartam generationem'; *MF*, p. 96. The information here is not quite accurate, for example Fountains had eight, not seven, daughters, all noticed by Hugh; see *MF*, p. 96 n. 5.

[198] For example Hugh notes that Alexander the first abbot of Kirkstall was one of the original monks at Fountains, from St Mary's, York; *MF*, p. 92.

[199] *MF*, p. 61.   [200] *MF*, p. 89.   [201] *MF*, pp. 36–45. See n. 187 above.

[202] See *MF*, pp. 73, 81, 107–8.   [203] See *MF*, pp. 75, 78, 123.

[204] For record of land acquisition see *MF*, pp. 54–7, 86. Hugh is equally brief on this subject; see *MF*, p. 125.

[205] The conventual church was completed soon before 1170 but is not mentioned by Serlo; see *MF*, p. lvi. Hugh gives a very brief mention (*MF*, p. 128) of the rebuilding of the choir and building of the Lady Chapel by Abbot John (1203–11); see *MF*, p. lxiii.

[206] *MF*, pp. 111–13.

Abbot Ralph well because Ralph ruled Kirkstall before his election to Fountains in 1190, hints that Ralph was bad at business.[207] However, Hugh tried to maintain the *Narratio*'s pious tone by describing at length visions Ralph had as a boy.[208] But the troubles of Fountains were increasing. Hugh records that Abbot John (who succeeded Ralph in 1203), was accused by his monks of extravagant spending (again there is no analysis).[209] Hugh ends with a bitter attack on King John, 'a tyrant, depraved by evil counsellors', oppressing Fountains with such heavy financial exactions that the abbot had to buy him off with a lump sum.[210]

Hugh of Kirkstall also probably wrote the first part of the chronicle of Kirkstall abbey (it has a later continuation into the fourteenth century). It, like the *Narratio*, gives a picture of the abbey passing from an age of religious enthusiasm to one of preoccupation with quarrels and litigation. In the account of the abbey's foundation, it stresses the piety of the early community and the part played by its lay patron, Henry de Lacy, who gave the first site (at Barnoldswick) and laid the first stone of the abbey church at Kirkstall. The chronicle then gives brief sketches of the rules of the abbots, being primarily concerned in John's reign with recording the abbot's disputes with neighbouring landowners. Although, unlike the Fountains chronicle, it has no direct attack on King John, it blames him for the abbey's failure to regain one grange (he gave an unfavourable judgment), and for the loss of another grange ('by force of King John').

Note. Since this chapter went to press I have found another local history belonging to this period, the *Historia Selebiensis Monasterii,* an anonymous account of the foundation (in 1069) and early history, with hagiographical features, of Selby abbey, written in 1184. It is printed in J. T. Fowler, *The Coucher Book of Selby* (Yorkshire Archaeological and Topographical Assoc., record series, x, xiii, 1891, 1893, 2 vols), vol. 1, pp. 1-54.

---

[207] *MF*, pp. lix, 122. [208] *MF*, pp. 118–22 *passim.* [209] *MF*, pp. 125–6.
[210] *MF*, p. 126.

14

Sacred Biography from the Reign of Henry II to John

Besides both national and local history, ecclesiastical biography also flourished in the latter half of the twelfth century and in the early thirteenth century. Most of the biographies were written at centres which had established biographical and historiographical traditions – at Canterbury, Durham and Lincoln.

The biographers had various and mixed motives for writing. Some wrote partly because they wanted to record contemporary history. Some wrote partly to record the history and promote the interests of the cathedral or religious house with which their subject was connected. But the biographers' principal reason for writing was religious. The authors wanted to express and share their religious feelings which were moved by the lives of saints and good men. The importance of religious sentiment is shown by the number of biographies connected with the new orders, that is the Cistercians and Carthusians. The piety and austerity of the Cistercians in Ailred's time are reflected in his biography by Walter Daniel. In the next generation the Carthusian order was, generally speaking, regarded as the most austere and observant, and Carthusians became the subjects of biographies: Lives were written of St Hugh of Avalon, who, before becoming bishop of Lincoln (1186–1200), had been prior of the Carthusian priory of Witham in Somerset, and of Adam, a monk of Witham. But the strongest incentive to biographical writing was the martyrdom of Thomas Becket. The shock, and the fame of his tomb for working miracles, elicited at least ten biographies of Becket by the end of the twelfth century, five of them within a year or two of his death.

Many of the biographies produced at this period are of little literary and historical interest. Exceptions are the excellent series of Becket Lives and the long *Life of St. Hugh* by Adam of Eynsham. The Becket Lives will be discussed first because of their importance. Then the minor works will be briefly described, and finally Adam of Eynsham's *Life of St. Hugh*.

The primary purpose of the Lives of Thomas Becket[1] was to promote the

---

[1] The Becket Lives in Latin are printed in vols 1–4 of *Materials for the History of Thomas Becket*, ed. J. C. Robertson and J. B. Sheppard (RS, 1875–85, 7 vols). For the French and Icelandic Lives see p. 301 nn. 38–9 below. Excellent surveys of the Lives are in D. C. Douglas and G. W.

cult of the saint and to edify readers. But the authors also intended to provide a historical record of the most significant event, to the authors' knowledge, in church–state relations which had ever happened in England. Becket himself had realized the importance of preserving for posterity documents relating to the quarrel with Henry II.[2]

Moreover, the biographers were encouraged to concentrate particularly on the historical, non-hagiographical elements in their subject, because Becket's only claim to sanctity was his martyrdom. As Professor Knowles writes: 'the canonization of St. Thomas was due directly to his murder and to his posthumous fame, not to his personality'.[3] Although Becket abruptly changed his way of life on his appointment to the archbishopric, resigning the chancellorship and abandoning worldly pleasures, this merely entitles him to be regarded as a good churchman, not a saint. He underwent neither sudden religious conversion (like the conversions of St Paul, St Augustine or John Wesley), nor perceptible slow improvement in his spiritual life. He worked no miracles when alive and, apart from a reputed vision experienced by his mother before his birth,[4] the biographers had a hard time finding parallels from other saints' lives for events in Becket's. Therefore they only tried to prove that he was personally a good man, frugal and chaste,[5] and that he lived in great austerity when with the Cistercians at Pontigny.

Therefore the Becket Lives are fairly free from the hagiographical stylization which limits the value to the historian of many saints' Lives. The importance of some of the Becket Lives as historical sources is increased because they were written by men who knew Becket and had worked for him. Moreover, though most of the Lives are textually interrelated, each has information not in the others, much of it no doubt derived from oral

---

Greenaway, *English Historical Documents*, vol. 2 (London 1953), pp. 698–702 (extracts from the Lives are printed in an English translation in ibid., pp. 702–69 *passim*), and in *The Life and Death of Thomas Becket Chancellor of England and Archbishop of Canterbury based on the account of William Fitz Stephen his Clerk with Additions from other Contemporary Sources*, translated and edited by G. W. Greenaway (Folio Soc., 1961), pp. 28–33 (extracts from the Lives are printed in an English translation, to form a consecutive biography of Becket, ibid., pp. 35–160). For a useful monograph on the Becket Lives (their authors, dates, interrelationships, etc.) see Emmanuel Walberg, *La Tradition hagiographique de Saint Thomas Becket avant la fin du XIIe siècle* (Paris 1929). I have adopted the dates given by Walberg for the composition of the Lives; for a summary of his conclusions on the dates see ibid., pp. 133–4.

2 See Becket's letter of 1170 to Gratian, one of the papal officials appointed for the reconciliation of Becket with Henry II. The letter ends: 'Provideat etiam vestra discretio ut urgentiores et efficaciores litteras, quas dominus noster pro ecclesia regi Anglorum transmisit, registro inserantur; quia posteris magnum incitamentum est virtutis, quotiens eos animaverint exempla majorum. Ad negotium vero nostrum spectantes quas accepimus remittimus vobis, ut si forte editorum exemplaria desint, ea mutuare possitis a transcriptis': Epistola no. 695, printed in *MTB*, vol. 7, p. 353. I owe this reference to Professor C. N. L. Brooke. It will be noticed that Becket wanted documents relative not only to his side of the case, but also to Henry's, to be recorded. Similarly Gervase of Canterbury recorded *both* sides of the dispute between Archbishop Baldwin and St Augustine's; see pp. 153–4 above.

3 Knowles, 'Becket', p. 100.

4 See *MTB*, vol. 3, pp. 13–14; vol. 4, p. 3.

5 *MTB*, vol. 3, pp. 21–2.

tradition. Thus the Lives supplement and complement each other, and the best do not eclipse the historical value of those of poorer quality.

Two early Lives were by Edward Grim and Benedict of Peterborough. Grim, who wrote in 1172, was a secular clerk born in Cambridge where he may have lived.[6] Out of admiration for Becket he went to see him on his return from exile and was at the martyrdom, receiving a wound in the arm when he tried to shield the archbishop.[7] Benedict was a monk of Christ Church, Canterbury. He became prior in 1175 and abbot of Peterborough in 1177.[8] His work, written in 1173 or 1174 at the request of the community, is not strictly speaking a *Life* of Becket, but a Passion, as it deals only with the martyrdom itself.[9] He also wrote a book on the miracles worked at Becket's tomb and at his intercession.[10] Before the end of 1175 four more Lives were written. Another Christ Church monk, William of Canterbury, wrote a *Life* in 1173 or early in 1174.[11] He had become a monk during Becket's exile and on his return Becket vested him and ordained him a deacon. William was in the church at the time of the martyrdom but fled, fearing a general slaughter.[12] Like Benedict he also made a collection of miracles:[13] he seems to have held some office connected with Becket's tomb and so could record pilgrims' stories. His collection was, as it were, the 'official' one of the cathedral. It was read in chapter and a copy was presented by the monks to Henry II, at his request.[14] At about the same time another *Life* was written by an unknown author (called the Lambeth Anonymous because the only known text is in the library of Lambeth Palace),[15] and John of Salisbury wrote a brief one some time between 1173 and 1176.[16]

Also to this period belongs a *Life* in French verse by a wandering clerk called Guernes, or Garnier, of Pont-Sainte-Maxence, who met Becket on the continent and after the murder visited his tomb at Canterbury.[17] This work

[6] For what is known about him see *MTB*, vol. 2, p. xlv. His *Life of St. Thomas* is printed in ibid., pp. 353–450. For its date see Walberg, *Tradition*, pp. 105–7.

[7] *MTB*, vol. 2, p. 437. The incident is also mentioned in the Lives by William Fitz Stephen, Herbert of Bosham and the Lambeth Anonymous (for which see below and n. 15): *MTB*, vol. 3, pp. 141, 498; vol. 4, p. 130.

[8] See *MTB*, vol. 2, p. xix.

[9] Printed in ibid., pp. 1–19.

[10] Printed in ibid., pp. 21–281.

[11] For his life and works see *MTB*, vol. 1, pp. xxviii–xxx. The *Life of St. Thomas* is printed in ibid., pp. 1–136. For the date of the *Life* see Walberg, *Tradition*, p. 73.

[12] *MTB*, vol. 1, p. 133.

[13] Printed in ibid., pp. 137–546.

[14] See ibid., pp. xxx, 137.

[15] See *MTB*, vol. 4, pp. xiii–xiv. The *Life* is printed in ibid., pp. 80–144. For the date of this *Life*, see Walberg, *Tradition*, p. 59.

[16] See *MTB*, vol. 2, p. xlii. The *Life* is printed as part of Alan of Tewkesbury's *Life* (see below, p. 299 and n. 20) in ibid., pp. 301–22. For the date of John's *Life* see Walberg, *Tradition*, pp. 116–31.

[17] Printed, with a useful introduction, in *Guernes de Pont-Sainte-Maxence, La Vie de Saint Thomas Becket*, ed. Emmanuel Walberg (Les Classiques français du Moyen Age, vol. 77, Paris 1936, reissued 1964).

is evidence of the spread of St Thomas's cult.[18] Another Frenchman to write Becket's Life was a monk of Pontigny, perhaps called Roger, who was Becket's personal servant during his exile, and wrote late in 1176 or early in 1177.[19] Between 1176 and 1179 a monk of Christ Church, Alan of Tewkesbury, supplemented John of Salisbury's *Life* and added a collection of Becket's letters: Alan had studied at Benevento, returning to become a monk of Christ Church in about 1174; he was made prior in 1179 and elected abbot of Tewkesbury in 1188.[20] And then after 1183, probably in 1184, a monk of St Albans called Benedict wrote a Life in French verse.[21] He seems to have derived most of his information from an earlier Latin Life, now lost, by Robert of Cricklade, prior of the Augustinian priory of St Frideswide's in Oxford, who probably wrote at a date between 1172 and 1180.[22]

The two most authoritative Lives were by William Fitz Stephen and Herbert of Bosham. Fitz Stephen was a secular clerk in Becket's household.[23] As he himself says, he was Becket's confidant.

> I was a secretary in his chancery, and subdeacon in chapel when he celebrated. When I sat with him at the hearing of cases, I read out the letters and documents which were presented, and, at his command, I presided over other cases. When the Council of Northampton was held, where things of great importance were done, I was with him; and I saw his passion at Canterbury.[24]

Fitz Stephen was not with Becket in exile. The date of his work is not certain, but it was composed some time between 1173 and 1175 (probably between 1173 and 1174[25]) and certainly draws largely on the author's memory of what he himself saw and heard. Fitz Stephen had a lively, rather worldly mind and treats his subject widely, putting the controversy between Becket and Henry II in its contemporary context and occasionally digressing from his theme altogether (for example in his description of London[26]).

---

[18] However, there is no evidence that Guernes's work became popular in France; see Legge, *A-N Lit.*, pp. 249–50.

[19] The *Life* is printed in *MTB*, vol. 4, pp. 1–79. The author states in the preface (ibid., p. 2) that he served Becket and was ordained priest by him. For the identity of the author see *MTB*, vol. 4, pp. xi–xiii; Douglas and Greenaway, *Documents*, p. 700; E. Walberg, *Tradition*, pp. 78–9.

[20] See *MTB*, vol. 2, pp. xliii–xliv. The *Life* is printed in ibid., pp. 299–352 (see p. 298 n. 16 above for its incorporation of John of Salisbury's *Life of St. Thomas*).

[21] Printed (from a defective manuscript) by F. Michel as an appendix to his *Chronique des Ducs de Normandie* (Paris 1836–44, 3 vols) in *Collection de documents inédits sur l'histoire de France*, vol. 3, pp. 461 et seq. For the work see Walberg, *Tradition*, pp. 11–33.

[22] For Robert of Cricklade see ibid., p. 25 and p. 301 below.

[23] For Fitz Stephen see *MTB*, vol. 3, pp. xiii–xvi. The *Life* is printed in ibid., pp. 1–154.

[24] Ibid., pp. 1–2.

[25] Greenaway, op. cit., p. 29, states that it was probably composed between 1173 and 1175. Walberg, *Tradition*, p. 58, places it before 1176, probably 1173–4.

[26] See pp. 307–8 below.

The other authoritative *Life*, written comparatively late (it was not completed before 1186), was by Herbert of Bosham, a member of Becket's household who was with him at the Councils of Clarendon and Westminster and also accompanied him in exile.[27] Herbert was a learned but an overbearing and fanatical man,[28] and on occasion exhorted Becket to increase his already great intransigence towards Henry II.[29] He writes in a heavy, bombastic style,[30] full of edificatory exhortations, but had a penetrating, perceptive mind, making good use of his excellent information. Besides the *Life* he wrote the *Liber Melorum* (the *Book of Melodies*), a hagiographical study of Becket, which has some historical matter.[31] After Becket's death Herbert lived abroad, depressed and resentful because his work had received inadequate appreciation.[32]

The Lives by William Fitz Stephen and Herbert of Bosham are original, in the sense that the authors did not borrow from the other Lives. Alan of Tewkesbury's work also seems to be independent (apart from the fact that it reproduces John of Salisbury's *Life*). The interrelation of the other Lives is not entirely clear. No one Life extracts word for word from another, and the problem of their interrelationship is made harder because of the uncertain dating of some of them. Moreover, a common oral tradition, besides literary borrowing, could account for some similarities between the Lives: immediately after Becket's murder the Canterbury monks shared and promoted an accepted verbal version of events, and information was exchanged by word of mouth as well as in writing.

Nevertheless it is certain that some of the Lives are textually related.[33] Guernes used Grim[34] and William of Canterbury, and perhaps Fitz Stephen. 'Roger of Pontigny' used Guernes, Grim, John of Salisbury and William of Canterbury. And Benedict used John of Salisbury and Grim. Particularly surprising is the strong probability that John of Salisbury, Becket's close companion, relied on earlier writers rather than personal observation: he apparently used William of Canterbury and the Lambeth Anonymous (for the account of the murder itself he used his own letter to the bishop of Poitiers).[35] Some other Lives have not been mentioned above because they

[27] See *MTB*, vol. 3, pp. xvii–xxiv. The *Life* is printed in ibid., pp. 155–534.
[28] His overbearing behaviour is described by William Fitz Stephen; ibid., pp. 99–101.
[29] For example he advised Becket against compromise at the conference at Montmirail; ibid., p. 422.
[30] He justifies his verbosity, which, he says, tends 'rather to theological edification than to the historical exposition of Becket's acts', by asserting that it was his purpose not to write a bare record, but to examine the causes of events and Becket's motives; ibid., pp. 247–8 and see p. 302 below.
[31] For the *Liber Melorum* see *MTB*, vol. 3, pp. xxv–xxvi. Extracts are printed in ibid., pp. 535–54.
[32] Ibid., p. 553.
[33] For the following textual relationships see Walberg, *Tradition*, pp. 92–134.
[34] Guernes wrote two versions of Becket's *Life*, the first of which survives only, apparently, in a fragmentary form. This partially lost first version seems to follow Grim more closely than the second version: see Legge, *A-N Lit.*, p. 249.
[35] See Walberg, *Tradition*, pp. 173–85.

are entirely or mainly derivative: for example there is the *Quadrilogus* (so called because it was compiled from the writings of four authors) which was probably compiled by Elias of Evesham at the end of the twelfth century and recast in 1212 or 1213 by Roger, a monk of Crowland, for presentation to his abbot.[36] It is a conflation of the works of Edward Grim, Benedict of Peterborough, William of Canterbury and Herbert of Bosham.

By 1200 or soon after, Latin Lives of Becket had reached Iceland[37] (St Thomas became one of Iceland's most venerated saints) and soon versions appeared in Icelandic. Early in the thirteenth century the *Quadrilogus* was translated into Icelandic,[38] and in the first half of the fourteenth century a long *Thómas Saga* was composed,[39] based on the Passion by Benedict of Peterborough and Robert of Cricklade's work.[40]

The interrelation of the Lives is not of primary importance because the authors usually preferred their own observations and what they heard at first-hand to any written source. And it is clear when they are writing from their own knowledge. Thus William Fitz Stephen knows the most about Becket's early life and his conduct as chancellor. He gives a brilliant eye-witness account of the Council of Northampton, and, as he was not with Becket in exile, he was able to describe events in England during that period. Then he describes Becket's return and murder. Other accounts of the murder, also by eye-witnesses, are by Edward Grim, William of Canterbury and John of Salisbury. Fitz Stephen was not at the Councils of Westminster and Clarendon; the best authority for them is Herbert of Bosham who attended both. He gives a full, first-hand account of Becket's exile, including the meetings at Montmirail, Montmartre and Fréteval. He came back with Becket but was not at the martyrdom. 'Roger of Pontigny' is of value mainly for his details of Becket's appointment to the chancellorship, his election to the archbishopric of Canterbury and for the hours before his death. Alan of Tewkesbury, presumably because of his Italian contacts, is especially full on the negotiations with the papal curia in 1164.

The Lives will be discussed from four angles. First, what they convey of Becket's character and personal appearance, to what extent they bring him alive. Second, the account they give of the issues between Becket and Henry II. Third, the importance of the Lives for general history, and, fourth, their information about local history.

[36] For the *Quadrilogus* see *MTB*, vol. 4, pp. xix–xxi. It is printed in ibid., pp. 266–430.
[37] See Walberg, *Tradition*, pp. 22–9.
[38] Printed in *Thómas Saga Erkibyskups. Fortælling om Thomas Becket erkebiskop af Canterbury. To bearbeidelser samt fragmentter af en tredie*, ed. C. R. Unger (Christiania 1869). See Walberg, *Tradition*, pp. 22 et seq.
[39] Printed *Thómas Saga Erkibyskups*, ed., with an English translation, E. Magnússon (RS, 1875, 1883, 2 vols). For this work see Walberg, *Tradition*, pp. 23 et seq. For the cult of St Thomas in Iceland see *Thómas Saga*, vol. 2, pp. v et seq.
[40] For the sources see *Thómas Saga*, vol. 2, pp. liv, xcii–xciv.

Becket's character presents many problems. Professor Knowles has written: 'for all that historians and hagiographers and poets have written and sung, the character and personality of St Thomas elude us like a wraith each time we start forward to grasp them.'[41] And yet there is no lack of information. Herbert of Bosham specifically claims an interest in psychological motivation: 'Our purpose is not only to record the works of the archbishop, but the causes of these works, not only the facts, but the mind of the doer.'[42] The Lives by Edward Grim and William Fitz Stephen and the *Thómas Saga* all give character-sketches. But Grim's sketch is too hagiographical to be of value.[43] Those in Fitz Stephen[44] and the *Thómas Saga*[45] are more lifelike and include descriptions of Becket's physical appearance, but are also predominantly eulogistic. Fitz Stephen writes:

> He was brisk in his movement, eloquent in speech, acute in intelligence, great of heart, ever pursuing the path of virtue, showing kindness to all, compassion to the poor, and resisting the proud, intent on promoting his fellows, not from insincerity but from duty, and revering all good. He was generous and witty, guarding against either deceiving or being deceived, at once a prudent son of the world and destined to be a child of light.

The *Thómas Saga* says that he stammered a little. It also mentions his charm and remarkable memory which enabled him to 'repeat at any time he chose whatever legal judgments or awards he had heard'. Fitz Stephen says of Becket's physical appearance that he was 'handsome and good looking, tall, with a prominent rather aquiline nose'. The *Thómas Saga* gives a similar description, adding that he was slightly built, and had a pale complexion and dark hair.

The accounts of Becket's behaviour give the best idea of his character. These clarify some aspects of his personality: his tendency to go to extremes and to behave in a dramatic way at the expense of moderation, his obstinacy and intractability, and finally his heroism. His lack of moderation is illustrated by comparing Fitz Stephen's description of him as chancellor with that of him as archbishop. Fitz Stephen tells how as chancellor Becket lived like the grandest noble, hunting and hawking and lavishly entertaining guests at table. He was on the most familiar terms with the king, riding and dining with him.[46] But when he became archbishop he put on 'a hair shirt of the coarsest sort, reaching to his knees and swarming with vermin'. He ate little and drank water in which hay had been boiled, and often submitted to

---

[41] Knowles, 'Becket', p. 98.   [42] *MTB*, vol. 3, p. 248. Cf n. 30 above.
[43] *MTB*, vol. 2, pp. 363–5.
[44] For Fitz Stephen's character-sketch and description of Becket's appearance see *MTB*, vol. 3, p. 17.
[45] See *Thómas Saga*, vol. 1, p. 29.   [46] *MTB*, vol. 3, pp. 20–1, 24–5.

corporal discipline.[47] Herbert of Bosham describes how his austerities increased in severity at Pontigny where he tried to lead the life of this most strict Cistercian community, wearing the habit, lying on a rough pallet, and eating the meagre, vegetarian diet[48] (Grim adds that he immersed himself in cold water to suppress the desires of the flesh[49]). Bosham remonstrated with him for endangering his health by excess.[50] Moreover Bosham, usually an advocate of uncompromising measures, was dumbfounded by Becket's ill-timed publication of the excommunications at Vézelay.[51]

There is a good example of Becket's love of dramatic effect in Fitz Stephen's account of the Council of Northampton. He relates how on the way to court Becket said to Alexander, his cross-bearer,

> 'I would have done better to have come in my vestments.' For he had meant to approach the king with bare feet, fully vested and bearing his cross, in order to plead with him for the peace of the church. But his clerks dissuaded him from this plan and they did not dream that he would carry the cross himself. When he had entered the hall of the castle and dismounted from his horse, he took the cross which Alexander the Welshman had carried before him. Gilbert bishop of London had come to the door of the hall. Hugh of Nonant archdeacon of Lisieux, who had come with the archbishop and was a member of his household, said to him, 'Lord bishop of London, why do you allow him to carry his cross?' The bishop replied, 'My good man, he always was a fool and always will be.'

So Becket entered the council chamber, still bearing the cross, to everyone's astonishment and to Gilbert Foliot's annoyance.[52]

Becket's penchant for acting on his own initiative, without taking advice, appears in a number of contexts. Bosham remarks that the excommunications were published at Vézelay without any consultation.[53] 'Roger of Pontigny' gives an account, apparently preserving the original talk, of how John of Salisbury remonstrated with Becket, just before his martyrdom, for courting death.[54] It was when the four knights burst in on Becket while he was sitting with his monks and clerks after dinner. After an uproar, in which

---

[47] Ibid., p. 37. [48] Ibid., p. 376.
[49] *MTB*, vol. 2, pp. 412–13 and cf. pp. 417–18.
[50] *MTB*, vol. 3, pp. 377–9. [51] Ibid., p. 392.
[25] Ibid., p. 57. A translation of Fitz Stephen's account of the Council of Northampton is in Douglas and Greenaway, *Documents*, pp. 724–33.
[53] '[Thomas] quidem, sicut cito post nobis ipsemet indicavit, sciens et prudens hoc a nobis celavit, per supradictam causam se excusans quod nobis inconsultis hoc fecisset'; *MTB*, vol. 3, p. 392.
[54] *MTB*, vol. 4, p. 74. Guernes, ll. 5361–80, describes the same incident and may be the source of 'Roger''s account (see Guernes, p. xi). The scene is mentioned by Knowles, 'Becket', pp. 125–6.

Becket refused to leave, the knights left and Becket sat down again calmly, John of Salisbury remonstrated with him:

> 'It has always been your practice and still is, that you have persis-
> tently acted and spoken entirely on your own.' The saintly man
> said to him, 'What would you have then, Master John?' And
> John said, 'You ought to have taken advice, knowing for certain
> that these knights seek nothing from you but the excuse to kill you.'
> The saintly man said, 'We all must die, nor must we be turned
> from justice by fear of death. I am more prepared to bear death for
> God and the justice of the Church and the freedom of God than
> they are to inflict it.' 'And we', said John, 'are sinners and are not
> ready to die. I see no one who wishes for death except you.' And
> he replied, 'God's will be done.'

The description of the martyrdom by Edward Grim not only portrays Becket's heroism.[55] It illustrates the biographer's historical and literary skill. Apart from some typical medieval imagery, the account of what happened is detailed and factual, and its substantial truth is corroborated by three other independent witnesses (William of Canterbury, John of Salisbury and William Fitz Stephen.)[56]

Grim relates that Becket stood near the altar, holding on to a pillar and praying, when the knights approached. The first blow (which wounded Grim in the arm as he tried to shield the archbishop) struck the crown of his head.

> Next he received a second blow on the head, and still he remained
> immovable. At the third blow he fell on his knees and elbows,
> offering himself as a living sacrifice, saying in a low voice 'For the
> name of Jesus and the protection of the Church I am prepared to
> embrace death.' The third knight inflicted a terrible wound as he lay
> prostrate, at which blow the sword struck the stone paving, and
> the crown of the head, which was large, was separated from the
> rest, so that the blood, whitened by the brains, and the brains
> reddened with blood, stained the floor of the cathedral with the
> white of the lily and the red of the rose, the colours of the
> Virgin Mother of the Church and of the life and death of the
> confessor and martyr. . . . And, so that a fifth blow should not be
> lacking for the martyr, who in other things had imitated Christ,
> a clerk who had entered with the knights, put his foot on the

---

[55] *MTB*, vol. 2, pp. 437–8. A translation of Grim's account of the martyrdom and of the scenes leading up to it is in Douglas and Greenaway, *Documents*, pp. 761–8.

[56] See the comments in Douglas and Greenaway, *Documents*, p. 761. Cf. Knowles, 'Becket', p. 124 and n. 1.

neck of the saintly priest and precious martyr, and horrible to relate, scattered the blood and brains on the pavement.

Whatever the original cause of the quarrel between Becket and Henry II, whether personal animosity or conflict of jurisdictions, at the end Becket died, as he said in his last words, for the freedom of the church. And no medieval biographer tried to tell the story of his life divorced from the background of the issues between church and state. Most of the authors either gave extracts from or the full text of the Constitutions of Clarendon,[57] and Herbert of Bosham gives Becket's own objections to the clauses: he includes his famous comment on article three, that a clerk should not be judged twice for the same offence. William Fitz Stephen's account of the Council of Northampton is partly a record of the legal proceedings. It starts: 'The king decreed that another general council should be held at Northampton on Tuesday, 6 October, being the octave of St Michael. On the day appointed we came to Northampton.' It goes on to describe each day in turn, beginning 'On the second day', 'On the third day', and so on. Fitz Stephen explains in detail the technicalities discussed, how the archbishop resented having been summoned by a general summons of the sheriff of Kent, instead of by a personal one,[58] how he was accused of contempt for ignoring the summons to answer John the Marshal,[59] how he was sued for £300 which he had received as keeper of the castles of Eye and Berkhamsted, and for other debts binding the king.[60]

The biographers, like the general and local historians, appreciated the value of a document quoted *verbatim* to authenticate the narrative. This not only appears in the inclusion of the text of the Constitutions of Clarendon, but also in the use of Becket's correspondence. Edward Grim and William Fitz Stephen quote isolated letters.[61] Herbert of Bosham goes further, specifically referring the reader for more details to the collection of letters made by Alan of Tewkesbury: he omits, for the sake of brevity, a number of letters about Becket's exile because they are in Alan's great collection now owned 'by many people and many churches'.[62] Alan himself was an innovator in his creation of a separate volume of documents to illustrate a narrative source (here he was a precursor of Matthew Paris[63]). He regarded John of Salisbury's work as too brief, as merely introductory to the subject,[64] and explains that he added the collection of letters so that the reader could fully understand Becket's 'life, the manner of his exile, and the progress and

---

[57] The Constitutions of Clarendon or extracts from them are in William of Canterbury, Alan of Tewkesbury, Edward Grim, William Fitz Stephen and Herbert of Bosham: *MTB*, vol. 1, pp. 18–23; vol. 2, pp. 352 n. 1, 380; vol. 3, pp. 47, 280–4, respectively.

[58] *MTB*, vol. 3, pp. 50–1.   [59] Ibid., p. 50.   [60] Ibid., pp. 53–4.

[61] See *MTB*, vol. 2, pp. 408–12; vol. 3, pp. 90–2. Cf. Grim who states that he quoted the letters to give the reader additional details: *MTB*, vol. 2, p. 409.

[62] *MTB*, vol. 3, pp. 395–6.

[63] For Matthew Paris's collection of documents see p. 367 below.

[64] *MTB*, vol. 2, p. 300.

conclusion of the controversy'.[65] He gathered the letters from scattered sources and arranged them in chronological order, in five sections, asking anyone who could improve the position of those of doubtful date to do so. He not only regarded the letters as illustrative of, and supplementary to, the *Life* itself, but also saw the *Life* as elucidating the letters. Thus, because John of Salisbury wrote practically nothing about the period from the Council of Clarendon to the death of Pope Alexander III (1181),[66] Alan wrote a narrative appendix, as it were, to John's work, to provide a historical background to the correspondence.

The Lives have little information about general history, beyond the relationship between church and state. On the whole the biographers keep narrowly to the point, though William of Canterbury denounces Henry II's Irish wars,[67] and Fitz Stephen, who treats the subject more diffusely than the other writers, has an excursus on the office of chancellor.[68] And yet Becket came to be regarded as the personification, as it were, of the primacy of Canterbury – and to some extent Canterbury personified England. Becket's life therefore could not entirely be extricated from national events. A tendency to give him a generalized, almost mystical role in national history appears in the biographers' treatment of his posthumous power. The latter was regarded as a factor determining events in the years following his martyrdom: God avenged the murder with thunder and lightning and with the desolation of the cathedral for one year; and He avenged it by bringing defeat on Henry II through his rebellious sons. When Henry was finally reconciled with the church, having done penance at St Thomas's tomb and abrogated the objectionable clauses in the Constitutions of Clarendon, he was rewarded with victory over the Scots.[69] The attitude of the biographers to Henry was not fanatically hostile throughout, but decidedly restrained. Both Grim and Herbert of Bosham thought his act of penance wiped out the sins of the past. Herbert had a friendly conversation with him, in which Henry denied complicity in the murder,[70] and William Fitz Stephen solicited his favour with a small composition, a metrical prayer for the king.[71]

Nor do the Lives have much about the local affairs of Canterbury. The biographers did not imitate Eadmer's aim in the *Life of St. Anselm*,[72] to

---

[65] He added the letters 'ut qui desiderat et ad id suffit, totum habeat, si quis vitam viri modum exsilii, causae processum, vel ipsius rei requirit exitum'; ibid., p. 300. For Alan of Tewkesbury's use of documents see M. D. Knowles, A. J. Duggan and C. N. L. Brooke, 'Henry II's Supplement to the Constitutions of Clarendon' in *EHR*, lxxxvii (1972), pp. 757–71 *passim*.

[66] For Alan's explanation why he added a historical narrative for the period from the Council of Clarendon see ibid., pp. 322, 347, 351–2.

[67] See his *Miracles of St. Thomas: MTB*, vol. 1, pp. 180–1, 364, 378, 457, etc.

[68] *MTB*, vol. 3, p. 18.

[69] This is the interpretation of events given by William of Canterbury in the *Miracles of St. Thomas*, by Herbert of Bosham in the *Liber Melorum*, and (in a general way) by Edward Grim: *MTB*, vol. 1, pp. 487–93; vol. 3, pp. 544–8; vol. 2, p. 447, respectively.

[70] *MTB*, vol. 3, pp. 541–2.   [71] Ibid., pp. 78–81.

[72] Fitz Stephen refers to Eadmer's *Life of St. Anselm* in his discussion as to whether Becket deserved to be called a martyr (he cites Anselm's views on St Elphege); ibid., p. 61.

record the history and increase the reputation of Christ Church. There is a little on the history of St Thomas's shrine in Benedict of Peterborough (he records that a wall was built round the tomb[73] and that phials of lead were substituted for wooden ones, to hold the diluted blood of St Thomas on sale to pilgrims[74]). And both Benedict's and William's *Miracles of St. Thomas* concentrate on proving how great were the saint's posthumous powers, particularly in favour of pilgrims to Canterbury (the other biographers were interested in fostering the cult in a general, non-localized way). Moreover, none of the biographers was especially concerned with the claims of the primacy (as Eadmer had been). They describe Becket's assertion of the rights of Canterbury, on the occasion of the coronation of the young Henry in 1169 by the Archbishop of York, but they do not give the incident undue emphasis.

In fact the most remarkable local touch is William Fitz Stephen's famous description of London.[75] He introduces it with the excuse that Becket was his fellow citizen, and because Becket was born in London the city had as great a claim to glory as Canterbury, where he died. This is the earliest literary account of London and a good example of the contemporary taste for the realistic portrayal of places and social customs. First he describes the city's topography (St Paul's, the Tower, the Thames 'that mighty river, teeming with fish', the suburbs with gardens planted with trees, and excellent wells full of clear, clean water). Then he writes of the institutions and customs of London, the schools where scholars dispute, and the public cook-shop on the river bank, 'where every day you may find all sorts of food, roast, fried and boiled, large and small fish, coarse meat for the poor and the more delicate for the rich (such as venison and birds of all sizes)', a great convenience, he remarks, if friends arrive unexpectedly and there is no food ready at home. He describes the horse fair, where light palfreys were sold 'with shiny, glistening coats', and also heavier riding horses, cart horses, mares and foals. He ends by writing about the various entertainments and sports enjoyed by the Londoners, the miracle plays, cockfights and a ball-game. The ball-game was very popular: 'the scholars of each school have their own ball, and most of the workers in the trades have theirs. The older men, fathers and rich citizens, come on horseback to watch the contests of the young, reliving their own youth, as it were.' And then there were winter sports on the frozen marshes north of the city. Some people slide, some are dragged along on blocks of ice by a number of people 'who run along at great speed holding hands'. Others lash the shin-bones of animals to their feet and, using iron-tipped poles, project themselves along 'as fast as a bird

---

[73] *MTB*, vol. 2, p. 81.
[74] Ibid., p. 134. For these phials see also Herbert of Bosham; *MTB*, vol. 3, p. 552.
[75] *MTB*, vol. 3, pp. 2–13. For an English translation see H. E. Butler, 'A description of London by William Fitz Stephen' in F. M. Stenton, *Norman London* (Historical Association leaflets, nos 93, 94, 1934), pp. 25–35.

in flight or a bolt from a mangonel'. Sometimes two such skaters challenge one another, hitting each other with their poles as they glide and meet: there were nasty accidents when they fell and slid along distances from their own volition and broke an arm or leg, or got a badly grazed face, for 'wherever the ice touches the head, it scrapes and skins it entirely'. But the young, 'greedy for glory, craving for victory', don't mind.

The Cistercian order in Henry II's reign still retained its early enthusiasm. Its idealism was an important motive for the writing of the *Life of Ailred, Abbot of Rievaulx*, by Walter Daniel.[76] It also contributed to the continuance of the historiographical tradition at Durham which produced the three biographies of St Godric of Finchale.[77] Both at Durham and at Rievaulx the religious incentive to record the lives of the saints was strengthened by the Bedan tradition. The Cistercian and Northumbrian traditions were not separate, but inextricably involved. One of the Lives of Godric, by Reginald, prior of Durham, was written at the direct request of Ailred.[78] Bedan studies were cultivated at Rievaulx. Ailred's patron saint was St Cuthbert,[79] and his predecessor as abbot of Rievaulx, Maurice (1145–7), was regarded as a second Bede, 'refreshed by the bread of St. Cuthbert'.[80] The Durham writers and Walter Daniel alike portrayed their subjects as saints who rivalled the seventh-century Northumbrian ones in holiness and austerity: a vision of St Cuthbert appeared to St Godric,[81] and Ailred immersed himself in cold water, to subdue the desires of the flesh, just as St Cuthbert[82] – and Drythelm[83] – had done.

Like Bede, Walter Daniel and two of the biographers of St Godric wrote from first-hand information collected during the saint's lifetime. Germanus, prior of Durham from 1162 to 1168, knew Godric well (for the last seven years of Godric's life the saint placed himself under Germanus's jurisdiction).[84] Unfortunately Germanus's work has not survived, though some of its contents are known from the *Life* by Geoffrey who borrowed from it.

[76] The most recent edition is *The Life of Ailred of Rievaulx by Walter Daniel*, ed., with an English translation, F. M. Powicke (Nelson's Medieval Texts, 1950).

[77] The Lives were by Prior Germanus, Geoffrey and Reginald of Coldingham. Reginald's work is printed in *Libellus de Vita et Miraculis S. Godrici, heremitae de Finchale, auctore Reginaldo Monacho Dunelmensi*, ed. Joseph Stevenson (Surtees Soc., xx, 1845).

[78] *V et M SG*, p. 19. Cf. ibid., pp. ix–xii.

[79] *VAAR*, pp. xxxvii–xxxviii, xcv. See another of Reginald of Coldingham's works, *Reginaldi Monachi Dunelmensis Libellus de admirandis Beati Cuthberti Virtutibus*, ed. J. Raine (Surtees Soc., i, 1835), pp. 176–7. This work, mainly a collection of miracles relating to St Cuthbert, has some value to the historian because of the picture it gives of life in the north country in Reginald's time. For an English synopsis of passages bearing on social history see ibid., pp. 293–325.

[80] *VAAR*, pp. xxx and n. 3, l, xci, 33. Before entering Rievaulx, Maurice was a monk of Durham. See also F. M. Powicke 'Maurice of Rievaulx' in *EHR*, xxxvi (1921), 17–25.

[81] *V et M SG*, pp. 52–3.

[82] *VSC* (Anon.), c. 3 (pp. 81, 319 n.).

[83] *VAAR*, p. 25. See Bede, *HE*, v. 12.

[84] See *V et M SG*, p. vii.

Geoffrey, a monk of Durham, wrote a biography of Godric after the saint's death. Although he remembered as a boy seeing Godric and gives an account of his appearance from his own observation, he otherwise relies for information on the earlier Lives, that by Germanus and also the one by Reginald.[85] Reginald wrote at the instigation not only of Ailred, but also of Thomas, prior of Durham (1161/2–3).[86] He visited Godric to collect facts about him. At first Godric would not co-operate, but subsequently supplied the required information and Reginald sent him the finished book on his deathbed.[87] Reginald gives an interesting account of Godric's career (lasting for sixteen years) as a merchant and seaman before he became a hermit.[88] However, he mainly concentrates on the hagiographical aspects of his subject and is not concerned either with local or general history.

Walter Daniel's *Life of Ailred* has a wider interest. Walter had become a monk of Rievaulx in about 1150 and wrote soon after Ailred's death in 1167.[89] Though he wrote primarily as a hagiographer (he says little about Ailred's competent administration of Rievaulx[90]), he has some good realistic passages about Ailred, notably the extremely vivid account of his death. Walter was also interested in the spread of the Cistercian order in the north. He gives a eulogy of Rievaulx[91] and records the succession of the abbots before Ailred, with biographical details.[92] And he describes the foundation of one of Rievaulx's daughter houses, Revesby,[93] and mentions another, Dundrennan (here he has some reflections on the barbarous people of Galloway[94]).

Walter has one passage throwing light on general history. It describes the disordered condition of the north in Stephen's reign, and it helps to explain why nevertheless the Cistercians prospered and increased their possessions.[95] He tells how the anarchy affected Ailred's attitude to lands offered in free alms by knights to his monastery. Ailred, he says,[96] accepted these gifts

> because he realized that in this unsettled time such gifts profited knights and monks alike. For in those days it was hard for any to lead the good life unless they were monks or members of some religious order, so disturbed and chaotic was the land, reduced almost to a desert by the malice, slaughter and harryings of evil men. And so he desired that the land, for which almost all men were fighting to the death, should pass into the hands of the monks

[85] For Geoffrey's *Life of St. Godric* see *V et M SG*, pp. viii–ix. It is printed by the Bollandists, *Acta Sanctorum*, Mens. Maii, v. 70.
[86] *V et M SG*, p. 269.
[87] Ibid., pp. 315–17.
[88] Ibid., pp. 25, 28–33 *passim.*
[89] For its date see *VAAR*, pp. xxix–xxx.
[90] See *VAAR*, p. xvi.
[91] Ibid., pp. 36–8.
[92] Ibid., pp. 32–3.
[93] Ibid., pp. 27–8.
[94] Ibid., p. 45.
[95] For the phenomenal growth of the Cistercian order in the British Isles in Stephen's reign until the prohibition by the general chapter of the order in 1152 of further foundations see M. D. Knowles, *The Monastic Order in England* (2nd ed., Cambridge, 1963), pp. 245–6, 346.
[96] *VAAR*, p. 28.

for their good; and he knew that to give what they had, helped the possessors of goods to their salvation, and that, if they did not give, they might well lose both life and goods without any payment in return.

A generation later in the south of England, biographical writing was promoted by two partially interrelated factors, the historiographical tradition at Lincoln and the Carthusian order. Gerald of Wales wrote a number of biographies connected with Lincoln cathedral, where he stayed from 1196 to 1199.[97] He wrote probably to please, or at the direct request of, the cathedral chapter, and was apparently influenced by a previous Lincoln writer, Henry of Huntingdon. Between 1196 and 1200 he wrote the Lives of the bishops of Lincoln, revising the work between 1210 and 1214, and in about 1213 he composed his *Life of St. Hugh* of Avalon, adding a collection of miracles some time before 1223. He presented both books to Archbishop Stephen Langton.

The Lives of the bishops of Lincoln was ostensibly a *Life of St. Remigius*. Gerald wrote Remigius's biography for hagiographical reasons: Lincoln needed more saints connected with it, so Gerald, perhaps using the cathedral martyrology, concocted a *Life* representing Remigius (probably unjustifiably) in a hagiographical light.[98] This part of the work has no value to the historian. But then Gerald continued the work by appending the Lives of subsequent bishops of Lincoln up to the rule of St Hugh of Avalon. This part of the work is virtually the history of the cathedral. It records the lands acquired by the bishops, their gifts to the church and their building activities. It is apparently based on some now lost cathedral records. This is suggested by the fact that a later Lincoln historian, John de Schalby, a canon of Lincoln, writing in the first half of the fourteenth century, seems to have used a common source: he gives some of the same information as Gerald but has additions to, and omissions from, Gerald's work.[99] The account of St Hugh, written during his lifetime, is not like Schalby's probably because the common source used by both authors did not yet have an entry for St Hugh when Gerald wrote.[100]

Gerald gave a first-hand account of Hugh, which, though in general brief, has a remarkable description of St Hugh's pet swan. This passage

---

[97] Gerald of Wales's *Life of St. Remigius*, including the Lives of the bishops of Lincoln from Remigius to St Hugh, is printed in *GW*, vol. 7, pp. 3–80. His *Life of St. Hugh* is printed in ibid., pp. 83–147. For the dates of these works see J. F. Dimock in ibid., pp. xi–xii, xlix–l, respectively.

[98] For the dubious value of the *Life of St. Remigius* see ibid., pp. xvi–xxiii.

[99] For John de Schalby's work and its common source with Gerald see ibid., pp. xv–xvi. His Lives of the bishops of Lincoln are printed in ibid., pp. 193–216 (Appendix E). For an English translation with a useful introduction and notes, see J. H. Srawley, *The Book of John de Schalby Canon of Lincoln (1299–1333) concerning the Bishops of Lincoln and their Acts* (Lincoln Minster Pamphlets, no. 22, reprint 1966).

[100] *GW*, vol. 7, p. xl.

shows Gerald's acute powers of observation at their best: such an application of personal observation to natural history is in marked contrast to the accepted superstitions of the contemporary bestiaries.[101] This swan lived on Hugh's manor of Stow. Gerald describes its habits ('it would fly over the surface of the river, beating the water with its wings, and giving vent to loud cries'), and its appearance. The latter description is so realistic that the bird can be identified as a whooper swan:[102]

> It was about as much larger than a swan as a swan is than a goose, but in everything else, especially in its colour and whiteness, it closely resembled a swan, except that in addition to its size it did not have the usual swelling and black streak on its beak. Instead that part of its beak was flat and bright yellow in colour, as were also its head and the upper part of its neck.

Finally Gerald added to the *Life of St. Remigius* a section on six contemporary ecclesiastics (he included St Hugh again, but the rest belong to other dioceses) arranged in pairs: that is – Thomas Becket, archbishop of Canterbury, and Henry of Blois, bishop of Winchester (1129–71); Bartholomew, bishop of Exeter (1161–84) and Roger, bishop of Worcester (1164–79); and Baldwin, bishop of Worcester (1180–4) and archbishop of Canterbury (1184–90), and St Hugh. This part of the books is in Gerald's anecdotal style and is not serious history. However, it has some interesting facts, for example that the prince-like Bishop Henry of Blois kept a private zoo.[103] Such a section, appended to a work which up to this point had a unifying theme, is stylistically reminiscent of the *De Contemptu Mundi* which Henry of Huntingdon added to his history of England. Gerald's other Lincoln work, the *Life of St. Hugh*, is, like the *Life of St. Remigius* (so far as the latter relates to Remigius), primarily hagiographical. He added some miracles specifically to please Hugh of Wells, bishop of Lincoln (1209–35)[104] and some to please Roger, dean of Lincoln (1195–1223).[105] In a sense his *Life* is supplementary to that by Adam of Eynsham: Gerald concentrates on Hugh's career as bishop of Lincoln rather than his life as a Carthusian. But this biography is disappointingly thin and written as if Gerald did not care much about his subject.

In the south a generation later the Carthusian order provided an incentive for biographical writing. The order, the only one not made fun of by

---

[101] M. R. James writes of the medieval bestiary, 'Its literary merit is *nil*, and its scientific value (even when it had been most extensively purged of fable, and reinforced with soberer stuff) sadly meagre'; *The Bestiary: being a reproduction in full of the manuscript Ii. 4. 26 in the University Library, Cambridge*, ed. M. R. James (Roxburghe Club, 1928), p. 1.

[102] *GW*, vol. 7, p. 74. Mr Yealland, formerly Curator of Birds at the Zoological Society of London, informed me in a letter of 2 October 1967 that on the evidence of Gerald's description, 'the swan must be either the Whooper swan or Bewick's swan and I think it is probably the former'.

[103] *GW*, vol. 7, p. 45.　　　　[104] Ibid., pp. 1, 136.　　　　[105] Ibid., pp. 1, 137.

Walter Map, was introduced into England in 1178 or 1179 by Henry II who founded Witham priory.[106] The order attracted many men who were already monks but wished to lead more austere lives. It no doubt had the effect of stimulating biographical writing partly because the piety of its members deserved record. Moreover, the order had already produced a biography: Guigo de Castro wrote a *Life of St. Hugh* of Grenoble in about 1134. The Carthusian biographical tradition was strengthened by the literary tradition at Lincoln. As will be seen, Gerald of Wales's biography of St Hugh of Avalon was known to St Hugh's principal biographer, Adam of Eynsham. And it is almost certain that the Witham biographer of Adam, a monk of Witham, knew Adam of Eynsham personally. For the latter visited Witham with St Hugh on more than one occasion and undertook St Hugh's biography at the request of the Witham community.[107]

The Witham biographer, who wrote soon after 1214,[108] claims to have been Adam of Witham's close companion ('or rather pupil and disciple') for over ten years and to have been a bearer at his funeral.[109] Adam himself was a pious and scholarly monk who had joined the Carthusians because he wanted to follow their strict observance, having previously been abbot of the Premonstratensian house of Dryburgh. The Witham biography only survives in a fragmentary form. From what remains it seems that the *Life of Adam* was mainly hagiographical in tone, emphasizing Adam's piety. Nevertheless it has some local history of the priory (for example an account of a dispute between the prior and the king's officials over rights of pasture[110]), and one passage of wider interest, an eye-witness description of a visit to Witham of Hubert Walter.[111]

In its lack of interest in general events the Witham biography resembles the north-country ones: it is mainly of value for the study of religious life. The case with Adam of Eynsham's *Life of St. Hugh* is different.[112] Like Becket, Hugh was a national figure. He too opposed the king (but unlike Becket with moderation and humour), and travelled abroad (but as a voluntary exile, for spiritual reasons). Therefore though Adam of Eynsham is mainly concerned with Hugh's spiritual qualities, he had to follow his career in public affairs, and describes in detail his encounters with Henry II, Richard I and King John. Adam himself was a Benedictine monk of Eynsham abbey

---

[106] For the foundation of Witham see *VSH*, vol. 1, p. 46. Cf. M. D. Knowles, *The Monastic Order in England*, p. 381 and n. 3.

[107] See p. 313 below.

[108] The Witham biography is described and printed by André Wilmart, 'Maître Adam chanoine Prémontré devenu Chartreux à Witham' in *Analecta Praemonstratensia*, ix, fasc. 3–4 (1933), pp. 207–37. For its date see ibid., pp. 210–12.

[109] Ibid., p. 129.　　　　[110] Ibid., p. 225.　　　　[111] Ibid., pp. 225–8.

[112] The most recent edition is *Magna Vita Sancti Hugonis. The Life of St. Hugh of Lincoln*, ed., with an English translation, D. L. Douie and Hugh Farmer (Nelson's Medieval Texts, 1961, 1962, 2 vols). For Adam's career see ibid., vol. 1, pp. viii–xxi *passim*, 45.

in Oxfordshire, who at Hugh's request became his chaplain in the last three years of Hugh's life. The bishops of Lincoln had a close connection with Eynsham abbey because they were its patrons owing to the circumstances of its re-foundation (Bishop Remigius had re-founded it with monks from Stow in 1086).[113] After Hugh's death, Adam returned to Eynsham where he became sub-prior and then abbot (1213/14–28) from which office he was deposed for inefficient administration.[114] Although Adam wrote the *Life of St. Hugh* at the request of the whole community at Witham[115] and dedicated the work to the prior,[116] he seems to have wanted particularly to please two ex-Benedictines there, Robert who had been prior of St Swithun's, Winchester, from 1187 to 1191, and Ralph, formerly the sacrist of St Swithun's.[117]

Adam of Eynsham finished the biography of St Hugh soon before 1214.[118] He wrote primarily as a hagiographer. Besides Guigo's *Life of St. Hugh* of Grenoble and Gerald of Wales's *Life of St. Hugh* of Avalon,[119] he had studied a number of other saints' Lives.[120] He himself was the author of another hagiographical work: he recorded the vision which Edmund, his brother, a monk of Eynsham, had of the next world.[121] But though a hagiographer, Adam was not a blind one, and produced a convincing, lifelike portrait of Hugh's character, with minor criticisms. Nor does St Hugh dominate the *Life* in the same way as St Thomas dominated his biographies. Unlike the Becket biographers, Adam did not write for all England, to promote a cult of European fame, but he wrote in the first place for the small community at Witham. Therefore he included the local history of Witham, besides giving information about Lincoln and his own house of Eynsham.

Adam came under other literary influences as well as hagiographical ones, notably those prevalent in the cathedral school of Lincoln. He apparently acquired a taste for naturalistic descriptions from Gerald of Wales. He copies Gerald's description of St Hugh's pet swan, adding touches of his own: for example he describes St Hugh's devotion to the swan, which 'he fed with big fingers of bread', and the swan's devotion to St Hugh (whenever St Hugh came to the manor of Stow, where the swan lived, 'it gave a very loud cry and went to meet and greet him', accompanying him everywhere, even into his bedroom).[122] And Adam gives a realistic description of a six-months-old baby's response to St Hugh:[123]

[113] For Eynsham as the *Eigenkloster* of the bishops of Lincoln see Knowles, op. cit., p. 631.

[114] *VSH*, vol. 1, pp. xi–xiii. See also the *Eynsham Cartulary*, ed. H. E. Salter (Oxford Historical Soc. Publications, xlix (1907); li (1908)), i. xix–xx.

[115] *VSH*, vol. 2, p. 226.   [116] *VSH*, vol. 1, p. 1.   [117] Ibid., pp. 88–9.

[118] See ibid., pp. xii, xxi.

[119] He used Gerald's character-sketch of Hugh (*GW*, vol. 7, pp. 73–80) in the *Life of St. Remigius*; cf. p. 310 above and *VSH*, vol. 1, p. xiv and n. 1.

[120] See *VSH*, vol. 1, pp. xiv–xv and n. 1.

[121] See ibid., p. ix. The vision is printed in Salter, op. cit., ii. 285–371. It is also printed by H. Thurstan, 'Visio Monachi de Eynsham' in *An. Boll.*, xxii (1903), pp. 225–319.

[122] *VSH*, vol. 1, pp. 107–8. Cf. pp. 310–11 and n. 102 above.   [123] Ibid., pp. 129–30.

The tiny mouth and face relaxed in continuous chuckles. . . . It then bent and stretched out its little arms, as if trying to fly, and moved its head to and fro. . . . Next it took St Hugh's hand in both its small ones, and using all its strength raised it to its face, immediately licking rather than kissing it.

Moreover, Adam of Eynsham's *Life* has some features in common with Walter Map's *De Nugis Curialium*. It is possible that he knew Map personally, for he records that St Hugh had contact with Map, refusing to promote him or his nominee to the see of Hereford.[124] Like both Map and Gerald of Wales, Adam adopted the Suetonian method of using anecdotes to illustrate character (this feature is well illustrated by the descriptions quoted below of St Hugh's encounters with royalty). And Adam's satirical dislike of the royal court and courtiers could have partly derived from Map's influence. Adam comments, when recording with approval that Hugh refused to help Richard I raise an aid: 'thus by God's favour Hugh escaped the snares of courtiers'.[125] And he says of a royal messenger that 'his insolence had been greatly increased by his position at court'.[126]

Adam's character portrait of Hugh, his value as a local historian, and his accounts of Hugh's dealings with the kings of England, will be discussed in turn. Adam's primary objective was to depict Hugh as a saint. He relates at length the miracles worked by St Hugh, notably cures of the blind and sick. He is compared in the last pages to St Martin of Tours, and there are hints that Adam regarded him as the equal or superior of St Thomas: he indicates that on two occasions Hugh preferred his own judgment to Becket's, once when he opposed the building of a church dedicated to St Stephen, as Becket proposed,[127] and once when he forbade his archdeacons and others to impose fines on offenders, which had been Becket's practice.[128]

Nevertheless Adam does not produce a stylized portrait, but a convincingly lifelike one of a good man and conscientious bishop. He describes Hugh's assiduity over the burial of the dead,[129] in reforming the morals of his clergy,[130] and in the choice of clerics for the benefices in his gift.[131] He shows Hugh to have been warm-hearted and human, approving of family life. Hugh not only liked babies, but also regarded the married state with more favour than most churchmen of that generation. Adam writes:[132]

[Hugh] said, 'The kingdom of God is not confined only to monks, hermits and anchorites'. . . . He taught that even married people, who never rose above the natural obligations of their state, should not be considered devoid of the virtue of chastity, but

---

[124] *VSH*, vol. 2, p. 131.
[125] Ibid., p. 106.
[126] Ibid., p. 113.
[127] *VSH*, vol. 1, p. 122.
[128] *VSH*, vol. 2, p. 38.
[129] Ibid., pp. 75 et seq.
[130] Ibid., pp. 95-7.
[131] Ibid., pp. 96-7.
[132] Ibid., pp. 46-7.

equally with virgins and celebates would be admitted to the glory of the heavenly kingdom.'

Adam emphasizes the fact that Hugh, although involved in the affairs of the world, remained remote at heart, in communion with God. Hugh was often so lost in thought when riding that 'he saw nothing beyond the mane of his horse'.[133] Like St Anselm he hated business. He regarded judicial duties as unworthy of a bishop and the execution of them a cross and penance rather than a good work.[134] He absolutely refused ever to attend the audit of accounts in his exchequer.[135] On the other hand this disregard for worldly business meant that he was uncorruptible.[136] He never allowed his seal to be used on any letter unless what it said was true.[137] He refused to promote unsuitable candidates to prebends or livings, even if backed by the king.[138] And he refused to allow the king to employ the canons of Lincoln on diplomatic missions abroad.[139] Hugh's detachment was perhaps the cause of a fault mentioned by Adam, his irritability: St Anselm had slept through meetings; St Hugh when presiding over chapter snapped at the company.[140]

Adam relates that Hugh thought news of public events unsuitable for the ears of monks: the bishop of Bellay asked Hugh, when in France, to tell the monks of Arvières, with whom he was staying, about the treaty between 'our kings'. But Hugh replied: 'It is not right to bring such reports into the cloister or the cell, to forsake the cities in order to discuss secular matters in the wilderness.'[141] Hugh identified himself with the Carthusians even after he became bishop. Adam accompanied him in 1200 when he revisited La Chartreuse, and gives a paean on life in this 'holy community'.[142] He also describes Hugh's affection for Witham which he visited once or twice a year.[143] It was a centre of true Christian philosophy and its monks and lay brothers were like Elijah and Enoch, 'the two protagonists of justice and innocence'.[144]

Hugh's interest in monasticism gave Adam the excuse for including local history. He has a considerable amount of information about La Chartreuse, about the mode of life there, the solitary site, 'almost in the clouds',[145] the separate cells and the monks' hours of unbroken prayer and study. And he records how the monastery was founded by Bruno,[146] whose relics Adam saw.[147] Such facts no doubt interested the Witham monks. For them too Adam included the history of their house. He records how Henry II founded

---

[133] Ibid., p. 201. [134] Ibid., pp. 149–52. [135] Ibid., p. 152.
[136] Ibid. [137] Ibid., p. 48.
[138] See *VSH*, vol. 1, pp. 113–15, 119–20; vol. 2, p. 131. [139] *VSH*, vol. 2, p. 112.
[140] *VSH*, vol. 1, p. 124. For Anselm see pp. 134, 139 above.
[141] *VSH*, vol. 2, p. 174. For Hugh at La Chartreuse see ibid., vol. 1, pp. 22–59, 98–101 *passim*; vol. 2, 164–5.
[142] *VSH*, vol. 1, pp. 31 et seq.
[143] *VSH*, vol. 2, p. 44. For accounts of Hugh's visits to Witham see ibid., pp. 49–54, 62–4, 70–3.
[144] *VSH*, vol. 1, p. 77; vol. 2, p. 44. [145] *VSH*, vol. 1, p. 22.
[146] *VSH*, vol. 2, pp. 160–1. [147] Ibid., p. 162.

Witham and chose Hugh as prior, how the foreign monks were dismayed by the unfamiliar food and customs in England, and became unpopular in the neighbourhood.[148] He describes the community's early poverty (its wooden buildings and lack of lands) which Hugh remedied partly by persuading King Henry to give money.[149] Henry also gave the monks a very fine bible which greatly delighted them, for 'the correctness of the text and even more for the delicacy of the penmanship and general beauty'.[150] But Hugh discovered that the king had acquired the bible by false pretences from the monks of St Swithun's, Winchester, and therefore returned it. This bible was the Winchester bible which still survives today, one of the best illuminated manuscripts of the twelfth century. Adam continues to give facts about the priory's history after Hugh became bishop. For example he describes how on one of Hugh's visits the kitchen caught fire so that a number of the buildings were burnt (the account has information about the architecture of the priory buildings).[151] Moreover, Adam does not neglect his own house at Eynsham. In the course of recording that Hugh recovered his patronage over the abbey in the king's court against the crown, he gives a sketch of its early history.[152] His information about Lincoln is disappointingly slight, no doubt partly because Adam was only with Hugh during his last three years which were partly spent abroad and at Witham. He says practically nothing about Hugh's diocesan administration or building of the church, or about the famous cathedral school.[153]

Some of Adam's liveliest passages are about Hugh's meetings with the kings. Hugh angered Henry II by excommunicating the king's chief forester (for oppressing his tenants) and by refusing to collate a courtier to a prebend at Lincoln.[154] Henry summoned him to answer for his recalcitrance. When he knew Hugh was coming, he went into the neighbouring forest and sat down with his court. He ignored Hugh on his approach and began stitching a bandage on to his finger. Hugh, realizing that the king could not speak for anger, made a joke to the effect that such boorish behaviour and such a love of sewing were to be expected from a man descended from the bastard son (William the Conqueror) of a tanner's daughter (William's mother, Arlette, was the daughter of a tanner of Falaise, which was celebrated for its leatherwork). Henry burst out laughing, rolling on the ground in amusement at this 'courteous mockery', and they made friends. Hugh's quarrel with Richard I was more serious. In 1197 at the Council of Oxford Hubert Walter asked for an aid for Richard's war against the king of France. Hugh refused on the ground that Lincoln was only bound to provide knights to serve in England.[155] As a result of Richard's anger Hugh visited him in France. Adam describes how he overcame the king's rage by making Richard

[148] *VSH*, vol. 1, pp. 46–7.   [149] Ibid., pp. 60–72.   [150] Ibid., pp. 85–6.
[151] *VSH*, vol. 2, p. 72.   [152] Ibid., pp. 39–41.
[153] For the cathedral school at Lincoln see *VSH*, vol. 1, pp. xxix–xxx.
[154] Ibid., pp. 115–19.   [155] *VSH*, vol. 2, pp. 98–9. Cf. vol. 1, pp. xlii–xliv.

give him the kiss of peace. At first Richard refused and turned away, but Hugh argued (Adam gives his words) and twice, seizing the king's cloak, shook him violently, until Richard, 'overcome by his courage and determination, kissed him with a smile'.[156]

Adam has quite a lot to say about King John. He was clearly committed to the cause of the church in the political circumstances of the time and was preoccupied with John's rule. His attitude, like that of Hugh, was in theory uncompromisingly antagonistic to the king, though the tone of his writing, through personal observation, sometimes gives John a touch of pathos. Adam's sketches of John's behaviour seem exceptionally realistic and free from the exaggeration and bombast of the chroniclers. He introduces John's reign with the remark that 'we have now endured him for fourteen years three months', and that Hugh foresaw his folly.[157] When John visited Hugh on his deathbed, the latter, having 'no illusions about him', refused to answer his kind words so that 'the king was obviously much distressed and said he was ready to do anything he wanted.'[158] Not long before John's accession (the circumstances of which are fully described[159]), Hugh had met him, then count of Mortain, at Fontevrault. Adam gives a brilliant account of the visit, during which Hugh tried to persuade John to improve his behaviour. John showed him an amulet he wore round his neck to bring him good luck in defending his domains. Hugh immediately reprimanded him for putting his trust in an inanimate stone rather than in God.[160] He criticized him again for his behaviour at mass: John hesitated to make his offering of twelve gold pieces, which the chamberlain had given him, saying that if he had had them a few days earlier he would have pocketed them.[161] He offended Hugh again by telling him to cut his sermon short so that he could have lunch.[162] And Adam describes how Hugh showed John the carvings on the tympanum of the abbey door, using the pictures of the Last Judgment ('a magnificent example of the human sculptor's art') to impress on John the terrors of eternal damnation. Hugh added that 'such sculptures or pictures were at the entrances to churches for a very good reason, namely that those about to enter and pray to God in their need, should understand what would be their last and final extremity and so would pray for forgiveness for their sins.' But John turned aside and pointed out to Hugh some carvings of kings, saying that it was them he wished to emulate.[163]

[156] *VSH*, vol. 2, p. 101. [157] Ibid., p. 74. Cf. p. 140. [158] Ibid., p. 188.
[159] Ibid., p. 137. [160] Ibid., p. 139. [161] Ibid., p. 142.
[162] Ibid., p. 143. [163] Ibid., pp. 140–1.

15

Historians of King John's Reign

In the reign of King John the historiographical trends of the late twelfth century continued. The north-country style of the Augustinian William of Newburgh, with its excellent narrative, good stories (especially about the supernatural) and independent judgments, was paralleled in the work of Ralph of Coggeshall written soon after John's death. The satirical tradition of Lincoln reappears in Gerald of Wales's strictures on King John. And a 'romance' history was written to commemorate the activities of William the Marshal. But in no case were the earlier styles reproduced without change.

The most notable development in the early thirteenth century was the emergence of annals as the commonest form of historical writing. The annalistic tradition, going back to early Anglo-Saxon times and revived after the Conquest at Worcester, had been adopted in the late twelfth century at Winchester[1] and Winchcombe.[2] In about 1200 Gervase, or a continuator, had written annals at Canterbury.[3] Early in the thirteenth century annals were written in a number of religious houses, for example in the Augustinian priories of Southwark, Merton, Dunstable and St Osyth's, and in the Benedictine abbeys of Worcester, Bury St Edmunds and Winchester.[4] But the best, the fullest and most sophisticated annals are those attributed (on slender evidence[5]) to a canon of the Augustinian priory of Barnwell in Cambridgeshire.

The fuller, more detailed, annals constitute the typical monastic chronicle (the annals of Dunstable, Worcester, Winchester and 'Barnwell' fall into this category). The term 'monastic' is not, strictly speaking, applicable to the chronicles of the regular canons (as the Augustinians were not monks). However, it can be appropriately used of those of their chronicles which are indistinguishable in form from the normal monastic productions.

Many of the chronicles are mutually interdependent. The fashion developed of lending the chronicle of one house to another, where they would be copied (with the addition and omission of material in accordance with the interests of the copyist) and continued. The exact relationship between them

[1] See pp. 252 and nn. 46, 47, 253.
[2] For the Winchcombe annals see pp. 260 n. 97, 405 n. 13. They were apparently compiled fairly contemporarily with the last few years they record.
[3] See pp. 254, 260.   [4] See pp. 331 et seq.   [5] See pp. 339-42.

is hard, often impossible, to determine, because some chronicles have been lost. This pooling of chronicles was done regardless of the order to which the houses concerned belonged: a Cistercian house would borrow Benedictine annals and a Benedictine one those of the Augustinian canons, and *vice versa*.[6] Most chronicles are anonymous: even if the name of a compiler is known, we may not be certain how much of the work he wrote. And his own personality is submerged in the chronicler's overriding purpose of providing a record of local and national events. Unlike the 'romance' historian, the chronicler did not try to amuse. And unlike dedicated historians such as William of Newburgh, he rarely commented on events: he reported news, without editorial comment.

The keeping of a chronicle had become part of routine business in some houses. The chronicles are a mixture of local and national affairs, the proportion varying from house to house. The style is often poor, and the changes of hand in the surviving contemporary manuscripts suggest multiple authorship in some cases. The Winchester chronicler attributes the literary imperfections of chronicles to changes of authorship. His preface also makes it clear that he regarded chronicle-keeping as a quasi-official duty:[7]

> As chronicles are necessary in religion, for various reasons, we have extracted these things for you from old rolls and neglected charters, collecting them like crumbs from the Lord's table lest they perish. The rough and unpolished Latin should not offend your cultured taste as you are accustomed to rely more on the sense than the words of the Scriptures, to consume the fruit rather than the pages themselves! Nor is [its lack of style] to be wondered at,

[6] A good example still survives of a chronicle lent to a neighbouring house at this period. The monks of St Albans lent their copy of Ralph Diceto to the Augustinian canons of Dunstable. The manuscript is now BM MS. Royal 13 E VI (C in Stubbs's edition; see *RD*, vol. 1, p. xci). It also contains annals from 1199 to 1213 added to Diceto at St Albans. Both Diceto and the additional annals were copied to provide the basis for the Dunstable annals; see Cheney, 'The Dunstable annals', pp. 84–8. For the similar lending of the chronicle of Bury St Edmunds (to Peterborough) see p. 403 below.

[7] This passage is printed as the preface to the Worcester chronicle (*Ann. Mon.*, vol. 4, p. 355), and is attributed by Professor Galbraith to the Worcester chronicler; see V. H. Galbraith, 'The St. Edmundsbury chronicle, 1296–1301' in *EHR*, lviii (1943), p. 53. But the Worcester writer copied it from Vespasian E IV which descends from a lost Winchester chronicle; see Denholm-Young, 'Winchester-Hyde chron.', p. 88. For an excellent example of a monastic chronicle written by a number of authors (from the mid-twelfth century to the late thirteenth century) see *The Chronicle of Melrose*, facsimile, ed. A. O. Anderson and M. O. Anderson (limited edition, London 1936). This edition shows the numerous changes of hand in the manuscript of the chronicle (BM MS. Cotton Faustina B IX), the spaces left between annals for additions, the early corrections, etc. The Melrose chronicle, covering the years from 781 to 1275, is Scotland's principal monastic chronicle; the contemporaneous portion has much information not found elsewhere, and is particularly useful for the history of Scotland and northern England in the thirteenth century. The chronicle is printed in *Chronica de Mailros*, ed. Joseph Stevenson (Bannatyne Club, Edinburgh 1835). See also Denholm-Young's review of the Andersons' edition in *Medium Ævum*, v (1936), pp. 129–31, and A. O. Anderson's rejoinder in ibid., vi (1937), pp. 72–5.

since the book is added to every year, and, being therefore composed by various people, it may fall into the hands of someone who writes barbarously. So let it be your responsibility that a sheaf of loose leaves be added to the end of the book, on which should be noted in pencil the deaths of illustrious men and anything memorable you hear concerning the state of the kingdom. At the end of the year let he who is ordered (not just anyone who likes) record for posterity what he thinks truest and best, writing briefly in the book itself. Then the old sheaf of pages should be taken away and a new one substituted.

Historiographical tradition was one reason for chronicle-keeping. There were two other reasons, one domestic, the other political. The domestic reason was the development of monastic archives, the collection of charters and the composition of cartularies. Chronicles were a near necessity to provide chronological guides to the monastery's business affairs (its acquisition of property, lawsuits and the like). And once the framework of a local history was constructed, the national history was fitted into it. It will be shown below[8] how at Bury St Edmunds the record of local events generated general chronicles. In the same way the chronicles of Canterbury, Dover and Worcester began primarily as local histories. Archive consciousness permeates the chronicles, profoundly affecting the treatment of general as well as local history. Documents are copied in full in most chronicles. Some of these documents are unique and of first-rate importance for thirteenth-century history. The chroniclers were no doubt encouraged to copy documents not only by the archive tradition of their own houses, but also by the example of Matthew Paris and Roger of Howden.

The official nature of these chronicles had advantages. It encouraged the continuity of historical writing, obviating the risks and uncertainties inherent in individual composition. As the chronicles were regarded as records, they tended to be accurate.[9] Furthermore a monastic chronicler profited from the status of his monastery. As a result of his relative security *vis-à-vis* the outside world (he was not dependent for his livelihood on the king or on any great magnate), he could criticize the government with comparative impunity. As an inmate of an abbey he benefited from the information it attracted as a centre of communications. But the chronicles have the disadvantages of official histories. They reflect corporate self-interest, and their outlook is narrow and their scope circumscribed. The author took his stand on the welfare of his house: he saw the outside world through a distorting lens whenever it impinged on the monastery's interests. And when the monastery's affairs were not concerned he was inclined to ignore external events.

The nature of annals is one reason why the attitude of contemporary historians to King John tended to be veiled and reserved. It was left to Roger

[8] See pp. 380–1.   [9] On the value of annals in general see also p. 31.

of Wendover and more especially to Matthew Paris to attack King John's character with full-blooded, homiletic invective, and to attempt a coherent interpretation of the constitutional issues of the reign.[10] The St Albans historians were helped by knowledge of later events. But though sometimes they were, perhaps wilfully, misled by the myth which developed round King John, they said remarkably little which is not in embryo in the earlier chroniclers.[11]

I have already shown that Richard of Devizes[12] and the biographer of St Hugh of Lincoln[13] did not like John in early life, and have discussed the evolution of a quasi-constitutional view of John's reign by Gervase of Canterbury (or his continuator).[14] But neither Gervase nor the other contemporary historians attempted an exhaustive analysis of the reign for a number of reasons. They lived too near events to see them in perspective and to interpret them in the light of later developments. Some were restrained in their criticism of John by discretion – by fear of alienating valuable friends.[15] Nor were they all equally concerned with politics. Ralph of Coggeshall had wide and varied interests, and of the annalists only the 'Barnwell' chronicler wrote primarily about political issues. The other annalists divided their attention between local history, the history of their order, church affairs – and politics. Moreover, their comments were circumscribed by the succinct, factual and, on the whole, objective type of historiography they had adopted.

Gerald of Wales attacks John bitterly in De Principis Instructione (On the Instruction of a Prince).[16] But here he was writing as a satirist, not a historian, and did not hesitate to turn the evidence topsy-turvy to prove his point. He tried to show that God punished a prince who ruled contrary to His precepts. John was the worst of tyrants, the wickedest of his dynasty, punished

---

[10] See pp. 367 et seq.

[11] I here agree with Bishop Stubbs, who asserted that Matthew Paris's view of King John was corroborated by the earlier writers (see WC, vol. 2, pp. xi–xiv and notes). Professor Galbraith, although he pointed out that Matthew Paris's views are to be found in Roger of Wendover, overemphasizes, I think, the novelty of the St Albans estimate of King John (see V. H. Galbraith, Roger Wendover and Matthew Paris (Glasgow 1944), pp. 17–19). However, Stubbs's opinion that Matthew Paris gave a just and accurate assessment of King John cannot be maintained in the light of modern research on the non-literary records of John's reign. The conclusions of the contemporary historians were based on incomplete evidence. Moreover, John's contemporaries judged him by their own values (they praised good 'lordship', success in war, etc.) and not by the standards of modern historians (who base their assessment on efficient administration and the like). For a modern assessment of King John, and the extent to which recent research has confirmed or contradicted the views of the contemporary chroniclers see J. C. Holt, King John (Historical Assoc., 1963), passim. Professor Holt includes chronicles written in the generation after John's death, and those of the continental writers, which we do not discuss here.

[12] See p. 250.   [13] See p. 317.   [14] See p. 258.

[15] See pp. 347, 431 and n. 265.

[16] De Principis Instructione, ed. G. F. Warner in GW, vol. 8, pp. 309–11, 328–9. For the date of the work, and for a suggestion that Gerald's invectives against John were due to John's failure to give Gerald the bishopric of St David's, see ibid., pp. xv–xvi, l–lii.

by the rebellion of the barons. Gerald criticizes the barons because their opposition was too late to save the church from the king's oppression and the country from degradation by foreign mercenaries. Nor, Gerald says, could the barons have succeeded without the help of the French. By way of contrast Gerald extols the French kings who had been rewarded by God with victory over the English, because of their humility and love of peace. These views show no attempt at objective political analysis: Gerald was trying, even perversely, to prove that it was necessary at all costs to preserve God's law and defend the interests of the clergy.

The author of the *History of William the Marshal* was also prevented by his historiographical genre from offering a comprehensive view of politics. John's actions were only incidental to the main theme, the career of William the Marshal. Moreover, as the author wrote in the tradition of chivalric romance, one of his aims was to demonstrate his hero's loyalty to his lord – King John was the Marshal's lord. The desire to emphasize the Marshal's loyalty was of course reinforced by the fact that he was in reality one of John's supporters. And as a trouvère the author's object was to amuse: and political discussion and the record of sad events were not entertaining. Therefore, though the author of the *History* clearly disliked John, he limited his criticism to personal disparagement.

Thus none of these writers undertook a reflective analysis either of John's character or of the baronial opposition. Nevertheless a marked similarity of attitude to king and politics can be detected. John was condemned by the standards of all his contemporaries. The ecclesiastics hated him for his treatment of the church. The author of the *History of William the Marshal* condemned him for his lack of chivalry (his treachery and cowardice). And all condemned him for involving the country in civil war. Historians could praise a decisive victory or a gay tournament, but none approved of the suffering inflicted on ordinary people. All the writers regarded the accession of Henry III as the beginning of a new era. They, like the barons, could not hate an innocent child, especially one under the protection of the Church.

I shall discuss the chronicles in turn: first, the chronicle of Ralph of Coggeshall; second, the monastic annals; third, the 'Barnwell' chronicle; and last, the *History of William the Marshal*.

Ralph of Coggeshall was abbot of the small Cistercian abbey of Coggeshall in Essex from 1207 to 1218 when he resigned because of ill-health.[17] His succession as abbot is recorded in the chronicle under 1207:[18]

---

[17] The standard edition of the chronicle is *Radulphi de Coggeshall Chronicon Anglicanum*, ed. Joseph Stevenson (*RS*, 1875). For his resignation from the abbacy see ibid., p. 187. See also G. Morin, 'Le Cistercien Ralph de Coggeshall et l'auteur des *Distinctiones Monasticae*' in *Revue Bénédictine*, xlvii (1935), pp. 348–55.

[18] *RC*, pp. 162–3.

Dom. Thomas, the fifth abbot of Coggeshall, died. To him succeeded Dom. Ralph, monk of the same place, who wrote this chronicle from the capture of the Holy Cross until the eleventh year of King Henry III, son of King John, and took care to record faithfully certain visions which he heard from venerable men, for the edification of many.

The chronicle as we have it does not correspond to this description. It begins in 1066, not 1187, and ends in 1224, not 1227. Moreover, it is not certain that the chronicle is all the work of one man.[19] The earliest surviving manuscript, which looks like an early draft (there are numerous marginal additions, corrections and erasures), has changes in handwriting and shades of ink throughout.[20] Not all these changes indicate a new scribe (though the annals for 1206 to 1212 are certainly not in the same hand as the rest of the text);[21] they could merely mean that Ralph was writing sporadically,[22] or that he employed a number of scribes to copy his autograph. From 1187 to 1206 and from 1213 to 1224 the chronicle has a stylistic unity (the sections from 1066 to 1186 and 1206 to 1212 are not in the graphic narrative style of the rest of the chronicle but consist of brief annals). Therefore it is likely that the entry under 1207 quoted above means that Ralph was the original author from 1187 and that he, or someone else, prefixed the annals from 1066 to 1186 en bloc. It seems probable that the section from 1206 to 1212 is distinctive because Ralph's original text was lost, and that the present text was interpolated after some of the subsequent chronicle had been written.[23] Why

---

[19] F. M. Powicke writes that 'it is difficult to estimate [Ralph of Coggeshall's] responsibility for the [work]'; F. M. Powicke, 'Roger of Wendover and the Coggeshall chronicle' in *EHR*, xxi (1906), p. 286 n. 1.

[20] BM MS. Cotton Vespasian D X. Joseph Stevenson takes this manuscript as the basis of his text, giving variant readings in the footnotes from two other early texts, College of Arms MS. XI and Bibl. Nat. MS. St Victor 476 (now MS. Lat. 15076; see *RC*, pp. xvi–xvii). Hardy, *Catalogue*, vol. 3, pp. 66–7, states that the Arundel and St Victor's MSS. are copies, or copies of a copy, of Vespasian D X which is very near a first draft (see n. 23, p. 326 n. 51 below). Arundel XI is very little later in date than Vespasian D X: this is shown by the fact that some of the almost contemporary marginal additions in Vespasian D X are in the margins of Arundel XI, also in nearly contemporary hands (see e.g. *RC*, pp. 8 n. 7, 9 n. 4, 17 n. 4, 21 n. 1, 26 n. 1); however, Arundel XI incorporates into the text some of the marginalia in Vespasian D X (see e.g. *RC*, pp. 8 n. 5, 9 n. 4).

[21] See note 23.

[22] Powicke, 'Roger of Wendover', p. 286, suggests that one such pause in the composition of the chronicle occurred in 1194. He bases this supposition partly on the evidence of a change of hand in the manuscript (there is certainly a change of ink, but I am not sure there is a change of hand) and on the fact that Roger of Wendover uses Coggeshall up to this point (Powicke, op. cit., p. 287, disputes Luard's contention that Wendover used Coggeshall after 1195).

[23] The annals from 1206 to 1212 start at the top of a new leaf (Vespasian D X, f. 112) and end at the bottom of the verso of the same leaf. Collation of the gatherings shows that the one to which folio 12 belongs had at least eight leaves, the first four of which are now missing (folio 12 is pasted to the stub of the fourth leaf of the gathering). This, combined with the new hand on folio 12, 12ᵛ, and the annalistic style of the entries, suggests that the text here replaces some earlier, now lost, text by Ralph. These annals were supplied soon after the date of the last (1212): this is proved by the fact that (1) the handwriting is of the early thirteenth century,

the entry under 1207 states that Ralph continued to 1227 is not clear: probably this was simply a mistake. From Richard I's last years the chronicle has passages which were written up with the help of more or less contemporary information (there is for example the contemporary account of Richard's capture). By 1223 at latest it was composed within three years or so of the events recorded.[24]

Although Coggeshall was a comparatively unimportant house, Ralph was in close touch with contemporary events. Coggeshall was within fifty miles of London, and as a member of the Cistercian order it was in communication not only with Cîteaux but also with other Cistercian houses on the continent. So Ralph was kept well informed. He heard about Richard I's engagement with the Saracens in 1191 from one of the combatants, Hugh de Neville.[25] He heard about Richard's capture by the emperor from another eye-witness, the king's chaplain Anselm.[26] Milo, abbot of the Cistercian abbey of Le Pin (near Vienne) and the king's almoner,[27] gave him the details of Richard's death: Milo heard the king's last confession and administered extreme unction. Ralph also got information from abroad from the *littérateur* Gervase of Tilbury (concerning the catharist heresy in France), who belonged to the household of William archbishop of Rheims.[28] Master W. de Argenti, 'who lived in those parts', told him the story of how the bishop of Chartres imposed a fitting penance on some of the French king's castellans for hanging a converse of the Cistercian abbey of Preuilly.[29]

Ralph names a number of informants for home affairs. Sir Richard de Colne told him about the two 'green' children found in Suffolk,[30] John de Savigny described the hurricane at Newark after King John's death,[31] and

---

and (2) they are in the hand of the rest of the text in Arundel XI (for which see note 20). The St Victor MS. does not have this section, as it breaks off in 1201 and does not start again until 1213 (see Powicke, 'Roger of Wendover', p. 286 n. 2, and *RC*, pp. 117 n. 3, 165 n. 3).

[24] The comparative contemporaneity of the chronicle at latest by 1223 has been established by Francis Wormald, 'The rood of Bromholm' in *Journal of the Warburg Institute*, i (1937-8), p. 36. Professor Wormald shows that Ralph of Coggeshall's account of the rood of Bromholm *s.a.* 1223 was written in about 1226, as it mentions that beautiful new buildings replaced the old ones at Bromholm (as a result of the prosperity brought to Bromholm by pilgrimages to the rood). An entry on the Close Rolls, *Rotuli Litterarum Clausarum* (Record Commission, 1833, 1844, 2 vols), vol. 2, p. 1406, shows that these buildings were erected in *c.* 1226.

[25] *RC*, p. 45. Hugh de Neville (d. 1222) accompanied Richard I on the crusade and was at the siege of Joppa. In 1198 he became chief justice of the forests, and was one of King John's principal advisers.

[26] *RC*, p. 54. The account of Richard I's capture (ibid., pp. 54-5, part of which is quoted on p. 330 below) was fitted into a gap left in the text after the subsequent passage was written (see ibid., p. 54 n. 4).

[27] Ibid., p. 98.   [28] Ibid., pp. xiii, 122.

[29] Ibid., pp. 200-1. Preuilly is in the diocese of Sens. It is noteworthy that Ralph of Coggeshall is a valuable authority for Anglo-French relations. He is 'the best and almost the only authority' for the forfeiture by John of the Angevins' continental possessions to Philip Augustus in 1202; see R. Fawtier, *The Capetian Kings of France*, translated by L. Butler and R. J. Adam (London and New York 1960), p. 147.

[30] Ibid., p. 119. See pp. 330-1 below.   [31] Ibid., p. 184.

Robert, a converse at Coggeshall ('a good man') provided information about a vision he had had.[32] Presumably Ralph obtained the details of the siege of Bedford in 1223 from the monks of the Cistercian abbey of Wardon, 'who suffered great and irreparable loss because their magnificent woods, especially the trees around the abbey, were cut down to make siege-engines.'[33] The interconnections of the order must have enabled Ralph to obtain his full information about the quarrel between the Cistercians and King John in 1200, over the king's attempt to tax the monks.[34] And presumably Ralph knew about the ecclesiastical council held at Oxford in 1222 because either he himself or someone he knew attended it.[35]

However, although Ralph had a good supply of oral evidence, he does not seem to have been able to obtain many documents: he transcribes into his chronicle only three letters (one of Richard I on his French war,[36] one of King John ordering the sheriffs to protect the Cistercians' property,[37] and one of Pope Innocent III urging support for the crusade[38]). Ralph admits that he does not have the text of the letter of the Cistercian general chapter to King John on the taxation issue in 1200, and so can only give the gist of it.[39]

Ralph, though he had his own individual characteristics as a writer, was influenced by a number of contemporary literary and historiographical conventions. Romance literature helped to determine the style of his work. He gives long sections of colourful narrative, with apostrophes to the reader, and imaginary speeches and conversations. To some extent he regards Richard I as a romance hero. He describes him as renowned,[40] warlike[41] and generous,[42] and says he was universally mourned at his death.[43] He emphasizes that Richard was a good Christian knight, assiduous in his attendance at mass (taking an interest in the music and encouraging the cantors),[44] and beneficent to the church (at his coronation Richard gave an annuity of 20s. to the Cistercian general chapter and was the benefactor of a number of religious houses, including the Cistercian ones at Le Pin and Pontigny).[45]

But Ralph also describes another side of Richard's character. Possibly it was the influence of romance literature which led Ralph to expatiate on Richard's avarice (one of the worst vices in the chivalric code), but more likely it was the recognition of reality. Ralph writes that no one could enter

---

[32] Ibid., pp. 134–5.
[33] Ibid., p. 207.
[34] For the quarrel see ibid., pp. 102–10.
[35] Ibid., pp. 190–1.
[36] Ibid., pp. 84–5.
[37] Ibid., p. 110.
[38] Ibid., pp. 113–16.
[39] Ibid., p. 106.
[40] 'rex inclytus'; ibid., p. 47.
[41] 'rex ille bellicosus'; p. 49; cf. p. 94.
[42] 'ob excellentis animi liberalitatem et praeclarae militiae strenuitatem, omnium Normannici generis regum unicum fore speculum sperabimus'; ibid., p. 91.
[43] Ibid., p. 91.
[44] Ibid., pp. 96–7. For the relationship between chivalry and Christianity see Sidney Painter, *French Chivalry* (Baltimore 1940), chapter III.
[45] *RC*, p. 97.

his inheritance without paying an exorbitant sum[46] and that Richard made a profit from the resealing of charters when he changed the royal seal.[47] 'No age can remember or history tell of any king, even one who ruled for a long time, who demanded and took so much money from his kingdom, as this king extorted and amassed within the five years after his return from captivity.'[48] Ralph admits that Richard's need for money, which was due to political circumstances, provided him with some justification. But in the end God struck him down with a death unworthy of such a warlike king, to punish him for his sins. Moreover, Ralph describes Richard's terrible temper, how he scowled at anyone who interrupted him at business, and how his fury could only be appeased by money and promises.[49]

Romance literature had no apparent influence on Ralph's attitude to King John (though Ralph may have regarded him as the antithesis of the chivalric knight). Ralph's dislike of John was probably the result of quick disillusionment. It would not be true to attribute his disillusion to ill-feeling engendered by John's treatment of the Cistercians. Ralph's detailed account of the quarrel between John and the Cistercians in 1200 ends on a note of amity: the king forgave the abbots, asked for the prayers of the general chapter, and promised to found a Cistercian house and to protect the order.[50] Ralph became disillusioned because of John's political behaviour.[51] He seems to have begun by being fairly favourable to John who 'restored peace abroad and loved peace at home', and deplored the damage done to the kingdom by the frequent wars of his father and brothers.[52] Ralph also says that John was pleased that Hubert de Burgh did not carry out the cruel

---

[46] Ibid., p. 92.   [47] Ibid., p. 93.   [48] Ibid., p. 93.   [49] Ibid., p. 92.
[50] Ibid., pp. 109–10.
[51] Powicke, 'Roger of Wendover', pp. 287–93, argues that Roger of Wendover preserves three anti-John passages which were originally in Coggeshall but which Ralph rewrote in order to mitigate the aspersions on John. In each case the passage now in Coggeshall is on an erasure in Vespasian D X, the earliest text. The first passage, *s.a.* 1192, in Wendover (*RW*, vol. 1, p. 217) says that John tried to subdue England and 'later events proved that this was his intention'. For the sentence in inverted commas Coggeshall (*RC*, p. 52) has 'because he had thrown out his chancellor on account of his excessive tyranny'. The second passage in Wendover (*RW*, vol. 1, p. 229), *s.a.* 1193, also accuses John of treachery. He says that John plotted to have himself crowned king: Coggeshall (*RC*, p. 61) has instead a notice of the succession to the bishopric of Bath. The third passage (*RW*, vol. 1, p. 230) says that King Philip took the city of Évreux in 1193, and put it in John's custody. Coggeshall (*RC*, p. 62) says that Philip took Évreux and committed great tyranny there. Powicke argues that an early recension of Coggeshall, to 1195 (where there is a change of hand in Vespasian D X), reached St Albans before Ralph's revision. This proposition cannot be proved. The variant passage *s.a.* 1192 in Wendover would fit in the erasure in Vespasian D X (f. 64), but the two variant passages *s.a.* 1193 in Wendover are too long for the erasures in Vespasian D X (f. 67). However, Wendover may have expanded Ralph's sentences. On the present evidence it is not possible to be sure that Ralph was responsible for these anti-John passages. It should be noted that Powicke's transcript of the variant passages in Coggeshall does not correspond to the readings in Vespasian D X in a number of places. Stevenson's transcript is more accurate, but also has errors.
[52] *RC*, p. 101. Gervase of Canterbury says that at the beginning of the reign John preferred peaceful negotiations to war; *GC*, vol. 2, pp. 92–3.

sentence against Arthur of blinding and castration.[53] But Ralph's attitude soon changed. By 1203 he is commenting on John's fear of treachery.[54] This, and John's lack of decisiveness, are emphasized under 1205 (with reference to the proposed Poitevin campaign).[55] During John's negotiations with the barons which culminated in the granting of Magna Carta, Ralph twice accuses John of acting with duplicity, 'as was his custom'.[56] Ralph in particular accuses John of forging letters.[57] He accuses him of cowardice in the face of Louis in 1216: on seeing Louis's army John 'fled in terror, weeping and lamenting'.[58] Ralph implies that the English army could easily have captured Louis if John had not acted so ignobly.[59] Ralph apparently blamed John's counsellors for some of his failures. When John abandoned the Poitevin campaign in 1205, Ralph says that the disbanded army 'cursed the archbishop and other counsellors of the king'.[60] And when John fled in 1215, it was 'on account of the stupidity of his counsel'.[61] Ralph mentions John's quick temper[62] and gluttony ('his belly was always insatiable, guzzling to repletion'[63]).

Like the other historians, Ralph was on the side of the barons. Their army was the army of God[64] and they were fighting 'to protect the liberty of the church and of the whole realm'.[65] But he deplored the depredations of the civil war. He relates the suffering of Coggeshall abbey, how the royal army broke into the church during terce and drove away twenty-two horses belonging to the bishop of London and others.[66] Ralph records the ravaging of East Anglia,[67] the north,[68] and Kent (which the king's army 'cruelly depopulated'). He describes the treatment of Rochester cathedral: the army 'stabled its horses in the church, cloisters and monastic offices, while the soldiers feasted and drank regardless of the monks.'[69] Such chaos was one reason why Ralph became a 'royalist' on the accession of Henry III (God was now on the side of the king's army). Another reason why Ralph sup-

---

[53] *RC*, p. 141.

[54] Ibid., p. 144. 'Rege vero Johanne nullum praesidium ferre obsessis volente, eo quod suorum proditionem semper timeret'.

[55] Ibid., pp. 152–3.

[56] 'Rex quoque Johannes, fraudulosam pro more suo stropham commentatus, literas jam direxerat Philippo regi Franciae'; ibid., p. 176; cf. p. 173.

[57] He accuses John of forging papal letters (to get armed help from Flanders against the barons), and letters from the barons (to the king of France asking him not to allow Louis to interfere in English affairs); *RC*, pp. 174, 176–7 respectively.

[58] '[Lodowici] appulsione visa, statim Johannes rex perterritus fugit, flens et lamentans, et omnis exercitus eius cum eo. . . . Rege sic ignaviter fugiente'; *RC*, p. 181; cf. p. 182.

[59] 'Et quidem cum sola navis domini Lodovici, aliis a longe remigantibus, applicuisset, nisi fata regem urgerent, facillime illum cum omnibus suis cepisset, utpote per biduum in mari procelloso valde fatigatos'; *RC*, p. 181.

[60] Ibid., p. 153.   [61] Ibid., p. 175.   [62] 'Rex igitur indignatus'; ibid., p. 167.

[63] Ibid., p. 183.   [64] Ibid., p. 171.   [65] Ibid., p. 167.

[66] Ibid., p. 177. The use of churches as places of safe-keeping was widespread. See the account of the use of Lincoln cathedral during the siege in 1217 in the 'Barnwell' chronicle; see pp. 340–1 below.

[67] Ibid., pp. 177–8.   [68] Ibid., p. 180.   [69] Ibid., p. 176.

ported Henry III was patriotism: he identified the barons' cause with that of Louis, a Frenchman. On Louis's defeat in 1217 he comments: 'Thus God struck his enemies who had come to destroy the English people.'[70] This shows the development of a patriotic, anti-foreign feeling which reached an almost hysterical pitch later in Henry III's reign.

Ralph was interested, as one would expect of a Cistercian monk at that period, in religious history, especially when it concerned his order. He has long accounts of various contemporary religious personalities, of whom some were Cistercians and others had connections with the order. He describes the life and works of the Cistercian mystic and biblical scholar Joachim of Flora[71] and of another well-known biblical scholar Peter Cantor (he died in a Cistercian abbey).[72] There is an account of the preacher, Foulque of Neuilly-sur-Marne,[73] who attended the Cistercian general chapter in 1201 to preach the crusade.[74] And there is a section on Master Rener, Innocent III's confessor, who tried to dissuade the pope from taxing the Cistercians.[75]

Ralph's interpretation of events corresponds with the conventional Christian ethic of his day. He is doctrinaire, even cruel, and lacks the humanity of William of Newburgh. He regarded both Richard I's capture and his death as God's judgment for his uncorrected sins,[76] and the death of Hubert Walter as a good example of the transitory nature of all earthly success.[77] Ralph was intolerant of heretics, apostates and Jews (attitudes not fully shared by William of Newburgh[78]). He tells without repugnance the story of the death of a girl belonging to the catharist sect which Philip count of Flanders was persecuting mercilessly, 'with just cruelty'.[79] She was brought before the archbishop of Rheims and questioned concerning her beliefs. She was very well informed on the scriptures but, refusing to recant, was condemned to be burnt and died as bravely as any martyr.[80] Ralph

---

[70] Ibid., p. 185. Ralph also comments adversely on John's use of foreign troops; ibid., p. 204.

[71] Ibid., pp. 67–70. For a different opinion on this passage on Joachim of Flora, c. 1132–1202, see Marjorie Reeves, *The Influence of Prophecy in the Later Middle Ages* (Oxford 1969), pp. 12–14. It seems likely that Ralph was here using some Cistercian collection of pious tracts similar to that produced in the first half of the thirteenth century by the Cistercian Caesarius of Heisterbach (see nn. 72, 75 below). For a similar passage on St Alpais, a holy woman in the diocese of Sens, see *RC*, pp. 125–8: this passage in Coggeshall is not mentioned in the notice of St Alpais in A. B. C. Dunbar, *A Dictionary of Saintly Women* (London 1904, 1905, 2 vols), i. 48.

[72] *RC*, pp. 79–80. Peter Cantor's sanctity is mentioned by Caesarius of Heisterbach; *Caesarii Heisterbacensis Monachi Ordinis Cisterciensis Dialogus Miraculorum*, ed. Joseph Strange (Cologne 1851, 2 vols), xii. 48.

[73] *RC*, pp. 80–3. Cf. pp. 133–4. [74] *RC*, pp. 129–30. Cf. pp. 133–4.

[75] For this incident which is described by Coggeshall (*RC*, pp. 131–3) see H. K. Mann, *The Lives of the Popes in the Middle Ages* (London 1902–32, 18 vols), vol. 11, p. 238 and n. 5 (which quotes Coggeshall). Rener is called Innocent's confessor by Caesarius of Heisterbach who gives substantially the same account of the affair as Coggeshall though with more specific details; *Caesarii . . . Dialogus*, vii. 6.

[76] *RC*, p. 57.   [77] Ibid., p. 161.   [78] See pp. 265–6.

[79] *RC*, p. 122.   [80] Ibid., p. 124.

records without comment how an apostate to Judaism was burnt at the ecclesiastical council at Oxford in 1222, where also an unbelieving man and woman were immured until they died.[81] He gives a detailed account of the attack on the Jews of York by the citizens in 1190, saying that they deserved it.[82]

Ralph devoted much space to, and is well informed about the Fourth Crusade, a concern he shared with the whole Cistercian order. As he points out, some Cistercian abbots accompanied the crusaders in 1201.[83] He records that loot from the Greeks (a golden shield and an icon of the Virgin Mary) was sent by the crusaders to the Cistercian general chapter in 1204,[84] and that in 1205 there was some question of founding a Cistercian house at Nicaea.[85] Ralph attempts a topographical description of Constantinople which he apparently constructed from information supplied by people who had been there:[86]

> The city of Constantinople seems to be triangular, being six miles wide, so they say. The circumference of the city is about eighteen miles, that is from one corner of the triangle to the next is six miles. The walls are fifty feet in height and the towers on the wall are twenty feet apart. In the city is a magnificent imperial palace called Blakerna, and the palace of Constantine and that of Bohemund. And also in it is an incomparable church, that is St. Sophia, built by Justinian: wonderful and incredible things are said about the size of its construction and the splendour of its richness. The same emperor is said to have endowed this church very generously, establishing nine hundred and fifty canons. Those who know the population of this city assert with conviction that it has more inhabitants than live between the city of York and the river Thames.

Ralph is particularly remarkable for his narrative ability, which rivals that of William of Newburgh. A good example is his vivid account of the capture of Richard I by Leopold duke of Austria. Richard landed on Corfu

---

[81] Ibid., pp. 190–1.
[82] Ibid., p. 28. Cf. William of Newburgh's more tolerant attitude, pp. 265–6 above.
[83] Ibid., p. 130.   [84] Ibid., p. 149.   [85] Ibid., p. 161.
[86] Ibid., pp. 149–50. Ralph's information about Constantinople is inaccurate. The walls were about thirty-six feet high, not fifty, and the towers are various distances apart, from over forty feet to nearly seventy feet. The palaces of Blacherna and of Constantine (traditionally so called, actually the Tekfur Saray) are correctly identified. No trace now remains of the palace of Bohemund. Justinian established 425 priests in his four great churches (not just in St Sophia). Ralph (ibid., p. 150) also describes an antique column bearing carved heads of four emperors, but here he was misled by some baseless tale, as nothing in reality corresponded with it. I owe the information in this note to the great kindness of Professor R. Janin who wrote in answer to my query.

accompanied by some friendly pirates and by some of his own men, including 'the chaplain Anselm who told us what he saw and heard'[87] and a few Templars. After various adventures he reached Vienna,[88] having travelled without food for three days and nights. He had with him a boy who spoke German. Ralph continues:[89]

> The duke of Austria himself was in Vienna, to crown all evils. The king's boy went to the market in the town and when he offered some bezants, behaving in an excessively officious and pompous manner, he was seized by the citizens. On being asked who he was he said he was the servant of a certain rich merchant who would be arriving at the city in three days time. They then let him go and he secretly returned to the king's hide-out. He repeatedly exhorted the king to fly, telling him what had happened. But the king wanted to rest in the town for some days after the great hardships of the sea. And meanwhile the boy often returned to shop in the market. Then one day (the feast of St. Thomas the apostle) it happened that he carelessly took with him the king's gloves tucked under his belt. When the city officials saw them they again apprehended the boy and tortured him cruelly, applying various punishments and torments, inflicting wounds and threatening to cut out his tongue if he did not quickly confess the truth. The boy was compelled by terrible suffering to tell them what he was carrying. They at once told the duke everything, who surrounded the place where the king was staying and demanded that he should at once give himself up voluntarily. The king hearing such a tumult of barbarous voices remained imperturbed. As he thought that his defences could not withstand so many barbarians, he ordered the duke to present himself, undertaking to give himself up to him alone. The king came a little way to meet the duke when he arrived, and handed the duke his sword. The duke appeared overjoyed and escorted the king honourably. And then he handed the king over to the custody of his fierce knights, who closely guarded him everywhere, both day and night, with drawn swords.

Like William of Newburgh, Ralph loved good stories, especially about the supernatural. One of the stories he tells about supernatural beings is also told by William, although in different words. It concerns the two green children, a boy and a girl, who were found at Woolpit in Suffolk, living

---

[87] *RC*, pp. 53–4. For a lost biography of Richard I by his chaplain Anselm and Milo abbot of Le Pin see p. 239 and n. 156 above.

[88] The authorities are not agreed that Richard I was captured in Vienna; see Kate Norgate, *Richard the Lion Heart* (London 1924), p. 269 n. 7.

[89] *RC*, pp. 55–6.

in a pit. They were just like ordinary humans except that they were green. They were taken to the house of Sir Richard de Colne at Wakes in Essex. No one could understand their language and they would eat nothing that was given them until someone thought of beans. The boy soon died but the girl survived. She became accustomed to eating other food, lost her green colour, learned English and was baptized.[90] Another story is about a merman caught in a net off Orford in Suffolk. 'He was naked and looked like a human. He had hair but it seemed to have been pulled and torn out on top. His beard was full and pointed, his chest very shaggy and hairy.' He was kept in Orford castle for a long while and ate avidly, especially cooked or raw fish which he squeezed in his hands until dry. He could not or would not speak even if hung up by the legs and cruelly tortured. Nor would he show any reverence in church. Eventually he managed to escape back to the sea. 'Whether he was a mortal man, or a fish in human form, or an evil spirit . . . was hard to decide.'[91]

As stated above, the Coggeshall chronicle has some short annalistic entries (for example, from 1207 to 1213, and from 1219 to 1223). This illustrates the revived popularity of annals. Some annals from 1162 to 1178, which were added to the chronicle of Ralph Niger,[92] have been ascribed to the authorship of Ralph of Coggeshall himself.[93] But the references in them to St Osyth's in Essex[94] suggests that they were written in the priory of

---

[90] Ibid., pp. 118–20; for William of Newburgh's version see p. 267 above.

[91] *RC*, pp. 117–18.

[92] The annals are printed in *The Chronicles of Ralph Niger*, ed. Robert Anstruther (Caxton Soc., 1851), pp. 169–78. This continuation is notable for its revision of Ralph Niger's estimate of Henry II (ibid., pp. 169–70; see p. 222 n. 16 above). The author writes: 'Hucusque protraxit hanc chronicam magister Radulfus Niger, qui accusatus apud praedictum principem [Henricum] et in exilium pulsus, ob expulsionis injuriam atrociora quam decuit de tanto ac tam serenissimo rege mordaci stylo scripsit, magnificos ejus actus quibus insignis utique habebatur reticendo, atque prava eius opera absque alicujus excusationis palliatione replicando, quum pleraque de his quae commemoravit in pluribus articulis aliquantulam admittant excusationem si gestorum ejus intentio justo libramine ponderetur, si regiae potestatis lubrica libertas pensetur, quae fere cunctis potentibus dat licere quod libet, quorum vitiis favent inferiores, proni ad imitandum, prompti ad adulandum, quum et impunitas praestet audaciam, divitiae vero acuant et accendant culpam.' Cf. the panegyric on Henry II in the Coggeshall chronicle, *RC*, pp. 25–6.

[93] Hardy, *Catalogue*, vol. 2, p. 415, states that this attribution is 'on the authority of the Herald's MS' (i.e. Arundel XI in the College of Arms); for which see W. H. Black, *Catalogue of the Arundel Manuscripts* (London 1829, not published). In fact Arundel XI does not ascribe the continuation to Ralph of Coggeshall, though Lord Howard of Naworth has written a note ascribing to Coggeshall the annals from 1114 to 1158 which follow in the manuscript (ff. 40ᵛ–45; printed in Anstruther op. cit., pp. 178–91): Howard cites the *Catalogue* of John Bale; see John Bale, *Scriptorum Illustrium Brytannie . . . Catalogus* (Basle 1557–9), p. 275. There is no evidence that the annals from 1162 to 1178 or those from 1114 to 1158 were by Coggeshall: it is likely that Bale attributed the latter annals to Coggeshall because they occur in manuscripts containing Coggeshall's chronicle (i.e. Vespasian D X and Arundel XI in the College of Arms). However, in the earliest of these manuscripts, Vespasian D X, which is very near a first draft (see p. 323 and n. 20 above) neither continuation of Ralph Niger is in the same hand as Coggeshall's chronicle (ff. 46–128ᵛ).

[94] See Anstruther, op. cit., pp. 173, 177.

Augustinian canons there.[95] Another East Anglian religious house produced annals at about this time. Early in the thirteenth century, annals from the the Incarnation were compiled at Bury St Edmunds.[96] As these survive today they end abruptly in 1212 owing to the loss of leaves from the only known manuscript. To 1202 the annalist used such well-known authorities as Ralph Diceto. After that date, to 1211, he has passages in common with Roger of Wendover which seem to come from some source, now lost, used by both authors. The annal for 1212 is independent of all known authorities. It is fairly detailed and of some interest for King John's reign. Annals were also written in the Cistercian abbeys of Stanley in Wiltshire and Margam in Glamorganshire. The Stanley annals were appended as a continuation to William of Newburgh's history. From 1198, where William ended, to 1201 the author borrowed from Roger of Howden. Then various annalists, writing fairly contemporarily with events, continued the chronicle up to 1270.[97] The Margam annals are very brief; they cover the years from 1066 to 1232 (ending incomplete because one or two leaves are missing from the only known manuscript). They have some interest for general history, but are mainly valuable for their information on local affairs.[98]

Thus the revival of annalistic writing affected the Augustinian canons, the Benedictines and Cistercians. In the London area the Augustinian canons played a particularly important part in the revival. Dunstable priory produced annals from the Incarnation to 1297.[99] From the early thirteenth century they are detailed, combining local with general history, and are of considerable value to the historian. After 1210 they seem to have been written up close to events.[100] Two other Augustinian priories produced annals, Southwark and Merton. Both annals begin at the Incarnation, Southwark ending in 1240 and the Merton ones in 1242,[101] and both provide

[95] For another continuation of Ralph Niger's chronicle, to 1213, which is in BM MS. Royal 13 A XII (a thirteenth-century manuscript from the Carmelite convent in London), see Hardy, *Catalogue*, vol. 3, p. 22, and *Catalogue of Western Manuscripts in the Old Royal and King's Collections in the British Museum* (London 1921, 3 vols), vol. 2, pp. 81–2.

[96] See pp. 359 and n. 24, 395. Printed Liebermann, *U A-N G*, pp. 97–155.

[97] Printed in *Chrons. Stephen, Henry II, and Richard I*, vol. 2, pp. 503–58. From 1217 to 1220 the Stanley chronicle (ibid., pp. 524–7) seems to draw on a version of the Coggeshall chronicle (*RC*, pp. 185–8), or, as suggested by Howlett (op. cit., vol. 2, pp. lxxxix–xc), on a common source. For the Stanley chronicle as an authority for the reign of Henry III see pp. 406, 407, 421 below.

[98] Printed in *Ann. Mon.*, vol. 1, pp. 3–40. For their historical value see ibid., pp. xiii–xv.

[99] Printed in ibid., vol. 3, pp. 3–408. To 1201 the Dunstable annals use Ralph Diceto (see p. 319 n. 6 above) and other well-known authorities; see ibid., p. xiv. The part of the Dunstable annals up to 1242 is fully discussed by Cheney, 'The Dunstable annals', pp. 79–98. See also pp. 334 et seq. below. For the annals as an authority for the reigns of Henry III and Edward I, see pp. 424–9, 440 below.

[100] See *Dunst.*, p. xi and pp. 335–6 below. The manuscript (BM MS. Tiberius A X, ff. 5–113) is in various thirteenth-century charter hands apparently contemporary with the contents of the text.

[101] See M. Tyson, 'The annals of Southwark and Merton' in *Surrey Archaeological Collections*, xxxvi (1925), pp. 24–57, who describes and analyses the Southwark and Merton annals and prints (in the appendix) those for 1209–18, 1224, 1229, 1231–4, with the variants between the

contemporary accounts of events from the early thirteenth century. From 1207 the annals of Southwark and Merton appear to be independent of all other known sources, but not of each other. They seem to derive information from some common source, now lost. Thus the two sets closely resemble each other (except for the years 1216 to 1217 when the Merton annals have much independent material); from 1219 to 1240 they are almost identical.

The Southwark annals became a source of a chronicle from which a number of others emanated. This was the set of annals written at Winchester,[102] started perhaps by Richard of Devizes or by some other monk of St Swithun's.[103] The Winchester annals as they survive today cover the years from the Incarnation to 1277 and may have been written at Hyde abbey.[104] But these descend through some annals which went up to 1280 and were certainly compiled at Hyde, from a lost chronicle of St Swithun's, from the Incarnation to 1281.[105] The lost Winchester annals incorporated the annals sometimes attributed to Richard of Devizes (which were written soon after 1202), and then continued, using the Southwark annals and contemporary material. From these lost Winchester annals descend two sets from the Cistercian abbey of Waverley, one to 1285,[106] and the other to 1291.[107] The set of Waverley annals which reach to 1285 were used in the annals written by the Benedictines of Worcester cathedral.[108] The Worcester annals themselves have contemporary material, copied from no known annalistic source, from 1202 to 1261.[109]

Some of the annals written in religious houses are very brief for John's

---

two sets. Extracts relating to European history from the Southwark annals are printed in *MGH, Scriptores*, xxvii, 430–2.

[102] For the use of the Southwark annals at Winchester and elsewhere see Denholm-Young, 'Winchester-Hyde chron.', pp. 91–2 and Liebermann, *U A-N G*, pp. 178–9.

[103] See pp. 252–3 and nn.

[104] The Winchester chronicle (from 519) is printed in *Ann. Mon.*, vol. 2, pp. 3–125. For its value as an authority for Henry III's reign see pp. 411–12 below.

[105] See Denholm-Young, 'Winchester-Hyde chron.', pp. 86–9. Wint. dep. was written up contemporarily with the events recorded from 1264; ibid., p. 87.

[106] Long extracts are printed by Liebermann, *U A-N G*, pp. 182–202. As these Waverley annals were copied almost *verbatim* in the annals of Worcester, most of their text can be read in the latter (printed in *Ann. Mon.*, vol. 4, pp. 355–562). However, from 1202 to 1266 the Worcester annals are independent of all other known annals (see below and n. 109); for these years the Waverley annals are only to be found printed in Liebermann's text. For the two sets of Waverley annals see Liebermann, *U A-N G*, p. 174 and Denholm-Young, 'Winchester-Hyde chron.', p. 86.

[107] Printed in *Ann. Mon.*, vol. 2, pp. 129–411. For the Waverley annals as an authority for the reigns of Henry III and Edward I see pp. 412–16 below.

[108] The Worcester annals begin with the Incarnation and were continued in the thirteenth and fourteenth centuries to 1307 (with a few brief additional annals). For a printed text see n. 106. For their use of the Winchester/Waverley annals see Denholm-Young, 'Winchester-Hyde chron.', pp. 87–8 and n. 4 (where it is mistakenly asserted that Worcester does not use the Winchester/Waverley annals after 1202 until 1266; 1261 is the correct date; see *Worc.*, pp. xxxix, 447). For *Worc.* as an authority for the reigns of Henry III and Edward I see pp. 411, 421, 449–52 below.

[109] See above, n. 106 and Denholm-Young, 'Winchester-Hyde chron.', p. 88 n. 4.

reign and have little comment on his character or on constitutional issues. The annals of Southwark, Merton and Bury St Edmunds are virtually unadulterated records of events, expressing no point of view or feeling. The annals of Stanley abbey and Worcester are rather fuller and more reflective. Those of Dunstable are quite detailed and have some passages of good narrative with a few comments on events. In all the annals, what can be gathered about John and his reign is much the same. The Stanley and Dunstable ones mention John's cruelty. The Stanley writer comments on his cruel treatment of the de Braose family,[110] and the Dunstable one mentions his 'martyrdom' of 'the innocent and faithful Geoffrey of Norwich'.[111] The annals of Bury St Edmunds describe Geoffrey as 'a noble clerk', recording that he was captured at Nottingham 'and clothed in so much iron that he died.'[112] They also assert, under 1212, that everyone was terrified of John's ferocity.[113] The Stanley annals have a story illustrating both John's cruelty and his lechery: one of the northern barons, Eustace Fitz John, put a whore in John's bed instead of his wife: John, thinking she was Eustace's wife, broke her finger.[114] The Dunstable annalist thought John was excessively severe to the sheriffs.[115] The Stanley writer accuses him of cowardice[116] and duplicity,[117] of neglecting his 'natural and free subjects' in favour of foreigners,[118] and of failing to take counsel.[119] The Worcester annalist accuses John of tyranny.[120]

The Stanley, Dunstable and Worcester writers all have a bias against foreigners. The Stanley writer resents John's love and promotion of aliens[121] and says (under 1215) that his foreign mercenaries, 'whom he had promised to expel', brought harm to the kingdom.[122] The Worcester annalist calls Fawkes de Breauté 'both foreign and ignoble'.[123] The Dunstable annalist says that the king, in 1214, 'sent abroad to many barbarous nations, to foment war between himself and his subjects',[124] and he hates Louis and his supporters 'who began to grow proud, to thrust the nobles of England from their counsels and call them traitors, retaining the castles they had taken and not restoring their rights to the English.'[125] The Bury annals record (under 1212) that John promised to remove aliens from his intimate circle.[126] Particular invective is directed against the count of Nevers by the Dunstable writer. His tyrannous rule over the people of Wiltshire and Sussex 'made his own name and that of his lord [Louis] stink'.[127] Two of the annalists, those of Dunstable and Worcester, comment on the cupidity of the Roman church,[128] and there is considerable evidence that the annalists bitterly

---

[110] *Stan.*, p. 511. [111] *Dunst.*, p. 34. [112] *A St. E*, p. 155.
[113] *A St. E*, p. 154. [114] *Stan.*, p. 521. [115] *Dunst.*, p. 35.
[116] *Stan.*, p. 517. [117] *Stan.*, pp. 518, 520. [118] *Stan.*, p. 518.
[119] *Stan.*, p. 517. [120] *Worc.*, p. 402. [121] *Stan.*, p. 518.
[122] *Stan.*, p. 520. [123] *Worc.*, p. 416. [124] *Dunst.*, pp. 43–4.
[125] *Dunst.*, p. 47. [126] *A St. E*, pp. 154–5. [127] *Dunst.*, p. 46.
[128] *Dunst.*, p. 34; *Worc.*, p. 418.

resented John's treatment of the church in England. The Stanley annalist says that in 1215 John was acting for the destruction of the church, and equated John's supporters with the impious 'who ignored God and had no respect for men'.[129] The Dunstable annalist records the king's extortionate taxation of the clergy in 1210.[130] If the Dunstable writer has a hero it is Stephen Langton, who withstood the accusation made against him in Rome in 1215 of supporting the barons, because 'God knew his innocent conscience and so preserved his reputation untarnished.'[131]

The civil war is deplored by most of the annalists. For example, the Stanley writer says that when the barons chose Louis as king there was fighting everywhere, fathers against sons, sons against fathers, an unheard-of situation.[132] The annalists apparently regarded the barons as the only men able to check John's arbitrary rule. As the Stanley writer says, they were fighting for 'the laws and good customs of the realm which had been perverted by the obstinacy of the king and by the cruelty of wrongheaded foreigners.'[133] They were also struggling for the 'rights and liberties of the church'.[134] And the barons acted 'by common counsel' in their appeal to Louis.[135] The Dunstable annalist says of Magna Carta that it concerned 'the liberties of the realm of England'.[136] He explains how John's opponents began to support Henry III on his accession, 'because this king was young and innocent and had offended no one.'[137] And he points out that the barons in 1225 granted the king a tax specifically in exchange for the confirmation 'of certain liberties granted by King John'.[138]

The Dunstable annals are, unlike the other annals, not wholly anonymous. From 1210 the chronicle seems to have been by the prior, Richard de Morins, who had been a canon of Merton. This is indicated by a passage at the beginning which states that from the Incarnation 'until now are 1210 years, our eighth year'. Richard, the chronicle records, became prior in 1202, so his eighth year was 1210. It appears, therefore that he began writing in 1210. The annals have a number of entries about him. He was a man of some importance.[139] He was sent by King John to arrange peace with France in 1203, and was a visitor of religious houses in the diocese of Lincoln in 1206. In 1212 he travelled through the diocese to inquire about losses inflicted on the church by King John. In the same year he acted for three preachers sent by Innocent III to preach the crusade, in Huntingdonshire, Bedfordshire and Hertfordshire. He attended the Fourth Lateran Council and on the way back stayed a year studying in the schools at Paris. He was one of the

---

[129] *Stan.*, p. 520.   [130] *Dunst.*, pp. 32–4 *passim*.   [131] *Dunst.*, p. 45.

[132] *Stan.*, p. 522. A similar comment on family disruption engendered by the civil war is made in the 'Barnwell' chronicle and in the 'Merton' *Flores*; see pp. 345, 462.

[133] *Stan.*, pp. 517–18.   [134] *Stan.*, p. 518.   [135] *Stan.*, p. 522.

[136] *Dunst.*, p. 43.   [137] *Dunst.*, p. 48.   [138] *Dunst.*, p. 93.

[139] For a summary of the information about Richard de Morins in the annals and elsewhere see *Dunst.*, pp. x–xii.

commissioners in 1223 who settled the question of the exemption of Westminster abbey from the bishop of London. He was a visitor of the order in the province of York in 1223, and in the dioceses of Lincoln and Lichfield in 1228. And in 1239 he drew up the case on the right of the archbishop to visit monasteries in his suffragans' sees. He died in 1242. Richard was therefore a man of affairs. But whether he actually wrote the chronicle from 1210 to 1241 is not certain. Clearly he initiated it, but much of it is a piecemeal composition (including brief records of events and of the priory's business transactions) which could have been put together by a number of men.[140]

Something is known about an author of one other set of annals. The Worcester annals are anonymous but have some information about the monk responsible for at least the early part of them. The author records, under 1219, a lease to his brother of land belonging to his mother.[141] Under 1221 he mentions that he carried the cope and vestments of Thomas prior of Winchcombe when the latter dedicated the church of Dodderhill.[142]

All these annalists included local history with general history (anything that would interest the inmates of the house). The Worcester and Dunstable annals are particularly full on local history. Sometimes it was closely connected with general history. Thus the Worcester annalist, despite his support of the baronial cause, could not approve, for local reasons, when the citizens of Worcester adopted Louis's cause.[143] He records how they, following bad counsel, submitted to Louis in 1216 and received William the son of William the Marshal in Louis's name. But the king's army entered the city, notwithstanding the citizens' brave resistance, sacked it, and violently dragged the young Marshal from the cathedral 'where he had taken refuge, forewarned, it was said, by his father'. The knights locked the cathedral and fined the monks 300 marks. 'Moreover to crown our misfortunes we were suspended until nearly the feast of the Assumption [15 August], just as if we had been excommunicated, because we had celebrated mass in the presence of the king's enemies.' Whatever side the monastic annalists took in general, they always put local interests first.

---

[140] The question of the authorship and composition of the Dunstable annals is fully discussed in Cheney, 'The Dunstable annals', pp. 88–97. Professor Cheney conjectures, adducing internal evidence, that Richard de Morins wrote to 1210, and that the section from 1210 to 1219 was written up from contemporary notes in one piece, c. 1220, at Richard's order, after his return from Paris. Thereafter Richard supervised the keeping of the annalistic records in the priory, which were written up and added to the chronicle at intervals of three or four years. Professor Cheney's hypothesis would satisfactorily explain the fact that up to 1210, but not after, the chronicle reflects Richard's interests as a canonist. It would also explain the chronological confusion from 1210 to 1219 (though the information itself is excellent in this section), and the chronicle's subsequent chronological accuracy – and the references in this part to Paris university (see Cheney, op. cit., p. 97).

[141] *Worc.*, p. 411. I do not agree with Luard (*Ann. Mon.*, vol. 4, pp. xl–xli) that the man who wrote this and the following entry necessarily wrote all the annals to the late thirteenth century.

[142] *Worc.*, p. 413.   [143] *Worc.*, pp. 406–7.

Similarly, local history sometimes merges into national history in the Dunstable annals. For example under 1215 it is recorded that Louis captured Hertford and Berkhamsted castles 'and then, besides doing much damage to the borough of Dunstable, obtained two hundred marks from it.'[144] Under 1224 it is noted that as robbers and brigands overran the countryside, justices in eyre were appointed to restore law and order; 'in our county the justices were Simon de Hale and Richard Ducket.'[145] But usually the local entries are not related to the general ones. The Dunstable annals are a valuable source for local history. The author used oral information, and charters[146] and court rolls[147] stored in the priory. He notes that some of the records were enrolled at Westminster.[148] The local entries relate to the internal history of the priory (the succession of the priors and obedientiaries and the like) and to its lawsuits and property transactions. One such business transaction concerns an allegedly forged charter.[149] It reads:

> Moses, son of Brun, a Jew, plagued Richard prior of Dunstable and his church for £700, by means of a certain charter, which was proved to be a forgery by Sir Martin de Pateshull and other justices of the lord king, because the charter was said to be for a loan accepted by Prior Thomas but the seal bore the name of Richard. Moreover, the charter had been washed and had false grammar. So the Jew was imprisoned in the Tower of London for a year or more, because the other Jews gave the king a mark of gold to put off the judgement. And afterwards, since they could not defer the case longer, they gave the king £100 so that he would not be hanged, in mockery of his law.

Moses therefore abjured the realm and was outlawed.

The Dunstable annals have longer passages of narrative prose than the other sets of annals. Some of these are of considerable value for general history, and show that the author was capable of rational deductions. He explains, for example, how John's relations with Geoffrey de Mandeville were impaired by the latter's financial indebtedness to the king.[150] He explains why Louis lost the support of the barons in 1215 (due to the depredations and overbearing behaviour of the French in England),[151] and why Henry III gained it (because of the appeal of his youth).[152] The author

---

[144] *Dunst.*, p. 47.

[145] *Dunst.*, p. 95.

[146] See e.g. *Dunst.*, pp. 60–1, 106.

[147] See e.g. ibid., pp. 65–6.

[148] See e.g. ibid., pp. 58, 85, 93, 100.

[149] Ibid., p. 66. A full record of this case is preserved in the plea roll; see V. H. Galbraith, *Studies in the Public Records* (London and New York 1948), p. 51.

[150] *Dunst.*, p. 45. For Geoffrey de Mandeville's marriage and consequent debt to John, see J. C. Holt, *The Northerners* (Oxford 1961), p. 102. Professor Holt gives the indebtedness of the barons to the king as an important cause of their disaffection; ibid., pp. 174 et seq. Cf. p. 352 and n. 300 below.

[151] *Dunst.*, pp. 46–7.

[152] *Dunst.*, p. 48.

was well informed. Dunstable was within thirty-five miles of London and Prior Richard took an active part in church affairs. Information was obtained from documents: these are not cited in full, but either just referred to or extracted from. Thus Magna Carta is mentioned,[153] with the information that copies 'were deposited in safe places in each bishopric'.[154] Some of the terms of the 1215 treaty with Louis[155] and of the 1223 treaty between Henry III and Llewelyn of Wales are mentioned,[156] and extracts are cited from the letter of Pope Honorius III about Prester John.[157]

One of the most graphic passages in the annals is the account of the capture of Bedford in 1224.[158] The author's source of information is clear: he says townsmen from Dunstable took part in the siege, and they must have told him about it. Fawkes de Breauté had imprisoned one of the royal justices, Henry de Braybrook, in the castle, so that the king in anger laid siege to it.[159] Fawkes himself was not there and the castle was held for him by his brother William. It fell after one of the most considerable sieges of Henry's reign, lasting for eight weeks. The passage reads:

> The castle was captured in this way. On the east side was a stone thrower and two mangonels which daily attacked the tower. On the west side were two mangonels which battered at the old tower. There was a mangonel to the south and one to the north which made two entrances in the walls nearest them. Also there were two wooden structures, with metal work, erected overlooking the tower and castle, for use of crossbowmen and look-out men. There were besides many siege-engines in which both stone crossbowmen and slingers lay under cover. And there was a siege engine called the Cat under which underground diggers, who are called miners, had an entrance and exit while they dug under the walls of the tower and castle. The castle was taken in four assaults. The barbican was captured in the first assault, where four or five of those inside were killed. The bailey was taken in the second assault, in which many were killed: here our men gained, as plunder, horses with their harness, and shields, cross-bows, cows, bacon, live pigs and innumerable other things. They burnt the buildings with the corn and hay in them. At the third assault the wall by the old tower was brought down by the

---

[153] *Dunst.*, p. 43.

[154] This passage is mentioned in J. C. Holt, *Magna Carta* (Cambridge 1965), p. 249.

[155] *Dunst.*, p. 51. The treaty is in *Foedera*, vol. 1, pt 1, p. 148.

[156] *Dunst.*, p. 83. For this treaty see J. E. Lloyd, *A History of Wales* (London 1939, 2 vols), vol. 2, p. 663 and n. 48.

[157] *Dunst.*, pp. 66–7.

[158] *Dunst.*, pp. 87–9.

[159] For the siege see F. M. Powicke, *King Henry III and the Lord Edward* (Oxford 1947, 2 vols), vol. 1, pp. 63–5.

miners. Our men entered over the ruins and occupied the inside bailey at great peril: many of our men died occupying it. Ten of our men trying to enter the tower were shut in and held by the enemy. At the fourth assault, on the vigil of the Assumption, at about vespers, the tower was fired by the miners, so that the smoke filled the rooms in the tower where the enemy were. The tower was split so that cracks appeared on the side. And then the enemy despairing of their safety, allowed Fawkes's wife and all the women with her and Henry, the king's justice, to go out safe and unharmed, and submitted to the king's will, raising the royal standard on the top of the tower.

The so-called 'Barnwell' chronicle is a more sophisticated work than the annals so far discussed, and it was almost certainly by one author throughout. It has annals from the Incarnation to 1225 (with a brief and valueless continuation to 1307). To 1202 it is compiled from well-known authorities (mainly Florence of Worcester, 'Benedict' and Howden). From 1202 to 1225 it is independent of all known sources and was described by Bishop Stubbs as 'one of the most valuable contributions in existence to the history of that eventful period'.[160] The only known manuscript[161] (which dates from early in Henry III's reign) belonged to the Augustinian priory of Barnwell in Cambridgeshire and may have been written there. Its provenance is established by three marginal additions to the chronicle, two of them in a hand contemporary with that of the text, recording the succession of the priors of Barnwell.[162]

But there is no evidence that the chronicle itself was composed at Barnwell.[163] On the contrary, its centre of interest does not lie primarily in Cambridgeshire but in the Holland area. The author refers to Holland,

---

[160] *WC*, vol. 2, p. vii.

[161] College of Arms MS. Arundel X. This has never been published, though an edition by J.C. Holt is planned to appear in the series of Oxford Medieval Texts. At present the only printed text available (covering the years from 1202 to 1225) is in *Memoriale Fratris Walteri de Coventria*, ed. W. Stubbs (*RS*, 1872, 1873, 2 vols), vol. 2, pp. 196–279. Walter of Coventry (*floruit* 1293–1307, see ibid., pp. xiii et seq.) copied the 'Barnwell' chronicle indirectly, from a midthirteenth century compilation made in the Fenland (see *WC*, vol. 1, pp. xxxviii–xlvii *passim*, and F. Liebermann, 'Ueber ostenglische Geschichtsquellen des 12, 13, 14 Jahrhunderts' in *Neues Archiv der Gessellschaft für ältere deutsche Geschichtskunde* (Hanover–Leipzig 1892), xviii, pp. 233–4). Walter's text corresponds closely with the 'Barnwell' chronicle and Stubbs gives variants in Arundel X in footnotes.

[162] The nearly contemporary marginal notes relating to Barnwell are on ff. 81, 83 (by the annals for 1213 and 1214): these are printed in *WC*, vol. 2, pp. 212 n. 4, 218 n. 1. The other marginal entry is on f. 68ᵛ, by the entry *s.a.* 1093, recording the foundation of St Giles's at Cambridge. It is in a fifteenth-century hand and reads: 'Dominus Johannes Whaddu[m] canonicus et vicarius de Waterbeche plantauit cimitorium sancti Egidii de Bernwell viridibus arboribus. Anno Domini m. cccc.xl.iiij.' The Augustinian canons of Barnwell had had their priory (until they moved in 1112) at St Giles's, Cambridge (founded *c.* 1095); *VCH, Cambridge*, vol. 2, p. 235.

[163] *WC*, vol. 1, pp. xli–xliv, and Liebermann, 'Ostenglische Geschichtsquellen', p. 234.

between King's Lynn and Lincoln, as 'our parts'.[164] He has special notices about Crowland and Thorney. He records under 1216 that King John sent Savary de Mauléon and other soldiers to look for his enemies 'hidden in remote places'.[165] They came to Crowland and, not finding whom they sought, broke into the monastery, and dragged some men from the altar where they were hearing mass. The chronicler records the death of one abbot of Thorney, Ralph ('a religious and God-fearing man') under 1216,[166] and the deposition of another, Robert ('on account of certain excesses') under 1195.[167] A connection with the Fenland is suggested by the fact that the chronicle was incorporated in a compilation made in the Fens,[168] perhaps at Peterborough or Crowland, in the mid-thirteenth century.[169] But there is insufficient evidence to connect it with any one house. However the fairly numerous references to other Benedictine houses in this area and farther afield (Ramsey, Selby, Bardney, St Augustine's, Canterbury, Abingdon, and others),[170] suggest that the chronicle was written by a Benedictine.

Nevertheless, if the 'Barnwell' chronicle is a monastic production, its lack of local attachment is remarkable. It would be explicable if the author had entered religion late in life (a parallel example would be Thomas Wykes), when his opinions and loyalties were already formed.[171] If this was so, it is likely that the author, before becoming a monk, had had some connection with Lincoln. The chronicler knew a lot about and was interested in Lincoln, its bishopric and cathedral. He records the death of Roger de

---

[164] *WC*, vol. 2, p. 231.

[165] Ibid., p. 232. For references to Crowland (the succession of abbots and the like) in those parts of the 'Barnwell' chronicle not copied by Walter of Coventry (*s.a.* 1190, 1194, 1198 and 1228) see *WC*, vol. 1, p. xli n. 2. On the strength of these entries Liebermann, 'Ostenglische Geschichtsquellen', p. 234, stated that a monk of Crowland was author of the 'Barnwell' chronicle.

[166] *WC*, vol. 2, p. 234.   [167] Ibid., pp. 89, 244.

[168] For the intermediate compilation see p. 339 n. 161 above.

[169] Stubbs suggested a Crowland or Peterborough provenance for the intermediate compilation (*WC*, vol. 1, p. xliv), but Liebermann ('Ostenglische Geschichtsquellen', p. 234) thought this narrowed down the possibilities excessively and that some third Fenland abbey could equally well have been responsible.

[170] See e.g. *WC*, vol. 2, pp. 213, 216, 217, 246, 250.

[171] Professor Kathleen Major has called my attention to two clerks belonging to Robert Grosseteste's *familia* who entered religion fairly late in life. One was Benedict de Burgo, who was a subdeacon in 1231/2, became a canon of Lincoln in 1247, and in 1252 was admitted to Dunstable priory as a canon. The other was Master William of Pocklington who had entered Grosseteste's service by 1243 and became a Franciscan at Oxford in 1251. See K. Major, 'The *Familia* of Robert Grosseteste' in *Robert Grosseteste Scholar and Bishop*, ed. D. A. Callus (Oxford 1955), pp. 216–41. Professor Major suggests that other members of Grosseteste's household may have retired to religious houses though the evidence has not been discovered; see ibid., pp. 234, 240. It will be noted that Benedict de Burgo, like Thomas Wykes, entered an Augustinian house late in life, and the possibility cannot be discounted that the author of the 'Barnwell' chronicle was an Augustinian canon. This would fit in with the survival of the text in an Augustinian house, and would give added significance to the author's moderate political views, which resemble Wykes's.

Rolleston, dean of Lincoln from 1195 to 1223.[172] He mentions that King John took over the bishop's castles of Sleaford and Newark (where John died).[173] One of his most vivid passages describes the relief of Lincoln in 1217.[174] He gives details of how the royal army went to Lincoln to relieve Nicholaa de la Haye (wife of Gerard de Camville), 'to whom had been entrusted the custody of the castle in exchange for money',[175] because it seemed 'dishonourable not to help so brave a lady'. He explains how some of the royal army entered the city through a postern gate and surprised Louis's men, who ('scarcely able to move because of the narrowness of the place') made little resistance.[176] The chronicler lists some of the dead, gives the number of captured knights and says that it was not possible to count the lesser men taken. He describes the looting and sacrilege which followed:

> Those wanting loot violated each city church in turn, not sparing even the cathedral. For women, with their children and bedding, had taken refuge in it, and the burgesses and others had stored their property there. It was said that this was done with the con- nivance of the legate because the clergy of the city had stood in open rebellion to him; they were therefore excommunicated (including those who fled to the immunity of the church), and their churches defiled and when they were taken each was laden with chains by his captor.

The chronicler was also interested in places near Lincoln. He has special references to Bardney abbey, within ten miles of Lincoln, to Axholme less than twenty-five miles north of it, and to Belvoir less than twenty-five miles to the south. He notes that in 1214 the legate deposed the abbot of Bardney 'or rather, as the abbot had resigned, so it was said, he substituted another, according to his custom'.[177] In 1216 he records that the royal army laid waste the Isle of Axholme[178] and that King John ordered all castles to be demolished, 'including the famous and noble castle of Belvoir'.[179] More- over the author has a detailed and graphic description of the siege of Bytham castle in 1219: the castle was held by the Colvilles, members of which family were important tenants of the bishop of Lincoln.

The author had considerable talent as a historian. He had no taste for the

---

[172] *WC*, vol. 2, p. 252.　　　　[173] Ibid., 231.

[174] Ibid., 237–8. However it must be noted that there are also fairly detailed accounts of the sieges of Rochester (ibid., p. 227) and Bedford (ibid., pp. 253–4), although they are not quite so graphic as the account of the siege of Lincoln.

[175] Ibid., p. 230. Nicholaa was hereditary castellan of Lincoln; see J. W. F. Hill, *Medieval Lincoln* (Cambridge 1948), pp. 88–9.

[176] See F. W. Brooks and F. Oakley, 'The campaign and battle of Lincoln, 1217' in *Associated Architectural Societies' Reports and Papers*, xxxvi, pt 1 (1921), pp. 302–3, 305.

[177] *WC*, vol. 2, p. 217.　　　[178] Ibid., p. 231.　　　[179] Ibid., p. 230.

dramatic or for colourful exaggeration and, having no marked loyalty to any one man or place, he manages to be fairly objective. He concentrates almost exclusively on English affairs, giving a more comprehensive and comprehensible analysis of the political scene than any of his contemporaries.[180] He makes intelligent use of documents (some of which are now lost). Thus, for his unique account of the combination of barons against John in the autumn of 1214, he seems to have used the words of their written agreement (*conjuratio*) itself.[181] Similarly he knew the writ of 19 June 1215 ordering that Magna Carta should be carried through towns and villages and that everyone should swear to observe it.[182] He used documents for his account of John's submission to the pope in 1213,[183] for his discussion of John's grant of freedom of election to the church in 1214, and for the peace between Henry III and Louis in 1217.[184] In these cases he gutted the documents and did not cite them *in extenso*. Under 1219 he refers the reader for further information on the crusade to a letter addressed to Pope Honorius III by the patriarch of Jerusalem and others.[185] After 1224 the author quotes some documents in full, notably the long letter of Fawkes de Breauté to the pope justifying his opposition to the king and asking for a remission of his sentence. The chronicler used oral information with discretion. He often points out that he is using hearsay, with such expressions as 'so it was said'. He understood the unreliability of rumour. He says that the reputation of Peter of Wakefield (who prophesied that John would only reign fourteen years) was much increased by his imprisonment; 'daily, as is the custom, the common people added lies to lies, daily they imputed something new to him, and everyone, producing some new lie from his heart, asserted that Peter said it'.[186]

The author treats evidence rationally and often explains why he thinks events happened. He says that many barons fled in 1212 either because they feared the king's anger or because of guilty consciences.[187] He believed that King Philip of France agreed to help the barons because he hated John and hoped for financial gain (having heard that England was rich).[188] In places, he shows a touch of cynicism. He thought the people very fickle in their loyalty, easily swayed from one party to the other during the conflict between King John and the barons.[189] And he preferred to attribute acts to self-interest rather than idealism. He believed that John took the cross in

---

[180] Professor Holt describes the 'Barnwell' chronicle as the 'most perceptive' chronicle of the period; Holt, *Magna Carta*, p. 136 and cf. p. 129.

[181] *WC*, vol. 2, pp. 217–18. See Holt, *Magna Carta*, p. 136.

[182] *WC*, vol. 2, p. 222. See Holt, *Magna Carta*, p. 249.

[183] *WC*, vol. 2, p. 210. For the act of submission see Stubbs, *Charters*, pp. 279–81.

[184] *WC*, vol. 2, p. 239.   [185] Ibid., p. 242.

[186] Ibid., p. 208. Cf. ibid., p. 212 for the strength of the rumours started by Peter of Wakefield.

[187] Ibid., p. 207.   [188] Ibid., p. 209.

[189] Ibid., p. 209; 'Erat autem cor populi fluctuans, et quod facile in quamvis partem flecteretur, quasi arescentibus hominibus prae timore et exspectatione eorum quae in proximo superventura credebantur'. Cf. ibid., p. 228 ('cor populi fluctuantis...'), and ibid., p. 236 ('Et quoniam mobile vulgus facile mutatur...').

1215, not because of piety, but to mislead the barons so that they would abandon their opposition.[190] And in 1217 he ascribed the peace move between Louis and the 'royalists' to a desire to temporize: Louis was waiting for help from abroad and 'royalists' hoped for an opportunity to sack their opponents' property.[191]

The 'Barnwell' chronicle gives the fairest account of John of any of the contemporary annalists. The author gives a reasonable justification for John's submission to the pope in 1213.[192] Many, he writes, saw the submission as the most ignominious slavery, a monstrous servitude. But at the time, he explains, it was the best and only way of averting invasion: no one in the world would harm or attack John once he had put himself and the kingdom under apostolic protection, because Pope Innocent was universally feared, more than any of his predecessors. The author is the only chronicler to give a fair account of John's attempts in 1213 to check abuses by the sheriffs and other officials.[193] (The Dunstable annalist interprets the reform as yet another example of John's harshness.[194]) He records the reforms 'as worthy to be remembered and praised'. John, the chronicler writes, tried to check the greed and violence of the sheriffs, removing some from office and appointing others who would treat the people more justly. He showed pity to those who had suffered from the exactions of the forest officials and of the keepers of the ports, remitting their debts, and he was kind to widows. The chronicler asserts that John's good intentions were frustrated by the necessity of summoning an army to fight the French.

Nevertheless the 'Barnwell' chronicler's limited approval of John hardly extends beyond the king's official actions. His final assessment of John's character is unfavourable.[195]

> He was indeed a great prince, but rather an unhappy one, and, like Marius, experienced both good and bad fortune. He was munificent and generous to foreigners but a robber of his own people. He confided more in foreigners than in his subjects. And therefore he was deserted by his people before the end and was only moderately happy at the last.

The author writes in greater detail than his contemporaries, but attributes many of the same characteristics to John as they do. His views particularly resemble those of the Dunstable annalist. He mentions John's excessive fury with William de Braose[196] and his suspicious nature. In 1212 John 'heard some rumours, without certain authority, of a baronial conspiracy against him ... so he began to suspect everyone and went everywhere armed, with

---

[190] Ibid., p. 219.   [191] Ibid., p. 238.   [192] Ibid., p. 210.
[193] Ibid., pp. 207, 214–15. See Holt, *Magna Carta*, pp. 128–9, where a translation is given of the passage in the 'Barnwell' chronicle.
[194] *Dunst.*, p. 35.   [195] *WC*, vol. 2, p. 232.   [196] Ibid., p. 202

armed men'.[197] The chronicler mentions John's unhappy gift for arousing suspicion. For example in 1213, after the reconciliation with the papacy, John's failure to disband the army 'caused many to suspect his good faith',[198] and again in 1215, after the granting of Magna Carta, when John took the cross, his motives were questioned, especially as a rumour spread that he had appealed abroad for help.[199] The author resented John's treatment of the church, and records that John was regarded as a tyrant[200] and disturber of the realm.[201]

The author adopted the baronial standpoint. He evolved anti-papalist, anti-curialist and anti-alien views. The development of his anti-papalism can be traced. He begins by being pro-papal.[202] Then his dislike of the legate Pandulf, whom he accuses of supporting John 'more than was just' over ecclesiastical appointments,[203] began to affect his attitude to the pope. Under 1217, having recorded that those barons who sided with the king against Louis were allowed to commute their vows to go on crusade, he adds: 'not only the legate but even the pope were accused of being blinded by gifts and conquered by cupidity'.[204] By 1225 his attitude is clear. Pope Honorius wrote to Henry III demanding a prebend from each cathedral and collegiate church and certain revenues from every monastery. This demand, the chronicler said, not only removed but completely abnegated the liberties and rights of king and kingdom, clergy and people.[205] And he gives a full account of the ecclesiastical council which met at Lyons to counter the pope's demands. Similarly the chronicler's dislike of the king's intimate advisers and of his foreign mercenaries grew. He refers to *aulici* already under 1213,[206] and he resembles the Worcester writer[207] in his bitter attack on Fawkes de Breauté 'whom King John had raised with others from being a poor "satellite" into a knight, and then had made him the equal of an earl, because of his assiduous obsequiousness'.[208] The chronicler's anti-foreign feeling begins with dislike of John's mercenaries.[209] He attributes John's failure to resist Louis when he first landed in England to the fact that the royal army was mainly composed of Frenchmen,[210] and accuses foreigners of deliberately breaking the peace in Henry III's reign.[211] His sympathies lay with the barons. He calls the baronial army the 'army of God',[212] which was fighting for the liberties of the church and realm.[213] He agrees with the Dunstable annalist that the barons' financial debts to the king aggravated the

---

[197] Ibid., p. 207. [198] Ibid., p. 211. [199] Ibid., p. 219.

[200] Ibid., pp. 218, 225. [201] Ibid., p. 224.

[202] For an estimate of Innocent III see ibid., p. 210; 'non erat in orbe Romano princeps qui in sedis apostolicae injuriam vel illum infestare, vel illa invadere praesumeret, eo quod ab universis metuebatur papa Innocentius supra omnes qui eum a multis annis praecesserunt.'

[203] Ibid., p. 216. [204] Ibid., p. 235. [205] Ibid., p. 274.

[206] Ibid., p. 213. [207] See p. 334 above. [208] *WC*, vol. 2, p. 253.

[209] See ibid., pp. 224, 226, 232, 233.

[210] Ibid., p. 229. [211] Ibid., pp. 247, 251. [212] Ibid., pp. 220, 236.

[213] Ibid., pp. 218, 236.

struggle.[214] He gives a good account of the baronial party and of the shifting elements in it. For example he defines the meaning of the term 'northerners' ('they were called the northerners because most of them came from the northern parts').[215] He comments, like the Stanley chronicler,[216] on the divisions in families caused by the civil war; father fought son, nephew fought uncle. He remarks that the young men, hoping to make their names in battle, sided with the baronial opposition.[217] Such young men were presumably the landless knights, the 'bachelors', who play an important part, as the heroes of the chivalric ideal, in the *History of William the Marshal*.

L'Histoire de Guillaume le Maréchal, the biography of William the Marshal, ?1146–1219,[218] earl of Pembroke and Striguil, was written between 1225 and 1226 in Anglo-Norman verse by an unknown poet called John.[219] Like Jordan Fantosme's *Chronique de la Guerre entre les Anglois et les Ecossois* and Ambroise's *Histoire de la Guerre Sainte*, it is in the romance literary tradition. But it belongs to a different branch of romance writing. It emphasizes chivalric values: thus it is less concerned with heroism in real battles aimed at actual military advantage than with displays of bravery at tournaments.[220] It belongs to the artificial world of the knights errant who made their fortune going from tournament to tournament in France, collecting prize money (in the form of ransom, horses and equipment from their defeated opponents).

The chivalric tone of the *History* does not detract from its historical value. On the contrary, the *History* gives a unique picture of chivalric society (just as Jocelin of Brakelond gives a unique account of life in the cloister). Besides having considerable literary ability,[221] John had a good sense of historical evidence and records William the Marshal's acts fairly accurately. The Marshal was a typical product of chivalric society. He started his career as a knight errant, making enough money to marry a rich heiress, Isabel de Clare, countess of Pembroke and Striguil. By his marriage (which

---

[214] See ibid., p. 225. Cf. p. 337 and n. 150 above.

[215] Ibid., p. 219. For other specific references to parties see ibid., pp. 225, 235–7 *passim*. See Holt, *The Northerners*, p. 9.

[216] See p. 335 and n. 132.

[217] *WC*, vol. 2, p. 200. For the part played by young men in chivalric society and in the baronial opposition in thirteenth-century England see A. Gransden, 'Childhood and youth in mediaeval England' in *Nottingham Mediaeval Studies*, xvi (1972), pp. 8–19 *passim*.

[218] Printed *L'Histoire de Guillaume le Maréchal*, ed. Paul Meyer (Société de l'Histoire de France, 1891–1901, 3 vols). The text is in vols 1 and 2, with a glossary. A translation of the text, slightly abridged, into modern French, an index and Meyer's introduction are in vol. 3. The passages translated into English below are based on Meyer's modern French translation, except for the passage on pp. 353–4 below which is from the original text.

[219] *HGM*, vol. 3, pp. vii–ix.

[220] For the attitude that glory, not military advantage, was the chivalrous knight's objective, see *HGM*, ll. 4481–4, 16388–91; cf. Sidney Painter, *French Chivalry*, p. 36.

[221] For the literary value of the *History* see Legge, *A-N Lit.*, pp. 306–8.

took place in 1189) he become one of the greatest landowners in England, Ireland and Wales. His importance steadily grew in the reigns of Richard I and John, and on the latter's death he was made regent of England.

Unlike the works of Jordan Fantosme and Ambroise, the *History* was a family production. The Marshal's eldest son William commissioned it[222] at the suggestion of his father's esquire, John of Earley (the village of Earley is in Berkshire). This John entered the Marshal's service in the 1180s and died in 1230 or 1231.[223] He was moved 'by the love he bore his lord ... to put his heart, thoughts and money'[224] into the *History*. He not only contributed to the trouvère's fee, he also provided the information,[225] either verbally or in the form of a written memoir.[226] He had the work written to please the Marshal's children ('it ought to be heard with love and joy');[227] and ends:[228]

> When the family, both brothers and sisters, learn that the good Marshal, their brother William, has had such a work as this one done concerning their father, they will be touched to the heart. And may God give them joy concerning him, for I know well that they will rejoice greatly in this book when they hear it, on account of the notable good things and the honour which they will hear concerning their ancestor! God rest his soul!

The author digresses little from the Marshal's actual life, which limits the value of his work to the political historian today. He will not, he says, discuss Richard I's crusade, because 'it is not my subject'.[229] For the same reason he bypasses King John's negotiations with King Philip in 1202,[230] John's successes on the continent in 1213,[231] and the battle of Bouvines.[232] He dismisses the causes of the civil war between John and the barons in a few words: 'the king had wronged some who opposed him, and their example was followed by barons to whom he had done no wrong.'[233] He adds that 'this is not the place to speak of these quarrels in which both sides went to

---

[222] *HGM*, ll. 19181–3.

[223] For John of Earley see *HGM*, vol. 3, pp. xiv–xix. The *History* itself gives an excellent picture of the duties of John as an esquire. It shows his responsibility for his lord's weapons and armour, which he handed to the Marshal in battle (*HGM*, ll. 7947–8, 8587–8; for a story of how the Marshal had to go to a blacksmith to have his helmet removed see ll. 3102 et seq.). It shows his responsibility for the Marshal's horses (e.g. ll. 8693), and his great interest in horses – he recounts their bravery in battle, wounds, accidents, etc. (see e.g. ll. 5015–18, 7976–96, 8033–44, 8697–702, 16913–21). The *History* has a number of witty horsy stories; e.g. ll. 4197–274, 4339–430.

[224] *HGM*, ll. 19185–91 *passim*.   [225] *HGM*, ll. 19186–7.

[226] See *HGM*, vol. 3, p. x.   [227] *HGM*, l. 19168.

[228] *HGM*, ll. 19201–10. For another history in Anglo-Norman verse having a tenuous connection with the Marshal's family, see Appendix A (p. 518). For the intellectual interests of some members of the Marshal's family see p. 349 and n. 272.

[229] *HGM*, l. 9741.   [230] *HGM*, ll. 12055–8.   [231] *HGM*, ll. 14729–31.

[232] *HGM*, l. 14801.   [233] *HGM*, ll. 14847–50.

extremes'[234] – and then proceeds to give an account of the Marshal's children 'as this is my subject'.[235] Moreover, his dislike of unhappy and contentious subjects is evident. He says, for example, that he will not give details about Richard I's death 'from which the world still suffers, as it is too sad a subject'.[236] Sometimes caution made him silent. He refrains from giving the names of those who plotted against the Marshal late in Henry II's reign, because 'their descendants still survive who would bear me ill will'.[237] And he justifies his cursory treatment of the war between John and the barons partly 'because it would not be seemly to narrate it and could do me harm'.[238]

Sometimes the author lacks information. This was partly because John of Earley was not admitted to the inner counsels of the magnates, and partly because much of the Marshal's life had passed before John of Earley joined him, so for this period the *History* relies on hearsay. Some of the gaps in the information relate to the Marshal. He does not mention the Marshal's visit to England in 1199,[239] nor the honours with which John loaded him.[240] In the account of the Marshal's affairs in Ireland, notably his quarrel with the justiciar Meiler, he makes no reference at all to the part played by the Irish nobility.[241] He omits the Marshal's diplomatic mission to King Philip in 1215, to try to dissuade him from allowing Louis to interfere in England.[242] And he makes no mention of the reissue of Magna Carta in 1217, for which the Marshal was partly responsible.[243]

The author's integrity as a historian and his sense of evidence appear in the *History* in a number of contexts.[244] He quite often admits that lack of knowledge had forced him to be silent on a particular topic. He cannot, he says, describe the Marshal's acts on the Third Crusade because he did not accompany him.[245] Nor can he relate the negotiations between Henry II and King Philip in 1188 ('because they did not call me to their counsels'[246]) or in 1189 because he did not know what was said or agreed on.[247] And he cannot describe the coronation of King John, 'as I was not there',[248] nor name all the French participants in the naval battle off Sandwich in 1217 because he only had the names of those taken prisoner.[249] Similarly, on refusing to estimate the exact number of Frenchmen in the same battle, he says: 'I was not there and I would not take such responsibility', adding, 'the

---

[234] *HGM*, ll. 14852–5. [235] *HGM*, l. 14872. [236] *HGM*, ll. 11769–72.

[237] *HGM*, ll. 5142–7. [238] *HGM*, ll. 15034–6. [239] See *HGM*, vol. 3, p. lxxii.

[240] Ibid., pp. lxxii–lxxiii. [241] Ibid., p. lxxxi. [242] Ibid., p. lxxxviii.

[243] Ibid., p. lxxxi.

[244] Paul Meyer gives a careful analysis of the historical value of the *History*; ibid., pp. 287–8. It is the principal source used by Sidney Painter for his *William the Marshal* (Baltimore 1933). The value of its detailed account of the battle of Lincoln, 20 May 1217, is fully discussed by T. F. Tout, 'The fair of Lincoln and the "Histoire de Guillaume le Maréchal"' in *EHR*, xviii (1903), 240–65, reprinted in *The Collected Papers of T. F. Tout* (Manchester 1932–4, 3 vols), vol. 2, pp. 191–220.

[245] *HGM*, ll. 7296–301. [246] *HGM*, ll. 7377–80. [247] *HGM*, ll. 9033.

[248] *HGM*, ll. 11945. [249] *HGM*, ll. 17164–6.

world scorns those who digress from their subject to relate false or frivolous things'.[250] Although he wrote in the tradition of chivalric romance, his style is on the whole simple and he did not try to fill gaps in his knowledge with flights of fancy. He writes of Louis's campaign in 1217: 'I can say no more, for those who gave me the information do not agree and I can't follow everyone's account. I would lose the right way and would deserve to be believed less. It is not right to introduce lies into true history.'[251] Apparently he recognized the difficulty of adapting the style of romance literature to the needs of non-fictitious history, for he mentions the problem of putting a list of names into verse: 'there is not a clerk who does not find it hard to rhyme all the names he has to enumerate'.[252] But he records the names rather than leave them out for the sake of euphony.

Many statements in the *History* are confirmed by other authorities. For example the account of the truce between the English and the French in 1204 is confirmed by documentary evidence.[253] A charter confirms another statement: the *History* relates that the news of Richard I's death was brought to the Marshal while he was hearing a legal case between a certain Engeuier de Bohun and Sir Raoul d'Ardene at Vaudreuil; the charter made as a result of the suit has survived and corroborates details in the *History*.[254] A number of the chronicles, written both in England and Normandy, also provide confirmatory evidence. For example, Gerald of Wales corroborates the statement in the *History* that Richard I used to swear 'by God's eyes' and such like.[255] And Gerald, like the *History*, asserts that King Philip had contrived the ruin of all Henry II's sons in turn.[256] Ralph Diceto shares the *History*'s estimate of Richard's ransom at over £100,000,[257] while Roger of Howden confirms the story that Philip fell in a river when fighting the English in 1198.[258]

As mentioned above, it was not the author's purpose to discuss politics and, because of the type of work he was writing, he was hardly likely to adopt consistently anti-royalist attitudes. Therefore his incidental criticisms of King John are of considerable interest to the historian today because they confirm the views of the contemporary chroniclers. The author felt free to abuse King John because, though he was the Marshal's lord, he was a bad lord, mistrusting the Marshal's loyalty. The author says that John was blinded by pride and already in 1202 had lost the support of the barons who

---

[250] *HGM*, ll. 17496–500.   [251] *HGM*, ll. 16401–13.   [252] *HGM*, ll. 4447–50.

[253] *HGM*, vol. 3, pp. lxxvii, 177 and n. 1; ll. 12860–98.

[254] *HGM*, vol. 3, pp. 158 and n. 5, 159; ll. 11789–805. The arrangements made for the marriage of the Marshal's eldest son with the count of Aumale's daughter (see p. 518 below) is also confirmed by a charter; ibid., p. 208 and n. 2.

[255] See e.g. ibid., p. 89 n. 1; l. 7555.

[256] Ibid., p. 96 and n. 3; ll. 8099–114. Cf. *GW*, vol. 8, p. 308.

[257] *HGM*, vol. 3, p. 131 and n. 2; l. 9971. Cf. *RD*, vol. 2, p. 110, and Norgate, *Richard the Lion Heart*, p. 281.

[258] *HGM*, vol. 3, p. 146 and n. 2; ll. 11032–3. Cf. *RH*, vol. 4, p. 55.

were disgusted by his cruelty to prisoners.[259] He regards him as faithless,[260] unwarlike and unwise, and gives instances of his meanness,[261] nasty temper[262] and suspicious nature.[263] He remarks that he acted on his own, without taking counsel,[264] and kept the barons at a distance.[265] Commenting on John's thanks to God for the victories against the French in 1213, the author says, 'he would have been wise to give God return in good deeds.'[266]

The contents of the *History* were mainly determined by two factors: the chivalric ideal and love of the Marshal and his family. Both factors sometimes led to a biased historical viewpoint, but usually the author's sense of reality predominates. He depicts the Marshal as the perfect knight, a portrait which, as far as is known, corresponded with reality. He describes him as loyal, brave, strong and generous, and as a man of some culture. He emphasizes that (at least in 1205) King John regarded the Marshal as so loyal that he gave him permission to do homage to King Philip.[267] He insists that the Marshal's loyalty to the king was quite unshaken during the baronial revolt.[268] He asserts that when the Marshal accepted the care of the young Henry III, he said: 'I will carry him on my shoulders, one leg on each side, from island to island, from land to land, and I will not fail him, even if he never thanks me for my pains.' The author adds, 'May God help those who do good and act loyally!'[269] He mentions the Marshal's prowess on a number of occasions, and asserts that on his death William des Barres told the king of France that he had never known such a loyal and valiant knight.[270] The Marshal's generosity is also often referred to. For example when the English fleet defeated the French off Sandwich, it was the Marshal who ordered the booty to be distributed among the sailors, so that they had basins brimming with deniers and enough besides to found a hospital in honour of St Bartholomew.[271] The picture of the Marshal as a perfect knight is completed by references to his love of singing secular lyrics, particularly to ladies.[272]

---

[259] *HGM*, ll. 12499–512. The author also disapproved of John's cruelty to William de Braose (ll. 14143–53), and says that John failed to win the love of his people because of the cruelty of one of his mercenaries (ll. 12595–602).

[260] See e.g. the comment on John's failure to keep his promises to William des Roches; *HGM*, ll. 12522–3. He also states that John never repaid the Marshal for 500 marks he gave him; *HGM*, ll. 11969–82.

[261] The author remarks, for example, that after the death of Richard I the Normans had no effective leader; *HGM*, ll. 4649–52, and cf. F. M. Powicke, *The Loss of Normandy* (Manchester 1913), pp. 190–1. He considered that John's treatment of the Poitevins in 1202 was unwise (*HGM*, l. 12540) and that John's demands for hostages and pledges from the Marshal in 1210 was excessive (*HGM*, ll. 14395–9).

[262] See *HGM*, l. 14239.

[263] For John's suspiciousness in 1202 and 1203 see *HGM*, ll. 12635–6, 12799–804.

[264] *HGM*, ll. 12635, 13001.   [265] *HGM*, ll. 14480–2.   [266] *HGM*, ll. 14664–5.

[267] *HGM*, ll. 12958–66.   [268] *HGM*, ll. 15125–8, 15179–82.

[269] *HGM*, ll. 15692–8.   [270] *HGM*, ll. 19138–42.

[271] *HGM*, ll. 17515–34. See p. 353 below.

[272] *HGM*, ll. 3477–80; cf. ll. 18531–81 and p. 354 below. The Marshal's cultural tastes seem to have been preserved in his family. His grand-daughter, Isabel countess of Arundel, became a

The author's chivalric ideal was typical of the period. He believed that chivalry was best defended by the young, the landless 'bachelors', knights errant seeking fame and fortune at tournaments.[273] He personifies the chivalric virtues. Nobility was reared in the House of Largesse.[274] The champion of Chivalry was Henry II's eldest son, Prince Henry, and on his death its place was taken by Idleness and Sloth.[275] Like other such poets, the author had a nostalgic attitude to chivalry. And he believed that chivalry would one day flourish again: he hoped that Henry III would release it from prison.[276] His chivalric values were, like those of his contemporaries, modified by Christianity. He tells a story of how the Marshal robbed a monk who had absconded with a girl whom he intended to support on the interest of money lent at usury.[277] By breaking the laws of the church the monk had forfeited the sympathy of the author, who applauds the Marshal's act of robbery.

But in the last resort chivalry, not Christianity, determined the author's moral code. The author relates with approval how on his deathbed the Marshal preferred chivalric to Christian values. On being asked how he hoped to get to heaven without returning all the booty he had captured, the Marshal replied:[278]

> These clerks are too hard on us, they shave us too close. I have taken five hundred knights with their arms, horses and entire equipment. If because of this the kingdom of God is closed to me, there is nothing I can do about it, for I can't return these things. I can only give myself to God, repenting all my sins. Unless the clergy want my complete damnation, they must ask no more. But their teaching must be false, or no one would be saved.

And the Marshal chose that a final act of generosity should be to his knights, not the church. One of his clerks tried to persuade him to sell about eighty beautiful robes in order to spend the money for the salvation of his soul. But the Marshal said: 'Be silent, you tiresome fellow, you have not the heart of a gentleman. Pentecost is at hand and my knights should have their new robes. This will be the last time I will supply them, yet you try to stop me.' So he ordered John of Earley to distribute the robes and buy new ones if necessary.[279]

Nevertheless, although the author saw events from a chivalric viewpoint,

---

patroness of Matthew Paris. Moreover, it is possible that his second daughter Isabel countess of Cornwall and his daughter-in-law Maud countess of Winchester (widow of the Marshal's youngest son Anselm), were also patronesses of Matthew Paris. See pp. 358–9 and nn. 18–20 below.

[273] For these career knights see *HGM*, ll. 6391, 7030–1, 7185–94, 11252–6.

[274] *HGM*, ll. 5065–6.   [275] *HGM*, ll. 6872–8.   [276] *HGM*, ll. 2686–700.

[277] *HGM*, ll. 6676–864. This incident is discussed by Painter, *French Chivalry*, p. 88.

[278] *HGM*, ll. 18481–96. This passage is quoted by Painter, *William the Marshal*, pp. 285–6.

[279] *HGM*, ll. 18677–716. This passage is quoted by Painter, *William the Marshal*, pp. 287–8.

he did not distort historical truth. His chivalric interpretation of real events appears in a number of passages. He describes how Henry II 'sat in his pavilion which was strewn with grass and flowers'.[280] And his description of a skirmish near Drincourt in 1173 makes it sound more like a tournament than a battle (the Marshal fought under a window from which an audience of ladies, knights and burgers cried 'Oh! Norman lords! Go to help the Marshal. We are in agony watching him fight at such a disadvantage!' and meanwhile the heralds and minstrels proclaimed his bravery).[281] And when chivalry conflicted with patriotism or common sense, the author in most instances discarded his chivalric values without attempting to reconcile the two points of view. For example there was a potential conflict between the internationalism of chivalry and developing nationalism. Internationalism was an aspect of the travelling lives of the knights errant. Moreover, so far as chivalry was feudal, its internationalism had some political reality, for acts of homage could cut across territorial boundaries. Thus in 1205 the Marshal did homage to King Philip for his continental possessions and thereafter refused to fight him.[282] But this international concept ran counter to the growth of patriotism. The French monarchy was the rival of the English one. Therefore though the author of the *History* explicitly pays tribute to the pre-eminence of French chivalry,[283] he is usually outspokenly antagonistic to King Philip. He comments on Philip's poor following when he set out on the crusade[284] and accuses him of abandoning the crusade to annoy King Richard.[285] He repeatedly accuses Philip and the French of pride,[286] and charges Philip with provoking war against King John.[287] His account of Anglo-French peace negotiations in 1198 is unfair to the French. He asserts that the French king had bought over the papal legate, Cardinal Peter of Capua ('full of craft and plots'[288]), who acted as intermediary. In fact the legate, a learned scholar, was no friend of the French: he had been sent by the pope to restore Philip's lawful wife, with a threat of an interdict.

The chivalric virtue of largesse was particularly popular with the poets who relied on their patron's generosity. In real life, generosity can lead to extravagance, and extravagance to bankruptcy. This fact was recognized by the author. He speaks of the young Prince Henry as the flower of chivalry: when he died, largesse was forsaken.[289] But the author knew that Prince

---

[280] *HGM*, ll. 596–8.   [281] *HGM*, ll. 967–88.

[282] *HGM*, ll. 12958–66.

[283] See *HGM*, ll. 4481–3. The author's respect for French chivalry is perhaps shown by the fact that he puts the final praises of the Marshal's chivalry into the mouth of King Philip; *HGM*, ll. 19149–64.

[284] *HGM*, l. 9740.   [285] ll. 9800–2.

[286] e.g. *HGM*, ll. 10799, 11426, 15750.

[287] *HGM*, ll. 12035–42.

[288] *HGM*, ll. 11440–1. For the negotiations, which are described nowhere else in such detail, see ll. 11435–726. See also, for the value of this account and its bias, Powicke, *The Loss of Normandy*, pp. 183–5.

[289] *HGM*, l. 6876.

Henry's debts were a cause of his estrangement from Henry II,[290] and the *History* attributes the break-up of Prince Henry's party to bankruptcy. The young knights had not enough 'to give to a beggar' and had to sell their horses and equipment. So, the writer comments, 'when money's lacking, pride falls' and 'those raised to riches are shamed by poverty'.[291] And there is a story how after Henry the younger's death one of his creditors, a rich mercenary, tricked King Henry into paying his debts:[292] on paying, the king exclaimed, tears streaming from his eyes, 'my son has cost me more than anyone, and now it pleases God that he should cost me still more!'

The author's consciousness of money almost amounts to an obsession. He rarely mentions the beauty of a horse (as such poets often did) but frequently gives the price. He recounts with pleasure how on one occasion the Marshal got a superb horse worth £40 for £7,[293] and on another obtained one worth £40 or £50 for £30.[294] He remarks that the two horses which King Richard took as surety for a loan of £100 to the Marshal were in fact worth £100 each.[295] The author also records other exact sums of money. For example, in recording the Marshal's death-bed dispositions, he states that, at the persuasion of John of Earley, the Marshal gave his fifth son, Anselm, £40 worth of land ('so that he would at least have enough to shoe his horse'[296]). He states that the Marshal gave his fifth daughter, Joan, £30 worth of land and 200 marks to maintain her until she could make an advantageous marriage.[297]

The author's interest in money also appears in his comments on the poverty of kings. He tells how on Henry II's death the corpse lay almost stripped of clothing.[298] The Marshal could find no money to give to the poor because the king's steward, Stephen de Marçay, had hidden it.[299] He also mentions King John's poverty, recording that the Marshal once gave him 500 marks hoping for recompense ('and as for that recompense, I've never heard tell of it'[300]). He asserts that in 1215 John was penniless within five weeks of the beginning of the baronial war[301] ('which is inevitable for a man who spends without gain and keeps bad company'[302]), and therefore those serving him for wages left.[303] And he states that, in 1217, the Marshal thought his task as regent almost hopeless 'because the child [Henry] had no money'.[304]

The author's desire to please the Marshal's family, like his chivalric values, had a strong influence on the *History*. Usually the praises of the

---

[290] *HGM*, ll. 1971–2016. For the recognition by one chivalric writer (Philippe de Novare) of the fact that generosity could be excessive, see Sidney Painter, *French Chivalry*, pp. 31–2.

[291] *HGM*, ll. 2235–50. [292] *HGM*, ll. 7003–153. [293] *HGM*, ll. 4263–72.

[294] *HGM*, ll. 5965–8. [295] *HGM*, l. 7258. [296] *HGM*, ll. 18139–57.

[297] *HGM*, ll. 18158–68. [298] *HGM*, ll. 9138–43, 9413–32.

[299] *HGM*, ll. 9171–214. [300] See p. 349 n. 260. [301] *HGM*, ll. 15087–90.

[302] *HGM*, ll. 15092–5. [303] *HGM*, ll. 15118–21.

[304] *HGM*, ll. 15641–4. One reason why John of Earley tried to dissuade the Marshal from accepting the regency was the young king's poverty; *HGM*, l. 15453.

Marshal have little historical importance. The author says, for example, that the Marshal was chosen as regent because he was the greatest man in the kingdom.[305] Similarly the Marshal's chivalry and influence are emphasized throughout, and the virtues of his children extolled[306] ('there are none better').[307] And in the account of the siege of Lincoln a leading part is given to his nephew, John. The troops were led by John who was 'beautiful, and light as a bird, attacking the enemy as swiftly as a lion its prey'.[308] But sometimes the author's desire to eulogize the Marshal affects the historical sense. He probably exaggerates the part he played at the accession of King John.[309] It was, according to the *History*, on the Marshal's advice that John was chosen and Arthur's claim passed over (because Arthur had 'bad counsellors and is devious and proud'[310]). The archbishop of Canterbury, Hubert Walter, was not, according to the author, happy with the choice, saying 'Marshal, it shall be as you wish, but I tell you that never have you done anything you'll so repent.'[311] In fact John's own prompt actions were decisive. Similarly, the author overemphasized the Marshal's importance at the accession of Henry III as regent.[312] At this time legate Guala was also influential – and he is only briefly mentioned.

Nevertheless, the *History* does on the whole give a remarkably honest account of its subject. It even has some anecdotes at the Marshal's expense. For example, it tells how once, when the Marshal was with the young Prince Henry, he captured a mounted knight and led him, with Henry following, to their quarters. On the way the knight, as Henry saw, clambered on to an overhanging gutter of a house. When they arrived the Marshal said to an esquire, 'Take this knight.' Henry said, 'What knight?' The Marshal said, 'What knight? Why, the one I'm leading.' 'But you have no knight.' 'Where is he then?' asked the Marshal. Henry replied, 'He's remained behind hanging on to a gutter.' Everyone laughed.[313]

Social realism is one of the most remarkable features of the *History*. There are numerous vivid accounts of contemporary life. There is, for example, the realistic description of the delight of the sailors of Sandwich with the booty they captured from the French fleet in 1217:[314]

> In the morning the sailors walked about dressed in scarlet, and silk, boasting to each other. 'My robe is the best' said one. 'Bah!'

---

[305] *HGM*, ll. 15310–11.   [306] *HGM*, ll. 14860–15016.   [307] *HGM*, l. 14868.

[308] *HGM*, ll. 16606–12. The account of the siege and battle of Lincoln in the *History* is discussed by Brooks and Oakley, 'The campaign and battle of Lincoln', pp. 295–312 *passim*, and more fully by T. F. Tout, 'The fair of Lincoln', pp. 240–65.

[309] *HGM*, ll. 11837–908. For the historical value of this account of John's accession see *HGM*, vol. 3, pp. lxxi, 160 n. 6. For the circumstances of the accession see A. L. Poole, *From Domesday Book to Magna Carta* (Oxford 1951), p. 378. Powicke, *The Loss of Normandy*, pp. 194–5, cites the account in *HGM*.

[310] *HGM*, ll. 11885–7.   [311] *HGM*, ll. 11903–6.   [312] *HGM*, ll. 15255 et seq.

[313] *HGM*, ll. 2840–71. Earlier the author mentions that the Marshal as a young man had a reputation for spending his time eating, drinking and sleeping; ll. 775–6.

[314] *HGM*, ll. 17541–68.

said another, 'mine is all fur, coat and surcoat, mantle and cape. There's no better this side of Aleppo.' 'And mine', said a third, 'is all ermine and thread of gold.' And while they bantered in this way, others unloaded the ships of their provisions (meat, wine and corn), and iron and steel utensils, to the benefit of all.

The most moving passage in the *History* is the eye-witness account of the Marshal's death. As a deathbed scene it is only rivalled in English medieval literature by the anonymous description of Bede's last hours and by Walter Daniel's account of the death of Ailred of Rievaulx. The Marshal fell ill in the middle of March 1219, and died on 13 May. During this time the Marshal distributed his property.[315] He was moved to his manor at Caversham because he 'did not wish to stay in an unhealthy town'[316] and would be happier dying at home. He put his charge Henry III under the protection of the legate because of the mutual jealousy among the English magnates ('in no country are the people so divided by passion as in England'[317]). He said to Henry, 'Sire, I pray God that if ever I have done anything pleasing to Him, He may give you grace to be a good man. If it happens that you follow the example of a certain villainous ancestor, may God not grant you a long life.'[318] When the Marshal sent John of Earley to Wales on business, he told him to bring back two lengths of silk which he had deposited there and wished to be buried in.[319] On their arrival, the Marshal showed them to one of his knights, Henry Fitz Gerold.[320]

> 'Henry, look at these beautiful silks.' 'Certainly sire, but they seem a little worn, if I see right.' 'Lay them out,' said the earl, 'then we can judge them better.' When unfolded, the garments looked beautiful. The Marshal, having called his sons and knights, said: 'Lords, look at these. I have had them for thirty years. I brought them back when I returned from the Holy Land for the use I now intend them, that is to be spread over me at my funeral.'

The Marshal was growing weaker and could only eat button mushrooms.[321] One day he said to his wife: 'dear love, come and kiss me; it will be for the last time.'[322] They both wept, and the countess and their daughters had to be taken from the room because of their grief. His daughters visited him daily. On one occasion the Marshal was very anxious to sing as he used to do. John of Earley encouraged him, as it would restore his appetite, but he could not. So his daughters were asked to sing for him. He said, 'You sing first, Maud.' She had not the heart but nevertheless sang a couplet from a chanson to

---

[315] See p. 352 above. For a full account of the Marshal's death, based on the *History*, see Painter *William the Marshal*, pp. 276–89.

[316] *HGM*, ll. 17920–1. [317] *HGM*, ll. 18041–3. [318] *HGM*, ll. 18071–88.

[319] *HGM*, ll. 18183–5. [320] *HGM*, ll. 18204–25. [321] *HGM*, ll. 18445–52.

[322] *HGM*, ll. 18369–70.

please him, in a simple, soft voice. 'Joan, now it's your turn,' he said. She
sang a line of a lyric, but timidly. 'Don't sing in such a shamefaced way,' the
earl said, 'that isn't how you should sing.' And he showed her how she
should do it. When they had sung he said, 'Daughters, go to Jesus Christ.
I pray that He will keep you.'[323]

When the Marshal knew that he was actually dying, he told John of
Earley to summon his family and knights and the various ecclesiastics who
had come to see him. John of Earley supported him in his arms. He lost
consciousness and then revived.[324]

> 'John, did I lose consciousness?' John replied, 'Yes.' The Marshal
> said, 'I have never seen you so remiss. Why haven't you taken some
> of that rose water and bathed my face with it, so that I will have
> time to talk to these good people, as I have not long now?'
> John hurriedly took the rose water, which was in a phial, and
> washed his face, for he was pale with the agony of death.

And so, after absolution by the abbot of Reading, the Marshal died.

---

[323] *HGM*, ll. 18528–84.   [324] *HGM*, ll. 18848–64.

16

Matthew Paris and the St Albans School of Historiography

Matthew Paris did not possess the wisdom of Bede, or the mental acumen of William of Malmesbury. But he deserves to be ranked with them as a great English historian on account of the comprehensiveness of his work and because he developed historical method; and he was the first historian in England, writing on a grand scale, who had a sustained and consistent attitude to authority.

Matthew was probably born soon after 1200, and took the habit at St Albans in 1217, where he died, probably in 1259.[1] While a monk of St Albans (as far as is known he held no office in the abbey) he attended the feast of St Edward in Westminster abbey in 1247, and may have gone to other important functions at Westminster, Canterbury, Winchester and elsewhere. On one occasion he went abroad: in 1248 he was sent by Pope Innocent IV to St Benet Holm, an abbey on the island of Nidarholm in Norway, to reform the observance of the Benedictine Rule there. The monks of St Benet's had specifically asked for Matthew to be sent, perhaps because previously, in 1246, he had, at the request of King Haakon, helped them reach an agreement with some Cahorsin moneylenders in London concerning the abbey's debts.[2]

Matthew spent most of his life at St Albans writing history. He wrote general histories of the world which narrow down to concentrate on English history as he nears his own times. His great work was the *Chronica Majora* (*Greater Chronicle*),[3] begun in 1240 or soon after,[4] which covers the period from the Creation to 1259 (it fills five volumes in the Rolls Series). In 1250 Matthew began a shorter work, the *Historia Anglorum* (*History of the English*), a chronicle from the Norman Conquest to 1253.[5] He also wrote two other short chronicles, the *Abbreviatio Chronicarum* (*Epitome of*

---

[1] For Matthew's career and work see the excellent scholarly book by Richard Vaughan, *Matthew Paris* (Cambridge 1958).

[2] Ibid., pp. 4–6.

[3] The standard edition is *Chronica Majora*, ed. H. R. Luard (RS, 1872–83, 7 vols). For an English translation see J. A. Giles, *Matthew Paris's English History* (London 1852–4, 3 vols).

[4] For the date of *CM* see Vaughan, op. cit., pp. 59–61.

[5] The standard edition is *Historia Anglorum*, ed. F. Madden (RS, 1866–9, 3 vols). For its date see Vaughan, op. cit., p. 61.

Chronicles) [6] and the *Flores Historiarum (Flowers of History)*.[7] And in, or just before, 1250 he compiled a book of documents, the *Liber Additamentorum (Book of Additions)*[8] supplementary to the *Chronica Majora*. Matthew was also a local historian. By 1250 he had finished the first part of a history of St Albans, the *Gesta Abbatum Monasterii Sancti Albani (Deeds of the Abbots of the Monastery of St. Albans)*. This covered the period from the supposed foundation of the abbey in 793 to 1255 when John of Hertford (1235–63) was abbot.[9] Interest in local history also gave Matthew a motive for writing the *Vitae Offarum (Lives of the Offas)*. For (according to Matthew) Offa, king of Mercia, founded the abbey of St Albans in fulfilment of a vow made by a remote ancestor, another Offa.[10]

Another group of works by Matthew is a series of saints' Lives. As these are of limited interest to the historian today they can be briefly discussed. Matthew wrote two Lives in Latin, one of Stephen Langton[11] and the other of Edmund Rich.[12] Only fragments survive of the *Life of Stephen Archbishop of Canterbury* which was apparently mainly hagiographical. On the other hand the *Life of St. Edmund* is complete and has some historical matter. Matthew also wrote hagiographies in Anglo-Norman verse.[13] One was a translation of his own Latin *Life of St.*

---

[6] Printed in *HA*, vol. 3. Matthew's authorship has been disputed, but see Vaughan, op. cit., pp. 37–41.

[7] The standard edition of Matthew's *Flores* with its continuations to 1327 is *Flores Historiarum*, ed. H. R. Luard (RS, 1890, 3 vols): for an English translation, see C. D. Yonge, *Matthew of Westminster's Flowers of History* (London 1853, 2 vols). For this edition and translation see p. 377 n. 167 below. In the past, Matthew's authorship of the *Flores* to 1259 has been questioned, but the evidence adduced in favour of his claim by Professor Galbraith, *Roger Wendover and Matthew Paris* (Glasgow 1944), pp. 25, 31–2, 45–6 and by Professor Vaughan, op. cit., pp. 37–41, is virtually conclusive.

[8] Printed *CM*, vol. 6. For its date, see Vaughan, op. cit., p. 69.

[9] The most recent edition is *Gesta Abbatum Monasterii Sancti Albani*, ed. H. T. Riley (RS, 1867–9, 3 vols). But Riley printed the version of the *Gesta* by Thomas Walsingham, who in the late fourteenth century continued it (see p. 377 and n. 165 below) and continued it. Matthew's original work is printed in *Vitae Duorum Offarum sive Offanorum, Merciorum Regum: Coenobii Sancti Albani fundatorum. Et Viginti trium Abbatum Sancti Albani: una cum Libro Additamentorum, per Mathaeum Parisiensem. Omnia nunc primum edita, ex MSS. codicibus: Vitae, scilicet, ex duobus Cottonianis, unoque Spelmanniano . . .* ed. [William Wats], (London 1639), pp. 35–145, bound at the end of *Matthaei Paris . . . Historia Major . . .* ed. William Wats (London 1640). The references below are to Riley's edition, with those to Wats's edition in brackets. The test of the *GASA*, Book I, given by Wats is substantially the same as that by Riley (*GASA*, vol. 1, pp. 3–324) who gives variants from Wats in footnotes, and in Appendix D (ibid., pp. 505–21). For the date and composition of *GASA*, see Vaughan, op. cit., pp. 86–7, 184–5.

[10] The *Vitae Offarum* is published by Wats, op. cit. For the legendary origins of St Albans see H. F. R. Williams, *History of the Abbey of St. Alban* (London 1917), pp. 9–16.

[11] Printed in Liebermann, *U A-N G*, pp. 318–29. For this *Life* see Vaughan, pp. 159–61, and C. H. Lawrence, *St. Edmund of Abingdon* (Oxford 1960), p. 73.

[12] Printed in Lawrence, op. cit., pp. 222–89. Cf. ibid., pp. 73–100, and Vaughan, op. cit., pp. 161–8.

[13] For these verse Lives see Vaughan, op. cit., pp. 168–81, M. D. Legge, *Anglo-Norman in the Cloisters* (Edinburgh 1950), pp. 20–31 and her *A-N Lit.*, pp. 268–9.

Edmund.[14] Another was a *Life of St. Alban*, which includes an account of St Amphibalus, St Alban's supposed teacher:[15] it is apparently a translation of a Latin *Life* written at St Albans.[16] He also wrote a *Life of St. Edward the Confessor* (translated from Ailred of Rievaulx's *Life*), and a *Life of St. Thomas Becket* (of which only four leaves are extant; it seems to have been a translation of the *Quadrilogus*).

These verse Lives are of no historical value but are interesting because they show that Matthew could command an audience at court and in noble families. His historical works were intended for monks (the *Gesta Abbatum* and the *Lives of the Offas* were for the monks of St Albans, and his general histories and, presumably, his Latin hagiographies, were primarily meant for a monastic audience, at St Albans and elsewhere). On the other hand, though perhaps Matthew wrote the *Life of St. Alban* for his fellow monks, the rest of the verse Lives were written for the laity. They catered for the taste among lay noblewomen for saints' legends in vernacular verse enlivened with pictures (as will be seen, Matthew's verse Lives were profusely illustrated). The *Life of St. Edward* was written for Henry III's queen, Eleanor of Provence,[17] and the *Life of St. Edmund* for Isabel, countess of Arundel.[18] Moreover, it is known that Matthew had executed a book of verse, with pictures, for the countess of Winchester,[19] and arranged for the loan of his

[14] For the verse *Life of St. Edmund* see, besides the works cited in the previous note, Lawrence, op. cit., pp. 74–8. It is edited by A. T. Baker, 'La Vie de Saint Edmond' in *Romania*, lv (1929), pp. 332–81.

[15] For the legend of St Amphibalus see Williams, op. cit., pp. 78, 81.

[16] This Latin *Life of St. Alban* was by William, monk of St Albans, and was written between 1155 and 1168. See *Illustrations to the Life of St. Alban in Trinity College, Dublin, MS. E.1.40*, facsimile ed. W. R. L. Lowe and E. F. Jacob, with an introduction by M. R. James (Oxford 1924), p. 13.

[17] See *La Estoire de Seint Aedward le Rei*, facsimile ed. M. R. James (Roxburghe Club, Oxford 1920), pp. 12, 17. As a writer for lay noblewomen Matthew can be compared with the English Franciscan Nicholas Bozon, who in the late thirteenth (or early fourteenth) century wrote a *Life of St. Elizabeth* (of Hungary) in Anglo-Norman verse; see Louis Karl, 'Vie de sainte Elisabeth de Hongrie par Nicholas Bozon' in *Zeitschrift für romanische Philologie*, xxxiv (1910), pp. 295–314.

[18] See Baker, op. cit., pp. 338–42. Isabel countess of Arundel is wrongly identified by Lawrence, op. cit., p. 75, as Isabella de Fortibus (who was countess of Aumale). Isabel countess of Arundel, wife of Hugh d'Aubigny earl of Sussex and Arundel (1224–43), was daughter of William de Warenne earl of Surrey and his wife Maud, the eldest daughter of William Marshal, earl of Pembroke. Isabel died soon before 1282; see GEC, *Peerage*, vol. 1, pp. 238–9.

[19] See the note by Matthew Paris, on a fly-leaf on his *Life of St. Alban*. M. R. James transcribes the note in his introduction to Lowe and Jacob, op. cit., pp. 15–16, and in *La Estoire de Seint Aedward le Rei*, p. 23. Cf. Vaughan, op. cit., p. 170. The countess of Winchester, wife of Roger de Quency, earl of Winchester (1219 or 1235–64) may have been Maud, widow of Anselm Marshal (the youngest son of William Marshal and 9th earl of Pembroke) and daughter of Humphrey de Bohun, who had a previous and a subsequent wife. He married Maud in 1250. She died in 1252. It is impossible to be sure that Maud was the countess of Winchester to whom Matthew lent the books as the date of these Lives in uncertain. Vaughan, op. cit., p. 178, suggests that the *Life of St. Edward* was written soon after 1240 and the *Life of St. Thomas* after 1250 or 1257. If the *Life of St. Edward* is as early as Vaughan suggests, the countess must be identified as Helen, daughter of Alan lord of Galloway, whom Roger married some time after 1245.

Life of St. Edward and *Life of St. Thomas* first to Isabel countess of Arundel, and subsequently ('until Whitsun') to the countess of Cornwall.[20] The fact that Matthew wrote for these ladies illustrates his wide circle of secular acquaintances, which had an important influence on his historiography. Both his mobility (shown by his fairly frequent travels) and his many connections with the laity were unusual for a medieval Benedictine, and have never been satisfactorily explained.

I shall discuss Matthew's general histories first, then his local history, and, last, the influence he had on subsequent historiography.

The *Chronica Majora* was the most comprehensive history yet written in England. But less than half was, strictly speaking, Matthew's own work. To 1234[21] Matthew used the chronicle of another St Albans monk, Roger of Wendover. Little is known about Roger. He became prior of the cell of Belvoir, from which office he was deposed in 1219 or soon after for squandering the resources of the priory.[22] He began writing his *Flores Historiarum* after 1204 and possibly as late as 1231, and continued until 1234 (he died in 1236).[23] The *Flores* is a compilation of well-known authorities from the Creation to 1202, when Diceto's chronicle on which Wendover had relied for Richard I's reign, came to an end. Wendover from then on used no surviving literary authority, though he did use some annals which are now lost and which were also used by the thirteenth-century chroniclers of Bury St Edmunds.[24] But for John's reign and for the early years of Henry III,

---

[20] Probably Sanchia, daughter of Raymond Berengar count of Provence, who married Richard earl of Cornwall in 1243 and died in 1261. Richard's previous wife was Isabel, widow of Gilbert de Clare and second daughter of William Marshal earl of Pembroke. She died in 1239 or 1240. See ibid., vol. 3, p. 431.

[21] For the date when Roger of Wendover's *Flores Historiarum* ended see Richard Kay, 'Wendover's last annal' in *EHR*, lxxxiv (1969), pp. 779–85.

[22] See *GASA*, vol. 1, p. 270.

[23] There is no complete edition of Wendover's chronicle. It is edited from A.D. 447 onwards by H. O. Coxe, *Rogeri de Wendover Chronica sive Flores Historiarum* (English Historical Soc., 1841–5, 5 vols), and from 1154 by H. G. Hewlett, *The Flowers of History by Roger of Wendover* (RS, 1886–9, 3 vols). The latter edition is cited here. Matthew's version of Wendover's *Flores* is in the first three volumes of Luard's edition of the *Chronica Majora* (Matthew's borrowings are distinguished by small type). For the date of the *Flores* see *RW*, vol. 3, pp. ix–x, and Galbraith, *Roger Wendover and Matthew Paris*, pp. 16–17.

[24] The lost source was also used by the *Annales S. Edmundi*; see p. 395 below and Vaughan, op. cit., p. 24. The *Annales S. Edmundi* end abruptly, owing to loss of leaves from the only known manuscript, in 1212, and therefore they, and presumably their lost source, extended beyond that date. It may be suggested that the account of the meeting of the barons at Bury St Edmunds in 1214 which is only mentioned by Wendover (*RW*, vol. 2, p. 111) and, copying Wendover, by Matthew Paris (*CM*, vol. 2, pp. 582–3) derived from this lost source; for the incident see J. C. Holt, *Magna Carta* (Cambridge 1965), p. 138, *The Customary of the Benedictine Abbey of Bury St. Edmunds in Suffolk*, ed. A. Gransden (HBS, xcix, 1973), p. xxiv n. 5, and p. 387 and n. 50 below. I have not here discussed the suggestion put forward by some scholars that Wendover used a twelfth-century St Albans chronicle, perhaps by Abbot John de Cella (1195–1214), as even if Wendover did use such a work, it can only have been a compilation and not a piece of original historical writing: for a summary of the evidence and further reference see Vaughan, op. cit., pp. 22–3.

Wendover is a primary authority. In the *Chronica Majora* Matthew followed Wendover closely, but he was not a slavish copyist. He cut out some passages in Wendover and added new material. When he reached the thirteenth century, these additions become important; they reflect Matthew's own views, and some are authentic information which in the course of time had reached St Albans. From 1236 the *Chronica Majora* is independent of all known literary authorities. For these twenty-three years Matthew wrote within a year or so of the events he described, and provides a detailed record of events unparalleled in English medieval history. For this period the historian today is well informed: after Matthew ends, the historian's problems increase.

Matthew had excellent means of obtaining information. St Albans was within twenty miles of London, and had close connections, through its cells at Tynemouth, Belvoir, Binham and Wymondham, with the north, the midlands and East Anglia. Its guest-house served as a hotel for visitors from all over England and from abroad (in 1228 an Armenian archbishop, and in 1252 a group of Armenians, stayed in the abbey[25]). Henry III visited the abbey at least nine times before 1259. On one occasion (in 1257) Matthew claims to have been his constant companion and to have dined at his table. Henry gave him some information (a list of the sainted kings of England, and of the English baronies) for insertion into his chronicle, and Matthew interceded with the king on behalf of some visiting masters from Oxford.[26] Matthew had previously (in 1247) met Henry in Westminster abbey at the feast of St Edward: Henry had told him to take note of what passed so that he could record it, and invited him to dinner.[27]

Matthew had numerous other informants, many of them important public figures. They included such men as Richard of Cornwall, Hubert de Burgh and Alan de la Zouche. He knew the royal officials John Mansel and John of Lexington, the royal justice, Roger of Thurkelby, and Alexander of Swereford, a baron of the Exchequer.[28] And he may have known Elias of Dereham, steward successively of Hubert Walter, Stephen Langton and Edmund of Abingdon.[29] He also knew a number of bishops, including Peter des Roches, bishop of Winchester, and Robert Grosseteste, bishop of Lincoln. And he had friends in the mendicant orders (he received material from at least two Dominicans and one Franciscan – the artist William).[30]

---

[25] *CM*, vol. 3, p. 161; vol. 5, pp. 340–1, respectively.

[26] *CM*, vol. 5, pp. 617–18. Matthew also records his conversation with the king under 1251; ibid., pp. 233–4.

[27] *CM*, vol. 4, pp. 644–5. Cf. Vaughan, op. cit., p. 3, for a translation of the passage.

[28] These and the following (except Elias) are included in the list of Matthew's informants in Vaughan, op. cit., pp. 13–17.

[29] See J. C. Holt, 'St. Albans chroniclers' in *TRHS*, 5th series, xiv (1964), pp. 85–7. Professor Vaughan does not list Elias among Matthew's informants though he mentions that Matthew copied a picture of a wind rose designed by Elias; Vaughan, op. cit., p. 255.

[30] For reproductions and a discussion of a picture of Brother William by Matthew Paris and one by William which Matthew inserted into the *Liber Additamentorum*, together with drawings by

Through his contacts Matthew obtained information and documents. He had an omnivorous appetite for documents and used his acquaintance with men at the centre of affairs to obtain them. It is likely, for example, that he acquired the authentic text of Magna Carta and other documents (which were unknown to Wendover) relating to events in 1215 from Elias of Dereham who had taken an active part, as Langton's assistant, in the crisis.[31] Matthew also had access to records of the royal Exchequer; he used the Red Book of the Exchequer and others (some of which are now lost). And he obtained information from the Exchequer officials, notably from Alexander de Swereford.[32] Matthew copied many documents into the *Chronica*, as well as into the *Liber Additamentorum*, preserving some unique texts and some excellent ones. For example, he has the only known copy of the so-called 'Paper Constitution' of the barons, which he inserts (probably correctly) under 1244,[33] and he has the only known original of the 1253 confirmation of Magna Carta.[34] Moreover he alone preserves a copy of the papal letter ordering the visitation of the exempt monasteries in 1232,[35] and he has the best text of the decrees of the provincial chapter of the Black Monks held at Bermondsey in 1249.[36] But although Matthew realized the value of documents in substantiating his narrative, he had little critical sense about them. This is illustrated by his treatment of Magna Carta, for he conflates the text of Magna Carta with the 1217 and 1225 reissues, and fails to distinguish one reissue from another.[37]

In fact Matthew's critical powers are less remarkable than his wide range of interests and almost unlimited curiosity. Since the Norman Conquest historians in England had shown an increasing interest in European history. But their interest was nearly always in events connected however tenuously with English affairs. Matthew expanded this interest to such an extent that European history became in the *Chronica* a subject in its own right, and he himself an important authority. He was the only contemporary historian in Europe to give a full account of the Council of Lyons held in 1245.[38]

Matthew of St Francis (feeding the birds and receiving the stigmata), see A. G. Little, 'Brother William of England, companion of St Francis, and some Franciscan drawings in the Matthew Paris manuscripts' in his *Franciscan Papers, Lists and Documents* (Manchester 1943), pp. 16–24.

[31] See Holt, 'St. Albans chroniclers', pp. 85–7.

[32] See *The Red Book of the Exchequer*, ed. H. Hall (RS, 1896, 3 vols), vol. 1, pp. xix, xxi–xxx (and nn. for further references); F. Liebermann in *MGH, Scriptores*, xxviii, 82; Vaughan, op. cit., pp. 17–18.

[33] *CM*, vol. 4, pp. 366–8. See C. R. Cheney, 'The paper constitution preserved by Matthew Paris' in *EHR*, lxv (1950), pp. 213–21.

[34] See Holt, *Magna Carta*, p. 82.

[35] *CM*, vol. 3, pp. 238–9. Mansi prints a set of decrees of the Council of Lyons, 1245, from Matthew Paris, *CM*, vol. 4, pp. 462–72. Cf. n. 38 below.

[36] See *Documents of the General and Provincial Chapters of the English Black Monks*, ed. W. A. Pantin (Camden Soc., 3rd series, xlv, xlvii, liv, 1931–7, 3 vols), vol. 1, p. 32.

[37] See Holt, 'St. Albans chroniclers', pp. 76–7 and *passim*. Cf. Vaughan, op. cit., p. 132.

[38] *CM*, vol. 4, pp. 430–72. Matthew's account of the Council of Lyons, together with his copy of a set of its decrees, is printed in J. D. Mansi, *Sacrorum Conciliorum nova et amplissima collectio* (Florence *et al.*, 1759–1962, 55 vols), vol. 23, coll. 633–47. For the importance of Matthew's

Particularly notable are the documents and information he has about the Mongol invasions of eastern Europe in the 1240s:[39] as the invasions in no way affected England, Matthew's details illustrate well his objective curiosity about continental events. He records under 1238 the mission of the Ismailis to the French king to ask for help against the Mongols, and the first diplomatic contacts between the Mongols and the West in 1248, and gives copies of eleven documents[40] concerning the invasions.

Besides his interest in European history, Matthew increased the scope of history in other ways. The *Chronica* has an encyclopaedic quality. Matthew added details about art, architecture, heraldry and natural history to the annals and good stories characteristic of a chronicle. Previous historians, notably William of Malmesbury, had shown an interest in architecture, describing churches from personal observation. Matthew took a lively interest in the building activity of his day. He notices Henry III's rebuilding of Westminster abbey,[41] and the building of a new west front at Binham by Prior Richard de Parco.[42] He was interested in painting and goldsmiths' work: he lists the works of Richard, the painter, a monk of St Albans, and describes in detail the rings and gems owned by St Albans.[43] He was himself an artist and saw the world with an artist's eye: he has a particularly vivid description of a wash-bowl given by Queen Margaret of France to Henry III: it was 'in the shape of a peacock. It had a precious stone, commonly called a pearl, and other ornaments in gold and silver and sapphires, cleverly worked into the body, so that it looked just like a real peacock when he spreads his tail'.[44] Whenever Henry came to St Albans, Matthew regularly recorded the gifts he brought of silk hangings and the like (he gives a list describing the hangings owned by the abbey).[45] He shows his visual sense in his interest in heraldry. He describes how the Templars' hall in Paris was decorated with shields (including that of Richard I),[46] and he painted numerous armorial shields of English (and some foreign) nobles in the margins of his chronicles.[47] His interest in natural history appears in his notice of the

account see C. J. Hefele, *Histoire des Conciles*, ed. H. Leclercq (Paris 1869–78, 12 vols), vol. 5, pt 2, pp. 1633–79 *passim*.

[39] For this subject see J. J. Saunders, 'Matthew Paris and the Mongols' in *Essays in Medieval History presented to Bertie Wilkinson*, ed. T. A. Sandquist and M. R. Powicke (Toronto 1969), pp. 116–32.

[40] See ibid., pp. 124–7.

[41] *CM*, vol. 4, p. 427. Matthew's interest in art and architecture is particularly marked in the *Gesta Abbatum*. See p. 376 below.

[42] *CM*, vol. 6, p. 90. Richard ruled from 1226 to 1244. Therefore if the existing west front at Binham was that built by him, it must be earlier than 1244 and is the earliest example of bar tracery in England (earlier than Westminster Abbey); see N. Pevsner, *North-East Norfolk and Norwich* (Buildings of England series, Penguin Books, 1962), pp. 89–90.

[43] *CM*, vol. 6, pp. 202–3; 383–9.

[44] *CM*, vol. 5, p. 489. Matthew also gives a graphic description of the grand houses in Paris; ibid., p. 481.

[45] *CM*, vol. 6, pp. 389–92.

[46] *CM*, vol. 5, p. 480. For Matthew's interest in heraldry see Vaughan, op. cit., pp. 250–3.

[47] Matthew used the marginal shields as *signa* (p. 364 and n. 56). They and the pages of shields in

first arrival in England of cross-bills, buffaloes (which were given to Richard of Cornwall), and of an elephant (a gift to Henry III).[48] He briefly describes a buffalo in the *Chronica Majora* ('a kind of ox, very suitable for carrying or dragging loads, a great enemy of the crocodile and lover of water, armed with great horns'). Matthew did more than one painting from life of the elephant,[49] and also, in the *Liber Additamentorum*, gives a realistic description of it, presumably from his own observation.[50] He describes its colour as dirty grey, remarking that its skin is rough and has no fur, and he notices that its eyes are small and that it uses its trunk to get food.

The result of treating history in such depth and breadth was that Matthew Paris accumulated an almost uncontrollable amount of data in the *Chronica Majora*. He tackled this problem in two ways. First, he tried to increase the impact on the reader of the annals. Second, he isolated some material according to its nature, and he compiled epitomes of his own works. He tried to increase the chronicle's impact on the reader partly by stylization, and partly by pictorial illustrations in the margins. Matthew inherited some stylistic features from Wendover, notably the record at the beginning of each annal of where the king spent Christmas (Wendover may have adopted this practice from Roger of Howden, one of his principal sources[51]). Matthew also, like Wendover, decorated his text with tags of verse. Matthew added two new features: he often gave summaries of a man's character after the notice of his death, and gave a summary or 'characterization' of a year on its expiration. Moreover, after the annal for 1250, where Matthew originally meant to end, he gave a summary of important events of the last half century. The practice of summarizing people's characters may well have been borrowed from Henry of Huntingdon.[52] The practice of summarizing the year,

---

the *Liber Additamentorum* are also of great importance for the early history of heraldry. Matthew's shields are exhaustively edited in T. D. Tremlett, *Rolls of Arms, Henry III* (printed for the Society of Antiquaries and for the Harleian Society, cxiii–iv, 1961–2, Oxford 1967), pp. 3–86. For examples of shields painted in the margins of the *Historia Anglorum* see Plate IX a, b, c and f.

[48] *CM*, vol. 5, pp. 254–5, 275, 489. For Matthew's interest in natural history see Vaughan, op. cit., 256–7. Professor Vaughan also discusses Matthew's other scientific interests; ibid., pp. 253–8 *passim*.

[49] The merits of Matthew's realistic representation of the elephant is well illustrated by comparing one of his sketches with a traditional picture of an elephant in a medieval bestiary.

[50] Matthew's tract on the elephant is not in the printed text of the *Liber Additamentorum* but is in the manuscript (BM Cotton MS. Nero D I, f. 168[v] and attached slip) and on the fly-leaves of the Chronica Majora in Corpus Christi College, Cambridge, MS. 16. See F. Madden, 'On the knowledge possessed by Europeans of the elephant in the thirteenth century' in *The Graphic and Historical Illustrator*, ed. E. W. Brayley (London 1834), pp. 335–6, 352. One of Matthew's sketches from life of the elephant is reproduced by Vaughan, plate xxi, and another in *The Drawings of Matthew Paris*, facsimile ed. M. R. James (Walpole Soc., xxi, 1942–3), no. 26.

[51] See p. 225.

[52] See *HH*, p. 280, for a summary of the character of Alexander bishop of Lincoln after the notice of his death (for such character summaries by Matthew see e.g. *CM*, vol. 3, pp. 43, 205–6, 334, 391). Henry was one of Wendover's principal sources for the first half of the twelfth century. Matthew may have borrowed the idea of the wheel of fortune (to which he refers in *CM*, vol. 3, pp. 64, 279; cf. vol. 4, pp. 423, 479) from Henry (see p. 199 and n. 125 above).

which Matthew started as soon as Wendover ended, could possibly have been adopted from 'Benedict of Peterborough'. But the annual summaries given by 'Benedict' are of the *events* of the year:[53] Matthew begins by summarizing the *character* of the year (its weather, harvest, plagues and the like): only from 1243 does he include political events. It seems likely that he adopted the practice on the analogy of his character-sketches of recently deceased persons (the year, too, 'died'). The summary of the past half-year was presumably a development of the type of annual summary which included events.

Matthew's use of signs and pictures was no doubt partly due to his aesthetic taste and his artistic talent, but was primarily intended to help the reader. He used signs to distinguish passages on particular subjects: for example the coronation of a king was indicated by a crown and a shield, the succession of a bishop by a mitre and a staff (the staff was inverted to denote a bishop's death), and the death of a noble was indicated by his shield reversed.[54] After 1247 Matthew also used signs to help the reader to find easily cross-references from the *Chronica Majora* to the *Liber Additamentorum*.[55] Matthew's use of signs was probably the result of the influence of Ralph Diceto who had adopted the system to isolate passages in his chronicle,[56] which was an important source of the *Chronica Majora*.[57]

The series of marginal drawings with which Matthew illustrated his chronicles were intended to amuse the reader, catch his interest and stir his imagination. The number of these drawings, in pen and ink, some with tinted outlines, is unique in English historiography. John of Worcester has four excellent pictures in his chronicle[58] – three illustrating a vision of Henry I and one of Henry crossing the channel. An early and authoritative manuscript of Henry of Huntingdon has a graphic marginal pen-drawing of Baldwin Fitz Gilbert exhorting the troops before the battle of Lincoln in 1141,[59] and Roger of Howden has a sketch of the *rota* of King William of

---

[53] See p. 225.

[54] For examples from the *Historia Anglorum* see Plate IX. See also *CM*, vol. 3, pp. 1 n. 1; 77 n. 1; 74 n. 3; 60 n. 2, respectively.

[55] See Vaughan, op. cit., pp. 65–6.

[56] For Diceto's use of signs see p. 234 and n. 124. The suggestion in Vaughan, op. cit., p. 18, that Matthew Paris borrowed the system of *signa* from the Exchequer cannot be substantiated as there is no evidence for the use of *signa* in the Exchequer before the end of the thirteenth century (the best collection is in Liber A and Liber B, E 36/274, 275, in the Public Record Office, both of the late thirteenth century). This point has been kindly verified for me by Dr Patricia Barnes of the Public Record Office. The Exchequer system is explained in F. Palgrave, *Ancient Kalendars and Inventories* (Record Commission 1836, 3 vols), vol. 1, pp. xxvi–xxvii, with reference to Bishop Stapleton's Calendar (*c.* 1323).

[57] See p. 359. For the St Albans copy of Diceto (now BM MS. Royal 13 E VI) see p. 319 n. 6. Notes in Matthew's hand occur in this MS.; see R. Vaughan, 'The handwriting of Matthew Paris' in *Transactions of the Cambridge Bibliographical Society*, i (1953), pp. 381, 391.

[58] Reproduced as the frontispiece in *JW*. For two of the pictures see Plate VI.

[59] BM MS. Arundel 48, f. 168ᵛ; see *HH*, pp. xxxviii n. 2, xxxix n. 1, 271 n.a. This is the manuscript, which came from St Mary's, Southwark, which T. Arnold used as the basis of his text.

Sicily, under 1177.[60] And there is an early text of Gerald of Wales's *Topographia Hibernica* with marginal sketches of Irish life.[61] But there was no precedent in historiography for the profusion and high quality of Matthew's illustrations. He probably derived the idea of including numerous pictures from contemporary bibles, psalters and saints' Lives. But, despite the influence of his historical works, Matthew failed to establish a lasting tradition of the illustrated chronicle.[62]

A number of Matthew's works survive in his own handwriting, with pictures by him and his pupils (it is not always possible to distinguish their work). The best example of an illustrated work is his autograph of the *Chronica Majora*,[63] but the *Lives of the Offas*, the *Life of St. Alban*,[64] and the *Life of St. Edward the Confessor* (the extant copy is illustrated by Matthew's assistants)[65] also have numerous pictures. These are a lively reportage of events recorded in the texts. Matthew liked spectacular and sensational rather than pious or edificatory illustrations. He had of course no sense of historical dress (for example in the *Chronica Majora* King Canute appears in the armour of Matthew's own time[66]), but to avoid confusion he often labelled the principal figures and gave scenes descriptive captions. And sometimes the principal figures have their spoken words written next to them, as in modern strip-cartoons.[67] Thus the reader with little time or little Latin was able to learn from and enjoy Matthew's works.

Matthew has some importance in the history of English art because he popularized a revival of the Anglo-Saxon style of line drawing. He recaptured the liveliness of the Anglo-Saxon illustrators, intimately relating the marginal drawings with the text itself, both in subject-matter and in format. It is true that line drawing occurred in France in the second quarter of the thirteenth century, notably in the model-book of the architect Villard de

---

[60] See *RH*, vol. 2, p. 98 and p. 224 n. 36 above.

[61] BM MS. Royal 13 B VIII (a late twelfth-century MS. from St Augustine's, Canterbury). See Plate VIII, and T. S. R. Boase, *English Art 1100–1216* (Oxford 1953), p. 197 and plate 31e.

[62] However, the early fourteenth-century continuation of Matthew's *Flores Historiarum* from Rochester has rough marginal sketches of people, events and buildings; BM MS. Nero D II, for which see *FH*, vol. 1, p. xxvi.

[63] For surviving autograph manuscripts by Matthew Paris see Vaughan, op. cit., pp. 35 et seq. For examples of his drawings see Plate X. Many of his drawings and those of his pupils are reproduced in *The Drawings of Matthew Paris*, facsimile ed. M. R. James (Walpole Soc. xiv, 1925–6) and by F. Wormald, *More Matthew Paris Drawings* (Walpole Soc., xxxi, 1942–3) and a few by Vaughan, op. cit. For an assessment of the importance of Matthew as an artist, and of the St Albans school, see Peter Brieger, *English Art 1216–1307* (Oxford 1957), pp. 135–58, M. Rickert, *Painting in Britain: the Middle Ages* (London 1954), pp. 119–20, and Vaughan, op. cit., pp. 205–34. Matthew was also a skilled sculptor and metal worker; see *GASA*, vol. 1, p. 395, and John Amundesham, *Annales Sancti Albani*, ed. H. T. Riley (RS, 1870–1, 2 vols), vol. 2, p. 303.

[64] For a facsimile edition see p. 358 n. 16.

[65] For a facsimile see *La Estoire de Seint Aedward le Rei* (n. 17 above). Cf. Vaughan, op. cit., p. 168.

[66] James, *Drawings*, no. 2.

[67] See e.g. *La Estoire de Seint Aedward le Rei*, pp. 56, 64, 65.

Honnecourt.[68] Nevertheless, though Matthew may have used similar *exempla* material, he was probably more influenced by the Anglo-Saxon tradition of line drawing. The latter technique had survived the Norman Conquest,[69] and had subsequently been adapted to romanesque taste. It appears, for example, in the *Life of St. Cuthbert* probably executed at Durham *c.* 1120–30, in the Eadwine Psalter executed at Canterbury in the mid-twelfth century, and in the *Life of St. Guthlac* executed at Crowland *c.* 1200.[70] Even more significantly the twelfth-century copy of Terence's *Comedies* illustrated with numerous pen-and-ink drawings belonged to St Albans and was probably made there.[71] However, the style remained comparatively rare until the thirteenth century when its revival was mainly due to Matthew Paris.[72] He established a flourishing school of artists at St Albans who helped him illustrate both his own works and other books, notably psalters and apocalypses.[73] The influence of the St Albans school spread: it reached Westminster abbey and finally contributed, together with other provincial monastic styles, to the style of the new court school under Edward I.[74]

Matthew adopted his second expedient for making his work comprehensible to readers (the compilations of epitomes and the isolation of material according to type) in 1250. He planned to end the *Chronica* with the annal for 1250,[75] and meanwhile re-appraised his achievement up to date. The idea of abstracting from one's own work to produce a shorter one on a particular subject had been adopted by Diceto.[76] Matthew decided that the *Chronica* was too long and deviated too much from English history. So he went through it marking some passages as 'irrelevant to English history'. Then he made an epitome of the *Chronica*, an English history from 1066 to 1250,

---

[68] See H. R. Hahnloser, *Villard de Honnecourt* (Vienna 1935). For similarities between two figures drawn by Matthew Paris and two by Villard which suggest that Matthew may sometimes have used similar models (however no direct relation between the two artists, whose styles are in many respects very different, can be proved), see B. Kurth, 'Matthew Paris and Villard de Honnecourt' in *Burlington Magazine*, lxxxi (1942), pp. 227–8.

[69] For the survival and revival of the Anglo-Saxon style after the Norman Conquest see F. Wormald, *English Drawing of the Tenth and Eleventh Centuries* (London 1952), pp. 53–8.

[70] This copy of Bede's *Life of St. Cuthbert* is University College, Oxford, MS. 165; the Eadwine Psalter (Trinity College, Cambridge, MS. R. 17.1), is reproduced by M. R. James, *The Canterbury Psalter* (London 1935); for the Guthlac Roll (BM Harley Roll Y.6) see J. A. Herbert, *Illuminated Manuscripts* (London 1911), p. 140 and Plate xvii, and E. G. Millar, *English Illuminated Manuscripts from the tenth to the thirteenth century* (Paris–Brussels 1926), p. 37 and Plate 53.

[71] MS. Auct. F. 13 in the Bodleian library, Oxford.   [72] See Millar, op. cit., p. 60.

[73] For apocalypses illustrated in the St Albans style see Millar, op. cit., p. 60 and Plates 91, 92. For the 'Westminster' Psalter in the St Albans style see ibid., p. 60 and Plate 90 and James, *Drawings*, pp. 24–6 and Plates xxvii–xxix.

[74] See Brieger, op. cit., pp. 153–4.

[75] See the verses at the end of the annal for 1250 in *CM*, vol. 5, p. 198 (cf. Vaughan, op. cit., pp. 61, 65):

> Siste tui metas studii, Matthaee, quietas,
> Nec ventura petas quae postera proferet aetas.

[76] See p. 234.

omitting most of the marked passages[77] and some others, and adding new material.[78] This was the *Historia Anglorum* (which he later continued to 1253). It is likely that he also compiled the *Flores Historiarum* from the *Chronica* at about this date (he intended it to end in 1249).[79] At the same time he conceived the idea of relegating documents to a separate book. This was a development of existing trends in historiography. Already Henry of Huntingdon, whose work was a source of the *Chronica Majora*, had intended to put documents in a book of their own.[80] And Alan of Tewkesbury arranged the letters of Thomas Becket in a supplementary volume to his *Life of St. Thomas*, a work known to Matthew.[81] Moreover, Matthew's archive consciousness was probably stimulated by the production of monastic cartularies and registers, which reached its zenith in the thirteenth century. Chronicles themselves were becoming overcrowded with documents, which eclipsed the historical narrative. Roger of Howden's chronicle was an example of such overcrowding, and towards the end of his work the historical narrative petered out, so that the last pages were almost exclusively documents. Matthew Paris had appended a collection of documents to his annal for 1250, where he had originally meant to end.[82] Now he removed this into a new book, the *Liber Additamentorum*, adding more documents. In fact he created a cartulary, linked by cross-references to the *Chronica*: henceforth in the *Chronica* he gave references to the *Liber Additamentorum* where documents could be found substantiating and corroborating the *Chronica*'s statements. But Matthew did not stop copying documents into the *Chronica*: he simply reduced their number.[83]

These developments in technique helped to give unity to the *Chronica*. But undoubtedly its principal unifying factor was its theme. From beginning to end Matthew has a consistent attitude to centralized authority in church and state. He opposes it. He criticizes the king and government and he criticizes the pope and any ecclesiastic who interfered with established privileges. Not since the days of William Rufus had a chronicler had such an implacable attitude to royal power. Then the chroniclers' views were largely the immediate result of William's misrule. But Matthew had a more theoretical, almost detached, attitude. Sometimes he seems to complain for the sake of complaining, so that his invective has a homiletic ring. But he must have developed his ideas primarily under the provocation of contemporary politics,[84] and he must certainly have been influenced by the

[77] For these marked passages and Matthew's method of abridgment see Vaughan, op. cit., pp. 61–3, 112–13.
[78] For a list of Matthew's chief additions see *HA*, vol. 3, pp. xxxv–xlv. [79] *FH*, vol. 2, p. 361.
[80] See p. 198 and n. 120. [81] See pp. 299, 305–6.
[82] See Vaughan, op. cit., pp. 69–70. [83] Ibid., pp. 66–7.
[84] For public opinion against king and pope in Matthew's day see O. A. Marti, 'Popular protest and revolt against papal finance in England from 1226 to 1258' in *Princeton Theological Review*, xxv (1927), pp. 610–29, and H. MacKenzie, 'The anti-foreign movement in England, 1231–1232' in *Anniversary Essays in Mediaeval History . . . presented . . . to Charles Homer Haskins* (Boston–New York 1929), pp. 183–203.

climate of opinion which had grown up in the late twelfth century and in King John's reign. Walter Map had criticized satirically both king and court, and other members of the establishment. Gerald of Wales had become bitterly hostile to royalty, and Gervase of Canterbury had evolved ideas of limiting royal power.[85]

However, the most powerful intellectual influence on Matthew was Roger of Wendover. He was the originator of Matthew's hostility to king and pope; Matthew took over and elaborated his views. Roger criticized John for his angry temper[86] and arbitrary cruelty,[87] his taking of bad counsel,[88] his financial extortions[89] and interference with episcopal elections.[90] He took his stand on Magna Carta and the communal action of the barons.[91] Already when Roger wrote (perhaps after John's death), a myth had grown up about the king. Roger gives the story of how after the granting of Magna Carta, John, 'dumbfounded and in great consternation', went to the Isle of Wight. There he stayed for three months, 'on the sea-shore, in the company of sailors, cut off from the turmoil of the kingdom', planning vengeance on his enemies.[92] But the public records make it clear that John never went near the Isle of Wight during this period. Roger has an equally critical attitude to Henry III. He calls him 'simple'[93] and attacks the favour Henry showed to foreigners in general and to his alien counsellors in particular, at the expense of his natural subjects,[94] and intimates that he should be able to live off his customary revenues.[95] Moreover, Roger attacks the papacy for providing Italian clerks to livings in England,[96] for its financial exactions,[97] and for interfering with the autonomy of the Benedictine houses (by ordering a general visitation of them in 1232).[98]

Matthew developed Roger's ideas. When he copied Roger's chronicle to 1236 he added phrases to increase the dramatic effect and to underline the political moral. The added emphasis Matthew gave to Roger's 'constitutionalism' was partly due to the fact that he saw Roger's times in the light of his own: the continued conflict between king and barons, and between the English church and the papacy, made Matthew develop and clarify his ideas and give added significance to the events of John's reign.[99] Thus Matthew

---

[85] See p. 258.   [86] *RW*, vol. 2, pp. 48, 115, 148.

[87] Ibid., p. 57 (the starving to death of Matilda de Braose and her son); cf. ibid., p. 63.

[88] Ibid., pp. 53, 59–60.   [89] *RW*, vol. 1, pp. 318–19; vol. 2, pp. 35, 54.

[90] *RW*, vol. 2, pp. 37 et seq., 153 et seq., 309.   [91] Ibid., pp. 111–12, 113, 172.

[92] Ibid., pp. 135–6. This example of Roger's love of a good story against John at the expense of the truth is quoted by V. H. Galbraith, *Studies in the Public Records* (London and New York 1948), pp. 138–9.

[93] *RW*, vol. 3, p. 48.   [94] Ibid., pp. 48, 51.   [95] Ibid., p. 30.

[96] *RW*, vol. 2, pp. 295–6, 302; vol. 3, p. 16.

[97] *RW*, vol. 2, pp. 290, 299, 375 et seq.   [98] *RW*, vol. 3, p. 44.

[99] Matthew's additions to Wendover are easily isolated in *CM*, vols 1–3, because they are in large type. For Matthew's treatment of Wendover's account of King John, with excellent examples, see Galbraith, *Roger Wendover and Matthew Paris*, pp. 34–8. For Matthew's tendency to anachronism see Holt, *Magna Carta*, p. 290: Professor Holt admits that Matthew's views had some historical justification.

embellished Roger's account of John's stay on the Isle of Wight. Roger says that John 'pondered' how he could revenge himself on the barons; Matthew says that he 'plotted' and adds that he was burning with rage. Matthew also adds that John was unmindful of the solemn oath he had recently taken to the barons, that he was acting to the great damage and confusion of his kingdom, and was contemplating treachery. Similarly he adds a comment to his statement that the barons agreed in 1214 to seize John's castles if he broke his oath to them 'which was very likely because of his duplicity'[100] (Matthew also charges Henry III with duplicity[101]). He adds that John acted 'impudently, on the advice of Richard Marsh and similar men of his household (*aulici*)'[102] by taking 4,000 marks from the Cistercians during the Interdict. And where Roger records that Henry III removed Hubert de Burgh from office, Matthew adds 'although it is said he held his office by royal charter in perpetuity'.[103]

In the rest of the *Chronica* Matthew reiterates his criticisms of king and papacy, and his belief in the community of the realm, its liberties and customs, against any encroaching authority.[104] He depicts Henry as politically naïve and weak,[105] neglecting his 'natural' counsellors,[106] and imposed on by the pope.[107] He is particularly outspoken about the influence of Henry's Poitevin and Savoyard relatives, men such as Archbishop Boniface and Guy de Lusignan. Under 1251 he writes:[108]

> at this time the king daily, and not just slowly, lost the affection of his natural subjects. For like his father he openly attracted to his side whatever foreigners he could and enriched them, introducing aliens, and scorning and despoiling Englishmen. . . . And so in England there arose many kings to carry off carts and horses, food and clothes and all necessities. Moreover, the Poitevins occupied themselves in oppressing the nobles of the land and especially the monks in a thousand ways.

Matthew accused Henry of unnecessary extravagance (for example over the celebrations in London welcoming him back from Gascony in 1243),[109] and of avarice (he was a 'new Crassus' and the lynx of Merlin's prophecy).[110]

---

[100] *CM*, vol. 2, pp. 583, 588. [101] *CM*, vol. 3, p. 92; vol. 5, p. 293.

[102] *CM*, vol. 2, p. 581.

[103] *CM*, vol. 3, p. 220. One of the objectives of the early baronial opposition to Henry III was to secure the independent status of the chancellor and treasurer: see F. M. Powicke, *The Thirteenth Century* (Oxford 1953), p. 66. Under 1238 Matthew notes that Henry 'violently' deprived Ralph Neville of the seal although it had been committed to him by the baronage: *CM*, vol. 3, p. 495. Cf. *CM*, vol. 4, pp. 20–1.

[104] For Matthew's use of such terms as 'communitas regni', 'universitas barnagium' and 'libertas regni' see *CM*, vol. 3, p. 495; vol. 5, pp. 21, 504.

[105] *CM*, vol. 5, pp. 533, 546. [106] *CM*, vol. 3, p. 395. [107] *CM*, vol. 5, p. 361.

[108] Ibid., p. 229. Cf. ibid., pp. 316–17. [109] *CM*, vol. 4, p. 255.

[110] *CM*, vol. 5, pp. 274, 451.

Matthew also accused him of deceit, and of violating his coronation oath,[111] Magna Carta and John's charter of the church's liberties[112] (he regarded Edmund of Abingdon as a second Thomas Becket, dedicated to the defence of the church's liberties).[113]

Henry's oppression of the church took the form of interfering with episcopal and abbatial elections and exploiting his rights over vacant bishoprics and abbeys: and he allowed the pope to tax the English church. Ostensibly these papal taxes were for a crusade, but Matthew rightly diagnosed that in fact they were to help the pope against the emperor.[114] Matthew could see no religious justification for such taxes. One of Matthew's objections to the Franciscan and Dominican friars was that they acted as royal and papal agents for taxation.[115] He also objected to papal provisions, to procurations collected by papal legates, and to the expense of litigation in the Roman court, in fact to the corollaries of expanding papal authority. He writes (under 1241):[116]

> At this time, with the permission or by the instrumentation of Pope Gregory, the Roman church was so weakened by insatiable greed, confusing good with evil, that (putting shame aside like a common and brazen harlot exposed for hire to everyone), it considered usury as a trivial offence and simony as no crime at all. And so it infected the neighbouring regions, and even the purity of England, with its contagion.

Maybe Matthew, as he grew older, realized that such language was more suitable for a sermon than a history, and that his complaints had a limited relation to reality. Or perhaps he modified his views and became less censorious partly because he found Henry, on personal acquaintance, more congenial than he had imagined. Certainly he became more prudent and was afraid of alienating the abbey's friends. Possibly he had some general fear of reprisals against the abbey by offended parties. Already under 1232 Roger had cautiously omitted the names of Henry's evil counsellors 'because it would be wrong to include them'; Matthew altered this to 'because it would be unsafe'.[117] Later he suppressed some facts for fear of making enemies, lamenting the dilemma of the contemporary historian: 'truth offends man, falsehood is unacceptable to God'.[118] Therefore, Matthew decided, as early as 1250, to modify the invective in the *Chronica* against king, aliens, papacy and friars. He went through the text and from the annal

---

[111] Ibid., p. 567.
[112] Ibid., pp. 362, 381, 449, 451, 467.
[113] *CM*, vol. 4, pp. 14–15, 31–2.
[114] Ibid., pp. 10–11; vol. 5, p. 452.
[115] See e.g. *CM*, vol. 3, pp. 287, 627; vol. 4, pp. 9, 599–600.
[116] *CM*, vol. 4, p. 100.
[117] *CM*, vol. 3, p. 220.
[118] *CM*, vol. 5, p. 470. For similar revision in favour of greater moderation by William of Malmesbury see pp. 181–2 above.

for 1241 onwards marked some passages as 'offensive', or 'offensive to friends', or 'not false but provocative'. He also erased some invidious passages, substituting milder ones.[119] For example, he originally wrote under 1241 that Boniface of Savoy was elected archbishop of Canterbury with the connivance of bishops and abbots who feared the king more than God, despite the adamant opposition of some monks of Christ Church. He described Boniface as insufficient in learning, morals and years for such a dignity. On revision Matthew, while admitting that the Canterbury monks were distressed at the appointment, emphasized that the bishops and abbots supported him gladly, of their own free will, because he was particularly suitable for the office. Matthew describes him as 'of noble stature and elegant bearing' instead of as 'insufficient'.[120] When a copy of the *Chronica* was made at St Albans in 1250 or soon after, the scribe, copying the revised version of the text, omitted many of the passages marked as offensive.[121]

Matthew's panacea for the ills of his times was to limit royal and papal power. The king's power was to be limited by the observance of his coronation oath,[122] of Magna Carta and other charters of liberties and privileges,[123] and of the traditional customs of the kingdom. This observance was to be enforced by the community of the realm represented by the baronage. Papal encroachments were to be limited by adherence to custom and written privileges (Matthew was particularly opposed to the papal use of the 'non obstante' clause to override privileges previously granted to churches and monasteries[124]). It is clear to historians today that Matthew's ideas offered no solution to the clash between vested interest and the growing power of monarchy and papacy. And it would be anachronistic to describe Matthew as a 'constitutionalist' or a 'conservative'.[125] Though he believed that central authority should be limited by the community of the realm, he did not conceive of the community exercising authority instead of the monarch, or permanently supervising the monarch's activities. All would be well, he thought, if the *status quo* were scrupulously observed. But he was not a conservative in the modern political sense which presupposes conflict, actual or conceptual, with more progressive forces. On the contrary Matthew's view was typically medieval. He believed in a static hierarchic form

---

[119] Matthew revised the *Historia Anglorum* even more drastically. For his revision of *CM* and *HA* see Vaughan, op. cit., pp. 64–5, 117–24.

[120] *CM*, vol. 4, pp. 104–5.

[121] BM MS. Cotton Nero D V, pt ii. See Vaughan, op. cit., pp. 65, 110, 117.

[122] See n. 111 above.

[123] For references to passages in which Matthew accuses Henry of violating Magna Carta and John's charter to the church see p. 370 n. 112. He also accused him of violating the charter of privileges of 'communities' smaller than that of the realm; for example of London (over the king's attempt to tax the citizens) and of Ramsey abbey (over the abbey's right to a market); *CM*, vol. 4, p. 95; vol. 5, p. 297, respectively.

[124] See e.g. *CM*, vol. 4, pp. 580, 619; vol. 5, pp. 688, 695.

[125] The so-called constitutionalism of the St Albans historians is a commonplace among historians today; see Galbraith, *Roger Wendover and Matthew Paris*, p. 20.

of society, consisting of pyramids of authority, small and great, but all on the same permanent pattern.

Rather than apply modern political terms to Matthew's views, it is more helpful to consider him as a typical Benedictine. His opinions evolved in the cloister and reflect the sort of authority he found there. Ultimate authority lay in the Rule of St Benedict; its day-to-day administration was in the hands of the abbot. Matthew's concern for the Rule and the Benedictine ideal is clear in his writings. It is easy to exaggerate Matthew's worldliness and underestimate his religious feeling,[126] because he wrote about contemporary politics and society. Nevertheless the very homiletic tone of much of his writing had a religious origin. The fact that he came to dislike the mendicant orders should not blind the reader to his profound admiration for St Francis.[127] Similarly, though most of Matthew's line illustrations are lively and dramatic, a few show genuine piety: there is the picture of St Francis receiving the stigmata, and one of the Virgin Mary, with Matthew kneeling at her feet, of almost Byzantine splendour and grandeur.[128]

Matthew intended in the *Gesta Abbatum Monasterii Sancti Albani* to show that before his time the Rule of St Benedict was strictly observed at St Albans.[129] Moreover, in the *Chronica Majora*, on recording the exhumation of thirty monks during building operations in 1251, Matthew is careful to point out that these monks had lived very austerely. For they wore the most primitive shoes, such as were still worn by the poor, 'round at the back and front, with leather thongs sewn in all round and bound over the top, and so made that they could be worn on either foot'. Matthew adds that the monks who saw the bodies exclaimed at the holiness of their predecessors and were ashamed of their own comfortable lives.[130] Matthew objects to some contemporary developments in the religious orders. He criticizes the use of Benedictine monks as royal justices in eyre, because this was contrary to the Rule.[131] He also criticized the friars because their lives violated the

---

[126] My estimate of Matthew's intellectual motivation differs slightly from that given by Vaughan, op. cit., pp. 139–51, in so far as I stress his Benedictinism. Professor Vaughan attributes Matthew's 'constitutional attitude' to 'his own material interests and those of his house'. Such interests obviously weighed heavily with Matthew, but this view neglects, I think, Matthew's genuine piety and concern for the Benedictine observance.

[127] Matthew copied Wendover's account of St Francis and notice of his canonization (*CM*, vol. 3, pp. 131–5), and added an account of the pope's limitation of the order, and a copy of the Rule of St Francis; ibid., pp. 135–43.

[128] Reproduced by Vaughan as a frontispiece.

[129] See *GASA*, vol. 1, pp. 58–61 *passim*, 211–12. Matthew's meticulous specification of meat-eating regulations may have been due to the interest in the subject shown by the general chapters of the Benedictines in Matthew's day; see M. D. Knowles, *The Religious Orders in England*, vol. 1, *1216–1340* (Cambridge 1956), pp. 18–19. Matthew also records the reduction of elaborations of the liturgical observance at St Albans under Abbots Warin, John de Cella and William of Trumpington (*GASA*, vol. 1, pp. 212–13, 235, 295); such liturgical retrenchment was another feature of the statutes of the general chapters: Knowles, *Religious Orders*, vol. 1, p. 20.

[130] *CM*, vol. 5, pp. 243–5.   [131] Ibid., p. 466.

ideal of stability.[132] Of all the new orders Matthew preferred the Cistercians because their rule had the closest affinities with that of the Benedictines.[133] But he criticized the Cistercians for founding a house at Paris university in competition with the mendicants: the duty of a monk, he said, was to cultivate religion, not learning.[134]

It was presumably partly because Matthew was considered an authority on the Rule that the monks of St Benet Holm in Norway asked him to reform the observance in their house.[135] It is likely that Matthew's preoccupation with the Rule was increased by the circumstances of the times. In the twelfth century the Benedictines had suffered from the competition of the new monastic orders, and in the thirteenth century they suffered from the competition of the friars, notably the Dominicans and Franciscans. Moreover, in the thirteenth century the papacy challenged the autonomy of the individual Benedictine monasteries. The Fourth Lateran Council instituted provincial and general chapters of the Benedictine order on the model of those held by the Cistercians,[136] and Gregory IX promoted the visitation of the Benedictine houses, sending legates to visit the exempt ones.[137] Matthew, therefore, was on the defensive. He thought that the Rule held all the answers, and he was on his guard against any interference with the autonomy of the Benedictine monasteries.

This attitude helps explain Matthew's political views because he believed that monastery, kingdom and papacy represented the same static pattern of government on a progressively large scale. He regarded the ideas he had as a Benedictine as equally applicable to all parts of this hierarchic system. A kingdom therefore was a macrocosm of a monastery, and, conversely, a monastery was a microcosm of a kingdom.[138] The interests of the community (the convent) were protected from the executor of authority (the abbot) by the Rule of St Benedict, by the customs of the house, and by any charters that the abbot and convent had mutually agreed on for the definition of their duties, rights and property. Very roughly these defences of the convent corresponded to the liberties, customs and charters of the realm. Like the abbot, the king should take his subjects' advice,[139] and live on his own income. The organization of the monastery was static, each element, the

---

[132] Ibid., p. 529. For other examples of Matthew criticizing the friars because their lives were incompatible with the precepts of the Rule of St Benedict see *CM*, vol. 4, p. 625; vol. 5, p. 79. Matthew also disapproved of begging: *CM*, vol. 5, p. 52.

[133] *CM*, vol. 5, p. 529.   [134] Ibid., pp. 79–80.   [135] Ibid., p. 44; *HA*, vol. 3, p. 40.

[136] Fourth Lateran Council, canon 12.

[137] For the visitation of exempt houses in England by papal legates in 1232 and 1234 see *CM*, vol. 3, pp. 234–9, and R. Graham, 'A papal visitation of Bury St. Edmunds and Westminster in 1234' in *EHR*, xxvii (1912), pp. 728–39. Cf. Knowles, *Religious Orders*, vol. 1, p. 80.

[138] Professor Galbraith points out that Matthew's interest in the internal politics of St Albans may have led to his interest in general history; *Roger Wendover and Matthew Paris*, p. 6.

[139] Matthew stresses in the *Gesta* that an abbot who was led astray by flatterers, neglecting good counsel, was at fault; *GASA*, vol. 1, pp. 196, 198, 215 (Wats, *Vitae Offarum*, pp. 94–5, 95, 102).

abbot and convent, being almost autonomous. In the same way, according to ancient tradition, a Benedictine abbey was autonomous in its relations with the outside world: Matthew thought that England should be similarly autonomous in its relations with the papacy (in temporal, not spiritual, matters). His belief in autonomy was increased by his natural feelings. Just as Matthew, the monk, loved the Benedictine monasteries, so Matthew the Englishman loved England. His patriotism increased his hatred of aliens, and also appears in his attitude to French institutions: he asserts that Oxford university was as good as the university of Paris,[140] and that barbarous Savoyard laws were unsuitable for the English.[141] One of the few occasions when he praises Henry III's extravagance was on Henry's visit to Paris: his generosity and magnificence greatly impressed the Parisians.[142]

If Matthew saw a Benedictine monastery as a microcosm of the kingdom, the monastery he had particularly in mind was St Albans. Although in his historical works he shows his indignation at the violation of the autonomy of any Benedictine house, he knew and cared most about his own monastery. He wrote the *Gesta Abbatum* to record its history. The *Gesta* makes clear both that the Rule had been strictly observed in the past, and also that Matthew sympathized with the community (the convent) and not with the ruler (the abbot). He records the struggle between the abbot and the convent over the latter's rights, particularly how the convent tried to stop Abbot Warin (1183-95) and Abbot William of Trumpington (1214-35) from banishing recalcitrant monks to the abbey's cells. The convent claimed that such exile was contrary to its customs, and tried to force Abbot Warin on his deathbed to seal a charter confirming their rights.[143] As he refused, they fraudulently sealed the charter, and attempted, unsuccessfully, to make Abbot William observe it.[144]

Matthew's historical method in the *Chronica* is reproduced in miniature in the *Gesta Abbatum*. The idea of writing a local as well as a national history was, of course, an old one, originating in England with Bede,[145] revived by the post-Conquest Durham historians,[146] and kept alive by Richard of Hexham and at Peterborough and Canterbury. Matthew knew the local histories written at Ely and Ramsey towards the end of the twelfth century.[147] Moreover, there was already a local history at St Albans itself. This was a

---

[140] *CM*, vol. 5, pp. 352-3.   [141] Ibid., p. 369.   [142] Ibid., p. 482.

[143] *GASA*, vol. 1, pp. 247-9 (Wats, pp. 111-12).

[144] *GASA*, vol. 1, pp. 255-7, 260 (Wats, pp. 114-15, 116, respectively).

[145] One of Wendover's sources was Bede's *History of the Abbots of Wearmouth*; see *CM*, vol. 1, p. xxxv.

[146] Wendover used the *Historia Dunelmensis Ecclesiae* (i.e. the *Libellus*, for which see pp. 115-21); see *CM*, vol. 1, p. xxxviii.

[147] Wendover used the *Liber Eliensis* (for which see pp. 271 et seq.), and the Ramsey chronicle (for which see ibid.); see *CM*, vol. 1, p. xxxvi.

history of the abbots to Robert (1151–66) by Bartholomew, clerk of 'Adam the cellarer' – presumably the cellarer who held office in Robert's time.[148] Matthew apparently used Bartholomew's chronicle (which was written, according to a note in the *Gesta Abbatum*, on an 'ancient roll').[149] The arrangement and style of the *Gesta Abbatum* in some respects resemble those of the *Chronica*. Thus it is in two sections, the first (which Matthew wrote soon before 1250)[150] is a narrative history of St Albans from its foundation to the death of Abbot William of Trumpington in 1235. It is divided, not like the *Chronica* by years, but by abbacies. After the notice of each abbot's death is an assessment of his achievements for the abbey, what he had done and more particularly what he had left undone (his 'negligences'). These summaries correspond both to the character-sketches in the *Chronica*, and also to the annual summaries, for like them they give each section a unity of its own. Then, in about 1255, Matthew added the second section of the *Gesta*. This is different in character from the first. The brief passages of creative historical writing are outweighed by documents and business records (Matthew had already included much of the narrative history of John's abbacy in the *Chronica*).

But Matthew's objectives in the *Gesta Abbatum* were wholly different from those in his general histories, though it too reflects the breadth of his interests and his visual sense. He wrote to edify his fellow monks and so improve their conduct, to commemorate the achievements of past monks of St Albans, and to provide a record of the abbey's rights and privileges. The *Gesta* is more specifically didactic than the *Chronica*. The latter was intended for a wide monastic audience, and though it has general denunciations of vice and sin, Matthew must have known it could have no immediate effect on those it criticized most (the king, magnates and the rest), because they would never read it. But as the *Gesta* was intended for the monks of St Albans, Matthew no doubt hoped they would find it edifying. He tried to improve the religious observance of the monks: he hoped, by recording the strict lives of their predecessors, to encourage them to emulation; and he may have intended, by recording the customs of the abbey, as codified by successive abbots, to help the monks to observe them properly.[151] And perhaps Matthew meant the abbots to read the *Gesta* as a salutary warning. He not only recorded the abbots' disputes with the convent, but also summarized their 'negligences': an abbot reading the work might hope to earn a good rather than a bad notice in the *Gesta*. Matthew explicitly suggests how an abbot should behave when visiting the cell at Tynemouth, so that his

---

[148] For Bartholomew's roll see Vaughan, op. cit., pp. 182–4, and C. Jenkins, *The Monastic Chronicler and the Early School of St. Albans* (London 1922), pp. 34–7.

[149] *GASA*, vol. i, p. xiv.

[150] Ibid., pp. 3–305 (Wats, pp. 35–134). Cf. Vaughan, op. cit., pp. 86–7.

[151] Matthew must have borrowed from a customary of the house and from chapter statutes. See *GASA*, vol. i, pp. 73–9, 206–14, 224, 234–5 (Wats, pp. 56, 98–101, 105, 109).

visit would be spiritually beneficial and not financially burdensome to the priory.[152]

Moreover, in the *Gesta*, Matthew instructed the monks about the abbey. His account of St Albans architectural and artistic history provided a historical background to the abbey's extant treasures and buildings. Therefore the *Gesta* served as a guidebook. But another reason why Matthew recorded such information was to preserve the memory of those who had contributed to the abbey's artistic and architectural achievements. He writes: 'We are led to commit these things to the immortality of the written word, so that those who adorned our church by their industry should be gratefully remembered among us, and with blessings'.[153] Thus the *Gesta* has considerable value for cultural history.[154] Matthew records, for example, that Abbot John de Cella (1195–1214)[155] started the west front, that Abbot William heightened the tower and roofed the aisles of the church with oak,[156] and (in the second section) that Abbot John of Hertford (1235–63) built the palatial guest-house, with its great hall (having fireplaces, chimney, vestibule and crypt), its two-storeyed entrance-hall and large bedrooms.[157] He records the artistic work of some of the monks, the paintings of William on the altar panels and his bas-reliefs behind the altars, done in the time of Abbot John de Cella.[158] And he notices the carvings on the pulpit by the sacrist Walter of Colchester, 'an incomparable painter and sculptor'.[159] He also records books given to or copied for the abbey,[160] including one which survives today.[161]

Finally, the *Gesta* provided the monks with a record of the abbey's defence of its privileges and property, and could have been used as a book of precedents. It has what is virtually a tract proving that the diocesan had no

[152] *GASA*, vol. I, p. 265 (Wats, p. 118).

[153] *GASA*, vol. I, p. 233 (Wats, p. 108). Of course the obits in the *Chronica* had a general commemorative intention.

[154] *GASA*, vol. I, p. 73 (Wats, p. 56). Matthew has one passage throwing light on the early history of liturgical plays: he records that before Abbot Geoffrey (1119–46) became a monk of St Albans, he had been a grammar master at Dunstable priory and had produced mystery plays of St Catherine there (he borrowed copes from St Albans for the actors which were unfortunately destroyed by fire, so Geoffrey, as recompense, took the habit at St Albans). The passage is noticed by E. K. Chambers, *The Medieval Stage* (Oxford 1903, 2 vols), vol. 2, pp. 64–5, 107, 366.

[155] *GASA*, vol. I, pp. 218–20 (Wats, pp. 103–4). For John de Cella's building of the west end see N. Pevsner, *Hertfordshire* (Buildings of England series, Penguin Books, 1953), p. 209.

[156] *GASA*, vol. I, pp. 280–1 (Wats, pp. 121–2). Much of the existing nave is by William, although it was begun by John de Cella: Pevsner, *Hertfordshire*, p. 209.

[157] *GASA*, vol. I, p. 314 (Wats, p. 142). For other references to buildings see *GASA*, vol. I, pp. 79, 285, 287–8, 290 (Wats, pp. 58, 123, 124–5, 125–6).

[158] *GASA*, vol. I, p. 233 (Wats, p. 108).

[159] *GASA*, vol. I, pp. 279–81, 286 (Wats, pp. 121, 124). He also notes that the artist Richard (see p. 362 and n. 43 above) painted on the walls of John of Hertford's new guest-house: *GASA*, vol. I, p. 314 (Wats, p. 142).

[160] *GASA*, vol. I, pp. 58, 192 (Wats, pp. 51, 93).

[161] See *GASA*, vol. I, pp. 233–4 (Wats, p. 108). The book, a copy of the *Historia Scholastica*, is now BM MS. Royal 4 D VII.

right to dedicate its altars, chapels and churches,[162] or to hold ordinations in the abbey.[163] It gives a list of the various bishops who performed such dedications and ordinations, emphasizing that the bishop of Lincoln had never performed these functions and had no right to. The section on the abbacy of Robert (mainly borrowed from Bartholomew's chronicle-roll) is almost wholly a record of the abbot's litigation in defence of rights and property, and, as has been seen, the section which Matthew added to the *Gesta* in about 1255 is almost entirely such a record: it has a detailed and fully documented account of the election of Abbot John, a record of an important lawsuit involving the abbey, and brief entries recording the abbot's business affairs.

The *Gesta Abbatum* became the official history of St Albans for the monks of the abbey. After Matthew's death it may have been continued contemporaneously at least during the rule of Abbot Roger (1263–90).[164] Subsequently, in the late fourteenth century, it was worked over by Thomas Walsingham, who, using the *Chronica*, the *Liber Additamentorum* and the abbey's archives, interpolated it and continued it to his own day.[165] Similarly, Matthew's general history was continued. He himself wrote to shortly before his death in 1259. A note at the end of the last annal in the *Chronica* reads:[166]

To this point wrote the venerable man Matthew Paris. Although the hand on the pen may vary, as the method of composition is the same throughout, the whole must be ascribed to him. What is added and continues from here must be ascribed to another brother who, presuming to approach the work of such a great predecessor and unworthily to continue it (as he is not worthy to undo the tie of his shoe), has not deserved even to have his name mentioned on the page.

This humble, anonymous monk did not in fact continue the *Chronica*, but he did continue the *Flores Historiarum*, Matthew's own abbreviation of the *Chronica*. He wrote apparently from 1259–65,[167] and at first imitated

162 *GASA*, vol. 1, pp. 147–8 (Wats, pp. 78–9). See also *GASA*, vol. 1, pp. 269–70, 282, 288–9 (Wats, pp. 119, 122, 125). For a tract similar to this passage, written at Bury St Edmunds, cf. p. 392 and n. 82 below.
163 *GASA*, vol. 1, p. 149 (Wats, p. 79). See also *GASA*, vol. 1, p. 388.
164 There are references in the existing text to 'the book of the acts of Abbot Roger'; *GASA*, vol. 1, pp. 480, 483.
165 This is the text printed by Riley: see p. 357 n. 9 above. Walsingham begins his continuation with Book II of the *Gesta*; *GASA*, vol. 1, pp. 327 et seq.
166 *CM*, vol. 5, p. 748, n. 1. See Galbraith, *Roger Wendover and Matthew Paris*, p. 12 and Vaughan, op. cit., p. 7.
167 The continuations, to 1326, to Matthew's *Flores* are printed in *FH*. For the St Albans continuation, 1259–65, see *FH*, vol. 2, p. 426 to vol. 3, p. 6. That this continuation was the work

Matthew's method: up to, and including, 1260, he gives an annual summary, and to the end of 1261 he notices where the king spent Christmas and frequently refers to the *Liber Additamentorum*, to which he relegates documents.[168] As will be seen, his political views are like Matthew's (he hates papal taxation and provisions, and Henry III's alien counsellors).[169] But he could not reproduce Matthew's homiletic fervour and breadth of knowledge and interest, and reduced the St Albans chronicle to much the same level as the monastic annals of other houses.

The anonymous author of the *Flores Historiarum* was succeeded at St Albans, after a brief interval, by a series of mediocre annalists.[170] It was left to Thomas of Walsingham late in the fourteenth century to revive the method and concepts of Matthew Paris's history. But though the *Flores* was only an abbreviation of the *Chronica Majora* with a second-rate continuation, it was eminently suitable for further continuation. It became the most popular of all Matthew's works and St Albans chief literary export. Matthew's own copy went to Westminster abbey soon after 1265, where it was continued to 1327.[171] By the end of the thirteenth century a copy of the *Flores* (containing the annals to 1296) was at St Swithun's, Winchester.[172] In the early fourteenth century, copies of the *Flores* were owned by the Augustinian

---

of the St Albans monk referred to in the note at the end of the *Chronica* was first pointed out by Sir Frederic Madden and has been accepted by subsequent scholars; see *HA*, vol. 1, pp. xxi–xxiv and nn. His conclusion was due to his discovery in the Chetham library, Manchester, of the St Albans copy of the *Flores* to 1327 (MS. 6712), which is partly (from 1241–9) in Matthew's own hand (*HA*, vol. 1, p. xxii; Vaughan, op. cit., p. 92). It should be noted that Yonge's English translation (see p. 357 n. 7 above), which is of the *Flores* to 1326, does not in all places correspond to Luard's text. This is because Yonge's translation, preceding Luard's edition, is of the conflated text originally printed by Archbishop Parker who did not know the Chetham MS. which Luard took as the basis of his text. (For Parker's editions of the *Flores* see *FH*, vol. 1, pp. xliii–xlviii; cf. Vaughan, op. cit., pp. 154–5.) Thus Yonge's translation of the account of the battle of Evesham is of the 'Merton' version of the text (see p. 379 and n. 173 below) and is not the same as that in Luard's text (Luard prints the variant 'Merton' version in an appendix, *FH*, vol. 3, pp. 251–68).

[168] See *FH*, vol. 1, pp. xl–xli for the references to the *Liber Additamentorum*. The change in method from the end of 1261 onwards could indicate that only the annals to 1261 were written at St Albans. This view would be corroborated by the fact that the last detailed reference to St Albans is under 1260 (*FH*, vol. 2, p. 460). Possibly the annals from the end of 1261 to 1265 were compiled at Westminster where the Chetham MS. was soon after 1265 (see p. 420 and n. 147 below). The conclusion that the whole continuation from 1259 to 1265 was written at St Albans is based on the fact that the text for these years is in the same hand in the Chetham MS. (see Luard, *FH*, vol. 1, p. xiv). However, it is possible that a scribe at Westminster copied in this section, incorporating annals from 1259 to 1261 obtained from St Albans.

[169] See pp. 418–19.

[170] See V. H. Galbraith, *The St. Albans Chronicle, 1406–1420* (Oxford 1937), pp. xxvii–xxxvi.

[171] This copy is now the Chetham MS. (see n. 167 above). Owing to a confusion of the evidence John Bale, followed by Archbishop Parker and subsequent scholars, thought that the *Flores* to 1307 was by 'Matthew of Westminster': the evidence adduced by Sir Frederic Madden as to the true provenance of the *Flores* makes it very unlikely that 'Matthew of Westminster' ever existed: see *HA*, vol. 1, pp. xx, xxi and nn. 1, 4.

[172] Bodleian MS. Laud Misc. 572. See *FH*, vol. 1, pp. xvii–xviii. For its provenance see N. R. Ker, *Medieval Libraries of Great Britain* (2nd ed., Royal Historical Soc., 1964), p. 201.

priory of Merton in Surrey,[173] St Paul's, London,[174] St Mary's, Southwark,[175] St Augustine's, Canterbury,[176] and the cathedral priories of Norwich[177] and Rochester.[178] A copy was also at St Benet of Hulme, in Norfolk, and this went to the Cistercian abbey of Tintern in Monmouthshire soon after 1304.[179] All these copies still survive. They differ in varying degrees from the St Albans *Flores* and from the Westminster continuation. They omit some passages and include new material, often relating to the houses for which they were written. They all end in the last years of Edward I, though two (those from St Paul's and Tintern) have continuations of their own (to 1341[180] and 1323[181] respectively).

[173] Eton College MS. 123. See *FH*, vol. 1, pp. xv–xvi. This copy of the *Flores* (printed in *FH*, vol. 3, pp. 239–327) has substantial variants from the Chetham MS., notably its account of the battle of Evesham, which is that translated by Yonge; see p. 377 n. 167 above. It provided an alternative textual tradition to that in the Chetham MS. and influenced a number of the copies of the *Flores* (see Luard's descriptions of the MSS., *FH*, vol. 1, pp. xvii–xxxiii *passim*, and pp. 456–8 and nn. *passim* below).

[174] Lambeth MS. 1106; see *FH*, vol. 1, p. xxvii. See n. 180 below. For the use made of the *Flores* by the author of the *Annales Londonienses* see pp. 508–9.

[175] Bodleian MS. Rawlinson B. 177; see *FH*, vol. 1, p. xxix.

[176] BM MS. Harley 641; see ibid., pp. xxxi–xxxiii.

[177] Bodleian MS. Fairfax 20; see ibid., p. xxix. Another Norwich copy, *c.* 1400, is BM MS. Cotton Claudius E VIII; see ibid., p. xxiv.

[178] BM MS. Cotton Nero D II; see ibid., pp. xxvi–xxvii. Additions to the *Flores* in it are printed in *FH*, vol. 3, pp. 327–8.

[179] BM MS. Royal 14. C VI; see *FH*, vol. 1, pp. xxii–xxiv.

[180] Printed as *Annales Paulini* in *Chronicles of the Reigns of Edward I and II*, ed. W. Stubbs (RS, 1882, 1883, 2 vols), vol. 1, pp. 255–370.

[181] Printed in *FH*, vol. 3, pp. 328–48.

17

Historical Writing at Bury St Edmunds in the Thirteenth Century

St Edmund's abbey is less known as a centre of historiography than St Albans. And yet historical writing started sooner at Bury (in the late eleventh century) and lasted longer (until the late fifteenth century). It produced one masterpiece, *Cronica Jocelini de Brakelonda* (*Chronicle of Jocelin of Brakelond*), besides numerous tracts on the abbey's history, and two world chronicles, one of which was widely used in other East Anglian monasteries. The comparatively great number of historical works surviving from Bury makes it possible to determine the motives for historical writing there.

As at St Albans, the initial incentive to write history was provided by an interest in the abbey's past. This curiosity was closely linked in its origin with the cult of the patron saint. The first attempt at abbatial history was by Hermann in his *Miracles of St. Edmund,* and the first known annals from Bury (the so-called *Annals of St. Neots,* compiled in the early twelfth century) have entries about St Edmund, king and martyr.[1] And the influence of hagiography on historical writing persisted at Bury well into the thirteenth century, notably in Jocelin of Brakelond's chronicle.

As a patron saint was regarded as the *persona* of his monastery, interest in hagiography led to the study of local history. Therefore piety was one motive for local historiography. But in the thirteenth century other incentives increased monks' interest in abbatial history. They wished to keep a record of their abbey's history (partly for practical reasons), they wanted to augment its prestige by historical propaganda, and they sometimes had a genuine antiquarian curiosity, a desire to understand the origin of their abbey's existing treasures and architectural features.

Hagiography and local history encouraged the study of general history. The *Annals of St. Neots* demonstrate the use of annals to provide a chronological framework for abbatial history. Towards the middle of the twelfth century the monks of Bury used a copy of Florence of Worcester's chronicle in the same way, inserting quite long passages about St Edmund and his

[1] For the *Annals of St. Neots* see p. 148 n. 77.

abbey.[2] In the thirteenth century the tendency of interest in local history to lead to the study of general history was accelerated because of the increasing involvement of the religious orders in the outside world. This involvement was due to the expanding authority of king and pope, in administrative, judicial and especially in financial matters. For example it was a short step from recording the assessment of an abbey for a royal or papal tax, to explaining the events leading up to the imposition of the tax.

The historical writings produced in St Edmund's abbey show the influence of these historiographical motives in varying degrees. They will be discussed in four sections; first, Jocelin of Brakelond's chronicle; second, the record-type tracts; third, tracts with propaganda and/or antiquarian features; and fourth, the two world chronicles.

Jocelin of Brakelond completed his chronicle soon after 1202.[3] He was strongly influenced by the hagiographical tradition. He himself was the author of a saint's life (now lost), the Life of St Robert, a boy allegedly martyred by Jews in Bury in 1181.[4] The chronicle is a biography of Abbot Samson with some features of an Anglo-Saxon hagiography. Jocelin used the work as a vehicle for conventual history for the period he covered, from the death of Abbot Hugh (1180) and the succession of Samson (1182), to 1202 (thus he stopped before Samson's death in 1211). Like the Anglo-Saxon and the twelfth-century biographers, he knew his subject intimately. Eadmer had been Anselm's chaplain, Adam of Eynsham was St Hugh's, Milo was chaplain to Richard I, and Jocelin was the chaplain of Abbot Samson for the six years following Samson's election to the abbacy. Thus Jocelin was with Samson 'night and day', acted as his secretary, and noted 'many things which he stored in his memory'.[5]

The influence of hagiography on Jocelin appears in two strands in the chronicle: preoccupation with the cult of St Edmund; and a tendency on occasion to treat Samson as a quasi-saint. Like any hagiographer, Jocelin is anxious to show that the patron saint's body lay in the church uncorrupt and complete – an anxiety increased by the recent fire in St Edmund's shrine.[6] Therefore he describes in detail the opening of St Edmund's coffin, before a number of witnesses (whom Jocelin names), by Abbot Samson in 1198. The uncorrupt body was found wrapped in a linen cloth 'of wondrous whiteness'.[7] Samson

---

[2] Now Bodley MS. 297 in the Bodleian Library. Most of the interpolations are printed in *Memorials SE*, vol. 1, Appendix B, pp. 340–56. Cf. p. 148 n. 77 above.

[3] The most recent edition is *The Chronicle of Jocelin of Brakelond*, ed., with an English translation, H. E. Butler (Nelson's Medieval Classics, 1949).

[4] *JB*, p. 16. For a record of his passion see the *Annales Sancti Edmundi* printed in Liebermann, *U A-N G*, p. 135.

[5] *JB*, pp. 26, 35, 36.

[6] *JB*, pp. 108–9.

[7] See *JB*, pp. 112–16.

touched the eyes and nose which was very large and prominent, and afterwards he touched the breast and arms and, raising the left hand, he touched the fingers and placed his fingers between the fingers of the saint; and, going further, he found the feet turned stiffly upward as of a man dead that selfsame day, and he touched the feet and toes, counting them as he touched them.

Moreover, Jocelin attributes posthumous power to St Edmund, which was exercised in defence of the abbey. He tells a story ('to spread abroad more widely the memory of the blessed king and martyr') of the defeat in a judicial duel of an opponent of the abbey, Henry of Essex, as a result of the unnerving apparition of St Edmund to Henry.[8]

Jocelin's occasional tendency to represent Samson as a saint appears in two prophetic visions. Jocelin asserts that Samson when nine years old dreamed that he would turn his back on 'the pleasures of this world' and enter St Edmund's monastery.[9] And he states that two monks had visions foretelling Samson's election to the abbacy.[10] Jocelin's occasional eulogy of Samson could be partly due to the influence of hagiography or secular biography. He praises 'the merits of his life and the depth of his wisdom', his ability in business matters and as a judge ('his glance was sharp and penetrating, and his brow worthy of Cato'); and his acts were 'worthy of immortal record and renown'.[11]

But the influence of the traditional form of hagiography was severely limited in the chronicle by Jocelin's strong sense of reality and acute powers of observation. Both Eadmer and Adam of Eynsham had given realistic touches to their biographies, but Jocelin surpassed his predecessors. He gives a portrait of his subject unique in English monastic literature. He gives a full description of Samson's appearance and personal habits, and, in the course of the work, throws light on other aspects of his character. He writes:[12]

> Abbot Samson was of middle height, and almost entirely bald; his face was neither round nor long, his nose prominent, his lips thick, his eyes clear as crystal and of penetrating glance; his hearing of the sharpest; his eyebrows grew long and were often clipped; a slight cold made him soon grow hoarse. On the day of his election he was forty-seven years old, and had been a monk for

---

[8] *JB*, pp. 68–71. This story was told by 'Jocelin the almoner' to the author. From this H. E. Butler, p. xiii, concludes that the story was told by Jocelin of Brakelond who was then almoner to someone who then interpolated it into Jocelin of Brakelond's own work. This is most unlikely as the story is in the text in the only known manuscript and there is no evidence that Jocelin of Brakelond was ever the almoner. Here I agree with R. H. C. Davis, *The Kalendar of Abbot Samson* (Camden Soc., 3rd series, lxxxiv, 1954), p. liv.

[9] *JB*, p. 37.

[10] *JB*, pp. 19, 20.

[11] *JB*, pp. 34, 36–7, 47.

[12] *IB*, pp. 39–40.

seventeen. He had a few white hairs in a red beard and a very few in the hair of his head, which was black and rather curly; but within fourteen years of his election he was white as snow. He was a man of extreme sobriety, never given to sloth, extremely strong and ever ready to go either on horseback or on foot, until old age prevailed and tempered his eagerness. When he heard of the capture of the Cross and the fall of Jerusalem, he began to wear drawers of haircloth, and a shirt of hair instead of wool, and to abstain from flesh and meat; none the less he desired that meat should be placed before him when he sat at table, that so our alms might be increased. He preferred fresh milk and honey and the like to any other food. . . .

As has been said above, Jocelin used the biography of Samson as a means of recording abbatial history. He applied his sharp eye and ear to the life of the cloister, and gives an unrivalled picture of it. He was obviously susceptible to gossip and tale-bearing, which flourished particularly at blood-letting time when 'monks are wont to reveal the secrets of their hearts'.[13] He reflects conventual opinion, for example the monks' rather disgruntled reaction to a visit by King John:[14]

We indeed believed that he would make some great oblation; but he offered nothing save a single silken cloth which his servants had borrowed from our sacrist – and they have not yet paid the price. And yet he received the hospitality of St. Edmund at great cost to the abbey, and when he departed he gave nothing at all to the honour or advantage of the saint save thirteen pence sterling, which he offered at his mass on the day when he left us.

Jocelin's interest in conventual affairs deepened after 1187 when he stopped being Samson's chaplain. In 1200 he became the convent's guest-master,[15] and consequently his loyalties changed. He devotes more space to the convent and becomes increasingly critical of Samson, his tendency to hagiographical eulogy being totally obliterated. He specifically defends

---

[13] *JB*, p. 14.

[14] *JB*, pp. 116–17.

[15] *JB*, p. 129. For the guest-master's connection with the cellarer's office see ibid., pp. 88, 89. I do not agree with Prof. Davis's view, op. cit., pp. li–liv, that Jocelin of Brakelond is to be identified with Jocellus the cellarer who appears in Jocelin's chronicle. Davis himself realizes the difficulties which such a view involves. One objection which he does not mention is that Jocelin of Brakelond's account of the opening of St Edmund's tomb was apparently obtained from a certain John of Diss who witnessed the scene from where he was perched up in the rafters, but Jocellus the cellarer was one of the monks present with Abbot Samson (*JB*, pp. 114–15; cf. the disappointment of most of the monks at not being allowed to attend; *JB*, p. 113). Moreover, the account of Jocellus in the chronicle is not entirely flattering, as he is represented as an extremist; *JB*, p. 118.

himself from the charge of being a flatterer,[16] and towards the end of the work states that in a certain case 'the abbot is not to be commended for what he did'. He calls another of his acts a 'stain of evil-doing, which, God willing, the abbot will wash out with the tears of penitence'.[17]

Therefore the chronicle is an important source for the history of St Edmund's abbey. And it does more than reflect monastic trivialities. It is a record of the constitutional struggle between Abbot Samson and the convent over Samson's financial and administrative reforms.[18] Jocelin obviously intended to provide a record of the conflict. His record-consciousness appears throughout the chronicle. He liked lists and documents. For example he gave Samson, as a New Year's gift, a list he had made of all the churches, together with their annual value, belonging to the abbot.[19] He notes the compilation of Abbot Samson's Kalendar, as a result of an inquiry into the abbot's tenants and the rents and services due to him. Jocelin also gives a list, made in 1200, of the knights and fiefs of St Edmund.[20]

The record-aspect of the chronicle also appears in Jocelin's careful account of the customs of the abbey (for example those relating to the abbot's obligation to entertain certain categories of visitors[21]), and Samson's administrative reforms. Jocelin explains how Samson stopped the sacrist and cellarer from contracting debts or selling the property of their offices without the knowledge of the convent, by stipulating that all charters should be read in chapter.[22] He explains how Samson appointed clerks to supervise the work of these two obedientiaries and even deposed them and lesser officials for maladministration.[23] He clearly indicates the reasons for Samson's policy and equally clearly the reasons for the convent's resentment. Samson claimed that as a tenant-in-chief he was responsible to the king for the good government of his barony.[24] The convent objected, because his encroachment on its property and privileges would, during a vacancy of the abbacy, be to the convent's detriment: for then the king took the abbot's barony into his hands and therefore would also take over whatever the abbot had usurped from the convent.[25]

Moreover, Jocelin makes it clear that conflict in the abbey was not only due to bad relations between abbot and convent: the convent itself was divided by faction. There were those who supported learning and education, and those who believed that the latter were unnecessary for a good monk, and even for those holding high office in the monastery.[26] Samson himself had

---

[16] *JB*, p. 105.　　　　　　　　　　[17] *JB*, pp. 130–1.

[18] I have discussed fully the struggle between Abbot Samson and the convent, and the resultant agreement drawn up between the abbot (either Samson or his successor Hugh of Northwold) and convent in *The Customary of the Benedictine Abbey of Bury St. Edmunds in Suffolk*, ed. A. Gransden (HBS, xcix, 1973), pp. xvii–xxi.

[19] *JB*, pp. 63–4.　　　　　　　　　　[20] *JB*, pp. 28, 120–2.

[21] *JB*, p. 39.　　　　　　　　　　　[22] *JB*, p. 30.

[23] *JB*, pp. 30, 79, 80, 88–90.　　　　[24] *JB*, pp. 63, 74–5, 105–6, 136–7.

[25] *JB*, pp. 73, 81, 89–90.　　　　　　[26] *JB*, pp. 11–15, 124–30, *passim*.

been a compromise candidate for the abbacy.[27] He did not like the introvert, studious type of monk but preferred good administrators.[28] He preached in French, and in English with a Norfolk dialect, not in Latin.[29] Nevertheless he was far from illiterate. He had studied in Paris[30] and wrote Latin verses for inscription in the abbey church.[31] Jocelin also shows that there was tension between the young and the old in the convent,[32] and between the sacrist and cellarer and their supporters.[33] These factions gained decisive importance during the vacancy which followed Samson's death in 1211 and lasted until the summer of 1215.

The second group of historical works written at Bury, the record-type tracts, were intended to authenticate the abbey's rights and privileges, and to provide legal precedents if required. A good example of such a tract is the *Narratio quaedam de Processu contra Fratres Minores qualiter expulsi erant de Villa Sancti Edmundi* (*Account of the Proceedings against the Friars Minor and how they were expelled from the Vill of St. Edmund*).[34] This work tells the story of the abbey's struggle from 1257 to 1263 against the attempt of the Franciscans to settle within the *banleuca* (the area of St Edmunds exempt from spiritual jurisdiction). It records the details of the compromise ultimately reached between monks and friars, and may well have been begun for the information of the papal judges delegate appointed in 1262 to hear the case. A rather similar tract records the details of the revolt during the Barons' War of the young townsmen of Bury, organized in a 'Guild of Youth', against the abbey.[35] The young men's revolt led to a royal inquiry and the tract was written to present the abbot's case to the king's justices.

The tracts on the Franciscans and on the townsmen are written in vivid narrative and do not quote documents in full. But other tracts are little more than cartularies of documents relating to one subject, arranged in chronological order; and a few even have the notary's attestation to the authenticity of the copies. A tract of this type records the proceedings (1262–3) relating to the attempted Franciscan settlement in the *banleuca*, held before the papal

---

[27] M. D. Knowles, *The Monastic Order in England* (2nd ed., Cambridge 1963), pp. 503–4.

[28] *JB*, p. 40. But Samson did claim that he would rather have looked after the abbey's books than been abbot; *JB*, p. 36.

[29] *JB*, p. 40.   [30] *JB*, p. 44.

[31] *JB*, p. 9. Possibly these verses are those which still survive, copied on to the fly-leaves of Arundel MS. XXX in the College of Arms: they are described and extracts printed by M. R. James, *On the Abbey of St. Edmund at Bury* (Cambridge Antiquarian Soc., 8vo series, xxviii, 1895), pp. 131–2, 186–203.

[32] *JB*, p. 14.   [33] *JB*, pp. 100–1.

[34] Printed in *Memorials SE*, vol. 2, pp. 263–70. For this tract and other evidence for the Franciscans' settlement at Bury see A. G. Little, *Studies in English Franciscan History* (Manchester 1917), pp. 96–8.

[35] Printed and discussed by H. W. C. Davis, 'The commune of Bury St. Edmunds, 1264' in *EHR*, xxiv (1909), pp. 313–16.

judges delegate.[36] Equally typical are the records of abbatial elections (of Simon of Luton in 1257,[37] and of Thomas of Tottington in 1301[38]). An incentive to write election accounts was provided by the Fourth Lateran Council. The latter, by defining election procedure and asserting the pope's responsibility for elections in exempt abbeys, made election records desirable, in order to prove that the due canonical process had been observed.[39] Such records were particularly important if the elections were disputed. In this case the record is a *pièce justificative*, providing evidence that the abbot's title was beyond dispute. In fact by far the most remarkable election account written at Bury in the thirteenth century was of a disputed election.

The *Cronica de Electione Hugonis Abbatis postea Episcopi Eliensis* (*Chronicle concerning the Election of Abbot Hugh, later Bishop of Ely*)[40] is an account of the election of Hugh of Northwold to the abbacy in the summer of 1213 and the dispute which followed, lasting nearly two years until King John finally gave his assent to Hugh's election at Runnymede in June 1215. The *Electio* provides a very detailed narrative of the affair (with copies of some relevant documents), which, though written primarily for reference and not for the reader's amusement or edification, has considerable literary merit. It is a valuable source for conventual history: it both throws light on the internal factions, already made apparent in Jocelin's chronicle, and also contains the earliest known account of proceedings in a conventual chapter. Moreover, although it is a local and not a national history (national affairs are only obliquely referred to), the events it records were contemporary with a crucial period in political history. It has some incidental information about conditions in East Anglia during the civil war. And it contains eye-witness accounts of King John, in his dealings with the abbey. None of the chroniclers gives first-hand descriptions of the king (the only known parallel is in Adam of Eynsham's *Life of St. Hugh*[41]). As the *Electio* has received less attention from historians than it deserves, it will be discussed here in some detail.

King John's long delay in granting his assent to the election of Hugh of Northwold was partly because he thought that the monks, by not offering

---

[36] Printed in *Memorials SE*, vol. 2, pp. 271–85.

[37] Printed in ibid., pp. 253–9.

[38] Printed in ibid., pp. 299–323.

[39] For an election account by Matthew Paris in the *Gesta Abbatum* see p. 377 above.

[40] Printed in *Memorials SE*, vol. 2, pp. 29–130. A synopsis of the contents, with some extracts translated into English, is in ibid., pp. viii–xxiv. A new edition, by R. M. Thomson, is to be published in the series Oxford Medieval Texts. Mr Thomson kindly allowed me to read the thesis he prepared on the *Electio* for an M.A. degree at the University of Melbourne, on which his edition will be based. I read it after completing the above section on the *Electio* and was pleased to find that our general conclusions, notably on the authorship of the *Electio*, coincide. I am also indebted to Mr Thomson for reading my section and for making some valuable suggestions and corrections.

[41] See p. 317.

him a choice of candidates, had defied his customary rights.[42] And it was partly because the convent was not unanimous. The latter was fairly evenly divided,[43] one faction supporting the Elect, Hugh of Northwold, the other supporting the sacrist, Robert of Graveley, who had hoped to be elected himself.[44] The Elect's party defended the convent's right of election,[45] regarded the election as canonical[46] and felt bound by its oath to support the Elect.[47] The sacrist's party supported the king's rights, emphasizing the dangers of opposing John.[48]

The dispute was obviously a *cause célèbre*. Important public figures and ecclesiastics became involved before the ultimate settlement. Archbishop Stephen Langton, defending the abbey's right to free election, initially declared that Hugh's election was a victory for the freedom of the church.[49] And perhaps John finally agreed to the election at Runnymede, when he was negotiating with the barons, to win support against his opponents.[50] The reforming papacy took advantage of the dispute to attack lax observance in the abbey, instructing its representatives to inquire about bad customs.[51] And the legate, Nicholas, issued regulations forbidding meals to be taken outside the monks' refectory.[52] Moreover, during the dispute, appeals were made to the new papal constitutions on elections.[53]

Bury was visited, in attempts at a settlement, by various powerful people. Besides the legate, the pope appointed judges delegate (Henry abbot of Wardon, Richard prior of Dunstable and Richard dean of Salisbury)[54] to hear the case. And before King John finally came to Bury himself, he sent such men as Peter des Roches bishop of Winchester, William Marshal earl of Pembroke, Robert Fitz Walter, Eustace de Fauconberg (the king's treasurer)

[42] The king refused his assent 'audita forma sub una persona'; *EH*, p. 34. See M. D. Knowles, 'Essays in monastic history 1066–1215. I. Abbatial elections' in *Downside Review*, xlix (1931), p. 272 and n. 1.

[43] For a division list see *EH*, pp. 75–6.

[44] The *Gesta Sacristarum* (for which see p. 301 below) asserts that Robert was actually elected: 'Mortuo autem abbate Sampsone, a quibusdam Hugo de Northwolde, a quibusdam Robertus praedictus ad abbatiam fuerat electus'; *Memorials SE*, vol. 2, p. 293. The *Electio* records that Robert and his party disputed the election process because Robert, though chosen one of the seven 'compromissarii' to elect the abbot, was removed from their number and another monk substituted; *EH*, pp. 32, 98.

[45] *EH*, pp. 45–6, 77, 100. For the abbey's right to elect its abbot see D. C. Douglas, *Feudal Documents from the Abbey of Bury St. Edmunds* (London 1932), p. 69.

[46] *EH*, p. 46 (cf. ibid., p. 120).

[47] e.g. *EH*, pp. 47, 78.

[48] *EH*, pp. 60–1.   [49] *EH*, p. 34.

[50] See *EH*, p. 127, and J. C. Holt, *Magna Carta* (Cambridge 1965), pp. 154–5. There is a possibility that Bury had been used as a centre of resistance to King John, which is discussed in *The Customary of . . . Bury St. Edmunds*, ed. A. Gransden, p. xxiv n. 5.

[51] *EH*, p. 72.   [52] *EH*, pp. 56–7, 62–3.

[53] *EH*, pp. 75, 80. Apparently references to *Quia requisitis* (see *Quinque Compilationes Antiquae* ed. E. Friedberg (Leipzig 1882), p. 67) and *Quum terra* (ibid., and Decret. Greg. IV, lib. 1, tit. VI, 14 in *Corpus Juris Canonici*, ed. E. Friedberg (Leipzig 1879, 1881, 2 vols), vol. 2, p. 54), respectively.

[54] *EH*, p. 69.

and Richard Marsh (the chancellor).[55] Meanwhile the Elect and his opponents travelled to France and Rome, and followed the English court, in search of a settlement.

The author of the *Electio* was probably Master Nicholas of Dunstable, a monk of Bury.[56] He frequently appears in the narrative, taking an active part in the dispute: he acted as the convent's spokesman and go-between with the judges delegate and others.[57] And whenever his views are recorded, they are identical with those expressed by the author. It was he who originally opposed the inclusion of the sacrist, Robert of Graveley, among the seven monks chosen by the convent to elect an abbot, by way of compromise.[58] And he led the Elect's party in its opposition to the use of the convent's seal by the sacrist's supporters.[59] He also played an important part in preventing the sacrist's party from presenting only its supporters to the bishop of Ely for ordination.[60]

Master Nicholas of Dunstable was the spokesman of the Elect's party in its objection to the deal offered it by John: the king offered his assent to the election in return for a release from his debts contracted with the abbey during the Interdict.[61] Master Nicholas gives eye-witness accounts of proceedings in the conventual chapter, probably from the actual minutes. Particularly vivid is the description of a chapter meeting in 1213, when the parties disputed as to whether a letter should be sent, without the assent of all the monks, recalling the Elect from the king's court.[62] It gives details of quarrels in other chapter meetings: one over the convent's right to control the use of its seal;[63] another, culminating in the deposition of the subcellarer, over the convent's beer allowance.[64] And it has a lively account, with speeches cited *verbatim*, of King John's appearance in the chapter on 4 November 1214.[65] He told the monks of the danger they ran in upholding Hugh of Northwold's election: the prolonged dispute would antagonize him and reduce the abbey's wealth and prestige. He called for a division of the monks, listened to the arguments, some serious, some frivolous, and, amazed at the strength of opposition to his wishes, left with threats.

A strong argument in favour of Master Nicholas's authorship is the fact that the *Electio* is especially detailed about events which took place in his presence. For example the *Electio* only has a brief and obviously second-hand

---

[55] See e.g. *EH*, pp. 74–5, 90, 107–8.

[56] Davis, *Kalendar*, pp. lvi–lvii, suggests that Jocelin of Brakelond was the author of the *Electio*. However, his hypothesis depends on the identification of Jocelin of Brakelond with Jocelin of the altar, one-time cellarer, in the *Electio*. As I reject the identification of Jocelin of Brakelond with the cellarer (see p. 383 n. 15 above), Prof. Davis's argument loses its force for me. In one place in the *Electio* (p. 54) Master Nicholas is called the cellarer; but as Peter was cellarer at this time, this must be a scribal error.

[57] See, e.g., *EH*, pp. 43, 51, 71, 72, 80, 111. [58] *EH*, p. 32.

[59] *EH*, p. 51. [60] *EH*, pp. 87–8.

[61] *EH*, pp. 107–8. [62] *EH*, pp. 35–6.

[63] *EH*, pp. 51–2. [64] *EH*, pp. 67–8.

[65] *EH*, pp. 95–101.

notice of the Elect's visit to John in Poitou in 1214, but it gives a detailed eye-witness account of the opening of Abbot Samson's tomb which happened at the same time. Clearly the author had not accompanied the Elect to Poitou. And it is known that Master Nicholas stayed at home; for the *Electio* carefully records that, because of the opposition of the sacrist's party, Nicholas, though chosen for the mission by the party of the Elect, was unable to go.[66] Moreover the *Electio* notes that Master Nicholas was with the Elect on four occasions, fully described in the *Electio*, when Hugh met King John.

The Elect, accompanied by Master Nicholas and other supporters, saw the king at Windsor in October 1214. This is the graphic account in the *Electio*:[67]

> When [Hugh] had eventually managed to see the king and had spoken to him about his election, he got this reply, 'Go to the bishop of Winchester. He will explain my wishes to you.' Having approached but got no satisfactory answer, [Hugh] returned to the king. Thus three times on that day, I don't know why, [the king] sent the Elect to the bishop of Winchester, without result. In the morning the Elect went to the king in chapel where mass was being celebrated. When it was at last finished the Elect said, 'Oh lord king, I have persistently tried to gain your grace and get a reply from you or the bishop of Winchester, since up to now I have received no reply at all.' The king answered, 'What do you want me to say? I love my crown more than you or your honour. You stir up war against me which cannot have any good result.' When Hugh instantly denied this, as he ought, the king added, 'I am not speaking of you in particular, but of certain other people.' Therefore as Hugh could achieve nothing more in his attempt to get the king's grace he returned home on All Saints' Day [1 November].

The Elect met John again in March 1215, in Sherwood, near Nottingham. Again, as appears from the full description in the *Electio*, the king prevaricated:[68]

> When [Hugh and his party] came to Sherwood outside Nottingham and had seen the king approaching from a distance, they got off their horses, that by meeting the king on foot they would obtain his favour more easily, and on nearing him they did obeisance before him on bent knees, imploring the royal grace and favour. The king was pleased to a remarkable degree by this show of humility before him, and, not allowing the Elect to lie long on the ground, he raised him up, and then expressed himself

[66] *EH*, pp. 84–5.　　　　[67] *EH*, pp. 94–5.　　　　[68] *EH*, pp. 123–4.

in these words. 'Welcome, lord Elect (saving the law of my kingdom!).' And they walked about together for a long time talking confidentially with no one else there. And as the Elect could on that day get no proper answer from the king about his business, he went on the next day into the chapel where the king was to hear mass. When it was over the king said to the Elect, 'Go to William Brewer who will explain my wishes to you more fully.'

The meeting between the Elect and the king, in June 1215, 'in Staines meadow' (that is Runnymede) was more successful and Hugh was finally admitted to favour. The *Electio* says of it:

> When [the king] had arrived and stayed a long time on the meadow [between Windsor and Staines], after considerable discussion and the intervention of nobles sent frequently from one party to the other by the king, at last he admitted the abbot to his favour with a kiss, putting off the oath of fealty he owed the king until the next day. When this was done the king immediately said, 'Father abbot, there remains one request to be made, which must be satisfied by your goodness. It is that your prayer should prevail, so that we should not be deprived of the company at our table of him whom the divine mercy restored to our grace.'

The *Electio* goes on to tell how, while the king and abbot 'were sitting after dinner on the royal couch in the king's chamber, talking of many things' the sacrist came to thank the king for his favour to the Elect, but the king angrily turned on him, saying that if it had not been for the sacrist's plots at court the royal grace would have been granted half a year earlier.[69] However, the ambitions of the sacrist Robert of Graveley were not long frustrated, for in 1217 he became abbot of Thorney.[70]

The preceding tracts and Jocelin's chronicle concern contemporary history. But the next group of tracts are mainly about past history. Though they were primarily intended to enhance the abbey's reputation and satisfy antiquarian curiosity, some were also meant, like the record tracts, to establish precedents. To this group belong: a tract on the abbey's architectural history, probably written in about 1234, with additions;[71] an account of the foundation of the abbey, and a tract on the origin of the Douzegild (the duodene), the guild of twelve secular priests in the borough of Bury St

---

[69] *EH*, pp. 128–9.
[70] See *VCH, Cambridge and the Isle of Ely*, vol. 2, p. 214, and p. 391 and n. 76 below.
[71] Printed in *The Customary of . . . Bury St. Edmunds*, ed. A. Gransden, pp. 114–21. The tract is noticed and extracts printed by James, op. cit., pp. 161–2 (but it is not printed, as James asserts, in *Mon. Angl.*). It was used by G. M. Hills, 'The antiquities of Bury St. Edmunds' in *Journal of the British Archaeological Association*, xxi (1865), pp. 32–56, 104–40 *passim*, and see p. 392 n. 81 below.

Edmunds, both probably written in the last half of the thirteenth century;[72] and the *Gesta Sacristarum* (*Deeds of the Sacrists*) covering the period from the rule of Abbot Baldwin (1065–97) to 1280, with a continuation from 1294 to 1297 (the period from 1280 to 1294 is omitted).[73]

The *Traditiones Patrum* (*Traditions of the Fathers*),[74] the monastic customary of St Edmunds compiled in about 1234, will also be considered, because the early part contains historical material. This was because an inquiry into the existing customs of the house involved study of their original introduction or evolution. A problem had arisen at Bury because new customs had been allowed to succeed the old ones.[75] How this could lead to historical inquiry is well illustrated by a letter, written a little before the compilation of the *Traditiones*, by the sacrist to Robert of Graveley, then abbot of Thorney, to ask about certain customs which had been observed when he was sacrist of Bury.[76] The *Traditiones* was probably written in preparation for, or as a result of, the visitation of the abbey by delegates appointed by the pope in 1234 to reform the observance in exempt abbeys.[77]

It is likely that the *Traditiones* was by the same man who wrote the tract on architectural history. This is suggested by a similarity in method between the two works. They both sometimes record various opinions on the subject at issue. For example the *Traditiones* states, giving reasons, that some say that the first monk to be blessed at matins on Sunday should be the officer for the week (the hebdomadary); others say those setting out on journeys should have priority; and some say it does not matter who is first; 'however, the first opinion is the most sensible'.[78] Similarly the architectural tract states that, according to some people, the cross in the abbey church by the altar of St Peter existed long before the introduction of monks at Bury while, according to others, Abbot Leofstan (1044–65) had it put there.[79] The *Traditiones* and the architectural tract, in its present form, belong to the

---

[72] The foundation story occurs in a late thirteenth-century confraternity drawn up between St Edmund's abbey and St Benet of Hulme in Norfolk, in BM MS. Cotton Galba E II, f. 36ᵛ (printed *Mon. Angl.*, vol. 3, p. 135), and in BM MS. Harley 1005, ff. 35, 35ᵛ. The story of the foundation of St Edmunds by Hulme monks also occurs in the *Cronica Buriensis*, written *c.* 1328 (printed *Memorials SE*, vol. 3, pp. 1–2); see A. Gransden, 'The "Cronica Buriensis" and the abbey of St. Benet of Hulme' in *BIHR*, xxxvi (1963), p. 78 and n. 6. The tract on the Douzegild is printed in *The Customary of . . . Bury St. Edmunds*, ed. A. Gransden, pp. 123–4.

[73] Printed in *Memorials SE*, vol. 2, pp. 289–96.

[74] Printed *The Customary of . . . Bury St. Edmunds*, ed. A. Gransden. The *Traditiones Patrum* is so called from its *incipit*.

[75] See, e.g., ibid., pp. 22, 32. This problem of new customs *versus* ancient ones arose during the papal visitation of the abbey in July 1234; see R. Graham, 'A papal visitation of Bury St. Edmunds and Westminster' in *EHR*, xxvii (1912), p. 731 (novices are warned not to neglect the Rule in favour of 'newly introduced customs').

[76] The letter is printed in *Memorials SE*, vol. 2, pp. 133–4.

[77] For the visitation see Graham, op. cit., pp. 728–37. The evidence for the date of the *Traditiones* is discussed in *The Customary of . . . Bury St. Edmunds*, pp. xxxii–xxxiii.

[78] Ibid., pp. 28–9; cf. p. 5 (opinions on who was responsible for entertaining the various categories of visitors).

[79] See ibid., pp. xxxix–xl.

same period (the architectural tract has no reference, except in what is obviously a later addition, subsequent to Abbot Samson's time).[80]

The primary purpose of the *Traditiones* was to facilitate the observance of customs, by codification. The architectural tract was also concerned with recording precedents. It was probably partly derived from an earlier work, now lost, written early in Henry II's reign to prove that the bishop of Norwich had no right to dedicate an altar, chapel or church within the *banleuca* of St Edmunds.[81] There is some evidence that at this time the abbey was under renewed attack from the bishop of Norwich – certainly the abbot and prior supported the abbot of St Albans against his diocesan, the bishop of Lincoln.[82] Therefore the author of the tract probably wrote to prove St Edmunds' exemption from episcopal control (a similar tract was written at St Albans);[83] for the same reason Hermann had produced evidence proving that the bishop of Norwich could not claim the right to consecrate the abbot of Bury.[84]

Another work of this group which was partly written for record purposes was the *Gesta Sacristarum* which records, presumably for convenient reference, the sacrists' acquisitions and administrative acts. For example it states that when Nicholas of Warwick was sacrist (*c.* 1234–52), the oblations from the church were finally removed from the sacrist's care and entrusted to treasurers.[85] The section of the *Gesta* from 1280 to 1294 shows preoccupations different from the earlier part: the author was concerned only with the financial problems and the administration of his office. He records, for example, the tax of a half of temporal and spiritual revenues imposed on the clergy for the French war in the autumn of 1294, and the consequent impoverishment of the sacristy at Bury.

The architectural tract, the account of the abbey's foundation and the tract on the origin of the Douzegild were partly intended to prove that Bury St Edmunds was of venerable antiquity. For example the architectural tract connects the earliest parish church in the borough with Bedan times. It asserts that the church was dedicated to St Mary, in the time of Felix, the first bishop of the East Angles (*c.* 630–47). Abbot Baldwin pulled it down, replacing it with a larger one dedicated to St Denis. This was demolished by

---

[80] The author states that he had seen a tower on the site where in his day stood the new infirmary; see ibid., p. 120. The new infirmary was built by Abbot Samson; *Memorials SE*, vol. 2, p. 291.

[81] This lost twelfth-century work, and not the thirteenth-century tract, was probably that used for the *Registrum Alphabeticum* compiled in the cellarer's office in the fifteenth century, now Cambridge University Library MS. Gg. 4. 4, extracts (including some from the work in question) from which are printed by John Battely, *Opera Posthuma, viz. Antiquitates Rutupinae et Antiquitates S. Edmundi Burgi ad Annum 1272 perductae* (Oxford 1745), pp. 57–76 *passim*.

[82] See *GASA*, vol. 1, p. 145, and M. D. Knowles, 'Essays in monastic history. IV. The growth of exemption' in *Downside Review*, l (1932), pp. 212–13, 214 et seq. For the struggle between St Edmunds abbey and the bishop of Norwich in the late eleventh and early twelfth centuries see ibid., pp. 208–12 and pp. 126–7 above.

[83] *GASA*, vol. 1, pp. 147–8.

[84] *Memorials SE*, vol. 1, p. 66. Cf. p. 126 above.

[85] *Memorials SE*, vol. 2, p. 294.

Abbot Anselm who built a church which was dedicated to St James by Richard be Beaufou, bishop of Avranches (1135–42).[86] The account of the foundation of the abbey embellished the pre-existing story. The earliest authority, Hermann, merely said that the abbey was founded by King Canute on the advice of Ælfric bishop of Elmham and Earl Thurkill.[87] By the mid-eleventh century the detail was added that the original settlement was by a group of monks from St Benet of Hulme in Norfolk.[88] The thirteenth-century foundation account adds more details:[89] it states that the original foundation numbered twelve monks, besides the abbot, and that six came from St Benet's and six from Ely, and it names the abbot (Uvius)[90] and monks concerned.[91] It also states that the monks from St Benet's had constituted half the total community in the mother house, from which they brought half the books, vestments and church ornaments. The story was further elaborated in the fourteenth century.[92] The tract on the Douzegild shows a similar desire to increase the venerability of Bury St Edmunds. It claims that the guild of twelve priests was founded in the time of King Canute and that its first members were the secular clerks whom the monks replaced as guardians of St Edmund's shrine. The author borrows the passage from the architectural tract on the building of St Denis's church by Abbot Baldwin, asserting that the church was given to the guild.

The truth of the details added in these three thirteenth-century works has proved impossible to verify: but they read more like legend than history. However, many passages in the *Traditiones*, the architectural tract and the *Gesta Sacristarum* show a genuine desire for historical inquiry. The author of the *Traditiones*, weighing one opinion about a custom against another (he is not always dogmatic as to which is correct) was trying to discover the truth. Moreover, if possible he says when and by whom a custom was instituted.[93] Similarly in the architectural tract the author not only weighs evidence but also sometimes admits his ignorance. For example he says that it is 'buried in oblivion' whether or not Abbot Leofstan obtained a papal privilege, and that he will say nothing, because of his ignorance, about certain chapels which have been destroyed without trace.

The most remarkable feature of the architectural tract and the *Gesta Sacristarum* is the antiquarian interest they reveal. Their authors show an

---

[86] See *The Customary of . . . Bury St. Edmunds*, ed. A. Gransden, pp. 116, 118.

[87] Hermann, *De Miraculis Sancti Eadmundi* in *Memorials SE*, vol. 1, p. 47.

[88] See *Memorials SE*, vol. 1, pp. 341–2. According to an early tradition at Ely, monks from Ely were also among the original colonists; see *LE*, p. 155 and n. 2.

[89] For this foundation story see p. 391 n. 72.

[90] For Abbot Uvius see Hermann, op. cit., p. 48.

[91] Alfric, Bondo, Agelwin and Edric are among the monks listed in the confraternity. Alfric, Bundi, Egelwin and Eadric occur in Hermann, op. cit., pp. 30, 32, 34, 69, respectively.

[92] For the foundation story in the late fourteenth century see the extract from Bodley MS. 240 printed in *Memorials SE*, vol. 1, pp. 358–9.

[93] For examples where the author states who instituted a custom see *The Customary of . . . Bury St. Edmunds*, ed. A. Gransden, pp. 10, 105.

objective intellectual curiosity and visual sense comparable to Matthew Paris (though their works are much slighter than his *Gesta Abbatum*). The author of the architectural tract notes, for example, that the parish church of St Denis was pulled down to make room for the nave of the abbey church, and that the church of St James was built to the west of the south corner of the cemetery. He records that the small chapel of St Andrew was demolished because, though 'venerable', it was badly situated, surrounded by water. Moreover, he has information about the tall tower dedicated to St Benedict which was no longer standing in his day (it had been pulled down to make room for the new infirmary built by Abbot Samson): he states that 'people say that Abbot Baldwin had his rooms next to [the tower], and that the entrance-hall (*porticus*) was built by Alfric son of Withgar, whose son was in the infirmary under Abbot Uvius and Abbot Leofstan, and who gave the manor of Melford'. The author mentions that Abbot Anselm had a painted altar erected, and that the altar of St Cross, dedicated by Alberic bishop of Ostia, was painted 'by the painter Wohancus'.

The antiquarian material in the *Gesta Sacristarum* is in the section to 1280. There is, for example, the account of the building done by Hugh, sacrist under Abbot Samson:[94]

> [Hugh] completed the great tower towards the west, roofing and leading it, and the lord abbot devoutly provided the panelling and beams and all other necessary wood. He finished the chapel of St Faith in respect to the stonework, and added a story to another tower by the chapel of St Catherine. Hugh built the greater part and completed the new infirmary ([begun] in the time of the sacrist William at the instance of Abbot Samson), and the chapel of St Andrew, the lord abbot Samson supplying the beams and all the timber from his woods.

The *Gesta* notes that Hugh's successor William of Banham completed the tower and brought water in lead pipes to the cloisters from springs two miles away.[95] It mentions the decoration of the abbey church, for example, the pictures and the bas-reliefs, and the painting of the abbot's chair in the choir 'by the painter Symon'.[96]

The *Gesta* is particularly detailed on Hervey, sacrist under Abbot Anselm, and includes a valuable account of the activities of Master Hugh, the craftsman and painter he employed. It records that Master Hugh carved the west doors of the church ('in his other works Hugh excelled all others, but in this work he wonderfully excelled himself').[97] These doors no longer survive, but another of Hugh's works is extant, the illuminated bible from Bury St Edmunds now in Corpus Christi College, Cambridge.[98] The *Gesta* provides

[94] *Memorials SE*, vol. 2, p. 291.   [95] Ibid., p. 292.   [96] Ibid., pp. 291, 293.
[97] Ibid., p. 290.   [98] Corpus Christi College, Cambridge, MS. 2.

the evidence proving that Hugh was the artist of the Bury bible. The relevant passage reads:[99]

> Hervey, brother of Prior Talbot, found all the expenses for his brother the prior for writing a great book, and he had it incomparably painted by the hand of Master Hugh. He, since he could not find in our neighbourhood calf-skins suitable for his purpose, bought parchment in the region of Scotland.

The Bury bible bears out the author's claim that Hugh's work was incomparable. Moreover, it confirms the inference that Hugh obtained particularly fine parchment, for the illuminations are on pieces of parchment almost as thin as tissue-paper: they are sewn on to the pages of the bible which are of ordinary parchment.

The earliest of the two general chronicles written at Bury in the thirteenth century, the *Annales Sancti Edmundi*, is of little value to the historian today. To 1199 it is a compilation from well-known authorities and, just when it begins to give a full contemporary account of events, it ends incomplete, in 1212, owing to the loss of leaves from the only known manuscript. However, from the early thirteenth century to 1211 the annals have some interest because they partly derive from a lost source also used by Roger of Wendover.[100]

The other chronicle from the Creation of the world to 1301 is of greater value.[101] From about 1265 to the end it provides a fairly full account of English history written up more or less contemporarily with the events recorded. It is particularly valuable for East Anglian affairs, but is also well informed about events in the north (Bury was on the road from London to Scotland), in London and about Anglo-Flemish relations (news no doubt was obtained from the sailors of Yarmouth). Henry III visited St Edmund's abbey at least fifteen times during his reign, and Edward I was also a frequent visitor. Other important people stayed there, and as the abbey administered one-third of Suffolk it was brought into close touch with the central government. Therefore the chroniclers had access to excellent sources of information.

The Bury chronicle was the work of at least three men: there is proof of changes of authorship in 1265 and 1296. To 1265 the author was, as the chronicle itself states, John de Taxter, who took the habit at Bury in 1244.[102]

---

[99] *Memorials SE*, vol. 2, p. 290. This passage is cited by E. G. Millar, *English Illuminated Manuscripts from the Tenth to the Thirteenth Century* (Paris–Brussels 1926), pp. 30–2. Possibly 'in Scotiae partibus' refers to Ireland (see ibid., p. 31).

[100] See pp. 332, 359 and n. 24.

[101] Printed *The Chronicle of Bury St. Edmunds 1212–1301*, ed., with an English translation, Antonia Gransden (Nelson's Medieval Texts, 1964).

[102] 'Hoc anno scriptor presentis uoluminis habitum suscepit monachicum dictus I. de Taxter die sancti Edmundi'; *Bury*, p. 13 n. *b*, *s.a.* 1244.

He used well-known sources up to 1202 (mainly Florence of Worcester and Diceto), and then the *Annales Sancti Edmundi* to some time after 1212.[103] Taxter interpolated his secondary material with original matter, and continued the chronicle using documents, oral information and his own observations to 1265. The vivid and obviously eye-witness account of the storm and darkness following the battle of Evesham ('those who sat down to dinner could scarcely see the food before them'),[104] suggests that Taxter wrote close to events in 1265.

The author of the continuation from 1265 to 1296[105] first revised Taxter's work.[106] For example, he added passages on classical history to the early part; he omitted the entry about Taxter, and modified Taxter's statement that Simon de Montfort's corpse worked miracles with the phrase 'so men say'; and he added a complaint to Taxter's notice of the fine of 800 marks imposed on the abbey by the king in exchange for his good will after the Barons' War: the continuator considered it unfair that the convent had to pay half the sum since only the abbot, as the king's tenant in chief, had been accused in the royal court and so should have paid the total.[107]

The author of the continuation from 1265 to 1296 has never been identified. However, there is enough evidence to suggest that he may have been William of Hoo, sacrist of Bury St Edmunds from 1280 to 1294:[108] and there is certainly enough to prove that even if the sacrist himself was not the author, the chronicle was by someone in his office. The sacrist's office was obviously history-conscious at this period, for it produced the *Gesta Sacristarum*, and almost certainly the tract on the 'Guild of Youth' at Bury, the one on the Douzegild, besides a tract on the controversy between the abbey and the king's clerk of the market in 1285, over the abbot's right to hold the assize of weights and measures in the borough.[109]

The sacrist of Bury was a man of consequence. As the most important obedientiary, a large proportion of the convent's property was allocated to his use, and, as the abbot's deputy, he was virtually lord of St Edmund's borough; he drew revenues from it, presided over its court, enforced the

---

[103] For Taxter's sources see *Bury*, p. xviii.   [104] Ibid., p. 31.

[105] The possibility cannot be ruled out that this continuation was the work of more than one man. However, as will be seen, the preoccupations shown in this section are the same throughout.

[106] For the revision see ibid., p. xix.   [107] Ibid., p. 32 and n. *a*.

[108] I expressed the views stated below in the introduction (pp. 72–85) to my edition of the complete Bury chronicle done for a Ph.D. thesis of London University (a typescript is in the Institute of Historical Research, Senate House, London W.C.1). I was not at the time sufficiently convinced by the evidence for Hoo's authorship to publish it in my printed edition. However, the researches of Professor E. L. G. Stones and Dr Roy establishing the astronomical accuracy of the chronicle (p. 398 and n. 125 below) have provided confirmatory evidence for the authorship of Hoo or one of his subordinates, as the sacrist was the monastic time-keeper.

[109] The tract on the dispute (which involved William of Hoo) is printed in *The Letter-Book of William of Hoo Sacrist of Bury St. Edmunds 1280–1294*, ed. Antonia Gransden (Suffolk Records Soc., v, 1963), pp. 125–30.

assizes of weights and measures, and bread and ale, supervised the mint, and was in charge of the grammar school, the song school and the Douzegild.[110] Also acting on behalf of the abbot he performed the functions of archdeacon within the *banleuca*. In the abbey itself the sacrist was, as was customary, responsible for the fabric and furnishing of the church, for the buildings belonging to his office, and for time-keeping.

The chronicle itself records the appointment of William of Hoo, the chamberlain, to the sacristy in 1280,[111] in succession to Simon of Kingston. And it mentions under 1287 that he presented a moneyer, Richard of Lothbury, to the treasurer and barons of the Exchequer,[112] for acceptance in his office. More details about his career can be discovered from Hoo's letter-book and from other documents relating to him from the abbey's archives.[113] These show him at work, enforcing his authority in the borough, keeping his buildings in repair and administering his estates. They also prove that Hoo was intimately concerned with both papal and royal taxation. He was an agent of Geoffrey de Vezzano, a papal collector from 1276 to 1299.[114] And in 1273 he was probably one of the five monks of Bury who assessed the abbey's obedientiaries before the papal tax assessor, Master Raymond de Nogaret.[115] Moreover, in 1290 Hoo went, on behalf of the abbot and convent, to the Exchequer to compound with the treasurer and barons for the fifteenth imposed on St Edmunds.[116]

William of Hoo, therefore, had two reasons for being interested in taxation: as sacrist he received a substantial proportion of the convent's revenues; and, as an important obedientiary, he was used by the abbot and convent, and by the papal agent, to deal with financial business. The evidence that Hoo, or one of his subordinates, wrote the chronicle from 1265 to 1296 is partly in this section of the chronicle itself. The preoccupations evinced by the author coincide with those one would expect of someone closely connected with the sacristy. Moreover, most of the author's interests are also found in the *Gesta Sacristarum*.

The author's principal preoccupation, amounting to an obsession, was with taxation, particularly when it effected Bury St Edmunds.[117] There are

---

[110] For an account of the duties of the sacrist of Bury see M. D. Lobel, *The Borough of Bury St. Edmunds* (Oxford 1935), pp. 31–59.

[111] *Bury*, p. 71.   [112] Ibid., p. 90 and n. 1, and Gransden, *Letter-Book*, pp. 33, 158.

[113] The letter-book and related documents are printed in *Letter-Book, passim*.

[114] *Letter-Book*, pp. 17, 47, 48, 57, and nn.

[115] The assessment of 1274 of Bury for the tenth granted by the Council of Lyons, was, according to the extant record (College of Arms MS. Arundel XXX, f. 213) carried out by the sacrist, cellarer and chamberlain (perhaps Hoo, though it is not known when he took office as chamberlain) and two other monks. For the assessment see R. Graham, 'The taxation of Pope Nicholas IV' in *EHR*, xxiii (1908), p. 449, and W. E. Lunt, *Financial Relations of the Papacy with England to 1327* (Cambridge, Mass. 1939), p. 319 n. 7. For Raymond de Nogaret, papal tax collector in England 1272–7, see ibid., p. 618. Cf. *Bury*, p. 55.

[116] *Letter-Book*, p. 138.

[117] For the importance of the Bury chronicle for the history of taxation see *Bury*, pp. xxv–xxvi and nn.

notices of some papal or royal tax under nearly every year, and under 1268, 1276 and 1292 the chronicler gives full details of the assessment for the papal tenths of the convent. This obsession with taxation is quite explicable if the chronicle for these years was written in the sacrist's office, especially as the sacristy was in serious financial difficulties, the result, according to the author of the *Gesta Sacristarum*, of taxation.[118]

The chronicle from 1265 to 1296 has some specific references to the sacrist's office. It records under 1268 that £100 due for the papal tenth was taken by the king's clerks 'under the sacrist's seal', after the convent had tried to evade payment by bribing the papal collectors with 20 marks.[119] Under 1279 the chronicle recounts that the royal justices indicted certain goldsmiths in the borough for clipping the coin and 'compelled even the sacrist to pay 100 marks as a fine'.[120] It gives a full account of the dispute between the abbey's right to hold the assize of weights and measures: and it records that a compromise was eventually reached 'by the counsel of the lord king and the sacrist'.[121] The chronicle has another reference to the assize under 1275, recording the king's confirmation of the abbey's right to hold it.[122]

The chronicle has a passage reminiscent of the antiquarian tastes apparent in the *Gesta Sacristarum*. It mentions the discovery in 1275 of the foundations of an ancient round church during the demolition of St Edmund's chapel in the abbey church, to clear the site for building the Lady Chapel. The ancient church 'was much wider than the chapel of St Edmund and so built that the altar of the chapel was, as it were, in the centre. We believe that this was the chapel first built for the service of St Edmund.'[123]

The chronicle has a few other entries showing an interest in affairs connected with the sacristy. Though most of these occur in the 1265 to 1296 continuation, they are not exclusively confined to this section. However, this does not invalidate the argument that the first continuation was produced by the sacrist's office. There is no evidence that Taxter was connected with the sacristy, but neither is there evidence to the contrary. And the author of the second continuation (from 1296 to 1301) could have obtained information from the sacristy. Entries concerning the mint at Bury occur both under 1247 and 1280[124] (under 1287 is the entry about the appointment of Richard of Lothbury as moneyer). More interesting are the chronicle's numerous and remarkably accurate observations of eclipses.[125] These

---

[118] See p. 392.

[119] *Bury*, p. 45. For a particular reference to the chamberlain's office, see ibid., p. 44.

[120] *Bury*, pp. 67–8.

[121] *Bury*, pp. 83–4. A tract on the dispute (printed Gransden, *Letter-Book*, pp. 125–30) records that it originated with a complaint delivered personally by the abbot and William of Hoo to the king, that Ralph of Middlington, the king's clerk of the market, had held the assize within St Edmund's liberty.

[122] *Bury*, pp. 57–8.   [123] *Bury*, pp. 59–60.   [124] *Bury*, pp. 14, 72.

[125] On the record of eclipses in the Bury chronicle see A. E. Roy and E. L. G. Stones, 'The record of eclipses in the Bury chronicle' in *BIHR*, xliii (1970), pp. 125–33.

suggest that someone was keeping a close watch on the sky, and as the sacrist was the monastic time-keeper,[126] it is likely that the observer was connected with the sacristy (he may also have been responsible for the many meteorological entries). One solar eclipse (under 1261) and eleven lunar eclipses (under 1258, 1265, 1270, 1276, 1280, two under 1281, 1287, 1288, 1291 and 1297) are noticed. All the chronicler's dates are accurate, and the solar eclipse is correctly described. Moreover, only one of the descriptions of the lunar eclipses (as total or partial) is wrong. It is possible that twenty-nine lunar eclipses were visible at Bury during the period from 1258 to 1297, but the observer's view must sometimes have been obscured by bad weather.

There is, therefore, enough evidence to prove that the chronicle was produced by the sacrist's office, and was perhaps by William of Hoo, writing before and while he was sacrist and after his retirement. The chronicler's obsession with taxation makes it likely that he was also the author of the section of *Gesta Sacristarum* from 1294 to 1297. The omission of Hoo from the *Gesta* may have been due to the fact that the author, having recorded some facts about Hoo's career in the chronicle, did not want to repeat himself.

There is another piece of evidence probably relating to William of Hoo. If it does relate to Hoo it proves that before becoming a monk of Bury he had been a monk of Norwich. The chronicle of Bartholomew Cotton, a monk of Norwich, records that in October 1272 William of Hoo, precentor of Norwich, installed the prior of Norwich, William of Kirkby.[127] It seems probable that this William of Hoo is to be identified with the later sacrist of Bury. Transference of monks from one monastery to another was by no means unusual in the middle ages.[128] If this identification is correct it would fully explain the vivid account (quoted below) in the Bury chronicle of the burning of Norwich cathedral by the townsmen in August 1272; this account closely resembles the graphic description of the same event in Cotton's chronicle, though neither chronicle here copies the other (this is shown by the fact that the Bury chronicle dates the ecclesiastical council held at Eye, which excommunicated the offenders, a day earlier than Cotton).[129] Perhaps after the revolt at Norwich, Hoo or his superiors considered his position as precentor untenable, and he moved to Bury for a quieter life.[130]

[126] For the sacrist as time-keeper see *The Monastic Constitutions of Lanfranc* (Nelson's Medieval Texts, 1951), pp. 82–3, and *Les Monuments primitifs de la Règle Cisterciennne*, ed. P. Guignard (Dijon 1878), p. 233. I owe these references to Professor M. D. Knowles.

[127] *BC*, p. 149. I overlooked this piece of possible evidence in my edition of the Bury chronicle.

[128] See M. D. Knowles, *The Monastic Order in England* (2nd ed., Cambridge 1963), p. 475. Cf. n. 130 below.

[129] *Bury*, p. 51; *BC*, p. 148.

[130] An example of a monk who moved monastery at least temporarily to avoid townsmen's rage is William of Stow, a sacrist of Bury St Edmunds, who took refuge at St Benet of Hulme because of the townsmen's animosity to him expressed in the revolt in St Edmund's borough in 1327; see Gransden, 'Cronica Buriensis', pp. 81–2.

It is worth noting that to 1290 Bartholomew Cotton copied a pre-existing chronicle written at Norwich.[131] This chronicle was apparently written contemporarily with the events it recorded from about 1270. A hypothesis fitting the historiographical facts would be that Hoo started this chronicle in 1272 to record the terrible events of the Norwich townsmen's revolt. He added to the annal the notice that he installed Prior William of Kirkby. Subsequently he moved to Bury, leaving the Norwich chronicle to be continued by another monk. And he himself continued the Bury chronicle, retelling the story of the revolt at Norwich (with slight revision). And Hoo may have maintained his connection with Norwich, exchanging historiographical material (from 1279 to 1284 the Norwich chronicle copied the Bury one).[132]

The second continuation of the Bury chronicle from 1296 to 1301 has been ascribed to the cellarer, John of Eversden. However, the evidence for his authorship is weak. It rests on a passage under 1300 that 'John of Everisdene, then the cellarer of St Edmunds, made a successful expedition to the manor of Warkton near Northampton on business concerning the pasture called Boughton as is recorded in the precentor's register'.[133] John Bale attributed the whole chronicle to 1301 to Eversden, probably on the basis of this passage, and, because of the authority of Bale's Catalogue, the attribution was unquestioned until modern times. However, this section of the chronicle should be regarded as anonymous. It shows no preponderant interest in any of the obedientiaries. And if the author were Eversden, it is odd that he should refer to the precentor's, and not the cellarer's register for a record of his own acts.

The chronicle (like the Annales) was written partly to provide a framework of general history for local events. And it is an important source for the history of St Edmund's abbey. As a source for general history the value of the chronicle lies in the accuracy of the facts it records, rather than in any intellectual distinction. It is possible to see how at least part of the chronicle (from about 1286 to 1296) was compiled, as an early draft survives.[134] This copy shows how blank lines were left at the end of each annal for the insertion of late news,[135] how small gaps were left in the text for names, and how additions were made in the margins.

The authors exploited their opportunities for accumulating data. They recorded oral information and used the abbey's archives. Moreover, they obtained news from the royal court when the king was staying in the abbey.

---

[131] See p. 444.

[132] See p. 402.

[133] Bury, p. 158. For the tradition that the chronicle to 1301 was by John of Eversden see ibid., p. xli.

[134] College of Arms MS. Arundel XXX. See Bury, pp. xl–xli. For evidence of the contemporaneity of the first and second continuations see ibid., p. xx.

[135] This feature, the blank lines between annals, is more marked in the copy of the chronicle now in the Moyses Hall Museum at Bury St Edmunds; see Bury, p. xliii.

Good examples of the value of contact with the king can be discovered by comparing the chronicle's statements with the public records.[136] Under 1245 the chronicle notes that Henry III named his second son Edmund after St Edmund the king and martyr:[137] a copy still survives of the letter Henry sent telling the abbot and convent of this.[138] The chronicle has details, which are found nowhere else, about the negotiations for the proposed marriage of Edward I with Philip of France's sister Blanche.[139] It describes the draft of the marriage agreement and ends that Blanche finally refused because 'she did not wish to marry any man, especially such an old one'. The source of the chronicler's information is clear: Edward I was at Bury during these negotiations and he summoned the chancellor to bring the seal from London to him at one of the manors of the abbot of Bury.[140] And again, the chronicle mentions, under 1295, a fire in Windsor castle:[141] the king issued instructions from Bury for the repair of the castle.[142] Finally, news of the surrender of the Welsh rebel Rhys in 1296 reached the king when he was at the abbey, and was duly recorded in the chronicle.[143]

Despite the authors' piecemeal method of compilation, all three were capable of writing good narrative. There is an excellent account of the Barons' War. The chronicle is fairly objective on the political issues, clearly because it was more concerned with problems at home. Nevertheless Taxter, like other monastic chroniclers, shows some veiled sympathy for the barons. Besides stating that Simon de Montfort's corpse worked miracles (a passage modified by his successor), he remarks that the fugitive bishop of Norwich would never have found safety from the barons in 1263 had he not come to Bury, 'for at this time St Edmund's liberty was exceedingly precious in the eyes of the barons'.[144] Concern for the abbey's own interests grew with the revolt of the townsmen in 1264 and the consequent trouble with Henry III, who, moreover, suspected the abbey of supporting the baronial cause.[145]

One of the most graphic passages is probably the eye-witness account of the attack by the citizens of Norwich on the cathedral priory in 1272. It illustrates well the prejudiced attitude of the author – he makes no attempt to discover the causes of the outbreak:[146]

> After many assaults had been made on the priory, the convent gates broken down forcibly by the rebels and much other outrageous damage done, immediately after the convent had dined,

---

[136] Professor E. L. G. Stones suggests that a monk from Bury St Edmunds attended the meeting summoned by Edward I on 10 May at Norham to hear the Great Cause of the competitors for the Scottish throne. This would explain the excellent account of the Great Cause given in the Bury chronicle. See E. L. G. Stones, 'The appeal to history in Anglo-Scottish relations between 1291 and 1401: Part I', *Archives*, ix, no. 41 (1969), pp. 11–21.

[137] *Bury*, p. 13.
[138] *Memorials SE*, vol. 3, pp. 28–9.
[139] *Bury*, pp. 118–20 and nn.
[140] *Cal. Chancery Warrants, 1244–1326*, p. 40.
[141] *Bury*, pp. 126–7.
[142] *CCR, 1288–96*, p. 498.
[143] *Bury*, pp. 135 and n. 5, 136.
[144] *Bury*, p. 27.
[145] For the chronicle's account of the Barons' War see *Bury*, pp. xxii–xxv.
[146] *Bury*, pp. 50–1. For this passage see p. 399 above.

some vile sons of holy mother church, that is the whole commonalty of Norwich city, numbering it is believed thirty-two
thousand men armed to the teeth, marched on their holy mother
church herself. Together with the women of the city they set fire
to various parts of the priory and reduced the church and whole
priory to ashes except for three or four buildings hardly worth
mentioning among all the rest; only the stone-work was saved
and even that not wholly. Nearly all the monks were driven out.
Some thirty or so of their servants, after tortures of various kinds,
were either done to death in the bosom of their mother church, or
torn from the church as from a mother's breast, dragged before a
special tribunal and condemned with the same sentence, without
respect for age or rank. The townspeople smashed to pieces and
plundered all the valuables in the treasury, vestry and refectory as
well as in the other offices of the church and in the cupboards. The
monks fled secretly one after another and scarcely escaped with
their lives.

The second continuation also has some good narrative. There is, for
example, a vivid description of Edward I's siege of Edinburgh castle in
1297,[147] and one of his battle in 1298 at Ghent ('a very strong and heavily
fortified city, an impregnable fortress and an invincible place of refuge,
surrounded by remarkable walls, ditches, palisades and moats, with a
thousand towers dominating the city which is fortified like a citadel').[148] It
has a memorable account of the king's visit to Bury in 1300, with his son
Edward of Caernarvon, on the way to the Scottish war. King Edward told
his justices to protect St Edmund's privileges so that the saint would help his
campaign and asked for the monks' prayers. When he resumed his journey he
left Prince Edward there for a while: the latter lived like the monks, was
admitted to confraternity, and enjoyed himself so much that he was reluctant
to leave to join his father.[149]

The Bury chronicle (to 1294) was used in the neighbouring Benedictine
houses. The Norwich chronicler copied Taxter's chronicle for the years from
1258 to 1263, and copied the first continuation of the Bury chronicle (in
the same version as that used at St Benet of Hulme) for the years from 1279
to 1284 (the Norwich chronicle is independent of all known chronicles from
1263 to 1278).[150] The chronicle of St Benet of Hulme, which goes under the
name of John of Oxenedes,[151] used the Bury chronicle for the years from
1020 to 1169 and from 1258 to 1290 (for the intermediate period its main
source was the St Albans chronicle). The Hulme chronicle's two final

---

[147] *Bury*, p. 132.
[148] *Bury*, pp. 143–7.
[149] *Bury*, pp. 156–7.
[150] *BC*, pp. lii–lviii.
[151] The chronicle of St Benet of Hulme is printed as *Chronica Johannis de Oxenedes*, ed. H. Ellis
(RS, 1859). For its relationship with the Bury chronicle see Gransden, 'Cronica Buriensis',
pp. 80–1.

annals, for 1291 and 1292, are related to the Bury chronicle but not copied from it in its present form. In about 1295 a copy of the Bury chronicle was made for the abbey of Peterborough.[152] The exemplar of the Peterborough text survives.[153] This text was adapted for the Peterborough copyist: in the margin by Edward I's letter of 1291, concerning the Scottish succession case, which is here addressed 'to the abbot and convent of St Edmunds', the revisor wrote 'of Peterborough' ('Sancti Petri de Burg') as a directive to the Peterborough scribe, who duly substituted 'to the abbot and convent of Peterborough' ('abbati et conventui S. Petri de Burg') in place of the original address.[154] Some time towards the end of the century the Bury chronicle was used either directly or indirectly by the chronicler of Spalding priory.[155]

The chroniclers plundering the Bury chronicle did not copy it blindly. They cut out some passages, particularly those about Bury, and inserted others, particularly about their own houses. As they neared their own time they became more and more independent, partly because they had their own sources of information and partly because the Bury chronicle itself was no more than a tentative draft when the up-to-date sections were distributed. An example of this fluidity is provided by the Hulme chronicle: it has a copy of Edward I's letter of 1291 on the Scottish succession case addressed to the abbot and convent of St Edmunds with the letters of submission of the competitors to the Scottish throne in Latin;[156] but in the Bury chronicle these same letters are in French.[157] Finally the chroniclers seem to be using the same material as the Bury chronicle rather than the chronicle itself. For example under 1295 the Peterborough version has a account of the treachery of Thomas de Turbeville[158] similar to but not identical with the Bury chronicle:[159] the resemblance is no closer than is to be expected between the chronicles of two Benedictine houses within forty miles of each other.

---

[152] The Peterborough version of the chronicle from 1152 to 1295, which follows a text of Florence and John of Worcester (Corpus Christi College, Cambridge, MS. 92), is printed in *FW*, vol. 2, pp. 136–279.

[153] College of Arms MS. XXX.

[154] See *Bury*, pp. xliv, 100 and n. *b*.

[155] The citations in the Spalding chronicle from the Bury chronicle are under 1265, 1267, 1269 and 1271. The Spalding chronicle is printed as *Chronicon Johannis abbatis S. Petri de Burgo* in Joseph Sparke, *Historiae Anglicanae Scriptores Varii* (London 1723), reprinted as *Chronicon Angliae Petriburgense* by J. A. Giles (Caxton Soc., 1845). For its provenance from Spalding see F. Liebermann, 'Ueber ostenglische Geschichtsquellen des 12, 13, 14 Jahrhunderts, besonders den falschen Ingulf' in *Neues Archiv der Gesellschaft für ältere deutsche Geschichtskunde*, xviii (Hanover–Leipzig 1892), pp. 235–6.

[156] *Bury*, pp. 100–3. For the inclusion of these letters in monastic chronicles see p. 442 below.

[157] *JO*, pp. 280–3.   [158] *FW*, vol. 2, pp. 278–9.   [159] *Bury*, pp. 128–9.

18

Chronicles in the Reign of Henry III

The reign of Henry III was the heyday of the monastic chronicle. Such chronicles, which were primarily records and comprised entries arranged in strictly chronological order, had increased in number in King John's reign,[1] and now became an omnibus type of historiography, subsuming not only general history but also local history and biography. As a result both local history[2] and biography[3] declined as distinct genres, and the influence of the romance tradition of historiography became minimal. Only Robert of Gloucester, in his chronicle in Middle English verse, was noticeably influenced by romance literature.

Record-type chronicles were written in numerous religious houses. Chronicles started in King John's reign and earlier were continued, and houses with established historiographical traditions influenced neighbouring ones, thus becoming the centres of historiographical complexes. As has been seen the *Flores Historiarum* from St Albans was the basis of annals in a number of houses, notably at Westminster.[4] The chronicle of Bury St Edmunds provided a stimulus to, and source for, a number of East Anglian chroniclers.[5] At Christ Church, Canterbury, the chronicle of Gervase was continued into the fourteenth century.[6] And the continuation is closely related to what can be called the official chronicle of St Martin's priory, Dover,[7] a cell of Christ Church (there is another chronicle, apparently composed at St Martin's by a monk of the priory, perhaps called Henry de

---

[1] See pp. 318–20.

[2] For local histories written in the thirteenth century see Appendix B.

[3] For the Lives of St Edmund Rich, which, though they contain material useful to the historian, are primarily hagiographical, see C. H. Lawrence, *St. Edmund of Abingdon* (Oxford 1960).

[4] See pp. 378–9.

[5] See pp. 402–3.

[6] The continuation, to 1327, is printed in *GC*, vol. 2, pp. 106–324. See also p. 216.

[7] The Dover chronicle, A.D. 1 to 1286, is unpublished. It is in BM MS. Cotton Julius D V, which was damaged in the Cottonian fire of 1731. The text from about the middle of 1263 is hard and in places impossible to read because of distortion, discolouring and partial destruction caused by the fire. For a description of the Dover chronicle see *GC*, vol. 2, pp. xxii–xxiii. For notices of the section from 1226 to 1228 in so far as it relates to Stephen Langton, see F. A. Cazel, jun., 'The last years of Stephen Langton' in *EHR*, lxxix (1964), pp. 679–97. For the relationship of the Dover chronicle to the Canterbury chronicle see pp. 422–3 below.

Silegrave, soon after Henry III's death).[8] At Winchester, the pre-existing annals were added to,[9] and the additional annals were used by the monks of Worcester cathedral priory.[10] Chronicles were also written in the Benedictine abbeys of Battle,[11] Burton-on-Trent,[12] Tewkesbury,[13] St Werburg's, Chester,[14] and perhaps at Gloucester (though as will be seen it is not quite certain that Robert of Gloucester's chronicle is a monastic production[15]).

[8] This chronicle, from the Anglo-Saxon invasions to the accession of Edward I (with brief notices to 1274) is printed in *A Chronicle of English History ... by Henry of Silegrave*, ed. C. Hook (Caxton Soc., 1849). The only known evidence for Silegrave's connection with the chronicle is in the only surviving manuscript, BM MS. Cotton Cleopatra A XII, a fair copy in a late thirteenth-century book hand. The title page (f. 4ᵛ) in a hand of the same period as the text, is headed 'Liber Henrici de Silegrave'. The manuscript came from St Martin's, Dover: it was no. 371 in the medieval catalogue of the priory; see M. R. James, *The Ancient Libraries of Canterbury and Dover* (Cambridge 1903), pp. 430, 484. There seems no reason to doubt that it was composed by a monk of St Martin's, whether Silegrave or not, because it has (Hook, op. cit., pp. 88–9) an account of the foundation of St Martin's which is substantially the same as the detailed account in the 'official' Dover chronicle (see *Cont. GC*, p. 287). Moreover, it has at least one citation from the 'official' Dover chronicle (compare the eulogy on the barons who fell at Evesham in 'Silegrave', Hook, op. cit., p. 105, with *Cont. GC*, p. 243). Therefore there seems no reason to accept C. Bémont's suggestion (*Simon de Montfort Comte de Leicester* (Paris 1884), p. xiii) that the chronicle was by a monk of the Cistercian abbey of Beaulieu: he suggests this because it records King John's association with the abbey 'quam a fundamentis construxit et egregie ditavit' (Hook, op. cit., p. 101); but the chronicle has notices of other abbeys in similar terms (e.g. see the notice of Stephen's burial at Faversham 'in abbatia quam a fundamentis construxerat, ut hodie cernitur'; ibid., p. 91).

[9] For the Winchester chronicle see pp. 252 and n. 47, 253, 333.

[10] For the Worcester chronicle, see p. 333 and nn. 108, 109. For its use of the Winchester/ Waverley chronicle see pp. 319 n. 7, 333 and n. 108.

[11] This chronicle of Battle abbey, Brutus to 1264 (with a continuation to 1286), is mainly unpublished. It is described and the annals from 1258 to 1265 printed by Bémont, op. cit., pp. xiv–xv, 373–80. It is not printed in E. F. Jacob's translation (Oxford 1930) of Bémont, for which see n. 8 above.

[12] The chronicle of Burton, 1004 to 1262 (*Burt.*) is printed in *Ann. Mon.*, vol. 1, pp. 183–500. See also pp. 408–11 below.

[13] The chronicle of Tewkesbury, 1066 to 1262 (here referred to as *Tewkesbury I*) and a short chronicle, 1258 to 1263 (here referred to as *Tewkesbury II*) which follows it in the manuscript, are printed in *Ann. Mon.*, vol. 1, pp. 43–174, 174–80, respectively. In the manuscript (BM MS. Cotton Cleopatra A VII) *Tewkesbury I* (on ff. 9–62ᵛ) is an untidy copy to the end of 1253 (f. 54ᵛ); from there onwards the spaces between annals for additions, and the increasing untidiness of the text from 1258, suggest that the whole was written in the time of the Barons' War, for which period it is contemporary with events. Apparently a lost Tewkesbury chronicle formed the basis of *Tewkesbury I* and also of the Winchcombe annals from 1182 to 1232; both may partly derive from some lost Worcester annals: for the hypothetical interrelation of these chronicles see the unpublished M.A. thesis for the University of Manchester by Dr Eric John, 'A critical study of the sources of the annals of Winchcombe, Faustina B I, ff. 21–29ᵇ (1182–1232)'. *Tewksbury II* (ff. 63–69ᵛ) is a fair copy in one hand, and stops incomplete owing to the loss of leaves in the manuscript. The text has no references to Tewkesbury but this copy was certainly made at Tewkesbury as it is on the same gathering of leaves as *Tewkesbury I*. However whether *Tewkesbury II* was originally composed there is an open question. See also pp. 416–17 below.

[14] The chronicle of St Werburg's, Chester, covering the period from the Incarnation to 1297, is so brief that it will not be discussed here. In its present form the text is late fifteenth or early sixteenth century, but it is based on a chronicle probably begun by, or at the order of, Abbot Simon of Whitchurch (1265–91). It is printed in *Annales Cestrienses*, ed., with an English

But the Benedictines were not the only chroniclers. Part of the Winchester chronicle was used by the Cistercians of Waverley abbey in Surrey, who also produced their own excellent annals.[16] The Cistercians of Stanley abbey, in Wiltshire, lent their chronicle to the monks of Furness abbey, in Lancashire, who copied, expanded and continued it.[17] And finally the Cluniacs of St Andrew's, Northampton, wrote a small chronicle.[18] Furthermore the Augustinian canons produced two good chronicles at this period, the Dunstable chronicle[19] and the Osney chronicle.[20] The canons of Dunstable continued their chronicle, started in King John's reign, throughout the reign of Henry III and the reign of Edward I. The canons of Osney began a chronicle in the 1250s: it starts with the mission of St Augustine and continues to 1293 (there is a fourteenth-century continuation, mainly copied from Higden's *Polychronicon*).

As stated above, the typical thirteenth-century chronicler tends to concentrate on the affairs of his own house. Some chroniclers ignore national events if they do not affect their houses, and most view them in the light of the interests of their own community. Nevertheless a few of the chroniclers had a deep interest in, and clear understanding of, general history. On the whole they all concentrated on general history when they thought it of

translation, R. C. Christie (Record Society of Lancashire and Cheshire, xiv, 1886). For its sources to 1250 see ibid., p. xiv. From 1250 it is original and contains mainly local material though it also has entries on general history, especially relating to Simon de Montfort (whom it favours). This chronicle and another even shorter thirteenth-century chronicle from St Werburg's are fully discussed in ibid., pp. v et seq. See also John Taylor, *The Universal Chronicle of Ranulf Higden* (Oxford 1966), p. 11, and p. 439 n. 1 below.

[15] The chronicle of Robert of Gloucester, Brutus to 1270, is printed *The Metrical Chronicle of Robert of Gloucester*, ed. W. A. Wright (RS, 1887, 2 vols). A rendering in modern English of the part on Henry III's reign is in Joseph Stevenson, *The Church Historians of England* (London 1853–8, 5 vols), vol. 5, pt i, pp. 351–81.

[16] For the Waverley chronicle see p. 333 and n. 107.

[17] For the Stanley chronicle see p. 332 and n. 97. The Furness chronicle is printed parallel to the Stanley chronicle, and its relationship to the Stanley chronicle is discussed, in *Chrons. Stephen, Henry II, and Richard I*, vol. 2, pp. lxxxvii–xc, 503–83.

[18] The chronicle of the Cluniacs of Northampton, A.D. 1 to 1339, is described and the annals from 1258 to 1268 are printed by H. M. Cam and E. F. Jacob, 'Notes on an English Cluniac chronicle' in *EHR*, xliv (1929), pp. 94–104. See also pp. 421–2 below. For a very brief set of annals written by various authors from the late twelfth to the late thirteenth century (with later additions) from another Cluniac house, Lewes, see F. Liebermann, 'The annals of Lewes priory' in *EHR*, xvii (1902), pp. 83–9.

[19] Printed in *Ann. Mon.*, vol. 3, pp. 3–408. See pp. 332–9 *passim* above.

[20] Printed in *Mon. Angl.*, vol. 4, pp. 3–352. For two unpublished Premonstratensian chronicles, of Barlings, 1066–1282 (Magdalen College, Oxford, MS. 199), and Hagnaby, 1066–1307 (BM MS. Cotton Vespasian B XI), see *Chronicles of the Reigns of Edward I and Edward II*, ed. W. Stubbs (RS, 1882, 1883, 2 vols), vol. 2, pp. xxxix–xli. The Barlings chronicle is based on the Hagnaby chronicle to 1252; its additions to the latter, and the section from 1252 to 1282 which is independent of the Hagnaby chronicle are printed in ibid., pp. cxiii–cxviii. The Hagnaby chronicle seems to be based on the Waverley chronicle to 1252, after which it is apparently original and contains brief annals relating to local and general history. From about 1293 the annals become longer, showing particular interest in Edward I's relations with Wales, Scotland and France and including copies of a number of official documents, letters, etc. There are also references to Lincoln and a few to Hagnaby.

overriding importance: patriotism could eclipse self-interest. They were inspired by the Barons' War to discard their usual materialistic criteria and consider wider national interests. It is likely that politics even induced historical writing. The number of chronicles which were written during the barons' dispute with Henry III suggests that it provided the incentive for composition. And many end during or soon after the baronial period. The Burton chronicle ends in 1261. The Tewkesbury chronicle (here called *Tewkesbury I*)[21] ends in 1262. Another short chronicle copied (and perhaps composed) at Tewkesbury (here called *Tewkesbury II*) ends (incomplete) in 1263. The Battle chronicle ends in 1264 (it has a continuation to 1284). The St Albans *Flores Historiarum* and the chronicle of John de Taxter end in 1265, and the Stanley and Dover chronicles in 1270. The close coincidence of these dates indicates that once the turbulent events of the revolt were over, chroniclers lost a strong motive for writing.

The sympathies of all except one of the chroniclers lie, when expressed, with the barons. They saw the barons as fighting for their right to be the king's counsellors and for the expulsion of the hated foreign relatives and favourites of Henry III. Simon de Montfort himself came to be represented as a martyr for the ancient laws and customs of England and the liberty of the church. The attitude of some chroniclers was emotional rather than rational. It was partly the result of contemporary propaganda disseminated especially by friars and clerks in minor orders who had wholeheartedly embraced Simon de Montfort's cause, exhorting the people with sermons and political verses.[22] Simon's reputation was augmented by the circumstances of his death. His posthumous fame seems to have owed more to the violence of his slaughter at Evesham (he died unshriven and his body was dismembered) than to his actual political objectives and beliefs.[23] He became a popular saint, and Henry on his restoration to power had to take steps to suppress the cult.[24] But the almost mystical attitude to Simon evinced by some of the chroniclers (for example those of Waverley, Battle, and Furness) only temporarily clouded their usual moderation and fairness. They do not blacken Henry III's character. On the contrary they try to find scapegoats

---

[21] For *Tewkesbury I* and *Tewkesbury II* see p. 405 n. 13.

[22] For the propaganda see R. F. Treharne, *The Baronial Plan of Reform 1258–1263* (Manchester 1932), p. 334. For the political songs evoked by the Barons' War ('The song of the Barons' and 'Lament for Simon de Montfort') see *Anglo-Norman Political Songs*, ed. I. S. T. Aspin (Anglo-Norman Texts, xi, Oxford 1953), and Legge, *A-N Lit.*, p. 354.

[23] Modern historians differ as to the extent of Simon de Montfort's altruism and idealism. Charles Bémont, *Simon de Montfort*, ed. and translated by E. F. Jacob (Oxford 1930), reaches a favourable verdict (see especially pp. 49–50), but C. H. Knowles, *Simon de Montfort 1265–1965* (Historical Association Pamphlet no. lx, London 1965), considers that Simon was motivated by self-interest. F. M. Powicke, *The Thirteenth Century* (Oxford 1953), pp. 114–15, 192 n. 2, takes a moderate view. For Simon's posthumous cult, see ibid., p. 203.

[24] The Dictum of Kenilworth, c. 8. See pp. 396, 401, Plate XI above on a possible alteration in the text of chronicle of Bury St Edmunds in response to this ordinance. See also p. 421 and n. 168 for the Furness chronicle's caution on the subject of de Montfort's miracles, because of fear of the king.

for his shortcomings – usually evil counsellors, or an unscrupulous papacy using him to promote its interests against the empire. The Furness chronicler, having stated that Simon de Montfort's body worked miracles,[25] later has a panegyric on Henry III after the notice of his death.[26] Henry's piety was generally recognized and, as the patron of Westminster abbey, he was assured of one consistently favourable chronicle, the Westminster continuation of the *Flores*.

The chief authority for the general history of Henry III's reign is, as has been pointed out in chapter 16, Matthew Paris.[27] The value of the chronicle of Bury St Edmunds for this period has also been discussed above.[28] And it should be noted that the chronicle of London attributed to Arnold Fitz Thedmar has a valuable account of the Barons' War in so far as it affected London.[29] More information about the period is to be found in some chronicles written in Edward I's reign (notably in Thomas Wykes,[30] Walter of Guisborough[31] and in the Lanercost chronicle[32]). Of the chronicles here under discussion the most important are those of Burton and Waverley, and the *Flores Historiarum*. The Winchester chronicle, though brief, has a good record of national events, and *Tewkesbury II* has a forceful account of the Barons' War. These will be dealt with first. Next the lesser monastic authorities will be discussed; that is, the chronicles of Canterbury, Dover, Battle, Norwich, Stanley, Furness and Northampton, and *Tewkesbury I*, all works of more limited interest, some of which are principally interested in local history (but local history itself is of value for general history when a neighbourhood becomes involved in national events). Then the Augustinian chronicles, of Dunstable and Osney, will be considered. The chronicle of Robert of Gloucester will be treated last because it has distinctive features of its own.

The Burton chronicle begins in 1004 with the foundation of the abbey and it ends, incomplete, in 1262 with a notice that Henry III was reluctant to observe the Provisions of Oxford.[33] To 1201 it consists of extracts from Roger of Howden's chronicle. Then there are very short annals for 1202, 1207 and 1208. Under 1211 is an account of an alleged dialogue between King John and the papal ambassadors, which occurs more briefly in the Waverley annals.[34] After that the chronicle acquires its own distinctive characteristics. It is a series of documents connected with sections of narrative, the work of an archivist rather than a historian. The value of the chronicle is mainly due to the fact that some of these documents are unique and others rare. Probably the technique of assembling documents in a

---

[25] *Furness*, p. 548.
[26] Ibid., p. 563.
[27] See p. 360.
[28] See pp. 401–2.
[29] See pp. 514–17.
[30] See pp. 464–70.
[31] See pp. 470–1.
[32] See pp. 500–1.
[33] For the construction of the Burton chronicle see *Burt.*, pp. xxviii–xxx.
[34] *Burt.*, pp. 209–17; *Wav.*, pp. 268–71.

meaningful historical order was adopted from Roger of Howden. The documents were obtained from the abbey's own muniments and from those of its diocesan, the bishop of Coventry and Lichfield (the records were at Lichfield, only twelve miles from Burton). The episcopal records at Lincoln (which was fifty-five miles away) were also used.

The Burton chronicle has documents valuable for the history of the ecclesiastical reform movement, led in Henry III's reign by Robert Grosseteste, bishop of Lincoln.[35] To take a few examples: it has the articles of inquiry by Roger Weseham bishop of Coventry and Lichfield into the conduct of the clergy, in 1252, 'following the example of Robert Grosseteste'.[36] It has a copy of a summons to the council of the province of Canterbury in London in August 1257,[37] and another to the council of the clergy at Merton in June 1258[38] (copies of both are also preserved among the muniments of the dean and chapter at Lichfield[39]). Robert Grosseteste played an important part in the Council of Merton.[40] Some of the documents in the Burton chronicle relate directly to Grosseteste. The chronicle has a copy of a letter of 1253 from Pope Innocent IV to the archdeacon of Canterbury ordering him to obtain a prebend at Lincoln for his nephew,[41] with a copy of Grosseteste's indignant reply.[42] It gives a copy of the privileges of the clergy drawn up by one of Grosseteste's clerks at his request.[43] Grosseteste as bishop of Lincoln was *ex officio* chancellor of Oxford university (and he had been a lecturer there before his promotion to the episcopate). The Burton chronicle shows an interest in the university: it has a unique copy of the university regulations drawn up in 1257 concerning the discipline of the regents[44] (it also has information about the university of Paris – concerning the latter's conflict with the Dominicans[45]). Particularly remarkable are the documents relating to the Barons' War. The chronicle has one of the two best surviving texts both of the Provisions of Oxford

---

[35] The Burton chronicle is followed in the manuscript (BM MS. Cotton Vespasian E III) by a collection of miscellaneous documents, including some important diocesan constitutions, apparently relating to the diocese of Coventry; see M. Gibbs and J. Lang, *Bishops and Reform 1215–1272* (Oxford 1934; reprinted F. Cass, 1962), pp. 108–9.

[36] *Burt.*, pp. 296–8.

[37] *Burt.*, p. 401. Printed from this and another text in *Councils and Synods*, vol. 2, pt i, pp. 531–2.

[38] *Burt.*, pp. 411–12. Printed from this and another text in *Councils and Synods*, vol. 2, pt i, pp. 571–2.

[39] See *Councils and Synods*, vol. 2, pt i, 531, 571.

[40] See Gibbs and Lang, op. cit., p. 37.

[41] *Burt.*, pp. 437–8.

[42] *Burt.*, pp. 311–13. Printed in *Roberti Grosseteste Episcopi quondam Lincolniensis Epistolae*, ed. H. R. Luard (RS, 1861), pp. 432–7, ep. cxxviii.

[43] *Burt.*, pp. 425–9.

[44] *Burt.*, p. 436. This passage is noticed as the authority for the regulations, by Anthony à Wood, *The History and Antiquities of the University of Oxford ... now first published in English ... by John Gutch* (Oxford 1792, 1796, 2 vols), vol. 1, p. 257. For the importance of the regulations see *Statuta Antiqua Universitatis Oxoniensis*, ed. Strickland Gibson (Oxford 1931), p. xliv.

[45] *Burt.*, pp. 347–8, 430–4.

(June 1258)[46] and of the Provisions of Westminster (October 1259),[47] and a unique letter, by an eye-witness at court, of the barons' negotiations with Henry III concerning his Poitevin relatives, in the summer of 1258.[48]

Nevertheless the Burton chronicle is more than a series of documents. Some of the narrative is long and detailed, showing literary skill and historical understanding. There is a graphic account of the persecution of the Jews of Lincoln following the alleged ritual murder of St Hugh in 1255.[49] As in the chronicle of Thomas Wykes,[50] the cessation of the slaughter of the Jews is attributed to the intervention of Richard of Cornwall. The chronicle evinces the intolerance of the Jews typical of most contemporary writers, and blames Richard for his interference which it attributes to the fact that Richard had the farm of the English Jewry for that year.[51] Some narrative passages show the chronicle's attitude to politics, notably to Henry III's struggle with the barons. On the whole it is moderate and objective rather than opinionated. It mentions Henry's 'astuteness and power'[52] and is obviously pleased at the honour done him by Louis IX when he visited Pontigny and Paris in 1254 (the warm welcome and state receptions are described at some length).[53] But the chronicle questions the motives for Henry's friendship with Pope Innocent IV. Having described the pleasantries they exchanged on their respective ages, it remarks that the friendship was based on love of money (as both parties planned to extort money from the people) rather than on love of heaven.[54]

The Burton chronicle appreciates the importance in English politics of the Sicilian venture, the expense of which aggravated relations between king and barons. It calls Henry's acceptance of the kingdom of Sicily for Edmund 'stupid and ill-considered', ascribing it to 'wicked counsel'.[55] It gives a full and valuable account of the ecclesiastical council in London in the spring of 1257, when the clergy negotiated with the papal legate Rostand on taxation for the proposed Sicilian campaign.[56] Moreover, the chronicle explains the baronial position. In 1255, it records, the barons demanded the right to choose the justiciar, chancellor and treasurer, 'according to the custom of the

[46] *Burt.*, pp. 446–53. For the importance of this text see Treharne, *Baronial Plan*, p. 82.

[47] *Burt.*, pp. 471–9 (the French versions: a Latin version is ibid., pp. 480–4). For the importance of the text see Treharne, *Baronial Plan*, pp. 164–5, 167, 390–1.

[48] *Burt.*, pp. 444–5. See Treharne, *Baronial Plan*, p. 78 and n. 1. The Burton chronicle also has the only known text of a letter of Pope Alexander IV to Richard of Cornwall, of 30 April 1259; *Burt.*, pp. 469–70 (printed from this copy in *Foedera*, vol. 1, pt i, p. 382).

[49] *Burt.*, pp. 340–8. For St Hugh's alleged martyrdom see C. Roth, *A History of the Jews in England* (Oxford 1964), pp. 56–7.

[50] For Wykes's view see p. 466. For Richard of Cornwall's part in stopping the execution of the Lincoln Jews, with reference to this passage in the Burton chronicle, see N. Denholm-Young, *Richard of Cornwall* (Oxford 1947), pp. 69–70.

[51] *Burt.*, p. 348. For the grant to Richard of the farm of the Jewry see *CPR, 1247–1258*, pp. 400–1.

[52] See *Burt.*, p. 339.   [53] *Burt.*, pp. 327–9.   [54] *Burt.*, p. 323.

[55] *Burt.*, p. 360.

[56] *Burt.*, pp. 386–91. Printed from this text in *Councils and Synods*, vol. 2, pt i, pp. 524–7.

realm', and they replied to the king's demands for money 'by common counsel'.[57] One of the most important passages, with information not found elsewhere, throws some light on the circumstances in which the 'community of the bachelors of England' presented a petition to the barons in the autumn of 1259. The chronicle states that the 'bachelors' (who exactly they were is obscure) were afraid that the barons would not fulfil their undertakings to carry out reforms 'for the public good', but were only seeking their own advantage. The Lord Edward took up their cause, swearing to stand by the *communitas* until death.[58]

Another chronicle of moderate tone is the Winchester chronicle, written at St Swithun's, and covering the period from A.D. 519 to 1277.[59] From 1202 it was written fairly close to the events recorded. This chronicle is a dry record of local and national events, disappointingly brief: a Winchester chronicler should have been able to give detailed information about important events because the king and court were often in the city. But the chronicler dismisses, for instance, the parliament held at Winchester in 1258 with a few lines, although the reconciliation of Henry III and Edward took place in the cathedral chapter-house itself.[60] The chronicle is mainly important because it is accurate and because its exemplar, a lost Winchester chronicle, was historiographically influential (it was copied at Hyde, Worcester[61] and Waverley[62]). It is primarily a record. Many paragraphs begin in a business-like way, with 'Item ...'. The preface (quoted above) emphasizes the record-aspect of the work. Moreover, the original chronicle had an appendix of documents illustrating the text,[63] like Matthew Paris's *Liber Additamentorum*. As the Winchester chronicle has citations from the

---

[57] *Burt.*, p. 336.

[58] *Burt.*, p. 471. For the 'bachelors', with reference to the Burton chronicle, see Treharne, *Baronial Plan*, pp. 160–4 and nn. for further references. The text of the Provisions of Westminster, framed on the demand of the 'bachelors', follows in the Burton chronicle: see above, n. 47.

[59] See pp. 252 and n. 47, 253, 333. This chronicle only survives in a version made for the monks of Hyde abbey; see Denholm-Young, 'Winchester-Hyde chron.', p. 88. For a full description of Bodley MS. 91 (1891), see F. Madan, H. H. E. Craster, and D. P. Record, *A Summary Catalogue of Western Manuscripts in the Bodleian Library of Oxford* (Oxford 1895–1953, 7 vols), vol. 2, pt 1, pp. 101–2.

[60] *Wint.*, p. 97.

[61] See p. 333 and n. 108.

[62] See p. 413 and nn. 78, 89.

[63] See the reference to the establishment of the council of nine under 1264, 'prout versus finem huius libri videbitis continuari' (*Wint.*, p. 102). The relevant documents are not in the manuscript printed by Luard (BM MS. Cotton Domitian A XIII). But Luard's text is itself derived from a text in Bodley MS. 91 (a Hyde book, which in its turn descends from the lost Winchester chronicle). Bodley MS. 91 does have an appendix of documents, to which the entry cited refers. For Bodley 91 and the appendix of documents see Denholm-Young, 'Winchester-Hyde chron.', pp. 87–9 *passim*. A calendar of the documents is printed as an appendix in ibid., pp. 94–5. For another reference 'ut patebit infra', for the constitutions of the Council of Lyons, 1274, see *Wint.*, p. 117 (but the constitutions are not in Bodley 91): the same reference is in the Waverley annals (again without the document) which is here copying the lost Winchester chronicle; see *Wav.*, p. 383.

St Albans chronicles,[64] it may here have been influenced by Matthew's example.

The attitude of the Winchester chronicle to the great crisis of the day, the Barons' War, is moderate, even muted. It asserts that, besides a thunderstorm, there was darkness, a token of divine displeasure, after the battle of Evesham.[65] It emphasizes that laws were made in parliament 'by common assent' and 'for the common utility of the whole realm'.[66] But it passes no judgment on Henry III. Indeed towards the end of his reign Henry was on fairly good terms with St Swithun's and a frequent visitor. The Lord Edward also went there: in 1270 he attended chapter and asked for the monks' prayers for his crusade.[67] The chronicle is very much preoccupied with the abbey's own troubles. The quarrel precipitated by Bishop Aymer over the appointment of a prior lasted over twenty years (until 1276),[68] and during the Barons' War the townsmen, taking advantage of the weakness of the central government, attacked the property of laymen and clergy in the city, including that of St Swithun's.[69]

More positive political views are expressed in the Waverley chronicle. Of all the chronicles under discussion it is perhaps the one which supports the baronial side most explicitly and intelligently. It covers the period from the Incarnation to 1291, ending incomplete.[70] It uses as sources various well-known authorities, including the Anglo-Saxon Chronicle, Geoffrey of Monmouth, William of Malmesbury, Henry of Huntingdon, Ralph Diceto and Roger of Wendover.[71] From 1157 it has original material. The dialogue under 1212 between King John and the papal ambassadors has some relationship to the similar passage in the Burton annals.[72] From 1219 to 1266 it is a series of more or less contemporary annals, 'one of the chief authorities for this period'.[73] The evidence for the near contemporaneity of this section is provided by the manuscript and by the contents of the chronicle. It is an early draft and while up to 1219 the text is obviously a fair copy, after 1219 there are frequent changes of hand, indicating that the work was added to from time to time.[74] The annals were written up a year or so after the events. This is demonstrated by a notice under 1264 that John Mansel, exiled in that year, died abroad;[75] he died in January 1265. Under 1223 the

[64] See *Wint.*, pp. 48–9 *passim*.

[65] *Wint.*, p. 103. Chroniclers almost certainly alluded to darkness following Simon de Montfort's death on the analogy of the darkness which allegedly followed the Crucifixion. As in neither case was there an eclipse of the sun, the darkness must be interpreted symbolically. Similarly the *Song of Roland* states that darkness followed Roland's death; *La Chanson de Roland*, ed. F. Whitehouse (Oxford 1946), cc. 179–80. I owe this reference to Miss Gay Clifford.

[66] *Wint.*, pp. 110, 119. [67] *Wint.*, p. 109.

[68] For a résumé of the quarrel, described in the chronicle, see *Wint.*, pp. xxiii–xxv.

[69] *Wint.*, p. 101. [70] See p. 333 and n. 107.

[71] For its sources see *Ann. Mon.*, vol. 2, pp. xxxi–xxxvi.

[72] See p. 408. [73] *Ann. Mon.*, vol. 2, p. xxxvi.

[74] BM MS. Cotton Vespasian A XVI, ff. 24–200ᵛ.

[75] *Wav.*, p. 355. For the date of Mansel's death see *DNB*, vol. 12, p. 971.

chronicle remarks that a boy who nearly drowned in the ditch by the abbey gate was restored to health 'and can to this day be found, at any time (even if not wanted), going in and out of the same gateway'.[76] And under 1247 it says that the meteorites which fell in Cheshire 'still survive, made like stones by the heat of the sun, it is believed, so hard that neither iron or any skill or human effort can break or dent them, as those who have seen them testify'.[77]

From 1266 to 1275 the Waverley chronicle is identical with the Winchester one, except that it has additions about Waverley and the Cistercian order. Similarities between the works continue until 1277 when the Waverley chronicle again becomes independent.[78] The chronicle not only used the lost Winchester chronicle from 1266 to 1277, it also drew on Winchester material for the previous period. It has some information about Winchester which is not in the Winchester chronicle.[79] For example the Waverley chronicle has a much fuller account of the opposition at Winchester to Bishop William Raleigh in 1243,[80] and to the young Simon de Montfort in 1265.[81]

Like the Winchester chronicle, the Waverley one is a record of local and national history. As a local history, it records gifts to the abbey, using charters as its source. For instance it explains the terms of a bequest by Matilda of London (d. 1263) to the abbey. Matilda was to be buried in the church and gave all her money, specifying the pittances which were to be supplied on her and her husband's anniversaries. The monks bought the manor of Surbiton with part of the legacy (if necessary the rent was to pay for the pittances).[82] The chronicle records a grant of land (in Neatham) by Henry III, referring the reader to the writ of seizin on the chancery rolls.[83] The chronicle also has entries about the liturgical history of the abbey (the regulations made in chapter by Abbot Giffard concerning masses to be said for benefactors,[84] the candles to be burnt at Christmas,[85] and the like).

Similarly, as a national history, the Waverley chronicle provides a business-like record of events, 'for the information of posterity'.[86] It gives documentary evidence (there are copies of King John's submission to the pope, 1213,[87] and of King Henry's submission to the barons in 1265[88]), and is deliberately brief in the annalistic manner. It says that it will record the

---

[76] *Wav.*, p. 298.   [77] *Wav.*, p. 338.

[78] For the relationship of the Waverley chronicle and surviving Winchester one, both descended from the lost Winchester chronicle, see Denholm-Young, 'Winchester-Hyde chron.', pp. 89–91.

[79] Mr Denholm-Young, ibid., pp. 90–1, asserts that the Waverley chronicle preserves information about Winchester which was in the lost Winchester chronicle, the latter being fuller than any of its surviving descendants.

[80] *Wav.*, pp. 330–3.   [81] *Wav.*, p. 363.   [82] *Wav.*, pp. 353–4.

[83] *Wav.*, p. 321. For the enrolment see *Cal. of Charter Rolls, 1226–1257*, pp. 246–7.

[84] *Wav.*, p. 316.   [85] *Wav.*, p. 317.   [86] *Wav.*, p. 355.

[87] *Wav.*, pp. 275–6.   [88] *Wav.*, pp. 358–61.

battle of Lewes succinctly,[89] and will say little about Henry III's expedition to Brittany in 1230 because 'the affair is so public that nearly anyone who wishes can learn about it'.[90] The idea that the reader already knows or can easily obtain the information for himself is often the excuse for brevity. The chronicle passes quickly over the quarrel between Archbishop Edmund and the monks of Christ Church partly 'out of reverence for so great a church,' but partly because 'the truth is hardly hidden at all from the knowledge of most people'.[91] And, with regard to the regulations drawn up by the legate Otho for the Cistercians in 1237, the chronicle gives one chapter (on meat-eating) and for the rest refers the reader to 'the text publicly recited within hearing of everyone'.[92] Nevertheless the chronicle, despite its attempted brevity, has literary pretensions. It cites a number of verses (for example one from an inscription on the abbey's new bell,[93] and two commemorating the deaths of Stephen Langton and Richard the Marshal[94]). It was intended to amuse as well as instruct, and has a few good anecdotes (for example the one about the boy who nearly drowned in the abbey ditch), and some excellent narrative, notably on Henry III's dispute with the barons and the civil war.[95]

The Waverley chronicle maintains a constant 'constitutional', anti-royalist point of view, identifying itself with Simon de Montfort and his party. Its attitude may have been partly determined by the abbey's friendship with Simon's wife, Eleanor. In 1245 Eleanor countess of Leicester, 'our most sincere friend', came to Waverley with her 'very pious husband, Simon de Montfort earl of Leicester, their two sons Henry and Simon, and three ladies in waiting'.[96] They entered the church just when the Host was being raised ('by divine disposition, it was thought'). Eleanor gave the abbey a precious altar cloth and money, and helped it acquire some lands. 'She attended the sermon in chapter, the procession, and high mass, and when she had kissed the holy cross, left, having been much edified.'

But personal considerations do not entirely account for the chronicle's attitude. It is likely that a more important influence on the annalist's outlook were the consultative and representative elements in the organization of the Cistercian order. The chronicle has a close interest in Cistercian affairs (it records the sessions of the general chapter, the foundation of new houses, and the like), and is in favour of the strict observance of the Rule.[97] It is

---

[89] *Wav.*, p. 355.   [90] *Wav.*, p. 308.   [91] *Wav.*, p. 320.

[92] *Wav.*, p. 318.   [93] *Wav.*, p. 321.   [94] *Wav.*, pp. 304, 315.

[95] See especially *Wav.*, pp. 349–50, 355–7.

[96] *Wav.*, p. 336. The Waverley chronicle is also very favourable to Richard of Cornwall, who was the founder of the Cistercian abbey of Hailes. It says for example that he was received on his return to England in 1242 'like an angel'; *Wav.*, p. 329.

[97] e.g. it cites Otho's constitution on meat-eating (see above and n. 92), and records the deposition of the prior and cellarer of Beaulieu in 1246 for infringing the Cistercian statutes by allowing a woman (in this instance the queen) to stay in the abbey, and meat to be served to seculars; *Wav.*, p. 337.

conscious that decisions at Waverley itself were made after consultation: in 1263 some business was settled 'by the sane counsel of the seniors of the house'. The order's alienation from the king had begun under King John. The chronicle notes John's persecution of the Cistercians, his financial extortions and depredation of their property in 1210. It records the dispersal of the Waverley monks and the nocturnal flight of the abbot.[98] This section of the chronicle is not contemporary (being written at least ten years later) and, perhaps because of a growing anti-royalist bias among the Cistercians, it does not mention that the English Cistercians as a body previously negotiated successfully with King John, as Ralph of Coggeshall relates.[99] It explains how, in 1256, the English Cistercians, fearing an infringement of the order's privileges, successfully resisted the king's financial demands. They refused to make a grant without the licence of the general chapter and 'the consent of all the abbots'. The chronicle comments: 'Thus the integrity and constancy of the Cistercian order were spoken of and praised nearly everywhere, and were so respected that, in many people's opinion, there was no other order under heaven comparable to this one in steadfastness, unity and religious fervour.'[100] The chronicle also mentions the arrangements made in 1261 by the general chapter to resist prelates who infringed the order's privileges (three senior abbots in the locality were to inquire about it, if necessary raising money for legal defence).[101] Thus the chronicle gives expression to ideas of consultation, consent and corporate action long accepted in the order. By association such ideas could well have been applied to the baronial opposition.

Simon de Montfort and his adherents are called 'the saner party' and are the would-be saviours of the kingdom[102] ('divinely awakened from sleep, they saw the misery of the realm and united'[103]). The chronicle emphasizes their right to counsel the king.[104] Henry III turned from their advice to that of aliens ('who made fun of the magnates').[105] The chronicle speaks bitterly about the aliens in England, and seems to have been influenced by popular rumours. It says:[106]

> numerous foreigners of various tongues have so increased over the years and are so richly endowed with rents, lands, vills and other benefits that they hold the English in contempt as inferiors. It is said by some who know their secrets that if their power prospers, all the magnates of England will be poisoned, Henry

---

[98] *Wav.*, p. 265.   [99] See p. 326.

[100] *Wav.*, pp. 348–9. Similarly when the chronicle records how in 1239 a homicide who worked as a shoemaker in the abbey was seized by royal officials in defiance of the abbey's privileges, it treats the abbey's consequent defence of its liberties as if it were the defence of the liberties of the whole order; *Wav.*, pp. 325–6. It again compares the Cistercians' constancy in resisting oppression with the other orders' lack of it, under 1281; *Wav.*, p. 397.

[101] *Wav.*, p. 352–3.   [102] *Wav.*, p. 356.   [103] *Wav.*, p. 350.

[104] *Wav.*, p. 351.   [105] *Wav.*, p. 355.   [106] *Wav.*, p. 349.

deposed and someone else put in his place, as they decide, and thus all England will at last be subject to them.

The chronicle states that the barons based their opposition to the king on an appeal to ancient law: in 1258 'they began industriously to renew and reform ancient laws and customs.'[107] The chronicler writes: 'These laws and customs had been either excessively corrupted or wholly quashed and reduced to nothing, and it was as if instead of the law, there was [the king's] tyrannical will; and no just judgement could be easily obtained except for money.' As this passage is very like one under 1215, the author must here have had King John in mind and have referred back to the chronicle's account of John's reign.[108] Simon and his party first tried to defend these ancient laws and customs and overthrow the new 'perverse' laws by negotiation.[109] Having failed, they resorted to war. Simon died – 'Alas! a glorious martyr for the peace of the land, and for the redemption of the realm and of mother church'.[110]

The same attitude to the crisis, though expressed in even more emotional, almost homiletic, language, is in *Tewkesbury II*, the short account of the baronial opposition from 1258 to 1263. The Provisions of Oxford were agreed 'by unanimous consent', their opposers were 'wicked Pharisees'. The aliens 'of whatever nation, whether Roman or others' were 'the owners, devourers and wasters of most of the property in England', they behaved 'like little kings' at Henry III's side. And some of the barons were seduced from the baronial cause 'by the wicked temptings of the Devil', and 'by the serpentine wiles of a woman' (that is Queen Eleanor).[111] There is an eloquent passage (put into the mouth of King Louis) on Henry's real need of baronial co-operation:[112]

> Just as a ship cannot be saved from the peril of the sea without the guidance of the oarsmen, so neither can any king govern his realm prosperously nor defend it from its enemies without the help of his own subjects: it is right and just that every kingdom should be governed by the king and the loyal men of the kingdom and not by aliens.

Tewkesbury II concludes with a curious letter of advice 'from a certain faithful Englishman' to the barons (it ends incomplete). The political views reflected in it are not those of the chronicle. They are apparently those of moderate men and waverers. The letter warns the barons of the dangers of failure. A legate, it says, the cardinal bishop of Sabina (Guy Foulquois), was to be sent with power to annul the barons' work. If he entered England

---

[107] *Wav.*, p. 350.
[108] *Wav.*, p. 282. This passage is cited in an English translation by J. C. Holt, *Magna Carta* (Cambridge 1965), p. 98.
[109] *Wav.*, p. 355.   [110] *Wav.*, p. 365.   [111] *Tewkesbury II*, pp. 174–5.
[112] *Tewkesbury II*, p. 176.

he would undo their achievements; if he were excluded, he would excommunicate the barons and call French aid to defeat them. Therefore the barons are advised to submit unless they are sure of victory. It also points out that Simon de Montfort has been unfair in his treatment of aliens (he has expelled some but allowed others to stay), and in his distribution of royalist property. The barons should appoint another leader, as Simon is old, and should find allies in Wales, Scotland and Ireland. They should work for the common good and not take spoil, if they want to succeed.[113] The purpose of this letter is not clear, but perhaps it was to promote the interests, by propaganda, of Richard de Clare, earl of Gloucester, the head of the moderate party.[114] The occurrence of such a document in a Tewkesbury manuscript could be accounted for by the fact that the Clares were patrons of the abbey.[115]

The continuation, from 1259 to 1265, of Matthew Paris's *Flores Historiarum*, written at St Albans,[116] combines the record-value of the Burton chronicle with the narrative quality of the chronicle of Waverley. And although it continues the pro-baronial, anti-royalist bias of Matthew Paris, it is less emotional in tone and less propagandist than *Tewkesbury II*. It is better informed, notably about foreign affairs and governmental administration, than either the Waverley chronicle or *Tewkesbury II*, and as the Burton chronicle ends at the beginning of 1262, it becomes the most important contemporary source for the period preceding the battle of Evesham. Local information occupies only a small proportion of space.

As a record the *Flores* at first continues Matthew Paris's technique, relegating documents to the *Liber Additamentorum*. One document preserved in this way is a good text of the Provisions of Westminster.[117] The *Flores* was intended to be brief: 'an uninhibited poet or a verbose *raconteur* would describe the various events [at the battle of Lewes], and the diverse modes of slaughter; but brevity limits us by a strict law and we are not allowed to say how it happened, only what happened'.[118] The *Flores* was written partly for reference, to provide precedents and guides for wise behaviour. Under 1262 it records that the laity and clergy refused to grant an aid to help Baldwin II, emperor of Constantinople, against the Greeks: they

---

[113] *Tewkesbury II*, pp. 179–80. Professor Treharne, *Baronial Plan*, p. 334, calls this letter 'one of the most skilful and insidious' attempts at propaganda to win supporters in the baronial period.

[114] *Tewkesbury II*, p. 334.

[115] There are a number of references in *Tewkesbury I* demonstrating the close connection between the Clares and Tewkesbury abbey – e.g. it records the burial of Richard de Clare, earl of Gloucester (1230–62), in the abbey; *Tewkesbury I*, p. 169.

[116] See pp. 377–8 and nn. 167–8.

[117] Printed in E. F. Jacob, *Studies in the Period of Baronial Reform and Rebellion, 1258–1267* (Oxford Studies in Social and Legal History, ed. P. Vinogradoff, vol. 8, 1925), pp. 370–6. For the value of this text of the Provisions of Westminster see Treharne, *Baronial Plan*, pp. 165–8, 390–1. *FH*, vol. 2, p. 474 and n. 1, refers to a copy of the Provisions of Oxford and to a royal writ 'in fine huius libri' but these are not in *Lib. Add.*

[118] *FH*, vol. 2, p. 497.

said that they would rather help their own prince than a foreigner: 'I have inserted this', the *Flores* remarks, 'for the instruction of posterity, so that future generations shall be forewarned and preserved from these sorts of imposts, because they have learnt a lesson from the past, on a united reply from one community with one will'.[119]

Modern research has shown that though the *Flores*'s account of the baronial administration from 1259 to 1260 is biased in favour of the barons, it is on the whole accurate and well informed. The *Flores* praises the barons' achievement. It writes, at the end of the annal for 1259: 'England, which had long suffered injuries and the tyrannies of many kings, as it were, in this year began to breathe with long-desired reforms, as a new spirit of justice rose within her'.[120] The *Flores* gives a reasoned account of the work of the baronial justiciar, Hugh Bigod, and his associates. Bigod was a man 'worthy of the greatest trust' who travelled 'from county to county and franchise to franchise, doing justice to all men according to their deserts. The community of the realm had chosen him and the other justices because they were the most skilled in English law and the most just in their judgements.'[121] They had sworn to do justice to all men, without fear or favour, and without taking bribes. The *Flores* states that the council established by the Provisions of Oxford was energetic in carrying out its programme of reform – and the records of the central government confirm this view.[122] The *Flores* shows detailed knowledge of the local conflicts caused by Henry III's attempt to regain power in 1261.[123] He sent out justices in eyre without the barons' consent. The *Flores* describes the methods used 'by certain men on behalf of the baronage' to oppose the eyre in some counties. They argued that the justices gave summonses of less than forty days, the period required 'according to English law beneficially decided on from ancient times'. Moreover, they pointed out that less than seven years (the interval required by custom and by the barons) had elapsed since the last eyre.[124] The *Flores* also notices Henry's dismissal of the baronial sheriffs and the local resistance to his nominees.[125]

In its treatment of the Barons' War, the *Flores* in general supports the barons, even unfairly, but it does admit to some of their shortcomings (especially as the civil war gained momentum) and to some of the problems

---

[119] Ibid., p 479.

[120] Ibid., p. 439. Professor Treharne, *Baronial Plan*, p. 212, cites this passage with which he substantially agrees.

[121] *FH*, vol. 2, pp. 426–7. See Treharne, *Baronial Plan*, p. 156.

[122] *FH*, vol. 2, p. 439. See Treharne, *Baronial Plan*, p. 209.

[123] See *FH*, vol. 2, pp. 463–4, and the next note. Professor Treharne, *Baronial Plan*, p. 250 n. 4 describes the *Flores* as 'the only good account of the events of the early part of 1261'.

[124] *FH*, vol. 2, pp. 468, 472. For the importance of these passages see Treharne, *Baronial Plan*, pp. 398–406 *passim*.

[125] *FH*, vol. 2, p. 473. For local resistance see Treharne, *Baronial Plan*, p. 273 n. 3, and pp. 437–8 below.

inherent in Henry III's situation. It represents the barons as striving with God's help for the prosperity of England.[126] They 'were bound together by one faith and one will, they all loved God and heaven, and were so united by fraternal affection that they did not fear to die for their country.'[127] The *Flores* implies that the barons had a right to counsel the king,[128] and accuses Henry III of scorning them and taking secret advice,[129] and of favouring aliens.[130] It also accuses Henry of trying to establish 'dominion over the whole realm'[131] and of following 'his own free will'.[132] Simon de Montfort is described as 'the wisest and bravest warrior in England',[133] the leader[134] and inspiration of the barons.[135] Sometimes the *Flores* shows unfair bias in the barons' favour. For example there seems to be no foundation for the story that by the spring of 1261 Henry had alienated even Edward by his untrustworthiness.[136]

But the *Flores*'s attitude underwent a modification as time passed. The reason for this was horror at the civil war. Even the *Flores*'s enthusiasm for the barons' 'glorious, God given'[137] victory at Lewes is almost outweighed by the thought of the number of the dead ('a miserable sight')[138] and of a nation torn by strife.[139] It was 'a detestable battle, such as was unheard of in all centuries',[140] and the day it was fought was one 'of bitter calamity and dire misery'.[141] The *Flores* mentions with disapproval the subsequent ravages of Simon de Montfort's army in the marches of Wales: 'the local people were struck with great terror and apprehension, so that wherever [the soldiers] came, the inhabitants fled to the churches and built huts in the cemeteries, to save themselves and their goods'.[142] Simon himself is criticized. The *Flores* attributes his breach with Gilbert, earl of Gloucester, to his high-handed behaviour and greed: he kept the king a prisoner just as he liked, and held castles and other properties which 'ought by law to have been held in common', and took ransoms for himself and his sons 'more than was fair'.[143] The *Flores* has traces of sympathy for Henry. It believes that he was deceived by bad counsellors.[144] Henry's point of view is expressed in a speech the *Flores* puts into his mouth, justifying his opposition (in 1261) to the Provisions of Oxford. He claims that he is no longer, as it were, the lord of the barons, but their servant.[145] And later, under 1264, the *Flores* remarks that

---

[126] *FH*, vol. 2, p. 496.

[127] Ibid., pp. 494–5.

[128] Ibid., p. 470.

[129] Ibid., p. 463.

[130] Ibid., pp. 463, 479.

[131] Ibid., p. 469.

[132] Ibid., p. 471.

[133] Ibid., p. 454.

[134] Ibid., p. 481.

[135] Ibid., p. 495.

[136] Ibid., pp. 466–7. See Treharne, *Baronial Plan*, p. 258 n. 1.

[137] *FH*, vol. 2, pp. 494–5.

[138] Ibid., p. 496.

[139] Ibid., p. 498.

[140] Ibid., p. 494.

[141] Ibid., p. 498: 'Cujus eventum belli, calamitatis, et miseriae, diei dirae nimis et amarae valde, motaeque seditionis et guerrae inter cives unius terrae, signa portendere possunt'.

[142] Ibid., p. 502. For a lamentation on the looting, etc., by Edward's army in 1264 see ibid., p. 489.

[143] *FH*, vol. 3, p. 1.

[144] For references to adulatory and frivolous counsel see *FH*, vol. 2, pp. 464, 466.

[145] Ibid., pp. 463–4.

the king had ruled for fifty years but was king only in name, so that he could not travel through his land, but was under the absolute control and guidance of another.[146]

In 1265, soon after the battle of Evesham,[147] a copy of the *Flores* went to Westminster abbey. The manuscript of this copy still survives.[148] It was probably made especially for Westminster (this is suggested by the passages in it which would have been of particular interest to Westminster monks).[149] At Westminster the *Flores* was revised: the additions about the abbey were made in the margin[150] and on erasures in the text.[151] Then it was continued contemporarily with the events described to 1306[152] (a further continuation was later added to the accession of Edward II[153]). The Westminster continuation of the *Flores* is different in political outlook from the St Albans *Flores*: it is royalist.[154] It supports Henry III partly no doubt from reasons of circumspection (the king's government was next door to the abbey – his treasury was in the abbey itself), and partly because Henry was the abbey's patron and builder of its new church. As patron, Henry had a close relation with the abbey: the *Flores* describes how, when Henry was ill in 1271, 'the monks of Westminster, fearing to lose their patron, processed with bare feet, in the rain, to the New Temple and there celebrated for him a mass to the Blessed Virgin Mary'; on his recovery, which they attributed to their prayers, the monks sang *Gaudent in caelis*.[155] The *Flores* calls Henry an innocent, God-fearing man, whose main desire was to end civil discord.[156] It gives a panegyric after the notice of his death: 'God and those who faithfully supported [Henry] know what an innocent, patient man he was, and with what devotion he worshipped the Saviour. And, above all, the miracles which followed his death show how God valued his life'.[157] This no doubt was the official attitude to Henry at Westminster.

But there is a copy of the *Flores*[158] which shows a very different political orientation from that in the Westminster continuation. The *Flores* itself has a

---

[146] Ibid., p. 505.

[147] It is not certain at exactly what point in the *Flores* the St Albans writer stopped and the Westminster one began. There are a number of changes of hand in Chetham MS. 6712 from 1265 to 1302: see *FH*, vol. 1, p. xiv. However, a change of hand occurs at 'Bello igitur Eveshamie viriliter consummato' (*FH*, vol. 3, p. 6): it seems likely therefore that the Westminster author started here. V. H. Galbraith, *Roger Wendover and Matthew Paris* (Glasgow 1944), p. 25, states that the manuscript went to Westminster 'soon after 1265'.

[148] Chetham MS. 6712. See p. 378 and nn. 167, 171 above.

[149] See e.g. *FH*, vol. 2, p. 289. Cf. Galbraith, op. cit., p. 25 and n. 2.

[150] See *HA*, vol. 1, p. xxiv n. 2.

[151] See e.g. *FH*, vol. 2, p. 471 and n. 2.

[152] Printed in *FH*, vol. 3, pp. 6–137.

[153] Printed in ibid., pp. 137–235. See n. 147 above.

[154] For a version of the continuation of the *Flores* written in the late thirteenth century with even more extreme royalist attitudes, see pp. 456–73.

[155] *FH*, vol. 3, pp. 22–3.

[156] Ibid., p. 15.   [157] Ibid., p. 28.

[158] MS. 24 in the Chapter Library, Westminster. Described J. Armitage Robinson and M. R. James, *The Manuscripts of Westminster Abbey* (Cambridge 1909), pp. 82–3.

brief account of the battle of Evesham and of Simon de Montfort's death. This version of the *Flores* substitutes a passionately pro-Montfortian account of these events.[159] The propagandist tone suggests that it was written soon after the battle. It is an eloquent eulogy of Simon, resplendent with biblical quotations. The circumstances of the battle are compared with those of the Crucifixion. Simon, deserted by Gilbert earl of Gloucester ('intoxicated by the devil, like Judas'), fought at Evesham and won the palm of martyrdom ('he will be received in heaven as a reward for his labours'). And then '"there was darkness over all the land"' [Matt. 27. 45]. Simon was 'the most faithful man "in deed and word before God and all the people" [Luke 24. 19], the most energetic and wisest warrior of all the English'.

The other monastic chronicles for Henry III's reign have one or a combination of shortcomings – extreme brevity, a lack of non-derivative material, obsessive concentration on local affairs. *Tewkesbury I*, starting in 1066 and ending in the middle of the period of the baronial opposition, is very brief and mainly interested in the abbey's affairs.[160] However, its sympathies are clearly with the barons (who are described as 'noble and energetic', protesting against 'the intolerable Poitevins').[161] It is a partisan of Richard de Clare, earl of Gloucester, the abbey's patron.[162] The Worcester chronicle,[163] which was apparently written up fairly close to the events recorded from early in Henry III's reign,[164] is from 1261 to 1280 a derivative, with hardly any additions of its own, of the lost Winchester chronicle.[165] For the years immediately preceding, it is brief on general affairs, being preoccupied with local matters. Nevertheless, its baronial sympathies are shown by its description of the Provisions of Oxford as 'good laws'.[166]

The chronicle of Stanley abbey, a continuation of the chronicle of William of Newburgh to 1270, is very short and factual. It was copied and supplemented at Furness abbey where it was continued to 1298.[167] The Furness chronicle's entries on the Barons' War show its pro-baronial bias. For example it mentions the miracles worked by Simon de Montfort's corpse, adding 'no one dared speak of such things for fear of the king and his men'.[168] It also has a local detail, a story of the looting by the royalists of a local knight's manor and his revenge (he shut the culprits up in one of his buildings and burnt them).[169] The chronicle of the Cluniac priory of St Andrew at Northampton, mostly unpublished,[170] covers the years from the Incarnation to 1339, and has an apparently contemporary account of the Barons' War. It

---

[159] Printed in *FH*, vol. 3, pp. 5 n. 1, 6 n. 2.
[160] See p. 405 n. 13.
[161] *Tewkesbury I*, pp. 163–4.
[162] See p. 417 and n. 115.
[163] See p. 405 and n. 10.   [164] See p. 336.
[165] See pp. 319 n. 7, 333 and n. 108.
[166] *Worc.*, p. 445. For a reference to the liberties of England see *Worc.*, p. 448.
[167] For the chronicles of Stanley and Furness see pp. 332 and n. 97, 406 and n. 17 above.
[168] *Furness*, p. 548.   [169] *Furness*, pp. 544–5.
[170] See p. 406 and n. 18.

is very short but makes a few intelligent observations, for example that the Poitevins were hated 'because of their overbearing government of their franchises' (most chroniclers merely attack them as 'aliens').[171] The short chronicle, from the Anglo-Saxon invasions to the accession of Edward I, written at St Martin's, Dover, by a monk probably called Henry of Silegrave, has little value.[172] The passages in the Norwich chronicle about general history from 1258 to 1263 are borrowed from the chronicle of Bury St Edmunds.[173] The Bury chronicle is also the source of the general entries in the Spalding chronicle, from 1269 to 1271,[174] and of most of the chronicle of St Benet of Hulme from 1259 to the end.[175]

The three chronicles of this group which are of the most value for general history are the chronicle of Battle abbey, the chronicle of Christ Church, Canterbury, and that of the priory of St Martin, Dover. The Battle chronicle (only the section on the Barons' War, from 1258 to 1265, has been printed[176]) starts with Brutus, and goes to 1265, with a continuation to 1286. For the reign of King John it resembles the Dover chronicle but it is independent of all known literary authorities for Henry III's reign.[177] The attitude to Simon de Montfort is typical of a Benedictine writer – he is regarded as a martyr: he died (his flesh already subdued by a hair shirt) in defence of the Provisions of Oxford, a Christian martyred by Christians.[178] The chronicle has colourful local details about the progress of the royal army through Sussex in May 1264, just before the battle of Lewes. Henry III led his army through the lands of Combwell priory, in Kent, and Master Thomas Cook[179] who 'incautiously went in front of his army' was killed by 'a certain fellow'. The king therefore executed a number of men from Flimwell, a manor belonging to the abbot of Battle. When Henry came to Battle he was met by a procession of monks, 'but he showed an angry face'. The abbot gave him 100 marks and gave Edward 40 marks. But Henry accused the abbot of sending men to Flimwell to kill his men. The abbot defended himself but Henry 'seemed determined to harass him'. The king went on to Winchelsea where he allowed his army to loot, while he drank wine.[180]

The relationship between the Dover and Canterbury chronicles is complex. The printed text is a continuation of Gervase of Canterbury to 1327, in a manuscript written at Christ Church, Canterbury, but including material from St Martin's, Dover.[181] The continuation of Gervase relates mainly to the affairs of Christ Church and to the archbishopric to 1241. Then from

---

[171] See Cam and Jacob, op. cit. (see p. 406 n. 18 above), pp. 98, 100.
[172] See pp. 404–5 and n. 8.   [173] See p. 402 and n. 150.
[174] See p. 403 and n. 155.   [175] See pp. 402–3 and n. 151.   [176] See p. 405 and n. 11.
[177] See Bémont, *Simon de Montfort*, pp. xiv–xv.   [178] Ibid., p. 380.
[179] For letters of protection, 8 July 1262, to Master Thomas the Cook to go to France with the king, see *CPR, 1258–1266*, p. 220.
[180] Bémont, *Simon de Montfort*, pp. 375–6.
[181] Corpus Christi College, Cambridge, MS. 438. For the printed edition see p. 404 n. 6 above. For the structure of the Canterbury chronicle and its relationship to the Dover chronicle see *GC*, vol. 2, pp. xxii–xxv.

1242 to 1270 it has annals on general and local history and is closely related to the unpublished chronicle of Dover priory.[182] The Dover chronicle, from the Creation to 1286, is an annalistic summary of English history from 1226 to 1234. It is very brief from 1234 to 1258 when it becomes full: presumably it was compiled soon after 1258. The Canterbury chronicle again uses Dover material for the period from 1270 to 1277. This section is mainly concerned with the troubles of Richard de Wenchepe, prior of Dover.[183] From 1278 to the end the preponderance of Canterbury material reasserts itself in the Canterbury chronicle.

The relationship between the Canterbury and Dover chronicles from 1242 to 1270 is obscure. Either the Canterbury chronicle borrowed from an early copy of the Dover chronicle, or both compilations used each other's material. The latter seems most likely as each has some information not in the other.[184] Obviously the contact between the houses was very close. St Martin's was a cell of Canterbury, and Prior Wenchepe himself had been a monk of Christ Church before he became prior of Dover.[185] The account of the foundation of St Martin's at the end of the section in the Canterbury chronicle on Wenchepe's priorate, was written explicitly for the information of the Canterbury monks.[186] The interrelation of the Canterbury and Dover chronicles from 1242 to 1277 makes it most accurate to refer to it as the Canterbury/Dover chronicle.

For the period, therefore, of the Barons' War the Canterbury/Dover chronicle is an independent, contemporary authority, though one much occupied with local events. It is pro-baronial, representing the barons in 1261 as acting against the aliens 'for the honour of God, the service of the king and the benefit of the realm'.[187] St Thomas himself appeared at the battle of Lewes in support of the barons, who won 'a most glorious victory'.[188] Simon de Montfort was killed at Evesham for the peace of the land, and 'it was said that innumerable miracles were worked through the Lord by the slain'.[189] The chronicle has valuable local information about the war. It records the surrender of Dover to the barons in 1263[190] and Henry III's subsequent attempt, while staying in Dover priory, to gain entry (there is a list of those in the castle), and gives the reasons for the barons' refusal to admit him.[191] Again in 1264 Henry stayed at the priory and was refused entry into the castle.[192] There is a graphic description of how Simon de Montfort captured Rochester in 1264. He got his men in by river under cover of 'a large bonfire which he made in a little boat, with pitch, coal, sulphur and pork dripping'.[193]

---

[182] See p. 404 and n. 7.
[183] GC, vol. 2, pp. xxv–xxvii; Cont. GC, pp. 250–91.
[184] This is Stubbs's conclusion; see GC, vol. 2, p. xxiii.
[185] Cont. GC, pp. 192, 247.
[186] Cont. GC, pp. 286–9. [187] Cont. GC, p. 213.
[188] Cont. GC, pp. 237–8.
[189] Cont. GC, p. 243. [190] Cont. GC, p. 223.
[191] Cont. GC, pp. 229–30.
[192] Cont. GC, p. 233. [193] Cont. GC, p. 235.

The Dunstable chronicle is primarily a record of domestic affairs, written by more than one author.[194] From early in Henry III's reign it was written more or less contemporarily with the events described. As has been pointed out, the prior, Richard de Morins (1202–42) either initiated or wrote the chronicle (or part of it) to 1241. The rest of the chronicle, to 1297, was probably the work of more than one man. A repetition of news under 1283 suggests a change of authorship.[195] The chronicle's meticulous record of the priory's agricultural building programme (for example, it records, under 1249, the construction of cowsheds at 'Stokes', a sheep-pen and cowsheds at Studham, a barn at Chalton, and a dairy at Ruxox,[196] and, under 1254, of a stable at Dunstable – which collapsed three years later[197]) peters out in the 1270s.[198] This again may indicate a change of author. The manuscript itself provides the evidence of contemporaneity from early in Henry's reign. It is in various untidy hands and spaces are left for information which has not yet arrived.

The Dunstable chronicle is an excellent source for the priory's domestic history. It makes good use of the priory muniments, personal observation and hearsay. It uses a variety of documents, charters,[199] and accounts,[200] and the records of itinerant justices[201] and of the royal Exchequer[202] and chancery[203] when relevant to the priory's affairs. It also cites the records of the priory chapter[204] and of visitations by the diocesan, the bishop of Lincoln, and his deputies.[205] Of all thirteenth-century chronicles it gives the most vivid picture of the predominantly agricultural economy of a religious house. There is, for example, a description of Prior William de Wederhore's visit to his manor of Bradbourne in November 1287.[206]

---

[194] For the annals in the Dunstable chronicle on King John's reign see pp. 332–9 *passim* above.

[195] *Dunst.*, p. 298 and n. 1.

[196] *Dunst.*, p. 179. For similar notices of building on the priory's estates see *Dunst.*, pp. 187, 188, 191, 205, 258. For the places mentioned see the index to and map in G. H. Fowler, *A Digest of the Charters preserved in the Cartulary of the Priory of Dunstable* (Bedfordshire Historical Record Soc., x, 1926).

[197] *Dunst.*, pp. 191, 207. It also mentions the construction of a carpenter's workshop *s.a.* 1252; *Dunst.*, p. 183.

[198] There is an entry *s.a.* 1273 on the construction of a dovecot at Dunstable (*Dunst.*, p. 258). However, there are entries relating to domestic building, etc., until the 1280s (see *Dunst.*, pp. 276, 294, 296, 299) and the construction of a mill is noticed *s.a.* 1295 (*Dunst.*, p. 402); see p. 425 below.

[199] For references to charters see e.g. *Dunst.*, pp. 138–9, 148, 277.

[200] e.g. *Dunst.*, p. 316. For information derived from accounts see the prices of corn, etc.; e.g. *Dunst.*, pp. 191, 192, 208. See p. 426 and n. 219 below.

[201] e.g. *Dunst.*, pp. 131–2, 155, 184–5, 213.

[202] e.g. *Dunst.*, pp. 336, 366.

[203] For a reference to an enrolment on the Fine Rolls see *Dunst.*, p. 300. See also p. 427 below for *Quo warranto* proceedings against the priory.

[204] e.g. *Dunst.*, p. 138.

[205] e.g. *Dunst.*, pp. 266, 283–4. The chronicle has a considerable amount of information about the activities of the bishops of Lincoln; besides recording the episcopal visitations of the priory, it has notices on the conflict between the Bishop Grosseteste and the cathedral chapter and other material; see e.g. *Dunst.*, pp. 147–8, 149, 168, 171.

[206] *Dunst.*, pp. 337–8.

He found in the granges there corn of every sort, because of the excellent harvest which was general in England in that year. There were also a total of nine hundred and sixty sheep. . . . [But] the place was burdened with debt because of the failure of crops and other misfortunes in previous years. The small wood to the north which canon Brother Henry de Newton had previously planted, of ash and various other trees, had grown tall and was a delight to see.

Under 1296 the chronicle records that beech-mast was particularly plentiful in the Chilterns, so the priory's pigs were grazed there until the following Easter, when they had consumed it all.[207] Under 1295 there is a graphic account of the failure of a novel 'and previously unheard-of' kind of mill constructed by Brother John the Carpenter. The latter had 'promised that it could be drawn by one horse on its own. But when the mill was completed and ought to have ground, four horses could scarcely move it. So it was taken away and the old horse-mill restored to use.'[208]

The chronicle also throws light on the priory's relations with the town. It gives the text of an agreement between the priory and town made in 1248 to settle certain jurisdictional matters in dispute between them.[209] It records occasions when the town was fined for breaking the assize of bread and ale.[210] And it notes that the prior and burgesses together had pulled down some sheds which the butchers built over their stalls, 'because they touched the ground: however, the prior allowed them to roof their stalls with leaves, so long as they did not reach the ground.'[211] It describes how the Dominicans secretly entered the town in 1259 and their subsequent rather strained dealings with the priory.[212] There is some information about one rich burgess, John Durant. The chronicle mentions that in 1284 Durant held a feast when his two sons, William and Richard, incepted at Oxford.[213] It notes that Durant paid half the expense of two pinnacles built by the parishioners on the north front of the church in 1289.[214] In the same year it records that he held 'an unprecedentedly grand funeral' for his wife.[215] And under 1283 it justifies the prior's dining with Durant, although it was

[207] *Dunst.*, p. 408.
[208] *Dunst.*, p. 402.
[209] *Dunst.*, pp. 173–4.
[210] *Dunst.*, pp. 267, 375, 399.
[211] *Dunst.*, p. 281.
[212] *Dunst.*, pp. 213, 278, 289, 336–7. For the early history of the Dominican priory at Dunstable, with references to the Dunstable chronicle, see W. A. Hinnebusch, *The Early English Friars Preachers* (Rome 1951), pp. 79–81, 322. Matthew Paris has numerous details in the *Chronica Majora* and *Gesta Abbatum* about the Dominicans at Dunstable; he is more biased against them than is the Dunstable chronicler.
[213] *Dunst.*, p. 313. Richard and William Duraunt (or Durant) are both listed, with reference to this entry, in A. B. Emden, *A Biographical Register of the University of Oxford to A.D. 1500* (Oxford 1957–9, 3 vols), vol. I, pp. 611, 612, respectively. John Duraunt was a rich wool merchant of Dunstable; see *CPR, 1266–1272*, pp. 613, 648, 699, 700, 704, 713.
[214] *Dunst.*, p. 358.
[215] Ibid.

'contrary to our customs', because the prior 'owed John a great deal of money and dared not offend him'.[216]

Like the chronicle of Bury St Edmunds, the Dunstable chronicle is pre-occupied with the house's finances. It frequently notes the prices it paid for corn, beer and other items.[217] It has considerable information about the priory's production of wool (it had sheep-runs in the Peak district[218]). It notes the annual yield (lamenting any failure of the wool-clip), and the price it fetched.[219] It notes the tax put on wool by the king in 1275[220] and the restriction imposed on the export of wool during the war with France.[221] The chronicle records with satisfaction the drowning at sea of a wealthy wool merchant, Lawrence of Ludlow, together with a royal clerk, in 1294 (the rest of those aboard, including Robert Frude of Dunstable, were saved): this was a divine judgment because Lawrence had persuaded the other wool merchants to grant the king 40s. on each sack.[222] The chronicle becomes increasingly concerned with the priory's debts as the century proceeds. It records the burden of debt and the repayment of loans,[223] and under 1280 mentions the economies imposed on the priory, in the interests of solvency, by the bishop of Lincoln.[224]

Local affairs often involved the priory in national issues. So the chronicle's interests expanded to include matters of general importance. The chronicle has, under 1246, a passionate invective against the papal practice of providing Italian clergy to English livings.[225] The pope, the chronicle says, not only in this way bypasses the right of patrons, but also gives the parishioners clergy who do not preach, give alms, supply books or vestments, or serve the church as they ought: and thus Italian succeeds Italian and the English are seriously oppressed, notwithstanding their rights and privileges. The chronicle's strong feelings about papal provisions may well be partly caused by the fact that one of the priory's churches was held by just such an Italian: the chronicle records that, in the mid-thirteenth century, Peter Vitelle of

---

[216] *Dunst.*, p. 302.

[217] See p. 424 n. 200. Cf. n. 219 below.

[218] See *VCH, Beds.*, vol. 1, p. 372.

[219] For entries on the sale of the priory's wool see, e.g. *Dunst.*, pp. 192, 195, 221, 265, 389. For disappointing wool-clips (1284, 1291) see *Dunst.*, pp. 315, 371.

[220] *Dunst.*, p. 258. For the tax imposed on wool in 1275 see N. S. B. Gras, *The Early English Customs System* (Cambridge, Mass. 1918), pp. 59 et seq., 223.

[221] *Dunst.*, p. 398 (for restrictions on trade in 1244 see *Dunst.*, pp. 163–4). For Edward I's manipulation of trade for political purposes see Edward Miller in *The Cambridge Economic History of Europe*, vol. 3, pp. 314–15.

[222] *Dunst.*, pp. 389–90. For Edward I's maltote of 1294–7 see E. Miller, 'The fortunes of the English textile industry during the thirteenth century' in *Economic Hist. Rev.*, 2nd series, xviii (1965), p. 81.

[223] See *Dunst.*, pp. 198, 221, 253, 264, 265.   [224] *Dunst.*, p. 285.

[225] *Dunst.*, pp. 169–70. Under 1231 the Dunstable chronicle (pp. 128–9) notes the seizure of Italian clergy in England; this entry is noticed in H. MacKenzie, 'The anti-foreign movement in England, 1231–1232' in *Anniversary Essays in Medieval History by Students of Charles Homer Haskins*, ed. C. H. Taylor and J. L. La Monte (Boston and New York 1929), pp. 194–6 and nn. *passim*.

Ferentino held the church at Steppingley which he farmed *in absentia* to a deacon for 2 marks a year.[226]

The chronicle is opposed to royal and papal taxation and other financial impositions which directly affected the priory. It records under 1257, 1282 and 1283 the amount of the priory's contributions to the king,[227] and under 1275[228] and 1291[229] its assessment for the papal tenths. Under 1294 it describes the search made by the king's officials for money hoarded in monasteries 'which greatly displeased the English church because such sacrilege was previously unheard of'.[230] The officials came to Dunstable where they looked everywhere, but 'found nothing except £40 deposited in our church by Walter de Rudham'. The chronicle, moreover, had reason to dislike Edward I's judicial policy because *quo warranto* proceedings involved the priory in expensive litigation in defence of its liberties.[231] And in 1286 the priory had to lop its trees and trim its hedges by the king's highway in order to conform to the regulations in the Statute of Winchester,[232] drawn up to stop the activities of highwaymen.

It is likely that the chronicle's attitude to the disinherited barons in 1267 and 1268 was largely determined by local factors. For Dunstable (like Bury St Edmunds) became a scene of disorder. In 1266 marauders looted some of the priory's estates and stole the almoner's horse ('worth 100s.').[233] In 1267 a band of robbers from the Isle of Ely, led by Sir Ralph Perot, came to Dunstable, extorted 10 marks from the priory as extortion money and 'took one good horse from the mill and all the horses they found in the town', before they joined Sir John de D'Eyvill at Wing (in Buckinghamshire).[234] Later in the same year Dunstable was again infested by thieves from the Isle, who lived in luxury on the proceeds of theft[235] until they fled and died miserably. Under 1269 the chronicle mentions a number of Ely robbers staying at Dunstable. One, John de Suthun, took refuge in the priory church

---

[226] See *Dunst.*, pp. 176, 181–2, 197. For other entries relating to papal provisions see *Dunst.*, pp. 214, 353.

[227] *Dunst.*, pp. 207, 294–5 *passim*.

[228] *Dunst.*, p. 267. For the assessment of Dunstable priory for the sexennial tenth imposed in 1274 see W. E. Lunt, *Financial Relations of the Papacy with England to 1327* (Cambridge, Mass. 1939), p. 318.

[229] *Dunst.*, p. 367. The assessment of Dunstable priory for the sexennial tenth imposed in 1291 is also in the Dunstable cartulary; see Fowler, op. cit., p. 248.

[230] *Dunst.*, p. 390.

[231] *Dunst.*, pp. 329–33, 335, 360.

[232] *Dunst.*, p. 335. The Statute of Winchester, c. 5, stipulated that 'highways leading from one market town to another shall be broadened, wherever there is ditch or underwood or bushes, so that there be neither dyke, tree, nor bush where a man may lurk to do hurt within two hundred foot of the one side and two hundred foot on the other side of the way' (see Stubbs, *Charters*, pp. 465–6).

[233] *Dunst.*, p. 241.

[234] *Dunst.*, p. 245. For Sir Ralph Perot (Pyroth in *Dunst.*) and Sir John de D'Eyvill (Dayville in *Dunst.*) see C. Moor, *Knight of Edward I* (Harleian Soc., lxxx–lxxxiv, 1929–32, 5 vols), vol. 4, pp. 48–9; vol. 1, pp. 283–4.

[235] *Dunst.*, p. 247.

when surrounded by the king's officers. He abjured the realm but was killed in Oxford. Three of his companions were imprisoned in Newgate and the prior got their horses and 'splendid arms'. One died in prison and two were delivered 'by a corrupt inquisition'. They reclaimed their goods from the prior but were subsequently imprisoned again.[236]

Thus self-interest probably accounts for the Dunstable chronicle's dislike of the disinherited barons. It may also partly account for its antagonism to the Lord Edward. For in 1264 the prior had to pay £10 as protection-money to stop Edward's army looting one of his manors.[237] The chronicle criticizes Edward for not negotiating a peace, as he had promised, between Henry and the barons in 1263.[238] It tells a discreditable story of how Edward robbed his mother's treasury in the New Temple on 29 June 1263, to save himself from the disgrace of bankruptcy.[239] But no doubt the principal reason for the chronicle's dislike of Edward was his desertion of the baronial cause in 1263.[240] The chronicle's unreserved support of the barons from 1258 to 1265 was probably due to political idealism, not self-interest. It is likely that its sympathy was an extension of attitudes developed under King John and a response to contemporary politics. The priory, despite a visit from Simon de Montfort in 1263 (he was granted confraternity in the priory)[241] had no materialistic reason for supporting the baronial cause. In fact the war involved the priory in expense: in 1264 it had to pay 30 marks and supply four armed and mounted soldiers and six foot-soldiers, to help the barons defend the coasts against the queen.[242]

The Dunstable chronicle regards Simon de Montfort as a hero and martyr. At the battle of Lewes he had 'God and justice before his eyes, preferring to die for the truth rather than violate his oath' and, 'following the counsel of bishops and other religious men', fought 'the battle of the Lord armed with faith'.[243] He won the battle miraculously (as his forces were outnumbered) with God's help. The chronicle also praises his ally, Llewelyn of Wales, 'a very handsome man, bold in war, who had as it were, bound all the Welsh to him'.[244] It asserts that Simon's supporters only looted the property of aliens and those opposing the baronial party.[245] The chronicle gives a full account of the Barons' War (local matters take a minor place) and attempts rational analysis. For example it tries to explain one of the principal causes for the conflict: the barons' refusal in 1256 to prosecute Henry's claim for the crown of Sicily on behalf of Edmund. It says that the barons refused because of lack of money, and because the route to Sicily was

---

[236] *Dunst.*, pp. 251–2.   [237] *Dunst.*, p. 230.   [238] *Dunst.*, p. 228.

[239] *Dunst.*, pp. 222–3. For the royal treasury and storehouse in the New Temple see T. F. Tout, *Chapters in the Administrative History of Medieval England* (Manchester 1920–33, 6 vols), vol. 1, pp. 245–6. For the queen's treasury there see ibid., vol. 5, pp. 240–1.

[240] For Edward's creation of a royalist party in 1263 see F. M. Powicke, *King Henry III and the Lord Edward* (Oxford 1947, 2 vols), vol. 2, pp. 430–4 *passim*.

[241] *Dunst.*, p. 226.   [242] *Dunst.*, p. 233.   [243] *Dunst.*, p. 232.

[244] *Dunst.*, p. 200.   [245] *Dunst.*, p. 222.

long and difficult, surrounded by enemies. Moreover, the barons emphasized the wealth and power of Manfred and the dangers which would threaten England in their absence.[246]

Nevertheless the chronicle takes it for granted that kingship is the only legitimate form of government. Its attitude to Henry III himself was not unfavourable (after the Barons' War Henry sometimes stayed in the priory,[247] and in 1277 a new chamber was built for his use).[248] It mentions with approval occasions when Henry followed baronial advice. It states under 1245 that Henry resisted demands for money because the barons had not agreed to them,[249] and that he opposed the pope's demands again in 1258, 'having taken the magnates' advice'.[250] The chronicle blames the queen for some of Henry's troubles,[251] and criticizes Louis IX for condemning the Provisions of Oxford (he 'exceeded the power granted to him and was unmindful of his honour').[252]

On the whole the chronicle's account of the baronial period (which is partially based on official documents) is accurate and has some useful information. For example it gives an exact summary of the proclamation issued by the baronial government on 20 October 1258 to redress grievances and regulate the conduct of local officials of the crown.[253] It appears to be the only authority stating that the barons established their sheriffs 'nearly all over England', though the fact that the public records mention them in only sixteen countries suggests that the chronicle may be exaggerating.[254] The chronicle also throws light on the reason for Simon's quarrel with the earl of Gloucester in 1258: it says that Gloucester had joined the royalist party 'as if by treachery'.[255] And under 1263 it seems to be the only authority for the statement that Henry promised a judicial commission for the restoration of confiscated baronial estates, 'as stipulated in the terms of the document'.[256]

The chronicle of Osney abbey also has a detailed account of the Barons' War. This chronicle, from the foundation of the abbey in 1016 to 1293, was written at Osney by various authors (as will be seen, Thomas Wykes almost certainly wrote the section from 1278 to 1293).[257] It is copied to the end of the twelfth century from an earlier chronicle of Osney which is mainly a compilation from well-known authorities such as Robert of Torigni and William

---

[246] *Dunst.*, pp. 199–200.
[247] For notices of his visits see *Dunst.*, pp. 173, 266, 274.
[248] *Dunst.*, p. 276.   [249] *Dunst.*, p. 168.   [250] *Dunst.*, p. 208.
[251] *s.a.* 1260 the Dunstable chronicle says that the queen was considered by some to be the cause of the king's quarrel with Edward; *Dunst.*, p. 215.
[252] *Dunst.*, p. 227.   [253] *Dunst.*, p. 210. See Treharne, *Baronial Plan*, p. 120 n. 3.
[254] *Dunst.*, p. 217. See Treharne, *Baronial Plan*, p. 267.
[255] 'quasi apostatavit'; *Dunst.*, p. 217. See Treharne, *Baronial Plan*, p. 271.
[256] *Dunst.*, p. 224. See Treharne, *Baronial Plan*, p. 321 and n. 6.
[257] For the structure of the Osney chronicle and its relationship to the chronicle of Thomas Wykes see *Osney*, pp. x–xv; N. Denholm-Young, 'Thomas Wykes and his chronicle' in *EHR*, lxi (1946), pp. 171–5; and p. 463 and n. 187 below.

of Newburgh.[258] It is mainly independent of known literary sources for the thirteenth century, though it borrows some facts from Matthew Paris.[259] It has the characteristics of a monastic chronicle, combining general with local information, though the proportion of local material is considerably smaller than in the Dunstable annals.

The Osney chronicle's value as a domestic record is well illustrated by the information under 1254 on the abbey's debt to Sienese merchants.[260] The chronicle gives a copy of Alexander IV's letter to the abbot and convent ordering repayment, and explains how the debt was contracted – by means of a fraud perpetrated by the bishop of Hereford. In order to raise money for the king's Gascon expedition, the latter obtained by a trick the seals of various bishops and abbots appended to blank leaves of parchment. He took these to Rome where he used them to enter into bonds with the merchants on behalf of the unsuspecting ecclesiastics. 'These things are recorded', the chronicle states, 'so that everyone, particularly prelates, should know with what care and discretion they ought to guard their seals and take precautions lest such things happen again.'

Besides notices about Osney (the succession of the abbots, burials in the abbey church and the like), the chronicle has information about Oxford, about a mile from Osney (the abbey held the church of St George in Oxford castle[261]). For example, it records the robbery of the Oxford Jewry by students in 1244,[262] and that the masters at Oxford obtained the king's permission, in 1256, to fix the rents of students' hostels in the town.[263] It records the quarrel in 1263 between the students and the townsmen (which was described at length by Robert of Gloucester): as a result Henry allowed the townsmen to imprison the students, contrary to the privileges of the university, and subsequently expelled them. The chronicle adds that the students later 'returned under the protection of Simon de Montfort'.[264] Like Robert of Gloucester, the chronicle mentions Henry's visit to St Frideswide's in the same year. And it praises Walter de Merton for the foundation of Merton college.

The Osney chronicle's sympathies in the baronial period are with the

---

[258] Only a burnt fragment (1066–1179) of this chronicle is known (BM MS. Cotton Vitellius E XV, ff. 1–2ᵛ). Noticed in *Osney*, p. xvi n. 1. For its sources see the account of the Osney chronicle in ibid., pp. xvi–xvii. An early thirteenth-century copy of Newburgh's chronicle from Osney abbey survives today (BM MS. Cotton Vespasian B VI, ff. 111–82); see N. R. Ker, *Medieval Libraries of Great Britain* (2nd ed., Royal Historical Soc., 1964), p. 140.

[259] See *Osney*, pp. xvii, 78–92 *passim*.

[260] *Osney*, pp. 107–10. See Lunt, *Financial Relations*, p. 266.

[261] See *Osney*, p. 120 and *Cartulary of Osney Abbey*, ed. H. E. Salter (Oxford Historical Soc., lxxxix–xci, 1929–31, 3 vols), vol. 1, pp. 2, 5.

[262] *Osney*, p. 91.

[263] *Osney*, p. 111. For the method by which the rents of students' hostels were fixed see Wood, *Oxford*, vol. 1, pp. 254–6.

[264] *Osney*, pp. 139–41. For the involvement of the Oxford students in national politics, with reference to this passage, see H. Rashdall, *The Universities of Europe*, ed. F. M. Powicke and A. B. Emden (Oxford 1936, 3 vols), vol. 3, p. 87 and n. 2.

barons, but they are moderate. Its moderation may have been partly due to the fact that caution was considered advisable, because this section of the chronicle was written fairly close to the events. Recording the battle of Lewes, it comments:[265]

> because of the malice of the times it is not safe to tell the whole truth, so at present we will be silent concerning the names of the magnates who fled and who were captured in the battle; and we have omitted from this history much else that was done in these days, for the sake of the readers' peace, because what perhaps might please the king's men would displease those who favoured the barons.

At this time there was 'no love without suspicion, no word without dissimulation'.[266] But the chronicle's moderation may also have been due to a connection, although a tenuous one, with the royal family. Philip of Eye, who was treasurer in turn of Richard of Cornwall, Henry III and Edward I,[267] became a canon of Osney on retirement and, the chronicle records, was buried in the abbey (he died in 1277).[268] Probably Philip's presence at Osney accounts for the chronicle's interest in Richard of Cornwall. It mentions the chief events of his life and seems to reflect his political outlook. For Richard was a moderate, an arbiter between king and barons (the chronicle notes his successful arbitration in 1267 which 'pleased Jesus Christ'[269]). This interest in Richard may have been reinforced by the fact that his third wife Beatrix of Falkenburg (called, according to the chronicle, 'the gem of womanhood because of her beauty') was buried with the Oxford Franciscans.[270]

The Osney chronicle's moderation appears particularly in its treatment of Henry III and Simon de Montfort: it criticizes the king, but with reservations, and it praises Simon, also with reservations. It blames Henry for favouring aliens and for financial oppression. 'He loved aliens more than all the English, and enriched them with innumerable gifts and possessions'.[271] The chronicle has an almost hysterical outburst against aliens under 1264, fearing they would invade England and overthrow 'the native inhabitants'.[272] It criticizes Henry's and Edward's financial impositions in 1267: 'much more was extorted from ecclesiastics and laymen in the tranquillity of peace than in the turmoil of war'.[273] Nevertheless it records with satisfaction that Henry

---

[265] *Osney*, pp. 148–9. For caution in other chronicles see pp. 370, 401, 421 and n. 168 above.
[266] *Osney*, p. 138.
[267] For Philip of Eye's service with Richard of Cornwall see Denholm-Young, *Richard of Cornwall*, pp. 73, 81 n. 3, 92, 149. For Thomas Wykes's interest in Philip of Eye see p. 463 below.
[268] *Osney*, p. 271.
[269] *Osney*, p. 209. For other references to Richard of Cornwall see ibid., pp. 102, 115–6, 146.
[270] *Osney*, p. 274.   [271] *Osney*, p. 254.   [272] *Osney*, pp. 150–1.
[273] *Osney*, p. 207.

celebrated Christmas at Osney 'with great joy and rejoicing'[274] in 1266, and on his death it comments that 'he loved the beauty of the house of God and the divine service more than any of his predecessors'.[275]

The Osney chronicle's attitude to Simon de Montfort is equally moderate. On the whole it favours Simon. He was 'a noble man',[276] 'a man of virtue, valour and fortitude',[277] and of 'great constancy',[278] 'a man of God',[279] who declared at Evesham that it was 'not for the soldiers of Christ to flee but to fall by the sword of the enemy of the truth'.[280] The enemy attacked him shouting, 'You old traitor! you old traitor! you can live no longer!', and he died commending his cause to God and the Virgin Mary.[281] His death was followed by divine portents (the darkness and the storm). But this partisan account is tempered by criticism. The chronicle asserts that in 1265 he alienated support (notably of the earl of Gloucester) by holding the castles himself: 'he fortified them according to his will and ordained concerning them just as he liked'.[282] The Osney chronicle has a few facts about the Barons' War not found elsewhere, for example the information that Simon de Montfort's body was exhumed, because he died excommunicate, and 'thrown into a remoter place which is hidden today and unknown except to a very few people.'[283]

The chronicle of Robert of Gloucester (from Brutus to 1270)[284] stands apart from the chronicles already discussed because it is in Middle English verse and is influenced by the secular romance tradition of historiography. This raises two questions: Who was Robert of Gloucester? And exactly what did he write? The latter problem will be discussed first. The chronicle attributed to Robert of Gloucester is a composite work, by more than one man, as it survives today. The present text is late thirteenth century,[285] but it has a contemporary account of the Barons' War. Moreover, the chronicle survives in two versions, a longer and a shorter one.[286] Both seem to incorporate a pre-existing chronicle.

This earlier work was, apparently, a history from Brutus to the death of Henry I.[287] The section in the chronicle for this period is similar in both the

---

[274] *Osney*, p. 197.
[275] *Osney*, pp. 253–4.
[276] *Osney*, p. 129.
[277] *Osney*, p. 172.
[278] *Osney*, p. 169.
[279] *Osney*, p. 170.
[280] *Osney*, p. 169.
[281] *Osney*, p. 170. Bémont cites a similar cry by the royalists from the chronicle of St Benet of Hulme attributed to John Oxenedes; Bémont, *Simon de Montfort*, p. 242 and n. 1.
[282] *Osney*, p. 162.
[283] *Osney*, pp. 176–7. For other information in the Osney chronicle on the baronial period see Treharne, *Baronial Plan*, pp. 74, 279 n. 1, 295 n. 6.
[284] See p. 406 n. 15.
[285] It refers to Louis IX as 'now saint' (*RG*, l. 10943); Louis was canonized in 1297. For the date of the present text see *RG*, vol. 1, pp. x–xi.
[286] For the two versions see ibid., pp. vii–ix. Wright prints the extra passages in the early part in the short version, and its continuation, in the Appendices; ibid., vol. 2, pp. 779–877.
[287] See ibid., vol. 1, pp. viii–ix.

long and the short version (the short version has a few additional passages). The two versions have different accounts, of almost the same length, of Stephen's reign. From then until the end the longer version is much more detailed than the shorter (the former ends in 1270 and the latter with the accession of Edward I). It seems most likely that Robert, using the early work to the death of Henry I, wrote the longer continuation soon after 1270 and that this chonicle was revised at the end of the century. Someone else probably wrote the shorter version, also using the earlier chronicle to 1135.

The evidence for Robert's authorship of the longer version (the one to be discussed here) is in the chronicle itself, under 1265. The relevant passages (there are corresponding lines in the shorter version) follow the account of the darkness after the battle of Evesham. They read:[288]

> This sign befell in this land   when these men they slew;
> For thirty miles from there   this saw Robert
> Who first made this book   he was right sore afraid.

Gloucester is about thirty miles from Evesham. But there is plenty of direct evidence in the chronicle justifying Robert's designation as 'of Gloucester'. The chronicle is in the Gloucestershire dialect and has a detailed knowledge of Gloucester.[289] There are, for example, the vivid descriptions (quoted below) of the conflict between the baronial sheriff and the sheriff appointed by the king in 1262, and of the capture of the city of Gloucester by the barons early in the summer of 1263 and of its recapture by Edward in the spring of 1264 (with details which surely only a local man could have known).

The author also knew a lot about Oxford. Most remarkable is his account of the riot in 1263 between the students and the townsmen.[290] The burgesses had shut the gates of Oxford to keep out Edward. When he left they opened them all except Smithgate. This angered the students because they used Smithgate to reach their recreation places 'towards Beaumont'. As the bailiffs refused the demand of 'a few wild fellows' that they open the gate, the students axed it down. The provosts (William the Spicer and Geoffrey of Hinksey) and the mayor, Nicholas of Kingston, imprisoned some of the students. The students immediately rioted; one rang St Mary's bell, others robbed the bowyers' shops, burned down the house of William the Spicer and the spicery, and looted the vintnery (because the mayor was a vintner). After an inquiry Henry III temporarily expelled the students.[291] Another reference to Oxford describes how in 1263 Henry III hesitated to enter the town, because, due to an old superstition, no king had done so since the

---

[288] *RG*, ll. 11747–9.   [289] See *RG*, vol. 1, p. xii.

[290] *RG*, ll. 11186–233. For an account of the riot, with a citation of this passage in Robert of Gloucester, see Wood, *Oxford*, vol. 1, pp. 263–7, and Rashdall, *The Universities of Europe in the Middle Ages*, vol. 3, p. 87 and n. 2.

[291] The reason for the expulsion of the students was partly political. See Rashdall, *The Universities of Europe*, vol. 3, p. 87.

time of St Frideswide (d. 735?). Eventually a Dominican friar, John of Balsham, persuaded the king to enter. Henry visited the Augustinian priory of St Frideswide, making an offering in the church ('and afterwards often when he came he made an offering there').[292]

The evidence connecting Robert with both Gloucester and Oxford has led to the suggestion that he was a monk of St Peter's, Gloucester, who went to study in Oxford, living in the hall for Gloucester monks which stood on the site later used by Sir John Giffard for the college he founded in 1283.[293] There is no conclusive proof of this theory. In order to corroborate it, two questions need answering: first, whether the chronicle has any evidence which could connect Robert with the Gloucester monks at Oxford and, second, whether it has evidence associating him with St Peter's. The answer to the first question is negative. As far as the chronicle shows a particular interest in a religious order at Oxford, it is in the Augustinians (there is the passage quoted above about St Frideswide's, and one, to be mentioned below, about Osney abbey[294]). With regard to the second question, the answer is a qualified affirmative (qualified because the evidence is not strong enough to prove that the author had a close association with St Peter's). There are a number of passages referring to St Peter's. For example the chronicle mentions the porch of St Peter's in the account of Edward the Elder's reign;[295] it says that Henry III, on his accession, was offered as king at the cathedral altar;[296] and under 1264 it records that in 1264 Reginald, abbot of St Peter's, with the bishop of Worcester, mediated between Edward and the barons occupying Gloucester castle.[297] Moreover it asserts that Edward and Gilbert earl of Gloucester took Gloucester in 1264 by breaching the 'long wall' of 'the abbot's orchard', which lay 'between Saint Oswald's gate and the north gate', where there 'was no folk their town to defend'.[298]

Any citizen of Gloucester would have been interested in St Peter's abbey, but the chronicle has internal evidence suggesting that it was a monastic production. Its contents show that the author had access to a large library and was record-conscious. The early part of the chronicle is compiled from a wide variety of sources[299] – such as Geoffrey of Monmouth, Eadmer, William of Malmesbury and Henry of Huntingdon – and it seems to be related to Roger of Wendover's chronicle, and to the chronicle of Waverley up to the accession of Henry III (when it becomes independent of all known literary authorities). The author's record-consciousness appears in his inser-

---

[292] RG, ll. 11313–27. The incident is mentioned in the Osney chronicle (Osney, pp. 142–3).
[293] See Robert of Gloucester's Chronicle, ed. Thomas Hearne (Oxford 1724), pp. lxxvi–lxxvii. W. A. Wright (RG, vol. 1, p. vii) accepts that Robert was probably a monk of Gloucester.
[294] See p. 436.   [295] RG, l. 5481.
[296] RG, ll. 10570–1.   [297] RG, l. 11263.
[298] RG, ll. 11585–8.
[299] Its sources and the chronicles related to it are listed in RG, vol. 1, pp. xiv–xxxii.

tion into the verse of many dates and lists of people (for instance of the baronial supporters at Bristol, of the fallen at Evesham, and of the men chosen in 1266 for the settlement of the kingdom[300]).

Moreover, the author's attitude to events is the same as that found in the typical monastic chronicle: it is pro-baronial. Henry III, misled by evil counsel, turned from 'the good laws and the old charter' and from the barons' Provisions.[301] He favoured aliens 'who annoyed the land sore'.[302] God favoured the barons, particularly Simon de Montfort,[303] a wise man[304] who 'wished to do right and no wrong'.[305] The chronicle regards Simon's 'murder' and the dismemberment of his body at Evesham as 'the most pitiful thing', and mentions that he was wearing a hair shirt, and (so it was said) that his body did not bleed.[306] Jesus showed his displeasure at Simon's death by 'terrible signs: as when He died on the cross, there was darkness throughout the world – men were terrified and could hardly see.'[307] The chronicle blames Simon's defeat on his son Simon the younger. The latter ('his proud heart destroyed him'[308]) would not sleep in Kenilworth castle but stayed in the town where he was surprised and nearly captured by Edward. And then when summoned to help his father on the eve of the battle, both he and the king 'would not set forth until they had eaten'.[309] He arrived at Evesham after his father's defeat and death: the chronicle remarks with dry humour: 'He might then as well have stayed at his dinner.'[310]

This touch of wit is typical of the chronicler's often secular tone, an aspect of the work which divides it from the normal monastic production. The influence of chivalric literature appears in the emphasis on the bravery of some men, notably of Richard the Marshal[311] and Edward.[312] Edward's creditable following of knights and his success in tournaments is also noted.[313] Misfortunes and the like are often attributed to treachery or cunning. Richard the Marshal was killed because of treachery,[314] the barons entered Gloucester city (in 1264) by a clever ruse,[315] and Gilbert of Gloucester took London in 1267 by cunning. Simon the younger was the antithesis of the chivalric knight. The chronicle says of his failure to help his father at Evesham:[316]

---

[300] *RG*, ll. 11498–500, 11718–24, 11945–55, respectively.

[301] See *RG*, ll. 10700–2, 11018, 11356.

[302] See *RG*, ll. 10992–11003 (the content of this passage is reminiscent of the invective against aliens in the Waverley chronicle; see pp. 415–16 and n. 106 above). For the unpopularity of Simon de Montfort's French soldiers see *RG*, l. 11451.

[303] See *RG*, l. 11537.

[304] *RG*, l. 11545.

[305] *RG*, l. 11461.

[306] See *RG*, ll. 11726–36.

[307] *RG*, ll. 11737–47.

[308] *RG*, l. 11643.

[309] *RG*, ll. 11679–81.

[310] *RG*, l. 11766.

[311] *RG*, ll. 10782–813 *passim*.

[312] See *RG*, ll. 10879, 11131.

[313] *RG*, ll. 11040–2.

[314] *RG*, ll. 10802–7.

[315] *RG*, ll. 11988–91.

[316] *RG*, ll. 11770–1.

> He might say when he came   'Little have I won
> I may hang up my axe[317]   weakly have I done.'

Like the author of the *History of William the Marshal*, this writer loves a good anecdote. For example he tells how when there was a riot at Osney against the legate Otho, one of his servants threw some broth at a clerk, and the legate fled for safety 'into the steeple'.[318] And he tells how, when the legate Ottobon excommunicated the disinherited at the siege of Kenilworth, the barons, against the advice of many, dressed up their surgeon, a clerk called Master Philip Porpeis ('an ingenious, bold fellow') as a mock legate, and he stood on the castle wall and cursed the king, the legate and all their men.[319]

The features of the chronicle belonging to the secular tradition of historiography make it impossible to say definitely that Robert was not a secular clerk, connected with both Oxford and Gloucester. The view that the chronicle was a secular production would be supported by the fact that of the twelve manuscripts listed by the editor,[320] not one is known to have come from a monastic library. There is even evidence in the chronicle suggesting that it was written to please a particular secular lord, Sir Warin of Bassingbourne. Sir Warin appears, always in a flattering light, rather more often than his importance justifies. He was one of Edward's knights who became a staunch baronial supporter, but subsequently made his peace with Henry III, receiving (in 1265) a reward, a grant of land, for his 'good services'.[321] In 1267 he was appointed keeper of the forests between Oxford and Stamford, and sheriff of Northamptonshire. He died in 1269. Sir Warin's activities from 1261 to 1266 are mentioned in the chronicle. Under 1261, the chronicler writes: 'All this while the Lord Edward was travelling abroad in Gascony, that was his, with a full noble company and he had good knights – such as Sir Warin of Bassingbourne – whom he led about with him.'[322] The chronicle lists Sir Warin among Edward's men who joined the barons, mentions him with those who attacked Wallingford in 1263,[323] and records that Warin, 'a man of great fame', was with the barons in Bristol.[324] Moreover, it has what purports to be a description of his (rather vocal) part in the battle of Evesham, relating that when Sir Warin saw many of the barons' enemies in flight,[325] he

---

317 Cf. *Sir Gawain and the Green Knight*, ed. I. Gollancz (EETS, ccx, 1940), l. 477: King Arthur says to Sir Gawain after the latter has beheaded the Green Knight and committed himself to an encounter in a year's time, 'Now Sir, heng vp þyn ax, þat hatʒ in-nogh hewen' – i.e. relax your military activities. I owe this reference to Miss Gay Clifford.

318 *RG*, ll. 10854–61.

319 *RG*, ll. 11923–31. Such behaviour was in the tradition of medieval 'misrule'; see N. Z. Davis, 'The reasons of misrule: youth groups and charivaris in sixteenth-century France' in *Past and Present*, l (1971), p. 42 and *passim*.

320 *RG*, vol. 1, pp. xl–xlv.

321 For a summary of facts in the public records about Warin's life see C. Moor, *Knights of Edward I* (Harleian Soc., lxxx–lxxxiv, 1929–32, 5 vols), vol. 1, pp. 56–7.

322 *RG*, ll. 11039–43.   323 *RG*, ll. 11418–19.   324 *RG*, l. 11498.

325 *RG*, ll. 11709–13.

Spurred on before them   and shouted on high
'Turn again traitors, turn back again   and have in your thoughts
How villainously at Lewes   you were to ground brought.
Turn again and remember   that this force is all ours,
And we shall, as if they were nothing,   surely overcome our foes.'

And the chronicle mentions Sir Warin as one of the men co-opted by the barons in 1266 to devise a plan for the settlement of the kingdom ('they could have chosen no better').[326]

However, the evidence in favour of secular authorship hardly outweighs that in favour of monastic provenance. A possible solution to the problem is that Robert of Gloucester became a monk of St Peter's late in life, having previously been at Oxford where he may have formed a friendship with Sir Warin.[327] Perhaps he wrote the chronicle to please Sir Warin, or perhaps it simply reflects an interest in him derived from a mutual connection with the neighbourhood of Oxford.

As a historical source the chronicle of Robert of Gloucester is chiefly valuable for the local details about the baronial period. The best passages combine the accuracy of detail, characteristic of monastic chronicles, with the dramatic power typical of the romance literature. Besides the already described notice of the Oxford riots, there are the two vivid passages on affairs in Gloucester and its environs. One concerns the conflicts resulting from the appointment by Henry III of a Frenchman, Sir Matthew Bezill, as sheriff of Gloucestershire and constable of Gloucester castle in 1261.[328] The barons, opposed to aliens, chose Sir William de Tracy, 'by common counsel',[329] giving him power to expel Sir Matthew. Sir William held the shire court, was attacked by Sir Matthew who dragged him from his chair, threw him in a puddle and rode over him and his esquire. Sir Matthew then imprisoned Sir William in the castle. Sir John Giffard therefore led an attack on the castle, and later attended one of Sir Matthew's courts, armed with his retainers, where he killed some of the officials – 'these wicked bailiffs, who to poor men frequently do great harm'.[330]

Equally circumstantial is the account of the barons' capture of the city of Gloucester.[331] Sir John Giffard, with Sir John de Balun,[332] managed to enter the city 'riding upon two woolpacks, as if they were merchants', both covered

[326] *RG*, l. 11955.
[327] A possible parallel would be Thomas Wykes whose chronicle reflects his connection with Richard of Cornwall, formed before Wykes became a canon of Osney; see pp. 464–5 below.
[328] *RG*, ll. 11060–165. Robert calls Sir Matthew Bezill, sheriff of Gloucestershire 1261–2 (see Public Record Office, *Lists and Indexes no. ix, List of Sheriffs for England and Wales* (London 1898), p. 46), 'Sir Basil de Macey' (presumably Massay in France). For Sir Matthew see also Moor, op. cit., p. 98.
[329] *RG*, l. 11065. For Sir William de Tracy, see Moor, op. cit., vol. 5, p. 38.
[330] *RG*, l. 11162.
[331] *RG*, ll. 11168–84.
[332] For Sir John de Balun see Moor, op. cit., vol. 1, p. 38.

with 'two Welsh cloaks'. Once inside the gates they leapt down, fully armed, and so frightened the porters that they handed over the keys with which Giffard admitted the baronial army. When Edward recaptured Gloucester he punished the burgesses for allowing the barons to take the city. The porters themselves, 'Hobbekin of Ludlow and his fellows', were executed,[333] having been shriven by 'Robert of Caumpdene, a married man, for he was a clerk in minor orders',[334] as there was no priest to do it.

---

[333] *RG*, ll. 11296–303.
[334] 'Roberd of Caumpedene, þat hosebonde was on,/Vor he was a lute clerc'; *RG*, ll. 11302–3.

19

Chronicles in the Reign of Edward I

Most of the monastic chronicles of Henry III's reign discussed in the previous chapter were continued in the reign of Edward I. But they were on the whole disappointingly meagre in their treatment of general history.[1] The chronicle of Winchester only covers, and very briefly, the first few years of Edward's reign (to 1277). The Waverley chronicle is independent of the lost Winchester chronicle from 1277, but its subsequent annals are short and have a fair amount of local material. The chronicle of St Benet of Hulme is almost valueless because it is so closely related to the chronicle of Bury St Edmunds. The chronicle of Furness, which is independent of all known chronicles from 1270 (when the Stanley chronicle ends) but entirely omits the years from 1276 to 1289, is not very well informed about national events. Its chief value is for the history of the Isle of Man;[2] its information is of particular interest because it does not occur in the chronicle of Man and the Isles, which becomes very brief after 1251.[3] Of more value to the historian today are the Westminster *Flores Historiarum* (the so-called 'Merton' *Flores Historiarum*[4] is a re-write of the Westminster *Flores* and has little value as a historical source), the chronicles of Canterbury and Norwich and the chronicle of Bury St Edmunds (which has already been discussed above).[5] A few chronicles were started in Edward I's reign. The chronicles of the Franciscan Richard of Durham and of the Dominican Nicholas Trevet will be discussed

---

[1] Two chronicles which relate to Edward I's reign will not be considered here: the chronicle of St Werburg's, Chester, to 1297 (see p. 405 and n. 14), which is so brief that it has little value though the annals for 1282–4 have some material relating to Anglo-Welsh affairs; the unpublished chronicle of Hagnaby, to 1307 (see p. 406 n. 20).

[2] See *Furness*, pp. 569–71.

[3] The chronicle of Man and the Isles, covering the years from 1015 to 1251, is very brief until 1247, but from 1248 to 1251 is a full contemporary account of events in, and relating to, the Isle of Man. Entries about the Cistercian abbey at Rushen in the Isle of Man show that it was written there. Later brief annals were added from 1252 to 1316 (many years, including those from 1276 to 1312, are omitted). The chronicle is printed, with a parallel English translation, in *Antiquitates Celto-Normannicae containing the Chronicle of Man and the Isles* ..., ed. James Johnstone (Copenhagen 1786). A translation is also in Joseph Stephenson, *The Church Historians of England* (London 1853–8, 5 vols), vol. 5, pt 1, pp. 386–405.

[4] Printed in *FH*, vol. 3, pp. 251–327. The 'Merton' *Flores* has short summaries of the annals from 1245 to 1264 in the St Albans *Flores*; printed in ibid., pp. 239–51.

[5] See pp. 396–401.

in the next chapter. A monk of Peterborough (probably the sacrist, William of Woodford) wrote a chronicle which has some use for general history though it concentrates primarily on local events.[6] But the most outstanding newcomer was Bartholomew Cotton, a monk of Norwich who began writing late in the thirteenth century (he died in 1298).[7]

Perhaps of all the monastic chroniclers only Cotton bears comparison with the Augustinian writers. Although the Dunstable chronicle is of little value for general history from the end of Henry III's reign, and the Osney chronicle is very brief, other Augustinian chronicles of first-rate importance were written during this period. Besides the already discussed (anonymous) chronicle of Osney, another chronicle was written in the abbey by a canon whose name is known – he was called Thomas Wykes.[8] In the north two long chronicles were written in Edward I's reign, in Yorkshire in the vicinity of Newburgh. One was by Walter of Guisborough (Guisborough is about twenty-five miles from Newburgh), covering the period from 1066 to 1312 (with later continuations).[9] The other chronicle was by Peter of Langtoft, a canon of Bridlington (within fifty miles of Newburgh): it is in French verse and covers the period from Brutus to 1307.[10] Bridlington produced another chronicle, in Latin, which is now lost.[11]

As was pointed out above, the chronicles of Dunstable and Osney are indistinguishable in type from monastic chronicles. The same is true of the chronicle of Thomas Wykes. The chronicle of Walter of Guisborough also resembles a monastic production and uses some pre-existing annals. But it has more imaginative touches, more dramatic reconstructions of events, and more good stories than the typical monastic chronicle. And Peter of Langtoft's chronicle belongs to a different historiographical genre from the monastic chronicle – it is a verse history written in the romance tradition.

The chronicles of Thomas Wykes, Walter of Guisborough and Peter of Langtoft cover at some length the conflict of Henry III with the barons. Their accounts do not have the value of contemporaneity, but they are nevertheless of interest. Both Wykes[12] and Guisborough[13] preserve facts not otherwise known. Furthermore their accounts clearly show the authors'

---

[6] The chronicle of Peterborough, 1122 to 1295, is printed in *Chronicon Petroburgense*, ed. Thomas Stapleton (Camden Soc., 1849).

[7] The chronicle, 449 to 1298, of Bartholomew Cotton is printed in *Bartholomaei de Cotton Monachi Norwicensis Historia Anglicana*, ed. H. R. Luard (RS, 1859). For the date of Cotton's death see ibid., pp. xvi–xviii, 418.

[8] Printed in *Ann. Mon.*, vol. 4, pp. 3–352.

[9] Printed in *The Chronicle of Walter of Guisborough*, ed. Harry Rothwell (Camden Soc., 3rd series, l, p. xxxix, 1957). The chronicle was previously known as that of Walter of Hemingford, or Hemingburgh; see ibid., pp. xxiv–xxv.

[10] Printed, with a parallel English translation, in *The Chronicle of Pierre de Langtoft*, ed. T. Wright (RS, 1866–8, 2 vols).

[11] An extract from the Bridlington chronicle was sent to the king in 1291 as evidence for his claim to overlordship over Scotland; see F. Palgrave, *Documents and Records illustrating the History of Scotland* (Record Commission, 1837), pp. 60–7.

[12] See pp. 468–9.   [13] See pp. 470–1.

attitudes to the opposing parties. Similarly the interpretation of events during the Barons' War given by the 'Merton' *Flores Historiarum* which differs in emphasis from that in the Westminster *Flores Historiarum*, clearly shows the author's political views.[14] As has been seen, the Augustinian authorities contemporary with the Barons' War, the chronicles of Dunstable and Osney, share the normal attitude of the monks to Simon de Montfort and the barons: they are pro-baronial, though moderately so. Walter of Guisborough is also moderately pro-baronial.

On the other hand the 'Merton' *Flores*, Thomas Wykes and Peter of Langtoft are remarkable for their strong royalist sympathies. The 'Merton' *Flores* is even more royalist than its original, the Westminster *Flores*. The reasons for its loyalty to Henry III and Edward I are not entirely clear. But a strongly pro-royalist bias is a feature of the two other Augustinian chronicles, by Thomas Wykes and Peter of Langtoft. And their royalism is easily explicable. Wykes became a regular canon late in life, after a career which had brought him into contact with the government (he seems to have had a particularly close connection with the household of Richard of Cornwall).[15] Therefore he brought with him to Osney preconceived loyalties and perhaps part of his chronicle already written. His royalism was rationally based, and his intelligent attitude is reminiscent of that in the 'Barnwell' chronicle. Langtoft's royalism was primarily due to the Scottish war. Bridlington was in a region which suffered from Scottish raids. Victory over the Scots was Langtoft's obsession,[16] and Edward was the king who was to achieve it. Moreover, Langtoft wrote in the tradition of romance historiography (like Gaimar, Jordan Fantosme and the author of the *History of William the Marshal*) and romance histories usually had the king (or an important nobleman) as hero.

Three political issues stirred strong feelings in Edward I's reign, and elicited the best narrative on national history in the chronicles. The first was Edward I's struggle with the church over taxation from 1296 to 1297; this issue touched monastic interest directly but the chroniclers saw it in a wider context, as a conflict between church and state. The second issue was the conflict between Edward and the baronage in 1297 over the confirmation of the charters. And the third emotive issue was Anglo-Scottish relations – and to a lesser extent Edward I's conquest of Wales.[17] Edward's aggressive policy roused men's patriotism, particularly in the north in opposition to the Scots. (The Furness chronicler, like Peter of Langtoft, strongly favoured Edward I, regarding him as a bulwark against Scottish border raids.)

Edward I himself promoted the study of history to provide precedents in

[14] See pp. 461–2. [15] See p. 464.
[16] See p. 477.
[17] For the information on Wales in the Peterborough chronicle see pp. 452–3, and in the chronicle of St Wesburg's, Chester, see p. 439 n. 1.

support of his Scottish policy. In March 1291, two months before the meeting at Norham to hear the case of the competitors for the Scottish throne (the 'Great Cause'), Edward wrote to religious houses ordering a search to be made in their chronicles for evidence supporting his claim to overlordship of Scotland.[18] Probably he intended the returns to supplement study on the chronicles already done by his clerks. Returns from a number of houses survive.[19] In view of the short time the monks (and regular canons) had to examine the chronicles it is not surprising that the returns do not show a high standard of research. Edward apparently held a preliminary meeting at Norham on 6 May to assemble the information produced by clerks and monks,[20] and when the Great Cause was heard on 10 May Roger Brabazon, in his speech setting out Edward's right to overlordship of Scotland, quoted chronicle evidence.[21] The latter was incorporated in the official account of the proceedings, the *Processus Scotiae*, completed by the king's clerk, John of Caen, some time before 1297. The *Processus* gave a version of Anglo-Scottish relations from 901 to 1252 strongly biased in favour of Edward's claims.[22]

Besides telling the religious to examine their chronicles, Edward sent them copies of the letters of the competitors to the Scottish throne, in which they submitted to his arbitration; he instructed the recipients to copy the letters into their chronicles, as evidence.[23] It has been suggested that as a result of this order the Furness chronicle, which originally ended in 1275, was taken up again, the Scottish letters inserted (the years from 1276 to 1289 were omitted), and then it was continued to 1298.[24] Thus Edward not only produced an official history of his own; he also interfered, for the sake of obtaining and recording historical precedents, with other people's historiography.[25] Edward again appealed to history when Boniface VIII challenged

[18] Edward I's appeal to historical precedent in the Great Cause is fully discussed by Professor E. L. G. Stones, 'The appeal to history in Anglo-Scottish relations between 1291 and 1401: Part I' in *Archives*, ix (1969), *passim*. For Edward I's letters to the religious house see ibid., p. 12 and n. 8: J. Bain, *Calendar of Documents relating to Scotland* (Edinburgh 1881–8, 4 vols), vol. 2, p. 110, n. 470; F. Palgrave, op. cit., pp. xcv, 89, 123.

[19] Some of the returns are printed by Palgrave, op. cit., pp. 56–134. For abridgments in English see ibid., pp. xcvii–cxv. For the use made of them by the royal clerks see *Foedera*, vol. 1, pt ii, pp. 769–71 (see also below and next note). Professor Galbraith, *Historical Research in Medieval England* (London 1951), pp. 35–6, accuses the monks of perfunctory research; but they are defended by Professor Stones, 'Appeal', p. 14.

[20] See Stones, 'Appeal', pp. 15–16 and nn.

[21] See ibid., pp. 16–17.

[22] *Foedera*, vol. 1, pt ii, pp. 762–84. Cf. Galbraith, op. cit., p. 36, and Stones, 'Appeal', pp. 17–19.

[23] See Bain, op. cit., vol. 2, p. 122, nos 503–4; Palgrave, op. cit., pp. xcvi–xcvii and n.; *Bury*, p. 103; *Furness*, p. 576.

[24] See *Chrons. Stephen, Henry II, and Richard I*, vol. 2, p. lxxxviii. For the hastily added material relating to the Scottish succession case see ibid., pp. 574–8. The manuscript of the chronicle of Furness (BM MS. Cotton Cleopatra A I) is a fair copy in book-hand written soon after 1298, the date of the last entry: there is no break in the handwriting at the lacuna in the text from 1276 to 1290 (f. 202ᵛ).

[25] For the possibility that an official history, in literary narrative, was written to please Edward I, perhaps at his command, see p. 459 n. 160.

his claim to overlordship of Scotland. He wrote to the English cathedrals, to the two universities and to some religious houses to collect evidence for the Lincoln parliament of 1301.[26] Two letters to the pope were drafted in the parliament, one from the barons and one from the king.[27] Edward's answer was the longest. It was based both on the *Processus* and on new material. Unlike the *Processus* it borrowed from Geoffrey of Monmouth, asserting that Brutus's eldest son Locrine was overlord of his two brothers who ruled Scotland and Wales. It also brought the history of Anglo-Scottish relations up to date. Finally, in 1315, a new version of the *Processus* was written by another royal clerk, Andrew de Tange, based on the original one and on Edward's letter to Boniface. This became the standard text to which later kings referred in their dealings with Scotland.[28]

The suggestion that Edward I's struggle with the church and with the barons, and his Scottish and, to a lesser extent, his Welsh policy, acted as stimuli to historical writing receives some support from the dates when most of the chronicles ended.[29] The political conflicts were resolved by the end of the century. Moreover, by that time Edward's Scottish policy had suffered a serious reverse – Englishmen could no longer feel triumphant patriotic fervour. So history became a duller and more depressing subject for study. A number of the chronicles stop either at or soon after the submission to Edward of the competitors for the Scottish throne, or towards the end of the century. The Waverley chronicle ends in 1291, in the middle of the competitors' letter of submission. The anonymous Norwich chronicle and the chronicle of St Benet of Hulme end just after the competitors' letter, and the Osney chronicle ends in 1293. Welsh affairs particularly stirred the interest of the Peterborough chronicler; he has virtually no interest in general history after the Welsh campaign of 1282–3 (though he does not end until 1295). The Dunstable chronicle ends in 1297 and Bartholomew Cotton and the Furness chronicle in 1298. Only six of the chronicles survived into the fourteenth century. The Bury chronicle ends in 1301, the Worcester chronicle and Peter of Langtoft end in 1307 with the accession of Edward II, and Walter of Guisborough ends in 1312; the *Flores Historiarum* and Canterbury chronicle continue to 1327.

The monastic chronicles will be considered first, starting with Bartholomew Cotton as the most important monastic chronicler, and following with

---

[26] See Stones, 'Appeal', p. 19.

[27] The barons' letter to Boniface VIII is printed in *Foedera*, vol. 1, pt ii, pp. 926–7. Edward I's letter is printed in *Anglo-Scottish Relations 1174–1328, Some Selected Documents*, ed., with English translations, E. L. G. Stones (Nelson's Medieval Texts, 1965), pp. 96–109. Cf. Stones, 'Appeal', pp. 19–20.

[28] See Stones, 'Appeal', pp. 20–1, and nn. for further references.

[29] The suggestion that Edward I's Scottish policy stimulated interest in history in the monasteries (as well as at the centre of government) is supported by the fact that St Albans preserved a long tract on the Great Cause (BM MS. Cotton Claudius D VI, ff. 138–84), described and printed in *Willelmi Rishanger Chronica et Annales*, ed. H. T. Riley (RS, 1865), pp. xxv–xxxi, 233–368.

the Canterbury, Worcester and Peterborough chronicles, and the *Flores*. Second, the Augustinian chronicles will be considered, taking in turn the 'Merton' *Flores*, Thomas Wykes, Walter of Guisborough and Peter of Langtoft.

Bartholomew Cotton's *Historia Anglicana (English History)* is in three books.[30] Book I is merely a transcript of Geoffrey of Monmouth, but Book II is a normal chronicle in two parts: the first part begins with the Anglo-Saxon invasions and goes up to the Norman conquest: it is compiled mainly from Henry of Huntingdon. Part two, with which we are concerned, is a chronicle from the Creation to 1298. Book III *De Archiepiscopis et Episcopis Angliae (Concerning the Archbishops and Bishops of England)*, is a tract on the history of the English archbishops and bishops from the time of St Augustine to Cotton's own day. Its account of the bishops of Norwich, with a continuation to 1299, is of some value.

Apparently Cotton started writing the chronicle in about 1292.[31] From that date until 1298 he seems to have written fairly close to the events he recorded. But first he probably copied an earlier chronicle written at Norwich, covering the period from the Creation to 1290. Cotton's modern editor has decided, mainly on stylistic grounds, that this chronicle was by another monk of Norwich, not by Cotton.[32] Therefore only the section from 1291 to 1298 is Cotton's work. The earlier Norwich chronicle is a compilation to 1263 of various well-known sources, such as William of Malmesbury, Henry of Huntingdon, Ralph Diceto, Roger of Howden, Roger of Wendover, Matthew Paris and John de Taxter. From 1264 to 1279 it is independent of all known sources and is particularly valuable for local history (for example for the citizens' revolt against the cathedral priory in 1272[33]). From 1279 to 1284 it uses the Bury chronicle. From 1288 to 1290 it is again original and has much of local interest.

Cotton himself belong to the archivist type of historian. He only once expresses his feelings: he says of the reconciliation between King Edward and the barons in 1297, 'and thus was a good peace made between the king, and his earls and magnates, and then they discussed the expedition against the Scots, may God be praised, Amen.'[34] In general, the chronicle consists of objective narrative and numerous documents. Cotton gives good texts of some documents, a few apparently unique. For example he has the summons

---

[30] Only the last two books are printed in the edition noted p. 440 n. 7 above.

[31] See *BC*, pp. xviii, 418.

[32] For this anonymous Norwich chronicle see *BC*, pp. xxi–xxv. For a suggestion as to one of its authors see p. 400 above. Its text from the Incarnation to 1291 corresponds with Cotton (*BC*, pp. 47–182). Its annals for most of 1291 and for 1292 are quite different from Cotton's (they are printed as an appendix in *BC*, pp. 428–33). For another variant passage see *BC*, pp. 427–8.

[33] *BC*, pp. 146–9. For entries of more general interest in the anonymous Norwich chronicle see pp. 445 n. 46, 449 n. 79 below.

[34] *BC*, p. 339.

to, and the official record of, the proceedings of the council of the province of Canterbury held at the New Temple, London, and at Lambeth, in 1292.[35] He copies the text of the treaty between Adolf of Nassau and Edward I in 1294, and related documents.[36] He gives a copy of the letter of the two papal nuncios, Berard cardinal bishop of Albano, and Simon cardinal bishop of Palestrina (who had been appointed in 1295 to make peace between England and France) on the method of collecting money for their expenses.[37] This particular letter was to the bishop of Norwich's official and to the sacrist of the cathedral church: Cotton also gives another, on the same subject, to the prior and convent of Norwich.[38] Cotton has the only known copy of a treasonable letter (1295) from Thomas de Turbeville to the provost of Paris and a unique eye-witness account of Turbeville's execution as a traitor.[39] And he has one of the only two early copies in French of the *Monstraunces* of the barons in 1297.[40]

Cotton obtained documents from the archive collection in the cathedral priory,[41] from the bishop of Norwich's muniments,[42] and from the sheriff of Norfolk.[43] Besides copying documents into the chronicle, Cotton tells the reader to see 'above' for some documents.[44] The existing manuscript does not have these documents, so it seems likely that originally Cotton prefixed to his work a collection of relevant texts (similar to Matthew Paris's *Liber Additamentorum*). Cotton was a competent archivist. He notes that John Balliol's letter of submission to Edward I (1296), which he transcribes, 'was without date'.[45] He describes the appearance of one of the many papal bulls he transcribes: 'This is a copy of some papal letters (with the leaden bull attached by a thread of hemp) not faulty or in any way damaged.'[46] His object here was no doubt to stress the authenticity of the bull – Nicholas IV's taxation of ecclesiastical benefices in aid of the Holy Land (1291).

Although Cotton aimed at writing a business-like record he has some good

---

[35] *BC*, pp. 199–210. Printed from Cotton's text in *Councils and Synods*, vol. 2, pt ii, pp. 1100–7.

[36] *BC*, pp. 240–5. The text is not identical with that printed in *Foedera*, vol. 1, pt ii, p. 812.

[37] *BC*, pp. 283–92. Noticed from Cotton's text, in W. E. Lunt, *Financial Relations of the Papacy with England to 1327* (Cambridge, Mass. 1939), p. 553.

[38] *BC*, pp. 292–3.

[39] *BC*, pp. 304–6 (see *BC*, pp. 437–9, for an English translation).

[40] *BC*, pp. 325–7. For the importance of this text see J. G. Edwards, '*Confirmatio Cartarum* and baronial grievances in 1297' in *EHR*, lviii (1943), p. 148.

[41] e.g. the just cited letter of the papal nuncios to the prior and convent of Norwich must have been in the priory's archives.

[42] e.g. the summons from the archbishop to the bishop of Norwich to the council of 1295 (cited *BC*, pp. 293–4) must have been kept with the bishop's archives.

[43] e.g. Edward I's writs to the sheriffs of Norfolk and Suffolk, cited *BC*, pp. 245–7, 303 etc., must have been in the sheriff's archives.

[44] For such references see *BC*, pp. 315 and n. 2, 316 and n. 2, 320 and n. 1.

[45] *BC*, p. 309.

[46] *BC*, p. 191. The previous Norwich chronicle seems also to have been interested in the problem of the authenticity of documents, for it tells the good story of how Adam de Statton, a clerk of the Exchequer, forged a charter in his own favour, for which he was convicted; see *BC*, p. 180.

narrative (often supplemented with relevant documents) which shows that he was a well informed and intelligent historian. He is interested in both local and general history. He writes at some length about the local merchants and sailors at Yarmouth, and their disputes with Norman, and other, sailors. Here he was continuing a subject which interested the anonymous Norwich chronicler (the latter mentions violent quarrels between the sailors of Yarmouth and the Cinque Ports in 1289, and the naval battle between sailors of Yarmouth and the Cinque Ports, and the sailors of Bayonne and Flanders, in 1290[47]). Cotton records that in 1295 some ships from Yarmouth plundered the Norman coast. French ships then attacked Dover and Winchelsea, from which they were expelled by a fleet from Yarmouth.[48] Cotton cites a royal writ to the prior of Norwich ordering him to co-operate with the king's officials in the defence of the coasts of Norfolk and Suffolk.[49]

Cotton was well informed about trade (the legitimate occupation of the Yarmouth sailors, who carried wool especially to Flanders and brought wine and other merchandise from France). He notes the effect on commerce of the war between England and France. He says that since the beginning of the war English merchants had landed in the territory of the count of Holland. Therefore when in 1295 the count allied with the king of France, Edward forbade merchants and seamen to land in the count of Holland's territory (Cotton cites Edward's writ, 24 January 1296, to this effect to the sheriff of Norfolk[50]). Cotton records that Edward forbade merchants to go abroad at all, but soon afterwards withdrew his prohibition (except in a few cases) provided the merchants swore not to trade with France or its allies.[51] Cotton has slightly pathetic details of the attempts of the royal officials to enlist foot soldiers in Norfolk for the French war. The officials enumerated many men to be in the infantry 'and had them bought white tunics, knives and swords at the common expense'. The prospective recruits were summoned to Newmarket, where many were found inadequate and were rejected – even those chosen were sent home within four days.[52]

But Cotton's interest extended beyond local news, and he was very well informed about national events. He shares some information with the chronicle of Bury St Edmunds.[53] Like the Bury chronicle he has a full account of Edward I's negotiations for a marriage with King Philip's sister Blanche.[54] Most important is his account of the conflict between Edward and

---

[47] See *BC*, pp. 171, 174–5. For an entry about building activity, etc., at Yarmouth, see *BC*, pp. 167–8.

[48] *BC*, pp. 295–6.   [49] *BC*, p. 296.   [50] *BC*, p. 303.

[51] *BC*, p. 304. For Edward I's manipulation of trade for political purposes see p. 426 and n. 221 above, pp. 513–14 below.

[52] *BC*, p. 307.

[53] The anonymous Norwich chronicle also has material similar to that in the Bury chronicle: see the account of the townsmen's attack on Norwich cathedral priory in 1272 (pp. 399–402 *passim* above), and the long account of the purge of royal officials and justices in 1290; *BC*, pp. 171–6.

[54] *BC*, pp. 232. For the entry in the Bury chronicle see p. 401 above.

the barons in 1297, when the barons refused to accompany the king on his Flemish campaign and demanded the confirmation of the charters.[55] A modern scholar on this conflict has written: 'Cotton is a first-class source, and his chronicle is not only independent both of Hemingburgh and of Trevet but is also more closely contemporary with the events of 1297'.[56] By inference it appears that Cotton's sympathies were characteristic of a monk – pro-baronial. He states that Roger Bigod, the earl marshal, and Humphrey de Bohun, the constable, claimed that they refused 'on behalf of the community of the realm' to accompany Edward to Flanders. Moreover, Cotton was interested in the development of parliament. He copies Edward's writ of summons to the prior of Norwich to attend parliament in August 1295.[57] He also gives the writ summoning parliament to discuss the French invasion of Gascony later in the same year,[58] the first writ to begin with the famous phrase asserting that, according to the most just principle of law, 'what touches everyone, should be approved by everyone'.[59] And Cotton is the only chronicler of the time to recognize the growing importance of the commons in parliament. In 1294 the chancery clerks at last evolved a formula in the writs of summons clearly specifying that the knights should come with full powers to bind their shires. Cotton records the summons of the knights in 1294, and, apparently citing the writ itself, says that they were to have 'full power of binding the shires'.[60]

Like other monastic chroniclers Cotton saw the clergy as the champions of England's charters of liberties and the defenders of the freedom of the church in England ('which was in decline and continually abused' in Edward's reign).[61] Perhaps his most vivid piece of narrative is the account of the conflict between the church and the king over the taxation of the clergy in 1296 and 1297. He gives the fullest descriptions of any chronicle of the meetings of the clergy at Bury St Edmunds in November 1296[62] and at St Paul's in January 1297.[63] These accounts are so circumstantial that Cotton must have obtained them from eye-witnesses.

He relates how the clergy met in 1296, after parliament had been held, in the chapter house at Bury and discussed the king's demand for money under four headings drawn up by the archbishop. Then he describes how the

---

[55] *BC*, pp. 325–30. For Cotton's text of the baronial *Monstraunces* see p. 445 and n. 40 above.
[56] J. G. Edwards, '*Confirmatio Cartarum* and baronial grievances in 1297' in *EHR*, lviii (1943), p. 148.
[57] *BC*, pp. 294–5.   [58] *BC*, p. 297.
[59] 'Quod omnes tangit.' See Antonio Marongiu, *Il Parlamento in Italia* (Milan 1962), pp. 43–4; an English translation and adaptation of Marongiu, op. cit., is by S. J. Woolf, under the title *Medieval Parliaments, a Comparative Study*, with a foreword by H. M. Cam (London 1968).
[60] *BC*, p. 254. For a discussion of the importance of the chancery formula, with a citation of the passage in Cotton, see J. G. Edwards, 'The *Plena Potestas* of English parliamentary representatives' in *Oxford Essays in Medieval History presented to H. E. Salter* (Oxford 1934), pp. 144–5. For a slight error in Cotton see ibid., p. 145 n. 3.
[61] *BC*, p. 327.
[62] *BC*, pp. 314–15. This account is printed in *Councils and Synods*, vol. 2, pt ii, p. 1150.
[63] *BC*, pp. 317–18. This account is printed in *Councils and Synods*, vol. 2, pt ii, pp. 1159–60.

clergy were divided into four groups which discussed the matter separately. These groups were: first, the archbishops, bishops and their proctors; second, the religious; third, all dignitaries; fourth, the procurators of the community of the clergy. Cotton says that the clergy sat in the same groups at the meeting at St Paul's. There the archbishop, Cotton records, told the clergy to find some middle way between the two dangers, on the one hand the papal bull (*Clericis laicos*), on the other 'the subversion of the whole kingdom'.[64] Edward's representative pointed out that to defend the land against its foreign enemies the king needed clerical (financial) assistance. In reply the archbishop read aloud the papal bull. Cotton then gives the threatening words of the royal official, Sir Hugh le Despenser, and the clergy's subsequent deliberations. He describes under 1297 how the king persecuted the clergy,[65] many of whom therefore compromised with him, 'notwithstanding the common reply of the clergy, and without consulting the archbishop'.[66] Edward's mood apparently softened, for he received two bishops, sent by the archbishop and other ecclesiastics to present certain proposals, 'with a kind face and in a modest manner, seeking their blessing', before he set sail for Gascony.[67]

As said above, the Canterbury continuation of Gervase from 1270 to 1277 mainly concerns the history of Dover priory.[68] But from 1278 to 1327 the annals are mainly of general history, with a Canterbury orientation.[69] The annals are short to the end of 1292 (they include a transcript of the letter of submission of the Scottish competitors to Edward I). Then, from 1293 to 1299 they are full and interesting (from 1300 to the end they are again brief). Like Cotton, the Canterbury chronicle is well informed about Anglo-French relations. It gives an account of the naval battle in 1293 between sailors from the Cinque Ports and elsewhere in England, and the Normans and French,[70] and has a copy of King Philip's letter to Edward I citing him to answer concerning the outrage.[71] It has similar details to those in Cotton of the negotiations for Edward's marriage with Blanche and his consequent forfeiture of Aquitaine.[72]

The Canterbury chronicle has much papal history (it benefited no doubt by access to the archbishop's archives). It has a first-hand account of the visit of two papal envoys, Berard bishop of Albano and Simon bishop of Palestrina, in 1295 to negotiate a peace between England and France.[73] It tells how they were met at Dover by the prior of Canterbury and the abbot of St Augustine's. Having visited the shrines in the priory church, they spent the night at Dover and left next day for Ospringe. They were met at Harble-

---

[64] *BC*, p. 317. [65] *BC*, pp. 318–35 *passim*. [66] *BC*, p. 321.
[67] *BC*, p. 335.
[68] See pp. 422–3. For the general value of the annals 1270–7 see *GC*, vol. 2, p. xxvi.
[69] *Cont. GC*, pp. 291–324. See *GC*, vol. 2, pp. xxvii–xxviii. [70] *Cont. GC*, p. 302.
[71] *Cont. GC*, pp. 302–5. [72] *Cont. GC*, pp. 305–6. [73] *Cont. GC*, pp. 311–12.

down by the archbishop and then travelled in stages to London. The chronicle gives an account of their unsuccessful negotiations with the king.[74] It was also able, because it was written at Canterbury, to give unique details relating to the wedding of Edward I and Margaret in 1299. It records that people quarrelled over who was to have the canopy which had been held above the couple when they were blessed. The archbishop, the prior of Christ Church, the clerks who held the archbishop's cross and the clerks of the king's chapel, all thought they had good claims, so the king ordered it to be kept by the earl of Lincoln until the dispute was decided. After the wedding Edward went to Chartham with only two knights, while the queen feasted in the archbishop's palace.[75]

The Worcester chronicle is independent of other chronicles from 1281 to 1307. This section may have been written by the sacrist, Nicholas of Norton (who is mentioned by name three times[76]), or at least at his order (there are numerous specific references to the sacrist's office[77]). The chronicle is fairly full until 1303, but mainly concerns local affairs (it is an excellent domestic history of the priory). Its attitude to local events illustrates the self-sufficiency and self-centredness of a rich Benedictine foundation. It devotes much space, for example, to the priory's frequent quarrels with the bishop of Worcester over his alleged encroachments on the monks' property and privileges.[78]

Particularly valuable is the light the chronicle throws on the causes of the bad relations between the Benedictines and the Franciscans at this period. Clearly the Worcester chronicler, like the authors of the Norwich[79] and Canterbury/Dover[80] chronicles, and of the Westminster continuation of the *Flores*,[81] hated the Franciscans. The activities of the friars clashed with monastic vested interest. The chronicle shows that the main cause of contention at Worcester was the wish of some laymen to be buried in the Franciscans' cemetery instead of in the cathedral (this deprived the monks of burial dues). The chronicle describes the quarrel from 1289 to 1290 between the Worcester monks and the Franciscans over the burial of a certain Henry Poche.[82] The latter was buried in the monks' cemetery despite the Franciscans' opposition. The friars obtained an order from the archbishop for his exhumation, and an inquiry was held which discovered that Poche had

[74] *Cont. GC*, pp. 312–14.   [75] *Cont. GC*, pp. 317–18.

[76] *Worc.*, pp. 480 (*s.a.* 1281), 510 (*s.a.* 1292), 546 (*s.a.* 1300).

[77] The numerous references to the sacrist's office (for example the record of his perquisites when a newly elected abbot was blessed by the bishop of Worcester) start early in Henry III's reign. See e.g. *Worc.*, pp. 424, 427, 433, 484, 489.

[78] See e.g. the quarrel over the Westbury prebends (*Worc.*, pp. 500–2 *passim*, 504, 523) and over the bishop's attempt to visit the cathedral priory (*Worc.*, pp. 503–4, 545).

[79] *BC*, pp. 429–30 (an account of the quarrel between the clergy of Yarmouth and the Franciscans over the right to hear confessions, 1291).

[80] *Cont. GC*, p. 281 (a disapproving reflection, *s.a.* 1275, on the introduction of a Franciscan as lector at Christ Church, Canterbury).

[81] *FH*, vol. 3, pp. 75, 108 (mainly general invective).

[82] *Worc.*, pp. 499–504 *passim*. The case is mentioned by A. G. Little, *Studies in English Franciscan History* (Manchester 1917), pp. 392 n. 3, 110 n. 2.

bequeathed his body to the Franciscans. The archbishop ordered the friars to bury him quietly. But 'to our confusion they carried [the body] with noisy chanting through the main market place, inviting everyone they could to the spectacle and expounding their privileges to the people in the mother tongue'.[83] Again, under 1298, it records that William de Beauchamp, having bequeathed his body to the cathedral, succumbed to persuasion and gave it to the Franciscans. And they 'buried it in a spot (I formerly saw nettles growing there) never used for burial before, where it was drowned rather than buried in winter-time'.[84] William's wife Maud was buried next to him, although while alive she had arranged to be buried elsewhere.[85] The chronicle shows its general antipathy to the Franciscans with an allegation of the betrayal of a confession by a Franciscan[86] (the friars' claim to hear confessions affected monastic interests indirectly because, through the system of appropriation, monasteries held parochial livings[87]). And the chronicle mentions Pope Boniface's bull *Super cathedram*, which prohibited friars from preaching in parish churches except by invitation of the parish priest or command of the bishop, and stipulated that the priest should have one-quarter of all offerings and legacies to friars.[88]

But the Worcester chronicle expresses some more laudable opinions. Its criticism of the work of the general chapters of the Benedictines arose from the introduction of modifications to the Rule. It records that the general chapter of 1300 allowed prelates and their servants to eat meat, and abolished prolix prayers between the hours – 'no doubt', the chronicle remarks, 'in the future the *Pater noster* will seem superfluous'.[89] Here the chronicler failed to appreciate that cuts in liturgical observance were partly intended to release time for study. In fact the Worcester chronicle shows a respect for academic learning, an interest in the development of Oxford university, and an admiration for Benedictines who graduated there, unique among contemporary monastic chronicles. It notes under 1283 the foundation of Gloucester college ('a spacious place') by Sir John Giffard ('who wanted his and his wife's soul to be perpetually blessed by monks of St. Benedict').[90] It records that in 1298 three monks of Malmesbury were sent to the new foundation permanently and that Giffard made one of them prior.[91] Under the same year it mentions the quarrel at Oxford between the clergy and the townsmen and specifies the terms of the settlement between the parties.[92] It records the inception, apparently at Oxford, of two monks of Gloucester, one William de

---

[83] *Worc.*, p. 504.   [84] *Worc.*, p. 537.   [85] *Worc.*, p. 549.
[86] *Worc.*, pp. 513–14.
[87] For the friars' claim to hear confession see Little, *Studies*, pp. 105–22 *passim*.
[88] *Worc.*, p. 545. See Little, *Studies*, pp. 114–15.   [89] *Worc.*, p. 547.
[90] *Worc.*, p. 488. For the early history of Gloucester college see V. H. Galbraith, 'Some new documents about Gloucester College' in *Snappe's Formulary*, ed. H. E. Salter (Oxford Hist. Soc., lxxx, 1924), pp. 341–51.
[91] *Worc.*, p. 539.
[92] *Worc.*, p. 539. For the full terms of the settlement see Anthony à Wood, *The History and Antiquities of the University of Oxford*, vol. 1, pp. 349–57 *passim* (s.a. 1297).

Beor ('who did not neglect his talents') in 1298,[93] and the other Lawrence (who 'deserved a place and honour among the doctors of theology') in 1301.[94]

Despite its preoccupation with local affairs and matters particularly concerning the Benedictine order, the Worcester chronicle has some information about general history. It derived its facts from the priory and episcopal archives, from the records of the sheriff of Worcestershire, and by ear. Some news came direct from the king's court, for Edward I was often at Worcester (*en route* for his Welsh campaigns). In places in the chronicle news of national importance immediately precedes a notice of a royal visit, which suggests that the chronicler obtained his information from the court. Thus there are details under 1294 concerning Anglo-French relations;[95] and the chronicle then records that Edward arrived at the priory 'late in the evening of 1 September' (details of his visit and gifts follow), and stayed until the following evening.[96] Under 1295 there is a valuable account of Edward's Welsh campaign in the spring of that year:[97] the chronicle describes a visit by Edward to the priory in July.[98]

The Worcester chronicle shows a particular interest in Edward's relations with Scotland, in the dispute between king and church over taxation, and in the barons' struggle for the confirmation of the charters. It has a copy of the writ to the prior and convent of Worcester enclosing copies of the letters of submission of the Scottish lords to Edward, together with the instructions to copy them into their chronicles.[99] And under 1296 are details of Edward's Scottish war.[100] The struggle between the king and the church is described in considerable detail, illustrated with copies of relevant documents (the bull *Clericis laicos*, a writ to the sheriff of Worcester to seize the property of the clergy, and the like).[101] And it records the exact amount paid, during the king's persecution of the church, by the prior of Worcester for the king's protection.[102] In the account of the barons' struggle for the confirmation of the charters, the chronicle's attitude to Edward is on the whole favourable. It remarks that in 1298 the king confirmed the charters, which previously he had granted to the barons and community of the realm, 'not from fear, but of his own free will and without payment. ... And so he deserves to be

---

[93] *Worc.*, p. 537. William de Beor is listed from this entry in A. B. Emden, *A Biographical Register of the University of Oxford to A.D. 1500* (Oxford 1957–9, 3 vols), vol. 1, p. 172.

[94] 'Nonis Junii Laurentius monachus Gloucestrensis inter doctores theologiae sedem meruit et honorem'; *Worc.*, pp. 49–50. Lawrence is not listed in Emden, op. cit.

[95] *Worc.*, pp. 515–16.   [96] *Worc.*, pp. 516–17.

[97] *Worc.*, pp. 519–20. For the value of the account in the Worcester chronicle of the Welsh campaign of 1294–5, see J. G. Edwards, 'The battle of Maes Madog and the Welsh campaign of 1294–5' in *EHR*, xxxix (1924), pp. 1–12 *passim*. Sir Goronwy Edwards points out that the Worcester annalist was 'a keen observer of Welsh affairs', and states: 'His narrative of the events in Wales in 1294–5 is about the longest in any chronicle, and contains a good deal of detail – especially chronological detail – which when tested proves him to have been a careful and well informed writer'; ibid., pp. 5–6.

[98] *Worc.*, p. 521.   [99] *Worc.*, pp. 507–9.   [100] *Worc.*, pp. 526–7.

[101] *Worc.*, pp. 528–35 *passim*.   [102] *Worc.*, p. 531.

loved at the present time and to be blessed in the future'.[103] And it mentions that the royal confirmation of 1299 was read publicly in the city of Worcester, 'in the mother tongue'.[104]

The Peterborough chronicle was written in the period from about 1273 to 1295, probably by the sacrist of Peterborough, William of Woodford, who became abbot in 1296, ruling until 1299.[105] He wrote to record the triumphs in the law courts of Abbot Richard of London (1274–95), an able defender of the abbey's rights. The chronicle, which starts in 1122, mainly concerns local history. But it does show some interest in general history, especially in Edward I's Welsh policy.[106] The chronicle's interest in Wales was partly the result of the king's demand for knight service and his financial impositions, made necessary by the Welsh campaigns, which affected Peterborough directly. It was also caused by Peterborough's proximity to Northampton, the venue of the council held in 1283 to discuss Edward's financial demands for the Welsh war. And of course the abbot of Peterborough would have attended this and other such councils, together with the heads of other religious houses.

Thus under 1277 the Peterborough chronicle notices Edward's Welsh campaign and the terms of the treaty of Conway. It also records the summons for military service and the repercussions at Peterborough.[107] The account of Welsh affairs and the related negotiations over money is even more detailed under 1282–3. The chronicle notices David's rebellion and Edward's expedition against the insurgents.[108] And it has copies of acquittances to the abbey for the fine paid in lieu of military service: there are two acquittances from Lucchese bankers, members of the Ricciardi, Henry of Podio and Bartholomew Walteri, to the abbey in part payment of the fine owed to the king for military service; and one acquittance from the king.[109] The chronicle gives copies of the summons (addressed to the sheriff of Northampton) of the knights of the shire,[110] and of the clergy of the southern province[111] to the Council of Northampton (January 1283) where a one-thirtieth for the war was negotiated. Moreover, the chronicle has a unique account of the king's requests to the clergy at the council and of the clergy's replies.[112] It also notes that one of Peterborough abbey's tenants, Peter de la

---

[103] *Worc.*, pp. 536–7.

[104] *Worc.*, p. 541.

[105] See G. A. Poole, *Diocesan Histories, Peterborough* (London 1881), p. 80. For the value of this chronicle for local history see Appendix B, p. 520 below.

[106] See also the passage relating to the king's attack on money-clippers etc. in 1278; *Pet.*, pp. 26–8, and the account of the translation of St Hugh of Lincoln; *Pet.*, p. 40.

[107] *Pet.*, pp. 24–6. Cf. W. Stubbs, *The Constitutional History of England* (5th ed., Oxford 1891–1903, 3 vols), vol. 2, p. 114.

[108] *Pet.*, pp. 55–6.

[109] *Pet.*, pp. 56–7. For Henry of Podio and Bartholomew Walteri (Bouruncus Gwalteri in *Pet.*) see Lunt, *Financial Relations ... to 1327*, pp. 643, 644.

[110] *Pet.*, pp. 60–1. See Stubbs, *Charters*, pp. 457–8.

[111] *Pet.*, pp. 58–9. This text is collated in *Councils and Synods*, vol. 2, pt ii, pp. 940–2.

[112] *Pet.*, pp. 59–60. Printed in *Councils and Synods*, vol. 2, pt ii, pp. 943–4.

Mare, was killed in the Welsh war, and that the abbot took seisin of his lands.[113] Under 1283 the chronicle has information about the ecclesiastical council summoned at Lambeth in May to finish business started at Northampton. It gives an account of the proceedings not found elsewhere,[114] which is followed by a copy of the writ, addressed to the sheriff of Northampton, summoning knights of the shire to the parliament at Shrewsbury.[115] This interest in writs of summons is reminiscent of Bartholomew Cotton.

The continuation of the *Flores Historiarum* from 1265 to 1327, written at Westminster, falls into two parts. To the end of 1306 it was by an anonymous Westminster monk (or perhaps by more than one monk). From 1307 to 1327 it was by a monk at Westminster called Robert of Reading.[116] Only the section to 1306 concerns us here. From 1266 to 1292 the annals are short. From 1293 they are longer. Although the chronicle shows an interest in documents (it describes one document as 'elegant, sealed with a hundred seals'[117]), it is not the work of a competent archivist such as Bartholomew Cotton. It quotes few documents in full and expressly omits some because they were 'too prolix'.[118] It does not even have copies of the letters of submission by the Scottish competitors to Edward I.

The *Flores* had excellent sources of information. Westminster abbey itself was often a centre of national affairs. Moreover, it was next to the king's usual seat of government (although the Exchequer and the court of King's Bench were in York from 1298 to 1304[119]), and near the capital city. Therefore the chronicle has some information at first hand and some on the authority of eye-witnesses. It has, for example, what is surely a first-hand account of the meeting of the clergy in the chapter house at Westminster in 1294 to discuss the king's financial demands.[120] Here a knight, John de Havering, put the king's point of view: the *Flores* gives his speech. Under 1306 the *Flores*, in one of its most colourful passages, describes the mass investiture of over 250 knights at Westminster by Edward I in 1306, which was followed by a banquet now known as the Feast of Swans, because swans formed the main dish. The ceremony and celebration are the strongest evidence of the chivalric tastes of Edward's court, tastes evinced especially in the cult of King Arthur.[121] However, the knighting of so many young men was intended to be more than a spectacle – new knights meant more money

---

[113] *Pet.*, p. 61.
[114] *Pet.*, pp. 62–3. Printed in *Councils and Synods*, vol. 2, pt ii, pp. 950–1.
[115] *Pet.*, pp. 63–4. See Stubbs, *Charters*, pp. 460–1.
[116] See *FH*, vol. 1, p. xliii.
[117] *FH*, vol. 3, p. 109.
[118] Ibid., p. 43.
[119] See F. M. Powicke, *The Thirteenth Century* (Oxford 1953), p. 688.
[120] *FH*, vol. 3, p. 90. This passage is printed in *Councils and Synods*, vol. 2, pt ii, p. 1131.
[121] See N. Denholm-Young, *History and Heraldry 1254–1310* (Oxford 1965), pp. 49–50, and the same author's 'The song of Caerlaverock and the parliamentary Roll of Arms' in *Proceedings of the British Academy*, xlvii (1961), pp. 251–62 *passim*.

for the royal treasury. The *Flores* begins by describing where the young men stayed:[122]

> When the three hundred young men ... had assembled, purple satins, silk and rich robes lavishly decorated with gold thread were distributed to each as was his due. And because the royal palace, although large, was too small for such a gathering, apple trees were cut down and walls levelled at the New Temple, and they erected tents and pavilions where the young men decked themselves in their cloth of gold. That night as many of the young men as possible kept their vigils in the Temple. But the prince of Wales at the order of the king, with a few of the most distinguished youths, kept his vigil in the church at Westminster. There was indeed such a noise of trumpets and pipes and so many loud, happy voices that the convent could not hear [its own words of] praise from choir to choir. Next morning the king knighted his son in his palace and gave him the duchy of Aquitaine. And the prince, now a knight, proceeded to the church of Westminster to knight his fellows in the same way. Then there was such a crush of people before the high altar, that two knights died and many fainted, although each had with him at least three knights to guide and look after him. The prince despite the pressing crowd, knighted his fellows from the high altar, the crowd having been broken up by war horses. Then two swans or cygnets, adorned with golden harness and gilded reeds (a wonderful sight to see), were carried with great pomp to the king.

In 1305 the *Flores* records that King Edward visited Westminster abbey, to give thanks to God and St Edward for his victory over the Scots.[123] It was perhaps to this occasion that the *Flores* owed the details of the siege and surrender of Stirling castle in the previous year.[124] The abbey's proximity to Westminster palace must account for the *Flores*'s details about a number of public transactions in the great hall. Under 1297 the *Flores* describes the king's interview in the great hall with the archbishop, bishops and barons, relating how the magnates opposed the king's expedition to Flanders (on the grounds that the Scots had revolted) and demanded the confirmation of the charters, and how Edward agreed to their demands in exchange for an aid.[125] Under 1298 it states that the king had recited at Westminster Pope Boniface's bull ordaining the peace between England and France, together with related bulls, 'to which all the people, with the clergy, gave their

---

[122] *FH*, vol. 3, pp. 131–2.
[123] Ibid., p. 121.
[124] Ibid., pp. 118–20.
[125] Ibid., pp. 101–2. For another account of transactions in Westminster hall see ibid., p. 95.

consent'.[126] And under 1306 it records that the Scottish prisoners were tried and condemned in the great hall.[127]

Sometimes the abbot of Westminster, Walter of Wenlock, had particular means of obtaining news. Wenlock was appointed in 1305 one of the English representatives to negotiate a peace with Scotland.[128] The *Flores* is very well informed about the negotiations, which, it records, began on 15 September at the New Temple and lasted for twenty days.[129] And the chronicler either himself saw or talked to someone who saw the executions of Scottish prisoners in London in 1305 and 1306. The *Flores* has gruesome descriptions of the executions of William Wallace (he was hanged, drawn and quartered)[130] and of John of Strathbogie, earl of Atholl (he was hanged and beheaded).[131]

On the whole the *Flores* is favourable to Edward I. In places it is even eulogistic in tone – but not uniformly so. It criticizes Edward for his financial demands on, and treatment of the church from 1296 to 1297. It considers the king's demands in 1294 oppressive,[132] and when in 1296 the clergy refused his request for an aid, the *Flores* says: 'therefore the king turned to cruelty, and the clergy were so constantly afflicted that it was as if the madness of Nero was revived in England.'[133] The monks of Westminster had their own causes of friction with the king. In 1303 some of the Westminster monks (including the sacrist) and abbey servants robbed the royal treasury of the king's wardrobe which was kept in the abbey.[134] Their imprisonment for the robbery elicited from the writer of the *Flores* a page of indignant protest (with biblical quotations). The monks were only released in 1305 when Edward returned from Scotland, pleased with his success.[135]

But any criticism of Edward was outweighed by enthusiasm for his Scottish policy. In 1297 Edward gave to Westminster abbey the regalia of the kings of Scotland, that is the golden sceptre and crown, and the stone of Scone. The *Flores* records the gift,[136] and from then onwards shows a close interest in Scottish affairs. The subject evokes some eloquent narrative. The account of the siege of Stirling castle, with its descriptions of heroism and military details, suggests that the *Flores* was here influenced by romance

[126] Ibid., p. 105.   [127] Ibid., p. 135.

[128] *Parliamentary Writs and Writs of Military Summons*, ed. F. Palgrave (Record Commission, 1827–34, 4 vols), vol. 1, p. 161. See *Documents illustrating the Rule of Walter de Wenlock, Abbot of Westminster, 1283–1307*, ed. B. F. Harvey (Camden Soc., 4th series, ii, 1965), p. 44 n. 1.

[129] *FH*, vol. 3, p. 124.   [130] Ibid.   [131] Ibid., p. 135.

[132] Ibid., p. 90.   [133] Ibid., p. 99.

[134] Ibid., pp. 115–17. The robbery and trial of the culprits are fully documented in the public records: see T. F. Tout, 'A medieval burglary' in *BJRL*, ii (1914–15), pp. 348–69. For an account of the same affair, told with more sympathy for the monks, see E. H. Pearce, *Walter de Wenlock, Abbot of Westminster* (London 1920), pp. 146–66. See also H. F. Westlake, *Westminster Abbey* (London, 1923, limited ed., 2 vols), vol. 2, pp. 430–46.

[135] *FH*, vol. 3, p. 121.

[136] Ibid., p. 101.

literature.[137] The treatment of Anglo-Scottish relations is literary and stylized. The situation is seen in almost Manichean terms, in black and white. Edward is good: the Scottish leaders are bad. Wallace, the murderer, was as cruel as Herod, and as debauched as Nero.[138] Bruce, the patricide and usurper, was crowned king by the conspirators just like Adonias.[139] Edward I, on the other hand is the hero, the lord and king of two realms,[140] the glorious victor,[141] the most fortunate king,[142] who in Scotland 'trampled on the horns of the proud, silenced the roar of rebels, conquered all the nobles of the kingdom of Scotland and forced them to submit to his judgement.'[143] And he was merciful: after the capture of Stirling castle 'he took pity on the tears and groans' of the garrison, and imprisoned the men instead of executing them.[144] The very walls of Stirling castle bore witness to his glory: the dents made by the besiegers' missiles were 'indelible tokens of the lasting victory and great triumph of this magnificent king'.[145]

The 'Merton' *Flores* presents problems. Though its contents suggest that it was compiled in Westminster abbey, the earliest extant text (Eton College MS. 123) was written in (or for) the Augustinian priory of Merton in Surrey – it has a copy of Edward I's letter on the Scottish succession case addressed to the prior and convent of Merton[146] and references in the margin to the priory's history.[147] In addition, the other manuscripts of the 'Merton' *Flores* apparently descend from the Eton College MS.[148]

Nevertheless there is evidence suggesting the possibility that the version of the *Flores* preserved in the Merton manuscript was compiled at Westminster. A Westminster provenance would satisfactorily explain the paucity of additions relating to Merton priory. Moreover, the 'Merton' *Flores* has no additions specifically relating to the Augustinian canons. But it does mention two wealthy Benedictine houses in Scotland, Dunfermline (in Fife) and Arbroath (in Angus), and describes the sack of the former by the Scots:[149]

---

[137] Ibid., pp. 118–20. [138] Ibid., p. 123.

[139] Ibid., p. 129. Adonias, fourth son of King David, tried to have himself proclaimed king in opposition to Solomon (3 Kings 1. 5–53). The *Flores* goes on to record Bruce's second coronation by Isabella countess of Buchan, and the alleged sceptical remark of his wife (Elizabeth de Burgh) that he would be a summer but not a winter king; *FH*, vol. 3, p. 130.

[140] *FH*, vol. 3, p. 121. [141] Ibid., p. 112.

[142] Ibid., p. 118. [143] Ibid., p. 118.

[144] Ibid. p. 120. [145] Ibid., pp. 119–20.

[146] *FH*, vol. 1, p. xvi; vol. 3, p. 74 n. 7. I have discussed the 'Merton' *Flores* and the chronicle of Robert of Reading (see p. 460 below) at greater length in 'The Westminster version of the *Flores Historiarum*' in *Mediaeval Studies*, xxxvi (Toronto 1974).

[147] See ibid., vol. 3, pp. 250 n. 1, 292, 302 n. 4. For an insertion in the text concerning the priory see ibid., p. 84.

[148] The manuscripts of the 'Merton' *Flores* are described in ibid., vol. 1, pp. xxix–xxxiii. All the known texts except two have Edward I's letter on the Scottish succession case addressed to the prior and convent of Merton. The exceptions are the so-called Tenison MS. and the chronicle of Ralph Baldock, for which see Appendix D.

[149] *FH*, vol. 3, pp. 311–13.

such additions could well have been made at Westminster where there was a close interest in and much information about Scottish affairs. And the homiletic and royalist tone of the 'Merton' *Flores* would fit a Westminster provenance. As has been seen, the Westminster *Flores* itself has a moderately 'royalist' point of view, mainly because the king was the abbey's patron.[150] Furthermore, it seems possible to detect a link between the 'Merton' *Flores* and the coronation service, a matter of particular interest to the Westminster monks (the abbey, the scene of the coronation, had custody of the regalia and of documents relating to the ceremony).[151] The 'Merton' *Flores*, unlike most contemporary chronicles, explicitly refers, in conjunction with biblical citations, to Henry III and Edward I as 'the Lord's anointed'.[152] (The Eton College MS., like the Chetham MS. of the Westminster *Flores*, marks the coronation of each king from William the Conqueror with a well-executed picture of the coronation ceremony.[153])

There is therefore a conflict of evidence. On the one hand the manuscript tradition suggests that the 'Merton' *Flores* was written at or for Merton priory. On the other hand the contents of the 'Merton' *Flores*, and the pictures in the Eton MS., suggest a Westminster provenance. A possible solution, which would fit the facts, can be very tentatively put forward. Perhaps the 'Merton' version was written at Westminster for presentation to Edward II at his coronation to commemorate the acts of his father. His coronation was important in the history of the ceremony because of the compilation of a new coronation *ordo*. This *ordo* included a prayer that the king should succeed against enemies and rebels (and against the infidel):[154] the 'Merton' *Flores* particularly emphasizes the defeat of Simon de Montfort and the barons (even at the time of his coronation Edward II was subject to baronial pressure[155]), and Edward I's Scottish victories. The 'Merton' *Flores*, in its treatment of the baronial period, is emphatic that whatever Henry III's shortcomings, they did not vitiate his heirs' monarchical rights. 'Even if', it asserts, 'the intolerable prodigality or other defect of the king

---

[150] See pp. 455–6.

[151] See P. E. Schramm, *A History of the English Coronation*, translated from the German by L. G. Wickham Legg (Oxford 1937), pp. 40, 75, 80.

[152] See e.g. *FH*, vol. 3, pp. 253, 317. When the coronation *ordo* was revised in 1308, a direction was added concerning the anointing; Schramm, op. cit., p. 131. Wykes calls Henry III Christ's anointed, in a phrase borrowed from the Book of Psalms; *TW*, p. 134.

[153] See Plate XII. The coronation pictures in the Chetham MS. are fully described and reproduced by A. Hollaender, 'The pictorial work in the *Flores Historiarum* of the so-called Matthew of Westminster (MS. Chetham 6712)' in *BJRL*, xxviii (1944), pp. 361–81. The Chetham MS. has pictures of the coronations of Arthur, Edward the Confessor and of the later kings from William I to Edward I (the picture of Henry III's coronation is missing owing to loss of a leaf); all were executed at St Albans except the picture of Edward I's coronation which is Westminster work. The pictures in the Eton MS. are not copied from those in the Chetham MS.

[154] *Foedera*, vol. 2, pt i, p. 34; 'Tribue ei, optimus Deus . . . ut sit fortissimus regum, triumphator hostium, ad opprimendas rebelles et paganas nationes; sitque suis inimicis satis terribilis, praemaxima fortitudine regalis potentiae'.

[155] See Schramm, op. cit., pp. 76, 207.

clearly demanded the appointment of a guardian [*curator*], nevertheless both divine and human law provide that once the fault or defect ceases, the punishment is never transmitted to the heirs, lest the iniquity of the father should attend the son and the punishment exceed the crime'.[156] That the author wrote 'heirs' not 'heir' indicates that he was thinking further ahead than Edward I.

It may be postulated that the exemplar of the Eton College MS. was a *de luxe* book written at Westminster containing the so-called 'Merton' version of the *Flores*. This would explain why the coronation pictures in the Eton College MS. are of a better quality than the rather mediocre handwriting of the text seems to justify.[157] One of these illustrations provides evidence which may corroborate our hypothesis. The picture of Edward I's coronation shows the king holding in his left hand the rod with the dove (in his right hand he holds, as was customary, the sceptre with fleur-de-lis and orb).[158] The dove is carefully delineated: a much less well drawn dove appears in the picture of King John's coronation. The rod with the dove does not appear in the coronation pictures in the Chetham MS. The rod with the dove is not generally represented in fourteenth and fifteenth century art (though it was probably normally used in the coronation service at least from the time of Richard I). Instead of a dove the rod is usually represented with a floriated finial as it is in the other coronation pictures in the Eton College MS. It is surely likely that the artist's exemplar was executed at Westminster soon after Edward's funeral when the rod with the dove must have attracted especial attention because of its burial with the king. When Edward I's tomb was opened in 1774 he was found, in full regalia, holding the rod with the dove. The actual rod bore a remarkable similarity to the artist's representation.[159]

---

[156] *FH*, vol. 3, p. 254. The coronation *ordo* of 1308 laid especial emphasis on Edward II's succession by hereditary right. See Schramm, op. cit., pp. 166–7.

[157] I am indebted to Mr Patrick Strong, librarian of Eton College, and to the College authorities, for depositing Eton MS. 123 in the British Museum for me to study. The text is in one hand at least until 1285 when there is a change of ink, perhaps of hand. This is followed by occasional changes of ink, or hand, until 1294 when the hand is again fairly even until the end of 1298, when there may be a change of hand, and thereafter to the end. I do not think the evidence of the handwriting indicates that the 'Merton' *Flores* from about 1285 was compiled fairly close to the events recorded. The slight unevenness merely suggests casual changes of pen, ink – and perhaps scribe. The manuscript ends incomplete in 1306, because of loss of a leaf, but there is no reason to suppose that it did not once extend to the beginning of 1307 where the Westminster *Flores* ends, as do the descendants of the Eton MS. See *FH*, vol. 1, p. xvi.

[158] See Plate XII. For the rod with the dove see L. G. Wickham Legg, *English Coronation Records* (Westminster, 1901), pp. lii–liii. This dove appears in none of the pictures reproduced in ibid.

[159] Joseph Ayloffe, 'An account of the body of King Edward the First, as it appeared on opening his tomb in the year 1774' in *Archaeologia*, iii (1775), p. 384; 'Between the two fore-fingers and the thumb of his left-hand, he holds the rod or scepter with the dove, which, passing over his left shoulder, reaches up as high as his ear. This rod is five feet and half an inch in length. The stalk is divided into two equal parts, by a knob or fillet, and at its bottom is a flat ferule. The top of the stalk terminates in three bouquets, or tiers of oak-leaves, of green enamel, in

If the postulated Westminster book, written for presentation to Edward II on the occasion of his coronation, once existed,[160] it would seem likely that it included the notice of Edward I's funeral and the assessment of his achievements, which occur in the chronicle of Adam Murimuth who used Westminster material.[161] The passage specifically attributes to him, as the Lord Edward, the defeat of Simon de Montfort and the barons, and praises him for his Scottish victories, both of which subjects particularly concerned the author of the 'Merton' *Flores*.[162] The production of such a work for Edward II, perhaps at his request, is not intrinsically improbable. Nicholas Trevet wrote a history for Edward I's daughter Mary.[163] And a number of books and works of art (including the coronation throne in Westminster abbey) were executed for Edward I and for members of the royal family.[164]

Presumably the Merton copy would have been made almost immediately after the completion of its exemplar – perhaps it was unfinished, stopping before the notice of Edward I's funeral, because of lack of time (the Westminster book must have been written and illustrated between Edward I's death on 7 July 1307 and Edward II's coronation on 24 February 1308). After the coronation the original Westminster book would have been in Edward II's hands. Therefore would-be borrowers were forced to use the Merton copy, directly or indirectly.

A possible candidate for authorship of the 'Merton' *Flores* is John of London, probably to be identified with John Bever.[165] John of London was the author of the account of the robbery of the king's treasury at Westminster[166] and of the Lamentation on the death of Edward I (a panegyric

---

alto relievo, each bouquet diminishing in breadth as they approach towards the summit of the scepter, whereon stands a ball, or mound, surmounted by the figure of a dove, with its wings closed, and made of white enamel.'

[160] An alternative hypothesis would be that the Westminster exemplar of the Merton MS. was written to please Edward I, perhaps at his request. But this view does not explain as satisfactorily as the hypothesis here adopted the coronation picture of Edward I, the two extra lines of verse in the assessment of Edward in the Tenison MS. (see n. 161), nor that the final assessment of Edward, with the notice of his funeral, emphasizes the same points as the 'Merton' *Flores*. It would, however, explain why the 'Merton' text ended before Edward's death.

[161] *Adae Murimuth Continuatio Chronicarum*, ed. E. M. Thompson (Rolls series 1889). *Murimuth*, pp. 9–10. This passage is in the Tenison MS. (see Appendix D below), where the concluding verse has an extra two lines (see *FH*, vol. 1, p. xxx).

[162] Archbishop Parker printed the passage on Edward I's funeral and achievements from Murimuth, with a few additions of his own, as part of the *Flores*. See *FH*, vol. 1, p. xlvi.

[163] See p. 504.

[164] See Peter Brieger, *English Art 1216–1307* (Oxford 1957), chapter XII *passim*.

[165] See *HA*, vol. 1, p. xxv n. 1, and, for a more cautious approach, *Chronicles of the Reigns of Edward I and Edward II*, ed. W. Stubbs (RS, 1882–3, 2 vols), vol. 2, pp. xii–xiii. T. D. Hardy (*Catalogue*, vol. 3, p. 325) and F. Madden (*HA*, vol. 1, p. xxiv–xxv) both suggested that John Bever wrote the Westminster *Flores* from 1265 to 1307, but produced no substantial evidence for this view. This attribution faces the problem that the Westminster *Flores* explicitly cites a work by 'John' for its account of the robbery of the royal treasury in 1303. See n. 166.

[166] John's account of the burglary of the royal treasury in the Westminster *Flores* (*FH*, vol. 3, pp. 115–17) appears in a considerably shortened version in the 'Merton' *Flores* (ibid., pp. 313–14), no doubt because the full text was unflattering to Edward I.

on Edward's virtues and achievements put in the mouths of various people, prefaced with an account of his appearance and character).[167] Both works have strong stylistic resemblances to the 'Merton' *Flores*, making lavish use of biblical citations. Furthermore, the Lamentation has numerous rhetorical questions, exclamations and evocations reminiscent of passages in the 'Merton' *Flores*.[168] Bishop Stubbs commented on part of the Lamentation that it might 'almost ... have been spoken at [Edward's] funeral';[169] it certainly shows John of London's close interest in the king. If the identification of John of London with John Bever is correct, there is confirmatory evidence that he was the author of the 'Merton' *Flores*. For one copy of the 'Merton' *Flores*, a fourteenth-century manuscript from St Augustine's, Canterbury, has a medieval note attributing the work to John Bever, monk of Westminster.[170]

It should be noted that Robert of Reading, the Westminster monk who continued the *Flores* from 1306 to Edward II's abdication and Edward III's accession in 1327, closely resembles the author of the 'Merton' *Flores*.[171] He too wrote in a strongly homiletic style, replete with biblical citations. His consistent criticism of, and bitter invective against, Edward II, contrasting with his partisan defence of Edward III, Isabel and Mortimer, suggest that he wrote to justify their seizure of power. The only manuscript known of his chronicle is appended to the Westminster *Flores*[172] (he gives a brief notice of Edward I's funeral, apparently independent of the account of the funeral and assessment of Edward's achievements preserved in Murimuth). If Robert's chronicle ever existed as a continuation of the 'Merton' *Flores*, we

---

[167] i.e. the *Commendatio Lamentabilis in Transitu Magni Regis Edwardi*. Printed Stubbs, op. cit., vol. 2, pp. 3–21. See Beryl Smalley, *English Friars and Antiquity in the Early Fourteenth Century* (Oxford 1960), pp. 11–12.

[168] See especially the invocation of England in the 'Merton' *Flores*, which even has phrases verbally reminiscent of the Lamentation. E.g. the latter reads 'Gladii nostri conflabuntur in vomeres' and 'pax vigescit' (Stubbs, op. cit., vol. 2, p. 16), and the 'Merton' *Flores* 'gladiis conversis in vomeres, pax et religio viguerunt' (*FH*, vol. 3, p. 267). The Lamentation, like the 'Merton' *Flores*, emphasizes the desirability of peace; Stubbs, op. cit., vol. 2, pp. 19–20.

[169] Stubbs, op. cit., vol. 2, p. xvii.

[170] BM MS. Harley 641; described *FH*, vol. 1, pp. xxxi–xxxiii. The note at the end of the text of the *Flores* (f. 115ᵛ) reads 'Cronica de edicione domini Johannis dicti [Be]vere monachi Westmonasterii. De libraria sancti Augustini extra muros Cantuarie'. (For a similar note at the beginning of the volume see *FH*, vol. 1, p. xxxi.) The version of the 'Merton' *Flores* in the volume is slightly abbreviated and no use is made of it before the Norman Conquest. The chronicle begins with Bever's abbreviated version of Geoffrey of Monmouth, interspersed with verses, which also survives in Rawlinson MS. B 150 in the Bodleian library, and in BM MS. Cotton Titus D XII; for these verses see Jacob Hammer, 'The poetry of Johannes Beverus with extracts from his *Tractatus de Bruto Abbreviato*' in *Modern Philology*, xxxiv (1936), pp. 119–32. The interpolated verses include pairs of hexameters similar to those which are characteristic of the 'Merton' *Flores* (cf. *FH*, vol. 1, p. xliii), though a few also occur in the Westminster *Flores*.

[171] Robert of Reading apparently knew John of London well; *FH*, vol. 1, p. xliii n. 1.

[172] Robert of Reading's chronicle, which I shall discuss more fully in my next volume, is printed in *FH*, vol. 3, pp. 137–235. The text, preserved in the Chetham MS., is in one hand to 1325 and then in a later fourteenth-century hand to the end; see ibid., vol. 1, p. xiv.

should in fact have an 'official' history of England covering the period from Henry III's later years to Edward III's accession.

To discuss the contents of the 'Merton' *Flores* in more detail: it gives a résumé of events culminating in the battle of Lewes. Here the views typical of other chronicles are reversed. The author denigrates the barons and justifies the monarchy. He calls the baronial leaders 'princes of faction', so many kings or governors (and England, like Rome, could not support many kings). Few were moved by patriotism, but most by hate, ambition and greed – when in power they left no money for God or Caesar.[173] They gave a specious appearance of equity and justice to the Provisions (here called *proditiones* instead of *provisiones*)[174] of Oxford. And they refused, contrary to canon law, to accept that the pope could absolve men from their oath to observe the Provisions, because they had been agreed 'by common consent', confirmed by oath, and no other consent could dissolve them.[175] But on the contrary, the author argues, the king could have annulled them 'by common consent' – only his scruples made him seek papal absolution. The author uses an ingenious argument to explain the support gained by Simon de Montfort. He accuses Simon of cleverly exploiting men's hatred of the bishop of Hereford (who was universally disliked for fraudulently involving monasteries in debt): Simon turned men into criminals dependent on his protection by encouraging illegal attacks on the bishop's and other aliens' property. Thus 'through hatred of the bishop, he bound people to him, paying his supporters with the spoils, and as they were therefore transgressors despairing both of papal and royal mercy, necessity compelled them to support him wholeheartedly.'[176]

The author defends Henry III. He praises his clemency, attributing his negotiations with the barons after the battle of Lewes to anxiety for the lives of prisoners held by the barons.[177] And he defends Henry's right to endow his relatives. But even this author could not condone all Henry's acts. He attributes baronial discontent partly to jealousy caused by royal gifts to foreign favourites and accuses him of 'intolerable prodigality' and other faults which necessitated the appointment of a guardian (*curator*) of the kingdom. But the author insists on the ultimate legitimacy of monarchy: both divine and human law stipulated that once a fault had been corrected the punishment should cease; certainly such punishment should not pass on to Henry's heirs. He attributes the civil war mainly to the bitterness aroused by papal provisions and by taxes for the Sicilian venture.[178]

The section in the 'Merton' *Flores* on the baronial period can be read as a paean on peace. It represents Henry as a man of peace and monarchical government as the custodian of peace. It regards Henry's restoration to due

---

[173] Ibid., vol. 3, pp. 252–4.
[174] Ibid., pp. 265–6. The 'Merton' *Flores* also attacks the pro-baronial bishops; ibid., pp. 262–3.
[175] Ibid., p. 255.
[176] Ibid., pp. 256–7.
[177] Ibid., p. 260.
[178] See ibid., pp. 252–3.

power in his 'perfect and spacious vineyard' as the restoration of peace.[179] The author praises peace both explicitly and (by contrasting it with the horrors of civil war) implicitly. He begins with a lamentation on the state to which the Provisions of Oxford reduced England.[180] They caused

> strife, looting and burning. The depredation of churches, the persecution of clergy, sieges of castles, the tribulations of cities, the disinheritance of great men, the groans of the poor, the oppression of ordinary folk, the ransoming of captives, the deaths of old people, the misery of orphans, the rape and groans of virgins, the tears and grief of widows, war and sedition, and other evils and ills.

After the notice of the battle of Evesham the author exhorts England, using historical arguments and patriotic appeal, to abandon civil war. He demonstrates the advantages of this course by comparing her then plight with her past prosperity. Now she is torn by internal anarchy which has destroyed ties of blood and bonds of honour, so that son rages against father, brother against brother, servant against master and flocks against their pastors. Formerly England had had every beauty of sky and earth, was blessed throughout the world. The sea was a wall and the ports guarded by strong castles were doors. Commerce with Europe, Africa and Asia prospered. Swords were turned into ploughshares, and peace and religion flourished.[181]

Peace in the north of England was to be achieved by Edward I, the architect of the aggressive policy against Scotland and the commander of the army. The laudatory attitude to Edward I, characteristic of the 'Merton' *Flores*, particularly appears in the account of the siege of Stirling,[182] an elaboration of the corresponding passage in the Westminster *Flores*.[183] Edward was brave, wise and just. He began by trying to 'kindle people's enthusiasm for the war' with a speech justifying his policy on historical grounds. During the siege the angel of the Lord protected Edward from blows of the devil. The description of the siege of Stirling is a good example of the author's propensity for weaving biblical quotations into the text, in order to embellish Edward's *persona* as the Lord's anointed. For example Edward's address to the soldiers ends: 'We undertook a just war in the name of the Lord, and on this account "I will not be afraid what man can do unto me" (Ps. 55. 11); "because He is at my right hand, I shall", therefore, "be moved" (Ps. 15. 8) very little.' And Edward's soldiers, reproving him for going unarmed too near the walls, said: '"Knew ye not that they would shoot from the wall? Who smote Abimelech the son of Jerubbesheth? did not a woman cast an upper millstone upon him from the wall, that he died at Thebez?" (2 Kings 11. 20, 21). Stay in the pavilions "for if we flee away, they will not care for us; neither if half of us die, will they care for us, but

---

[179] Ibid., p. 266. [130] Ibid., p. 248. [181] Ibid., pp. 266–8.
[182] Ibid., pp. 316–19. [183] Ibid., pp. 118–20.

[you alone] art worth ten thousand of us"' (2 Kings 18. 3). And when Edward's horse slipped and fell, it is compared with Balaam's ass.[184]

The author of the 'Merton' *Flores* can hardly be said to have based his royalist attitudes on careful historical analysis. However, the views of Thomas Wykes were founded on more rational principles. He was the best informed and the most intelligent of all the Augustinian chroniclers to be considered. His chronicle covers the years from 1066 to 1289. It has much in common with the Osney chronicle until 1256 (probably both chronicles used the same exemplar).[185] From 1256 to 1278 it is quite independent of the Osney chronicle. And from 1278 to 1289 it is again closely related to the Osney chronicle: it is likely that Wykes wrote this section of both chronicles[186] and continued the Osney chronicle to 1290 or 1293.[187]

How it happened that Osney abbey produced two chronicles with such a complicated relationship is not clear. But some facts are known about Wykes's life which suggest a partial explanation. His own chronicle records that he was born in 1222[188] and became a canon of Osney in 1282[189] – so he was already about sixty years old when he entered religion. The cartulary of Osney abbey has information about his private life.[190] He became rector of Caister St Edmunds before 1270 and owned property in Oxford, including a house called Elm Hall. He gave six cottages to Osney in 1269/70. Meanwhile he was living in London, only moving to Oxford in about 1274. In 1279 he gave a messuage in London to Osney. The Osney charters show that Wykes knew two well-known Dominicans, John Trussebut, a scholar of Cambridge, and Gilbert, former prior of Nuneaton who became a Dominican at Oxford in 1249.[191] The detailed notices in Wykes's chronicle concerning the career of Philip of Eye suggest the possibility that Wykes knew him.[192]

---

[184] Ibid., p. 318.

[185] For the structure of Wykes's chronicle and its relationship to the Osney chronicle see p. 429 n. 257.

[186] See N. Denholm-Young, 'Thomas Wykes and his chronicle' in *EHR*, lxi (1946), p. 173.

[187] Mr Denholm-Young, ibid., p. 178, suggests that Wykes wrote the Osney chronicle from 1278 to 1290 and that someone else continued it to 1293. However the similarity between the passage under 1292 condemning both the papal tax and the king's avarice (*Osney*, pp. 332–3) to the passage in Wykes on the papal tax granted to Henry III in 1269 (*TW*, p. 225) suggests that Luard's view that Wykes continued the Osney chronicle to 1293 may be correct; see *Ann. Mon.*, vol. 4, p. xv.

[188] This is the interpretation put by Mr Denholm-Young ('Thomas Wykes and his chronicle', pp. 157–8) on the entry under 1221, 'Natus est Thomas in vigilia sancti Gregorii'; *TW*, p. 62.

[189] *TW*, pp. 291–2. For references to members of Wykes's family in his chronicle see *TW*, pp. 96 (the death of Robert de Wykes *s.a.* 1246), 230 (the death of Edith de Wyks *s.a.* 1269), 295 (a notice that John de Wykes took his vows at Osney *s.a.* 1283).

[190] For references to Thomas Wykes in the Osney cartulary see the index to the printed edition (see p. 430 n. 261 above). The evidence in the cartulary and elsewhere about Wykes and his connections is fully described and discussed by Denholm-Young, 'Thomas Wykes and his chronicle', pp. 157–79 *passim*.

[191] See ibid., p. 159.

[192] See p. 431 and n. 268. For entries in Wykes concerning Philip of Eye see *TW*, pp. 247, 256, 271. Cf. Denholm-Young, 'Thomas Wykes and his chronicle', pp. 159–60.

Wykes therefore was a man of substance with important connections before he entered Osney. He had already formed his opinions and his loyalties. It seems likely that when he became a canon he used the existing Osney chronicle only up to 1256 because after that date it did not coincide with his own interests and opinions. For example his close interest in Richard of Cornwall's career was not fully shared by the Osney chronicle. And, unlike the Osney chronicle, he sympathized with the king, not the barons, during the baronial period (it should be noted that although Wykes's account of the Barons' War is a good piece of narrative it has not the contemporary value of the corresponding passage in the Osney chronicle). The section from 1256 to 1278 is virtually a secular chronicle (there are no references to Osney, but there is one to Oxford, under 1275[193]). Wykes may have written this section after 1282[194] when he had become a canon. Alternatively perhaps he completed it in London, between about 1275 and 1282, and took it to Osney. It seems likely that he was appointed official chronicler at Osney, and added the annals from 1278 to 1289 to both his own and the abbey chronicle.

Wykes's secular experience is reflected in his work. His detailed knowledge of Richard of Cornwall's public life[195] and tendency to eulogize him may indicate closer connections than any acquired through an acquaintance with Philip of Eye: perhaps he had been employed by him in some official capacity, possibly as his chaplain.[196] After a paragraph of general entries, Wykes begins the section of his chronicle independent of the Osney chronicle, with details of Richard's election as king of the Romans: he names the electors and gives the price paid by Richard for the election.[197] Under 1257 Wykes notes Richard's departure for Germany and describes his coronation at Aachen ('and with him was crowned his most serene wife Sanchia, whose inestimable beauty greatly adorned the ceremony: a solemn feast followed which in the opinion of the princes and great men present had no parallel in modern times').[198] Particularly remarkable is a long passage about Richard's tour of his kingdom in 1269, when he found that the German lords in the castles by the Rhine were terrorizing merchants on the river 'requiring or rather extorting money' and stopping at no sort of crime, 'without fear of God or respect for the royal dignity'. So Richard held a meeting of German magnates at Worms and abolished all tolls on the Rhine,

---

[193] *TW*, p. 264. This entry records that Edward entered Oxford despite the ancient superstition.

[194] For Wykes's dates and method of composition see Denholm-Young, 'Thomas Wykes and his chronicle', p. 177.

[195] See ibid., p. 160 n. 2.

[196] This is suggested by Denholm-Young, ibid., p. 160. However, the fact that Wykes records nothing personal about Richard or his family perhaps militates against the likelihood of the suggestion. There is of course the possibility that Wykes used some pre-existing biography of Richard.

[197] *TW*, pp. 111–16.

[198] *TW*, pp. 116–17.

except at Boppard and Kaiserwerth, in order to restore peace for necessary commerce.[199]

Wykes gives a detailed account of Richard's political influence in England. He deplores the fact that Richard was in Germany when the barons seized power in 1258: 'while he was in England he guided the king and the governing of the kingdom; all business of state had depended on his will'.[200] The barons acted, Wykes alleges, because they thought Richard would never return and saw Henry mismanaging affairs. Wykes is careful to point out that Richard subsequently submitted to the barons only under duress[201] (his shameful imprisonment was 'unfitting for a king'[202]). He also describes Richard's activities as mediator after the Barons' War. Richard was 'the most fervent enthusiast for the tranquillity of the realm',[203] negotiating peace between Henry III and the disinherited in 1269,[204] and between Edward and the earl of Gloucester in 1269 and 1270.[205] And Wykes records under 1269 that Richard, 'who always had enough money', was able to relieve Henry's impecuniousness by provisioning the royal army sent against the disinherited.[206]

One of the most graphic passages concerns the attacks on Richard's manor at Isleworth and his palace at Westminster by baronial supporters in 1263.[207] A 'furious crowd' from London led by Hugh le Despenser ('whom the barons called justiciar') went 'in the evening, by a straight route, with a few banners to the manor of the lord king of the Romans and burnt the manor, which he had surrounded with a ditch and fence, and some of his buildings, and seized for their own use all the movables they found there, with wicked daring. They emptied not only the water but also the fish from a certain pond which the king had had constructed with enterprising skill, having broken the dam providing a powerful barrier against the current of the water.' The rabble next went to Richard's mansion at Westminster, 'not leaving one stone upon another which they thought he needed, ripping out bushes, tiles and thatch, and taking all the stone they could from the towers.' Attacks followed on other houses in London and its suburbs, including the manor of Walter de Merton 'because he was chancellor' (he was also the founder of Merton college at Oxford).[208]

Wykes's residence in London is reflected in his detailed information

<hr />

[199] *TW*, pp. 222–4. See Denholm-Young, *Richard of Cornwall* (Oxford 1947), p. 140.
[200] *TW*, p. 118.
[201] *TW*, pp. 121–2.
[202] *TW*, p. 175.
[203] *TW*, p. 231.
[204] *TW*, p. 205.
[205] *TW*, pp. 229, 231–3.
[206] *TW*, p. 204. For Richard's loans to Henry III and Edward I see Denholm-Young, *Richard of Cornwall*, pp. 65–6, 157–61 *passim*.
[207] *TW*, pp. 140–1. For the attack on Isleworth and the mansion at Westminster see Denholm-Young, *Richard of Cornwall*, pp. 120 n. 4, 126, 132, 139.
[208] For other notices of him in Wykes see *TW*, pp. 260, 275. Cf. *Osney*, p. 275.

about the city. He has a vivid description of the attack on Queen Isabel in 1263 as she sailed up the Thames from the Tower to Westminster. When she reached London bridge, 'an infinite number of Londoners' shouted abuse at her, calling her a whore and adulteress and pelting her 'with stones, filthy mud, broken eggs and all sorts of disgusting projectiles'.[209] Wykes hated the London mob which supported the barons in 1263 and Gilbert of Gloucester in 1267. Under 1263 he speaks of the 'vast multitude of ribalds who call themselves bachelors',[210] who seized power from 'the seniors and wisest men in the city' and involved the whole community in trouble. In 1267 he accuses the Londoners of 'fantastic conceit' and describes how they flung the king's supporters from bridges and boats, and tore the doors and windows from the palace of Westminster, and looted as far afield as Kent and Surrey.[211]

But Wykes loved London itself, 'the city not unjustly called the capital of our kingdom.'[212] He respected the rich citizens and despite their involvement in the Barons' War, he thought that Henry III treated them too severely afterwards. He disapproved of the way the king persuaded the chief citizens to come to him at Windsor in 1265, promising a truce, and then 'less honestly than became the royal dignity' ignominiously imprisoned them.[213] Wykes also disapproved of the large sum of money Henry extorted from them in the same year: to make matters worse the money did little to replenish the king's treasury as most of it went abroad to pay the queen's creditors.[214] Moreover, Wykes respected the wealthy Jewish community in London. The Londoners attacked it in 1263: they were, Wykes said, not only 'forgetful of humanity and piety,' but moved more by greed (hoping 'to relieve their poverty with other people's money') than by 'zeal for the law'. Wykes expatiated eloquently on the Londoners' cruelty in murdering all those Jews who did not pay large sums or allow themselves to be baptized.[215] One of those killed was Kok son of Abraham,[216] 'the most famous Jew in the city and the richest in England'.

One reason why Wykes deplored this destruction of the London Jewry was financial. He says the damage done to the royal treasury was inestimable, as revenues from tallage on the Jews, from pleas, gifts, escheats, and the like,

---

[209] *TW*, p. 136.
[210] *TW*, p. 138. Wykes's hatred of such 'ribalds' extended to those in all cities and towns in England. He writes that on account of the wicked example of the Londoners 'per universum regnum Angliae consuetudo detestabilis inolevit, quod in omnibus paene civitatibus et burgis fieret conjuratio ribaldorum qui se bachilarios publice proclamabant, et majores urbium et burgorum violentis ausibus opprimebant'; *TW*, p. 138. See also p. 469 below.
[211] *TW*, pp. 203.
[212] *TW*, p. 260.
[213] *TW*, pp. 176-7.
[214] *TW*, p. 184.
[215] *TW*, p. 141-2. Wykes's attitude resembles that of William of Newburgh (see p. 265 above) who does not, however, mention the financial value of the Jews to the king.
[216] i.e. Isaac fil' Aaron. For him and the London massacre see C. Roth, *A History of the Jews in England* (Oxford 1964), p. 61 and n. 3.

greatly augmented the royal income. He makes the same point in his account of the expulsion of the Jews in 1290.[217] He states that some people said the sailors from the Cinque Ports who were ferrying the Jews across the channel attacked and robbed them, throwing some overboard. Again Wykes deplores the inhumanity of their treatment and again states that the royal treasury suffered (he alleges that the expulsion of the Jews made the tax of one-fifteenth on movables necessary).

Wykes's concern for the Jews as a capital asset may have been derived from his interest in Richard of Cornwall who obtained the farm of the English Jewry in 1255.[218] But it also reflects his interest in the king's finances and Exchequer. He has a number of entries on the subject, though no very profound knowledge of it.[219] He notes that the Exchequer moved from Westminster to the palace at St Paul's in 1261.[220] He records the resignation as treasurer of Philip of Eye in 1273 and the succession of Sir Joseph Chauncy, prior of the Hospital of St John of Jerusalem in England, 'who had cleverly borrowed money from merchants while the king was in Sicily and conscientiously repaid it.'[221] Under 1289 he deplores the alienation in fee of the chamberlainship of the Exchequer by the countess of Devon to Adam de Stratton.[222] And under 1290 he gives details on the death of John de Kirkby, bishop of Ely, who 'had energetically exercised the office of treasurer of the king's Exchequer',[223] and notices the election to the bishopric of Ely of William of Louth, who, he says, had been a good treasurer of the Wardrobe for a long time.[224]

Wykes criticizes the king's extravagance. He remarks that Henry and his associates distributed the property of the disinherited barons stupidly after the battle of Evesham, regardless of the country's future financial needs.[225] In 1268 he says that the royal treasury had little benefit from the tax on the clergy, because of Henry's habitual prodigality: the money 'was lavished on aliens through the ineptitude of the king; just as the mist passes away at dawn, or the clouds are dispersed in the face of the sun's rays, or smoke vanishes, it was squandered and allowed to slip through his fingers.'[226] And Wykes accuses Edward I of spending a vast sum of English money on the Gascon war to no purpose.[227]

---

[217] *Osney*, p. 327. For this incident see C. Roth, op. cit., p. 86, who adopts the account in Walter of Guisborough (see p. 472 n. 268 below).

[218] See Denholm-Young, 'Thomas Wykes and his chronicle', pp. 159–60.

[219] See ibid., pp. 161–2.

[220] *TW*, p. 125. See Denholm-Young, 'Thomas Wykes and his chronicle', p. 161.

[221] *TW*, p. 256.

[222] *Osney*, p. 321. See Denholm-Young, 'Thomas Wykes and his chronicle', p. 162.

[223] *Osney*, p. 323.

[224] *Osney*, p. 325.

[225] *TW*, p. 183.

[226] *TW*, p. 220. Similarly he remarks that the tax of a twentieth in 1269 seemed to add little to the royal treasury; *TW*, p. 228.

[227] *TW*, p. 256.

Wykes was interested in commerce: this appears in the mention of Richard of Cornwall's abolition of tolls on the Rhine and also in the account of the Barons' War and its aftermath. He points out that the prosperity of Northampton, Winchester and Norwich, 'very flourishing' cities, was ruined by the depredations of the barons.[228] And he has a powerful invective against the damage done by the baronial party to foreign trade in 1264. He alleges that Henry de Montfort won the name of 'wool merchant' by seizing the wool of English, Flemish and other merchants.[229] He accuses the men of the Cinque Ports of stopping trade by raiding the ships of foreigners and English alike, and by killing the merchants 'who bring us necessary goods'.[230] As a result, he says, the price of imports rose, the merchants were reduced to penury and export was impossible. He alleges that Simon de Montfort made public that the English 'could live comfortably on their own produce without foreign trade'. However, Wykes comments, 'this was impossible, as the mutual exchange of goods with foreign countries supplies all sorts of useful commodities'. He adds that 'many people wishing to please the earl wore only white cloth, scorning coloured materials in case he thought they were begging for foreign necessities.'[231] Again under 1293 Wykes laments damage to foreign trade caused by Philip IV's prohibition of commerce with England.[232]

In view of Wykes's interest in Richard of Cornwall and in the central government it is not surprising that he emphasized the importance of royal authority. He clearly states his position under 1258. He says that the barons took 'counsel together against the Lord' (Ps. ii. 2) and their king 'His anointed' and almost deprived him of power, appointing the twenty-four to govern the king and kingdom better and more happily than it used to be. 'And thus,' Wykes comments, 'the order of natural law was wrongly altered completely so that the king who was bound to rule his subjects was ruled by his subjects, and *vice versa*.'[233] Similarly, when describing Henry's dishonourable captivity, Wykes says that the order of law and nature were reversed: Simon de Montfort was not ashamed 'to rule his king' and elevated himself to such an extent that 'the name of earl quite overshadowed that of royal highness'.[234]

Wykes's dislike of Simon de Montfort and the other barons was almost unmitigated. He accuses Simon de Montfort of pride and greed (in the division of the royalists' property after the battle of Lewes),[235] and of

---

[228] *TW*, pp. 145, 169, 193. [229] *TW*, pp. 158–9. [230] *TW*, pp. 157–8.

[231] *TW*, p. 158. For this passage criticizing the doctrine of self-sufficiency which Wykes probably unfairly attributes to Simon de Montfort, see F. M. Powicke, *Henry III and the Lord Edward* (Oxford 1947, 2 vols), vol. 2, p. 515 and n. 3. Guisborough (*WG*, p. 186) states that the barons at Winchester in 1258 prohibited the export of wool and ordered only English cloth to be worn. Treharne, who accepts Wykes's statement, suggests that the 'statutes' mentioned by Guisborough are probably due to ante-dating Simon's legislation on these matters in 1264; R. F. Treharne, *The Baronial Plan of Reform, 1258–1263* (Manchester 1932), p. 80.

[232] *Osney*, pp. 335–6. [233] *TW*, p. 119. [234] *TW*, p. 153.

[235] *TW*, pp. 136, 153, 161.

recklessly promoting his sons' interests.[236] The barons were moved 'less by zeal for justice than by greed for temporal gain'[237] and were unstable in their loyalties (Simon's exploitation of their fickleness enabled him 'to subjugate the vulgar people more easily and freely').[238] Wykes particularly remarks on the youth of some of the baronial supporters, young noblemen 'whom we could truly call by the epithet[239] boys' and whom the barons could mould 'like soft wax'.[240] The spectacle of two noble youths killed at Evesham moved Wykes to pity. He asks who would not weep for the deaths of John de Mandeville and John de Beauchamp: 'both excelled their contemporaries in elegant appearance and were not unjustly excused by their rash youth.'[241]

Wykes (like the 'Barnwell' chronicle) had a strong dislike of the 'common people', which emerges in his comments on the London 'rabble'[242] and on the other townsmen 'who publicly proclaim themselves "bachelors" and violently oppose the civic authorities so that law loses its force.'[243] Like many other chroniclers he strongly expresses his hatred of civil disorder and love of peace. He has an eloquent passage in praise of the peace established in 1267. He compares the present plenty, from which the ordinary people greatly benefited (notably from the quantity of wine available), with the previous looting and confusion. Knights, he says, formerly engaged in war now go to tournaments for recreation.[244]

Wykes's conviction that royal power was the keystone of government did not prevent his criticizing Henry III and Edward I for their actual exercise of office (his personal loyalty was to Richard of Cornwall). As has been seen, he thought Henry's treatment of the Londoners in 1265 dishonourable and more than once condemns his extravagance. After the surrender of London to Henry in 1267 Wykes thought his continued stay there served no useful purpose, for he and his household merely consumed the last remnants of food in the city.[245] He considered Edward I's expulsion of the Jews damaging to English finances, and under 1290 and 1292 calls his taxes intolerable,[246] and also accuses him of insatiable avarice. But earlier in the reign Wykes praises Edward – he was 'the flower of the army',[247] 'of leonine courage'[248] and 'ignorant of fear'.[249] He particularly approves of his legislation: in 1275 he says that Edward summoned parliament, 'wishing, as he ought, to please the people and to revive and restore to their former state

---

[236] *TW*, p. 153.   [237] *TW*, p. 134.   [238] *TW*, p. 160.

[239] 'autonomatice' in *TW*, p. 134. For the meaning of this word see Murray, *New English Dictionary*, under 'Autonomasy' and 'Antonomasia', and C. Dufresne du Cange, *Glossarium mediae et infimiae Latinitatis*, ed. G. A. L. Henschel (Paris 1840–57, 8 vols), vol. 1, p. 507, under 'Authonomatice'.

[240] *TW*, pp. 133–4.   [241] *TW*, p. 174.

[242] See *TW*, pp. 138, 148, 150.   [243] See p. 466 and n. 210.

[244] *TW*, pp. 211–12.   [245] *TW*, p. 207.

[246] *Osney*, pp. 326, 333.   [247] *TW*, p. 150.

[248] *TW*, p. 173.   [249] *TW*, p. 173.

neglected laws which, on account of his predecessors' impotence and the disturbance of the realm, and indeed through the abuse of wrongful usage, had long lain dormant.'[250] He has a very similar comment under 1285, on the issue of the statute of Westminster II.[251]

Of the two north-country Augustinian chroniclers, Walter of Guisborough and Peter of Langtoft, only Walter wrote even approximately in the tradition of the monastic chroniclers. He, like the typical monastic writer, held moderately pro-baronial views. His attitude to politics is well illustrated by his account of the Barons' War. He favoured Simon de Montfort, comparing him with Simon Maccabeus (just as the latter had fought to the death for the people of the Lord and the law of the fathers, so de Montfort fought and died for the laws and liberties of England).[252] He was brave and indomitable and was 'martyred' asking for God's mercy.[253] But his sons are criticized. Walter attributes Simon's downfall partly to the pride of his sons.[254] Walter, in his assessment of Henry III, calls him artless (*simplex*) in temporal affairs, but appreciates his piety ('he was a devout, religious man . . . so profuse in pious gifts that many churches of the saints, and especially Westminster, benefited from his alms, in addition to his generous largess to the poor').[255]

Walter has some information about the battle of Evesham which, though in a highly dramatized form, seems quite credible. He describes how the barons made a mistake which contributed to their defeat, in identifying the approaching army. The mistake was due, he says, to a deliberate trick. The barons were misled by false armorial bearings into thinking that the forces were those of Simon de Montfort junior, brought from Kenilworth to relieve the barons: in fact they were royalist. Walter relates:

> When Nicholas, the earl [of Leicester]'s scout (he was his barber who was skilled in the knowledge of arms) saw the army approaching from afar he said to the earl: 'Look, soldiers are coming from the north, and, as far as I can see in the distance, the banners are yours.' And [Simon] said, 'It is my son. Do not be afraid, but go and look around in case we are surrounded.'

Then the scout went up the abbey tower and clearly saw ('for they had raised other banners by then') Edward's banner on the one side, the earl of Gloucester's on the other and, behind, Roger Mortimer's.[256] Walter also has a unique account of the capture of Henry III. The king was struck on the shoulder by Sir Adam de Mowhaut and, Walter says, 'he cried out loudly,

---

[250] *TW*, p. 263.
[251] *Osney* and *TW*, p. 304.
[252] *WG*, p. 185.
[253] *WG*, pp. 191, 201.
[254] *WG*, pp. 197, 201. Cf. pp. 435, 469 above, 479 below.
[255] *WG*, p. 212.
[256] *WG*, p. 200. For the importance of this reference to Nicholas the barber in heraldic history see A. R. Wagner, *Heralds and Heraldry in the Middle Ages* (Oxford 1939), p. 48, and N. Denholm-Young, *History and Heraldry 1254–1310*, p. 58.

"I am Henry of Winchester, your king. Don't kill me!" For he was an ingenuous man, of peaceful not martial ways.'[257]

However, Walter is not on the whole a reliable authority for the Barons' War, because he wrote in the next generation, either at the end of the thirteenth century or at the beginning of the fourteenth.[258] His chronicle is most important, particularly for north-country affairs, for the last years of Edward I's reign. He seems to have written the chronicle to 1301 'at a sitting', so to speak, and then to have continued it to 1305. He and others added further annals to 1312. He used various sources, including north-country ones.[259] His principal source to 1198 was William of Newburgh, supplemented by the *Historia post Obitum Bedae*. For the thirteenth century he used Martin Polonus's *Chronicon Pontificum et Imperatorum*, saints' Lives, a history of the founders of Guisborough priory, and probably a lost chronicle of Bridlington.

From 1198 to 1291 the chronicle is mainly thin and annalistic. It becomes more detailed from 1291 and in places seems to derive from the same source as Peter of Langtoft.[260] Walter treats a number of subjects of national importance *en bloc* rather than annalistically: these sections are, as it were, monographs, with flashbacks where necessary to elucidate the theme.[261] Walter treats in this way the account of Edward I's Welsh campaign in 1282,[262] Anglo-Scottish relations from 1291 to 1300,[263] the Gascon campaign in 1293,[264] and Edward's dealings with the barons from 1296 to 1297.[265] Another characteristic of Walter is his love of a good story, a predilection shared by Peter of Langtoft and the Lanercost chronicle. He particularly liked to dramatize events (as for example in his account of the battle of Evesham), making free use of direct speech. Such dramatization was not necessarily at the expense of accuracy. It can be proved that one formal speech is authentic – that delivered by Roger Brabazon at the meeting at Norham in 1291 when Edward tried the Scottish succession case. Walter gives the speech in Latin, remarking that it was delivered in French: the original French version has survived.[266]

---

[257] *WG*, p. 201.
[258] Walter originally intended the chronicle to go to 1300; *WG*, p. 2. For the evidence on the date of compilation see *WG*, pp. xxx–xxxi.
[259] For Walter's sources see *WG*, pp. xxv–xxvii.
[260] See pp. 475–6 and nn., 483 and nn.
[261] See the résumé of events leading up to the Scottish succession case in 1291; *WG*, pp. 232–7. For another example of a flashback see the account of the relations of the monks of St Cuthbert's, Durham, with the archbishop of York and the bishop of Durham; see p. 474 below.
[262] *WG*, pp. 218–22.
[263] See n. 261 above; and *WG*, pp. 323–45. Cf. ibid., p. 238 n. 1.
[264] *WG*, pp. 240–8.
[265] *WG*, pp. 284–94, 308–13. Professor Rothwell writes that these pages 'stand out quite clearly as units of a very deliberate composition'; *WG*, p. xxvii.
[266] *WG*, pp. 234–5 and n. 1.

Nevertheless Walter's love of the dramatic could lead him to sacrifice accuracy to literary effect. For instance the speech ascribed to Archbishop Winchelsey in the convocation of the clergy in January 1297 is most unlikely to be genuine, as it almost certainly contains an anachronism. As the other authorities do not confirm that the archbishop at this early date demanded papal permission before making a grant to the king, it looks as if Walter composed the speech in the light of later events.[267] Again, the account of the parliament at Salisbury in February 1297 is dramatized to the point of inaccuracy. Here Roger Bigod, earl marshal and earl of Norfolk, and the constable, Humphrey de Bohun earl of Hereford, are represented as making speeches in opposition to the king's demand that the barons should accompany him on his Gascon campaign. But it is improbable that Hereford was at this parliament at all.[268]

Walter tells a number of etiological stories of varying degrees of credibility. A clearly legendary story is the one he uses to explain how Anthony Bek came to lead an army against the Scots and burn Dirleton castle (in East Lothian) in 1298. The story's object was probably partly to justify Bek's military activities. King Edward, Walter relates, sent Sir John Fitz Marmaduke to Bek with instructions to order the bishop to burn three castles held by the Scots, and to tell him that though as a bishop he was a man of piety, piety had no place in this business. Apparently to underline the need for violence Edward said to Sir John himself: 'You are a bloodthirsty man and I have often rebuked you for rejoicing in the death of your enemies. But now go and exert all your cruelty; I shall praise not blame you.' And God helped the besiegers, for they were relieved by three boatloads of provisions.[269] Apart from the inherent improbability of the story, the recurrence of the numeral three betrays its legendary nature. And though Walter asserts that Bek fired three castles, he only names Dirleton.[270]

On the other hand, Walter tells what must surely be a true story to explain how the fire started which burnt Guisborough priory to the ground in 1289. He relates that a workman went up on to the church roof with two boys, to repair the leading. He put two iron braziers in the gutters above the dry woodwork of the vaulting and on the crossing. He came down after the convent had celebrated mass mistakenly thinking the boys had extinguished the fires. A lively wind rose at midday and the heat of the iron and the sparks melted the lead and lit the woodwork.[271] Walter's account of how the fire started at Boston in 1288 is less credible, though not impossible. According

---

[267] See *WG*, pp. xxviii, 287.

[268] See *WG*, pp. xxviii–xxix, 289–90. Similarly Walter's account of the ill-treatment of the Jews on their expulsion from England in 1290 appears to be over-dramatized; *WG*, pp. 266–7. A less highly coloured and more convincing account is in the chronicle of Thomas Wykes; see *Osney*, p. 327 and p. 467 and n. 217 above.

[269] *WG*, pp. 324–5.

[270] However for a contrary view see G. W. S. Barrow, *Robert Bruce* (London 1965), pp. 140–1.

[271] *WG*, pp. 225–6.

to Walter, some young knights who held a tournament there decided after the mock battle (in which one side was dressed as monks, the other as regular canons) to rob the fair, and set alight 'the small tents and huts' in three or four places.[272]

Another example of an etiological story which may or may not be true gives the immediate cause of the outbreak of war between England and France in 1293. The initial conflict between the English and the Norman sailors began because two English sailors from a ship anchored in a Norman port brawled with some local sailors when they went to draw water from a spring: 'being angered by them they were moved to words, then to blows, and at length swords being drawn, one was killed and the other fled.' The latter boarded his ship which immediately set sail, the Normans in pursuit, and got the help of some other English ships. And so war began at sea.[273]

Each story, therefore, must be judged for credibility on its merits. And in assessing Walter's reliability as a historian, his respect for documents and his excellent sources of information should be weighed against his love of the dramatic. As has been seen he drew on an authentic source for Roger Brabazon's speech at Norham in 1291. And he preserves good texts of documents relating to the quarrel between king and barons in 1297, that is of the baronial *Monstrraunces*[274] and of *De tallagio non concedendo*.[275] Walter drew his information from three main sources, his own priory, other religious houses, especially Augustinian ones, and apparently from people connected with important laymen holding lands near by or otherwise in contact with the priory.

Walter obtained his details about Scottish attacks in 1296 on the English living in Scotland from two canons from the Augustinian priory at St Andrews who took refuge at Guisborough.[276] They told him how the Scots 'bound old men, the religious and women, seated them on bridges, and then pushed them off', and killed three people who had taken sanctuary in the priory in St Andrews. Walter also has details about looting of the Augustinian priory of Hexham by the Scots in the same year, which was mitigated by the personal intervention of William Wallace (the text of his

---

272 *WG*, pp. 224–5. This passage is quoted by Thomas Allen, *The History of the County of Lincoln* (London 1834, 2 vols), vol. 1, p. 220. Walter says that the ringleader was a knight called Robert Chamberlayn who was executed for his part in the affair. No one of that name occurs in connection with the fire in the printed calendars of public records. For two Sir Robert le Chamberlains at this period, both of whom survived into the fourteenth century, see C. Moor, *Knights of Edward I* (Harleian Soc. lxxx–lxxxiv, 1929–32, 5 vols), vol. 1, pp. 189–90. For the commission of oyer and terminer dealing with the culprits see *CPR, 1281–1292*, pp. 319, 329, 330, 397, 401.

273 *WG*, p. 240. This alleged incident is not mentioned by G. P. Cuttino, *English Diplomatic Administration 1259–1339* (Oxford 1950), who, however, discusses piracy as a source of conflict between England and France from 1293 (ibid., pp. 50, 59 n. 4).

274 See *WG*, pp. xxix, 292–3.

275 See *WG*, pp. xxix, 311–13. For the text Walter used of the letters of 1291 relating to the Scottish succession case see *WG*, p. 235 n. 2.

276 *WG*, pp. 296–7.

letter of protection to Hexham is cited).[277] Moreover, he has a fair amount of information about Carlisle where there was a house of Augustinian canons. He tells how it was set alight in 1296, allegedly by a traitor, on the approach of the Scots army.[278] And he gives a detailed description of the parliament held at Carlisle in January 1307, where 'the barons and other magnates and the community of the whole realm' presented petitions on various 'intolerable complaints, oppressions, injuries and extortions' (the text of what is probably a preliminary draft of the grievances follows).[279]

Walter probably obtained some of the information on the quarrel between Anthony Bek and the cathedral priory of St Cuthbert's from the hospital of St Giles, Kepier, in Durham (which may have been a foundation of Augustinian canons).[280] This is suggested by a reference to the hospital in the historical recapitulation of the relations of St Cuthbert's priory with the bishops of Durham and the archbishops of York. Walter, arguing that if the monks had allowed the archbishop to visit them they would have avoided being visited by the bishop, describes the archiepiscopal visitation of 1280. The monks resisted violently and Archbishop William Wickwane's horse fell and broke its leg – 'it could never again carry a man, and the clerks, when the tumult had subsided, made the archbishop mount another horse and led him to the hospital of [St Giles], Kepier.'[281] It is very likely that Walter visited Durham, which is less than thirty miles from Guisborough. He gives what appears to be a first-hand description of the new cross Bek had borne before him on his return from Rome in 1304 (it was 'of silver and gilt, with two arms and a carving of the crucifixion in the centre').[282] Walter also got some news from the Franciscans: he comments that when Earl Warenne fled from the battle of Stirling Bridge he was in such a hurry to leave the country that his horse had no time to feed in the stable of the Friars Minor at Berwick.[283]

Among the important laymen connected with Guisborough priory were Bruces, its founders and patrons.[284] Robert Bruce IV ('glorious and rich in life and death'), who died in 1295, was buried in the priory church.[285] Although Walter had no good word to say for Robert Bruce's son Robert the Scottish patriot and king of Scotland from 1306 to 1329 (initially because he broke his oath of submission to Edward I[286]), the priory's association with the family must have increased Walter's interest in, and facilitated the

[277] WG, pp. 305–6.   [278] WG, pp. 272–4.

[279] WG, pp. 375–7. For references to Guisborough's account of the parliament held at Carlisle in January 1307, see H. G. Richardson and G. O. Sayles, 'The parliament of Carlisle, 1307: some new documents' in EHR, liii (1938), pp. 429 and passim, and W. E. Lunt, 'First levy of papal annates' in Am. Hist. Rev., xviii (1912), p. 53 and n. 43. Cf. Lunt, Financial Relations . . . to 1327, pp. 489–90 and n. 2.

[280] WG, pp. 346–51. For St Giles, Kepier, at Durham, see M. D. Knowles and R. N. Hadcock, Medieval Religious Houses of England and Wales (London 1953), p. 269.

[281] WG, p. 350.   [282] WG, p. 365.

[283] WG, p. 303. For another reference to the Franciscans see WG, p. 275.

[284] See WG, p. 33.   [285] WG, p. 259.   [286] WG, p. 296.

obtaining of information about Anglo-Scottish relations. Moreover, four powerful baronial families held lands adjacent to the priory's, the Mauleys, Latimers, Percys and Twengs.[287] Walter was very well informed, no doubt through his neighbours, on the activities of members of these families. For example he has a graphic description of the repulse of the English, Sir William Latimer among them, by the Welsh at Conway in 1282.[288] The English army crossed the river at low tide to fight the Welsh in the mountains. The tide rose in the estuary and they were trapped between the water and the Welsh. Many were drowned, 'but on that day the Lord saved Sir William Latimer, a most energetic knight: he was carried by his charger through the midst of the water'. Walter also gives a detailed account of the Gascon campaign of 1293, in which Sir William served[289] – and of the 1295 Gascon campaign[290] in which two Mauley brothers, Robert and John, served.[291]

Particularly remarkable is Walter's description of the exploits of Sir Marmaduke Tweng at the battle of Stirling Bridge (1297). The English tried to storm the castle by sending an advance party over the bridge. Sir Marmaduke was in the lead. As the relief forces failed to support the advance party, many wanted to swim across the river rather than fight their way over the bridge. But Sir Marmaduke, 'a man of great strength and stature', exclaimed: 'Look here, friends, it shall never be said I got wet voluntarily. Forget the idea, but follow me and I will make a way for you through the middle of them right up to the bridge.' He then spurred his horse and hacked a passage through the enemy. His nephew's horse was killed and his esquire gave him his horse on which to follow Sir Marmaduke. 'And thus the bridge was held by this strenuous soldier.' Earl Warenne put Sir Marmaduke in charge of the castle, solemnly promising him help within ten weeks – but he failed to keep his promise.[292]

Walter probably drew on some lost north-country history also used by Peter of Langtoft. This is suggested by similarities of information and attitudes in his chronicle and Langtoft's. Like Walter Langtoft praises the heroism of Sir Marmaduke Tweng at the battle of Stirling Bridge. Both writers condemn the Scots in similar terms (though Langtoft's invective is far more passionate), as perjurors[293] and robbers (they often call Wallace 'the robber').[294] They both bitterly criticize Hugh Cressingham, Edward's treasurer in Scotland who had also been an itinerant justice in Yorkshire, and John de Warenne, attributing Edward's reverses in Scotland to their

---

[287] For a sketch map of the properties and lordships of these families adjacent to those of Guisborough priory see *WG*, p. xxviii.

[288] *WG*, pp. 218–21. For the errors in this account see J. E. Morris, *The Welsh Wars of Edward the First* (Oxford 1901), pp. 179–80.

[289] *WG*, p. 244.   [290] *WG*, p. 261.   [291] *WG*, pp. 260–4.

[292] *WG*, pp. 298–303. Peter of Langtoft also mentions Tweng's bravery at Stirling; see p. 483 below. For a modern account of the battle of Stirling Bridge see Barrow, *Robert Bruce*, pp. 123–6.

[293] *WG*, p. 296; *PL*, vol. 2, p. 370.

[294] *WG*, pp. 294, 299, 300. Cf. p. 483 below.

negligence. Walter calls Cressingham 'a pompous man, a son of death', guilty of levity, pride and avarice, 'known as a traitor rather than a treasurer'.[295] He considered Cressingham's advice at the battle of Stirling disastrous.[296] Recording Cressingham's death in the battle, Walter writes: 'he who was prebendary of many churches and had the cure of many souls, never wore spiritual arms or chasuble, but the helmet and shield in which he fell. And he who terrified many in his judgments by the sword of the tongue, at length fell by the sword of the wicked.' And Walter describes how the Scots cut up his skin, 'not as relics but in hatred'.[297] Both Walter and Langtoft accuse Warenne of inaction during the battle[298] and of precipitate flight afterwards.[299]

Moreover, there is a similarity between Walter's and Langtoft's attitudes to Edward's taxation of the church. Walter attributes a speech to Edward in which the king says that if the clergy do not help him financially to carry out his enterprises he will be 'only a poor guardian of your land of England; and not only your land itself but the whole English church will be placed in danger'.[300] As will be seen, Langtoft uses much the same argument, but more forcefully, to justify Edward's taxes.[301]

The chronicle of Peter of Langtoft, canon of Bridlington, belongs to a different tradition of historiography from Thomas Wykes's. The latter is one of the best monastic chronicles of the annalistic type, which, though short, bears comparison in quality with the works of Matthew Paris. Langtoft's chronicle, in French verse, belongs to the romance historiographical tradition. Langtoft wrote in the late thirteenth and early fourteenth century. Some facts about his life as an Augustinian canon are known.[302] He probably had some legal training because contemporary documents show that he acted from 1271 to 1286 as attorney for Geoffrey prior of Bridlington, and also represented the convent in the courts at Westminster and elsewhere. He was out of favour with the next prior, and went south without permission in 1293, because of an internal dispute in the priory.

Langtoft's chronicle, covering the period from Brutus to 1307, is in three parts. The first book is from Brutus to the Norman Conquest. The second is from the Norman conquest to the death of Henry III. The third deals with the reign of Edward I. Book I derives ultimately from Geoffrey of Monmouth but, unlike Wace, Peter omits some of Geoffrey's legendary material: he says he 'has left out the trifles, and stuck to the truth'.[303] This is an over-

---

[295] *WG*, pp. 301, 303. Cf. p. 483 below. For Hugh Cressingham's activities in Scotland see Barrow, *Robert Bruce*, pp. 100, 106, 110, 120–4 *passim*.

[296] *WG*, p. 301. [297] *WG*, p. 303. [298] *WG*, p. 300.

[299] *WG*, p. 303. [300] *WG*, p. 249. [301] See p. 479.

[302] For a convenient summary of the evidence about Langtoft's life, see M. D. Legge, *Anglo-Norman in the Cloisters* (Edinburgh 1950), pp. 70–1. For the history of Bridlington priory at this period see *VCH, Yorks.*, vol. 3, pp. 200–1.

[303] *PL*, vol. 1, p. 264.

statement. However, Langtoft omitted enough fiction to displease Robert Mannyng of Bourne in Lincolnshire, a canon of the Gilbertine house of Sixhills, who translated Langtoft's chronicle into English in 1338.[304] Mannyng, considering that Langtoft had deprived readers of amusement, substituted Wace's version of the *Historia Regum Britanniae* for Langtoft's.[305] Peter ends Book I with the prophecies of Merlin. It is not quite clear what sources he used for Book II and as this section was written a generation after the events it is not of much value to the historian today. Book III, as a contemporary account of events by an intelligent and observant writer, is an important authority especially for Anglo-Scottish relations. Langtoft seems originally to have written to 1296, ending on a triumphant note, for Edward I's victory over the Scots then seemed complete.[306] But he continued to write after Edward's subsequent reverses: his criticism of Edward increased and his hatred of the Scots deepened. So he revised his earlier text besides continuing it. His latest version ended with Edward II's accession, on which occasion Langtoft expressed sad doubts on the new king's ability to restore England's fortunes in Scotland.[307]

Langtoft's overriding concern was for England's victory over Scotland. This provided him with a recurrent theme. In the application of this theme he made extensive use of Geoffrey of Monmouth. As has been mentioned, some other chroniclers (for example the chronicler of Battle abbey[308] and Robert of Gloucester[309]) use the *Historia Regum Britanniae* for the early part of their chronicles. And a number of writers refer in a conventional way to the prophecies of Merlin.[310] But none of these writers used Geoffrey of Monmouth to provide precedents justifying the acts of the kings of their own day – nor to supply moral exemplars for the ruler's benefit. But Langtoft was different. He used Geoffrey primarily to provide a justification for Edward I's policy of subjugating Scotland. And to a lesser extent he used him to justify the defence of English rights in Gascony. According to Geoffrey, Brutus had ruled all Britain and King Arthur had tried with varying degrees of success to rule the same territory, as well as France. Merlin had prophesied that England, Scotland and Wales would be reunited at an unspecified time. Langtoft used Geoffrey's pseudo-history to provide precedents for Edward I's claims (he also quoted the historical fact that John Balliol had done

---

[304] See *The Story of England by Robert Manning of Brunne*, ed. F. J. Furnivall (RS, 1887, 2 vols), vol. 1, p. xii. For Mannyng see also Oskar Preussner, *Robert Mannyng of Brunne's Uebersetzung von Pierre de Langtoft's Chronicle* (Breslau 1891).

[305] See Legge, *A-N Lit.*, p. 279, and *PL*, vol. 1, pp. xii, xvii.

[306] See *PL*, vol. 2, p. 266. The recensions of Langtoft's chronicle are not made clear in Wright's edition; see Legge, *Anglo-Norman in the Cloisters*, p. 74 (in note 1, Professor Legge mentions that she had intended to make a study of Langtoft's revisions of his work, but she told me in a letter of September 1968 that the project is in abeyance).

[307] For a manuscript containing this postscript see M. D. Legge, 'A list of Langtoft manuscripts, with notes on MS. Laud Misc. 637' in *Medium Ævum*, iv (1935), p. 24.

[308] See p. 422.　　　　[309] See p. 432.

[310] See e.g. *Dunst.*, p. 293.

homage to Edward[311]). Here he was adopting an argument used to justify Edward by the royal clerks in Edward's letter of 1301, and in that of the barons, to Pope Boniface VIII.[312] It is likely that Langtoft was glossing the royal thesis, by writing a history of contemporary events adjusted to this view (a French rendering, probably by Langtoft, of the letter to Boniface survives[313]). Langtoft represents Edward as a second Brutus and as Arthur returned. In 1295 when Edward seemed successful in Scotland, Langtoft proclaimed the fulfilment of Merlin's prophecy: Albany was reunited; two kingdoms were made one. Edward also ruled Cornwall, Wales and Ireland – no other king had united them ('Arthur had never the fiefs so fully').[314] Nothing remained to be done for the conquest of his complete inheritance except to campaign against France (which King Arthur had given to Sir Bedevere).[315] Langtoft wanted the English to keep Gascony – so the barons, like King Arthur's knights, should loyally support Edward's Gascon campaign.[316]

Langtoft's obsession with conquest resulted in dislike of people hindering it. He attributed the failure of the 1294 expedition to the Welsh rebellion, which deflected Edward's resources,[317] and he hated the Welsh accordingly:[318]

> May Wales be accursed of God and of St Simon!
> For it has always been full of treason. . . .
> May Wales be sunk deep to the devil.

But Langtoft's bitterest hatred was of the Scots. He lived in an area where Scottish raids were a fearful reality and his feelings about the Scots rise to an almost hysterical pitch. He calls on Edward to remember the burning of Hexham and do vengeance ('Man ought to have mercy, but it ought not to avail a traitor').[319] He believed that the Scots planned to seize Northumberland and, in alliance with the French, to destroy England from the Tweed to Kent, leaving no one alive.[320]

As Edward I was the champion of north-country Englishmen against the Scots, as well as the protector of the English in Gascony, it is not surprising that Langtoft supported royal authority. He sides strongly with the king against the barons in the account of Henry III's reign. The king's friends, he asserts, told him that the barons had put Henry in dishonourable tutelage by the Provisions of Oxford ('You do dishonour to yourself and to your

---

[311] See *PL*, vol. 2, pp. 192–3.   [312] See p. 443.

[313] See pp. 482–3 and n. 356.

[314] *PL*, vol. 2, pp. 264, 266. In the same year Langtoft says Edward had 'Scotland entirely as Albanak had it at the beginning'; ibid., p. 254. For the parallel drawn by Langtoft, as by other contemporary writers, between King Arthur and Edward I see R. S. Loomis, 'Edward I, Arthurian enthusiast' in *Speculum*, xxviii (1953), pp. 126–7.

[315] See *PL*, vol. 2, p. 278.   [316] Ibid., p. 296.   [317] Ibid., p. 218.

[318] Ibid., p. 220.   [319] Ibid., p. 256.   [320] Ibid., p. 254.

blood, when you are guided by the will of another').[321] He accuses Simon de Montfort of acting without the king's advice[322] and his sons of overbearing pride.[323] He rejoices at Henry's resoration to power:[324]

> Now has King Henry land and lordship,
> And is king of his land, and of all that belongs to it.

He puts a speech into Edward I's mouth vindicating his right, in opposition to the barons (in 1300), to appoint his own treasurer; he says that they all have the power to organize their own households and appoint and judge their bailiffs and stewards, and that no one should 'push his lord lower than himself'.[325] He even supports Edward's claim to tax the clergy (in 1294). He admits that England 'is much poorer now than it was', but says that both church and laity would be poorer still if Edward were beaten by the French:[326]

> The proud French would bring us so low,
> And cause us to be honoured no more than dogs.
> One may seek money, money comes and goes;
> Then it is better worth to give it as long as one has it,
> Than to live like a caitiff in suffering so extreme.

In the 1296 parliament at Bury St Edmunds Langtoft puts a speech into Edward's mouth which stresses his importance as defender of the kingdom:[327]

> I am castle for you, and wall, and house,
> And you the barbican, the gate, and pavilion.

Langtoft even defends Edward's unpopular commission of trailbaston, by saying that if criminals were not punished, 'A man would not dare live in his house'.[328] He can find nothing to say in favour of the statute of mortmain – but he adds to his comments on it that Edward was very devout.[329]

Langtoft's chronicle belongs to the romance tradition of historiography started in England by Gaimar, and continued by Jordan Fantosme and in the *History of William the Marshal*. Langtoft may have known Jordan's work.[330] And although Langtoft adopted a different verse metre (he used Alexandrines in rhymed *laisses*, the metre of the *chansons de geste*, which was old-fashioned in his day)[331] from Gaimar, he imitated Gaimar's general scheme – a

---

[321] Ibid., p. 138.   [322] Ibid., p. 140.   [323] Ibid., p. 144.
[324] Ibid., p. 146.   [325] Ibid., p. 330.   [326] Ibid., p. 214.
[327] Ibid., p. 288.   [328] Ibid., p. 362.   [329] Ibid., p. 174.
[330] See Legge, *A-N Lit.*, p. 81.
[331] See ibid., p. 278, and Legge, *Anglo-Norman in the Cloisters*, pp. 71–2. Cf. p. 209 above.

national history based in its early part on Geoffrey of Monmouth, in Anglo-Norman verse. Furthermore, like Gaimar, Langtoft wrote for a lay patron. The latter was called Scaffeld[332] about whom nothing else is known (it has been suggested that he had some connection with Anthony Bek, bishop of Durham since Langtoft mentions Bek in consistently flattering terms).[333] Langtoft wrote his work for recitation, to amuse men and stir their bellicosity against the Scots. Since the work survives in a fair number of manuscripts (a recent scholar lists fifteen and mentions two more now untraced[334]) and was soon translated into English, it obviously had some success. It was especially popular in Yorkshire: copies are known to have been owned by the Augustinian canons of North Ferriby and Bolton, and also by the vicar of Adlingfleet.[335] Robert Mannyng was himself a Yorkshireman, and his English rendering of Book III of Langtoft's chronicle became the source for the English prose *Brut*.[336]

In order to amuse, Langtoft adopted many of the features of romance literature. He often wrote in chivalric terms and in places vividly reflects the courtly cult of King Arthur prevalent in the late thirteenth and early fourteenth centuries. He ascribes chivalric virtues to King Edward, 'the flower of chivalry', second only to King Arthur:[337]

> He was so handsome and great, so powerful in arms,
> that of him may one speak as long as the world lasts.

Of the festivities held on the occasion of the knighting of Edward of Caernarvon in 1306, he writes:[338]

> Never in Britain, since God was born,
> Was there such nobleness in towns nor in cities,
> Except Caerleon in ancient times,
> When Sir Arthur the king was crowned there.

Edward was courteous[339] – in fact too courteous, for Langtoft feared that his leniency to the Scots in 1303 jeopardized the prospect of English victory.[340]

Langtoft criticizes Edward in chivalric terms when he suffered reverses in Scotland and Gascony towards the end of his reign. A perfect knight should be generous, keep his word and live a disciplined, almost ascetic life in harmony with his vassals. Langtoft accuses Edward of lack of generosity

---

[332] *PL*, vol. 2, p. 164.
[333] See Legge, *Anglo-Norman in the Cloisters*, p. 72.
[334] Legge, 'A list of Langtoft manuscripts', p. 20.
[335] See Legge, *Anglo-Norman in the Cloisters*, pp. 72–3.
[336] See ibid., p. 73.   [337] *PL*, vol. 2, p. 380.   [338] Ibid., p. 368.
[339] Ibid., p. 318.   [340] Ibid., p. 350.

to his barons ('courteous vassals of noble kindred'[341]). He says that if Edward had distributed conquered land in Wales among his barons in 1294, he could have held the country and so been free to concentrate on the defence of Gascony.[342] In 1299 Langtoft asserts that Edward's failure to give lands in Scotland to his barons, and to keep his promise of holding a perambulation of the forests, alienated baronial support and thus damaged the prospects of his Scottish campaign.[343] Although he attributes the ultimate failure of Edward's policy in Scotland to treachery[344] (a typically chivalric explanation) he also blames Edward personally, in a comparison with the unsuccessful British kings, because he fell short of chivalric perfection:[345]

> Idleness and feigned delay, and long morning's sleep,
> Delight in luxury, and surfeit in the evenings,
> Trust in felons, compassion for enemies,
> Self-will in act and counsel,
> To retain conquest without giving distributions of gain,
> Overthrew [?] the Britons in old time.

The influence of chivalric culture also appears in his references to feminine goodness and beauty. Edward fell in love in 1293 with Philip IV's sister Blanche: 'A fairer creature is nowhere found.... In body, in face, in leg, in hand, in foot.'[346] But Edward married, as his second queen, not Blanche,[347]

> But the Lady Margaret, in whose least finger
> There is more goodness and beauty, whoever looks at her,
> Than in the fair Ydoine whom Amadas loved.

And like the *History of William the Marshal*, Langtoft gives prominence to the bond between lord and man, particularly to homage. He accuses the Scots of violating their homage to Edward I when they rebelled in 1295.[348] Similarly in 1297 when the English barons refused to accompany 'their liege lord' to Gascony, he writes:[349]

> Never in time back was such a sovereign served
> Thus by his people, when he was going to make war.
> He is too cowardly who draws back
> When he sees his lord going into danger.

---

[341] Ibid., p. 298. [342] Ibid., pp. 216, 218. [343] Ibid., pp. 326, 328.
[344] See e.g. ibid., pp. 310, 312, for the Scots' 'treacherous' approaches to Philip IV against Edward I.
[345] Ibid., p. 326. [346] Ibid., p. 198. [347] Ibid., p. 316.
[348] Ibid., p. 230. [349] Ibid., p. 292.

Moreover, Langtoft introduced an element not found in the earlier romance histories written in England. This is the idea of madness as the fate of his hero's enemies. He calls John de Balliol and his advisers mad in 1294[350] and has a particularly graphic passage on the 'madness' of Robert Bruce after his defeat in 1306. He compares him with Fulk Fitz Warin,[351] who took to the forests in adversity.[352]

> King Robin has drunk of the drink of dan Warin,
> Who lost cities and towns by the shield,
> Afterwards in the forest, mad and naked,
> He fed with the beasts on the raw grass.

Various factors, therefore, could detract from the value of Langtoft's chronicle as a historical source – its violent anti-Scottish bias, its royalist attitudes, and its romantic tone. Nevertheless Langtoft managed to give a fairly accurate record of contemporary affairs. He was observant and had a sound sense of evidence, and therefore his history has value to the historian today, particularly for its information about north-country affairs. Sometimes Langtoft's sense of reality spoilt his taste for chivalry. This appears for example in his love of peace and consequent interest in negotiated settlements. Thus, though he wanted Edward to win bloody victories, he hoped for the success of the peace negotiations with Philip IV in 1295 and 1297 which he described in detail.[353] And he was surprisingly well informed about relations between Scotland and France in 1298.[354] He is the only chronicler to record that some thirty Scots, whom Edward released from prison for service in Flanders, defected and went to Philip hoping for a renewed alliance with him: but Philip rebuffed them and they returned home.

Though Langtoft admits he had no inside knowledge of affairs of state,[355] he was interested in official documents. It was probably he who rendered into French verse correspondence between Boniface VIII and Edward I on the king's claim to overlordship of Scotland.[356] Besides giving in his chronicle a

---

[350] Ibid., p. 220.
[351] For the romance of Fulk Fitz Warin see Legge, *A-N Lit.*, pp. 171–4. The original poem was written after 1256 and probably before 1264, but the extant version is early fourteenth century; printed L. Brandin, *Fouke Fitz Warin* (in Les Classiques français du Moyen Age, lxiii, 1930).
[352] *PL*, vol. 2, p. 372.
[353] Ibid., pp. 274, 308. Cf. G. P. Cuttino, 'List of English embassies to France, 1272–1307' in *EHR*, xliv (1929), 271–2, and Cuttino, *English Diplomatic Administration 1295–1339*, p. 9.
[354] *PL*, vol. 2, p. 310. I owe this reference to Professor G. W. S. Barrow who discusses the incident in his *Robert Bruce*, p. 137 and nn. 2, 3. Professor Barrow informs me that to the references given in n. 2 should be added *The Gascon Calendar of 1322*, ed. G. P. Cuttino (Camden Soc., 3rd series, lxx, 1949), p. 39 no. 394.
[355] See *PL*, vol. 2, pp. 274, 336, 358.
[356] Printed in ibid., pp. 388–424. See pp. 442–3, 478 above. These verse translations are attributed to Langtoft by Legge, *Anglo-Norman in the Cloisters*, p. 73.

version of the submission of John de Balliol to Edward,[357] he refers to the actual document containing the treaty between Edward and Philip IV drawn up in 1294 for Edward's marriage with Blanche: Langtoft has the unique statement that the treaty was already sealed.[358]

Langtoft seems to have used some literary sources now lost. One may have been a Life of Anthony Bek. This is suggested by the numerous details about, and the consistent eulogy of Bek. Langtoft attributes a prominent part to him at Norham in 1291. He says that Bek ('blessed may he be by God the son of Mary') examined the chronicles 'with sense and great subtlety' to ascertain Edward's right to overlordship.[359] In 1294 he asserts that Bek had no part in the making of Edward's disastrous treaty with Philip IV and expresses the hope that the bishop will help in subsequent negotiations, 'for without you there is no remedy'.[360] Langtoft alleges that later it was Bek who advised Edward to fight for Gascony[361] and that Bek was mainly responsible for Edward's success in 1296.[362] He alleges that in 1297 Bek demonstrated to Edward the dangers of a quarrel with the barons[363] and worked for peace between England and France.[364] Possibly Walter of Guisborough, who also has much information about Bek (though not all of it is flattering)[365] used the same lost Life. Moreover, as mentioned above, Langtoft probably used some material in common with Walter, perhaps a lost north-country chronicle. This is suggested by remarkable similarities between the chronicles. Both authors justify Edward's taxation of the clergy in similar terms (though Langtoft is more forceful on the subject[366]). The resemblance is particularly noticeable in passages reflecting the chroniclers' attitude to the Scots and to Edward's officials in Scotland. Like Guisborough, Langtoft refers to William Wallace as a robber.[367] Moreover, in some passages Langtoft has small additions to Guisborough which suggest the use of a common source. For example in his account of the battle of Stirling Bridge, he says that the English were defeated partly because Warenne 'by his own folly' was in bed at the crucial time,[368] he alleges that the Scots cut Cressingham's skin into thongs 'to insult the king whose clerk he was',[369] and he describes how after the defeat at Stirling Bridge the Scots captured Marmaduke Tweng (who was holding the castle) by a ruse.[370]

But probably Langtoft's most important sources of contemporary information were his own observation and hearsay. For example he can give a

---

[357] *PL*, vol. 2, pp. 192, 194.
[358] Ibid., p. 198.
[359] Ibid., p. 190.
[360] Ibid., p. 200.
[361] Ibid., p. 202.
[362] Ibid., p. 260.
[363] Ibid., p. 290.
[364] Ibid., p. 296.
[365] See pp. 472, 474. Guisborough takes the monks' side in Bek's quarrel with his cathedral chapter.
[366] See e.g. *PL*, vol. 2, pp. 278, 304, 306. Cf. p. 479 and n. 327 above.
[367] See *PL*, vol. 2, p. 350.
[368] *PL*, vol. 2, p. 298. Cf. p. 476 above.
[369] Ibid., pp. 298, 300. Cf. p. 476 above.
[370] Ibid., p. 300. Cf. p. 475 above. For the proximity of Tweng's estates to those of Guisborough priory see p. 475 and n. 287 above.

graphic description of the problems of the English army in Galloway which Edward found insurmountable. On the army's approach the people drove their cattle into the bogs. Langtoft continues:[371]

> Into the moors and marshes of such depth,
> A stranger knows not where to put his feet.
> Then the weather changes, torrential rains come,
> They run down the mountains into the plains and valleys,
> Overflow the rivers, flood the ditches,
> King Edward knows not at what point to cross the fords,
> Changes his road, takes to the easiest.

In one respect Langtoft preserves unique information about the Scottish wars. He is the only writer to throw light on the attitude of ordinary folk, especially of the foot-soldiers. He introduces a popular element which had not appeared in English historiography before this date. This element appears particularly in the popular songs and short political ballads in French and English (some combine verses in each language) which he inserts.[372] These rhymes sound as if Langtoft actually heard and carefully reproduced what people were singing. They are untouched by literary convention and belong to a genuine popular art. Most are satirical and are at the expense of the Scots, rejoicing at their discomfiture and trying to inflame hatred against them. For example one English rhyme reads (rendered in modern English):[373]

> The foot folk
> Put the Scots in the poke,
>   And bared their buttocks.
> On all my journeys
> I never heard tell anywhere
>   Of readier boys,
> To rob
> The robes of the rich
>   That fell in the field.
> They took of each man;
> May the rough ragged fiend
>   Tear them in hell!

One of the French rhymes ends with two verses in English, one reading:[374]

---

[371] Ibid., p. 324.

[372] For these songs see Legge, *A-N Lit.*, pp. 352–3. For two rather similar verses evoked by Edward I's Welsh wars see the *Annales Cestrienses*, ed. Christie (see p. 405 n. 14 above), pp. 110–11.

[373] *PL*, vol. 2, p. 248. The modern English rendering unfortunately loses some of the rhymes and alliterative effect in the original verses.

[374] Ibid., p. 264.

And so may men teach
The Scots to run
    And begin war;
To some is left nothing
But his rough riveling [shoe]
    To hop in.

Langtoft reveals that the Scots had used a rhyme to mock Edward I on his capture of Berwick, beginning[375]

Let him pike,
And let him dike.

This rhyme was incorporated into an English one ending[376]

Scattered are the Scots,
Huddled in their huts,
    Never do they thrive.
Right if I read,
They are tumbled into Tweed,
    Who dwelt by the sea.

These rhymes influenced the style of Langtoft's own verse. An obvious instance is a passage in which he says:[377]

May our king Sir Edward be struck with madness,
If he does not take them and hold them so close in cage
That nothing remain to them after his taxing,
Except only their rivelings and their bare buttocks.

This passage shows that Langtoft shared the popular sense of humour evident in the satirical rhymes. He makes jokes elsewhere in the chronicle. For instance he says that the captive John de Balliol 'lodged in the Tower of London at another's expense'[378] and that as Llewelyn 'has lost his head he has no need of a hat'.[379] Langtoft's affinity with ordinary country people is shown by his use of rural images. He compares pride in a country with nettles in a garden, which choke the roses,[380] and he says he 'wouldn't give a garlic' for Edward's chances against the French without God's help.[381]

William of Rishanger, writing in the early fourteenth century, quotes one

---

[375] Ibid., p. 234. For the original Scottish song see William Rishanger, 'Annales Angliae et Scotiae' in *Willelmi Rishanger, Chronica et Annales*, ed. H. T. Riley (RS, 1865), p. 373. The earliest poem in *The Oxford Book of Scottish Verse*, ed. J. MacQueen and T. Scott (Oxford 1966) is by Thomas of Erceldoune, *c.* 1225–*c.* 1300.
[376] *PL*, vol. 2, p. 236.   [377] Ibid., p. 232.   [378] Ibid., p. 258.
[379] Ibid., p. 180.   [380] Ibid., p. 258.   [381] Ibid., p. 286.

topical verse like Langtoft's,[382] but it is not until Thomas Walsingham wrote at St Albans on the Peasants' Revolt that another chronicler thought popular material worth including.[383]

[382] See p. 485 n. 375 above.
[383] See *Thomae Walsingham, quondam Monachi S. Albani, Historia Anglicana*, ed. H. T. Riley (RS, 1864, 2 vols), vol. 2, pp. 32, 34.

20

Mendicant Chronicles

English historiography acquired two new elements in the thirteenth century. One was the chronicles by friars, the other was the first town chronicle (the chronicle of London, which will be discussed in the next chapter). In contrast to the monks and Augustinian canons, the friars were not prolific historians. They lacked the institutional roots and stability of the older orders, and therefore could not draw on established historiographical traditions, accumulated archives and large libraries. Nevertheless three English friars wrote histories in the thirteenth and early fourteenth centuries.[1] And one of these works, Thomas of Eccleston's *De Adventu Fratrum Minorum in Angliam* (*On the Coming of the Friars Minor to England*)[2] is unique. It is not a general chronicle but a history specifically of the Franciscan order in England, from its arrival in 1224 to the mid-thirteenth century. It has a purpose and a theme. It aimed at edifying the friars of Eccleston's own day and, by recording the praiseworthy endeavours of their predecessors, to inspire them to emulation.

The other two mendicant histories, the so-called Lanercost chronicle,[3] by a north-country Franciscan, and the *Annals* written by Nicholas Trevet (sometimes spelt Trivet),[4] a London Dominican, equate more nearly in form to the monastic-type chronicles. But they too reflect (though to a lesser extent) the friars' ideals. The Lanercost chronicle, like Eccleston, has *exempla*, that is moral stories for the edification of the reader. The inclusion

---

[1] For an excellent survey of mendicant (English and continental) historiography see A. G. Little, 'Chronicles of the mendicant friars' in his *Franciscan Papers, Lists, and Documents* (Manchester 1943), pp. 25–41. For the Franciscan narrative sources for the history of the minister general Elias of Assisi see R. B. Brooke, *Early Franciscan Government* (Cambridge 1959), pp. 8–55.

[2] Printed *Fratris Thomae vulgo dicti de Eccleston Tractatus de Adventu Fratrum Minorum in Angliam*, ed. A. G. Little (Manchester 1951). An earlier edition by Little is in *Collection d'études ... du Moyen Âge* (Paris 1898–1909, 7 vols), vol. 7. English translations are by Father Cuthbert, *The Chronicle of Thomas of Eccleston* (Edinburgh and London 1909), and E. G. Salter, *The Coming of the Friars Minor to England and Germany. Being the Chronicles of Thomas of Eccleston and ... Jordan of Giano* (London and Toronto 1926).

[3] Printed *Chronicon de Lanercost 1201–1346*, ed. Joseph Stevenson (Maitland Club, Edinburgh 1839). An English translation of the chronicle from 1272 to the end is by Herbert Maxwell, *The Chronicle of Lanercost 1272–1346* (Glasgow 1913).

[4] Printed *Nicholai Triveti Annales*, ed. Thomas Hog (English Historical Soc., London 1845) Trevet spelt his own name thus (Trivet is a modern spelling): see R. J. Dean, a review of E. Franceschini, *Studi e Note di Filologia Latina Medievale; Il Commento di Nicolo Trevet al Tieste di Seneca* in *Medium Ævum*, x (1941), 164.

of such stories, commonly used in popular preaching, illustrates the friars' participation in pastoral work. And the chronicle's pious tone is augmented by the frequent attribution of events to divine causation. The *Annals* of Nicholas Trevet are included here, because although they were written in Edward II's reign, they end with Edward I's death and have contemporary material for his reign. They do not include *exempla*, but have vivid anecdotes similar in style to stories found in the Lanercost chronicle.

All three mendicant historians illustrate their orders' international ramifications (only the Lanercost chronicle shows strong local attachments). And they all reflect the friars' devotion to learning – they note the lives and works of famous scholars, and are particularly interested in the history of Oxford university where they had studied. Moreover, the political views of the Lanercost chronicle and Trevet (Eccleston, absorbed in Franciscan history, ignores secular politics), though diametrically opposed, can nevertheless be regarded as typical of their orders. The Lanercost chronicle is a partisan of Simon de Montfort during the Barons' War: it is known that some Franciscans preached in favour of the baronial cause.[5] Trevet on the other hand reflects the fact that usually the king's association with the mendicant orders was close and friendly:[6] Trevet eulogizes Edward I, treating him as a hero.

Little is known about Thomas of Eccleston though the numerous references in the *De Adventu* to men from Norfolk suggest that he may have come from there.[7] He dedicated the work to a 'Brother Simon of Ashby' (there is an Ashby in Norfolk, though the name is fairly common). Thomas knew personally some of the earliest English Franciscans, for example Solomon, the first Englishman to become a novice of the order.[8] He studied at Oxford some time between 1235 and 1253 and was in the London convent when William of Nottingham, whom he knew, was provincial minister of England (1240–54).[9] The style of the *De Adventu* (which seems to have been influenced by the *cursus velox* used in the papal chancery) suggests the possibility that Thomas had notarial training.[10]

Thomas finished the *De Adventu* in 1258 or 1259,[11] but, as he states in the prologue, he had been collecting material for twenty-six years. He accumulated material mainly from oral sources, writing down what he heard, often from well-known people, about the sayings and doings of the Franciscans. Though he made some use of a Life of St Francis[12] and probably knew a few documents (papal bulls, privileges and the like)[13] bearing on Franciscan history, his work is essentially original and not derived from any other

[5] See R. F. Treharne, *The Baronial Plan of Reform, 1258–1263* (Manchester 1932), p. 334.
[6] The view that the Dominicans as a whole were more royalist than the Franciscans is disputed by W. A. Hinnebusch, *The Early English Friars Preachers* (Institutum Historicum Ff. Praedicatorum Romae ad S. Sabinae, Dissertationes Historicae, fasc. xiv, Rome 1951), pp. 465–9.
[7] For Eccleston's life, friends and acquaintances see *TE*, pp. xxi–xxix.
[8] *TE*, p. 12.   [9] *TE*, pp. 101–2.   [10] *TE*, p. xxiii.   [11] *TE*, p. xxii.
[12] *TE*, pp. xxvi, 75.   [13] *TE*, p. xxvi.

literary source. He arranged his material in fifteen collations (headed, for example, 'On the first coming of the friars minor to England', 'On the first divisions of the friars', 'On the reception of novices'). He is not very methodical (he gives only one date[14]): he was constantly adding to the work, writing extra passages in the margins and on loose leaves, and put a number of entries under headings to which they were irrelevant.

Nevertheless comparison of Thomas's information with public records and private charters shows him to be remarkably accurate.[15] For example he says that Brother Albert of Pisa (provincial minister from 1236 to 1239) indignantly restored to the monks of Reading a charter containing an agreement between them and the friars which stipulated that the monks could not expel the friars at their pleasure (Albert offered to remove the friars voluntarily). This entry is confirmed by the charter itself which survives.[16]

The *De Adventu* is a unique source for the early history of the Franciscans in England. It is of value for social history, showing the popularity of the friars in the towns, especially with the craftsmen class. One of the earliest English novices was a tailor, William of London,[17] and one of the patrons of the London convent was Sir William Joynier, a rich citizen, successively sheriff and mayor of London.[18] The men who gave the friars a site at Oxford were Robert the Mercer[19] and Richard the Mulliner,[20] and the property of both the London[21] and Canterbury[22] convents was held, Thomas records, by the community of citizens for the friars.

Besides being detailed, accurate and well informed about English Franciscan history, the *De Adventu* is an important source for the history of the Franciscans on the continent. Most remarkable is Thomas's account of the conflict from 1227 to 1240 between the minister general Elias (1221–7, 1232–9)[23] and the majority of the friars. The same events are described in two other Franciscan histories, both written in Italy, the *Speculum Vitae*, composed in the first half of the fourteenth century,[24] and the *Chronica XXIV Generalium Ordinis Minorum* composed in the mid-fourteenth century.[25] But Thomas's account is the best of the three: it is the earliest and the most exact, and may be the source from which the other two works derived part of their information. Perhaps Thomas heard about the 1230 general chapter from Agnellus of Pisa who attended it, or from Albert of Pisa who may also have been there.[26]

---

[14] *TE*, p. 3.   [15] On Thomas's accuracy see *TE*, pp. xxiv–xxvi.

[16] *TE*, pp. xxv, 80 and nn.   [17] *TE*, p. 14.   [18] *TE*, pp. 21 and n. 37.

[19] *TE*, pp. 9 n., 22.   [20] *TE*, p. 22.   [21] *TE*, p. 21.   [22] *TE*, p. 20.

[23] *TE*, pp. 65–9. For the value of this account see Brooke, op. cit., pp. 27–45, and J. Moorman, *A History of the Franciscan Order from its Origins to the Year 1517* (Oxford 1968), p. 88 n. 6.

[24] Printed in E. Lempp, *Frère Elie de Cortone, Étude Bibliographique* in *Collection d'études . . . du Moyen Âge* (Paris 1898–1909, 9 vols), vol. 3, pp. 163–9. Cf. Brooke, op. cit., pp. 28 et seq.

[25] Printed in *Analecta Franciscana* (Quaracchi 1885 etc.), vol. 3. Cf. Brooke, op. cit., pp. 29 et seq.

[26] See Brooke, op. cit., pp. 43–4.

Thomas probably heard about the 1239 general chapter from the provincial minister Haymo of Faversham (1239–40).[27] His account of Haymo's opposition to Elias in the chapter, in the pope's presence, is so vivid that it suggests first-hand information. Elias was accused of living luxuriously. He said in defence that the friars had meant him to spend money[28] and have a horse. At first the pope would not let Haymo reply. But, Thomas records, Cardinal Robert of Somercote remonstrated saying, 'Lord, he is an old man; it would be good if you heard him, because he speaks briefly.' So Haymo stood up 'as if timid and fearful', while Elias remained seated – 'imperturbable, it seemed, and undaunted'. Haymo said that of course the friars intended Elias to spend money and have a horse, but not to accumulate treasure and have a palfrey or charger. Elias lost his temper, and the pope told them to be silent, exclaiming, 'This is not how the religious should behave', and then 'sat brooding until they were all ashamed'.

Piety was Thomas's main motive for writing. He explains in the prologue that he wants to record 'edifying examples and words' from English Franciscan history for the benefit of his fellow friars, especially so that they would not be tempted to leave the order when they read or heard of the miracles of other orders. In fact Thomas was, as it were, writing a contemporary pious history to compete with the hagiographies of, for example, the Benedictines. The work is permeated with Thomas's love of the Franciscan order. He gives stories and visions showing the holiness of St Francis and his followers. For example he describes how St Francis appeared, looking out from the wound in Christ's side, to Gregory IX while the latter was trying to convert heretics at Assisi; and he describes how Jesus himself intervened to cure a sick Franciscan.[29]

Perhaps Thomas wrote partly because of a sense of rivalry with the order of Friars Preachers. He disliked the Dominicans, accusing them of materialism. He thought they cared more for building fine friaries than for the salvation of souls. Some were so preoccupied with the financial aspect of their building programmes that they lost their talent for preaching. Thomas tells of one, William of Abingdon, to whom Henry III said, 'Brother William, you used to speak in such a spiritual way, but now all you say is give, give, give.'[30] Thomas records a saying of Albert of Pisa, that the Franciscans ought to be grateful to the Dominicans for providing an object lesson ('they instruct us how to avoid future perils').[31] A more powerful incentive to writing was Thomas's love of England. Patriotic fervour appears in more than one passage. Thomas relates that Albert of Pisa on his deathbed 'commended the English nation above all others for its zeal for the order',[32] and that the minister general John of Parma (1247–57) said on a visit to England, 'Oh that such a province were placed in the middle of the world so that it could be an example to all!'[33]

---

[27] See ibid., p. 44. [28] 'quod comederet aurum', TE, p. 67. [29] TE, p. 90.
[30] TE, p. 46. [31] TE, p. 82. [32] TE, p. 70. Cf. p. 79. [33] TE, p. 98.

Thomas was deeply concerned for the edification of his readers: the stories and sayings he records were aimed at their moral improvement. His work is closely related to the homiletic tradition (he explicitly states that two of the pious stories were told in sermons[34]). The stories emphasize the virtues needed by a friar – obedience, chastity, devoutness and the abnegation of secular pleasures. To illustrate the virtue of obedience Thomas tells a story of how a recalcitrant novice was freed from temptation after seeing a pigeon permit itself to be captured at the command of a friar.[35] To illustrate the virtue of chastity, he tells how a young man murdered a girl whom he had failed to seduce, for 'those who love carnally often in the end begin to hate to the same extent as they once loved'.[36] To emphasize the merit of silence, Thomas recorded a story which Albert of Pisa used to tell the friars when gathered for blood-letting. It relates that St Peter admitted a certain peasant to heaven on condition that he observed the law of silence. But the peasant could not refrain from giving foolish people good advice (for example he told a man trying to get a long piece of wood through a door crossways, to turn it round). At the third offence St Peter expelled him.[37] Thomas tells a story to encourage the friars' austerity. One of the Oxford friars, he relates, wore sandals, contrary to the custom of the convent. When he was attacked on the road by robbers, they refused to spare him as a friar, because, they said, friars went barefoot.[38] Excessive laughter is discouraged by another story about the Oxford friars, who would not stop their hilarity until one dreamt that the crucifix in the church reproved them and tried to leave.[39] Similarly, Thomas tells stories to discourage friars from eating outside their convents with laymen,[40] and from visiting women.[41]

Thomas reinforces his moral purpose by recording pious sayings. Most are collected together in the last chapter and are by friars. Thomas records, for example, a number of sayings by William of Nottingham – how he said to a novice who tried to fast but then feared he would grow weak, 'In God's name, go quickly and eat and drink, or you will grow weak because your faith has already failed, for thus Peter sank when he feared',[42] and the like. Thomas also includes sayings of Robert Grosseteste, a close friend of the Franciscans at Oxford and, before he became bishop of Lincoln, their lector. For example he tells how Grosseteste imposed a penance on a gloomy friar, enjoining him to drink a tankard of the best wine; when the friar had unwillingly done so, Grosseteste said, 'My dear brother, if you took such penance frequently you would surely have a better conscience.'[43]

The edificatory element in the *De Adventu* is of historical interest. Thomas

---

[34] *TE*, pp. 37, 90. [35] *TE*, p. 33. [36] *TE*, p. 29. [37] *TE*, pp. 83–4.
[38] *TE*, p. 35. [39] *TE*, p. 26. [40] *TE*, p. 77. [41] *TE*, p. 52.
[42] *TE*, p. 99.
[43] *TE*, p. 92. On Robert Grosseteste's *dicta* see *Robert Grosseteste Scholar and Bishop, Essays in Commemoration of the Seventh Centenary of his Death*, ed. D. A. Callus (Oxford 1955), p. 31, and E. J. Westermann, 'A comparison of some of the sermons and *Dicta* of Robert Grosseteste' in *Medievalia et Humanistica*, iii (1945), pp. 49–68.

was a second-generation friar, writing at a period when the observance of the Rule of St Francis had lost its primitive rigour. One of his objects was to inspire the English Franciscans, by recording their predecessors' achievements, to recapture the order's original idealism. He emphasizes the hardships and austerities of the early days, how the four friars who arrived at Dover lodged in the local school at night, drinking the warmed-up dregs of scholars' beer,[44] how the beer in the London convent was almost too acid to drink,[45] and how Thomas's friend Solomon and others walked barefoot in the snow.[46] No pillows or slippers, he says, were used in the custody of Oxford, no cloaks in that of Cambridge. The custody of York was famous for its poverty, Salisbury for its mutual affection, and Worcester for its simplicity.[47] Apparently to illustrate the English Franciscans' non-materialistic values, Thomas recorded Elias's command that they should wash their breeches (the Scottish friars waited for Elias's instructions before washing theirs).[48] Thomas describes the friars' warm reception by Archbishop Stephen Langton, commenting, 'I record this instance to make known the great reverence with which learned men regarded the primordial simplicity of the friars.'[49] He stresses the importance of the friars' function as confessors, a pastoral duty which kept them in close touch with the laity, and describes their successes in inducing repentance and attracting recruits to the order.[50] And he mentions their work as missionaries abroad (recording for example the projected mission of Adam of Exeter to the Saracens).[51]

Thomas particularly emphasizes the English Franciscans' close adherence to, and active defence of the Franciscan Rule. He begins Collation V, 'On the primitive purity of the friars', with the remark that the early friars 'served the Lord not so much with human constitutions, but with the unlimited love of devotion, content with the Rule and the very few statutes which were originally instituted after the confirmation of the Rule, in the same year.'[52] Thomas describes the leading part taken by Haymo of Faversham against Elias, in the interests of strict observance, in the general chapter of 1239.[53] And he records that the English friars in 1241 sent, as requested, their comments on the interpretation of the Rule to the minister general, asking him 'by the overflowing blood of Jesus Christ, that he would allow the Rule to remain as written by St Francis at the dictation of the Holy Ghost' – a petition which greatly pleased the protector of the order (the cardinal bishop of Ostia) and the friars abroad.[54] He especially praises William of Nottingham for obtaining the suppression of the papal bull *Ordinem vestrum* (of 1245), in face of the opposition of almost the entire general

---

[44] *TE*, pp. 6–7. [45] *TE*, p. 8. [46] *TE*, p. 12. [47] *TE*, pp. 35–6.
[48] *TE*, p. 42. [49] *TE*, p. 12. [50] *TE*, pp. 62–4.
[51] *TE*, pp. xxvii, 17. [52] *TE*, p. 25.
[53] *TE*, p. 68. For the zeal of Haymo and his fellows for strict observance see also pp. 29, 30.
[54] *TE*, p. 71.

chapter:[55] the bull had provided for the relaxation of the Rule in regard to the receipt of money through procurators. Thomas was opposed to the acquisition of privileges by the order – public merit, not apostolic privilege, should be the chief defence against the encroachments of prelates and princes.[56]

Thomas was worried about the transition from simple austere friaries to larger more comfortable ones. He relates a vision told him by Brother Robert of Slapton. St Francis appeared to some friars lodged in temporary quarters before acquiring a permanent site for a house. He sat looking around and the warden said, 'Father, what are you thinking?' St Francis told him to look at the place, and the warden saw it was built of twigs, mud and dung. And St Francis said, 'This is what houses of the Friars Minor should be like.'[57] Thomas records that the austere Albert of Pisa destroyed the stone cloisters at Southampton (with great difficulty because of the citizens' opposition).[58] Similarly William of Nottingham tore down the stone buildings of the Shrewsbury friary 'with marvellous devotion, much trouble and at enormous expense'.[59] When a friar threatened to accuse William to the minister general for not enclosing the London convent with a wall, 'he replied with burning zeal "I will tell the general that I didn't enter the order to build walls".'[60] Thomas comments on the simple building of the early convents (for example he mentions the very low ceiling of the infirmary at Oxford[61]). And he describes a vision experienced by a warden in which the apparition of a dead friar said that 'although friars would not be damned for excessive building, they would be severely punished'.[62]

Nevertheless Thomas was not, so to speak, a primitive purist. He was moderate and reasonable. He understood that times had changed and the increased number of friars made new buildings necessary, and that such buildings should be adequate for future expansion. Often, as the first site of a convent could not be enlarged, a new site was necessary – and removal, even if it meant a better location, was not in itself bad. Thomas also argued that bigger premises enabled the friars to grow more of their own food; and it was better to be self-supporting by means of labour, than to beg. He even allowed the argument that the 'class' of some of the new recruits to the order justified more comfortable living conditions.[63] The same moderation appears in Thomas's attitude to debt, which was forbidden by the Rule. He mentions that William of Coleville preached against it,[64] but includes some less uncompromising sayings of William of Nottingham (friars could borrow

---

[55] *TE*, p. 42 and n. See M. D. Knowles, *The Religious Orders in England*, vol. 1, *1216–1340* (Cambridge 1956), vol. 1, pp. 142–3.

[56] *TE*, p. 74. On the value of example, rather than preaching, for conversion see *TE*, p. 27.

[57] *TE*, p. 46.   [58] *TE*, pp. 79–80 and n.   [59] *TE*, p. 23.

[60] *TE*, p. 45.   [61] *TE*, p. 44.   [62] *TE*, pp. 31–2.

[63] *TE*, pp. 44–6 *passim*. For the virtue of supporting oneself by one's own labour rather than by begging see also *TE*, p. 99.

[64] *TE*, p. 37.

money, provided the terms of the loan were left to their discretion; and it was lawful to contract debts for alms).[65]

Thomas's moderate position also appears in his attitude to learning. St Francis's ideal precluded learning for its own sake:[66] learning, unless it directly contributed to salvation, should be abandoned, like property, by one who sought the spiritual life. But Thomas, like the first English friars, greatly valued study. As, according to Thomas, Robert Grosseteste used to say, 'unless friars favour study and studiously concentrate on the divine law, it would without doubt happen to us, as to the other religious, whom, alas! we see walking in the darkness of ignorance'.[67] Thomas has a collation 'On the promotion of the lecturers', mainly concerning the growth of the Franciscan school at Oxford. He describes how the friars went to their studies barefoot in the cold and mud.[68] He praises Grosseteste's teaching 'both in questions and in subtle moralities suitable for preaching'.[69] And he tells a story about a famous lecturer who regarded the inattention of students at his lectures as a divine judgment for his own failure to concentrate as a youth.[70] Apparently Grosseteste was pleased if students stayed away from his lectures, because this saved him from the sin of pride.[71]

In contrast to the *De Adventu* which, despite its occasionally haphazard arrangement, has a unifying theme, the other two mendicant histories conform to the normal chronicle. The Lanercost chronicle, as it survives today, represents more than one stage of composition.[72] It covers the period from 1201 to 1346, being appended in the only known manuscript to the chronicle of Roger of Howden.[73] It was written by a canon of the Augustinian priory of Lanercost. Having copied Howden, he then copied two chronicles, one from 1201 to 1297 and the other from 1297 to 1346, both by Franciscans, interpolating some material of his own (for example entries relating to Lanercost and some verses).[74] Only the Franciscan chronicle from 1201 to 1297 concerns us here. In its extant form it is incomplete at the beginning:

[65] *TE*, pp. 101–2.

[66] For St Francis's attitude to learning see L. Wadding, *Annales Minorum* (2nd ed., Rome 1731—), vol. 1, p. 346: 'Quaerentibus tunc quibusdam Fratribus, utrum sibi placeret, quod litterati jam recepti ad Ordinem intenderent studio sacrae Scripturae, respondit: mihi quidem placet, dum tamen exemplo Christi, qui magis orasse legitur, quam legisse, orationis studium non omittant, nec tantum studeant, ut sciant qualiter debeant loqui; sed ut audita faciant, et cum fecerint, aliis facienda proponant.' Cf. A. G. Little, *The Grey Friars in Oxford* (Oxford 1892), p. 29.

[67] *TE*, p. 91.   [68] *TE*, p. 27.

[69] *TE*, p. 48. For the aptness of this description of Franciscan studies see S. H. Thomson, *The Writings of Robert Grosseteste* (Cambridge 1940), p. 134.

[70] *TE*, p. 52.   [71] *TE*, p. 94.

[72] For the composition of the Lanercost chronicle see A. G. Little, 'The authorship of the Lanercost chronicle' in *Franciscan Papers*, pp. 42–54.

[73] BM MS. Cotton Claudius D VII. Cf. *Lan.*, p. iii.

[74] See Little, 'Authorship', p. 45 and n. 1.

it starts towards the end of Book VII (probably the earlier books were merely compiled from well-known authorities).[75] It seems to have been written in stages from about 1285 to 1297[76] and almost certainly used some existing annals,[77] besides at least one other literary authority (Martin Polonus, who was also used by Walter of Guisborough),[78] documents[79] and oral information.[80]

The Franciscan chronicle from 1201 to 1297 (the original text of which is now lost) was by a Franciscan called Richard of Durham. His authorship is proved by references in the fifteenth-century register of the Franciscans of London to certain passages 'in chronicis fratris Ricardi de Dunelmo': these passages are to be found in the Lanercost chronicle.[81] These references also show that the original Franciscan chronicle was rather fuller for the period from 1201 to 1297 than the existing version in the Lanercost chronicle (the Lanercost writer not only interpolated his exemplar but also compressed it).

Possibly Richard of Durham is to be identified with Richard of Sleckburn (Sleckburn is a village in Northumberland but it was in the palatinate of Durham). Richard of Sleckburn was the Franciscan confessor of Dervorguila the wife of John de Balliol.[82] The latter undertook to found a college at Oxford as part of a penance imposed on him by the bishop of Durham, but it was Dervorguila who, in 1282, after her husband's death, made the foundation permanent. Her agent in the foundation was Richard de Sleckburn. The Lanercost chronicle is very well informed about the origins of Balliol college.[83] This suggests the identification of Richard of Durham with Richard of Sleckburn. The possibility is reinforced by the fact that Sleckburn wrote a book of *exempla*[84] similar to those characteristic of the Lanercost

---

[75] *Lan.*, p. 21. See Little, 'Authorship', pp. 44, 51 n. 1.

[76] See Little, 'Authorship', pp. 46–7.

[77] This is suggested by the fact that the Lanercost chronicle gives some information twice, each time in different words: see, e.g., the two entries on the battle of Lewes (*Lan.*, pp. 73–5) and on the battle of Evesham (*Lan.*, pp. 75 et seq., 79).

[78] For the use in the Lanercost chronicle of Martin Polonus (otherwise called of Troppau) see Little, 'Authorship', p. 47. For Guisborough's use of the same source see p. 471 above. The Lanercost chronicle cites by name Bede, *HE* (*Lan.*, p. 174), and the St Albans chronicle (*Lan.*, p. 57), and, without acknowledgment, Geoffrey of Monmouth (see *Lan.*, p. 182).

[79] See *Lan.*, p. 140 for the text of John de Balliol's homage to Edward I. For references to other documents see p. 146.

[80] For the Lanercost chronicle's oral sources see Little, 'Authorship', p. 48 and pp. 500–1 below.

[81] See the printed text of the register of the Grey Friars of London in *Monumenta Franciscana*, ed. J. S. Brewer (RS, 1858, 1882, 2 vols), vol. 1, pp. 539–40, and in C. L. Kingsford, *The Grey Friars of London* (British Society for Franciscan Studies, vi, 1915), p. 196. The identification of the chronicle referred to in the register by the phrase *in chronicis fratris Ricardi de Dunelmo* with the lost source of the Lanercost chronicle to 1297 was made by Little, 'Authorship', pp. 42–4.

[82] Little gives the evidence suggesting that Richard of Durham and Richard of Sleckburn were the same person (he considered the identification probable); 'Authorship', pp. 49–51.

[83] *Lan.*, p. 69.

[84] The book of *exempla* is now lost. For a citation from it in a later medieval work see Little, 'Authorship', p. 50.

chronicle. Moreover, he had studied at Oxford – and some of the anecdotes in the chronicle make it clear that Richard of Durham had been a student there.[85]

Richard has a considerable amount of information about Oxford university. He relates that Edmund of Abingdon, when a young student, espoused an image of the Virgin Mary ('which we, and the whole university, have often seen') by placing on her finger a gold ring ('which many afterwards examined with their own eyes').[86] Another story particularly concerns the Franciscan convent at Oxford, telling how the warden, 'distressed by scarcity of food for the brethren', miraculously obtained generous alms from a local farmer.[87] And besides mentioning the origin of Balliol college, Richard notes the expulsion of the scholars by King John in 1208,[88] and a plague which decimated the students in 1295.[89] He also mentions the academic careers and works of some famous Oxford scholars[90] – Robert Grosseteste,[91] Alexander of Hales[92] and John Pecham.[93]

However, the identification of Richard of Durham as Richard of Sleckburn is not certain. There must have been numerous north-country friars called Richard and any one of them might have been a student at Oxford and have known about the foundation of Balliol. And although Richard of Durham mentions Dervorguila with respect, he shows no personal knowledge of her.[94] On the other hand he seems to have known well, perhaps as her confessor, Euphemia countess of Dunbar, the mother of Patrick sixth earl of Dunbar (1248–89). He tells a story of how Euphemia, angered to hear of Patrick's pleasures away from home in the courts of English nobles, jealously cursed him in church. Richard alleges that Patrick did her many injuries, and that they were only reconciled on her deathbed, in his presence.[95]

The chronicle provides another indication about Richard of Durham. Its many references to Haddington in East Lothian suggest that he was an inmate of the friary there. For example Richard records an anecdote about a friar preaching in the town, and a vision of a burgess.[96] He mentions a woman, Agnes de Burnevyle of Spott (in East Lothian) who, with her daughter, took a vow of chastity in the friary, where she was subsequently buried.[97] He notes that Patrick of Atholl was also buried in the church, having been killed in a tournament in the town (in 1242)[98] and that the latter was sacked by Scots in 1297.[99] He has a detailed account of the Lord Edward's visit to his sister Queen Margaret of Scotland when she was staying at

---

85 See *Lan.*, pp. 31, 45, 80.   86 *Lan.*, p. 36.   87 *Lan.*, pp. 130–1.
88 *Lan.*, p. 4.   89 *Lan.*, p. 163.
90 See also the list of the works of Thomas Aquinas, after his obit; *Lan.*, pp. 87–8.
91 *Lan.*, pp. 43–6 *passim*.   92 *Lan.*, p. 53.   93 *Lan.*, pp. 100–1.
94 *Lan.*, p. 134 (cf. p. 133).
95 *Lan.*, pp. 82–3 (cf. p. 54). According to GEC, *Peerage*, vol. 4, p. 506, Euphemia, wife of the fifth earl of Dunbar, died in about 1267.
96 *Lan.*, pp. 68, 162–3.   97 *Lan.*, p. 90.   98 *Lan.*, pp. 49–50.
99 *Lan.*, p. 191.

Haddington in 1266.[100] And Richard mentions that he officiated at a funeral in the neighbouring village of Tynninghame in 1246.[101]

Though Richard's chronicle has, as will be seen, value as a source for political history, its main interest lies in the light it throws on social and cultural history. It provides evidence about the work and outlook of the Franciscans in the north in the last half of the thirteenth century, and it is an important authority for the lives of the parish priests and ordinary people. Richard has a number of preoccupations (some shared with Eccleston) typical of a Franciscan. His sympathies are with the parochial clergy and their flocks, not with the religious establishment. Above all he was concerned for the salvation of souls – of mankind in general and of his readers in particular. His work has a strongly edificatory strain and was much influenced by the popular homiletic tradition. But, unlike other contemporary chronicles, Richard is often intentionally amusing.

Richard's sympathy for parish priests and the ordinary people, and his antipathy for the religious establishment, reflect his order's preoccupation with pastoral ministry. He criticizes bishops for 'the sensual indulgence of their own bellies', and for living as 'feeders *on* their flocks, rather than feeders *of* them'.[102] He accuses them of extorting money from the parish clergy. When describing the burning of Carlisle in 1292, he says that the cost of the glazing and stalls of the destroyed cathedral 'had been extorted by a robber rather than a high priest, from the purses of the stipendiary priests'.[103] He accuses Bogo de Clare of selfishly exploiting his numerous livings, and of providing inadequately for their upkeep and the cure of souls. He quotes as an example Bogo's church of Simonburn in Northumberland. This famous church, Richard says, had 'plaited withies spread with fresh cow dung in place of a panel over the high altar – and this although the church was worth seventy marks!'[104] Richard has an anecdote at the expense of an archdeacon ('an assessor of crimes and lover of transgressors'), who preferred to draw a rich revenue in his court from the sins of the people rather than reform their morals.[105] And Richard tells a story to illustrate the greater comfort enjoyed by a parish priest, if he loves God, on a small stipend augmented with the alms of the poor, than by a priest with a larger income living at the court of a rich man.[106]

Richard's dislike of the old orders, an attitude characteristic of Franciscans at this period, appears in his account of the riot of the townsmen against Norwich cathedral in 1272. He is the only chronicler to sympathize with the townsmen, not the monks. Monks, he alleges, made overbearing by their possessions ('as Daniel prophesied of Antichrist, wealth of all things destroys most men'), deposed the good old prior and chose a conceited youth.

---

[100] *Lan.*, p. 81.   [101] *Lan.*, p. 53.
[102] *Lan.*, p. 168. For invective against the church in Scotland see *Lan.*, p. 165.
[103] *Lan.*, p. 145.   [104] *Lan.*, p. 158.   [105] *Lan.*, p. 100.
[106] *Lan.*, pp. 101–2.

[497]

The latter 'enlarged his stables and increased his carriages, and even lodged his whore within the precincts'. Finally he infringed the liberties of the burgesses, who therefore revolted. Thus the prior dishonoured the Holy Trinity and sacrificed the lives of the many citizens who were later condemned by the royal justices.[107]

Richard's concern for the salvation of souls is evident in his long passages on the Fifth Crusade, telling stories to illustrate Christian heroism.[108] And he attempts to explain the tenets of the Moslem religion[109] (perhaps this indicates that he shared the view of some Franciscans that conversion should, ideally, be by persuasion, not by force).

Moreover, Richard was anxious about the salvation of the rural population in his vicinity, and *en passant* reveals the survival of paganism in the north. He tells stories demonstrating the bad luck brought by the observance of pagan superstition. He recalls, 'so that the reader would preserve the integrity of the divine faith', how during a cattle plague in Lothian, 'certain bestial people' instructed 'the idiots of the countryside' to erect statues of Priapus to save the cattle. And a Cistercian lay brother not only did this at Fenton,[110] but also sprinkled a farmer's herd with holy water infused with the testicles of dogs: when the farmer was accused of idolatry he disclaimed all knowledge, and whereas formerly his cattle had remained healthy, now two or three died daily. Similarly, Richard alleges that a parish priest called John, of Inverkeithing (in Fife), 'revived the profane rites of Priapus': carrying a phallic symbol, he led the village girls in a bacchanalian dance. By divine justice he was murdered in the night by the outraged villagers.[111]

Richard's edificatory intention permeates the book. This was no doubt one reason why he included numerous *exempla*. However, as the latter were aimed mainly at the improvement of the laity, and as Richard's principal audience must have been his fellow friars, he presumably had another reason for including them. His additional reason was probably to provide friars with moral stories to illustrate their sermons.

Some of these *exempla* relate to the laity's religious obligations. For example Richard has stories illustrating the importance of the congregation concentrating during mass, undistracted by the surroundings and the music.[112] He tells a story to show that people should go to church on important feast days (by divine retribution a farmer of Stenhouse, near Stirling, who went out ploughing on the feast of the Virgin Mary, killed his son by mistake).[113] He has a story to encourage generosity to the church: the body of a man of Bywell (near Hexham), who had refused to bequeath money to

---

[107] *Lan.*, pp. 103–4. Here these events are placed *s.a.* 1280 though they happened in 1272.

[108] See *Lan.*, pp. 27, 128–31.

[109] *Lan.*, p. 28. For the Franciscans' belief in conversion by persuasion rather than by force see Little, *Studies*, pp. 210–18 *passim*.

[110] *Lan.*, p. 85. There is a place called Fenton Barns in East Lothian. The place-name Fenton is common – it occurs in Northumberland, Yorkshire and elsewhere.

[111] *Lan.*, p. 109.　　　　[112] *Lan.*, pp. 38, 68.　　　　[113] *Lan.*, p. 117.

the church for the redemption of his soul, was buried without proper rites because of a sudden fire in his house.[114] Richard attributes the misfortunes of Berwick (devastation by the Scots and decline in trade) to the burgesses' failure to give generous alms to the Franciscans.[115] And he describes a miracle worked by a rector to persuade a rich man to pay tithe.

Other *exempla* were intended to improve laymen's general conduct. 'To frighten publicans and check tipplers', Richard tells a story about a certain William of Cunningham in East Lothian, 'a disciple of Bacchus' who spent the working day drinking beer in pubs, until the hideous ghost of a publican showed him a tubful of alcoholic vomit.[116] Richard tells a story to discourage usury[117] and has, as 'an image of the covetousness of this world', an anecdote about two monkeys owned by Robert, bishop of Durham (1274–83), who kept them 'to lighten the burden of his cares'. The bishop ordered a spoonful of almonds to be given to the younger one, who hastily crammed them into her cheek to prevent the other monkey from having any. But as soon as the bishop's servant had gone, the other one set upon her, forcing every almond out of her mouth.[118]

Richard's sympathy for the poor appears in a story unfavourable to the enclosure of common land: the twelve jurors who decided a case concerning common pasture in favour of the Augustinian canons of Markby, in Lincolnshire, all came in turn to a bad end.[119] And Richard emphasizes the equality of all men before God. He tells how a bishop suspended a vicar for having a concubine. The vicar told his mistress what had happened and she said, 'I will get the better of the bishop.' So she took some pudding, chicken and eggs, and on meeting the bishop told him she was taking them 'to the bishop's sweetheart who was lately brought to bed'. The bishop repented immediately and absolved the vicar.[120]

Some of the *exempla* were intended for the edification of parish clergy. Richard was particularly interested in clerical celibacy. Besides the story just quoted he has one, for example, about a clerk of Well, in Yorkshire, who kept a mistress. He hid her in a vaulted room with the money when his master's steward came to collect the income due. The girl thought that she would take the chance of providing for herself for life, so she took the money and had herself released from the room on pretext of the necessities of nature. So the clerk lost his job because he could not render account.[121] Such yarns, showing an earthy sense of humour, were obviously meant to amuse as well as edify (and at least one of Richard's anecdotes has no apparent moral[122]). Richard, who was sometimes consciously witty,[123] included some stories 'as a joke',[124] and others because, he says, a chronicle should not be dull.[125]

[114] *Lan.*, p. 119. [115] *Lan.*, p. 186. [116] *Lan.*, pp. 136–7.
[117] *Lan.*, pp. 98–9. [118] *Lan.*, p. 114. [119] *Lan.*, pp. 125–6.
[120] *Lan.*, p. 93. [121] *Lan.*, p. 134. Cf. *Lan.* pp. 80–2. [122] *Lan.*, pp. 95–6.
[123] See the quip made by a baron after feasting on lampreys: on being told that it was Judgment Day he said, 'If this is Judgment Day, we shall soon rise with full bellies'; *Lan.*, p. 116.
[124] *Lan.*, pp. 84, 99–100, 134. [125] *Lan.*, p. 117.

Obviously Richard's chronicle was not primarily a record of political events. Nevertheless it has entries relating to general history. Thus Richard gives a full account of the Barons' War. But, though he quotes as informants a knight who fought at Lewes and one who fought at Evesham,[126] he is not a reliable authority for the crisis. He wrote a generation later and interpreted his material in a characteristically edificatory way. He is more apt than any contemporary chronicler to regard disasters as divine retribution, and this penchant is particularly marked in his treatment of the baronial period.

Richard's interpretation is based on moral values. The struggle began as one between good and evil. The barons were good: Simon was the bravest soldier and a pious man; he attended mass before the battle of Evesham and was prepared to die, saying to his men, 'We have breakfasted here and shall dine in heaven.'[127] And his body worked miracles 'to the present time'.[128] Simon's son Henry was also good – he was as amiable and handsome as Jonathan, and as devout as David.[129] The barons were strict in religious observance: before the battle of Lewes they kept vigil and confessed. On the other hand the king's men were bad. They drank and sang before the battle and amused themselves with loose women ('they enjoyed their beds, defiled with harlots, in front of the very altars of the church of St. Pancras').[130]

But Richard had to explain the barons' ultimate defeat. He did this by finding a moral flaw in Simon de Montfort. The latter had married Eleanor, Henry III's sister, although she had taken a vow of perpetual celibacy.[131] This, according to Richard, was the cause of his downfall. The obscene mutilation of Simon's body was divine retribution for the sin. He writes, with reference to the mutilation: 'what had violated a vow of continence should itself be violated, and that through which Simon had sinned should be punished'.[132] Similarly Richard ascribes Henry of Almain's subsequent murder to Eleanor's sin.[133]

Richard's value as an authority for political history increases as he nears his own time. His chronicle is particularly useful for the Anglo-Scottish wars.[134] For example Richard himself witnessed the burning of Carlisle by the Scots in 1292 ('I saw birds flying about half burnt attempting to escape').[135] And he is the only authority for the statement that the Scots, 'adding fresh insolence to folly', burnt 'the little scholars' of Hexham in 1296.[136] Richard knew people who could give him information: he quotes as informants the confessor of Margaret queen of Scotland,[137] the confessor

---

[126] Richard quotes witnesses for the battle of Lewes and the battle of Evesham; *Lan.*, pp. 74, 76.
[127] *Lan.*, p. 76. [128] *Lan.*, p. 77. [129] *Lan.*, p. 76. [130] *Lan.*, p. 74.
[131] *Lan.*, p. 76. For Eleanor de Montfort's vow of perpetual celibacy, from which Simon de Montfort obtained her absolution from the pope, see GEC, *Peerage*, vol. 7, p. 547 n. a.
[132] *Lan.*, pp. 76–7. For references to the mutilation of Simon's body see *Osney*, p. 170; *TW*, p. 174; *Wav.*, p. 365. Cf. C. Bémont, *Simon de Montfort* (Paris 1884), p. 242 n. 2.
[133] *Lan.*, p. 90.
[134] The Lanercost chronicle is used as a source by Barrow, *Bruce, passim*, who does not, however, consider it reliable in all respects (see ibid., p. 21 and n. 2).
[135] *Lan.*, p. 145. [136] *Lan.*, p. 174. [137] *Lan.*, p. 97.

of Alexander III[138] and a knight who attended the latter on his deathbed,[139] emissaries of the king of Norway,[140] a Franciscan who had been in Rome,[141] a Frenchman,[142] and a man who had drunk wine from the sixty hogsheads captured by the men of the Cinque Ports from the French in 1296.[143]

Some of Richard's information is also found in Walter of Guisborough and/or Peter of Langtoft, writers who drew on common sources. For example both Richard and Walter record the fire at Boston in Lincolnshire in 1288,[144] and in Guisborough priory in 1289.[145] Richard's attitude to the Scots closely resembles Guisborough's and Langtoft's: the Scots were insane robbers and perfidious perjurors.[146] And though he does not quote any of the political verses cited by Langtoft, he mentions corresponding Scottish ones with strong disapproval: 'the biting tongues of certain evil men, who either could not or dared not do injury by force, composed ballads stuffed with insults and obscenity, to the blasphemy of our illustrious prince and the dishonour of his race, which, though they are not recorded here, will never be blotted from the memory of posterity.'[147]

Like Eccleston's *De Adventu* and the Lanercost chronicle, Nicholas Trevet's *Annales Sex Regum Angliae* (*Annals of Six Kings of England*) reflect aspects of the mendicants' lives – but different aspects. Trevet was a well-known scholar in close touch with the royal court and papal curia. Though devout, Trevet's subject was not like Eccleston's a history of his Order. Though a friar, he was not like Richard of Durham primarily concerned with the saving of souls of ordinary people. He wrote a general history centred on the monarch, Edward I.

Much more is known of Trevet's life than about either Eccleston or Richard of Durham.[148] He was probably born in about 1258 and died soon after 1334.[149] His father was Thomas Trevet, a landowner in Norfolk and Somerset and probably a knight, who was of some importance in the king's

---

[138] *Lan.*, p. 111.
[139] Ibid.
[140] *Lan.*, p. 104.
[141] *Lan.*, p. 121.
[142] *Lan.*, p. 89.
[143] *Lan.*, p. 183.
[144] *Lan.*, p. 122. Cf. p. 473 and n. 272 above.
[145] *Lan.*, p. 123. Cf. p. 472 above.
[146] See *Lan.*, pp. 170, 171, 173, 190. Cf. pp. 475, 483 above.
[147] *Lan.*, p. 166. Cf. above.
[148] For an outline of the facts known about Nicholas Trevet's life see the introduction to T. Hog's edition. For his position as an Oxford scholar see A. G. Little and F. Pelster, *Oxford Theology and Theologians A.D. 1282–1302* (Oxford Historical Society, xcvi, 1934), pp. 283–5. For his work as a biblical scholar, etc., see F. Ehrle, 'Nikolaus Trivet, sein Leben, seine Quolibet und Quaestiones ordinariae', in *Festgabe Clemens Baeumker* (Beiträge zur Geschichte der Philosophie des Mittelalters, Supplementband ii, Munster 1923), pp. 1–63. For Trevet's connection with continental scholars see R. J. Dean, 'Cultural relations in the middle ages: Nicholas Trevet and Nicholas of Prato' in *Studies in Philology*, xlv (1948), pp. 541–64. For Trevet's classical studies see Beryl Smalley, *English Friars and Antiquity in the Early Fourteenth Century* (Oxford 1960), pp. 58–65 (and see the further references in the index to ibid.).
[149] Little and Pelster, op. cit., p. 285, place Trevet's death in *c.* 1328 or 1330. But his chronicle (for which see below) refers to the year 1334 so he must still have been alive then; see Legge, *A-N Lit.*, p. 300.

service.[150] As Nicholas himself records, Thomas was a justice in eyre in 1272.[151] He assessed tallage for the king in the west country in 1260, joined the barons in their revolt against Henry III, but was subsequently reconciled with the king, first acting as a justice in eyre in 1268. He was a justice of gaol delivery at Ilchester (in Somerset) in 1276 and 1279, and died in 1281.

Nicholas became a Dominican at Oxford and already had made a name by 1297. He probably incepted in 1303 and taught at Oxford until he went to study in Paris. By 1314 he was again teaching at Oxford, but left soon afterwards and spent the rest of his life as a lecturer in the Dominican friary in London (there is an unsubstantiated tradition that he was prior of the London convent).[152]

Nicholas Trevet's principal works, some of which are only known by bibliographers' references to them, can be roughly classified in three groups. First, there are university disputations and polemics (for example *quodlibeta* and *quaestiones*). Second, there are numerous commentaries on the bible, the fathers, the classics, and on other works. Third, there are three histories.[153] The commentaries can be subdivided into religious and secular ones. Trevet wrote, for example, commentaries on St Augustine's *De Civitate Dei* and on the Psalms, and commentaries on Livy[154] and Seneca's tragedies:[155] the latter are purely secular in subject.

At first, while at Oxford, Trevet concentrated on academic and religious topics and probably wrote partly to promote biblical studies in the Dominican order. The general chapter held at Strasbourg in 1307 approved Trevet's commentaries on Genesis and Exodus which he had submitted to it. One of Trevet's patrons was the master general of the Dominicans, Aylmer. The latter asked Trevet to write commentaries on the rest of the Pentateuch, and Trevet dedicated his commentary on Leviticus to him.[156] The prior provincial, John of Bristol, commissioned Trevet's commentary on the Psalms.[157]

Trevet had an international reputation. In fact his commentaries may have been better known in France and Italy than in England. His reputation abroad was partly due to the international organization of his order. Possibly he attended general chapters and certainly knew people who did. It was also partly due to his friendship with Nicholas de Prato, a Dominican who was

---

[150] For Thomas Trevet see C. Moor, *Knights of Edward I* (Harleian Soc., lxxx–lxxxiv, 1929–32, 5 vols), vol. 5, p. 48.

[151] *NT*, p. 279.   [152] See Dean, 'Relations', p. 545.   [153] See ibid., p. 547.

[154] For Trevet's commentary on Livy see R. J. Dean, 'The earliest known commentary on Livy is by Nicholas Trevet' in *Medievalia et Humanistica*, iii (1945), pp. 86–98.

[155] For Trevet's commentary on Seneca's tragedies, which has some textual value, see Dean, 'Relations', p. 560 n. 35; E. Franceschini, 'Glosse e commenti medievali a Seneca tragico' in his *Studi e Note di Filologia Latina Medievale* (Pubblicazioni dell'Università Cattolica del Sacro Cuore, serie quarta: Scienze Filologiche, xxx, Milan 1938), pp. 1–105; and Dean in *Medium Ævum*, x (1941), pp. 162–3. The commentary is edited by E. Franceschini, *Il Commento di Nicolo Trevet al Tieste di Seneca* (Orbis Romanus: Biblioteca dei testi medievali a curadell' Università Cattolica del Sacro Cuore, xi, società editrice 'Vita e Pensiero', Milan 1938).

[156] See Dean, 'Relations', p. 548.   [157] Ibid., p. 552.

bishop of Spoleto from 1299 to 1303, cardinal bishop of Ostia from 1303 to 1321, and dean of the College of Cardinals. It is not known when Trevet first met de Prato. It could have been as early as 1301 when de Prato came to England as a papal nuncio and possibly stayed with the Dominicans of Oxford (to whom he bequeathed one of his books in 1321). On the other hand Trevet may have met him at a general chapter. However they met, de Prato took a part in the dissemination of Trevet's works abroad. When a notary of Arezzo, Ser Simone, bequeathed his library in 1338, it included five of Trevet's books: it is likely that he obtained them from de Prato as he was an executor of de Prato's will.[158] Furthermore de Prato contributed to the involvement of Trevet in the European humanist movement. Trevet sent a copy of the commentary on Genesis to Pope John XXII who, having admired it, commissioned him to write the commentary on Livy.[159] Most of Trevet's subsequent commentaries are on secular works – on Cicero, Juvenal and Virgil.

Trevet's historical works belong to the period of his life when he was preoccupied with secular writings. He wrote his three histories after 1320 but his historical interests date back at least to the time in Paris, where, as he says in the preface of the *Annals*, he collected material relating to England 'from the acts of the French and the Normans'.[160] Trevet was already in contact with people at court, from whom he may have hoped to obtain documents and oral information. In about 1314 he dedicated his commentary on the Declamations of the elder Seneca to John of Lenham, the confessor of Edward II,[161] and at about this time he dedicated a treatise on the mass to John of Droxford, bishop of Bath and Wells (1309–29) who had formerly been keeper of the king's wardrobe (1295–1307, 1308–9) and acted as treasurer in 1295.[162] As neither of these men were Dominicans, the dedications show Trevet's wide connections.

Trevet's three historical works were: *Historia ab orbe condito ad Christi Nativitatem* (*History from the Creation of the World to the Birth of Christ*); a chronicle in Anglo-Norman (covering the period from the Creation of the world to 1285); and the *Annales Sex Regum Angliae*. The *Historia*, completed between 1327 and 1329, was dedicated to Hugh of Angoulême, archdeacon of Canterbury and papal nuncio.[163] It is a history of the world (of no value as a historical source today) written under the influence of another Dominican, Vincent of Beauvais, the author, or rather general editor, of the *Speculum Historiale*, a universal history compiled in the mid-thirteenth

---

[158] Ibid., pp. 562–3.
[159] For the evidence that Pope John XXII commanded Trevet to write the commentary on Livy see Dean, 'The earliest known commentary on Livy is by Nicholas Trevet', pp. 90–1.
[160] *NT*, p. 2.
[161] See Dean, 'Relations', p. 149.
[162] Ibid., p. 149. Cf. F. M. Powicke and E. B. Fryde, *Handbook of British Chronology* (Royal Historical Soc., 1961), pp. 78, 100.
[163] The *Historia* is unprinted. See Legge, *A-N Lit.*, p. 299.

century.[164] The chronicle in Anglo-Norman, the last of Trevet's historical works, was written in about 1334. Trevet dedicated it to Edward I's daughter Mary, a nun of Amesbury (she entered the convent in 1285), intending to provide her with a short amusing world history. In fact Trevet finished it after Mary's death (she died in 1332).[165]

The *Historia* and chronicle both illustrate aspects of Dominican historiography in general, and of Trevet's historical writing in particular. These two works, like other Dominican histories (and unlike Franciscan ones) were compilations, relying mainly on earlier authorities. And they were universal histories (the chronicle is the first such history in Anglo-Norman). The chronicle also illustrates a characteristic of Trevet, his affection for Edward I and the royal family. Trevet did not write easily in Anglo-Norman (his style is rather stilted) but he tried to write a courtly book to entertain the princess, interspersing amusing anecdotes. Various factors contributed to Trevet's affection for the Angevin royal house. As a Dominican he would have respected Henry III and Edward I because they were generous patrons of the order. Edward I was regarded as the founder of the London convent at Ludgate, besides being a benefactor of the Oxford Dominicans.[166] Moreover, Thomas Trevet's career in the royal service may have enlisted his son's sympathies with the ruling class.

Trevet probably wrote the *Annals* in about 1320.[167] They are a history of the kings of England from Stephen to Edward I, set in its European context (papal, imperial and French history are included). Much of the *Annals* is derived from earlier sources. Trevet rarely states his authority, but for English affairs he used William of Newburgh, Robert of Torigni, Ralph Diceto, the *Itinerary* of Richard I, Roger of Wendover, Matthew Paris, the *Flores Historiarum* and Walter of Guisborough.[168] For continental affairs he used Martin Polonus and Vincent of Beauvais. As his sources suggest, Trevet was much influenced by the historiography of the Benedictines and Augustinian canons, and the form of the *Annals* is very like a normal monastic chronicle. The arrangement is almost entirely chronological and the entries are short. The record element, typical of the monastic chronicle, appears in Trevet's use of documents. He cites a number in full, some at least of which he must have obtained through his contacts at court – for example

---

[164] For the *Speculum Historiale* (edited as *Bibliotheca Mundi* by the Benedictines of Saint Vast at Douai, Douai 1624, 4 vols) see Little, 'Chronicles', p. 37.

[165] Trevet's chronicle is unpublished. See Legge, *A-N Lit.*, pp. 299–302. The chronicle was popular in the fourteenth century (at least six complete manuscripts of it survive) and one anecdote in it, the Tale of Constance, was used by Chaucer for *The Man of Law's Tale*, and by Gower for *Confessio Amantis*; see ibid., p. 301 and n. 3, and, for a printed text of the story in Trevet, *Originals and Analogues of some of Chaucer's Canterbury Tales*, ed. F. J. Furnival, E. Brock and W. A. Clouston (Chaucer Soc., 2nd series, vii, 1872, etc.), pp. iii–xii, 1–53.

[166] See W. A. Hinnebusch, *The Early English Friars Preachers*, pp. 12, 15, 34–8 *passim*.

[167] The date of the *Annals* is indicated by the prologue (*NT*, p. 2) which says that '120 years and more' had passed from the accession of King John. Cf. Little, 'Chronicles', p. 39.

[168] See Little, 'Chronicles', p. 40.

the only copies of Boniface VIII's correspondence with Edward I and the magnates on the question of supremacy over Scotland.[169]

If in form the *Annals* are like a monastic chronicle, their content shows Dominican features. They are more European in outlook than the contemporary monastic productions. Moreover, Trevet gives information about the Dominican order, particularly in England, although he does not try to record its complete history.[170] His interest in learning is reflected in the notices and obituaries of famous scholars, especially Oxford graduates, with lists of their works.[171]

Trevet's royalist tendencies appear throughout. He says in the prologue that he collected material in Paris on English history because the writing of patriotic histories in England had been neglected since the accession of King John. The history of one's own country should, in his view, be patriotic. He was comparing English thirteenth-century historiography with contemporary French work, which, he says, praised the rulers in the style of the Greeks and the Romans. The neglect in England was, he suggests, the result of 'the viciousness which makes people hate their princes and delight rather in abusing than in praising them'. History he asserts, is here 'disgracefully blackened by detractions of preceding kings, while foreign customs are extolled to the skies'.[172]

It is hardly surprising, in view of Trevet's patriotic motive, that he to some extent whitewashes the Angevin kings. He is never fulsomely eulogistic but he is very brief about, or suppresses, discreditable information. For example he makes the briefest mention of the barons' revolt against King John. He deals with the baronial opposition to Henry III in a similar short, objective way. And when describing the battle of Evesham he is the only authority for the statement that the Lord Edward provided an honourable burial for the fallen barons,[173] and he says nothing about the mutilation of Simon de Montfort's body.

The most interesting and original passages in the *Annals* relate personally to Henry III and Edward I. They show that Trevet collected not only documents from his friends at court, but also verbal information – first-hand impressions of the kings and intimate anecdotes about them. Trevet describes Henry III's character and appearance after the notice of his death:[174]

---

[169] *NT*, pp. 379–94. For this correspondence see E. L. G. Stones, 'The appeal to history in Anglo-Scottish relations between 1291 and 1401: Part I', *Archives*, ix (1969), p. 19 and nn. 78–9, and pp. 442–3 above.

[170] Trevet's account (*NT*, p. 209) of the foundation of the Dominican convent at Oxford in 1221 is quoted by Hinnebusch, op. cit., pp. 3–4. On the value of Trevet's information on the early history of the Dominicans in England see Little, 'Chronicles', p. 40.

[171] See for example *NT*, pp. 221–3, 224–5, 227, 229–30, 278–9, 287–91, 364.

[172] *NT*, pp. 1–2.

[173] *NT*, p. 266.

[174] *NT*, pp. 279–80. This and the following passage are quoted by F. M. Powicke, *Henry III and the Lord Edward* (Oxford 1947, 2 vols), vol. 2, pp. 686–7 (who at the end of the next passage incorrectly translates 'venabulum' as 'trap or buckstall' instead of 'hunting-spear').

This king was considered to be as little prudent in secular affairs as he was great in devotion to the Lord. For he was accustomed to hear three sung masses a day, and, wishing to hear more, he assiduously attended masses celebrated privately. Indeed it happened that St. Louis, king of the French, when discussing this with him, said that he should not always spend his time at mass, but should listen to sermons more often. To whom [Henry] wittily replied that he preferred to see his Friend more often that to hear Him speak, although uttering good things. [Henry] was of medium height, of compact build, with the lid of one eye drooping so that it hid part of the black pupil; he was strong in build, but rash in behaviour.

Trevet describes Edward I's habits and appearance at his accession:[175]

He was a man of tried prudence in affairs of state. He was devoted in adolescence to the practice of arms by which he acquired a widespread reputation for chivalry – his fame excelled every prince of his time throughout the christian world. He was elegant in form, of commanding height, exceeding an ordinary man from the leg upwards. His looks were enhanced by a beard which in adolescence turned from a silvery colour to gold, became black, when he reached manhood, and in old age changed from grey to the whiteness of a swan. He had a broad forehead and regular features, except that the lid of the left eye was lower, recalling his father's appearance. He had a lisp but was nevertheless effectively eloquent in speech when persuasion was necessary in business. His arms were long in proportion to his agile body, and none was more able, with sinuous dexterity, to wield a sword. His stomach protruded, and his long thighs made it impossible for him to be unseated by the galloping or jumping of the most spirited horse. When he had finished with fighting, he indulged in hunting and hawking. He especially hunted the stag, which he pursued on a courser and when he had caught one, struck it with his sword, instead of using a hunting-spear.

Trevet thought that Edward I was divinely protected. He illustrates this with two anecdotes. Edward when a young man was playing chess one day 'in a vaulted chamber' and for no particular reason suddenly left the room. Immediately a large stone, which would certainly have killed him, fell on his place.[176] On another occasion (in 1297) Edward nearly had a fatal accident at Winchelsea. He was riding along the town wall to see the fleet when suddenly his horse shied at the turning sails of a windmill, and when Edward beat it and spurred it on, it leapt from the battlements. The king's

[175] *NT*, pp. 281–2.   [176] *NT*, p. 282.

companions and all onlookers thought he would be killed, but the horse landed on the road below which was thick with mud, softened by recent rain. The horse slid twelve feet but did not fall, and Edward was unhurt.[177]

Another of Trevet's stories shows Edward's bravery and good humour. He was hawking by a stream and saw one of his companions on the other side trying ineffectually to deal with a falcon which had attacked a duck. As the man ignored his criticism, Edward lost his temper, swam his horse across the stream, and, despite an overhanging bank, clambered out. He chased the man with his sword, but when the latter submitted Edward stopped his horse, sheathed his sword and returned amicably with the culprit.[178]

One story seems merely to illustrate Edward's quick wit. In 1281 Edward visited his mother at Amesbury, where she had become a nun. He found that she had had a visit from a disreputable knight who claimed to have been cured of blindness at the tomb of Henry III. Edward tried to dissuade his mother from believing such a tale, and she became angry with him, sending him from the room. As he left he met the prior provincial of the Dominican order, Hugh of Manchester (1279–82), and said to him, 'I know the justice of my father so well that I am sure he would have pulled out the eyes whole of such a scoundrel rather than have restored the lost light to so much iniquity.'[179]

These anecdotes show that Trevet wished to make his work amusing. In this he succeeded, for at least seventeen medieval manuscripts of the *Annals* survive today.[180] He was the only thirteenth-century mendicant historian to achieve popularity (only two complete manuscripts of Eccleston and one of the Lanercost chronicle are known), and was much used by later chroniclers.[181]

---

[177] *NT*, p. 359. Trevet precedes this passage with what is surely an eye-witness description of Winchelsea.

[178] *NT*, pp. 282–3. Cited Powicke, op. cit., p. 687.

[179] *NT*, pp. 302–3. Cited Powicke, op. cit., p. 726.

[180] See Hardy, *Catalogue*, vol. 3, pp. 295–6.

[181] For example by Thomas of Walsingham see *NT*, pp. ix–x.

21

The Chronicle of London

The mendicant chroniclers reflect the growing importance of towns in English life – the sympathies of Eccleston and Richard of Durham were with townspeople, and Trevet was himself a Londoner. By the last half of the thirteenth century, London had been a potent political and economic force for over a century. It had privileges of self-government, derived from ancient custom and royal charters. It had a rich oligarchy of merchants and financiers, a thriving population of craftsmen and shop-keepers, besides many poorer people.

Already in Henry II's reign, London had inspired one citizen, William Fitz Stephen, to write about it.[1] But his work is a description of the city's social life, not a chronicle. In Edward I's reign two of the chroniclers already discussed paid particular attention to London affairs – Thomas Wykes, who lived for a time in London, and the author of the Westminster version of the *Flores Historiarum*. Furthermore, three other chronicles, all continuations of the *Flores*, were written by Londoners. The earliest was a set of annals (the *Annales Sancti Pauli*) from 1064 to 1274 written at St Paul's, London.[2] The author made extensive use of the *Flores* but added his own material which appears to have been derived from his own observation from about 1250. He probably wrote fairly contemporarily with events from about 1260 and gives a useful, if brief, account of the civil war (he was a moderate sympathizer with Simon de Montfort). Another of the London chronicles, the *Annales Paulini*, was also written at St Paul's. It was a continuation of the *Flores* from 1307 to 1341, and falls outside our period.[3] The other London chronicle was the *Annales Londonienses*, written by someone closely connected with the Guildhall, perhaps Andrew Horn, fishmonger of Bridge Street and chamberlain of the city from about 1320.[4] Horn died in 1328 but the chronicle continues to 1330; however, the last two annals could well have been added

---

[1] See pp. 307–8.

[2] The *Annales Sancti Pauli* are described and extracts printed by F. Liebermann in *MGH, Scriptores*, xxviii (Hanover 1888), pp. 548–51.

[3] See p. 379 and nn. 174, 180.

[4] Printed *Chronicles of the Reigns of Edward I and Edward II*, ed. W. Stubbs (RS, 1882, 1883, 2 vols), vol. 1, pp. 3–251. For evidence that Andrew Horn might be the author see ibid., pp. xxii–xxviii. For Horn see G. A. Williams, *Medieval London: from Commune to Capital* (London 1963), pp. 268–70, 312–13 (and his index for further references); Williams, op. cit., *passim*, accepts Horn as the author of the *Annales Londonienses*.

by another author. The chronicle is based on an abbreviated version of the *Flores* to 1301, into which the author interpolated his own material. From 1274 these additions seem to have been written fairly close to the events recorded.[5] The chronicle is arranged like a monastic one: the entries combine local and general history and there are numerous copies of documents relating to national affairs. Although the account of national events from 1289 to 1316 is of some value today, its use is limited by a gap from 1293 to 1301 and by the fact that the documents it cites in the annal for 1302 are also in the *Flores*. Its interest in local history is particularly centred on the Court of Arches and the other ecclesiastical courts in London. Stubbs pointed out that some of its information on thirteenth-century London history must be derived from a lost London chronicle.[6]

The only chronicle in our period to concentrate almost exclusively on London was the *Cronica Maiorum et Vicecomitum Londoniarum (Chronicle of the Mayors and Sheriffs of London)*.[7] It covers the period from 1188 to the coronation of Edward I and was written in stages from about 1258 to 1272. It is of unique importance for the history of London and for the city's relations with the king. And, because London was a centre of national affairs, it is a valuable source for the history of the Barons' War. The author of the chronicle was probably Arnold Fitz Thedmar,[8] alderman of the Bridge ward, and possibly the holder of some other office in the city.[9] Fitz Thedmar belonged to a well-established London family and was himself rich, owning a great hall, a house and other properties in the parish of All Hallows Haywharf.[10] He had four sisters advantageously married in the city,[11] one to John of Gisors, a wealthy merchant and financier.[12]

The evidence that Fitz Thedmar wrote the chronicle is strong, but it is circumstantial and not conclusive. Some of the evidence is in the chronicle itself. The latter has explicit details about Fitz Thedmar. Thus it states that in January 1258 he, as an alderman, was summoned, together with the sheriff of London, Henry Walemund, to appear before Henry III in the royal

---

[5] Stubbs, op. cit., p. xviii.   [6] Ibid., pp. xxi–xxii.

[7] Printed in *De Antiquis Legibus Liber: Cronica Maiorum et Vicecomitum Londoniarum . . . cum Appendice*, ed. Thomas Stapleton (Camden Soc., 1846), pp. 1–177. The chronicle only survives today as one item in a composite volume, the *Liber de Antiquis Legibus*, for which see p. 510 and n. 17 below; other items are described and some printed (see e.g. p. 510 and n. 17 below) as an appendix in ibid., pp. 179–253. For an English translation of the chronicle and other items in the *Liber de Antiquis Legibus* see H. T. Riley, *Chronicles of the Mayors and Sheriffs of London, A.D. 1188 to A.D. 1274 . . .* (London 1863). Riley claims (ibid., p. xi) to have based his translation on 'a careful collation' of Stapleton's text with the original volume. Neither Stapleton's edition nor Riley's translation conforms with modern standards of scholarship. Although Riley realized that the author begins the year on 29 September (see Riley, op. cit., p. 61 n. 2), he headed his pages with the year-dates as calculated by the chronicler, with results which are confusing for the modern reader. Nor did Stapleton add year-dates calculated from 1 January. For a notice of the chronicle, putting it in the context of London's historiographical tradition, see Ralph Flenley, *Six Town Chronicles of England* (Oxford 1911), p. 8.

[8] This suggestion is made by Riley, op. cit., pp. viii–x.

[9] See p. 511.   [10] See Williams, op. cit., p. 54.   [11] *L de AL*, p. 239.

[12] Williams, op. cit., p. 69.

Exchequer, to answer charges of peculation and fraud. Accusations had been brought against the city authorities by certain citizens: but according to the chronicle, which gives a very full account of the affair,[13] Fitz Thedmar and Walemund had not been accused.[14] Later in the same year the chronicle records that when John Mansel, who held the royal enquiry into the charges, appointed new aldermen to replace the previous ones, he exempted Fitz Thedmar. This was because Fitz Thedmar 'had been accused of nothing, except with regard to weighing with the balance – the method of weighing had previously been rectified by him and others, as mentioned above in this record'[15] (a reference to the full description, under 1256, of the reform of weighing methods in the city[16]). The chronicle asserts that Fitz Thedmar's inclusion among the accused was due to malice, and records that his innocence was publicly testified by John Mansel in the folkmoot at St Paul's Cross on 6 November: the king was present and Fitz Thedmar was restored to favour and office.

More evidence supporting Fitz Thedmar's claim to authorship is provided by another work, a short biography of Fitz Thedmar which survives today in the same manuscript as the chronicle. Both are in the *Liber de Antiquis Legibus (Book of Ancient Laws)*, a composite volume of miscellaneous historical and legal material mainly relating to London, compiled in the late thirteenth and early fourteenth centuries, and preserved since it was written with the records of the corporation of London.[17] The presence in it of Fitz Thedmar's biography shows that the volume had some connection with him. Moreover if, as seems likely, the biography was in fact an autobiography, it proves that Fitz Thedmar was a writer. And part of the biography has a marked resemblance in content and style to the chronicle.

The biography falls into two parts. First, there is an account of Fitz Thedmar's grandparents and parents. The biography relates that his grandfather, Arnold, and grandmother, Ode, visited England as pilgrims to the tomb of St Thomas. They went to London before returning home, wishing to see 'such a noble and famous a city', and were so impressed that they remained. The biography records that the couple had two children: one, Juliana, married a native of Bremen[18] called Thedmar, by whom she had eleven children. Their fifth son was the Arnold Fitz Thedmar here under discussion. He was named Arnold after his grandfather and his birth was

---

[13] *L de AL*, pp. 30–7. For this enquiry see Williams, op. cit., pp. 209–10.

[14] *L de AL*, p. 34.

[15] Ibid., p. 37.

[16] Ibid., p. 25.

[17] The *Liber de Antiquis Legibus* is now in the Record Office of the Corporation of London, Guildhall, London, E.C.2. Fitz Thedmar's biography is printed *L de AL*, pp. 238–42 (for an English translation see Riley, op. cit., pp. 201–8).

[18] Arnold Fitz Thedmar, the subject of the biography, seems to have kept some connection with Bremen, for he employed a servant called Hermann of Bremen; see the letter of 1276 by the city of Bremen to Edward I printed in *Foedera*, vol. 1, pt ii, p. 534 (cf. Riley, op. cit., p. ix n. 4).

foretold by a vision (described at some length in the hagiographical fashion). Arnold outlived his brothers and sisters.

The second part of the biography is a record of Fitz Thedmar's struggle to obtain acquittance from contributions to the fine of £20,000 imposed by Henry III on the city in 1266 for co-operating with the barons in 1264.[19] The biography asserts that the assessment of the citizens for the fine, which was paid in instalments, was inequitable, and that those, including Fitz Thedmar, acquitted from further payment were nevertheless charged again by Walter Hervey, the mayor elected in 1272. The biography details the demands on Fitz Thedmar; and it gives the text of the acquittance ('enrolled on the rolls of the city and of the chamberlain') awarded him by jurors in 1267, and the texts of the acquittances, ignored according to the biography, by Hervey and his successor as mayor, Henry le Waleys, granted by Henry III and Edward I. The work ends with the text of the agreement between Henry le Waleys and Fitz Thedmar acquitting the latter of further payment. This section of the biography has the same justificatory tone as the account in the chronicle concerning Fitz Thedmar's vindication during the royal inquiry on fraud in 1258.[20] The chronicle itself does not mention Fitz Thedmar in connection with the 1266 fine, but it does indignantly record Hervey's collection of arrears despite royal acquittances to individual citizens.[21] And Hervey is the object of the chronicle's persistent criticism.[22]

The *Liber de Antiquis Legibus* has one further piece of evidence strengthening the case for Fitz Thedmar's authorship. It has a list of charters headed: 'On this leaf are set forth what charters were in the chest of the citizens in the year of our Lord 1270: this chest was at that time in the custody of Arnold Fitz Thedmar, under the keys of Robert of Cornhill, Robert of Rokesley and John Adrien, draper.'[23] In exactly what capacity Fitz Thedmar had charge of the city archives is not clear, but access to them would certainly have facilitated his work as a chronicler and could well have encouraged him to write.

The evident motives for writing the chronicle and the views it expresses are those to be expected of a member of the city oligarchy like Fitz Thedmar. The chronicle resembles a monastic production in that its centre of interest and loyalty was the institution to which the author was attached – here the city of London. Like a monastic chronicle, it is both an institutional record and a *pièce justificative* of the group of men it represents.

The record element is obvious. The idea of writing such a chronicle, a quasi-official production, may well have derived from historical notes

---

[19] For the payment of this fine, which proved troublesome, see Williams, op. cit., pp. 235–41 *passim.*

[20] See pp. 509–10, 513.   [21] *L de AL*, pp. 148–9.

[22] See e.g. *L de AL*, pp. 119, 159, 164–5, 169–70.

[23] *L de AL*, p. 253. For Robert of Cornhill, Robert of Rokesley and John Adrien, all prominent citizens, see the entries listed in the index to Williams, op. cit. Robert of Cornhill and John Adrien were royalists during the baronial period; see ibid., pp. 211, 212.

entered on lists of mayors and sheriffs. Each year in the chronicle begins with a notice of the election of the two sheriffs (of the city and Middlesex). It also records the appointment of the mayor, and his and the sheriffs' presentation at the royal Exchequer for admission to office: any unusual circumstance is recorded. For example in 1272 the sheriffs were admitted to office in 'the small chamber next to the Receipt by the Thames' and not in the Exchequer room as was customary.[24] It records regulations made in the Hustings court for the government of the citizens (for example concerning testamentary cases[25] and the like[26]).

The chronicle shows particular concern about the enforcement of the assize of weights and measures to stop bakers selling short weight (as has been seen, Fitz Thedmar was involved in the reform of the method of weighing in the city).[27] The chronicle, under 1259, criticizes the use of the tumbril instead of the customary pillory to punish delinquent bakers.[28] Under 1269 it complains that the bailiffs had allowed the pillory to fall into disrepair, so that the bakers escaped punishment.[29] The chronicle's interest in weights and measures also appears in the precise description of the corn measures introduced at the accession of Edward I: 'the top of each measure was bound with an iron hoop, fastened with iron nails so that they could never be falsified, and each measure (that is each quarter, half quarter and bushel) was sealed with the alderman's seal'.[30]

The chronicle was also interested in the regulations concerning the nets of the Thames fishermen (it is worth noting that Fitz Thedmar's ward was by the river). A net's mesh had to be a specific size; if it was too small the net was burnt – a regulation regarded by the chronicler, who records the burning of nets in 1269 and 1272, as too severe.[31] Moreover the chronicle has a detailed and fully documented record of litigation involving the city; such litigation was usually due to the city's defence of its privileges. For example the chronicle describes the city's dispute, in 1256, with the abbot of Waltham over payment of stallage by the citizens trading in Waltham,[32] and the dispute, in 1263, with the abbot of Westminster over the latter's liberties in Middlesex.[33] There is a particularly full account of the quarrel with the men of Southwark, who complained that the Londoners were illegally making them pay customs on their side of London Bridge.[34]

The chronicle is a valuable record of the citizens' clashes with the king, who offered the most serious threat to their liberties. If the city authorities defaulted in administration, royal officials intervened and the city might be taken into the king's hands. The chronicle has an excellent account of the

[24] *L de AL*, p. 161. [25] *L de AL*, p. 41. [26] *L de AL*, p. 70.

[27] *L de AL*, pp. 145, 159, 162. [28] *L de AL*, p. 41. [29] *L de AL*, pp. 121–2.

[30] *L de AL*, pp. 167–8. No corn measure of this early date is preserved in the Guildhall Museum. The earliest English corn measure preserved in the Victoria and Albert Museum is of Henry VII's reign: it is made of cast bronze (the earliest wooden grain bushel is of George I's reign).

[31] *L de AL*, pp. 115–16, 161. [32] *L de AL*, p. 29. [33] *L de AL*, pp. 57–8.

[34] *L de AL*, pp. 39–40. For a dispute with the men of Northampton see ibid., pp. 46–8.

dispute with the king in 1258[35] over the citizens' alleged oppression of the poorer people. It relates how a roll was found in mysterious circumstances in the king's Wardrobe. The roll contained accusations against the mayor for financial extortion and for abusing the assize of weights and measures. The king took the city into his hands and appointed John Mansel to hold an enquiry. But the principal citizens refused to give evidence on oath, because they said it was against their privileges, and demanded to clear themselves with compurgators. The chronicle has a graphic description of the noisy meeting of the folkmoot in which the king referred the citizens' demands to the people: the latter denied that the case should be tried by compurgators, shouting 'Nay, nay, nay'. The king therefore deposed the aldermen and sheriffs who were only to be reinstated by popular election.[36]

Nevertheless the city's relations with the king were often more amicable. The chronicle was well informed about the king's movements, no doubt because he spent much time in his palace at Westminster. It records the dates of his arrivals in, and departures from London, and it describes the citizens' customary celebration of important events connected with the royal family. For example the streets were decorated to welcome the Lord Edward in 1255[37] and Richard of Cornwall in 1259.[38] There was a public holiday to celebrate the birth of Edward's first son in 1266, with dancing and singing in the streets and general thanksgiving.[39] One of the chronicle's most vivid passages describes the preparations for Edward's coronation feast.[40] All the grounds of Westminster palace were built over with halls ('within which were tables firmly fixed to the ground') and kitchens 'without number': cauldrons were placed in the open, for boiling meat, in case the kitchens were too small, and a kitchen was specially built for roasting, without a roof so that the smoke could escape. And the Great and Lesser Halls were white-washed, repainted and repaired throughout, 'so that the eyes of those who enter and see such beauty must be filled with joy and delight'.

The chronicle shows the king's respect for the city's embryonic financial dominance. It records that Henry III asked for the citizens' opinion on the gold pennies he issued in 1257.[41] Their reply was unfavourable: the poor especially would suffer because few owned goods worth a single gold penny. Moreover, the chronicle has valuable information about Henry's commercial connections with the city. It explains at length, citing numerous documents, the course of the quarrel between the king and the countess of Flanders which

---

[35] *L de AL*, pp. 30–7. Cf. pp. 509–10, 511 above and Williams, op. cit., pp. 209–10. For another conflict with the king, because the citizens allowed a murderer to escape from Newgate prison in 1255, see *L de AL*, p. 22; *CCR*, 1253–4, pp. 54, 315–16; and *CCR*, 1255–6, pp. 145, 202, 438.

[36] One cause of dispute with the king was over the right claimed by the citizens to appoint and dismiss their sheriffs; see *L de AL*, pp. 162–3 and Williams, op. cit., pp. 26–9 *passim*.

[37] *L de AL*, p. 23.   [38] *L de AL*, p. 41.   [39] *L de AL*, p. 87.

[40] *L de AL*, pp. 172–3.

[41] *L de AL*, pp. 29–30. For Henry III's unsuccessful attempt to introduce a gold coinage in 1257 see *Cambridge Economic History*, vol. 3, p. 590.

resulted in a partial embargo on wool exports.[42] And it has a careful description of the mark to be put on sacks of wool which were exempted from the embargo.[43]

Besides an interest in the king, the chronicle was, like Thomas Wykes, very interested in Richard of Cornwall. It records, for example, his acceptance of the crown of Germany[44] and the looting of his manor of Isleworth in 1264.[45] The chronicler used some of Richard's correspondence, giving unique copies of three items from it. One is a letter written by Richard to the citizens of London (because of 'their loyalty to, and warm affection for him'), describing his coronation at Aachen and victory at Boppard over the archbishop of Trèves.[46] Another is a letter to Richard from Philip king of France telling him of the murder of his son, Henry of Almain, at Viterbo.[47] And there is a copy of Richard's letter to the Franciscans of London announcing the sad news and asking for prayers for Henry.[48]

The chronicle is therefore a record of the city's internal history and of its external relations. But it is also a *pièce justificative* of the city oligarchy. The author saw the ideal city as one unified whole, comparing it with the human body (the aldermen were the head, the populace the limbs).[49] But London was far from unified – though a corporation, it was not homogeneous and its elements were in frequent conflict. Rivalry could break out between the mayor, elected by the citizens annually, and the aldermen, elected for life. The aldermen, who were rich merchants and financiers, competed with the London trades and crafts (the bakers, goldsmiths, and the rest). And below the trades and crafts were the poor people, the 'mob', an unpredictable, generally inarticulate force which sometimes exploited opportunities to riot and loot. Alliances between the factions in the city were transitory, and external powers, both king and barons, exploited instability and discontent.

The chronicle gives a comprehensible picture of the factions, notably during the Barons' War. The author's outlook was determined by his identification with the oligarchy. He praised or blamed the mayor according to his treatment of the aldermen. He hated Thomas Fitz Thomas elected mayor by the people of the city in 1261, against the wishes of the principal citizens.[50] And he hated Walter Hervey, both for extorting money from the

---

[42] See *L de AL*, pp. 126–7, 135–40, 142–5 *passim*, 159–61 *passim*. For an account of the dispute based partly on this chronicle's evidence, see E. Lipson, *An Introduction to the Economic History of England* (9th ed., London 1947, 3 vols), vol. I, p. 449.

[43] *L de AL*, p. 145.   [44] *L de AL*, p. 26.   [45] *L de AL*, p. 61.

[46] i.e. Arnold of Isenburg. For the letter see *L de AL*, pp. 26–9, and Denholm-Young, *Richard of Cornwall* (Oxford 1947), p. 92 and n. 1.

[47] *L de AL*, pp. 133–4 and N. Denholm-Young, op. cit., p. 151 and n. 2.

[48] *L de AL*, pp. 134–5.

[49] See *L de AL*, p. 98; 'omnes de civitate, tam pauperes quam divites, essent quasi corpus unum et vir unus...'. Cf. ibid., p. 150: 'ipsi aldermanni sunt quasi capita, et populus quasi membra'.

[50] *L de AL*, p. 58. For Fitz Thomas's popular support see ibid., p. 86; cf. Williams, op. cit., pp. 216–17.

oligarchy to pay the 1266 fine and for championing the cause of the craft guilds. Hervey was elected by the commons (in the face of bitter opposition by the aldermen), having promised to save them from financial oppression.[51] He granted charters, the chronicle says, to various craft guilds without the aldermen's consent and to the detriment of the other citizens and the whole realm.[52]

Hostility to the self-styled 'commons'[53] (men of the craft guilds and lesser trades, and the poorer people) is a persistent characteristic of the chronicle. The commons, the author thought, should not have full citizenship because some were of servile origin, and others, born outside the city, did not have its interests at heart.[54] They were 'fools of the vulgar herd',[55] 'swollen with pride'.[56] Any attempt by them to preserve or extend their rights infringed oligarchic privilege. The chronicle notes with disapproval their efforts to preserve common land and to reopen closed roads.[57]

The chronicle particularly blames the commons for the city's troubles during the Barons' War. Though the commons, as the chronicle admits, organized themselves to police the city, there was an eruption of indiscriminate looting in 1264,[58] and the sack of Isleworth was 'the beginning of woes and the cause of the deadly war in which manors were burnt and innumerable men, rich and poor, were robbed and thousands perished.'[59] During the war the commons provoked Henry III's displeasure with the city, because they supported the barons.[60] And again, in 1267, the king was angry because the commons, against the wishes of the principal citizens, allowed the earl of Gloucester to occupy the city: on the restoration of royal authority, Henry made the Londoners tear down the earl's covered-way built from the city to the Tower, and level his fosse 'so that it might not be seen'.[61]

Therefore, because of the chronicle's predominant loyalty to the city oligarchy, it has no consistent attitude to national politics. Its views were pragmatic, not theoretical, and determined by the effect of events on the oligarchy. Until 1264 it tends to criticize Henry III (notably for his alliance with the populace against the oligarchy in 1258) and to favour the barons. It says that the barons issued Provisions in the parliament[62] of Oxford in

[51] *L de AL*, p. 148. Cf. Williams, op. cit., pp. 243–5. [52] *L de AL*, p. 164.
[53] *L de AL*, p. 91; 'populus . . . vocans se Communam Civitatis'.
[54] *L de AL*, pp. 36, 150. Cf. Williams, op. cit., pp. 40–1.
[55] *L de AL*, p. 86; 'fatui de vulgo'.
[56] *L de AL*, p. 55. [57] *L de AL*, p. 56.
[58] *L de AL*, pp. 55, 61. Cf. Williams, op. cit., pp. 223–4.
[59] *L de AL*, p. 61. [60] *L de AL*, pp. 79–80, 86. [61] *L de AL*, pp. 90–3.
[62] *L de AL*, p. 37. The manuscript of the chronicle at present reads: 'Hoc anno fuit illud insane Parlamentum apud Oxoniam'. Stapleton gives this reading without comment and Riley translated 'insane Parlamentum' as the Mad Parliament, with a note that 'this remark gives proof of the adverse tendency of the writer's opinions to the cause of the barons'. However, examination of the manuscript shows that at least the 'a' of 'insane' is on an erasure. This was first noted by A. G. Little who decided that the original text had 'insigne'; see R. L. Poole, 'The "Mad" Parliament, 1538 [*sic*]' in *EHR*, xl (1925), p. 402. Further examination of the manuscript, under ultra-violet light, indicates that the whole of 'insane' ('Isane' in MS.) is on

1258, to abolish 'bad customs which had excessively oppressed the kingdom for a long time' and 'to emend the usages and laws of the realm'.[63] And it states that the barons, unlike the London mob, did not loot indiscriminately but only attacked the property of those who broke the Provisions of Oxford.[64]

As a Londoner, the author had some grounds for sympathizing with the barons. The citizens shared the barons' dislike of aliens. They especially hated the Italian merchants in the city (whom they accused of infringing the assize of weights and measures[65] and of living in unlicensed lodgings). And when the citizens ratified the Provisions of Oxford in 1262, they told the king that they objected to the presence of foreigners in the city.[66]

But already in 1258 the citizens had cause to complain of the barons. The chronicle records their objection to the baronial justiciar, Hugh Bigod, for hearing pleas in the Guildhall contrary to the city's liberties; he used a new procedure in freehold actions, the *querela*, which deprived the citizens of reasonable, customary summons. He also made them answer suits outside the city walls, in Surrey.[67] The barons occupied the city in 1264 and finally lost the support of the oligarchy. Simon de Montfort allied with the commons in order to gain support, promising concessions to the craft guilds. And the mayor on the barons' instructions told the guilds to draw up whatever regulations they wanted.[68]

Therefore, like a monastic writer, the chronicler of London expressed the narrow views of his community. But also like a monastic historian he sometimes took an objective interest in important national events. For example he mentions the alliance of Simon de Montfort with Llewelyn, which he regarded as reprehensible apparently on patriotic grounds ('the Welsh never made an alliance with the English, either now or later, without cheating and deception'[69]). He has a few other notices about the Barons' War unconnected with London,[70] and also has information about the Lord Edward when on crusade.[71] Moreover, he gives a long and extremely

---

an erasure, and I am inclined to agree with E. F. Jacob (see C. Bémont, *Simon de Montfort*, a new edition translated by E. F. Jacob, Oxford 1930, p. 155 n. 1) that it is impossible to determine the original reading. It seems unlikely that it was 'insigne', for the third letter of the erased word appears to have had a serif and this was divided at the top, and the 's's by the original scribe elsewhere in the text are not divided. Nor do the 'f's have divided serifs – which makes 'infame' (suggested by E. F. Jacob in *History*, ix, 1924, p. 189 n. 3) an unlikely reading. The 'b's, 'h's and 'l's have divided serifs; see Plate XIb and, for an enlargement of the passage, *BIHR*, iii (1925–6), Plate I (opposite p. 110).

[63] *L de AL*, p. 42.   [64] *L de AL*, p. 55.   [65] *L de AL*, p. 118.
[66] *L de AL*, p. 54.
[67] *L de AL*, pp. 40–1. For this passage see R. F. Treharne, *The Baronial Plan of Reform* (Manchester 1932), pp. 139, 148–53 *passim*, and E. F. Jacob, *Studies in the Period of Baronial Reform and Rebellion, 1258–1267* (Oxford Studies in Social and Legal History, ed. P. Vinogradoff, vol. 8, 1925), pp. 52 et seq.
[68] *L de AL*, p. 56. For Simon de Montfort's alliance with the populace of London see Treharne, op. cit., pp. 311–12, and Williams, op. cit., pp. 219–22.
[69] *L de AL*, p. 74.   [70] See e.g. the notice of the battle of Evesham; *L de AL*, p. 75.
[71] *L de AL*, pp. 156–7.

graphic account of the revolt at Norwich against the cathedral priory in 1272, strongly biased in favour of the citizens.[72] His attitude to the citizens of Norwich is the opposite to that expressed by the monastic chroniclers (who strongly support the priory). Perhaps it indicates that the London writer had concern for other growing urban communities besides his own.

The London chronicle, the first of a series, considered in conjunction with the mendicant chronicles, is symptomatic of the ending of the monastic monopoly of historiography which had dominated the earlier years of the thirteenth century. This trend was to be accelerated in the reign of Edward II. Then, while the monastic chronicle continued to decline, the next London chronicle was written, and secular clerks, who had made an important contribution to historiography in the twelfth century, re-emerged as historians. Furthermore, later in the fourteenth century, some laymen (for example, the knight, Sir Thomas Grey, and the herald of Sir John Chandos) wrote history. Nevertheless, the monastic tradition did not die; after a tenuous existence in the first half of the century it was revived and flourished, notably at St Albans, until the early fifteenth century.

[72] *L de AL*, pp. 145–8. The passage on the Norwich revolt reads like an attempt to vindicate the citizens for burning the cathedral, and it is so detailed as to suggest that here the chronicle incorporated a pre-existing tract.

Appendix A

Note on *The Song of Dermot and the Earl* and *L'Histoire des Ducs de Normandie et des Rois d'Angleterre*

The Song of Dermot and the Earl has some connection, though an indeterminate one, with the family of William the Marshal (cf. p. 349 n. 272). It recounts the exploits of Dermot MacMurrough, king of Leinster, and Richard de Clare earl of Pembroke and Striguil (1148/9–1176). Richard, invited to Ireland by Dermot to help him reconquer his land, married his daughter Aoife. Richard's and Aoife's daughter was Isabel, the wife of William the Marshal. The *Song* is printed as *The Song of Dermot and the Earl*, ed., with an English translation, G. H. Orpen (Oxford 1892). The edition was reviewed by Paul Meyer in *Romania*, xxi (Paris 1892), pp. 444–51. Meyer suggested (ibid., p. 447) that Isabel may have been in some way responsible for the commemoration in the *Song* of the deeds of her father and grandfather. However, she died in 1220 and the *Song* was composed in the second quarter of the thirteenth century (though it was based on earlier material): see Legge, *A-N Lit.*, pp. 306–8; J. F. O'Doherty, 'Historical criticism of the Song of Dermot and the Earl' in *Irish Historical Studies*, i (Dublin 1939), pp. 4–20; and a rejoinder to O'Doherty by M. J. de C. Dodd in ibid., pp. 294–6. The Marshal's family was also connected by marriage to another family which may have been responsible for the production of a historical work, i.e. *L'Histoire des Ducs de Normandie et des Rois d'Angleterre* . . . (ed. F. Michel, Société de l'Histoire de France, 1840). This is mainly a history, in Anglo-Norman prose, of Anglo-Norman relations from the death of Richard I until 1220 (it is valuable for its account of Louis's expedition to England), showing particular interest in Artois and the Boulonnais. P. Meyer (*HGM*, vol. 3, p. xci) believed that it was written by a minstrel of William de Forz, titular count of Aumale (1214–41). This family was connected with the Marshal by the marriage in 1214 between Alice, the daughter of William de Forz's predecessor as count of Aumlea, Robert de Bethune, and the Marshal's eldest son William; but the lady soon died (see *HGM*, ll. 14957–15012). For the counts of Aumale see GEC, *Peerage*, vol. 1, pp. 353–5.

Appendix B

Local History in the Thirteenth Century

Thirteenth-century monastic chronicles all contain information about local events. In some (for example the Canterbury/Dover chronicle, for which see pp. 422–3), local history almost eclipses the record of general events. In addition monks produced a number of tracts on local history (for examples see pp. 385–95) and a few chronicles exclusively devoted to the history of their houses. The most notable local history is Matthew Paris's *Gesta Abbatum*. Another abbatial history was Thomas of Marlborough's continuation of the Evesham chronicle (for the late eleventh-century Evesham chronicle, to 1077, see pp. 111–12). Thomas was successively sacrist, prior, and, from 1229 to 1236, abbot of Evesham. He revised the previous Evesham chronicle and continued it; his purpose was primarily to substantiate the abbey's claim to exemption from the control of the bishop of Worcester. Thomas's preoccupation with the abbey's exemption was caused by the conflict between the abbey and Mauger bishop of Worcester (1200–12) over Mauger's attempted visitation of the abbey in 1201; for this dispute see *Eve.*, pp. 100 et seq., C. R. Cheney, *Episcopal Visitation of the Monasteries in the Thirteenth Century* (Manchester 1931), pp. 38–9, 90–1, 101; *VCH, Worcs.*, vol. 2, pp. 117 et seq. and M. D. Knowles, 'Essays in monastic history, 1066–1216. IV: The growth of exemption', *Downside Review*, l (1932), pp. 398–401. Probably the original Evesham chronicle had no bias against the bishop of Worcester (see the very favourable mention of Wulfstan bishop of Worcester 1062–95; *Eve.*, p. 89). It is likely that Thomas inserted the statements that Hethomme (the name of the site of the earliest foundation) did not belong to Worcester (*Eve.*, p. 71), and that Evesham's privileges were not destroyed when the abbey was subjugated by the bishop of Worcester in about 1016 (*Eve.*, p. 82), and the notice of the appointment of a prior of Evesham as dean of Christianity in the Vale of Evesham for the first time since the subjection of the abbey to the bishop of Worcester – 'quam nunquam libertatem ecclesia ista postea amisit'. Thomas's continuation starts with brief entries concerning the abbots but becomes fuller after the succession of Abbot Adam in 1160. He gives a very full account of the dispute with Mauger and of his own achievements as sacrist, prior and abbot. The chronicle was continued, in less detail, after Thomas's death until 1536 (it is very brief from 1418). For a translation of the Evesham chronicle see D. C. Cox, *The Chronicle of Evesham Abbey* (Evesham 1964).

Durham had a well-established tradition of local history (for local histories written at Durham in the eleventh and twelfth centuries see pp. 114–23). In about 1214 Geoffrey of Coldingham, sacrist of the priory of Coldingham (a cell of Durham), previously a monk of Durham, wrote a history of the bishops of Durham from 1152 to 1214, as a continuation of the history of Durham attributed to Symeon of Durham (see pp. 114–21) and its continuation by an unknown monk of Durham (printed in *SD*, vol. 1, pp. 135–69). Coldingham's history was continued to 1336 by Robert of Graystanes, a monk of Durham, and his chronicle in its turn was continued by William de Chambre up to the episcopate of Bishop Tunstall (1530–59). These three histories are printed in *Historiae Dunelmensis Scriptores Tres, Gaufridus de Coldingham, Robertus de Graystanes et Willielmus de Chambre,* ed. James Raine (Surtees Soc., ix, 1839). Coldingham's history is related to, and Graystanes's history is partly based on, another Durham chronicle which is edited and described by F. Barlow, *Durham Annals and Documents in the Thirteenth Century* (Surtees Soc., clv, 1945), pp. xxv–xxxii, 1–84. This chronicle covers the history of Durham cathedral priory from 1202 to 1285–6. It includes numerous business and legal documents relating to the priory's affairs.

Peterborough also produced a number of local histories in the thirteenth century – the best survey of historical writing at Peterborough is by F. Liebermann, 'Ueber ostenglische Geschichtsquellen des 12, 13, 14 Jahrhunderts, besonders den falschen Ingulf' in *Neues Archiv der Gesellschaft für ältere deutsche Geschichtskunde* (Hanover–Leipzig 1892), xviii, pp. 228–36. Some time between 1250 and 1262 Robert of Swaffham, cellarer of Peterborough, continued the abbatial history by Hugh Candidus (for which see above, pp. 272–83 *passim*) from 1177 to 1245. His chronicle was continued in the fourteenth century by Walter of Whittlesey, to 1321. Swaffham's and Whittlesey's chronicles are printed in Joseph Sparke, *Historiae Anglicanae Scriptores Varii* (London 1723), pt iii, pp. 97–216. The Peterborough chronicle from 1122 to 1295, probably by William of Woodford (for which see pp. 440 and n. 6, 452–3 above), is primarily a local history though it has entries on national affairs. It is particularly valuable from 1273 for its record of legal cases involving Peterborough abbey.

At Glastonbury, as at Evesham, the abbey's conflict with its diocesan prompted the composition of a chronicle. The conflict originated with the annexation of the abbey by Savaric bishop of Bath (1192–1205). Adam of Domerham, author of the *De Rebus Gestis Glastoniensibus* (ed. T. Hearne, Oxford 1727, 2 vols), who entered Glastonbury abbey some time between 1235 and 1252, becoming successively cellarer and sacrist, gives a full account of the dispute (Hearne, op. cit., vol. 2, pp. 352 et seq.; see also M. D. Knowles, 'Essays in monastic history. V: The cathedral monasteries', *Downside Review,* li (1933), pp. 94–6). As sacrist, Adam was involved in a quarrel with Robert Burnell, bishop of Bath and Wells (1275–92), over the lordship of the abbey on the death of Abbot Robert; he excluded the bishop's officials and admitted the king's, thus vindicating the monks' claim to direct dependence on the crown (Hearne, op. cit., vol. 2, pp. 536–40). He wrote his chronicle as a continuation of William of Malmesbury's *De Antiquitate Glastoniensis Ecclesiae* (ibid., p. 302), to encourage readers to protect and augment the abbey's prosperity and privileges which had been so gravely diminished by the attacks of the diocesan (see Adam's preface in ibid., pp. 303–4).

Appendix C

Two Manuscripts of the 'Merton' Version of the *Flores Historiarum*

There are two copies of the *Flores Historiarum* (see pp. 453–63) which have exceptional features: the text in the 'Tenison' MS., and that in the chronicle of Ralph Baldock, bishop of London 1304–13.

1. The 'Tenison' MS. This manuscript was successively Clarendon MS. 93 and Phillipps MS. 15732. It was acquired by the Beinecke Library at Yale University, where it is MS. 426, from H. P. Kraus of New York (Cat. 117, item 29), and is briefly described in *FH*, vol. 1, pp. xxx–xxxi. It is written in a text hand of the first half of the fourteenth century, in two columns, with medieval marginalia. It covers the years from 1058 to 1327; it lacks leaves at the beginning and for the annals from 1322 to 1325. It is an abbreviated text of the *Flores* to 1305, and it is a conflation of the Westminster and 'Merton' versions (some annals belong to one version, some to the other). Edward I's letter on the Scottish succession case is addressed to the abbot and convent of Westminster. The annal for 1306 and the first part of that for 1307 derive from Nicholas Trevet's *Annales*. The last part of the annal for 1307, the characterization of Edward I and his reign, derives from Adam Murimuth's chronicle. It adds two extra lines to the verses given in Murimuth (printed in *FH*, vol. 3, p. xxxi). Murimuth is the source of the remaining annals. The chronicle ends rather abruptly with the deposition of Edward II, concluding with the verses (which are not in Murimuth):

> Carneruam natus, princeps Edwardus amatus;
> Ingratis gratus, est morte gravi cruciatus.

2. The chronicle of Ralph Baldock. It is now MS. Lat. hist. d. 4 in the Bodleian Library, Oxford. Baldock's chronicle is unprinted; the copy in this composite volume was owned in the middle ages, at least from the mid-fourteenth century, by the abbey of Bury St Edmunds and acquired by the Bodleian Library in 1965 from the Phillipps collection; see Sotheby's Sale Catalogue, 30 November 1965, where the contents are listed. Baldock's chronicle seems, after cursory examination, to comprise a copy of the 'Merton' *Flores* from the Creation to the end in 1306, but has Edward I's letter on the Scottish succession case addressed to the dean and chapter of St Paul's; ff. 76–202^v; and also annals for 1307 and 1308, corresponding to the text in the continuation of the *Flores* in the *Annales Paulini* (printed in

Chronicles of the Reigns of Edward I and Edward II, ed. W. Stubbs, vol. 1, pp. 255–66, which were probably compiled at Westminster (see ibid., pp. xlvi, lxxvi, and H. G. Richardson, 'The *Annales Paulini*' in *Speculum*, xxiii (1948), p. 631); ff. 202^v–205^v. At the end of this section a fourteenth-century annotator has written 'Explicit cronica Radulphi Baldok'. There follows a copy of Adam Murimuth's chronicle for the years from 1310 to 1334 (ff. 205^v–218) and annals, in a cursive hand, from 1335 to 1340 (ff. 218–19). Baldock's chronicle was no. cxxv in the list of 'libri scolastici' which he bequeathed to St Paul's cathedral and no. xxiv in the list of his books at the manor of Stepney in 1313; see A. B. Emden, *A Biographical Register of the University of Oxford to A.D. 1500* (Oxford 1957–9, 3 vols), vol. 3, p. 2148. It was seen by Leland but was lost by the time of Henry Wharton; see H. Wharton, *Historia de Episcopis et Decanis Londoniensibus* ... (London 1695), p. 110.

Appendix D

Chronological Index of the Principal Literary Sources[1] for English History to *c.* 1307

Arranged under Reigns from 1066

I THE ANGLO-SAXON PERIOD

[1] I have not distinguished between the different versions of the Anglo-Saxon Chronicle in this list, or between the various works of Gerald of Wales. It should also be noted that this list is selective (only the principal sources are given), not comprehensive, and that some chronicles are listed only under the reign for which they are primarily important: they may well have some (though less) value for earlier or later times. For a similar list see C. Gross, *The Sources and Literature of English History, from the Earliest Times to about 1485* (2nd ed., London 1915), pp. 712–15, and A. Potthast, *Bibliotheca Historica Medii Aevi* (Berlin 1896), vol. 2, pp. 1718–21.

II FROM 1066 TO *c.* 1307

Index

Post-Conquest people are indexed under their second names if the second name can be regarded as a surname. However, if a person is commonly known by his first name, he is indexed under his first name, with a cross-reference. Moreover, if the second name is purely descriptive (e.g. Hugh Candidus), the person is indexed under his first name.

Classical names (e.g. Constantius Chlorus) and names of the Anglo-Saxon period (e.g. Eadric Streona) are indexed under first names.

References to pages and notes are in italics if they cite printed editions of the works under discussion.